Introduction to

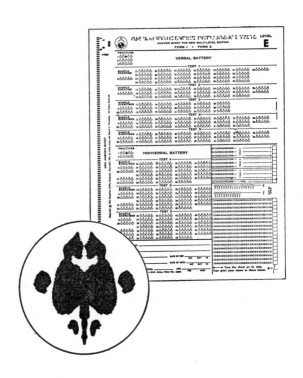

Educational Measurement

SECOND EDITION

Victor H. Noll
MICHIGAN STATE UNIVERSITY

HOUGHTON MIFFLIN COMPANY · BOSTON

TO MY FATHER AND MOTHER

Editor's Introduction

The opportunity to write an introduction for the second edition of a popular text is an obvious pleasure for an advisory editor. Such is the case with *Introduction to Educational Measurement,* which, since its initial appearance eight years ago, has won and held a position of leadership among textbooks in the field of educational measurement.

Although measurement is as old as man, its refinement and usefulness for educational purposes is a modern achievement. In the schools of today it meets a wide range of needs: facilitation of learning, improvement of instruction, effective counseling and guidance, and educational placement. Pupil, parent, teacher, supervisor, principal, superintendent, and school board member all find measurement indispensable to the total educational programs of both elementary and secondary schools. And, consciously or unconsciously, it is employed by the general public in its evaluation of our schools.

If the purpose of education is to achieve desirable change, then it is necessary to know with some degree of exactness the relationships among various educational procedures, the aptitudes of learners, and the resulting changes in human behavior. Accurate prediction and control in the educational process thus become prime considerations. What changes in behavior are desirable? How may these changes be measured? What aptitudes are essential to the development of an accepted form and level of behavior and the crucial elements in the educative process? The contribution and value of educational measurement are inextricably interwoven with the validity of the answers to these questions.

In this thoroughly revised edition of *Introduction to Educational Measurement,* Professor Noll has greatly improved an already excellent book. New developments and trends that have occurred since the first edition was published in 1957 are discussed and evaluated, chapter bibliographies are brought up to date, and the learning exercises within each chapter reflect new points of view and emphasis. The text remains both scientific and practical, one that is useful and understandable both to the experienced educator and to the beginner. The discussions of the applications of measurement and its contribution to the educational program will interest and serve the entire corps of school personnel and laymen who wish to know more about this important educational tool.

HEROLD C. HUNT

Preface

In the interval since publication of the first edition of this volume, much has happened in the field of measurement. The use of tests in the schools has increased and users have become more knowledgeable. In addition, testing has become a somewhat controversial issue. These facts, plus the warm response received by the first edition, have prompted author and publisher to produce a thorough revision that will meet current needs and interests.

Much of the material in the first edition has been revised and some sections or chapters have been wholly rewritten. In this category are the materials dealing with statistical methods, validity, reliability, norms, construction of classroom tests, measurement of capacity, and uses of measurement. New tests are described and descriptions of older ones are revised wherever appropriate. Lists of available tests and test publishers and annotated chapter bibliographies have been revised and brought up to date. Appendix B has been added to give the student who needs it help in extracting square root.

As before, this book attempts to provide an orientation to the field of measurement and evaluation in education, a foundation in measurement theory and elementary statistical methods, an acquaintance with published, standardized tests and sources of information about them, a basic understanding and skill in constructing tests for local use, and instruction in the interpretation and applications of the results of measurement. The author believes that the above still represent the fundamental needs of teachers, counselors, and others concerned with educational measurement who have no special training in the field.

As before the text is designed for use in the first or introductory course. No previous study or experience in educational measurement by the student is assumed. For most students in education this assumption and approach have proved appropriate. It is hoped that those who used the first edition will find the second substantially improved though still in familiar and agreeable form.

My indebtedness to the many authors and publishers who gave permission to reproduce materials from their works is gratefully acknowledged. Appreciation is expressed also to my students and colleagues for their many helpful suggestions, and to the instructors in other colleges and universities who sent many valuable suggestions in answer to an inquiry addressed to a sampling of staff members in various institutions in which the first edition has been used. Most of these suggestions have been incorporated into the revision. Finally, it is a pleasure to acknowledge the assistance of my wife, Rachel, who typed much of the revised manuscript and correspondence relating to it and carefully read and checked all proofs. Her encouragement and willingness to help have been unfailing.

Victor H. Noll

Contents

List of Tables

List of Figures

1

Educational Measurement:

An Overview

WHY MEASUREMENT IN EDUCATION?

Measurement goes on constantly everywhere, and it seems reasonable to suppose that the process has been used for a long time. In making his first suits of clothes, primitive man undoubtedly performed crude measurements when he selected and cut a large animal skin for himself and smaller ones for his mate and children. When he built a shelter, he probably used his own height as a measure, or if he sought a cave, he looked for one large enough for him and his family. As man came into contact with other men and began to exchange and share, it is likely that he devised crude standards of measure for purposes of barter.

Earliest records indicate that by the dawn of recorded history man had developed some systems of measurement. The ancient Egyptians must have had fairly accurate methods of measurement to build the pyramids. The Book of Genesis states that Noah built his ark three hundred cubits long, fifty cubits in breadth, and thirty cubits high.[1] There is also reference in the same source to the weighing of gold and silver.

The ancient Greeks and Romans had well-developed systems of measurement and performed very exact work in constructing roads, bridges, buildings, arches, and monuments. Before modern times, units were developed and adopted which have come down to this day, in name at least. The foot was based on the length of the human foot, the pennyweight (weight of a penny) was equal to thirty-two wheatcorns in the midst of the ear, and the ounce was twenty pennyweights.[2]

Some early attempts at standardization were necessary. For example, the foot unit came to be not the length of just any man's foot, but of one particular foot — that of the king. Naturally, if the king died or was deposed and a new one came to the throne, the length of the foot might change also. The sheer inconvenience of having variable units and, of course, the development of scientific methods made constant units and exact measurement a necessity. Since natural units tended to vary, it became the usual practice to arbitrarily fix unit measures by law or royal decree. Ultimately this process reached its highest level in the development and general acceptance in most European countries and in scientific work everywhere of the metric system of weights and measures. In this system natural but stable measures formed the basis for units which were adopted and made permanent standards by international agreement.[3]

All of us, every day, practice measurement in countless ways. Nearly everything — gasoline, potatoes, lumber, yard goods, etc. — is sold and purchased by measured amounts. When we travel, distances are expressed in units of measure; the growth of plants or animals can be measured accurately; the passage of time is measured in hours, days, years, or centuries; when we make estimates of time, distance, weight, size, color, texture, or countless other traits, qualities, or amounts, we are making measurements.

The remarkable scientific discoveries and advances of the past few hundreds of years have brought about and depend squarely upon accurate measurement. The work of the chemist, the physicist, the biologist, and the astronomer could not be done without accurate measurement. Volumes, weights, temperatures, pressures, speed, time — all are measured

---

[1] A cubit was the distance from a man's elbow to the tip of his outstretched middle finger, a distance of about eighteen inches.

[2] William Hallock and Herbert T. Wade, *The Evolution of Weights and Measures and the Metric System* (New York: The Macmillan Co., 1906), Chap. 1.

[3] For example, the meter, the unit of length in the metric system, equals one ten-millionth part of the distance measured on a meridian of the earth from the equator to the pole.

with great accuracy in scientific work. The astronomer calculates and predicts the exact time to the second, years in advance, of the solar eclipse; the chemist weighs quantities so small that they can be seen only under magnification; he determines the composition of substances with methods of analysis that are amazingly precise; every scientific worker employs measuring techniques and instruments that are, on the whole, sufficiently accurate and dependable for the purposes at hand. And some of these are surprisingly close. For example, as complicated a mechanism as an automobile is manufactured in thousands of parts, each made to such exact specifications that millions of cars are assembled without need for any major adjustment before they are driven off the end of the assembly line.

As measurement became more accurate and more commonly used it was inevitable that refinements in technique would affect educational measurement also. To be sure, teachers have had the responsibility of judging and appraising ever since teaching began. They could not fail to note that some individuals learned more easily and rapidly than others; that some learned more of what was taught and retained what was learned far longer than others. It has long been part of the responsibility of teachers not only to note and estimate the amount of such differences, but also to make reports on them and on pupil progress. As new and more refined methods of measurement were discovered and developed in natural science they gradually influenced method and thinking in other fields, including education. This development in education is of comparatively recent origin, but it has had tremendous effects on learning and teaching and all that concerns the school.

In order to judge the attainment of his pupils accurately and fairly a teacher must have accurate measurement techniques at his disposal, must know how to use them properly and how to interpret results obtained by their use. For example, in order to make satisfactory judgments of a child's achievement one must know accurately both his past achievement and his probable ability to achieve. A child whose achievement is low may be doing all that he is capable of doing, though actually achieving less than one whose accomplishment is much greater but who may not be using nearly all of his ability. Again, a pupil may have special abilities or aptitudes that result in great irregularity or unevenness in his day-by-day attainment. He may do good work in language, history, and literature, but his work in arithmetic and science may be distinctly below average. Accurate, dependable measurement is indispensable to interpreting and dealing with such situations. And, of course, teachers must make daily, or at least frequent, appraisals of the work of every pupil in terms of the objectives set up in order to see what progress each pupil is making toward such objectives in the light of his abilities. To do this a teacher should have at his disposal the widest possible range of dependable, accurate measuring instruments and techniques.

It is important that every teacher, counselor, or school psychologist have a thorough knowledge of available measuring devices and techniques as they apply to his work and that the appropriate and proper use of these be well understood. Moreover, especially in the case of the teacher, there will be many situations in which he will want to devise tests and examinations of his own, particularly where none is available that meets the needs of his situation accurately. Then he will have use for knowledge and skill in the construction of appropriate measurement devices so that the requirements inherent in his particular situation can be accurately appraised. Measurement devices or techniques prepared by the teacher are often the best, and sometimes the only, means of determining how well classes or individual pupils are progressing toward the objectives of instruction. For example, when it is desirable to know how well a child is learning to work and play with others, or what changes have taken place in his attitudes toward the other children, the teacher must often devise his own methods of evaluating the child's progress toward such goals.

Today measurement touches upon and influences every phase of education. Whether it is marking, promotion, guidance and counseling, curriculum development, instruction, or some other aspect of the work, measurement enters the picture and usually plays an important role. However, while recognizing the pervasiveness and usefulness of measurement in education, the student and teacher must always keep in mind that measurement is a tool, a means to an end, not an end in itself. We do not generally measure anything just for the sake of knowing how long or how heavy it is. We have a use for the knowledge, or some reason for acquiring it. We measure the dimensions or weight of an object to see whether it fits, whether we can carry it, or how much it will cost. Perhaps more important, we measure the object to determine whether it will serve a specific purpose. In education we measure the capacity (or fit) of an individual so that we can help him evaluate his strengths and weaknesses as he develops skills and knowledge in acquiring his place in life, or we measure to see to what degree the purposes, goals, or objectives of education have been attained and the extent of the student's progress toward them. Measurement in this field should always serve to help us do a better job of educating people.

▶ LEARNING EXERCISES ◀

1. One of our earliest written records is the Bible. Try to find what seems to you authentic evidence of the use of weights and measures in the first books of the Bible. What was the basis of such standards?

2. Compare the English and the metric systems of weights and measures. Which is more scientific? Which is easier to use?

3. Analyze the responsibilities of a second-grade teacher in the area of measurement. Compare them with those of a teacher of English in the ninth grade. A teacher of homemaking in senior high school. A student teacher majoring in your own field of study.

EDUCATIONAL MEASUREMENT TODAY

At the turn of the century standardized tests as commonly used today were unknown.[4] The first such school-subject test to be published or made generally available was one in arithmetic by Stone.[5] By 1920 the first standardized tests of intelligence and of personality, a number of tests in school subjects, some aptitude tests, and some general survey tests of school achievement had made their appearance. Also, the first books on educational measurement and on statistical methods as applied to education were published during this period. Some of the significant developments in the field of educational measurement during these early years will be described in the next chapter, but at this point it will suffice to say that by 1920 the use of tests and scales, including rating scales, score cards, check lists, and other measuring instruments, had become well established in the schools and colleges of the United States. In 1930, Odell[6] cited data collected several years prior to publication (perhaps 1925–26) indicating that somewhere between thirty and forty million standardized tests were sold in the United States during one of these years. A recent survey[7] estimates that in 1961 more than one hundred million commercially pro-

[4] A standardized test is one that has been carefully constructed by experts in the light of acceptable objectives or purposes; procedures for administering, scoring, and interpreting scores are specified in detail so that no matter who gives the test or where it may be given, the results should be comparable; and norms or averages for different age or grade levels have been pre-determined.

[5] C. W. Stone, *Arithmetical Abilities and Some Factors Determining Them*, Contributions to Education, No. 19 (New York: Teachers College, Columbia University, 1908).

[6] C. W. Odell, *Educational Measurement in High School* (New York: Appleton-Century-Crofts, Inc., 1930), 641 pp.

[7] David A. Goslin, *The Search for Ability* (New York: Russell Sage Foundation, 1963), p. 54.

duced ability tests were administered. This figure does not include personality tests.

Another kind of evidence for the increasing use of tests is the number of organizations engaged in the business of developing, standardizing, and distributing such instruments. Buros[8] lists more than 150 organizations in this country which publish tests; for some twenty of these, the development and publication of tests constitutes the major or at least an important part of their business.

Standardized tests of ability, aptitude, achievement, and personality also find wide use in business, industry, and the military services. Scarcely any large business organization or industrial concern could function today without a personnel manager or director and a staff of trained personnel technicians or psychologists. Much use is made of standardized and special tests in selecting persons for employment, determining what type of work they are fitted for, and measuring their efficiency. In addition to educational, business, and industrial use of measurement materials, the armed services use large quantities of tests, rating scales, and other measuring instruments. Men and women are tested at pre-induction centers and during recruit training for selection purposes, for special training, for fitness for unusual kinds of duty, for adjustment to the service, and for countless other purposes. The first group tests of intelligence, *Army Alpha* and *Army Beta,* were devised especially for use in World War I, and the development and use of all kinds of measuring devices were greatly expanded in World War II.

In addition to those uses already mentioned, tests have an important function in the so-called "external" testing programs. These include the College Entrance Examination Board, National Merit Scholarship, and the National Teacher Examination programs, to name but a few. Many states maintain one or more statewide testing programs, the oldest and best known being the New York State Regents' examinations. Among other states having well-established statewide testing programs are California, Illinois, Kansas, Kentucky, Minnesota, Ohio, and Texas. Tests of their own devising or choosing are also widely used by colleges and universities for admission purposes. Included among these are testing programs for admission to professional schools such as law, medicine, nursing, and graduate schools, as well as admission to undergraduate programs.

It is difficult to imagine how education, business, industry, the military, or any program of research in these fields could function today without measurement. Measurement has assumed the proportions of "big busi-

---

[8] O. K. Buros, *The Sixth Mental Measurements Yearbook* (Highland Park, N.J.: The Gryphon Press, 1965).

ness," both in usefulness and in size. No other development of modern times has contributed so much to our understanding of the nature and extent of individual differences among boys and girls, men and women. The structure and procedures of modern education rest upon the knowledge that individuals differ in every conceivable way, and upon the realization that it is the responsibility of the schools to identify these differences, measure them, and try to fit the educational program to them. The ideal is an education fitted to the individual, and not the individual to a set program of education. Progress toward this goal without measurement is at worst impossible and at best an intolerable hit-or-miss process.

ESSENTIAL CHARACTERISTICS OF MEASUREMENT

According to *Webster's New International Dictionary,*[9] to measure is "to ascertain the extent, degree, quantity, dimensions, or capacity of, by a standard. . . ." All of these terms imply a result expressed in numbers rather than descriptive phrases. When we measure something we express our findings in units of length, weight, etc. To say merely that an object is flat or round or green or heavy does not satisfy the *quantitative* aspect of the definition. Since measurement is a quantitative process, the results of measurement are always expressed in *numbers* — so many feet long, so many degrees of temperature, so many quarts or pounds.

In the second place, measurement is expressed, insofar as possible, in *constant units*. When the yard was the distance from a man's nose to his outstretched finger tips, it was not a constant unit. Some men had longer arms or noses than others. The English stone could be a large stone or a small one. Men soon came to realize that such variation in measuring units led to endless trouble and confusion, and they eventually reached agreement on certain units. Two systems of measurement came into existence: the English system, with which we are all familiar, and the metric system, which is used in most European countries and in scientific work the world over. Units are constant in both systems. An inch is an inch everywhere and a gram is the same in Paris as it is in Chicago. Standards such as the standard meter bar in Paris are used to calibrate or check other measuring instruments. Varying conditions sometimes affect the constancy of the unit measure. An object weighing a pound at sea level weighs less on top of a mountain, and a steel rule is longer at 100° C. than it is at 20° C. Therefore, in order to have strictly constant units we must have constant conditions. However, for all except the most

[9] Second Edition, unabridged (Springfield, Mass.: G. & C. Merriam Co., 1957).

exact scientific work such fine distinctions are not necessary. Ordinary measurement requires that the units be only relatively constant.

The idea of constant units also implies that the unit of measurement is exactly the same at all points on the scale. The difference between 95° and 96° must be the same as the difference between 10° and 11°; a centimeter is the same at all places on a single meter stick and on all meter sticks. In other words, the unit of measurement does not vary in different parts of the scale.

These two characteristics, quantitativeness and constancy of units, are fundamental to all measurement. It must be recognized, of course, that the degree to which they are attained varies from one field or area to another. They can be obtained in physical measurements, for example, to a higher degree than in the measurement of mental or emotional traits, at least at the present stage of development of measuring techniques. It is also well to keep in mind that the degree of constancy of units is governed in large part by the situation. Constancy is often a relative term. There is less need for exact equivalence of units on a carpenter's rule or a household thermometer than on the extremely fine instruments used in laboratory research.

▶ LEARNING EXERCISES ◀

4. Define the terms "quantitative" and "qualitative," as used, for example, in chemistry. Apply the distinctions thus expressed to educational measurement.

5. What is implied by the phrase, "constant unit"? Give some illustrations of the concept as it applies in educational measurement.

ERROR IN MEASUREMENT

Occasionally everybody makes mistakes in arithmetic, or in reading a scale or measuring the dimensions of a room. However, the concept of error in measurement has a somewhat different connotation. Suppose one were conducting an experiment which required the recording of temperatures. One might read the thermometer as accurately as possible and follow all directions closely, and yet there would be some degree of error in the results. Why would this be so? To answer this question let us consider the nature and sources of error in measurement. They are chiefly of three types.

The first is the error of observation, sometimes referred to as the human equation. This type of error has not always been recognized. It is said that one observer in a world-famous astronomical observatory in the late 1700's was discharged because his observations consistently differed from those of his co-workers. It was not known then that such differences, though possibly the result of carelessness on the observer's part, were often due to differences in how the independent observers actually "saw" the instrument readings. It is now a well-known fact that even highly trained observers may observe the same phenomenon at the same time and yet differ in their reading of a scale or in their description of what took place. Moreover, a single observer's own readings will commonly be found to vary from one observation to the next, even though the actual conditions are unchanged.

The second source of error is inherent in the measuring device or instrument. Variations from one instrument to another — slight and perhaps imperceptible variations in units of the scale and similar mechanical variations — result in measuring instruments which are something less than infallible. In spite of all the painstaking care with which scientific measuring tools are made and calibrated, there is none that is perfect. However, the more carefully the device is made and the better the materials used, the smaller the amount of error is likely to be. This source of error is especially significant in educational testing devices for reasons that will be discussed later.

The third source of error in measurement stems from lack of uniformity in what is being measured. Whether one is measuring the strength of a piece of twine or the performance of a child in arithmetic, some degree of uniformity is vital to accurate measurement. The strength of the twine varies in different segments of the samples and according to age, moisture, and other factors; the behavior of the child varies somewhat according to his motivation, the physical conditions of the room, and perhaps his health and mood at the time. For practical reasons it is generally impossible to measure all of a product or material such as a carload of ore or all of an individual's behavior or knowledge under all conditions. Therefore, an attempt is always made to measure a representative or typical sample of the material or behavior.

A knowledge and understanding of the possible sources of error is essential to an intelligent use of measuring instruments in any field, and through such knowledge and understanding we improve our methods of measuring. We can also make more intelligent use of the results of measurement, for knowing the limits of accuracy is very helpful in making proper interpretations.

▶ LEARNING EXERCISES ◀

6. Bring a thermometer to class and hang it on the wall for ten or fifteen minutes. (If the classroom or laboratory has a thermometer already installed, use it.) Have the temperature read by a dozen members of the class, each one estimating as accurately as possible to the nearest tenth of a degree. Have each person write down his reading but not show it to anyone. When all have finished, list the readings on the board. How do you explain the results?

7. Compare the readings of two thermometers, two yardsticks, two balances, or other pairs of measuring instruments. Do they agree? How closely?

THE NATURE OF EDUCATIONAL MEASUREMENT

In the light of the foregoing discussion of some of the chief characteristics of measurement in general, it might be well to consider how they apply or do not apply to measurement in education.

First, it may be said that measurement in education is quantitative, otherwise it cannot properly be called measurement. By use of educational measurement we get scores, norms, I.Q.'s, averages, etc., all of which are numerical expressions. Not all methods of appraisal or evaluation in education are quantitative, but those which are not cannot properly be classified as measurement.

Second, in the development of educational measuring devices substantial progress has been made toward constancy of units. This aspect of the problem cannot be discussed without getting into technical matters which are out of place in this chapter. It may be said, however, that the development of certain types of derived or transmuted scores such as *T*-scores or standard scores represents at least an approach to the establishment of constant units of educational measurement. It should be said again, however, that "constant" in this case is a relative matter and that there are few *absolutely constant* units of measurement in any field.

Third, error is present in educational measurement as it is in all fields of scientific research. Yet no sensible person would advocate discontinuing measurement in astronomy, physics, or even in biology or psychology because error of measurement is known to exist. Instead, the scientist determines the causes of error and tries to eliminate them; knowing that he cannot do this entirely or completely, he tries to determine the amount of error or the degree of accuracy in his measurements. When this has been determined he proceeds to use measurement to the best advantage with full recognition of the limits of accuracy of his results.

As we gain knowledge and experience in a field, our measurement techniques improve, the margin of error decreases, and the results become more exact. Also, as workers in any subject area learn more about measurement they develop an attitude of suspended judgment and caution which helps them to avoid rash statements or conclusions not justified by the data or the degree of accuracy of their measurements. Moreover, knowledge of the probable limits of the error of their measurements makes it possible to specify the degree of accuracy quite closely. Instead of saying that a child's I.Q. is 115 one learns that it is more accurate and just as useful to say that it is highly probable that his I.Q. is between 105 and 125, or that there is a 50–50 probability that his I.Q. is between 110 and 120. This may seem like rather rough or approximate measurement, and, compared with results in some other fields, it is. On the other hand, even with that degree of possible error the results are still much more accurate than any other known methods of estimating the intelligence of children, and what is perhaps equally important, the degree of accuracy or probable limits of error are known.

Fourth, educational measurement is generally indirect rather than direct. The weight of an object can be determined *directly* in pounds and ounces or other units by use of a balance or scale. By contrast, educational measurement is indirect. We do not measure such traits as intelligence or mechanical aptitude directly, but rather by inference. As an individual is able to perform designated tasks, we are able to draw from the results of his performance certain conclusions about his intelligence or aptitude. The same is true with measurements in the fields of school achievement or personality or interests. In these fields the pupil's knowledge, adjustment, or motivation are measured indirectly by inference based on his behavior and especially his performance on tests.

Fifth, educational measurements are relative; they are not in any sense absolute. There is no unit of achievement in arithmetic, no unit of aptitude in music, no unit of school intelligence which is comparable to absolute zero, or centigrade, or the time of the earth's rotation. Standards in educational measurement are based on observed performance of typical subjects. The evaluation of the performance of an individual or a group is made by comparing it with that of a typical group. To be more specific, performance on educational and other tests is interpreted in terms of norms which are generally averages of typical groups on the test in question. A child's score on a reading test may be 40, which has no immediately clear meaning comparable to 40 minutes or 40° centigrade. However, if we know his age and we find that the average score of children of the same age on this test is 35, his score takes on meaning. Furthermore, if we know that 15 per cent of the children of his age make scores above 40, his score takes on added meaning. It is for these reasons that measurement in education is said to be relative.

From the foregoing discussion it may be concluded that measurement in education is faced with many of the same problems and difficulties as measurement in other fields. However, it may seem that these difficulties are greater in education than in the more exact fields. One of the main reasons for this is the fact that the materials being measured — human beings — are constantly changing and sometimes difficult to control. A chemist, on the other hand, is able to handle most of his samples in any way he chooses. Most of them remain fairly constant and uniform, and can be divided or mixed. With children such uniformity of sample and control of conditions is extremely difficult to attain. And yet great progress has been made in a relatively short period. We do measure human beings in many ways already, and the biologist is able to control and measure animals and plants — organisms that grow and change also. No one would say that measurement in biological science is impractical or useless. The biologist leans heavily upon quantitative methods for research and for practical work. Yet he deals with living, growing, changing organisms — a guinea pig or a cow or a tomato plant — which differ from boys and girls, as far as measurement is concerned, only in degree of complexity and susceptibility to control.

It should be said again that measurement is only a tool. It is a means to an end. Yet it is valuable to the extent that it helps teachers, counselors, administrators, and others connected with the schools to do a better job of educating children and adults. Few would question that measurement has done much to help appraise what we do in education, to take education out of the realm of opinion and provide many valuable facts, and to point out ways in which the job can be done better.

Much more remains to be done and can be done toward improving our existing instruments and techniques and helping teachers and others to make more effective use of what is already available. Many difficulties in educational measurement have already been overcome, and new progress is being made every day. Those obstacles and imperfections that remain should be regarded as a challenge to the ingenuity, resourcefulness, and competence of those who work in this field.

▶ LEARNING EXERCISES ◀

8. What are some common sources of error and difficulties in educational measurement? What can be done about them?

9. Compare measurement in education with measurement in physics. With measurement in biology. What are the important similarities? Differences?

10. What attitude should a teacher or counselor take toward the problems and difficulties of educational measurements?

TESTING — MEASUREMENT — EVALUATION

The three terms mentioned above are widely used, sometimes interchangeably, and are the source of some confusion. "Testing," as seems obvious, means the use of tests. It may mean testing the strength of materials, as in the case of textiles; it may mean testing a class in arithmetic, or it may mean testing an individual's intelligence. It usually involves the use of some specific instrument or set of instruments to determine a certain quality or trait, or a series of such qualities or traits. For example, one may use a test battery to measure achievement in a variety of school subjects. As generally used in education, the term "testing" has come to have a rather specific and somewhat limited connotation and, in some instances, a slightly unfavorable one. A tester is regarded by some persons (whether rightly or wrongly) as a technician who is more interested in the scores and statistics of the results of tests than in what the results mean in relation to the boys and girls who made them. There is probably some justification for this attitude on the part of teachers if, for example, the tests are given to their pupils by administrative order, and they have no voice in the matter. Often tests get a bad name undeservedly, since the fault usually lies in the way they are used.

"Measurement" is usually conceived of somewhat more broadly than testing. It is thought of as including a greater variety of instruments than testing. Rating scales, check lists or score cards, any devices which yield or can be made to yield quantitative results may be regarded as measuring instruments. Also, measurement often implies a somewhat broader interpretation of results than testing, though this difference is very difficult to define. It might be said that a measurement program generally is thought of as having broader and more pupil-centered objectives than a testing program.

"Evaluation" is conceived of as being the broadest of the three terms. It generally includes and often uses predominantly qualitative as well as quantitative instruments. That is, an evaluation program may include such devices and methods as anecdotal records, observation of children without any special attempt to make such observations quantitative, children's work samples, and the like. Such methods are not actually measurement as it has been defined above. They are dependent upon and largely limited to qualitative judgments, descriptive accounts, and opinions. An evaluation program may and often does include quantitative methods such as tests and scales, but it is not limited to these. Basically, the purpose of evaluation is to judge the worth of a program or procedure, usually in terms of how well it has achieved its objectives. For this purpose all appropriate techniques of gathering evidence may be used.

Hagen and Thorndike[10] define evaluation in education as "describing something in terms of selected attributes and judging the degree of acceptability or suitability of that which has been described." This "something . . . is typically (a) a total school program, (b) a curricular procedure, or (c) an individual or a group of individuals." Thus, in evaluating a method of teaching, one would first determine the attributes or criteria upon which its worth was to be judged. Next, one would develop and apply procedures for describing or measuring these attributes truly and accurately. Finally, the evidence yielded through the use of these procedures would be analyzed and synthesized as a basis for judging the worth of the teaching method. The procedure to be followed in evaluating individuals or a school would be essentially the same.

The term "evaluation" has found much favor at the elementary school level where conditions for the use of anecdotal records, qualitative judgments, etc. are more favorable. An outstanding characteristic of some evaluative techniques is that they are very time-consuming. If a teacher is to keep his records in a way that will give meaningful and fairly reliable results, a great deal of his time will be required. A teacher of an elementary grade with the same thirty-five pupils in his class daily for a year is in a much better position to make anecdotal records, to chart participation, observe behavior, and examine work samples than a high school teacher of mathematics or of English who meets as many as 150 or more different pupils for five periods per week.

The distinctions between the three terms may be more apparent than real. There is little doubt that testing programs have often been narrowly conceived. There can be little doubt, also, that tests have often been given and nothing done with the results. On the other hand, it seems equally true that the term "evaluation" is sometimes thought of as some magical and simple process which, without much effort or work on the part of anyone, provides answers to the most difficult and baffling educational problems. One important and basic principle should underlie all such programs or activities: the instruments or techniques should be chosen to fit the objectives to be measured or evaluated. Whether the

---

[10] Elizabeth P. Hagen and Robert L. Thorndike, "Evaluation," in Chester W. Harris (ed.), *Encyclopedia of Educational Research,* Third Edition (New York: The Macmillan Co., 1960), pp. 482–485.

process is called testing, measurement, or evaluation is not nearly so important as whether the progress or status of the learner with respect to the desired goal is being determined. A second principle of equal importance is that no technique is worth using unless the results it yields can be depended upon in every sense. An evaluation procedure, like any test, is useful only to the extent that it yields data which are accurate and which mean what they seem or are believed to mean.

As a greater number and variety of tests, scales, etc., have been produced, the importance of using different kinds of instruments and relating data from one to another has become more and more evident. The broad concept of evaluation has contributed materially to the development of this point of view. It has emphasized the need for a great variety of measures or samples of an individual's behavior and it has stressed the interrelatedness of such information in understanding and helping the individual. Evaluation has also called attention to the importance of traits or qualities or conditions not easily measured by objective tests.

The term "measurement" is used throughout to express the area or field with which this book is concerned. The instruments commonly used in education today — tests, scales, inventories, rating scales — are all considered and discussed. The major share of space is given to tests since they greatly exceed in number and variety all other types of instruments. Some attention is given to evaluation procedures also, but this is limited to consideration of the applications of measurement in such procedures. A more complete treatment of the subject would go beyond the scope of this book. However, it is considered in more detail in some of the references at the end of this chapter.

▶ LEARNING EXERCISES ◀

11. As a curriculum specialist, you wish to evaluate the program or curriculum in your high school for training stenographers. How would you proceed?

12. The expression has been used in some comparisons that "differences are of 'degree' rather than 'kind.' " What does this mean? Does it have any application to the question of distinctions between the three terms, "testing," "measurement," and "evaluation"? To what was said earlier about the terms "quantitative" and "qualitative"?

PURPOSES OF THIS BOOK

Basically, the purpose of this book is orientation. It is presumed that most students in a first course in educational measurement have had little or no systematic presentation of the principles and practices in this field. Consequently, the book assumes no background other than the usual introductory courses in education required of those preparing to teach. It does assume a professional attitude and a willingness to work and learn in a field that is perhaps more technical than most undergraduate courses in education.

Another important purpose of this book is to assist teachers and others who devise their own tests and evaluative devices. Every teacher makes tests and examinations of his own. This is a part of the job of teaching — a necessary and important part. It is essential that this be done as well as possible, if only to insure that the least possible injustice be done to the individual pupil. More positively, adequate measurement skills are important because without them it is impossible to determine whether or not we are making progress toward our educational goals. If we are making progress we must know how much progress is being made, not only by groups but also by individuals. The skill of the teacher, counselor, or school psychologist in devising and using measuring instruments plays an important role. Therefore, one of the major purposes of this book is to provide the principles and the "know-how" so that those who have the responsibility of making examinations and other measuring instruments will be helped to do this better.

A further purpose of the book is to present in an elementary way the tools and techniques for the intelligent use and interpretation of the results of standardized and other measurements. Moreover, it is the particular aim of this book to show how such results can be put to practical use in the school for the benefit of boys and girls and for the improvement of the educational process. Too often a testing program is undertaken with great enthusiasm, and considerable time and money are given to it — only to have the tests selected, administered, and scored, and then filed away or tied up neatly in bundles, scarcely to be looked at again. Unless the results of tests are put to use the testing process becomes wasteful and pointless.

In order to use tests and measurements effectively, it is necessary to know what materials are available. This book does not pretend to make an exhaustive survey of all available educational measuring instruments since such a survey would be quite impractical. However, it does include descriptions and discussions of methods and devices in the major areas such as achievement, intelligence, and personality. Again, let it be understood that no attempt is made to describe or even list all available tests in such subjects or areas. The purpose here is simply to describe prototypes or typical examples so that the beginner in this field will be able to gain some knowledge and understanding of the kinds of instruments that have been developed and found useful.

ANNOTATED BIBLIOGRAPHY

1. Gerberich, J. Raymond; Greene, Harry A.; and Jorgensen, Albert N. *Measurement and Evaluation in the Modern School.* New York: David McKay Co., Inc., 1962. Chapter 1. A brief introduction to the field of educational measurement and evaluation. Definitions of terms, the background and status of measurement, the relationship of outcomes to measurement, and the significance and scope of educational measurement are discussed.

2. Jordan, A. M. *Measurement in Education.* New York: McGraw-Hill Book Co., Inc., 1953. Chapter 1. A brief discussion of the problems involved in educational measurement. Includes a description of the major types of measuring instruments used in education.

3. Leeper, Robert R. (ed.). "Testing and Evaluation," *Educational Leadership,* 20:2–37, 43, 55, 57, 76, 80; October, 1962. This issue of the official journal of the Association for Supervision and Curriculum Development of the National Education Association is given over entirely to the subject of testing and evaluation. A series of articles by measurement and curriculum specialists, administrators, and researchers discuss significant and timely aspects of this topic in a practical and objective way.

4. Remmers, H. H.; Gage, N. L.; and Rummel, J. Francis. *Practical Introduction to Measurement and Evaluation,* Revised Edition. New York: Harper & Row, Publishers, 1960. Chapter 1. A discussion of the purposes of evaluation and measurement in the schools.

5. Ross, C. C., and Stanley, Julian C. *Measurement in Today's Schools,* Third Edition. New York: Prentice-Hall, Inc., 1954. Chapter 1. A discussion of measurement in science and in education with comparisons and contrasts interestingly presented.

6. Thorndike, Robert L., and Hagen, Elizabeth. *Measurement and Evaluation in Psychology and Education,* Second Edition. New York: John Wiley & Sons, Inc., 1961. Chapter 1. A brief historical and philosophical introduction to modern concepts of educational measurement. Emphasizes the need for formulating objectives before attempting to measure, and for interpreting test results, no matter how precise measurement may make them.

7. Weaver, Warren (ed.). *The Scientists Speak.* New York: Boni and Gaer, 1947. Chapters 4 and 5. Outstanding scientists discuss new methods of observation and measurement in the physical and biological sciences.

8. Wrightstone, J. Wayne; Justman, Joseph; and Robbins, Irving. *Evaluation in Modern Education.* New York: American Book Company, 1956. Chapters 1, 2, 3, and 4. A complete and thorough presentation of the background and nature of the evaluation concept, including descriptions of techniques and discussions of the administrative aspects of an evaluation program.

2

The Development of

Educational Measurement

It may be assumed that teachers have always measured or evaluated the work of their pupils. Evidence of early records indicates that this was generally done through personal observation, oral questioning, and subjective judgment by the teacher. However, some responsibility for evaluating the progress of pupils has traditionally been shared by citizens other than the teachers. It has been customary, in this country at least, to have a school committee of lay citizens in each community who would be responsible for the local schools. From such committees have evolved our present-day school boards. One of the functions of the early school committees was to visit the schools in their communities or districts at least once a year for inspectional purposes. During these inspections it was customary for the members of the committee to examine the pupils by asking them questions.

The Boston Survey

The report of a school committee which visited the English High School in Boston in 1845 indicates that the members of the committee examined the pupils in algebra, geometry, and French, and reported that "the public have no reason to be dissatisfied with its [the school's] present condition."[1]

A few years before this time Horace Mann had been appointed Secretary of the Massachusetts State Board of Education. He soon was going about the state pointing out weaknesses as he observed them in the public ("common") schools. Naturally, the schoolmasters and the local school committees resented his criticisms, and some thirty teachers and committee members in Boston banded together for the purpose of resisting and refuting him. The upshot of the quarrel was an agreement to prepare written examination questions in history, arithmetic, geography, definitions (vocabulary), grammar, natural philosophy (science), and astronomy, to be answered by the pupils. A total of 154 questions were prepared, and these were answered in whole or in part by 530 pupils selected from a total of 7,526. It is said that this group of 530 pupils represented "the flower of the Boston Public Schools."[2] The average age of the pupils examined was thirteen years and six months.

Listed below are some typical questions, chosen at random, from this examination:

    [1] What do you understand by the Norman Conquest?
    [2] What is the square root of $\frac{5}{6}$ of $\frac{4}{5}$ of $\frac{4}{7}$ of $\frac{7}{8}$?
    [3] Name the principal lakes in North America.
    [4] Define "monody."
    [5] What is the difference between an active and a neuter verb?
    [6] Explain the hydrostatic press.
    [7] What causes an eclipse of the sun?

Giving the same written examinations to a sample of all pupils at the same school level in Boston was a novel procedure. Indeed, it appears that this was the first recorded instance of such a survey anywhere.

The results were eagerly awaited. We are told that the committee scored the papers under uniform conditions and tabulated the answers "question by question and school by school."[3]

The results fully justified the criticisms by Mann and were a keen disappointment to the school committee. They revealed great inequalities among

---

[1] Otis W. Caldwell and Stuart A. Courtis, *Then and Now in Education, 1845–1923* (New York: Harcourt, Brace & World, Inc., 1925), p. 4.
  [2] *Ibid.*, p. 171.   [3] *Ibid.*, p. 7.

schools and startling ignorance on the part of many pupils. We are told that Mann did not take advantage of his opportunity to ridicule or castigate his critics, but retained an impeccable professional attitude in commenting upon the findings. He did recognize the value of the method employed in examining the pupils, though it was to be almost half a century before this method of evaluation would again be a focus of real interest among educators.

Although there seems to be no record of anything like the Boston Survey in the United States for nearly fifty years thereafter, we are told of an English schoolmaster, one Reverend George Fisher, who reported having constructed what he called a Scale Book. The account of this is given in an article published in 1864 by E. B. Chadwick.[4] In his Scale Book the Reverend Mr. Fisher included a scale of handwriting against which samples of children's handwriting could be graded, a standard list of spelling words, and questions in mathematics, navigation, Scripture knowledge, grammar and composition, French, general history, drawing, and practical science. Thus he provided examinations by which any pupil could be tested and graded, not only in each subject or area, but also on the total and the average of all or any combination of subjects.

The work of Fisher, as in the case of Mann and the Boston School Committee, made no great impression or had no immediately discernible or lasting effect on practice in the schools, either in England or in the United States.

Measurement of Individual Differences

The next important figure in the development of measurement in education was an English scientist, Sir Francis Galton (1822–1911). He was one of the first to sense the implications of the fact that individuals differ intellectually and emotionally as well as physically. It is hard to believe today that the schoolmaster of colonial times had so little appreciation or understanding of individual differences in children. If one child did not learn as easily and as well as another the difference was explained as "laziness," and the way to cure that was by the use of corporal punishment. Galton's work was very influential in changing such ideas. He demonstrated both by ingenious tests and by statistical methods that individuals differ in physical, sensory-motor, and personality traits. He also laid the groundwork for modern statistical methods, without which progress in

---

[4] E. B. Chadwick, "Statistics of Educational Results," *The Museum, a Quarterly Magazine of Education, Literature and Science,* 3:429–84, January, 1864. Original not seen. Taken from a report entitled "Educational Measurements of Fifty Years Ago," based on a communication from E. L. Thorndike, *Journal of Educational Psychology,* 4:551, November, 1913.

educational measurement, and particularly in standardized tests, would have been impossible.

An American psychologist, James McKeen Cattell, contributed a great deal to the measurement movement in the United States toward the end of the nineteenth century. He became intensely interested in the problem of individual differences and made a number of experiments in sensory-motor abilities. For example, he developed a variety of simple tests to measure the length of time it takes a given individual to press down a telegraph key after a light flashes, the rate of tapping, keenness of hearing and vision, etc. Cattell worked on the theory that differences in sensory keenness, speed of reaction, and similar abilities or traits would reflect differences in intelligence. The results were disappointing in that no clear relationship was found between scores on such tests and intelligence as judged by success in school or college. He is credited, however, with being one of the pioneers in the measurement movement and the first to use the term "mental tests." Cattell and Galton both were more interested in measuring intelligence than in school achievement, but their ideas and work had significant and lasting influence on developments in the entire field of educational measurement.

In 1895, almost fifty years after the Boston experiment, J. M. Rice,[5] in an endeavor to determine what teachers in the schools were actually accomplishing, made up a list of fifty spelling words to be used as a test. These were given to more than sixteen thousand pupils in Grades 4 to 8. The results showed such wide variation that Rice devised another test in which the spelling words were used in sentences; more than thirteen thousand children were examined under his personal direction. Finally, a further test was devised by Rice whereby a story, accompanied by a picture, was read to the pupils, after which they were asked to write a composition about it. Their papers were then checked for spelling errors. Although our interest here is in the measurement aspects of his researches, it is interesting to note that Rice found great variation from class to class, school to school, and city to city, regardless of such factors as time devoted to study, location of the school, and efficiency of the teacher.

Rice conducted similar studies with tests of his own in arithmetic and language over a period of nearly a decade. Because of the scientific objectivity of his approach and his skill in devising measuring instruments, he stands as a pioneer in the field of measurement, though the significance of his contributions is not always fully appreciated.

The work of men like Mann, Galton, Cattell, Rice, and others, the grad-

---

[5] J. M. Rice, *Scientific Management in Education* (New York: Hinds, Noble, and Eldredge, 1914), Chaps. 5–11.

ual application and adaptation of scientific methods of measurement in the social sciences, the great increases in school and college enrollment, and the development of a body of knowledge and principles for the training of teachers — all these, as well as other factors, combined to make the time ripe for new methods of measurement in schools and colleges toward the beginning of the twentieth century.

It is impossible to say which of these factors were causes and which were effects. Certainly the greatly increased enrollments rendered almost impossible the oral and individual examining of the early days. Now that the typical secondary school teacher met 150 pupils a day instead of fifty, the older, more personalized methods of appraisal had to be abandoned. Indeed, it is unusual if today's high school teacher is able to learn the names of all his pupils before he gets a new group.

The scientific movement has influenced education as it has everything else in our world today. It has given us new techniques of measurement and appraisal to meet changing conditions in the schools. New practices in measurement have affected curriculum and methods, and changes in these have in turn encouraged improvements in measurement. Today, teaching and measurement are complementary, interdependent, and almost inseparable.

▶ LEARNING EXERCISES ◀

1. What ideas or procedures used in the Boston survey are exemplified in present-day educational measurement?

2. What is your reaction to the sample questions used in the Boston survey? Could today's eighth-graders answer them?

3. Name one contribution to educational measurement of each of the following: Galton, Cattell, Rice.

FROM 1900 TO WORLD WAR I

The field of measurement was dominated and shaped by the work of a few great minds in the first two decades of this century. One of the most outstanding contributors to the field was Edward Lee Thorndike. Arriving at Columbia University just before the close of the nineteenth century, he soon gained a position of leadership which he held for more than thirty years in the field of educational psychology and measurement. His first important contribution to the measurement field was a book on statistical methods.[6] Though no longer in use today as a textbook, it was the first of its kind. In this book Thorndike presented a compendium of available knowledge on the uses of statistical methods as applied to the measurement of human abilities and traits. It is perhaps significant that no other book on the subject appeared for more than ten years.

As in the case of Galton and of Cattell, Thorndike's interest in measurement grew out of his appreciation of the significance of individual differences. In addition to this interest, he possessed to an outstanding degree the ability to see clearly the implications and essentials of a problem or situation, and a wealth of ideas for designing experiments and tests. Thorndike produced a number of tests and scales, including a scale for measuring quality of handwriting, another for measuring quality of drawings, an intelligence test for use at the high school level, and several other tests. In addition to these contributions and his many articles and books on measurement, Thorndike inspired and guided many graduate students to significant contributions in the field. Among the early contributions made by his students were an arithmetic test devised by Stone in 1908,[7] the Hillegas scale for measuring quality in English composition,[8] and Buckingham's spelling scale.[9]

The First Successful Intelligence Test

It was during this same period that one of the most significant contributions in intelligence testing was made by a French psychologist, Alfred Binet. Binet had become interested in mental measurement through his work with children in the schools of Paris. He had observed the great differences in mental acuity or learning ability existing among these children, and he believed that it should be possible to devise some easily administered tests that would give accurate data on the extent of these differences. He became especially interested in finding some simple, rapid, and precise method of identifying mentally retarded children and measuring the degree of such retardation. Although many psychologists, both in this country and abroad, were interested in the measurement of in-

---

[6] Edward L. Thorndike, *An Introduction to the Theory of Mental and Social Measurements* (New York: The Science Press, 1904), 212 pp.

[7] C. W. Stone, *Arithmetical Abilities and Some Factors Determining Them,* Contributions to Education, No. 19 (New York: Teachers College, Columbia University, 1908).

[8] M. B. Hillegas, "A Scale for the Measurement of Quality in English Composition by Young People," *Teachers College Record,* 13:331–84, September, 1912.

[9] B. R. Buckingham, *Spelling Ability: Its Measurement and Distribution,* Contributions to Education, No. 59 (New York: Teachers College, Columbia University, 1913).

telligence, none had succeeded in devising adequate measurement techniques or methods.

After years of study and experimenting, Binet and his assistant, Théodore Simon, published an article in 1905 in which they presented a series of tests to measure the level of mental development in children. The article aroused world-wide interest, and many workers at once began experimenting with Binet's tests and corresponding with him about them. In 1908 Binet and Simon published an improved version of their scale, and in 1911 Binet published another revision. Unfortunately, he died soon thereafter.

In another chapter there is a more adequate discussion of the theoretical considerations underlying the work of Binet and some of its implications for mental measurement. At this point it is enough to say that his work constituted one of the most important milestones in the development of mental tests. His was the first successful method for measuring intelligence and expressing individual differences in accurate, quantitative terms. Indeed, Binet's methods and materials for the measurement of intelligence form the basis of the general approach in use today.

Tests of Personality and Character

While the work in measuring school achievement and intelligence was going on, early attempts toward the measurement of emotions, interests, and personality were also being made. Although many writers suggest that such endeavors came later than those in the measurement of intelligence and achievement, this apparently is not the case. There is evidence that Galton used rating scales as early as 1883. There is also some indication that a rating device was known of and used, in much the same manner in which rating scales are used today, even earlier than 1883.[10]

The so-called "free association" tests have also been known for nearly a century.[11] In these tests, the person tested is presented with a number of stimulus words, to each of which he responds by naming the first word that comes to mind. His responses are analyzed for emotional coloring and also for variations in the speed of response. That is, a response to the word "teacher" of "kind" or "nice," reveals something different from the response, "ugly" or "mean." Also, a response which comes slowly or hesitantly may indicate an emotional block which is perhaps significant, and

[10] Douglas G. Ellson and Elizabeth Cox Ellson, "Historical Note on the Rating Scale," *Psychological Bulletin,* 50:383–84, September, 1953.
[11] Galton outlined experiments using the free association technique as early as 1879.

which is probably not present in the subject who responds in the normal amount of time.

Other methods which, though unreliable, have been used for some time in judging personality are based on physical and motor attributes. For example, elaborate systems of evaluating personality and intellect on the basis of body size and proportions have been devised. Many persons, among them some psychologists, are intrigued by the idea of using handwriting as a measure of personality, and few persons can say that they never judge an individual's personality by his face. It is but a short step from such systems to the pseudo sciences of palmistry and phrenology. None of these systems has ever become established or accepted by reputable psychologists, at least in the United States, for the advocates of these questionable methods have never succeeded in demonstrating that their methods can produce reliable and valid results. In fact, when such methods have been subjected to objective, empirical tests the results have been consistently disappointing.

By 1915 the basic principles and techniques of educational and psychological measurement were beginning to become established. The fundamentals of statistical method were known, at least to the leaders in this field, and would soon be widely disseminated. Some important pioneering had been done, notably by a few outstanding men such as Thorndike and Binet. The stage was set for a new era in the development of testing, and as the United States entered World War I in 1917 real progress was being made.

▶ **LEARNING EXERCISES** ◀

4. Thorndike wrote, "Whatever exists at all exists in some amount. To know it thoroughly involves knowing its quantity as well as its quality." (See page 16 of *The Measurement of Educational Products,* listed in the annotated bibliography at the end of this chapter.) What are the implications of this statement for educational measurement?

5. Binet at one time studied medicine, but became a psychologist. Of what value might his medical training have been to him in his great work of measuring intelligence? Might it have been a handicap in some respects? If so how?

6. Graphology, phrenology, and palmistry have certain objectives and techniques in common. What are they? How would you test the validity of claims made for these systems?

FROM WORLD WAR I TO 1930

The Army Tests

When the United States entered the War in 1917, it soon became apparent that methods in use up to that time for appraising and classifying men were hopelessly inadequate. Hundreds of thousands of men were being drafted and within the short time of a month or two they had to be examined and assigned to duty. No instruments were known which would serve the purpose quickly and accurately. The Binet scale and its American revisions were individual examinations which required the complete time and attention of a trained examiner for an hour or more to test one man. Obviously, this was too slow. Out of the need for a more expedient procedure came *Army Alpha,* the first group test of intelligence. The War Department requested a number of prominent psychologists to produce such a test, and this was accomplished within the remarkably brief time of a few months.

The committee was fortunate in having placed at its disposal without reservation the work of Arthur S. Otis. Dr. Otis had made considerable progress in the development of a group test of intelligence, and it was largely his work which became the basis for *Army Alpha. Army Alpha* was a verbal test requiring approximately sixth-grade reading ability. Since many of the drafted men could not read at that level — some not at all — and others could not write, read, or speak English, another group test, *Army Beta,* was devised. This test required no reading, and even the directions could be given in pantomime. Nearly two million men were tested by one or the other of these examinations in 1917 and 1918.

At the same time, rating scales were devised for the army's use in classifying officers and men according to various qualities, and a personality test known as the *Personal Data Sheet* was devised by R. S. Woodworth for use by the army in identifying and studying neurotic draftees.

Some attempts were also made by the armed forces to develop tests for determining mechanical, clerical, and various other aptitudes, though these efforts did not receive the same attention that the other types of tests did, and the results were therefore less satisfactory.

The work in test development for the armed forces in World War I gave tremendous impetus to the development and use of tests in the schools. After the War, *Army Alpha* and *Army Beta* were released for general use and administered to many thousands of high school and college students. Within a few years a number of group tests of intelligence appeared, some patterned quite closely after the army test, others showing much originality. Among these new tests were the *Otis Group Intelligence Scale*,[12] the *Miller Mental Abilities Test*,[13] and the *Terman Group Test*.[14]

Important Early Publications on Measurement

During this period numerous books and monographs on educational measurement also began to appear. The first such book was published in 1916.[15] This was quickly followed by a more comprehensive volume in 1917.[16] At the same time other books on statistical methods in education began to appear. The first of these, by Rugg,[17] was published in 1917.

In 1918 there appeared a report that presented a stock-taking of the accomplishments of the early period and some predictions for the future.[18] This volume, assembled by leaders in the field — each one contributing a chapter dealing with some significant area or problem, such as the uses of measurement in the schools, existing tests and standards, etc. — was probably the most significant publication in educational measurement up to that time.

Survey Tests

Another important contribution of this period was the development of survey tests. Such tests consist of batteries of achievement tests in several common branches of instruction, particularly language, arithmetic, social studies, and science. The first standardized survey test was the *Stanford Achievement Test*.[19] Designed primarily for use at the elementary level, this test has continued through various editions and revisions to the present day. Not long after its publication a similar survey test for high schools[20]

[12] Arthur S. Otis, *Otis Group Intelligence Scale* (New York: Harcourt, Brace & World, Inc., 1918).

[13] W. S. Miller, *Miller Mental Abilities Test* (New York: Harcourt, Brace & World, Inc., 1921).

[14] Lewis M. Terman, *Terman Group Test of Mental Ability* (New York: Harcourt, Brace & World, Inc., 1920).

[15] Daniel Starch, *Educational Measurement* (New York: The Macmillan Co., 1916).

[16] W. S. Monroe, J. C. DeVoss, and F. J. Kelly, *Educational Tests and Measurements* (Boston: Houghton Mifflin Company, 1917).

[17] Harold O. Rugg, *Statistical Methods Applied to Education* (Boston: Houghton Mifflin Company, 1917).

[18] National Society for the Study of Education, *The Measurement of Educational Products,* Seventeenth Yearbook of the Society, Part II (Chicago: The Society [distributed by the University of Chicago Press], 1918).

[19] Truman L. Kelley, Giles M. Ruch, and Lewis M. Terman, *Stanford Achievement Test* (New York: Harcourt, Brace & World, Inc., 1923).

[20] G. M. Ruch, *Iowa High School Content Examination* (Iowa City, Iowa: Bureau of Educational Research and Service, University of Iowa, 1925).

made its appearance. These tests were followed in a few years by a number of others.

Personality Tests

Some significant beginnings in the measurement of personality were made during the period from World War I to 1930. Woodworth's *Personal Data Sheet,*[21] previously mentioned, consisted of a list of questions based on common neurotic symptoms, and was useful in identifying maladjusted men. This was a prototype of many of the so-called personality inventories.

One of the best known early measures of personality was the *Rorschach Ink Blot Test,* which was first published in Bern, Switzerland, in 1921, under the title of *Psychodiagnostics: A Diagnostic Test Based on Perception.* The *Rorschach* is still widely used today. Also among the early personality tests was the *Downey Will Temperament Test.*[22] In this test, Downey attempted to explore certain aspects of personality such as flexibility, finality of judgment, and interest in detail, by having the subject write or copy materials under different conditions. For example, the subject was asked to write as fast as he could, disguise his handwriting, or write with his eyes closed. Another early test, by Pressey,[23] was designed to measure emotional tone or feeling.

A number of tests of character or ethical discrimination also appeared during this period, such as the tests of trustworthiness by Voelker.[24] These tests were designed to measure the effect of special training and instruction in trustworthiness through testing the tendency toward overstatement, the resistance to opportunities for cheating, and so forth.

Aptitude Tests

During the period under review some tests of aptitude also made their appearance. Some of the earliest work was done in musical aptitude by

---

[21] R. S. Woodworth, *Personal Data Sheet* (Chicago: C. H. Stoelting Company, 1918).

[22] June E. Downey, *The Will Temperament and Its Testing* (New York: Harcourt, Brace & World, Inc., 1923).

[23] S. L. Pressey, "A Group Scale for Investigating the Emotions," *Journal of Abnormal Psychology,* 16:55–65, 1921.

[24] Paul F. Voelker, *The Function of Ideals and Attitudes in Social Education,* Contributions to Education, No. 112 (New York: Teachers College, Columbia University, 1921).

Seashore,[25] in mechanical aptitude by Stenquist,[26] and in clerical aptitude by Thurstone.[27]

During the 1920's a number of aptitude tests in the fields just mentioned and in other fields appeared in various forms. Without going into detail about such tests at this point, it may be said that generally they consist of exercises of a type familiar respectively to the musician, the artist, the mechanic, the clerk. For example, the *Seashore Test* consists of exercises dealing with such elements as pitch discrimination, rhythm, and duration and intensity or loudness of tones. It may be said that by 1930 the fundamentals of the approach to the measurement of aptitudes in specific areas or fields had become fairly well established.

A number of other factors contributed to the development of educational measurement during this period. Among those which might be mentioned is the educational survey. Beginning in the 1920's, some of the larger cities and a few states employed teams of experts to make thorough surveys and appraisals of the school systems. Although these surveys were largely concerned with school plant, administrative organization, qualifications of staff, and related matters, many of the surveys made use of tests of intelligence and achievement to measure the efficiency of curriculum and methods, amount of retardation, and comparative achievement. This use of tests encouraged the development of new instruments and extended the use of existing ones.

Statewide testing programs also stimulated the development and use of the objective, standardized test. A number of states began, and have continued to the present, testing programs involving most, if not all, of the pupils enrolled in the elementary grades.

Other developments that originated during this period and which undoubtedly contributed to the growth of the modern measurement movement were the establishment of educational journals devoted at least in part to articles dealing with measurement; the organization of professional societies whose membership included many persons interested and working in the field of measurement; and the development of bureaus of educational research in larger universities, city school systems, and state departments of education. These bureaus, especially the ones in higher institutions, contributed much to the development of new instruments and

25 C. E. Seashore, *The Psychology of Musical Talent* (New York: Silver, Burdett and Company, 1919), 288 pp.

26 J. L. Stenquist, *Stenquist Mechanical Aptitude Tests* (New York: Harcourt, Brace & World, Inc., 1922).

27 L. L. Thurstone, "Standardized Tests for Office Clerks," *Journal of Applied Psychology,* 3:248–51, 1919.

techniques of measurement through research carried on by staff members and graduate students.

In a sense, this period represents some of the best and some of the worst in the era of modern educational measurement. It was characterized by great activity, both in the development of measuring instruments, and in their widespread application. In the use of the new instruments educators tended to be impressed with the values and advantages of the instruments and were less aware than we are today of their inherent limitations. Probably the same thing may be said of many new ideas or inventions; the early stages are nearly always characterized by great enthusiasm and a lack of awareness of shortcomings. The latter usually become evident with time and extensive use. If the new ideas have real merit, they will be constantly refined and improved through trial, experimentation, and critical study.

▶ LEARNING EXERCISES ◀

7. By 1930, most of the types of educational and mental tests known and used today were quite well established. Name and briefly describe these early models.

8. What factors during the 1920's contributed substantially to the development of, and growth of interest in, educational measurement?

9. Name some factors or occurrences during this period, which, while related to the area of measurement, failed to advance or improve measurement techniques.

FROM 1930 THROUGH WORLD WAR II

The 1930's may be regarded as a period of questioning and doubt. As more and more objective tests, both teacher-made and standardized, were used, some unfavorable reactions were inevitable. Many test specialists and users began to raise questions about the new tests, particularly regarding the limitations of scope. There was a feeling that although the tests were generally good, they failed to measure some of the most fundamental educational objectives. Some tests were criticized for being too specific and for not testing the pupil's ability to organize his knowledge and present an acceptable written statement of it.

Although objective, standardized tests continued to be published in great quantities and one of the largest organizations devoted to such activities, the Cooperative Test Service, was established about 1930, the movement to develop other kinds of measures made steady progress. A number of leaders in this field, together with such organizations as the Progressive Education Association, became strongly identified with the evaluation movement. The new work in evaluation emphasized the importance of measuring more than knowledge and skills. More attention was focused on measurement of such outcomes of instruction as attitudes, interests, appreciations, and the ability to use the scientific method. Furthermore, the newer techniques emphasized the importance of supplementing standardized tests with locally made tests in order to measure fairly those areas emphasized by the individual teacher — areas which the standardized test might treat inadequately or not at all.

It is likely that Gestalt psychology, which emphasizes the interrelatedness of the parts of a whole, also had a marked influence on teaching and measurement during this period. Although few teachers are likely to have had a thorough knowledge of the wide implications of the Gestalt school of psychology, most of them assimilated something of the basic principles of the Gestalt school and formed therefrom a concept of "the whole child," which became almost a cliché.

Nevertheless, this concept has had a generally beneficial effect on educational measurement. It has served to remind all who deal with human beings that each person is an individual unlike any other and that there are many different facets and aspects of his personality, all of which combine to make him the person he is. In order to help an individual we must understand him, and in order to understand him we must know as much about him as possible — about his knowledge, interests, health, family, ability, and experience. It is essential, moreover, to try to understand the relationship of these various aspects to each other. Thus, it can be argued that in order to know as much as possible about a person, *more,* not *fewer,* tests and measurements should be used. The more aspects of an individual we are able to measure, the more complete and rounded will be our knowledge and understanding of him, and, therefore, the better we should be able to appraise his capabilities and potentialities and help him to realize them.

Measurement and World War II

As in World War I, the use of measurement was greatly stimulated by World War II. Though no contributions comparable in originality and uniqueness to *Army Alpha* and *Army Beta* were produced as a result of the Second World War, testing became widespread in all the armed forces, both in amount and variety. A great deal of work was done in devising effective aptitude tests for the placement of personnel in such specialties as radio, navigation, and radar. The procedures set up for appraisal and assignment of men and women were far more systematic than those which had been developed in the First World War. A large amount of research on the nature of human abilities was conducted by the armed services, and much experimental work in the development of tests, rating scales, and other assessment techniques was carried on.

The War also stimulated interest in the use of clinical instruments, especially projective tests like the *Rorschach*. Following the War, the federal government approved and supported the establishment of programs for the training of clinical psychologists in many universities.

The Guidance Movement

As early as 1920 and even before, some tests were devised for use in educational and vocational guidance. Some of these, such as the aptitude tests, have been mentioned. The establishment of federal-aided vocational programs in agriculture, trade, industry, and homemaking stimulated the guidance movement, as did the expansion of the high school curriculum. As more and more adolescents entered secondary school, and as the curriculum became more varied, the need for more systematic and effective counseling increased.

Probably the greatest impetus to guidance and counseling came as a result of World War II, however. With millions of men and women being inducted into military service, the task of classifying and assigning each to the kind of duty which he or she could perform efficiently with a minimum of training became of paramount importance. It was imperative that rapid and reasonably accurate classifying methods be devised. As a result of this need, thousands of men and women became classification officers or specialists. Considering the number of cases they had to deal with, the great variety of specialties which had to be filled, and the inevitable lack of knowledge and precedent, these specialists did a remarkable job.

All this — the changes in the secondary school population and curriculum, the development of tests of aptitude, and the demands of the War — gave to guidance practices a momentum and growth which have continued to the present time. Such growth is reflected in the vastly increased use of and need for tests and measuring instruments of all kinds in counseling, as well as in other areas.

▶ **LEARNING EXERCISES** ◀

10. What were some of the main criticisms of tests and testing which developed in the 1930's and 1940's?

11. Compare the contributions to the measurement field of World War I and World War II.

12. The guidance movement of today is a fairly recent development. Has the improvement of measurement techniques influenced this? If so, in what ways?

FROM WORLD WAR II TO THE PRESENT

Since 1945 the development and use of standardized tests has continued to increase. Their use in education, business and industry, the civil service, and the armed forces grows without ceasing. However, it would be difficult to mention a significant breakthrough in method or technique that could be clearly ascribed to this period. Research has been directed primarily to the exploration of the possibilities of refining and extending existing methods and the application of rather technical statistical techniques to current instruments. Nevertheless, a number of potentially important developments should be mentioned. One of these is the increasing use of factor analysis, a statistical technique based on intercorrelations between presumably related tests. The method is not new. One of the earliest if not the first published record of its use appeared in 1904. In this interesting paper, the English statistician, Spearman,[28] reviewed previous work on the measurement of intelligence and advanced for the first time his theory of a "factor" of *general intelligence* and some specific "factors" of *special abilities*. Forty years later the *Chicago Tests of Primary Mental Abilities*[29] were published. They represented another milestone in the development and application of factor analysis to mental testing.

We shall have more to say about this in a later chapter. In recent years the technique has been used with various types of tests, including intelligence, aptitude, and personality tests and in measurement in areas of great current interest, such as creativity. It seems safe to predict that the uses of factor analysis will expand in the search for ways of refining existing tests and in the development of new ones.

[28] Charles Spearman, " 'General Intelligence' Objectively Determined and Measured," *American Journal of Psychology,* 15:201–93, April, 1904.
[29] L. L. Thurstone and Thelma Gwinn Thurstone, *Chicago Tests of Primary Mental Abilities* (Chicago: Science Research Associates, Inc., 1941–47).

Another recent development, under government leadership, has had, and will probably continue to have, substantial influence on testing by schools. In 1958, Congress passed the National Defense Education Act, which provides federal funds for the establishment of programs of testing, counseling, and guidance in secondary schools. The purpose of the testing programs, as stated in the Act, is to identify students with outstanding aptitudes and abilities. Obviously, this requires wide-scale testing. There can be no doubt that this law has encouraged and stimulated many schools to inaugurate testing programs where none at all or perhaps haphazard and unsystematic ones existed before. In addition, money is provided for programs of guidance and counseling in the schools and for grants to institutions of higher education to establish institutes for the training of guidance and counseling personnel. Since the work of such personnel requires the use of tests, these provisions too will almost certainly stimulate the use of such instruments in the schools.

Still another factor in the use of measurement that has assumed increasing importance is the large-scale testing program. This type of program may be national or statewide in scope. It may be carried out by public or private agencies, and for a variety of purposes. One of the earliest of such programs, previously mentioned, was the Regents' examinations in New York. Of long standing also is the work of the College Entrance Examination Board. More recent samples of programs of this nature are the *National Teacher Examinations,* the National Merit Scholarship Program, and the American College Testing Program. The state legislatures of California and Pennsylvania have recently enacted laws requiring annual mental and achievement testing in certain grades in all public schools, both elementary and secondary.

Increasing enrollments and the growing pressure for admission to college and university have contributed substantially to the development of such programs. As pressures have mounted, higher education institutions have become increasingly selective and have turned more and more to the use of standardized tests as an aid in selection. This is particularly true of professional schools — medical, dental, nursing, to name some outstanding examples — which regularly use the results of examinations, generally comprehensive and objective in nature, along with other data, to select applicants who will be admitted.

This great increase in the use of objective, standardized tests has not gone unchallenged. The tests have been criticized as being inadequate, limited in scope, and, at best, imperfect. The programs have been attacked for placing too much reliance on scores determined by a few hours of testing. Critics have complained that our students are being "tested to death"; that some tests, such as personality tests, constitute an invasion of privacy; and it has even been suggested that we should have the use of all standardized tests regulated by a national board.[30]

As a result of such attacks, many thoughtful persons, including educators, have begun to examine the desirability and propriety of such extensive use of tests and, even more, the dependence placed on the results.

Undoubtedly such criticisms are having and will continue having some effect. However, it is only fair to say that reputable test publishers, specialists in measurement, and writers in the field have consistently stressed that the tests *are* fallible and must be used with full regard for their limitations. Furthermore, statistical techniques have long been known and used in assessing the extent of error in such measurements or conversely their reliability and validity. That these cautions have sometimes been ignored is unfortunate, but such neglect is the fault neither of the tests nor those who develop them. It is the responsibility of the critics (most of whom are laymen or non-professionals), on the other hand, to use great care in informing themselves fully and thoroughly on the entire subject before formulating and expressing their views. They should also make certain that these views are based on fact and that they deal with major issues.

In summary, it seems evident that a number of important developments in the field of measurement have been taking place since World War II. Among these are (1) the increasing application of factor analysis to problems of test planning; (2) the support, both financial and promotional, by the federal government of testing programs at the local level under the National Defense Education Act of 1958; (3) the increase in the so-called external testing programs, sponsored by both public and private agencies; and (4) the growing public interest in the testing movement and the clamor of its critics.

In measurement, as in life in the world today, this is an interesting and challenging time. The age in which we live is characterized by rapid change, by conflicting views and goals, and by many new and interesting ideas. Measurement must change and grow, must keep pace with the times, or fall into limbo. It has been equal to the challenge in the past. It can and will be in the days ahead.

---

[30] See, for example: Joint Committee on Testing of the American Association of School Administrators, National Education Association, *Testing, Testing, Testing* (Washington: The Association, 1962); Banesh Hoffman, *The Tyranny of Testing* (New York: The Crowell-Collier Publishing Co., 1962); and Hillel Black, *They Shall Not Pass* (New York: William Morrow and Company, 1963).

▶ **LEARNING EXERCISES** ◀

13. What are some of the significant developments in educational measurement since World War II? Do they suggest trends for the future? If so, what do you foresee as the nature of these trends?

14. Describe briefly a few applications of factor analysis as you understand it. Can you think of other ways in which the technique might be useful in educational measurement?

15. List a few of the current "problems" in the field of measurement. Select one and discuss how you think it might best be dealt with.

ANNOTATED BIBLIOGRAPHY

1. Caldwell, Otis W., and Courtis, Stuart A. *Then and Now in Education, 1845–1923*. New York: Harcourt, Brace & World, Inc., 1925. Chapters 3, 7. A report on the work of Horace Mann and particularly on the Boston survey of 1845. Contains data comparing the achievement of pupils of 1845 with that of similar pupils of 1919.

2. Garrett, Henry E. *Great Experiments in Psychology*. New York: Appleton-Century-Crofts, Inc., 1930. Chapters 1, 2, 8, 9. Interesting accounts of outstanding contributions in psychological method. Includes accounts of the work of Binet, Galton, Thorndike, and Cattell in measurement and of the development of *Army Alpha*.

3. Goslin, David A. *The Search for Ability*. New York: Russell Sage Foundation, 1963. Chapter II. A brief account of discoveries in the nineteenth century which helped to lay the foundation of modern measurement. Continues with a discussion of events and developments in the twentieth century to the present. Includes a brief comparison of educational testing in Russia, Great Britain, and the United States.

4. Murphy, Gardner. *An Historical Introduction to Modern Psychology*. New York: Harcourt, Brace & World, Inc., 1929. Chapters 21, 22. A general work on the history of modern psychology. Contains accounts of the beginnings and modern development of intelligence and personality tests.

5. National Society for the Study of Education, *The Measurement of Educational Products,* Seventeenth Yearbook of the Society, Part II. Chicago: The Society (distributed by the University of Chicago Press), 1918. 192 pp. An overview of the background and status of educational measurement by the leaders in the field of that time. Surveys available tests, the uses of tests in the schools, the work of higher institutions in the research and development of tests, statistical terms and methods, courses in measurement, and other problems.

6. ————. *The Scientific Movement in Education,* Thirty-Seventh Yearbook of the Society, Part II. Chicago: The Society (distributed by the University of Chicago Press), 1938. Chapters 29, 30, 31. Chapter 29 presents a good discussion of factors influencing the development of achievement testing during the first thirty years of the present century. Chapter 30 is a similar presentation with respect to tests of intelligence, aptitudes, and personality. In Chapter 31 observation, questionnaires, and rating scales are discussed in historical perspective.

7. Odell, C. W. *Educational Measurement in High School.* New York: Appleton-Century-Crofts, Inc., 1930. Chapter 1. An excellent chapter on the history and status (as of 1930) of the educational measurement movement.

8. Peterson, Joseph. *Early Conceptions and Tests of Intelligence.* New York: Harcourt, Brace & World, Inc., 1925. 320 pp. A fine historical account of the background and development of modern concepts of intelligence and methods of measuring it, up to and including the work of Binet.

9. Ross, C. C., and Stanley, Julian C. *Measurement in Today's Schools,* Third Edition. New York: Prentice-Hall, Inc., 1954. Chapter 2. An interesting account of the development of the scientific movement in education with special reference to measurement. Cites many references and interesting facts from the history of educational measurement.

10. Thorndike, Edward L. *An Introduction to the Theory of Mental and Social Measurements.* New York: The Science Press, 1904. 212 pp. The first book on the use of statistical methods in education. Now largely of historical interest, it reveals clearly the foundations of present statistical methods in educational research and measurement.

3

A Little Statistics

Although most of us probably make no claim to extensive statistical knowledge or training, we all have at least an elementary understanding of statistics. For example, most men are familiar with batting and fielding averages as a measure of the skill of the professional baseball player; most housewives are able to read and understand reports in which price ranges and average prices of various articles are discussed; most of us understand weather bureau reports on the average rainfall, temperature, and barometric pressure. In addition, vital statistics such as birth and death rates have some meaning for all of us.

As students and teachers or prospective teachers we know well the significance and importance of the class average in the assignment of marks. Few of us are totally unfamiliar with the meaning of such terms as "rank in class," "percentiles," "medians," "quartiles," and "correlation." So, while we may not be statisticians in any formal or learned sense, most of us are users of statistics in our work and in our recreational activities.

Any teacher or counselor who uses tests or measuring instruments in his work soon learns that some systematic treatment of scores is necessary to assure maximum benefit to all pupils and teachers concerned. The degree to which the results of measurement are useful is in part proportional to the accuracy and thoroughness with which those results are analyzed. This does not mean that every set of test scores must be subjected to exhaustive analysis, but it does mean that test scores in themselves have no significance except when some statistical analysis of them has been made. For example, to say that John's score on an arithmetic test is 36 does not tell us anything about his achievement in arithmetic. Before we can interpret such a figure we need more information. Taken by itself it is merely a number. Likewise, if we wish to use the results of a test to make comparisons between classes or groups or to do a better job of teaching or counseling it is necessary to make some analysis of the test scores. Such analysis can be performed only by statistical methods, however elementary these may be. Statistical methods are simply tools to help us acquire understanding of pupils from scores or numbers which, in themselves, are of little or no value to the teacher.

As most of us are already more or less familiar with some common statistical terms, it is the purpose of this chapter to round out our understanding of basic statistical ideas and techniques, and to show how statistical analysis of a very elementary nature can be applied by any teacher or counselor to scores on tests so that the scores can be made meaningful and therefore useful.

For those who are interested, a more extensive treatment of the techniques of simple statistical analysis, together with examples and guides, is given in Appendix A.

▶ LEARNING EXERCISES ◀

1. What uses does the average consumer make of statistics? The government? The classroom teacher?

2. Make a list of statistical terms or concepts that you know. How many can you define?

3. Examine a daily newspaper for articles using or quoting statistics. How many do you find?

INTERPRETATION OF TEST SCORES: SIMPLER METHODS

Simple Ranking

There are a good many ways to approach the interpretation of a test score. Let us consider one of the more elementary ones, using John's score of 36 on arithmetic as an example. It is apparent that we need more information to make any interpretation of the score of 36. One rather easy and quite useful method is that of *ranking*. If we know the scores of the other members of the class we can place John according to his relative position. This may be done by arranging the scores in order, from highest to lowest, and assigning each score a number according to its position. Usually we give the highest score a rank of 1, the second highest a rank of 2, etc.

In order to find John's rank in arithmetic we must know all the scores in his group or class. Let us suppose they are as follows:

ARITHMETIC TEST SCORES

Pupil	A	B	C	D	E	F	G	H	I	J	K	L
Score	44	21	14	18	46	45	52	30	39	36	31	22

Pupil	M	N	O	P	Q	R	S	T	U	V	W	X	Y
Score	23	38	33	33	29	38	32	29	42	28	26	33	25

John's score is 36, but we cannot tell anything about his rank until the scores are rearranged in order from highest to lowest. When this has been done the scores look like this:

Pupil	G	E	F	A	U	I	N	R	J	O	P	X
Score	52	46	45	44	42	39	38	38	36	33	33	33

Pupil	S	K	H	Q	T	V	W	Y	M	L	B	D	C
Score	32	31	30	29	29	28	26	25	23	22	21	18	14

When the scores are ranked we have the following array:

Pupil	G	E	F	A	U	I	N	R	J	O	P	X
Score	52	46	45	44	42	39	38	38	36	33	33	33
Rank in Class	1	2	3	4	5	6	7.5	7.5	9	11	11	11

Pupil	S	K	H	Q	T	V	W	Y	M	L	B	D	C
Score	32	31	30	29	29	28	26	25	23	22	21	18	14
Rank in Class	13	14	15	16.5	16.5	18	19	20	21	22	23	24	25

Note that where two or more scores are alike, the places they would otherwise hold have been averaged and the average thus obtained has been given as a rank to those pupils with the same scores. Thus, N and R both have a score of 38. I, with a score of 39, ranks sixth and so N and R would occupy seventh and eighth place. By averaging these ranks (7 and 8), each score receives a rank of 7.5. Similarly with O, P, and X, and Q and T.

John's score of 36 in arithmetic places him ninth in his class, or, to put it another way, there are eight pupils whose scores on the test are better and sixteen whose scores are poorer than his. This gives definite meaning to his score, which it did not have before.

Percentile Rank

The method of ranking just described has certain disadvantages which sometimes are rather troublesome. The most important of these arises from the fact that the procedure takes no account of differences in the size of groups. For example, a rank of 15 in a group of fifteen is quite different from a rank of 15 in a group of one hundred. In the first case the rank is the lowest in the group, whereas in the second it is one of the best. As long as the comparisons of individual ranks are based on groups of the same size this is no problem. Where the groups are quite different in size, however, some other procedure must be employed if a person's standing in one group is to be compared with his standing in another one. One method which eliminates this difficulty is that of *percentile ranks*. Percentile ranks differ from simple ranks in that they express the position of any score in the group in terms of the percentage of the group *below* that score. In our earlier example we said John's score of 36 gave him a rank of 9 in the class of twenty-five. We can also say that his score of 36 or rank of 9 places him above sixteen others. Putting this in another way we can say that $\frac{16}{25}$ or 64 per cent of the class made a lower score than John on the arithmetic test. This is his percentile rank. By the use of percentages, the ranks of individuals in groups of unequal numbers are made comparable.

Now John might take a history test with his whole grade of several hundred pupils. If his rank on this test were 44 it would be meaningless to compare this with his rank of 9 in arithmetic. Even if we knew that John's rank of 44 on the history test were based on a group of two hundred, it would still be difficult to compare it with his rank of 9 in a group of twenty-five. However, we know his percentile rank in arithmetic to be 64. In order to calculate his percentile rank on the history test we find first the number who make lower scores than John; $200 - 44 = 156$. $\frac{156}{200}$ equals .78, giving John a percentile rank of 78. In other words, 78 per cent of the class made lower scores than he did on the history test. Thus we can compare his standing on the two tests directly and say that his achievement on the first test (arithmetic) is apparently not as good as his achievement on the history test.[1]

---

[1] Percentile rank and percentile are sometimes confused. For example, the median score in a distribution has a percentile rank of 50; the actual *score*, whatever its amount, constitutes the 50th *percentile*.

Central Tendency or Averages

We may go beyond ranking and ask about the average of the class. Knowing this will assist us in further interpreting John's score. Determining the class average introduces another concept, that of *averages,* or *central tendency.* An *average* is a number, not always an actual score, which is taken as the most likely or typical value for a group of numbers or scores. There are several kinds of averages,[2] but those most often used in educational work are the *arithmetic mean* and the *median.*

The *arithmetic mean* is obtained by adding all the scores and dividing by the number of scores. Thus, in the case of John's class in arithmetic we would add the scores of all the pupils and divide by 25, the number of pupils. The sum of the scores is 807. Dividing this number by 25 gives a quotient of 32.28, which is the arithmetic mean. In a similar manner we determine the mean (or average) height of a group of ten-year-old boys, or the average cost of a pound of butter, or the average annual rainfall in a particular locality. In the first instance we measure each boy, add the heights, and divide by the number of boys; in the second, we determine the cost of a pound of butter over a period of time, or in a given locality in different markets, and proceed to find the average cost in the same way; in the third instance we measure the rainfall in inches over many years and find the average amount per year.

The other common measure of central tendency is the *median.* This is most simply the middle score or the one in a series which has an equal number of scores above it or higher than it is, and an equal number below it or lower than it is. Thus, to illustrate, if the heights of five pupils are respectively 60, 55, 52, 50, and 48 inches, the mid-score or median is 52, since two children are taller than that and two are shorter. If the number of cases is even, the median is midway between the lowest score of the upper half of the group and the highest score of the lower half. In our example, if we had six children instead of five, with heights of 60, 58, 55, 52, 50, and 48 inches respectively, we would say the median was midway between 55 and 52, or 53.5.

To return to John and his arithmetic, if we arrange the twenty-five scores in order from highest to lowest we find the median or middle score (the thirteenth one in this case) to be 32, almost the same as the arithmetic mean. (See Appendix A for a more exact method of calculating the median.) Another way of defining the median is to say that it is the 50th percentile or that it is the score or point that has a percentile rank of 50.

---

[2] The word "average" is often used synonymously with "arithmetic mean," but this usage is not precise, since all measures of central tendency are averages.

Comparison of Mean and Median

Know

With larger numbers of scores or cases, the median is a little simpler to calculate than the mean. The chief difference between them can be shown by the following example. Suppose one wishes to find the average salary of a group of executives whose annual salaries were $50,000, $20,000, $15,000, $13,000, and $12,000. The arithmetic mean would be calculated thus:

$$\begin{array}{r} \$50,000 \\ 20,000 \\ 15,000 \\ 13,000 \\ 12,000 \\ \hline 5\,)\overline{110,000} \\ 22,000 \end{array}$$

The median would be the mid-score or mid-salary, namely $15,000. Which of these would be the more representative or more typical average? It requires no technical knowledge to answer this question since it is obvious that the median — $15,000 — is much more representative of four of the five salaries than the arithmetic mean, which is $22,000. There are situations in which the two measures give the same or nearly the same value. The arithmetic test scores presented earlier are a case of this kind. Here it really makes little difference which measure is used.

In certain situations in which it is important from a statistical standpoint to give every score or measure its full weight according to its magnitude, the arithmetic mean is the average to use, but in nearly all ordinary situations encountered in school work the median serves equally well, and it has the advantage of being simpler to calculate and understand.

To return to the question of the meaning of a test score, and to sum up what has been said so far, a score has no meaning except in comparison to other scores in the same series, or to the central tendency or average of all scores in the series.

▶ LEARNING EXERCISES ◀

4. The following scores were made on a test of word meaning by twenty-four ninth-grade pupils: 45, 50, 41, 39, 45, 33, 42, 44, 38, 44, 25, 24, 44, 50, 32, 42, 40, 49, 60, 29, 50, 37, 47, 55. Rank them.

5. Find the percentile ranks of scores 33, 42, and 60 in Problem 4. Can a score have a percentile rank of 100? Justify your answer.

6. Find the mean and the median of the twenty-four scores. Are they the same? If not, why not?

INTERPRETATION OF TEST SCORES: MORE REFINED METHODS

Inadequacy of Central Tendency or Averages

Although central tendencies or averages provide a meaningful reference point for interpretation of individual scores in a series, such as the scores of a specified class, grade, or age, they are limited in what they reveal about the group as a whole. They do not tell us anything about the form of the distribution of scores. In other words, it is quite possible to have two or more groups whose averages are the same but which are quite unlike in their range or spread. For example, consider the following:

	A	B	C	D
	100	80	70	60
	80	70	65	60
	60	60	60	60
	40	50	55	60
	20	40	50	60
Mean =	60	60	60	60

Here we have four sets of scores whose central tendencies are identical but which are quite different in their composition or spread.

To make the point even clearer, let us suppose that a teacher has two classes in general science and has given both of them a test. He has calculated the mid-scores of Class 1 and of Class 2 and they are exactly the same, namely 47. To make the illustration very simple, let us assume that there are just nine pupils in each class and that the scores on the test in the two classes are as shown in Table I.

An inspection of these scores shows that the mid-score of the two groups is 47, as has been stated; the arithmetic mean of the two is also the same, namely 46. A teacher or counselor who made no further breakdown of these scores might easily conclude that the two classes are comparable in all respects as measured by the test. However, a closer study shows a marked difference between the groups, not in central tendency but in spread or variability. No informed teacher would handle two such classes in the same way! Whereas Class 1 has a score range of 51 points, from a low of 19 to a high of 70, Class 2 has a range of only 30 points, from 31 the normal curve, bears an exact relationship to the area under the curve which represents the number of scores or cases. These percentages will vary somewhat, depending on the degree of skewness or asymmetry of the curve.

Referring again to the nine scores in Class 1 and the nine in Class 2, we may make the following interpretation:

In Class 1 the mean is 46 and the standard deviation is 16.1. Adding this value to 46 gives 62.1; subtracting it from 46 gives 29.9. Between these points, approximately two-thirds of the nine scores in Class 1 should be found. (Check this.)

In Class 2, the mean is again 46, but the standard deviation here is 9.1. Adding this value to 46 gives 55.1; subtracting from 46 gives 36.9. Again, between these points, approximately two-thirds, or six, scores should lie. (Check this.)

Further details of calculating the standard deviation are shown in Appendix A. Going back to John's arithmetic class on page 40, when we determine the standard deviation for the twenty-five scores, we find that $\sigma = 9.2$.

The student will recall that the mean of the arithmetic scores in John's class was 32.3. If we now subtract one standard deviation from the mean we get 23.1. Likewise, by adding one standard deviation to the mean we get 41.5. Between these two points, each a distance of one standard deviation from the mean, we should find approximately 68.26 per cent of our twenty-five arithmetic scores. We find that the score nearest to 41.5 is 42, and the one nearest to 23.1 is 23. Beginning with the score of 23 on page 40, and counting each score up to and including 42, we find seventeen scores lying between the two points. What proportion of twenty-five is seventeen? $\frac{17}{25}$ equals 68 per cent exactly. In this case the calculated standard deviation value of 9.2, when actually applied to the distribution by adding and subtracting it from the mean, gives us two points on the scale between which 68 per cent of the cases lie. Results will not always conform so closely to the theoretical since many distributions in practice are less symmetrical than the one used here.

To illustrate one of the chief uses of the standard deviation in interpreting scores on tests, let us assume that the class of which John is a member has been given another test, this time in reading. As the teacher, we wish to know how the individual pupil's achievement in reading compares with his score on arithmetic. Since we have already done some work on the arithmetic scores, let us now consider the results of the reading test. We find that the scores of John and his classmates on the reading test are as follows:

TABLE I • Comparison of Groups Having Same Average but Differing in Spread or Range of Scores

Pupil	Class 1	(in order)	Pupil	Class 2	(in order)
A	51	(B) 70	L	40	(M) 61
B	70	(I) 64	M	61	(N) 55
C	32	(F) 59	N	55	(R) 53
D	44	(A) 51	O	38	(P) 50
E	47	(E) 47 (mid-score)	P	50	(Q) 47 (mid-score)
F	59	(D) 44	Q	47	(L) 40
G	28	(C) 32	R	53	(S) 39
H	19	(G) 28	S	39	(O) 38
I	64	(H) 19	T	31	(T) 31
	9) 414			9) 414	

Mean equals 46. Range equals 70 − 19 equals 51.	Mean equals 46. Range equals 61 − 31 equals 30.

to 61. In other words, we can say that on this test, Class 2 is more homogeneous than Class 1, or that Class 1 is more heterogeneous than Class 2. This difference would have considerable bearing on the methods used in handling the two classes.

Common Measures of Variability

The range is a very crude or rough measure of variability since it is based on only two measures, the highest and lowest scores. It is used here for the sake of simplicity in bringing out the main point, that is, the importance of the concept of variability in interpreting test results. In comparing groups or classes it is sometimes more important to know something about their respective spreads or variabilities than to know what their averages are. Generally speaking, knowledge of both types of measures is necessary for adequate comparisons of test scores.

There are several other measures of variability, two of which every teacher should know about. These are the *semi-interquartile* range and the *standard deviation*. The former is a measure of the spread of the middle half of the scores in any distribution. If we cut off the highest 25 per cent and the lowest 25 per cent of the scores in a class, the middle 50 per cent remains. Half the difference between the point which cuts off 75 per cent of the scores from the bottom of the distribution and the score which cuts off 25 per cent from the bottom, is the semi-interquartile range, designated by the capital letter Q. There is a formula for this, $Q = \dfrac{Q_3 - Q_1}{2}$, where Q = semi-interquartile range, Q_3 = 75th percentile, and Q_1 = 25th percentile. If we compare the Q's of two groups or classes on the same test and find Q to be larger in one group than the other, it tells us how much more varied, diverse, or heterogeneous one group is than the other. The semi-interquartile range is a refinement of the crude range. It eliminates the highest and the lowest 25 per cent of the scores, which are likely to be more scattered and unreliable, and expresses variation in terms of the more stable and concentrated middle 50 per cent of the scores. Whereas the range would be strongly affected by one score at the top or bottom of the distribution, the Q would not be affected at all by a single extreme score.

It is often helpful in thinking about averages and measures of variability to remember that an average is always a point or score, whereas a measure of variability is always a distance. For example, in the nine scores made by Class 1 and shown in Table I, the mean score is 46 — a single score or point on the scale; the range is 51 score points, a distance between the highest score of 70 and the lowest score of 19. Similarly, in Class 2, the mean is 46, while the range is the difference between the highest score and the lowest score, in this case, $61 - 31 = 30$.

From a statistical standpoint, the best all-around measure of variability is the *standard deviation,* usually designated by a sigma (σ).[3] The standard deviation is a true measure of variability in that it is based on the deviations of scores from a measure of central tendency, in this case the arithmetic mean, and it is the most reliable one because it takes into account the actual variation of each score from the mean of the series.

To illustrate how the standard deviation is calculated we shall use the two sets of scores shown in Table I (see Table II). The formula for the standard deviation is $\sigma = \sqrt{\dfrac{\Sigma\, d^2}{N}}$. In this formula Σ stands for sum; d stands for deviations from the mean; and N stands for the number of scores or cases.

Substituting in this formula the values shown in Table II, we get:

For Class 1:

$$\sigma = \sqrt{\frac{2348}{9}} = \sqrt{260.88} = 16.1$$

For Class 2:

$$\sigma = \sqrt{\frac{746}{9}} = \sqrt{82.88} = 9.1$$

[3] The standard deviation is represented by various symbols (S, $S.D.$, and σ). We use σ here, since it is the most common one.

TABLE II • Calculation of Standard Deviation

Pupil	Score	$d =$ Score–mean	d^2	Pupil	Score	$d =$ Score–mean	d^2
A	51	5	25	L	40	−6	36
B	70	24	576	M	61	15	225
C	32	−14	196	N	55	9	81
D	44	−2	4	O	38	−8	64
E	47	1	1	P	50	4	16
F	59	13	169	Q	47	1	1
G	28	−18	324	R	53	7	49
H	19	−27	729	S	39	−7	49
I	64	18	324	T	31	−15	225
			2348				746
Mean = 46 N = 9				Mean = 46 N = 9			

To recapitulate, what we have done can be described thus:

1. Determined the difference (deviation) between each score and the mean, giving those of scores below the mean a negative sign;
2. Squared each deviation (to get rid of negative signs);
3. Found the sum of these squared deviations;
4. Divided the $\Sigma\, d^2$ by N, the number of scores in each class (in this case, $N = 9$);
5. Extracted the square root of the quotient obtained in Step 4. (We do this because we squared the deviations in Step 2.)[4]

The obtained values for σ, namely 16.1 and 9.1, tell us that Class 1 is substantially more variable or heterogeneous than Class 2.

To further understand the significance of this statistic we may refer to the so-called normal or bell-shaped curve. This is the form of distribution approximated by measurements of many human traits such as height, weight, intelligence quotients, and scores made by random samples of children on many standardized tests. In such a "normal" distribution the standard deviation, laid off above and below the mean, will include 68.26 per cent of the scores or cases. Between the points two standard deviations above and below the mean, 95.44 per cent of the cases will fall, and between the points three sigmas above and below the mean, 99.74 per cent will fall. Thus, the standard deviation, a linear distance on the baseline of

[4] For method of extracting square root, see Appendix B.

READING TEST SCORES

Pupil	A	B	C	D	E	F	G	H	I	J	K	L	M
Score	86	68	48	70	94	102	92	72	91	80	69	62	56

Pupil	N	O	P	Q	R	S	T	U	V	W	X	Y
Score	73	66	77	75	65	87	46	111	81	59	77	76

When these are arranged in order and ranked, we get the following results:

Pupil	U	F	E	G	I	S	A	V	J	P	X	Y	Q
Score	111	102	94	92	91	87	86	81	80	77	77	76	75
Rank in Class	1	2	3	4	5	6	7	8	9	10.5	10.5	12	13

Pupil	N	H	D	K	B	O	R	L	W	M	C	T
Score	73	72	70	69	68	66	65	62	59	56	48	46
Rank in Class	14	15	16	17	18	19	20	21	22	23	24	25

If we try to compare the scores of individuals on the two tests directly we find it rather confusing. For example, pupil A makes a score of 44 on arithmetic and 86 on reading. Does that mean he is almost twice as good in reading as in arithmetic? Pupil B scores 21 in arithmetic and 68 in reading. Is his reading three times as good as his arithmetic? Careful inspection of the scores on the two tests shows that all pupils make higher scores in reading than they do in arithmetic. Does this mean that all pupils are better in reading than in arithmetic? Or does it show that the reading test is easier than the arithmetic test? Actually, we cannot answer any of these questions without further information. A comparison of ranks shows that A has a rank of 4 in arithmetic and 7 in reading; B ranks twenty-third in arithmetic and eighteenth in reading. We can see some tendency toward agreement in the ranks on the two tests, but not much more can be learned from them. A better method than simple ranks or percentile ranks for comparing such scores is now rather widely used. It is based on the respective means and standard deviations of the two sets of scores.

Standard Scores

Table III shows the means and standard deviations of the class, and John's scores on the two tests. The means are comparable since they represent average achievement of the same pupils on the same examinations. Likewise, the standard deviations are comparable and scores can be compared in terms of these values. For example, a point one standard

TABLE III • Comparison of Results of Arithmetic and Reading Tests

	Arithmetic	Reading
Class Mean	32.3	75.3
Standard Deviation	9.2	15.4
John's Score	36	80

deviation below the mean on the arithmetic test would be 32.3 − 9.2, or 23.1. A similar point on the reading test would be 75.3 − 15.4, or 59.9. These two points or scores represent the same levels of achievement on the two tests since they represent the same relative attainment on each test. Similar points can be worked out all along the scale, both below and above the mean, in standard deviation units.

Thus, in the case of John, his arithmetic score is 3.7 points above the mean (36 − 32.3 = 3.7). Dividing 3.7 by the standard deviation yields a value of .40 (3.7 ÷ 9.2 = .40). This tells us that on the arithmetic test John's score is .40 of a standard deviation above the mean of his class. On the reading test, John's score is 4.7 points above the mean (80 − 75.3 = 4.7). Since the standard deviation in this case is 15.4, we divide 4.7 by 15.4, which yields a value of .30 (4.7 ÷ 15.4 = .30). Since both these values, .40 and .30, are expressed in the same units — namely, the means and standard deviations of the two distributions — they may be compared directly. Therefore, we can say that John's score on the arithmetic test is slightly better than his score on the reading test.

The calculation of these standard scores, which are usually called z-scores, can be generalized in a formula: $z\text{-score} = \dfrac{X - M}{\sigma}$, where $X =$ actual score, $M =$ mean, and $\sigma =$ standard deviation.

It will be readily seen that a score below the mean will yield a negative z-score. For example, in reading, K's score is 69. Substituting in the formula, we get $z\text{-score} = \dfrac{69 - 75.3}{15.4} = \dfrac{-6.3}{15.4} = -.41$. From this value we know that K's reading score is .41 of a standard deviation *below* the mean.

It is often inconvenient to work with decimals and negative values, as is necessary with z-scores. These may both be eliminated by converting the z-score to a score with an arbitrary value for the mean and sigma or standard deviation. If we assume a mean of 50 and a standard deviation of 10, this will be accomplished. It is necessary simply to multiply the z-score by 10 and add the product to 50. Thus, John's z-score in arithmetic is .40. Multiplying .40 × 10 = 4. Adding this to 50 yields 54. In the example of pupil K in reading, we proceed thus: K's z-score on reading is −.41. Multiplying, −.41 × 10 = −4.1. We drop the decimal from −4.1, which gives −4. Adding this (algebraically), 50 − 4 = 46.

Now these values, 54 and 46, show that John is four-tenths of a standard deviation above the mean and K is four-tenths of a standard deviation below the mean. This is precisely what was said before, but our values, 54 and 46, are whole, positive numbers. These scores are sometimes erroneously called *T*-scores. We shall refer to them simply as *sigma* scores[5] to distinguish them from z-scores.[6]

There are two reasons for going into detail with respect to z-scores and *sigma* scores. We have already said that these scores are the best that have been devised for comparison of results on tests by individual pupils. The second reason is that an increasing number of the makers and publishers of standardized tests are expressing and interpreting results in terms of standard scores, usually in some form of what we have designated as *sigma* scores. Although not many teachers may have occasion to determine standard scores from their own tests, it is essential that all prospective users of standardized tests understand standard scores. Such an understanding is the primary purpose of the explanation given here.

One other type of standard score deserves mention. It is called a "stanine," a condensation of the words "standard nine." The term derives its name from the fact that each stanine represents a band or distance on the baseline of the normal curve of one-half of a standard deviation and that the entire range is divided into nine such bands. The middle stanine is the band including one-fourth of a standard deviation on each side of the mean. This is numbered the fifth stanine. On either side of this are four stanines, each a half a standard deviation. Those below the middle stanine are numbered from 1 to 4 and those above, 6 to 9. Scores are interpreted according to the band or stanine in which they fall. Stanines have certain advantages of convenience and ease of statistical manipulation.[7]

The relationship of the types of scores we have discussed and some additional ones are shown very clearly in Figure 1.

[5] They are also sometimes designated as *Z*-scores.

[6] A *T*-score is based on a normalized distribution with a mean of 50 and a standard deviation of 10.

[7] For a more detailed discussion, see Walter N. Durost, *The Characteristics, Use, and Computation of Stanines,* Test Service Notebook, No. 23 (New York: Harcourt, Brace & World, Inc., 1961).

FIGURE 1 • Normal Curve, Percentiles, and Standard Scores

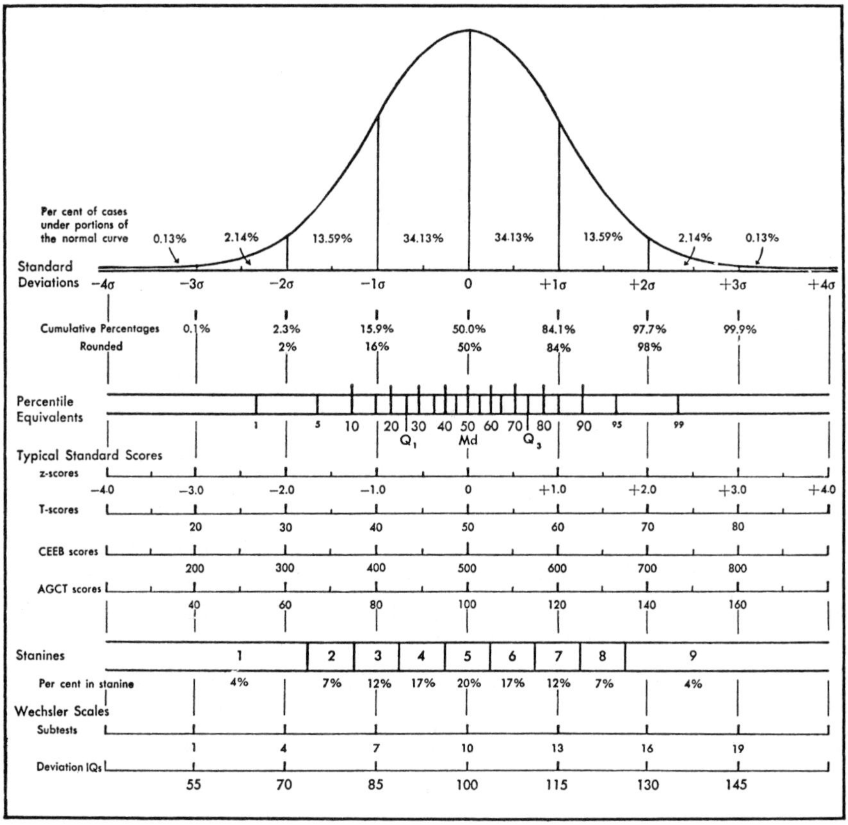

Note: This chart cannot be used to equate scores on one test to scores on another test [unless both tests were taken by the same group]. For example, both 600 on the *CEEB* and 120 on the *AGCT* are one standard deviation above their respective means, but they do not represent "equal" standings because the scores were obtained from different groups.

From *Test Service Bulletin,* No. 48, p. 8. Reproduced by permission. Copyright January, 1955, The Psychological Corporation, New York, N.Y. All rights reserved.

▶ **LEARNING EXERCISES** ◀

7. The same twenty-four ninth-grade pupils (see Learning Exercise 4, page 43) made the following scores on a test of English fundamentals: 35, 31, 28, 33, 40, 24, 21, 26, 29, 24, 31, 27, 32, 26, 25, 28, 22, 30, 26, 38, 30, 23, 18, 31. What is the mean of these scores?

8. Compare the ranges of the two sets of scores. Which is larger?

9. Calculate the semi-interquartile range of each set of scores. Suggestion: one-fourth of each series is six scores. Cut off the top six and lowest six, and find Q from the remainder. What do the two Q values tell you?

10. For the two sets of scores assume the following:

	WORD MEANING	ENGLISH
Mean	41.9	28.2
σ	8.7	5.1

Calculate (*a*) percentile ranks, (*b*) z-scores, and (*c*) *sigma* scores for the following raw scores:

PUPIL	SCORE WORD MEANING	SCORE ENGLISH
X	37	25
Y	60	40
Z	45	30

Compare these three types of scores. Which is simplest to calculate? Which type gives the most meaningful comparisons? Justify your answer.

MEASURES OF CORRELATION OR RELATIONSHIP

We often hear the term "correlation" used, or see it in print, in educational and psychological discussions and literature. Reference is made to a "high correlation" or a "low correlation" or to "no correlation." If such phrases are to have meaning it is necessary that the term "correlation," and the use of "high," "low," or "no" with reference to this term, be given some meaning.

Meaning of Correlation

Correlation is a method of determining the degree of relationship between two traits or quantities that can change or vary in amount. For example, people vary in height, weight, intelligence, industry, and in countless other ways. Each of these qualities is a variable. If two of the variables, height and weight, are selected for study it is possible to say on the basis of observation that there seems to be a degree of correspondence between them. That is, tall persons tend to be heavier, short persons tend to weigh less. The correspondence is not perfect because there are short, stout and tall, slender people, but generally it can be said that there appears to be a definite relationship between height and weight. Correlation is a mathematical procedure for determining and expressing quantitatively the closeness of the relationship between two variables. The measure of this relationship is called the *coefficient of correlation*. It ranges from a *maximum* of +1.00 through zero to a *maximum* of −1.00. If the two measured variables tend to vary together, as in the case of height and weight, the relationship is direct and positive, and approaches +1.00 as a maximum. If the relationship is negative, that is, if an increase in one variable tends to be accompanied by a decrease in the second, the coefficient will be negative, approaching −1.00 as a maximum. If there is no tendency for the traits or qualities to vary simultaneously either directly or inversely, the correlation is zero, or we say there is no correlation, or that there is absence of relationship.

The correlation of +1.00 denotes a perfect positive relationship. This exists when a change in one trait is *always* accompanied by a *commensurate* change in the *same direction* in the other trait. Likewise, a correlation of −1.00 denotes a perfect negative correlation which means that a change in one trait is *always* accompanied by a *commensurate* change in the *opposite* direction in the other trait. Perfect correlations, either positive or negative, are rarely found in educational measurements, and negative correlations of any size are quite uncommon.

An illustration of a positive correlation has already been given. The correlation between age of automobiles and their cash value would be negative since, as age increases, value will decrease. The correlation between age of school children and intelligence quotient would be zero since we will obviously find no relationship between age and I.Q. in children.

One of the most useful and easily understood devices for showing relationship between two variables is called a *scatter diagram*. In such a diagram the individuals who are being measured are located or plotted with respect to both variables at the same time. This kind of chart may also be used as the basis for one of the best methods of determining relationship, the *Pearson Product-Moment Correlation,* or *r.* The details of calculating *r* from such an array are explained in Appendix A.

To make clearer the nature of correlation and different values of the coefficient several scatter diagrams are shown below. In each case, there are two variables involved. In the first and second, the results are based on measurements of university students; in the third, on measurements of weather conditions and fuel.

In Figure 2 the scatter diagram shows what would be called a moderate positive correlation. There is a distinct tendency for high scores on one test to be accompanied by high scores on the other, and vice versa. However, some individuals who make high scores on the reasoning test make average or even low scores on the factual test, and the opposite is also true in some instances. If such exceptions did not occur, the correlation would be +1.00. This moderate positive correlation is quite typical of what is found when mental measurements are correlated. The correlations be-

Know

FIGURE 2 • Scatter Diagram Showing Positive Correlation

SCORES ON REASONING TEST	30-31	32-33	34-35	36-37	38-39	40-41	42-43	44-45	46-47
65-69					///	//	///	//	
60-64			/	/	////	//	╫ /	///	
55-59	/	//	///	///	╫	//	/	/	
50-54	/			╫	////	///	/	//	/
45-49	/	/	/	//		/			
40-44	/		/	/	/				
35-39	/								

SCORES ON FACTUAL TEST

Each tally represents a person located according to his score on a
factual test and his score on a reasoning test in educational measurement. $r = .51$

tween scores on tests in various school subjects, and between I.Q. and
achievement test results, tend to be in the general vicinity of .30 to .50.

Figure 3 shows the relationship between two other variables — in this
case, scores on a test of manual dexterity and scores on a vocabulary test.
The correlation is almost zero, indicating that there is no evident relationship. In other words, knowing an individual's score on either test would
provide no basis for estimating or predicting his score on the other.

Figure 4 shows a negative correlation of −.74 between average daily
temperature and tons of coal burned per day, a fairly high degree of inverse relationship. The data are hypothetical and serve only to illustrate
a negative or inverse relationship. Such a relationship is obvious in this
case, since the higher the mean temperature for any given day, the lower
would be the amount of coal burned for heating purposes. What the
true correlation would be is not determined. It would, of course, be affected by other atmospheric conditions such as wind, humidity, and
amount of sunshine, as well as other factors.

It should be clear that theoretically one may have high negative or

FIGURE 3 • Scatter Diagram Showing Negligible Correlation

SCORES ON MANUAL DEXTERITY TEST	50-59	60-69	70-79	80-89	90-99	100-109	110-119	120-129	130-139	140-149
40-44				/	/					
35-39				/	//	///	//			/
30-34	/		//	///	////	////	//	⁄⁄⁄⁄⁄		/
25-29			/	////	//	////		//	/	
20-24	/			////	//		⁄⁄⁄⁄⁄	/	/	/
15-19				/	//	////		/		
10-14		/		/	/	/	///	//		
5-9			/	//		//				
0-4						/			/	

SCORES ON VOCABULARY TEST

Each tally represents a person located according to his score on a test of manual dexterity and his score on a vocabulary test. $r = .06$

even perfect negative correlations, just as high or perfect positive correlations are possible. In actuality, however, as previously mentioned, perfect correlations are rarely found in educational measurement. It should also be noted that a negative correlation designates just as close a relationship as its positive counterpart. A correlation of $-.70$ is just as high for predictive purposes as one of $+.70$. It is the size of the correlation, not its direction, that determines how close the relationship is.

Further Ideas about Correlation

The coefficient of correlation is an index or pure number which gives a measure of the degree of relationship between variables. Most commonly, only two traits or quantities are considered at one time, though there are methods of determining correlation between more than two. The correlation coefficient is *not* a per cent. A correlation of .60 does

FIGURE 4 • Scatter Diagram Showing Negative Correlation

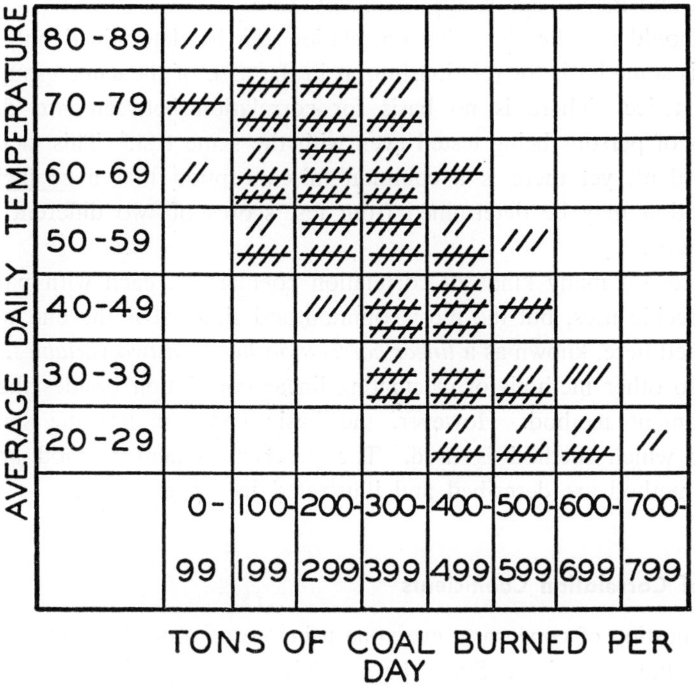

Each tally represents one day located according to average temperature and tons of coal burned in a community during the twenty-four hour period. $r = -.74$

not mean 60 per cent of perfect correlation. As has been said, it is simply a number or index which can vary from $+1.00$, through zero, to -1.00. We may repeat here for emphasis that the amount or size of the correlation coefficient expresses the degree to which two traits tend to vary simultaneously, or the extent to which increases (or decreases) in one tend to be accompanied by increases (or decreases) in the other.

It may be appropriate to mention one or two additional cautions concerning correlation. The student should remember that a relationship between two variables does not prove them to be *causally* related. They may vary together or tend to do so because of a third factor that affects both. Age is frequently such a factor. For example, a substantial positive correlation might be found between height or weight and mental maturity among school children. Such a correlation would be the result of the effect of age on physical growth and mental growth, and not evidence that increase in height or weight causes mental growth. When the factor of age is eliminated or "held constant," the correlation between height or weight and mental age is approximately zero.

It should also be clear that correlation can be determined only where there is some basis for relationship, as in the case of the same group being tested twice. There is no basis for correlation between two different groups of persons being tested even with the same test.[8] This fact seems self-evident, yet there is a common misconception that a coefficient of correlation may be determined from test scores of two different classes or groups.

There are many kinds of correlation coefficients, each with particular and specific uses, but the most common and simplest is the one we have discussed here, known as a *linear correlation between two variables*. There are also other methods of calculating linear correlation besides the product-moment method. However, the basic concepts are the same, no matter which method is used. The product-moment method and one other method are described and illustrated in Appendix A.

Size of Correlation Coefficients

A question of concern to everyone using correlations has to do with the size of the coefficient. Since the coefficient can vary in either direction from zero to 1.00, it is important that we try to determine what is a *high* correlation, a *moderate* one, and a *low* one. No simple and rigid rules or answers to such questions can be given. A correlation may be high in one situation and only moderate or even low in another. Correlations between two equivalent forms of a test of achievement or intelligence may be .90 or higher, sometimes as high as .98. On the other hand, correlations between I.Q. and school marks will ordinarily not be higher than .50. Correlations between measurements of physical traits or abilities such as rate of tapping or strength of grip, and scores on mental tests, will usually be not far from zero. Therefore, the interpretation of a coefficient of correlation depends on the situation.

Perhaps a more useful method of interpreting the size of the correlation coefficient is one which involves forecasting or predictive value. For example, if we know a pupil's level of intelligence, how accurately can we predict his achievement in algebra? Knowledge of a given pupil's I.Q. score will never tell us exactly what his score will be on an algebra test.

---

[8] The only common exceptions are to be found in the study of twins' or other relatives' resemblance in specific traits, or in educational experiments in which individuals in one group are paired or matched with individuals in another group on some basis such as intelligence.

But if both tests have been previously administered to the same group of pupils, then the size of the correlation coefficient between the scores on the two tests will give us some idea of how confident we can be later in predicting an algebra score from the score on the intelligence test. If the two tests prove to have a correlation of .90 or higher, then we would be fairly safe in predicting that a given individual will have roughly the same relative score on the algebra test as on the intelligence test. For *individual prediction,* the correlation must be very high — at least as high as .90.

On the other hand, if we wish simply to have some assurance of being right more often than wrong in *group prediction,* then correlations of .50 or even less are often quite useful. In such cases it is also possible to say with considerable assurance that one group will do better or worse than another.

Another problem in correlation is this: if we measure a group of children on a test today, how closely will the results agree with those obtained from the same test given to the same children several days later? Here, where we are interested in knowing how consistent the results of a test are, correlations of .80 or better are usually considered necessary to assure acceptable stability or consistency.

These matters will be considered further in the discussion of reliability and validity in the next chapter and again in Appendix A.

▶ LEARNING EXERCISES ◀

11. Cite three illustrations each of (*a*) positive correlation, (*b*) approximately zero correlation, (*c*) negative correlation.

12. Would you expect positive, negative, or no correlation in each of the following comparisons? (*a*) I.Q. and marks in algebra; (*b*) speed and accuracy in addition; (*c*) scores on two equivalent forms of an achievement test; (*d*) age and I.Q. within a school grade; (*e*) age and I.Q. over a range of grades; and (*f*) cost of a product and the supply.

13. Make a scatter diagram of the scores on arithmetic and reading given for the first group in this chapter. (See pages 40 and 49.) Suggestion: write down the pupils' letter designations and then, in parallel columns, each one's score on arithmetic and reading. From this arrangement make a plot locating each pupil with respect to both scores simultaneously. Comparing the result with the three diagrams given, what do you estimate the correlation to be?

14. By referring to Appendix A you can calculate the correlation between reading and arithmetic scores. Does the result agree with your estimate?

15. Knowing the size of the coefficient of correlation in this case, what can you say about predicting reading scores from arithmetic scores, and vice versa?

QUOTIENTS AND NORMS

The point has already been made that a single score on a given test is merely a number and has no meaning in and of itself. Such a score, called a *raw score,* must be related to something to give it meaning. We have also discussed several kinds of relative scores: ranks, percentile ranks, and standard scores. However, there are a number of other kinds of relative scores, derived scores, or transmuted scores, two of which should be familiar to every teacher and counselor. These are *quotients* and *norms*. Both will be briefly defined and discussed here, and more detailed discussion of each will be found at appropriate points throughout the remainder of this book.

Intelligence Quotient — Ratio I.Q.

The "intelligence quotient," or I.Q., has become a familiar term to the layman as well as to professional educators and psychologists. The term is frequently found even in newspapers and popular magazines. It is doubtful that the average person could give a precise definition of I.Q., however; most people know that it is supposed to be some indication of degree of intelligence, but that is as far as their knowledge goes.

The I.Q. or intelligence quotient is a ratio of mental age to chronological age or life age. The equation is written I.Q. $= \dfrac{M.A.}{C.A.}$. This theory assumes that the individual grows or develops mentally at a steady rate from birth to a few years before maturity, and that different individuals may develop mentally at the same or different rates. There are other assumptions of a more technical nature which will be discussed later in connection with the material on intelligence tests, but for present purposes the foregoing should suffice.

The rate at which an individual develops mentally is measured by determining first the level of difficulty of the tasks he can perform. For example, if A can do as much (that is, tasks as difficult) as the average child of twelve, he is said to have a mental age or level of mental development of twelve years. Thus, if A is only ten years old, it is obvious that he is developing at a rate which is faster than average, since he has reached the level of mental maturity in ten years which the average child requires twelve years to attain. The rate of his mental development is then determined by comparing his mental *level* with his chronological or life age. So we say his I.Q. is twelve years divided by ten years:

$$I.Q. = \frac{M.A.}{C.A.} = \frac{12}{10} = 1.20$$

To express the result in terms of the rate of mental development, we say that for every year A has lived he has added or grown 1.2 years mentally. It is common practice to multiply the result by 100 to eliminate the decimal (move the decimal point two places to the right), and say his I.Q. equals 120:

$$\text{I.Q.} = \frac{\text{M.A.}}{\text{C.A.}} \times 100 = \frac{12}{10} \times 100 = 120$$

It is generally assumed that mental growth or development as measured by tests ceases on the average somewhere between sixteen and eighteen, just as physical growth ceases at a slightly later age. Consequently, A does not continue to add 1.2 years indefinitely; instead, it is believed that this rate begins to decline at about twelve to fourteen years, and beyond sixteen to eighteen the *average* scores on intelligence tests do not continue to increase. From then on, the I.Q. is less useful than some other measures for indicating the degree of intelligence. However, there is some evidence indicating that while the rate of mental growth declines and finally becomes zero as stated, it may not cease entirely or reach its maximum until age twenty. The question is controversial and authorities disagree on the exact age, but there seems to be rather general agreement that the *average* maximum growth is reached somewhere between ages sixteen and twenty. It should also be noted that there is a wide range in the age at which mental maturity is reached. Of course some individuals reach maturity much earlier than others, but our figures here pertain to averages for the general population.

Theoretically, the range of I.Q.'s is from zero to 200 or more. Since the norm or standard is the level of development of the average child of a given age, it follows that the average I.Q. must always be 100 so long as these norms or standards are kept up to date. I.Q.'s in the range between 90 and 110 are generally designated as average. This includes, in a normal distribution, approximately one-half the population. (See Figure 1, page 52.) Those between 110 and 120 are referred to as above average, those between 120 and 140 as superior, and those above 140 as very superior. On the other side of the distribution, I.Q.'s between 80 and 90 are referred to as below average, those between 70 and 80 as borderline defective, and those below 70 as feeble-minded. Persons with I.Q.'s between 50 and 70 are referred to as mildly retarded (for many years they were termed morons); between 25 and 50 as moderately retarded (imbeciles); and below 25 as severely retarded (idiots). These classifications are, of course, arbitrary, and the limits are not fixed and rigid. It is probably more helpful to think of the retarded in terms of what they can be taught to do rather than in terms of labels.

Deviation I.Q.

The concept of the I.Q. has been a very useful one, although it has always been more or less controversial. For various reasons it has fallen into disfavor with some measurement experts, counselors, and psychologists, and there is a tendency to replace the I.Q. concept with some other measure such as standard scores. Although this change would eliminate a number of vexing problems, it is likely to take some time since the I.Q. is so well-established; standard scores as yet are not nearly so well-known or generally understood.

The so-called deviation I.Q. is gaining increasing acceptance as a measure which expresses information concerning an individual's mental ability but which avoids the technical weaknesses inherent in the ratio I.Q. The deviation I.Q. is simply a standard score obtained like our *sigma* scores with an arbitrarily assumed mean and standard deviation for all age levels. The typical values assumed are 100 and 16 respectively since these are the values found for the *Stanford-Binet* intelligence scale. Thus by changing obtained I.Q. distributions to this scale we automatically equate them to the *Stanford-Binet*.

For example, let us assume that a particular group test given to a representative sample of ten-year-olds yields a mean raw score of 60 and a standard deviation of 18. A score of 60 then would automatically represent an I.Q. of 100; a score of 78, an I.Q. of 116; one of 42, an I.Q. of 84; etc. Any intelligence test can thus be converted to the same scale when the mean and standard deviation have been determined for each age group.

It should be remembered in using I.Q.'s that any single test result is only an approximation. Every measurement, even in such exact sciences as physics and astronomy, is always subject to some error, and this fact must always be recognized in measuring human traits, particularly mental or psychological ones. Therefore, an I.Q. based on a single measurement or test should be regarded as only an approximate value which must remain tentative until it is substantiated or corrected through additional testing. A good rule to follow is that when we have an I.Q. based on a single test we should consider that the chances are only fifty-fifty that the true value is within a range of about five points on either side of the obtained value. In other words, a measured I.Q. of 108 represents a probability of 50 per cent that the true value is somewhere between 103 and 113. Moreover, there is a 25 per cent chance that the true I.Q. is more than 113 and an equal probability that it is less than 103. This should certainly not be taken to mean that a single measurement of a child's I.Q. is of no value, but it does mean that such an I.Q. must be regarded as an approximation which further testing and other facts about the child may or may not support and confirm.

Educational Quotient

Not so well-known or widely used as the I.Q. is the E.Q. or "educational quotient." This is calculated by the formula

$$E.Q. = \frac{E.A.}{C.A.} \times 100.$$

Educational Age (E.A.) is the age which corresponds to the score made by a pupil on an achievement test or battery. For example, if the score made by the individual pupil is equal to the average score on the test of pupils nine years and six months of age, his educational age on that test is nine and one-half years. If his chronological age is eight years and three months his

$$E.Q. = \frac{9-6}{8-3} \times 100 = \frac{114 \text{ (months)}}{99 \text{ (months)}} \times 100 = 115.$$

The educational quotient is usually based on a survey test or battery rather than a single test such as a reading test or an arithmetic test. In the latter cases, the quotients would more properly be called the "reading quotient" or the "arithmetic quotient."

$$\text{Reading Quotient} = \frac{\text{Reading Age}}{\text{Chronological Age}} \times 100.$$

$$\text{Arithmetic Quotient} = \frac{\text{Arithmetic Age}}{\text{Chronological Age}} \times 100.$$

One of the obvious limitations of the educational quotient arises from the fact that it is based on a pupil's average performance on a battery of achievement tests. His scores on the separate subjects might be distinctly above the norm in some and even below in others. Though the pupil's educational age would reveal the central tendency, it would not reveal these variations, which might be the most significant facts about his achievement.

Norms

Although, as will shortly be apparent, there are several kinds of norms, a norm is typically the average performance on a test by a defined group, e.g., a given age or grade. If the norms are based on groups of children of

TABLE IV • Mental Ages Corresponding to Scores on *Otis Quick-Scoring Mental Ability Test: Beta,* Forms Em and Fm

Score	M.A.	Score	M.A.	Score	M.A.	Score	M.A.
1	7–1	21	10–0	41	13–0	61	16–0
2	7–3	22	10–1	42	13–2	62	16–2
3	7–5	23	10–3	43	13–3	63	16–4
4	7–7	24	10–5	44	13–4	64	16–6
5	7–8	25	10–7	45	13–6	65	16–8
6	7–10	26	10–8	46	13–8	66	16–10
7	8–0	27	10–10	47	13–10	67	17–0
8	8–2	28	11–0	48	14–0	68	17–2
9	8–3	29	11–1	49	14–2	69	17–4
10	8–5	30	11–2	50	14–4	70	17–6
11	8–7	31	11–4	51	14–6	71	17–8
12	8–9	32	11–6	52	14–8	72	17–10
13	8–10	33	11–8	53	14–10	73	18–0
14	9–0	34	11–10	54	15–0	74	18–2
15	9–2	35	12–0	55	15–1	75	18–4
16	9–3	36	12–2	56	15–2	76	18–6
17	9–5	37	12–4	57	15–4	77	18–8
18	9–7	38	12–6	58	15–6	78	18–10
19	9–8	39	12–8	59	15–8	79	19–0
20	9–10	40	12–10	60	15–10	80	19–2

the same age they are called *age norms;* if based on groups in the same grade they are called *grade norms.* As a rule, intelligence tests have age norms while achievement tests have grade norms. It is not difficult to see the reason for this. In calculating a child's I.Q. we need to know his mental age and his chronological age. Mental age is determined by the average performance of children of given ages. Thus, if it is found that the average score on an intelligence test of children exactly ten years old is 42, then a child who makes a score of 42 on this test is said to have a mental age of ten years, since he can perform on this test as capably as the average ten-year-old. Reproduced in Table IV above is a table of norms for a well-known intelligence test.

For achievement tests, the type of norm commonly used is the grade norm. Here we are interested in knowing the average performance of children at certain grade levels. For example, in establishing norms on a test of achievement in American history we may wish to set up norms for Grades 4 to 8, inclusive. The simplest approach to the problem would be to determine the average score on the test for representative samples or groups at each grade level.

An illustration of an achievement test for which both age and grade norms are provided is shown in Table V. In this instance — the *Gates Basic Reading Tests,* Type GS — both grade and age equivalents are given for each score in terms of the number of paragraphs correct. For subjects such as reading, both types of norms are useful, whereas for those such as algebra or chemistry, age norms would probably be useless and possibly even misleading.

It will be noted in Tables IV and V that both age and grade norms are classified in terms of units smaller than a whole year. In many tables of norms one month is used as the unit, both in age and grade. In age norms the divisions include the entire twelve months of the year, while in grade norms the range is usually from the exact year, such as 9.0, to 9.9 representing the last month of the school year. Thus, in mental age norms one finds values like 7–10 or 9–11; these represent seven years, ten months and nine years, eleven months, respectively. In tables of grade norms one might find 5.4 and 7.7 representing the fourth month of the fifth grade and the seventh month of the seventh grade, respectively.

In addition to age and grade norms we find percentile norms and stand-

TABLE V • Grade and Age Scores for Type GS (*Reading to Appreciate General Significance*) — Time, 10 Minutes

Raw Score	Reading Grade	Reading Age	Raw Score	Reading Grade	Reading Age
0	2.5	7–8	13	5.4	10–6
1	2.6	7–10	14	5.6	10–8
2	2.7	7–11			
3	2.9	8–1	15	6.0	11–2
4	3.2	8–5	16	6.4	11–8
			17	6.8	12–1
5	3.4	8–7	18	7.2	12–6
6	3.6	8–9	19	7.4	12–8
7	3.8	9–0			
8	4.0	9–2			
9	4.3	9–6	20	7.6	12–11
			21	8.1	13–5
10	4.6	9–9	22	8.7	13–11
11	5.0	10–2	23	9.2	14–5
12	5.2	10–4	24	9.8	15–1

Reading grades are in years and tenths; reading ages in years and months.

Reproduced by permission of Teachers College, Columbia University, publisher.

ard score norms provided with many tests of achievement, particularly those intended for use at secondary and higher levels. An example of a set of such norms is given in Table VI for the *Cooperative English Tests*.

Several points should be noted in regard to Table VI. First, the table does not show raw score norms. The test is scored by determining the number of correct answers. This is the raw score. By means of a conversion table on the scoring stencil the raw score is converted to a "converted score," which is a standard score. The mean of the standard scores is set at 150 and the standard deviation at 10. Raw scores on all sub-tests of the *Cooperative English Tests* as well as those for different grade levels are converted to this same standard score scale. Thus scores on different sub-tests and those of different grade levels are made comparable.

Second, it should be observed that Table VI provides "percentile bands." These bands represent a range of values between which the theoretical true value for an actual score is likely to fall. Thus, if the converted score of student X in Grade 10 is 160, we can say with some confidence that his true score would lie between percentile ranks 86 and 93. The authors and producers of the *Cooperative English Tests* believe that percentile band norms are more realistic and useful in interpreting individual scores on a test than the usual percentile rank because, they maintain, the latter gives a false, or at least questionable, impression of accuracy. In other words, the percentile band is a more cautious, conservative interpretation.

Standard scores and percentiles are not averages as age and grade norms are, but serve to represent the relative standing or position of individual scores in a distribution of scores on a particular test. The distribution may apply to a group in a particular grade or a particular age, but this is not necessarily so. Such norms have advantages where age or grade have less significance (as in the case of an adult population) than they do with elementary school pupils.

Norms — Some Further Considerations

The subject of test norms includes important and rather complex problems which have not yet been mentioned. The purpose of the discussion to this point has been to present the basic facts which the user of standardized tests needs in order to interpret scores. The problems referred to concern mainly the test specialist and the producer of standardized tests and are only of secondary importance to the classroom teacher or counselor using the tests. However, a brief discussion of some of the problems in connection with the norming of standardized tests should be appropriate before leaving the subject.

TABLE VI • Converted Score (Standard Score) and Percentile Band Norms for 1960 Cooperative English Tests — Total English

Converted Score	Percentile Band					
	Grade 9	Grade 10	Grade 11	Grade 12	Grade 13	Grade 14
182–183					99.7–99.9	99–99.9
180–181				99.7–99.9	99.1–99.9	98–99.7
178–179				99.4–99.9	98–99.7	96–99.2
176–177				99–99.7	96–99.1	93–98
174–175		99.6–99.9	99.5–99.9	98–99.4	93–98	88–96
172–173	99.8–99.9	99.2–99.9	99–99.8	96–99	89–96	84–93
170–171	99.4–99.9	98–99.6	97–99.5	95–98	83–93	78–88
168–169	99–99.8	97–99.2	95–99	92–96	77–89	70–84
166–167	98–99.4	96–98	92–97	89–95	71–83	61–78
164–165	97–99	93–97	88–95	85–92	63–77	53–70
162–163	94–98	90–96	83–92	79–89	56–71	44–61
160–161	92–97	86–93	78–88	74–85	48–63	35–53
158–159	88–94	81–90	72–83	68–79	39–56	27–44
156–157	84–92	76–86	65–78	61–74	32–48	21–35
154–155	79–88	69–81	58–72	54–68	26–39	16–27
152–153	73–84	62–76	51–65	47–61	21–32	11–21
150–151	66–79	55–69	44–58	40–54	16–26	7–16
148–149	59–73	48–62	37–51	33–47	12–21	5–11
146–147	52–66	40–55	30–44	27–40	8–16	3–7
144–145	44–59	32–48	23–37	20–33	6–12	2–5
142–143	36–52	26–40	18–30	14–27	4–8	1–3
140–141	28–44	19–32	13–23	10–20	2–6	0.8–2
138–139	20–36	14–26	9–18	6–14	1–4	0.5–1
136–137	14–28	10–19	6–13	3–10	0.8–2	0.5–0.8
134–135	8–20	6–14	3–9	2–6	0.4–1	0.4–0.5
132–133	4–14	3–10	2–6	1–3	0.2–0.8	0.3–0.5
130–131	2–8	2–6	0.7–3	0.5–2	0.1–0.4	0.2–0.4
128–129	0.9–4	0.6–3	0.4–2	0.2–1	0.1–0.2	0.1–0.3
126–127	0.3–2	0.2–2	0.1–0.7	0.1–0.5		0.1–0.2
124–125	0.1–0.9	0.1–0.6	0.1–0.4	0.1–0.2		
122–123	0.1–0.3	0.1–0.2				
120–121						
Median	144	147.2	150.2	151.3	159.1	161.8
Lower Quartile	137.7	140.3	143.1	144.0	152.1	155.7
Upper Quartile	151.3	154.3	157.7	158.9	165.8	167.8

Adapted from Clarence Derrick, David Harris, and Biron Walker, *Manual for Interpreting Scores, Cooperative English Tests* (Princeton, N.J.: Educational Testing Service, 1960), Tables 9–14. Reprinted by permission.

One of these is the selection of the population on which the norms are based. Theoretically, and perhaps ideally, national norms are most desirable since truly national norms have the widest base and are most generally applicable. However, the obtaining of a truly representative national sample presents many difficulties. For example, such factors as sex, socio-economic status, size and type of community, racial origin, and other individual characteristics as well as sectional and/or regional differences, the quality of education available, and other factors should all be taken into account in selecting the normative sample. Also, some critics maintain that national norms cannot be truly representative because a norm based on widely varying groups must be an average which is not truly representative of many of them.

In order to avoid some of the difficulties encountered in establishing national norms, sectional, regional or perhaps more broadly differentiated norms are sometimes established. This means simply that norms are based upon a defined group from a particular geographical region, a defined type of community, a particular ethnic or racial group, and the like. This procedure does not get rid of the problems encountered in trying to establish national norms but merely segregates them, so that for any defined group fewer factors need be taken into account. On the other hand, such a procedure requires the establishment of norms for many different groups and purposes.

Larger communities or school systems may set up local norms based on their own school population. This may be done with locally constructed tests or with standardized tests. Local norms are restricted by definition to a particular community or area. Where the school population is small and perhaps of an atypical nature, they probably are of quite limited value and may even be misleading. Local norms, of course, do not permit comparison with schools or populations outside the local community, which is one of the chief advantages of norms based on a broader sampling.

It may be appropriate to emphasize here that *norms* are not *standards* of achievement. A standard is a goal which a pupil may be expected to attain. Goals or standards may vary with the abilities, interests, and the needs of the individual pupil. A norm, on the other hand, is an average or typical score which may be attained by some, exceeded by others, and not reached by quite a few. To assume that every pupil should reach the norm in his measured achievement or growth is like saying every boy should be five feet tall and weigh one hundred pounds at age twelve, or that every girl should know how to make a party dress using a pattern and sewing machine before she can graduate from high school.

In dealing with the problems of norming standardized tests, publishers continue to strive for a representative sampling of the appropriate population for a particular test or battery. However, problems of securing cooperation in the standardization process from selected schools or school systems also present difficulties, and schools invited to participate in such programs often have good reasons for finding it impossible to cooperate. This leaves the test producer with holes, sometimes irreparable, in his carefully chosen sample. Yet he must try as best he can to put together an acceptable population on which to base his norms. One way to safeguard against this eventuality is to start with a very large sample and thus allow some leeway for adjustment by careful selection from those who do agree to cooperate. This does not mean that schools who accept an invitation are later "dis-invited" but simply that certain ones may not be included in the population on which the norms are based. The inclusion of such schools could introduce imbalance into the sample because they do not meet the criteria of size, socio-economic status, or some of the other factors required.

To a considerable degree test producers are moving in the direction of obtaining the most representative sample they can and then carefully defining this sample in the test manual. In this way the user is fully informed of the nature of the sample upon which the test norms are based and is free to make such adjustments or allowances for his own students as seem appropriate.

▶ LEARNING EXERCISES ◀

16. Using the table of norms for the *Otis Beta Test* (page 64), determine mental ages for the following scores: 12, 30, 49, 55, and 61. If the ages of these individuals are respectively 6–9, 11–8, 14–0, 14–6, and 15–5, what are their I.Q.'s?

17. Referring to the table of norms for the *Gates Reading Test* (page 65), (a) what reading grades and reading ages would correspond to scores 9, 16, and 23? (b) Reading grade 5.6 corresponds to reading age 10–8; reading grade 7.6 corresponds to reading age 12–11. How do you explain this apparent discrepancy?

18. By referring to Table VI, page 67, answer the following questions:

a. What is the percentile band of a converted score of 143 for ninth-grade students? For eleventh-grade students? For college freshmen?

b. What converted score does a student in the tenth grade have to make in order to be in the percentile band, 69–81? What converted score is required in the twelfth grade to achieve approximately the same standing?

c. Between what two grades does the greatest average improvement on this test occur? How do you account for this?

ANNOTATED BIBLIOGRAPHY

1. Blommers, Paul, and Lindquist, E. F. *Elementary Statistical Methods.* Boston: Houghton Mifflin Company, 1960. A general introductory treatment of statistical methods for students in psychology and education. A scholarly and comprehensive presentation which the worker in measurement will find a valuable reference.

2. Cronbach, Lee J., *Essentials of Psychological Testing,* Second Edition. New York: Harper & Row, Publishers, 1960. Chapter 4. A rather condensed presentation emphasizing theoretical aspects of statistical methods. The computing guides, on the other hand, are practical and helpful, though not easy for a beginner to follow.

3. Darley, John G. *Testing and Counseling in the High School Guidance Program.* Chicago: Science Research Associates, Inc., 1943. Chapter 3. One of the best discussions and presentations of fundamental statistics needed by counselors in using tests. Most of the chapter is just as good for teachers as for counselors.

4. Durost, Walter N., and Prescott, George A. *Essentials of Measurement for Teachers.* New York: Harcourt, Brace & World, Inc., 1962. Chapter 11 and Appendices A, B, C, D, and E. A practical discussion of basic statistical techniques applicable to test scores. Appendixes contain tables of squares, square roots, reciprocals, and other statistics useful in calculations.

5. Garrett, Henry E. *Statistics in Psychology and Education,* Fifth Edition. New York: David McKay Co. Inc., 1958. One of the most widely used testbooks in statistical methods for workers in psychology and education. Replete with illustrations and applications in clear, readable style.

6. Gerberich, J. Raymond; Greene, Harry A.; and Jorgensen, Albert N. *Measurement and Evaluation in the Modern School.* New York: David McKay Co., Inc., 1962. Chapters 13, 14. A discussion of the interpretation of test scores and an explanation of basic statistical procedures for analysis of scores. Appropriate for beginners.

7. Ross, C. C., and Stanley, Julian C. *Measurement in Today's Schools,* Third Edition. New York: Prentice-Hall, Inc., 1954. Chapters 3, 9; Appendixes A, D. Good, practical treatment of simple statistical analysis and graphical presentation. Also presents problems and exercises in Appendix A, and computation of square roots in Appendix D.

8. Smith, G. Milton. *A Simplified Guide to Statistics for Psychology and Education,* Third Edition. New York: Holt, Rinehart & Winston, Inc., 1962. In less than one hundred pages all the statistics that most teachers, counselors, or beginners in research will need. Lucid and practical. Includes a table of squares and square roots.

9. Walker, Helen M. *Elementary Statistical Methods,* Revised. New York: Holt, Rinehart & Winston, Inc., 1958. A good basic textbook for beginners. Not too advanced or technical, but sound and thorough.

4

Finding and Selecting

Good Measuring Instruments

The title of this chapter poses a problem of concern to all people who
want to use a test[1] for a specific purpose or in a certain situation. What
is a good test of intelligence for fifth-grade pupils? Is there a reliable test
for measuring the interests of high school youngsters? How can I find out
what tests and other measuring devices are available? How can I tell
whether or not a measuring instrument is suitable for my purpose? These
and similar questions confront teachers, counselors, and administrators
who are responsible for measurement in the schools. Unfortunately, the
answers are too often based on hearsay or the opinion of an individual
who may have little actual knowledge on which to base his statements.
Undoubtedly a test is often chosen, purchased, and used on no better
basis than the casual word of a fellow teacher, principal, or counselor.
When a test is selected in this manner, there is at least a fair chance that
it will not prove to be entirely appropriate and satisfactory. In most cases,

[1] Although the discussion in this chapter deals largely with published, standardized
tests, it should be understood that the principles presented also apply to a considerable extent to measuring instruments and devices of all types.

if the test is not successful, there is a danger that the test itself may be condemned when actually its failure to do the job properly is the result of its misuse.

How then does one go about the intelligent selection of a test for a specific purpose? This question really should be considered in two major divisions: (1) sources of information about available measuring instruments, and (2) characteristics of a good measuring instrument.

Each of these topics will be considered in some detail in this chapter, although the main part of the discussion will be concerned with the latter — the characteristics of a good measuring instrument.

SOURCES OF INFORMATION

Publishers' Catalogs

For a first or preliminary survey of the available tests for any purpose, publishers' catalogs are invaluable. Most catalogs supply enough information to give the prospective purchaser a rather complete overview of each test without going into great detail. These catalogs are free upon request. All the publishers listed in Appendix C are reputable firms which will gladly send catalogs or lists of tests upon request. When corresponding with publishers about tests or test literature, one should write on school stationery, stating one's official connection or position, because publishing firms do not usually send such materials to unauthorized persons.

The catalogs and other advertising material distributed by the test publishers generally contain fairly objective and reliable information about each test. Usually included are brief statements concerning such matters as the purpose for which the test is intended, cost, number of equivalent forms, the grade level for which the test is appropriate, and the type of norms available. Most test publishers are restrained from making false or exaggerated claims for a test by the very keen competition in this field and by the certainty that a test must prove itself to be good during a period of several years if it is to show a profit. Critical reviews by test specialists who are often in a position to recommend tests constitute another factor which leads publishers to be conservative in advancing claims for the quality of their tests.

The sample entry on the following page, taken verbatim from the catalog of a publisher, will serve to illustrate the type of statements usually found in test publishers' catalogs.

Barrett-Ryan-Schrammel English Test:
New Edition, Grades 9–13

E. R. Barrett, Teresa M. Ryan, H. E. Schrammel

Contains five subtests covering *Functional Grammar, Punctuation, The Sentence* (parts of speech), *Vocabulary*, and *Pronunciation*. **Time:** 60 minutes. **Scoring:** *Hand score* detachable answer sheet or IBM Answer Sheet with IBM Machine Key. *Machine score* IBM Answer Sheet either locally or through HB&W's Scoring Service. **Norms:** Percentiles.

BARRETT-RYAN-SCHRAMMEL ENGLISH TEST	FORMS	NET PRICE
Test Booklet	DM, EM	$4.00 pkg/35
IBM Answer Sheet (Optional)	DM-EM	1.75 pkg/35
IBM Scoring — Basic Service (Optional. See page 86.)		.30 per student
Specimen Set		.40 each

Test package contains Directions, IBM Machine Key, and Class Record. IBM Answer Sheet package contains Class Record.

Specimen Sets

Although test publishers' catalogs provide valuable information about their tests, they do not make possible a thorough and adequate comparison when a choice must be made between several tests presumably suitable for a given purpose. For example, let us suppose that a search of several catalogs for available reading tests for intermediate grades has revealed at least three on the market. It would not be possible to make an intelligent choice without more information than is provided in the respective publishers' catalogs. The best way to obtain more information is to ask the publisher of each of the three tests for a specimen set. Such a set, costing perhaps fifty cents, will include a copy of the test, the manual, a scoring key, and perhaps other accessory material such as a class record sheet. Now it is possible to examine the test for content, length, and appropriateness for local conditions. The prospective user may even want to take or at least run through each test himself to become thoroughly familiar with it.

Although the test itself is perhaps the most interesting item in a specimen set, it is the manual which provides the data for a critical evaluation. A good manual will contain information about the following matters pertaining to the test: (1) purposes; (2) selection of content; (3) plan of organization; (4) directions for administering and scoring; (5) validity and reliability; (6) norms; (7) interpretation of scores; and (8) use of results.

All of the above are useful criteria in making comparisons of standardized tests and arriving at a choice. Lack of information regarding or inadequate meeting of any of them may be sufficient basis for eliminating a test from consideration.

With specimen sets in hand one can make a careful appraisal and comparison of each test under consideration. There is no better way to do this short of actual experience in the use of a test over a period of time.

Other Publications

Some test publishers distribute to school personnel series of short articles dealing with practical problems of testing. A sample list of these articles follows:

CALIFORNIA TEST BUREAU

Educational Bulletin No. 9: Identifying Difficulties in Learning Arithmetic. Willis W. Clark.
Educational Bulletin No. 18: Educational Diagnosis. Ernest W. Tiegs.
Educational Bulletin No. 22: Using Test Results to Identify Students' Needs for Corrective Instruction. Robert J. Darling, Raymond T. Eddy, and Jack R. Matlock.

EDUCATIONAL TESTING SERVICE

Selecting an Achievement Test. Evaluation and Advisory Service Series, No. 3.
Making the Classroom Test. Evaluation and Advisory Service Series, No. 4.
Short-Cut Statistics for Teacher-Made Tests. Evaluation and Advisory Service Series, No. 5.

HARCOURT, BRACE & WORLD, INC.

Test Service Notebook No. 13: A Glossary of 100 Measurement Terms. Roger T. Lennon.
Test Service Notebook No. 25: How Is a Test Built? Kenneth F. McLaughlin.
Test Service Bulletin No. 93: Test Interpretation in the High School Guidance Program. George E. McCabe.

HOUGHTON MIFFLIN COMPANY

Testing Today, No. 6, Winter, 1962. "Project Talent." John C. Flanagan.
Changes in the Intelligence Quotient. Samuel R. Pinneau. Ohio Norms Compiled for the Iowa Tests of Basic Skills.

PSYCHOLOGICAL CORPORATION

Test Service Bulletin No. 50: How Accurate Is a Test Score? Jerome E.
Doppelt.
Test Service Bulletin No. 54: On Telling Parents About Test Results.
James H. Ricks, Jr.
Test Service Bulletin No. 50: The Identification of the Gifted. Harold
G. Seashore.

Such articles apply the results of test research to the problems of teacher,
counselor, or administrator. Copies of the articles are usually free and,
although intended to help the sales of the respective publishing houses,
they are worth the thoughtful consideration of every person interested in
problems of measurement.

University Research and Service Bureaus

Most universities have an office or bureau to which prospective users of
tests may turn for advice and help. The members of the staff of such an
organization are frequently able to lend copies of available tests from their
files and give advice on the strengths and weaknesses of various tests. They
are usually willing to meet with and help committees of school personnel
authorized to choose tests for particular purposes. Such bureaus nearly
always have files of test publishers' catalogs and specimen sets or copies
of many published standardized tests. The persons in charge of these organizations are generally experienced test technicians and supervisors who
can help inexperienced school people avoid mistakes and save time and
money.

However, one should not place too much reliance upon the help of such
individuals, expert though they may be. Ideally, every teacher and counselor should be qualified to appraise tests objectively in the light of his own
situation, and, in the final analysis, be competent to select his own tests.

The persons connected with test and research bureaus, the instructors in
courses in measurement, and even representatives of test publishers, whose
job it is to help people select the best tests for the purpose at hand, will
seldom try to force the choice of a particular test on anyone. These specialists will usually follow the more ethical procedure of making available
several different tests with information about each, permitting the prospective user to choose the one best suited to the needs of his own situation.

Mental Measurements Yearbook and other Periodical Reviews

The meticulous user of tests will often want even more information than
that obtainable from the sources already mentioned. Having examined

catalogs and specimen sample sets of tests and talked with colleagues and perhaps even with an expert, he may still be undecided and want more facts. The best and most complete source of evaluative data on tests is the *Mental Measurements Yearbook,*[2] new editions of which are published at frequent intervals. The *Yearbooks* have earned for themselves a unique position in measurement literature. Each edition contains impartial, critical reviews of the majority of available standardized tests. Moreover, the more widely used tests are reviewed in successive editions of the *Yearbook* to show how the tests compare over a period of years. No equally objective, reliable, and comprehensive source of information and expert opinion concerning published tests is available.

Certain journals, such as *Educational and Psychological Measurement,* publish reviews which, generally speaking, are more useful to the test specialist or research worker than to a classroom teacher or guidance counselor. However, when the prospective user of a test is undecided, the reviews found in such periodicals and those in one or another edition of the *Mental Measurements Yearbook* may help materially in reaching a decision. It is much easier to find commentary on a particular test in the *Yearbooks* since the reviews are contained in one volume. In the periodicals, of course, the reviews appear in various issues.

Having consulted all or most of the above-described sources of information about tests, the prospective user should be in a favorable position to make a choice. He has first found out what is available to meet his needs; he has then gathered all the information he can from different sources about the tests which seem to hold possibilities for his purposes; he has related all this information to the situation in which the test is to function and the purposes for which it is to be used. In taking these steps, the prospective user has done everything possible, short of actually using the test, to insure success and efficiency in accomplishing his purposes.

▶ LEARNING EXERCISES ◀

1. Examine several catalogs of test publishers. How complete are the entries for each test? How do they compare in different catalogs?

2. Ask your instructor for a specimen set of a standardized test. Examine it for information concerning the criteria listed on page 74. Do you consider it adequate? In what respects (if any) do you consider it inadequate?

[2] Oscar K. Buros (ed.), *The Sixth Mental Measurements Yearbook* (Highland Park, N.J.: The Gryphon Press, 1965).

3. Read the reviews of a particular standardized test (perhaps the one used in Exercise No. 2, above) in the latest edition of the *Mental Measurements Yearbook*. Write a short evaluation of the test, basing it upon the *Yearbook* reviews.

CHARACTERISTICS OF A GOOD MEASURING INSTRUMENT

After studying the information available from the sources described above, how does one proceed to select for use one of two or three tests, all of which are available from reputable publishers? For the sake of this discussion we shall assume that the tests under consideration appear to be equally suited to local conditions and that the strengths and weaknesses of the tests are fairly well balanced as far as the obvious and non-technical features are concerned. What, then, are the basic criteria of a more technical nature that may be used as guides in the selection of a test or other measuring device?

All good measuring instruments have certain primary qualities in common. These are the universals — the qualities which differentiate good tests from inferior ones — whether they are for the use of the educator, the psychologist, the medical technician, the physicist, or people in other fields. A test which lacks a known and substantial degree of these primary qualities is not a measuring instrument in any true sense, and little or no dependence can be placed upon results obtained by its use. The two universals generally agreed upon are *validity* and *reliability*.

Besides these two universal requirements for a good test, whatever the field, there are certain secondary characteristics which are desirable in all good educational and psychological tests: *objectivity, ease of administration, ease of scoring,* and *ease of interpretation.* These characteristics are far less crucial than validity and reliability, but they affect validity and reliability to some extent and in any event make the use of a test much simpler.

In addition to these secondary characteristics, which are valuable in all educational and psychological tests, there are certain other attributes which are present in good standardized tests and which distinguish such tests from the informal, unstandardized or teacher-made tests. These attributes or criteria are *adequate norms, equivalent forms,* and *economy.* They are important for any good standardized test, though seldom applicable to unstandardized tests.

The rest of this chapter is devoted to a discussion of each of the above-mentioned characteristics of measuring instruments.

Validity

Of the two primary requisites of good measurement — those just referred to as universals — validity is generally regarded as the most important. Validity is the degree to which a test measures what it purports to measure. The definition of validity in a testing situation may be elucidated by such questions as these: What does this test actually measure? To what extent does it measure a particular ability, quality, or trait? In what situation or under what conditions does it have this degree of validity? In short, the question is essentially, To what degree does the test do the job it was intended to do? For example, in constructing achievement tests, an attempt is usually made to measure important outcomes of instruction, such as computation ability in arithmetic. To the extent that a test does measure the degree of attainment of this objective, it is considered to have validity. To the extent that it measures something else, perhaps reading ability, its validity as a measure of computational ability is lessened.

A test designed to predict success in college or university work is valid to the extent that those who make higher scores on it get better marks, stay in school longer, and more often graduate than those who get lower scores. A test designed to measure musical aptitude is valid to the extent that it distinguishes between persons who will succeed in varying degree in musical careers.

From the foregoing it is clear that validity is specific to the purpose and situation for which a test is used. A test might be a highly valid measure of intelligence for third-grade children and decreasingly valid for this purpose for fifth-graders, ninth-graders, high school graduates, and college seniors. Again, a test of manual dexterity might be a highly valid measure of probable success in assembling parts of small electric motors, but decreasingly valid for predicting success in farming, selling automobiles, managing a printing establishment, or teaching higher mathematics. A test which measures the thinking ability of seventh-grade pupils might well be almost a pure memory test for older persons who have been out of school for a long time. Thus, a test may be highly valid for one purpose and almost wholly lacking in validity for another. In the same way that a thermometer is used to measure temperature only, and a barometer to measure atmospheric pressure only, each testing instrument provides valid measurement for specific purposes.

Furthermore, it should be noted that validity is a matter of degree. That is, we would not ordinarily speak of a test as being completely valid or entirely invalid. Our concern is, rather, *how* valid is it or how well does it serve the purpose it is intended to serve? Does it do so extremely well, to a reasonable degree, or very little? To answer this question, in educational and psychological measurement we often employ the correlation techniques described in the preceding chapter. How this works, we shall explain more fully later in this chapter.

With these preliminary and basic considerations in mind, we may proceed to a discussion of different concepts of validity and of methods of determining the degree of validity of a particular technique of measurement or test. As conceived here, there are three types of validity, namely *curricular, empirical* or *statistical,* and *logical.* Each of these will be defined and illustrated and appropriate methods for determining each will be explained. Before doing so it will be desirable to refer to pronouncements on this matter by a national committee.[3] In its discussion of validity the Committee has suggested four types of validity information which it has named content validity, concurrent validity, predictive validity, and construct validity. Although this terminology has not been universally or uncritically accepted by test specialists, it has been widely adopted and used. To avoid confusion we shall proceed in this discussion on the basis that our curricular validity and the Committee's content validity have the same meaning; that our empirical or statistical validity includes both concurrent and predictive validities; and that we use logical validity with essentially the same connotation as the Committee's construct validity. With this frame of reference it will be possible for those who prefer the Committee's terminology to equate it directly and easily to that used here.

Curricular (Content) Validity

When a teacher gives a test which deals with the material and with the objectives of instruction in a particular class, his test is said to have curricular validity. Let us suppose that he has been teaching the rules for writing formulas of chemical compounds and has illustrated those rules with a variety of actual formulas showing how each one is written in accordance with the system of chemical symbols, the valence of the elements, etc. After perhaps a week of such instruction he makes a test, the questions of which are based on the same rules and on the same or similar formulas that he has been teaching. Under such circumstances the curricular validity of this test is taken for granted.

If achievement tests are based on what has been taught, they may be assumed to have curricular validity. Some tests purport to go beyond the

[3] Committee on Test Standards of the American Educational Research Association, National Education Association and National Council on Measurements Used in Education, *Technical Recommendations for Achievement Tests* (Washington: NEA, 1955).

knowledge, skills, and other immediate goals of instruction and attempt to measure more remote or ultimate goals, such as behavior in a situation in which the student must apply what he has learned. The validity of such tests is broadened to the extent that this attempt to measure applied knowledge or some other remote or ultimate quality is successful.

In constructing achievement tests and batteries it is common practice to give careful consideration to analyses of textbooks, courses of study, and other instructional materials to insure that the tests will have curricular validity. The degree of such validity is proportional to the extent to which the tests measure the goals of instruction and content that are common to courses of study and textbooks on the subject.

The efforts to construct tests measuring the ability to understand, interpret, and apply — rather than the ability to memorize facts — emphasize the problem of verbalism, concerning which much has been said and written in recent years. A test which measures only the ability to parrot what has been memorized will have less curricular validity than one which measures understanding — the ability to interpret and to apply — unless, of course, memorization of facts is all that has been taught.

Students who criticize an examination on the grounds that it measures only the capacity for memorizing facts may have a legitimate complaint. On the other hand, it may be argued that a student cannot understand or apply what he has not learned. If the ultimate objectives of instruction go beyond the memory of facts, then our tests, to be valid in a curricular sense, must also go further in what they attempt to measure. If and when they do, the gain for education will be in two directions at once. The tests will be better because they will have greater curricular validity, and instruction will be improved because teachers will tend to go beyond mere verbalism to stress broader and more functional outcomes.

Empirical (Concurrent and Predictive) Validity

This type of validity generally is based on agreement between scores on a test and some outside criterion, such as teacher's marks, or some future measure of success as graduation from college. Correlation between test scores and some other measure (marks, another test, ratings) taken at or near the same time is called concurrent validity. Correlation between test scores and some measure of performance or success obtained later (graduation, success on the job), is called predictive validity. Since the distinction between the two is not always easy or even possible, and since they represent essentially the same approach to validation, we lump them under the term empirical.

Empirical validity is appropriate wherever some other measure or criterion of the same quality, ability, or trait as that which the test being validated purports to measure is available. It is widely used with tests of achievement, intelligence, and aptitude, since many other criteria of what these tests are designed to measure are readily available. The basic procedure is to determine the correlation between scores on the test and some criterion judged to be a valid measure of the same ability, quality, or trait. In the case of an achievement test in arithmetic, for example, one type of empirical evidence of validity would be a comparison of marks given in arithmetic with scores made by the pupils who took the test. It would be possible to work out a coefficient of correlation between the teacher's marks and the actual test scores as a measure of the validity of the test. However, it is necessary to recognize the limiting factors in such a comparison. These are, first, the reliability of both the test and the teacher's marks (criterion) and, second, the validity of the teacher's marks (criterion). If the teacher's marks are perfectly reliable and valid measures of achievement in arithmetic, and the test scores are perfectly reliable, the resulting correlation between marks and test scores will be an accurate measure of the validity of the latter. The less reliable and valid the teacher's marks and the less reliable the test, the lower will be the maximum validity which the test can show empirically.

With intelligence tests, correlations between I.Q.'s and various measures of scholastic success are frequently cited as evidence of the validity of the tests. Similarly, correlations between test scores and ratings by teachers, between test scores and job success, and between test scores and results of other tests or measures judged to have validity — all are commonly used as empirical evidence of the degree of validity of tests.

Know

Logical (Construct) Validity

We might begin our discussion of logical validity by stating that this type of validation is employed where curricular or empirical validity either cannot be employed or to supplement them. As the joint committee's report[4] suggests, construct validity may be thought of as embracing all types of validity. The same may be said of our concept of logical validity. Certainly one would not wish to suggest that some types of validity or validation procedures are illogical. However, in the sense in which we use the term here, logical validity usually applies where the others are not applicable. It is quite natural to think of curricular validity in connection with achievement tests which are designed to measure the results of teaching a

[4] *Ibid.*

defined body of content as in English or science. Likewise, as has been explained, empirical validity is most useful where outside criteria are readily available. However, neither of these is always appropriate. An example or two will illustrate and clarify such situations.

The well-known *Seashore Measures of Musical Talents* consists of a series of records presenting tasks dealing with pitch discrimination, time intervals, rhythm patterns, and other basic musical abilities. These are not generally the subject matter of instruction in music classes, yet the author by logical analysis has resolved the ability to perform well, musically speaking, into a few fundamental aptitudes and has incorporated in his test objective methods of measuring these aptitudes. The validity of this test may be thought of in two ways: first, as a measure of ability in pitch discrimination, etc., and second, as a measure for predicting success in a musical field or career. Validity is logical in both aspects of the test, since both depend on the degree of success attained in logical analysis of musical talent. Similar examples can be drawn from such fields as mechanical aptitude and clerical aptitude. In each case the test is based on an analysis of those abilities, qualities, or traits that enter into successful performance. The logical validity of the tests is proportional to the degree that the analysis is accurate and complete, and to the degree that the tests reproduce and measure the actual skills involved.

In the case of intelligence tests, logical validity is attained to the extent that the tests contain tasks which actually require intelligence to perform successfully. The nature of these tasks is usually arrived at by introspective, logical analysis. Alfred Binet, the originator of our present-day approach to the measurement of intelligence, was the first person to arrive at a logical analysis of what an intelligent act involves, psychologically speaking. He came to the conclusion that "to judge well, to comprehend well, to reason well, these are the essentials of intelligence." Binet and his co-worker, Théodore Simon, proceeded to devise tests which seemed to them to measure these abilities. Their efforts were so successful that the basic approach they used has scarcely been improved upon to the present time.

Again, in the case of the intelligence test a logical criterion (a construct) of intelligence is that scores on such a test should increase with increase in age, at least to the point of maturity. Thus we would expect the average score of ten-year-olds on an intelligence test to be higher than that of nine-year-olds, that of nine-year-olds to exceed that of eight-year-olds, and so on. This idea is consistent with all our theories of intelligence and our knowledge and observation of child growth and development. Therefore, a test whose scores show such a progression would be deemed to have logical validity.

Another technique in which logical validity is relevant is in the use of what are sometimes referred to as widely spaced groups. Let us suppose that we wish to have some evidence of the validity of a so-called adjustment or personality inventory. We might proceed, under this plan, to have a group of persons rated according to individual adjustment by those who know members of the group intimately. The result would probably be a spread or distribution of the individuals from one extreme (very well adjusted) to the other (very poorly adjusted). Next, we might take the highest 10 per cent and the lowest 10 per cent of this distribution and give those persons the test we are attempting to validate. We would then score the papers of the two groups and compare them as groups. If our test is valid as a measure of the adjustment of individuals, we should expect the highest 10 per cent to make a much better average score than the lowest 10 per cent. Furthermore, we should expect to find little or no overlapping between the two groups.

In concluding the discussion of validity we should consider the question of the interpretation of validity data. What is an acceptable coefficient of validity? The answer to this question depends on the situation in which it is determined. For example, the correlations between scores, or I.Q.'s on an intelligence test and teacher's marks will usually range from the .30's to the .50's. This is not very high, numerically speaking, and one might ask why this is so. The reason is not difficult to find. For one thing, teacher's marks are influenced by many factors other than intelligence. These, such as the attitude of the teacher toward the student and his industry, interest, and previous preparation all influence his mark, and they are not measured by the intelligence test at all. Furthermore, since, as we shall see shortly, validity is influenced or determined in part by reliability, and since the intelligence test is not perfect with respect to reliability, and teacher's marks are notably unreliable, no matter how well our test actually measures pure intelligence, the correlation between it and marks will always be less than perfect.

The correlations between standardized tests of achievement and teacher's marks in the same subject will generally be somewhat higher, and the correlation between a standardized achievement battery and grade point average or rank in class will generally be found in the .60's or even .70's. In both instances the correlation will be higher because of greater similarity between what the test measures and teacher's marks; in the first instance the grade point average will be a more reliable measure of a student's scholarship than a mark in a single subject.

The correlations between two tests of intelligence or two standardized tests of achievement will generally range from the .60's to the .80's. Similarly, the correlations between good intelligence tests and standardized achievement tests may often be in the same range.

In interpreting validity coefficients it is necessary therefore to take into account the situation in which the correlation has been determined. The less similar the measures and the less reliable, the lower such coefficients will be. One of .35 may be all that can reasonably be expected in one case, whereas in another, a coefficient of .65 or .70 may be quite in order.

▶ **LEARNING EXERCISES** ◀

4. Classify each of the following as content, empirical, or construct validity:
   a. The correlation between scores on a standardized test in arithmetic and success in first-year algebra.
   b. A teacher-made test covering the work assigned and covered over a six-week period in class.
   c. On a test of musical aptitude, a mean score of 85 for music majors and a mean score of 40 for an unselected group of freshmen.
   d. A table showing the chances of success in a particular curriculum for different levels of performance on a test.

5. Approximately what would you expect the correlation to be between the following:
   a. Scores on an intelligence test and freshmen grade-point average?
   b. Job ratings of machinists by their foreman and a test of manual dexterity?
   c. Scores on an achievement battery for ninth-graders and their I.Q.'s?
   d. Rank in class of high school graduates and marks in first-year college work?

Reliability

In discussions of the two universal criteria of a good test it is customary to think of validity as the most important quality and to discuss it first, as we have done. However, it is worth noting that reliability is essential to validity but the opposite is not so. A test may be reliable without being valid, whereas the validity of a test depends in part on its reliability; therefore, a test is only as valid as it is reliable. Reliability refers to the consistency of measurement. The meaning of consistency may be best clarified by the use of a few illustrations. It was observed long ago that when an individual measured the diameter of a very accurately turned steel ball several times with an exceedingly accurate pair of calipers, he did not get exactly the same result every time. Even with the most accurate instruments available and the best possible control of conditions, the successive measurements of the diameter of the steel ball always varied somewhat. The extent of such variations is a measure of the consistency, or the lack of it, in this measuring situation.

In educational and psychological measurement we have another way of expressing and gauging consistency. In measuring the qualities of human beings it is seldom possible or even appropriate to determine the consistency of measurement by many repeated measurements of the same thing as was done in the illustration of the steel ball. Since we are dealing with living, changing organisms, we cannot expect numerous repeated measurements to show nearly such close agreement. Therefore, when dealing with people, we determine consistency by measuring a number of individuals — only twice as a rule — and comparing the relative standards of the individuals on the two sets of measurements or scores. It should be noted that the two successive measurements are usually not more than a few days apart.

To illustrate with a simple example, let us suppose we have given a group of seven children a test of clerical aptitude and ranked them according to their scores. A day or two later we repeat the test *on the same group* of seven children and rank them again. The results might be as shown in Table VII.

The degree of consistency of measurement can be judged here by the extent to which the pupils tend to hold the same relative positions in their group. We can see that this tendency is high in this case since all pupils except F and G hold the same rank in both applications of the test, and even those two pupils shift only slightly.

It should be pointed out that in this example all the children show a gain in score between the first and the second testing, but their relative standings or ranks change in only two cases. If all individuals made the same score

TABLE VII • Comparison of Scores Made by
Seven Children on the Same Test
Administered Twice

Pupil	First Testing		Second Testing	
	Score	Rank	Score	Rank
A	52	4	55	4
B	60	2	65	2
C	45	5	48	5
D	68	1	69	1
E	57	3	60	3
F	29	7	40	6
G	31	6	35	7

both times, or made lower scores the second time, the test would still show a high degree of consistency provided that the ranks of the individuals did not change. This, then, is what we mean by consistency. Conversely, a lack of consistency is shown by the degree to which individuals do not hold the same or similar relative positions in a group when measured twice with the same test.

In determining the reliability or consistency of measurement of a standardized test the number of individuals tested would usually be much larger, probably several hundred in all, but the principle would be the same. While there are various methods of estimating the reliability of educational or psychological tests, those most commonly used are based upon two measurements (or what is considered an equivalent procedure) of the same individuals.

Although we generally speak of reliability with reference to tests, this quality is equally important in other measuring and evaluating techniques. Rating scales, personality tests, interest inventories, or even questionnaires are of little value unless we can be sure that the results obtained by their use are reasonably reliable.

Unreliability or inconsistency in a measuring instrument stems from two sources. These are, first, the situation in which it is used, including the physical and psychological state of the individuals tested, and second, the test itself. Such variable factors as conditions of testing, time limits, and directions can be fairly closely controlled provided that the persons using the test are willing to study directions carefully and follow them exactly. Conditions of the individual, such as fatigue, motivation, illness, and similar temporary factors, though not always as serious as sometimes imagined, are harder to control. There is no doubt that these conditions tend to reduce the reliability of measurement, but it is also a fact that most of our good standardized tests show remarkably high reliability in spite of the operation of such factors.

The principal factors in the measuring instrument itself which may affect the reliability of a test are the quality of the individual questions or items and the length of the test. Concerning the individual items, there are many ways in which the quality of the questions can affect reliability. For example, a question may be ambiguous; that is, it may be subject to more than one interpretation or it may be so worded that its meaning is simply not clear.

The avoidance of ambiguity in test items contributes materially to the attainment of high degree of reliability, though even the most skillful test makers cannot always avoid this fault. In preparing a test one should guard against vagueness and eliminate those items which prove on tryout to be

ambiguous. Practice and experience in making tests and a thorough knowledge of the subject matter are the best preventives against ambiguity in test
items.

A second factor which is inherent in the test itself and which affects the
consistency of measurement is the number of questions or the length of the
test. Other things being equal, the reliability of a test is proportional to its
length; that is, the longer a test is, the more reliable it tends to be. If we
stop to consider the implications of this statement we see that it seems perfectly logical. It means simply that the more samples we take of a given
area of knowledge, behavior, or material, the more reliable our appraisal
of that knowledge, behavior, or material will be. A chemist would not
think of basing his analysis of a carload of iron ore on a half dozen samples
taken at one end, or at one or two levels as the car is unloaded. Instead, he
systematically samples the iron ore at all locations and depths, and then, by
a system of "coning and quartering," reduces these many samples to one
of a few ounces which he can take into the laboratory for analysis. Here
he samples once more, basing his final judgment not on the analysis of one
sample, but on duplicate or even triplicate samples which are carefully
checked against each other for agreement.

If we represent the areas of knowledge, behavior, or material to be sampled or tested by circles, as in the diagram below, the effect of more adequate sampling (or more items or questions) is evident:

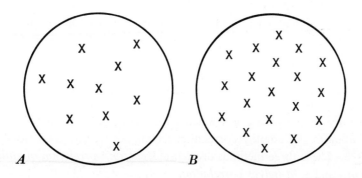

In *A* we have a sampling of the area by ten items; in *B* by nineteen. It
should be obvious that, other things being equal, the sampling in *B* will
yield more consistent and reliable results than that obtained in *A*.

Eventually we may reach a point of diminishing returns when sampling
is so thorough and reliability so high that additional sampling or testing
does not improve reliability enough to justify the extra time and effort required. There is a formula for determining the relationship between the
increased length of a test and its consequent increased reliability. Known

as the Spearman-Brown Prophecy Formula, it is very useful in showing how much the length of a test must be increased to attain a desired reliability, or conversely, how much the reliability of a test will be increased if its length is doubled, tripled, etc. The formula is $r_{nn} = \dfrac{nr}{1 + (n-1)r}$ where

r_{nn} = estimated reliability when the length of the test is increased n times, and r = the reliability of the test in question.

Thus, if a test of one hundred items was found to have a reliability of .80 and one wished to know what its reliability would be if the number of items were doubled, then $n = 2$, and $r = .80$, and

$$r_{nn} = \frac{2 \times .80}{1 + (2-1)\,.80} = \frac{1.60}{1.80} = .888.$$

This tells us that if the number of items were increased from one hundred to two hundred, the reliability of the test would be increased from .80 to .888 (or .89). The formula can also be used to determine how much a test's length would have to be increased to attain a desired reliability. In this case one simply substitutes in the formula the desired reliability (r_{nn}), the obtained reliability (r), and solves for n.

▶ LEARNING EXERCISES ◀

6. Suppose you had determined the reliability of a fifty-item test to be .75. What would be the effect on its reliability of increasing the number of items to 150?

7. A test has a reliability of .80, but you desire a reliability of .90. By what factor would the length have to be modified to have the desired reliability?

Reliability of measuring instruments is usually determined by one of three methods. All employ correlation techniques as discussed briefly in Chapter 3. These three methods are *self-correlation, correlation of equivalent forms,* and *split-halves correlation.*

Self-correlation

The example cited earlier in this section (see page 85), in which a test was given twice to the same children with a day or so between testings illustrates the *self-correlation* or *test-retest* approach to the determination of reliability. By calculating the coefficient of correlation between the two sets of scores an estimate of the consistency of measurement called the *relia-*

bility coefficient is obtained. This test-retest method has the disadvantage of repeating exactly the same questions to the same individuals, a procedure which may operate differently in individual cases. Some pupils may remember many items and look up the answers they did not know, while others may forget the whole thing at once. Also, in this method of determining reliability, "practice effect" is generally at a maximum. By practice effect we mean the improvement of scores which results when the same pupils take the same test a second time. However, if this effect is uniform for all persons taking the test a second time, it does not influence reliability.

Self-correlation is a generally used and accepted method of estimating reliability, and it is very valuable in situations where no other approach is possible. Whenever the self-correlation method is used, it is particularly important to use a test of adequate length and to provide an interval of several days between successive testings.

Correlation of Equivalent Forms

If two or more equivalent forms of a test are available, reliability is usually measured by giving both forms to the same individuals and then calculating the coefficient of correlation from the two sets of scores. The two forms may be administered at one sitting or two, depending upon the time required, the age and maturity of the person tested, the nature of the test materials, etc. In most cases it is customary again to allow several days to intervene between testings. For reasons which are not always pertinent to the question of consistency or reliability, longer intervals tend to reduce the correlation and thus give lower results than should properly be obtained.

By employing two forms of a test we are virtually using two equal halves of the same instrument. Equivalent forms are the same in degree and range of difficulty; they cover the same areas of knowledge, skills, etc., even though they use different items or questions. They are as near alike in every respect as it is possible to make them. Equivalent forms eliminate or reduce to a minimum the practice effect which is present when the same test is given twice.

Split-Halves Correlation

It is often impossible to employ either of the methods described above to determine reliability of a test. It may not be feasible to test twice, there may not be equivalent forms available, or there may be other valid reasons for not using either the self-correlation or the equivalent forms correlation methods. In such cases we generally use what is known as the *split-halves* technique. In this procedure, the test whose reliability we wish to measure is given in the ordinary manner, the papers are scored as usual, and then two scores for each individual are obtained by scoring alternate halves of the test separately. Such scoring can be done in several ways. Probably the most commonly used method of obtaining two scores for each person is to base one score on only the odd-numbered items of the test and the other on only the even-numbered items. Thus in a test of one hundred items one score for any individual would be based on the fifty items numbered 1, 3, 5, 7, . . . 99, and one on the fifty items numbered 2, 4, 6, 8, . . . 100. Therefore if a pupil missed ten of the fifty odd-numbered items and twelve of the fifty even-numbered items, his two scores would be 40 and 38. His total score would, of course, be 78, the sum of 40 and 38, or $100 - (10 + 12)$.

Sometimes the test is split by selecting pairs of items which are thought to be equivalent and allocating one of each pair to each half of the test. Again, the test may be divided in the middle and the scores based on the first and second halves, respectively. Finally, tests may be split by allocating groups of items to alternate halves. Each procedure has advantages and disadvantages, and the choice of which one to follow must be determined on the basis of which procedure will give *the most nearly equivalent halves of the test*.

Having obtained two scores for each person tested, we can then calculate the coefficient of correlation between the two sets of scores. This is, in effect, the correlation between the two equivalent halves of the test administered at one sitting. If the two halves are truly equivalent and if the test is a reliable one, the correlation thus achieved is likely to be fairly high. One step more is necessary to enable us to determine the reliability of the entire test, in this example a test consisting of one hundred items. The obtained correlation coefficient in our example is based on scores which represent only halves of the test, that is, scores on only fifty items. Since we wish to know the reliability of the one-hundred-item test, we now apply the Spearman-Brown Prophecy Formula, discussed on page 88, and calculate the estimated correlation for one hundred items, that is, for a test twice as long as our fifty-item odd-even halves. In this manner it is also possible to calculate the estimated reliability of a test three times as long (150 items), or one of any other desired length.

The split-halves method of determining reliability usually gives results which are higher than those obtained by either of the other methods. For this reason, reliability coefficients thus determined are generally regarded as approaching the maximum value which could be reached under ideal conditions. If this fact is kept in mind, the method may be used in obtaining estimates of reliability in a wide variety of situations, often where no other method is possible. It should be noted that the method gives spuriously high reliability coefficients whenever test scores are dependent largely on speed; the split-halves method should not be used in such cases.

Standard Error of Measurement

Once a coefficient of reliability has been determined by one of the three methods described it may be used to determine what is called the Standard Error of Measurement. This statistic is based on the reliability coefficient and the standard deviation of the test and gives a measure of the accuracy of any particular score on the test.[5] Thus if the $S.E._m$ on a particular test is 3 points, the probability is two to one that an individual's true score does not differ from his obtained score by more than 3. In other words, if he makes a score of 56 on the test, the chances are two to one (or two out of three) that his true score is not less than 53 or more than 59. The $S.E._m$ is a useful statistic in interpreting individual scores on a given test.

Interpretation of Reliability Coefficients

A very natural and important question concerns the desirable magnitude of reliability coefficients. Of course it is advantageous for tests to be as reliable as possible. As we have pointed out earlier, the degree of reliability is influenced by a number of factors, such as the condition of the subjects being tested, the length of the test, the nature of items, etc. Nevertheless, the best standardized tests of achievement quite consistently show reliability coefficients of .90 or higher. Standardized tests of intelligence commonly have reliabilities almost as good, generally .85 or higher. The reliability coefficients for instruments such as personality tests and interest inventories are usually lower, the average being most often in the .70's and .80's, although some have not attained a correlation as high as .70.

Another consideration in interpreting reliability coefficients is the range or variability of the group. A test will have a substantially lower reliability when it is given to a group of children in a single grade than it will when administered to a group ranging over several grades. For practical purposes this means that the reliability of a test should be judged in terms of the circumstances under which its reliability was determined. A test whose

---

[5] The formula for the Standard Error of Measurement is $S.E._m = \sigma\sqrt{1-r}$. Details of calculation are shown in Appendix A.

reliability is suitable for a range of several grades or several years in chronological age may be unsuitable for use in discriminating among children in the same grade or of the same age. For such purposes a test with proven reliability in the narrower range should be sought.

Desirable reliabilities differ also according to purpose. When a test is intended only for use in studying groups, a lower reliability coefficient (around .75) may be sufficient to make fairly accurate comparisons. When individual differentiation is the goal, reliabilities of .95 or higher are very desirable.

▶ LEARNING EXERCISES ◀

8. A teacher gives a one-hundred-item objective final test to his students in high school biology (120 in five sections). He cannot give the same test again. Describe how he could proceed to determine its reliability.

9. The correlation between two equivalent forms of a standardized test given to the same students is .90. What is its reliability?

10. A test is given on two successive days to the same fifty students. On comparing the scores it is found that all improve their scores somewhat the second time but the ranks on the two testings remain the same. What would be the coefficient of stability?

11. The standard error of measurement of an I.Q. obtained from a well-known intelligence test is five points. Apply this fact in the case of a student whose score gives him an I.Q. of 110 and tell what it means.

12. Why are validity coefficients of standardized tests consistently lower than their reliability coefficients?

Aside from the two universally applicable criteria which have been discussed to this point, certain secondary attributes, important in all good tests in education and psychology, have already been mentioned and will be briefly discussed below. These characteristics are *objectivity, ease of administration, ease of scoring,* and *ease of interpretation.*

Objectivity

A test is objective to the extent that competent persons agree on the scoring of answers. In other words, a test may be said to be objective to the extent that the opinion or judgment of the scorer is eliminated from the scoring process. Objectivity is usually attained by (1) stating the questions specifically and precisely, (2) requiring specific, precise, short answers, and (3) scoring the test by the use of a previously determined scoring key. This key may be printed, in which case most of the scoring can be done by clerical workers; or, if properly prepared answer sheets are used, the test can be scored by a machine in a matter of a few seconds. In extensive testing which involves thousands of cases, the test-scoring machine is a means of saving much time and money.

Objectivity is a matter of degree; few, if any, tests are either wholly objective or wholly subjective. The conventional essay test, which consists of a few questions asking the student to "discuss," "describe," "give reasons for," etc., is relatively lacking in objectivity. Essay tests emphasize such matters as judgment, opinion, and interpretation, both on the part of the student and the person who evaluates his answers. It is inevitable that different persons, all judged to be competent in the field or subject, will evaluate the same examination paper quite differently. Yet much can be done to make this type of examination more objective by careful phrasing of the questions, prior preparation of ideal answers, prior agreement among readers or judges on rules for evaluating answers, and by other such precautions. The maximum change in the direction of objectivity is achieved by the use of objective questions designed to eliminate ambiguity in the answering of such items, and by the use of mechanical scoring with previously prepared scoring keys.

A questionable reliability is the most serious weakness of subjective tests, since, as has been said, reliability is directly affected by the degree to which the judgment, biases, and emotions of the scorer enter into his evaluation of the answers. It is only fair to the individual whose test is being evaluated that these personal factors be kept to a minimum.

Objective tests have often been severely criticized on the basis that they emphasize and measure only specific, unrelated bits of information instead of broader concepts, inter-relationships, understanding, and the ability to interpret. Too often, the critics claim, such tests encourage only the memorization of miscellaneous facts. Although the evidence on this point is not voluminous and is often conflicting, at least one thing seems clear: no one has ever demonstrated that the broader aspects of learning, such as interpretation and application of knowledge, cannot be measured objectively. In fact, there is much evidence to support the claim that objective tests can be and have been devised to measure some of these broader outcomes of education. If objective tests on the whole have been based on the narrower, more specific goals of instruction, it is largely because the makers of these tests have lacked the necessary skill, vision, and perhaps the motivation to base their questions on larger concepts. If a teacher sincerely believes in the importance of the broader goals he can do much to encourage their attainment by emphasizing them in his own tests.

Objectivity is essential to published standardized tests if the tests are to achieve maximum effectiveness. It would be very difficult, perhaps useless, to attempt any comparative interpretations of test results not arrived at objectively. Comparisons with norms, comparisons between individuals, classes, schools, sexes, regions, or grades, would be largely meaningless if each user of the test scored it according to his own independent ideas of the quality of the responses. One of the chief values of the standardized test is that personal judgments and biases are largely eliminated in the scoring and in the interpretation of results.

Ease of Administration

It seems reasonable to assume that the simpler a test is to administer, the less the probability of making mistakes which will affect the results. Contrast, for example, two well-known older group intelligence tests, the *Army Alpha* and the *Otis Self-Administering*. Both tests were at one time among the most widely used tests of intelligence.

The *Army Alpha* consisted of eight parts or sub-tests, each one precisely timed. The time limits were all short, varying from one and a half minutes to four minutes. Since each part had to be timed exactly with a stop watch and all participants were supposed to begin and stop work on each part of the examination at the same time, the administration of the test placed a great burden on the examiner, especially if he was not highly trained in the administration of group tests. The test lent itself to frequent errors in timing, misunderstanding of directions by examinees, and failure of individuals to begin and stop working at the right times.

The *Otis Self-Administering Test Series,* published about the same time as *Army Alpha,* presented a notable improvement over *Army Alpha* in ease of administration. The Otis tests were not subdivided; all questions were together in a single set or part. The preliminary directions explained thoroughly each type of item the examinee would encounter in the test and provided an opportunity for him to receive further explanations when needed. When all examinees were ready, the signal to begin was given and work proceeded uninterrupted until the time allowed for the entire test had elapsed. These tests were properly called "self-administering." Any intelligent, conscientious person could administer them correctly with just a little preliminary study of the directions. No additional equipment, not even a stop watch, was needed.

In the more than forty years since the *Otis-Self-Administering* tests were first published many changes have been made in group tests, but it is doubtful that any subsequent tests have been easier to administer. This criterion, while not of supreme importance, is nevertheless one that test authors should meet more adequately than they sometimes do. A little forethought and planning concerning the administration of the test will often eliminate difficulties which otherwise might plague thousands of users as long as the test is available.

Once the test is standardized there is usually nothing that can be done to improve directions for administering it. To simplify the administration of a test would be to change it, and this would invalidate the norms and other standardization data and procedures. Therefore the authors of tests should give careful thought to the nature and organization of the test, as these affect its administration, in order to eliminate all unnecessary complications and difficulties. Likewise, the prospective user of the test should carefully study each test under consideration, keeping this criterion in mind. *Other things being equal,* it is only common sense to choose the test which is the simplest to administer. This will generally save time, and the results will probably be more accurate since there is less likelihood of mistakes occurring in an easily administered test than in a more complicated one, especially when the test is to be used by persons not highly trained and skilled in test administration.

Ease of Scoring

Much of what we have said regarding ease of administration applies with equal force to ease of scoring. In fact, the test which is simple and easy to administer may also be easy to score, though this is not necessarily so. Sometimes administration and scoring are complicated because the test is designed to yield sub-scores or part-scores for diagnostic purposes. In such cases it is obvious that ease of administration and scoring must be sacrificed in order to achieve some other more important aim.

Another factor which affects ease of scoring is objectivity. One can work out the directions for a test ever so carefully, organize it as well as possible, and yet achieve only a difficult and burdensome scoring system because of the lack of objectivity of the test itself. If the items do not permit specific, objective answers, scoring will be difficult. Of course where scoring is done mechanically, nothing but objective types of items can be considered for use. Yet, surprising as it seems, a few widely used standardized tests still include such relatively non-objective types of items as completions or fill-ins. As anyone who has used such tests knows, these items always make scoring difficult.

The use of properly prepared stencils, scoring keys, etc., will also do much to simplify test scoring. Test publishers have developed various schemes for simplifying the scoring of standardized tests. For example, the *Clapp-Young Self-Marking Tests*[6] were, so far as the writer knows, the pioneers in the use of a double sheet. The pupil marks his answers on the front and back of the closed double answer sheet or booklet. Parts of the inside surfaces of the double sheet are printed with a carbon ink strip facing printed squares or other symbols which designate the correct answers. Thus, when the student pencils his markings on the front and back of the closed double sheet the carbon strip inside carries the impression of the mark to the area of the printed symbols indicating the correct answers. Upon completion of the test, the scorer, when he has separated the double sheet, can quickly tally the correct answers by counting the number of carbon impressions which coincide with the printed ones. Similar systems are used by other test publishers.

Where the new type of answer sheets are used, publishers generally provide with the test a perforated scoring stencil for hand scoring. This stencil fits over the answer sheet and has holes so placed that the pencil marks of correctly answered items are visible. Scoring can be done quite rapidly by fitting the proper stencil over the filled-out answer sheet and simply counting the number of marks that appear in the holes of the stencil. The same or similar stencils are also used for machine scoring. When scoring tests in this way it is necessary to check each answer sheet to see that no one has marked more than one space in answering any item. Teachers will often make their own scoring stencils, which greatly facilitate the task of scoring examinations.

In recent years a number of different systems for the rapid and accurate scoring of standardized tests by mechanical devices have been developed. These systems have made possible the scoring of thousands of answer sheets or cards in a few hours. Many test publishers provide such a scoring service to users of their tests for an additional fee. The user of a test can purchase the scoring service with the tests and answer media. At additional cost he can also get an analysis of the results, including distributions, means, standard deviations, percentile ranks, correlations — almost anything he wants and is willing to pay for. All this can be provided in a comparatively short time. For users of large quantities of standardized tests such services are not only very helpful but also economical both in the time saved and in the actual cost of doing the work.

There are a few other considerations that have a bearing on this point. The more complicated the scoring, the greater is the chance for errors, and

---

[6] Published by Houghton Mifflin Company, Boston.

the more time-consuming the job of correcting the work. Also, if scoring becomes too burdensome and time-consuming it may never be finished. Tests may even be enthusiastically purchased and administered, only to be placed on shelves somewhere, the scoring never completed. Certainly there may be other causes contributing to such a state of affairs, but lack of time and energy for the burdensome job of scoring must be reckoned with.

Finally, the success of the scoring process depends to some extent on having simple, accurate, and clear directions for scoring. There is some variation among manuals for standardized tests with respect to this point. Directions for scoring some tests are so clear that the scorer cannot go wrong; at the other extreme are directions which are a veritable puzzle, even for experienced testers. However, it must be recognized that the aim of test authors and publishers is to consistently make their directions as simple and intelligible as possible. It is not to be expected that this goal will be uniformly attained in all tests, mainly because of the variation in complexity and scope of different tests.

Ease of Interpretation

A test may meet all the criteria so far mentioned and yet present great difficulties when it comes to interpretation of the results. Ease of interpretation generally depends on two factors: first, the mechanics of interpretation, and second, the helps provided for giving meaning and significance to the scores.

The first point largely concerns the transmutation of the raw score on the test to some derived score. This is generally done through tables of norms. The best that can be done by way of simplification in this process is to set up these tables in such a way that they can be easily and accurately read. It often helps to present norms both in the form of tables and of graphs. A graph, such as a percentile curve, may make the transition from raw scores to percentile equivalents easier, faster, and more accurate than a table can, especially in those cases which require interpolation in a table. Where profiles, either individual or group, are used, sample profiles should be given to assist inexperienced test users in constructing some for their own cases.

It is also desirable for the sake of easy interpretation not to crowd too much into one chart or table. In their desire to have everything in one handy place, test authors and publishers will sometimes crowd so much into a small space and use such small type that the ordinary user of the tests will become confused and lost in the maze of different types of scores, percentiles, mental ages, chronological ages, deciles, grade norms, and diagnostic devices presented on one page or in one chart.

The second point is perhaps the most difficult problem in the entire process of using standardized tests. After the tests are given and scored, the inevitable question is, What do the results mean? It is a sad but true fact that too often the test experts themselves, although proficient in their knowledge and advice about tests and how to administer and score them, are less skillful in providing practical aids for interpreting and applying the results. This is not wholly the fault of the so-called experts. It is extremely difficult to establish general rules for interpreting and using test results, rules which will apply in all or even most situations. What may be right for one test may be entirely inappropriate for another. The test manual usually suggests a variety of ways in which the test scores may be interpreted and used, and from the manual accompanying each test or group of tests the prospective user of any given test will gain some suggestions that are appropriate and useful. This is the function of the test manual. Some of our best tests now have manuals which in themselves are small textbooks on testing. These manuals are usually written clearly and without unnecessarily technical language so as to appeal to teachers and other prospective users of the tests. Usually the manuals contain a profusion of aids for simplifying the use and interpretation of the tests and many suggestions of ways in which the results can be used for better learning by, and counseling of, pupils. When considering the criterion of ease of interpretation in relation to a particular test, the prospective user must examine the manual carefully to find evidences of how well the criterion is met.

▶ LEARNING EXERCISES ◀

13. What is meant by objectivity? Subjectivity? Illustrate. How are measuring instruments made more objective?

14. Why must standardized tests be as objective as possible?

15. Some tests are very difficult and time-consuming to administer. Can you think of any situations in which this would be justifiable?

16. If a test-scoring machine is available in your vicinity, try to see the machine in operation. What are the limitations on the use of such equipment?

17. Examine a specimen set of a standardized test with respect to its objectivity, ease of administration, scoring, and interpreting. Is it satisfactory in every respect? If not, in what ways could it be improved?

We shall next discuss a group of characteristics which apply as a rule only to standardized tests. In fact, they apply so rarely to unstandardized, informal, classroom, and teacher-made tests that they may be considered as representing perhaps the chief differences between the two groups. These characteristics are *adequate norms, equivalent forms,* and *economy.* An informal, locally made test seldom has norms in any general sense; it rarely has two or more equivalent forms, and the question of cost is not usually a crucial factor. In the case of standardized tests, these factors are all of importance.

Adequate Norms

Every good standardized test has norms. In fact, one of the main purposes of the process of standardization is to establish norms. These may be of many types, depending upon the type of test and the uses for which it is intended. The common types of norms have been illustrated and discussed in Chapter 3, so they need not be repeated here. Adequate, usable norms are essential to a good standardized test. There was a time when standardized tests were published with inadequate norms, but now no reputable test publisher will put a test on the market without norms of some kind, and the better tests will have norms based on a large and reasonably adequate sampling of a representative population. The prospective user of a test should satisfy himself that the norms are based on a population sample that is representative from the standpoints of geographic areas, rural and urban populations, grade level, sex, socio-economic status, and types of schools. At this point the considerations regarding norms discussed in Chapter 3 find application. Careful reading of the test manual, particularly those parts describing how the normative population was chosen, will generally reveal whether or not the norms are representative, dependable, and useful.

It might be well to emphasize here that the fact that a test is printed does not mean it is standardized, and that all tests which claim to be standardized do not necessarily have adequate or useful norms. Furthermore, a test with adequate norms for a certain group might not be usable with people to whom these norms do not apply. For example, a test which has been standardized mostly on culturally disadvantaged children would probably have limited use with children from very superior environments.

We have already pointed out that the way the norms are presented and the adequacy of instructions for their use are important factors in the ease of interpretation of test results. It should be mentioned again, however, that the prospective user of a test can easily determine these qualities by a careful examination and study of the test and the accompanying manual.

Equivalent Forms

As a rule, a standardized test should have two or more equivalent forms. Again, this is one of the common differences between standardized and unstandardized tests. However, the fact that a test has two or more forms is not always to be taken as satisfactory evidence that the forms are really equivalent, for it will sometimes be found upon careful scrutiny of test and manual that they are not. Alternate forms may cover quite different areas of subject matter so that they are not at all comparable in this respect. They may also be unequal in difficulty — either in range of difficulty, in average difficulty, or both. Or they may be equivalent at some levels and not at others. For example, in a test of achievement for use in several successive grades the two forms may show equivalent difficulty at one grade level but not at the next higher or lower level. Such situations are probably the exception rather than the rule, but it is well for the test buyers to know that these possibilities exist and to keep them in mind when examining tests for possible use. By studying the test and the manual it should be possible to determine whether or not the different forms of the test are really equivalent.

Economy

The factor of economy, which we have already discussed at several points, is a real consideration, and we should emphasize here, first, that it must be reckoned in broad rather than narrow terms, and second, that — as far as possible — economy should be a determining factor in selecting tests only if all other criteria are equally well satisfied.

In elaboration of the first point, we may point out that, as with automobiles, for example, the important consideration is not so much the initial cost as the upkeep. The price per copy of the test booklet and answer sheet may well turn out to be one of the minor items in the total cost of testing, and it is a good idea to try to make accurate estimates of the total cost per pupil before embarking on any testing program. This estimate should include, in addition to the cost of the test materials themselves, the expense of scoring the tests, analysis of the results, and follow-up. Sometimes a test which costs less initially will cost more in the long run. It may be made of cheaper materials and have to be replaced sooner; or it might not be set up for use with answer sheets, in which case it can be used only once; it may require more scoring time; or it might even be found to be inadequate for its intended purpose, once the results are available.

The cost per pupil of testing with a battery such as the *Stanford Achieve-*

ment Test may be estimated at anywhere from twenty-five to fifty cents per pupil, depending upon the initial cost of the test booklet, upon who does the scoring and how the cost of this work is figured. If the scoring is done by teachers and no allowance is made for the time thus spent, the cost will be near the minimum. If the scoring must be computed on an hourly basis, the cost per pupil will be substantially higher. On the other hand, in the case of a test which is quickly and easily scored, this part of the cost will be a minor item in the total expense per pupil. Thus, costs must be calculated on the basis of more factors than just the actual price of the testing materials.

The second point relating to the criterion of economy is that no test is a bargain in cost if it is inferior in other important respects. Only if two tests are equally good for the purpose at hand should cost be the deciding factor. The prospective purchaser must satisfy himself by all the information available that two (or more) tests will do a job equally well before he makes a cost comparison. This is not to say that one should disdain a test merely because it is cheap. In the days when all tests were consumable, that is, when pupils marked their answers on the test itself rather than on separate answer sheets, some test publishers used cheaper, smaller print and a less expensive format without any evident harm to the usefulness of the test. If a test is not to be used over and over again with separate answer sheets, a test in the cheaper format may answer the purpose just as well as a more expensive test.

To summarize, the factor of economy in testing is a matter that goes far beyond the list price of the test in the publisher's catalog. For most users of tests in small quantities a difference of a few dollars per year may not be of great importance. Those who use large quantities of standardized tests year after year, however, should calculate carefully, taking many factors into account. Where large numbers of tests are used, small differences in cost per pupil will become very considerable in the aggregate and over long periods.

▶ LEARNING EXERCISES ◀

18. Examine the tables of norms reproduced on pages 64, 65 and 67, with respect to the discussion of norms in this chapter. Do they seem adequate and easily usable? What evidence do you find in the manuals to support your answer?

19. What are the advantages of equivalent forms? How would equivalent forms of a standardized test be made?

20. Name several factors that affect the economy of a measurement program besides the actual cost of the tests or other instruments used.

ANNOTATED BIBLIOGRAPHY

1. Anastasi, Anne. *Psychological Testing,* Second Edition. New York: The Macmillan Co., 1961. Chapters 5, 6, 7. A clear, practical discussion of reliability and methods for determining and utilizing validity data. The applications and illustrations are taken primarily from psychological testing, but the principles presented are applicable to all types of measurement of human abilities.

2. Buros, Oscar K. (ed.). *The Sixth Mental Measurements Yearbook.* Highland Park, N.J.: The Gryphon Press, 1965. (See also the earlier volumes dating from 1938 to 1959.) Each yearbook contains critical reviews of all obtainable published tests and books on measurement written in English. Most publications are reviewed independently by two or more specialists. Reviews in earlier editions are cross-referenced in later ones. This is one of the most useful publications in educational and psychological literature for the user and student of measuring instruments.

3. Campbell, D. T. "Recommendations for A.P.A. Test Standards Regarding Construct, Trait and Discriminant Validity," *American Psychologist,* 15: 546–553, August, 1960. An excellent synthesis of much that has been written on a rather controversial topic. Somewhat technical for beginners but challenging to those who want to try more solid fare.

4. Committee on Test Standards, American Educational Research Association, National Education Association, and National Council on Measurements Used in Education. *Technical Recommendations for Achievement Tests.* Washington: The NEA, 1955. An authoritative statement concerning the kinds of information test manuals should supply. Written primarily for authors and publishers, but a useful reference for students.

5. Cronbach, Lee J. *Essentials of Psychological Testing,* Second Edition. New York: Harper & Row, Publishers, 1960. Chapters 5, 6. Validity is discussed in terms of the Technical Recommendations referred to in this chapter with many examples and illustrations. The consideration of reliability is centered around different approaches to determining reliability coefficients.

6. Gerberich, J. Raymond; Greene, Harry A.; and Jorgensen, Albert N. *Measurement and Evaluation in the Modern School.* New York: David McKay Co., Inc., 1962. Chapter 3. A discussion of seven important characteristics of good educational appraisal devices and techniques: validity, reliability, adequacy, objectivity, practicality, comparability, and utility.

7. Harris, Chester (ed.). *Encyclopedia of Educational Research,* Revised Edition. New York: The Macmillan Co., 1960. Contains excellent discussions of all the recognized criteria of a good test. Some are probably too technical for the easy comprehension of beginning students, but most are well within the grasp of capable beginners.

8. Lindquist, E. F. (ed.). *Educational Measurement.* Washington: American Council on Education, 1951. Chapter 15: "Reliability," by Robert L.

Thorndike. Chapter 16: "Validity," by Edward E. Cureton. The best theoretical and statistical discussions of these two criteria now available. Much of the two chapters is too theoretical and advanced for beginning students of measurement, however.

9. Ross, C. C., and Stanley, Julian C. *Measurement in Today's Schools,* Third Edition. New York: Prentice-Hall, Inc., 1954. Chapter 4.   A well-documented discussion of three criteria — validity, reliability, and usability — ending with a presentation of five generalizations regarding the problem of measurement in the schools.

10. Thorndike, Robert L., and Hagen, Elizabeth. *Measurement and Evaluation in Psychology and Education,* Second Edition. New York: John Wiley & Sons, Inc., 1961. Chapter 7. Qualities essential to every measurement procedure are discussed under the main headings of validity, reliability, and practicality. Somewhat technical for beginners in educational measurement.

11. Wrightstone, J. Wayne; Justman, Joseph; and Robbins, Irving. *Evaluation in Modern Education.* New York: American Book Company, 1956. Chapter 3. The second half of the chapter consists of a brief discussion of the qualities for judging evaluative techniques, including tests.

5

Objectives as the Basis of All

Good Measurement

IMPORTANCE OF DEFINING OBJECTIVES

Teaching involves five essential processes; namely, defining goals or objectives, choosing content, deciding on methods of instruction, the instruction itself, and measuring results. The order of sequence is not absolutely fixed, particularly in regard to content and method, but measurement ordinarily comes last and definition of goals comes first — as it must if teaching is to have direction and purpose. To try to teach and evaluate without defining objectives is like starting out on a journey without knowing where to go. It may be pleasant to wander around for a while, but it is doubtful that any sort of progress can be made without some direction.

The good teacher formulates his objectives, chooses methods and materials in accordance with his objectives, employs these methods and materials, and uses measurement to determine how well or to what degree the objectives have been attained. In a sense everything is determined by the objectives. If the objective is to teach how to multiply two-place numbers by two-place numbers, the methods and materials will necessarily differ from those employed for teaching long division or square root; they will differ even more from the methods and materials used in teaching the parts of speech, the names of the chemical elements, or the story of the writing of the United States Constitution.

Objectives or goals may be stated in different ways, some of which will be discussed and illustrated later in this chapter. It may be that some teachers will not consciously formulate any objectives at all, but will simply teach "by the book." Nevertheless, every teacher works toward some objectives, even if it is only to get through the textbook by the end of the term. Whatever the objectives and no matter how they are formulated or thought of, they constitute an essential step or part of teaching. We do not mean to imply here that one way of thinking about or formulating goals is as good as another. We are saying only that every teacher necessarily has some goals or objectives which give direction and purpose to his work. It is highly important that these objectives be stated clearly and explicitly so that their meaning and implications are clear and well understood.

What has been said about defining objectives for teaching applies with equal force to measurement and evaluation. In order to measure the results and effectiveness of instruction it is essential to know what the teacher has been trying to accomplish. When objectives are poorly defined or perhaps not defined at all, it is impossible to do an effective job of evaluation.

In the five-step description of the teaching process mentioned above, measurement is the fifth or final step. There are occasions when measurement may come earlier, as in the case of pre-testing, and sometimes measurement is followed by re-teaching as in the case of diagnostic testing, but as a rule measurement is the last step in the procedure for any given unit or period of instruction. It reveals the success of the teacher's and the pupils' efforts. Measurement is the best way to determine to what extent the objectives of instruction have been attained. Unless there is systematic and effective appraisal, the extent of progress attained in the classroom must remain a matter of subjective opinion or conjecture.

Certainly teachers' opinions are valuable in determining the status and growth of pupils with respect to educational goals. However, they are only one element in the total process and it is important to supplement them with systematic and more objective measures. The teacher should employ the widest possible variety of measuring and evaluative tools and techniques, as long as these devices and techniques are practical and appropriate for the given situation. The use of a wide range of measurement tools is essential, not only from the standpoint of making appraisal more reliable, but also because different objectives or goals require different techniques of appraisal. If we desire to know how well some of the facts about the early history of our country have been learned we use one kind of instrument, possibly an objective test; if we wish to know how well pupils can handle rulers, read thermometers, or weigh objects, another approach to measurement would be employed. Still other techniques would be needed to determine the extent to which some of the precepts of good citizenship carry over into out-of-school behavior.

To summarize what has been presented so far, it might be said that objectives and measurement complement each other and are integral parts of a whole. Unless objectives are defined, we do not know what to try to measure, and unless we can measure, it is impossible to tell whether or not, and to what degree, objectives have been realized.

ARRIVING AT A USEFUL STATEMENT OF OBJECTIVES

Objectives or goals may be stated in various ways. For example, there are immediate objectives and ultimate objectives. Immediate objectives are often stated in terms of something specific to be learned, some skill, knowledge, or understanding to be mastered. Ultimate objectives, on the other hand, are more often stated in terms of some long-term goal and are likely to be focused more on the learner than on what is learned. They tend to emphasize the *function* of what is learned rather than the knowledge itself. In civics, for example, immediate objectives may be to learn about the organization of government, the responsibilities and functions of its different branches, and the duties and responsibilities of citizens in a democracy. Ultimate goals in civics might be to establish a continuing interest in improving our government and a willingness to perform conscientiously and consistently the duties of citizenship — such duties as examining and comparing political platforms, candidates, and issues, and exercising the right to vote.

A large share of our teaching and measurement has concerned itself with the immediate goals rather than the ultimate ones — testing for recall of instructional materials rather than for the ability to apply the knowledge and skills learned. There are several reasons for this. One is that teaching and testing for immediate objectives is more practical. Of course it is every teacher's hope and desire that what is taught today may be remembered and, even more important, carried over into action tomorrow and the next day, and a year or two or ten years from now. Also, every teacher hopes that what is learned in the classroom will function on the playground, at home, and elsewhere. But it is often not practical to measure the achievement of these ultimate objectives.

Second, because of the nature of what we teach, testing for immediate objectives is easier than testing for ultimate ones. Much of our school learning and teaching comes from the printed word. Our immediate goal is to have the pupil learn and understand what he has read and do as well as possible what he has been taught. It is therefore simpler to measure his present comprehension than to measure his ability and disposition to apply his knowledge. It is much easier in the classroom or even in the shop or laboratory to measure John's knowledge of the parts and structure of a gasoline engine than to measure his ability to repair such an engine; it is easier to measure his knowledge of traffic regulations than to measure his respect for and adherence to them.

In the third place, most of our measurement in schools is limited to various types of paper-and-pencil tests for reasons of economy of time and effort. And since immediate learning is often "book learning," our efforts have been largely directed toward the measurement of book knowledge, to the neglect of those types of learning concerned with action and actual performance, which often cannot be measured at all by paper-and-pencil devices.

Yet we should never stop trying in our measurement and evaluation practices to get at these ultimate goals, for they are the final measure of our teaching success. We have accomplished little in our schools if we produce only verbalization of knowledge. Such verbalization is comparatively easy to measure, but it demonstrates little more than that the learner can recite what he has been taught or has read. Formulations of objectives can be very useful to the evaluation process if they emphasize the functions of knowledge as well as knowledge itself, and if the objectives are expressed in terms of the learner's performance and behavior rather than in terms of the facts he has learned.

A statement of instructional objectives which illustrates such an approach is the *Taxonomy of Educational Objectives* by Bloom and his co-workers.[1] In this analysis the authors present a general outline of major categories of objectives in what is referred to as "the cognitive domain." These categories are (1) "Knowledge"; (2) "Comprehension"; (3) "Application"; (4) "Analysis"; (5) "Synthesis"; and (6) "Evaluation." Each of these categories is further sub-divided. For example, "Synthesis" includes "Production of a Unique Communication," "Production of a Plan or Proposed Set of Operations," and "Derivation of a Set of Abstract Relations." It should be clear that this category of objectives refers to the original or creative outcomes in which the pupil develops a plan of work,

---

[1] Benjamin S. Bloom and others, *A Taxonomy of Educational Objectives, Handbook I, Cognitive Domain* (New York: David McKay Co., Inc., 1956).

writes a theme in which he attempts to convey original ideas, or develops an outline or table of organization. The *Taxonomy* provides a useful tool for the teacher or curriculum worker, both as a source of ideas for possible instructional objectives and as a list against which to check his own formulations of objectives.

What has been said so far suggests that formulating objectives for a field like science or social studies, or even for a single subject, is a rather intricate procedure. Because of the inevitable complexities involved, statements of objectives are usually the work of committees or groups which are formed on a local, state, or, more often, on a national basis. Such groups are chosen carefully to assure representation of different viewpoints and localities, and the resulting formulations generally represent the best, most forward-looking ideas that the group can produce at that time. On the other hand, such statements usually represent in some degree a compromise between various viewpoints, and may not, therefore, wholly satisfy either the very progressive or the very conservative members of the group. As a rule, however, the statements of objectives are acceptable to the majority.

An example of a statement for science teachers is as follows:

OBJECTIVES OF SCIENCE INSTRUCTION[2]

A. *Functional information or facts* about matters, such as
    1. Our universe: earth, moon, stars, weather, and climate.
B. *Functional concepts,* such as
    1. All life has evolved from simpler forms.
C. *Functional understanding of principles,* such as
    1. Energy can be changed from one form to another.
D. *Instrumental skills,* such as ability to
    1. Perform simple manipulatory activities with science equipment.
E. *Problem-solving skills,* such as ability to
    1. Sense a problem.
    2. Define the problem.
F. *Attitudes,* such as
    1. Open-mindedness: willingness to consider new facts.
G. *Appreciations,* such as
    1. Appreciation of the contributions of scientists.
H. *Interests,* such as
    1. Interest in some phase of science as a recreational activity or hobby.

This quotation gives only one or two examples under each category, and even the original statement of objectives is incomplete in that all the facts,

[2] Victor H. Noll, "The Objectives of Science Instruction," *Science Education in American Schools,* Forty-Sixth Yearbook of the National Society for the Study of Education, Part 1 (Chicago: The Society [distributed by the University of Chicago Press], 1947), pp. 28–29. By permission of the publisher.

concepts, skills, and interests pertaining to science could never be listed. In fields such as the language arts or the social studies the task of formulating educational objectives is perhaps even more complex. Nevertheless, it has been done by similar committees from time to time. An example of a typical statement of objectives for the social studies is given below:

OBJECTIVES OF SOCIAL STUDIES INSTRUCTION[3]

1. *Understandings*
   a. Of the democratic faith and its meaning for human welfare and happiness
   b. Of the application of democratic faith in the development of the American heritage
   c. Of the forces which have made for world interdependence and the need for world organization
   d. Of the historical and geographic reasons for the behavior of regional and national groups
   e. Of the local community and its problems, and the need for wide participation in community concerns by all citizens
   f. Of the significance in social problems of the mental health and emotional balance of individual human beings
2. *Attitudes*
   a. That all human beings regardless of race, national origin, color, or any matter over which they have no control are entitled to equal rights to life, liberty, and the pursuit of happiness
   b. That we concern ourselves with achieving and improving human welfare and democratic liberties everywhere in the world
   c. That all citizens should participate actively in working toward the solution of community problems for social betterment
   d. That reflective group thinking can serve as an approach toward the solution of social problems
3. *Skills or abilities*
   a. The ability to take part in group discussion
   b. The ability to take part in group planning
   c. The ability to think reflectively on social problems
   d. The ability to search out and use valid and adequate sources of information
   e. The ability to evaluate ideas and opinions on controversial problems offered by and through television, radio, movies, newspapers, periodicals, books, etc.

How does the classroom teacher arrive at useful statements of objectives in his own work? It is obvious that few teachers will have the breadth of view or knowledge represented by committees, local or national. Yet every teacher has his own ideas as to what objectives are important and

---

[3] Wisconsin Cooperative Education Planning Program, *Scope and Sequence of the Social Studies Program*, Bulletin No. 14 (Madison, Wis.: State Department of Public Instruction, November, 1947), pp. 6–7. Reprinted by permission.

useful for his pupils. He should therefore study such statements as those given above and modify and adapt them to his own purposes. In the process he will learn and grow, and the statements thus will serve their ultimate purpose, which is the improvement of instruction. Boys and girls in the classroom will be the beneficiaries eventually.

Many teachers find it useful to take specific portions or items from such statements and relate them to methods, content, and evaluation techniques. This practice may be illustrated as follows:

Objective or *Goal*	*Method-Content*	*Evaluation*
1. Ability to take part in group discussion	Committee appointed to plan for a field trip to local city hall	Check list, rating scale
2. Understanding of time concept in the geological sense	Study of table of geological eras; field trip to study rocks, fossils, etc.	Paper and pencil test: identification of rocks and fossils, pictures of animals and plants of prehistoric times

The value of any statement of objectives is determined by the extent to which the statement is accepted and incorporated into the thinking and practice of teachers. It is the responsibility of the alert, professionally minded teacher to read and ponder such formulations, to select those objectives which will best apply in his own situation, and, as far as possible, to relate his teaching and measurement practices to the objectives chosen.

It should be emphasized here that nothing that has been said above should be taken to mean that a classroom teacher should not attempt to formulate a statement of objectives for his own work. Indeed, this would be one of the most useful and thought-provoking activities in which he could engage. It would, in all probability, have the effect of vitalizing his teaching and would make him intelligently critical of his own procedures as a teacher. On the other hand, teachers should not be condemned if they adopt as their own objectives those which are expressed either explicitly or implicitly in a good textbook. Whatever the nature and source of his objectives, it is important that the teacher think about them, adopt whichever objectives seem good to him (or possibly his local curriculum committee), and incorporate them into his teaching.

No single test, examination, or procedure can measure all objectives, nor can one teacher do an adequate job of weighing all of the many possible objectives in a given field. He must choose from an adequate list of objectives those which he will attempt to achieve at any given time and then formulate his teaching and measurement program on the basis of the objectives selected; another time he will decide upon another goal or set of goals to be measured, and his teaching and measuring procedures may then be quite different. By the process of constantly re-examining and re-appraising his objectives the teacher will broaden his outlook on his work and will develop breadth and skill in measuring a variety of outcomes. This will inevitably result in a fairer, more adequate evaluation of the pupils' status, growth, and progress.

▶ LEARNING EXERCISES ◀

1. Select some phase of a subject, such as: (*a*) fractions in fifth-grade arithmetic; (*b*) from geography, customs of a people like the Eskimos; (*c*) rules of punctuation in language arts; (*d*) the writing of simple formulas for chemical compounds; or some other phase of a subject with which you are thoroughly familiar. State some of the objectives you would attempt to achieve or have your pupils achieve if you were teaching.

2. Criticize constructively one of the sample statements of objectives given on pages 108 and 109 of this chapter. Does the statement seem to you to be (*a*) sufficiently inclusive; (*b*) detailed enough; (*c*) applicable at all levels from first grade through twelfth; (*d*) of practical value to a classroom teacher?

HOW OBJECTIVES FUNCTION IN GOOD MEASUREMENT

We have already emphasized the importance of objectives in measuring the results of instruction, and we have given some sample statements of educational objectives in subject-matter areas, and some suggestions regarding how a teacher may adapt these to his own purposes or develop some objectives of his own. In the remainder of the chapter we shall see how objectives may actually function in the process of devising measuring instruments or techniques.

Once we have selected the objective to be measured, our chief task is to decide on the method of measurement and then construct suitable tests or other instruments. Of course, as has already been noted, the measurement of different kinds of goals presents problems of a widely varying nature. Immediate objectives, such as the ability to solve certain problems in addition, subtraction, multiplication, and division, are easier to measure than ultimate ones, such as the ability to keep accurate financial accounts in the home. Indeed, little of our measurement in the schools gets at these more remote yet very important outcomes. Again, it is easier to measure knowledge objectives than to measure attitudes or appreciations. It is possible to determine quite satisfactorily how well an individual has learned the principles of good sportsmanship, but it is quite a different matter to measure his disposition to follow these principles and adhere to them in athletic competition. However, the measurement of the more ultimate and intangible results of instruction should not be regarded as a hopeless task or one which teachers themselves should not undertake. Great progress has been made in the development of a wide variety of measuring and evaluative techniques. Teachers and others responsible for the evaluation of educational products should keep these difficult-to-measure goals always in mind and continually experiment with ways of measuring them accurately.

One of the steps in measurement which often presents difficulties is the relating of content or subject matter to educational goals. For example, just what is the purpose, from the pupil's standpoint, of learning this or that or the other specific thing? In the case of subjects like homemaking or auto mechanics the answers to such questions are fairly clear. However, in the case of the more academic subjects like algebra or Latin the answers are not so obvious, though they are available in such statements of objectives as have been cited above. In making tests of certain educational goals it is essential to relate course content to objectives. One device which has been found helpful in doing this is a two-way chart. An example of such a chart for high school biology is shown in Figure 5.

It will be seen that the major areas of course content are outlined at the left, while the educational objectives in terms of pupil behavior are listed across the top. The boxes in the main body of the figure represent the points of intersection of these two aspects of the work being tested. The numbers in those boxes represent the test maker's judgment as to the amount of emphasis that each area should receive in the total examination, in terms of the proportion of questions or items to be included in the test. For example, the proportion of content dealing with "life on earth" is 5 per cent. This means that 5 per cent of the items in the test should be based on this content. Now, under the major category of "objectives," and the sub-category, "to achieve skill in," the sub-division, "problem solving," is given a weight of 20 per cent. If we multiply .20 x .05 the product is .01. This tells us that 1 per cent of the items in the test should be based on life on earth and should be designed to measure problem-solving skill. Again, the processes of "reproduction and heredity" represent 25 per cent of the content, and the objective, "to achieve knowledge and understanding of biological principles," 25 per cent. Therefore we find that .25 x .25 or approximately 6 per cent of the test items deal with this matter.

FIGURE 5 • Chart Showing Distribution and Relationships of Content and Objectives for a Test in High School Biology

CONTENT	I. To achieve knowledge and understanding of		II. To achieve skill in			III. To develop scientific attitudes of	Total
OBJECTIVES	A. Biological facts and concepts 25%	B. Biological principles 25%	A. Interpretation of graphs, charts, data, maps, tables, etc. 15%	B. Problem solving 20%	C. Use of biological information in the appraisal of real situations 10%	A. Suspended judgment, open-mindedness, sensitivity to problems & to cause-effect relationships 5%	
Methodology of Science. 5%		1		1	1	2	5%
Characteristics common to living organisms. Cellular structure and functioning. Molecular biology. 15%	5	4	1	3	2		15%
Kinds of living things and their groupings. 5%	1	1	1	1	1		5%
Nature of processes essential to the life of individual organisms: food manufacture, circulation, excretion, coordination, and adjustment. 25%	7	6	5	4	2	1	25%
Processes associated with continuance of species: reproduction and heredity. 25%	6	6	4	6	2	1	25%
History of life on earth, theories of evolution. 5%	1	2	1	1			5%
Interrelationships: ecological, harmful organisms, parasites, disease, beneficial organisms, conservation. 20%	5	5	3	4	2	1	20%
Total	25%	25%	15%	20%	10%	5%	100%

Courtesy of Clarence H. Nelson, Michigan State University.

It should be noted that although the totals in the columns and the rows agree with the theoretical or desired percentages, those in the cells or boxes do not always do so. For example, there are no figures in some cells and in others the percentage varies from the amount produced by multiplication as illustrated above. This is because no items are produced for certain content which the test-maker finds does not lend itself to the measurement of certain objectives, and because some products are not whole numbers and therefore are rounded off.

The development of such a chart by a teacher or prospective teacher is one of the most useful and rewarding activities he may engage in. It requires facing up to and answering several of the following questions: What content shall I teach or attempt to cover? How shall our time and effort be apportioned? Why am I teaching this and why should my students study it? Specifically, what are our mutually understood goals of instruction? And, eventually, how will I measure the degree to which my students, individually and as a group, have attained these objectives? These are searching questions — questions which every one who wishes to be a good teacher should and must face and answer.

Another illustration showing how test items may be keyed to specific objectives is to be found in the *Iowa Tests of Basic Skills,* Multi-Level Edition, for Grades 3–9, Form 1.[4] Figure 6, on page 115, shows a page from the test of *Work-Study Skills.* Also reproduced here is a page from the *Teacher's Manual* corresponding to the map-reading section of the *Work-Study Skills* test (see Figure 7, page 116). Notice the statements of the various skills involved in map reading and the table showing the relationship of each test item to a specific skill-objective.

Altogether, the test includes eighty-nine map-reading items for Grades 3–9. Items 12–19, as shown in Figure 6, are for Grade 5. After the test has been taken and scored, the items answered correctly and those missed can be checked against the analysis of skills and the key. Thus, a teacher is able to determine which map-reading skills have been attained and which have not. This can be done for individual pupils as well as for the class as a whole.

Again, a teacher may wish to construct a test or some other device for measuring the results of instruction on a single objective such as problem-solving ability. This task likewise involves a breakdown of the objective into behavior elements which can be observed or tested and recorded as evidence of the learner's progress toward the desired goal.

---

[4] E. F. Lindquist and A. N. Hieronymus, *Iowa Tests of Basic Skills* (Boston: Houghton Mifflin Company, 1955).

FIGURE 6 • A Page from the Test of *Work-Study Skills, Iowa Tests of Basic Skills*

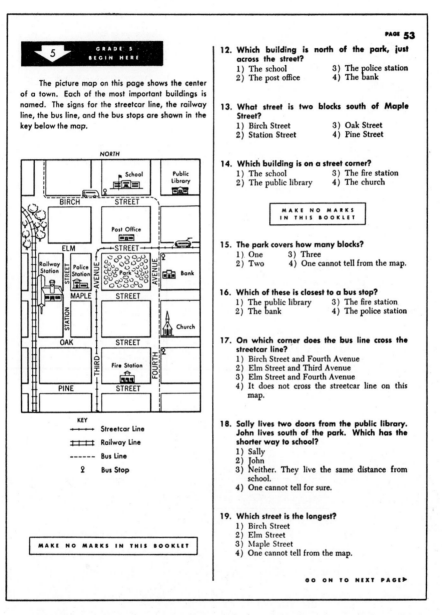

5 GRADE 5 BEGIN HERE

The picture map on this page shows the center of a town. Each of the most important buildings is named. The signs for the streetcar line, the railway line, the bus line, and the bus stops are shown in the key below the map.

NORTH

School | Public Library

BIRCH STREET

Post Office

ELM STREET

Railway Station | Police Station | Park | Bank

MAPLE STREET

Church

OAK STREET

Fire Station

PINE STREET

KEY
—+—+— Streetcar Line
+++++ Railway Line
------ Bus Line
Bus Stop

MAKE NO MARKS IN THIS BOOKLET

12. **Which building is north of the park, just across the street?**
1) The school
2) The post office
3) The police station
4) The bank

13. **What street is two blocks south of Maple Street?**
1) Birch Street
2) Station Street
3) Oak Street
4) Pine Street

14. **Which building is on a street corner?**
1) The school
2) The public library
3) The fire station
4) The church

MAKE NO MARKS IN THIS BOOKLET

15. **The park covers how many blocks?**
1) One
2) Two
3) Three
4) One cannot tell from the map.

16. **Which of these is closest to a bus stop?**
1) The public library
2) The bank
3) The fire station
4) The police station

17. **On which corner does the bus line cross the streetcar line?**
1) Birch Street and Fourth Avenue
2) Elm Street and Third Avenue
3) Elm Street and Fourth Avenue
4) It does not cross the streetcar line on this map.

18. **Sally lives two doors from the public library. John lives south of the park. Which has the shorter way to school?**
1) Sally
2) John
3) Neither. They live the same distance from school.
4) One cannot tell for sure.

19. **Which street is the longest?**
1) Birch Street
2) Elm Street
3) Maple Street
4) One cannot tell from the map.

GO ON TO NEXT PAGE▶

From E. F. Lindquist and A. N. Hieronymus, *Work-Study Skills,* in *Iowa Tests of Basic Skills* (Boston: Houghton Mifflin Company, 1955), p. 53. Reprinted by permission.

FIGURE 7 • A Page from the *Teacher's Manual* Corresponding to the Map-Reading Section of the Test of *Work-Study Skills*

TEST W-1 : MAP READING

Skills Involved

1. Ability to orient map and determine direction
   a) To determine direction from orientation
   b) To determine direction from parallels or meridians
   c) To determine direction of river flow or slope of land
2. Ability to locate places on maps and globes
   a) Through the use of standard map symbols
   b) Through the use of a key
   c) Through the use of distance and/or direction
   d) Through the use of latitude or longitude
3. Ability to determine distances
   a) Determining distance on a road map
   b) Determining distance by using a scale of miles

c) Determining distance on a globe
d) Comparing distances

4. Ability to determine or trace routes of travel
5. Ability to visualize landscape features
6. Ability to infer man's activities or way of living
   a) From physical detail
   b) Ability to recognize differences in seasons and hours of daylight in different latitudes
   c) Ability to determine differences in time zones
7. Ability to read and interpret facts from pattern maps
   a) To read and compare facts from a single pattern map
   b) To read and compare facts from two or more pattern maps
   c) To visualize landscape features
   d) To infer man's way of living

TEST W-1: MAP READING

Item No.	Form 1	Form 2	Item No.	Form 1	Form 2	Item No.	Form 1	Form 2
1	1a	3d	31	7a	7a	61	7a	7a
2	2c	3d	32	5	3b	62	7a	7d
3	3d	2a	33	3b	1c	63	7b	7a
4	4	1a	34	7d	5	64	7a	7a
5	2a	4	35	3d	7a	65	7d	7a
6	3d	3a	36	5	2a	66	7b.	7d
7	3a	1a	37	6a	1c	67	7c	7b
8	2b	2a	38	3a	2c	68	3b	7a
9	3a	3d	39	2b	2a	69	7d	7d
10	4	2b	40	1a	2b	70	7a	7b
11	2b	2c	41	4	4	71	7d	7b
12	2c	2a	42	4	2c	72	7a	7a
13	2c	2a	43	2c	3d	73	2d	7d
14	2a	2a	44	2b	3a	74	7a	7b
15	2a	2c	45	2a	3a	75	7b	7b
16	3d	3d	46	3a	6a	76	7b	3b
17	2b	4	47	4	4	77	1c	7d
18	2c	2a	48	2d	3c	78	7a	7b
19	2a	2a	49	2d	2d	79	3a	2b
20	2c	3d	50	6b	2d	80	2b	6a
21	2a	5	51	6b	2a	81	2b	3a
22	2a	2a	52	2d	6b	82	2a	4
23	3d	2a	53	6c	6b	83	3a	3a
24	5·	5	54	2d	2d	84	4	2a
25	3d	5	55	3c	6b	85	4	4
26	2a	3b	56	1c	1b	86	2d	2d
27	6a	2a	57	2d	6c	87	2d	2d
28	2c	3d	58	6b	3c	88	1b	1b
29	6a	7a	59	7d	7b	89	3c	1b
30	7a	6a	60	7d	7a			

31

From E. F. Lindquist and A. N. Hieronymus, *Teacher's Manual* for the *Iowa Tests of Basic Skills* (Boston: Houghton Mifflin Company, 1955), p. 31. Reprinted by permission.

Several examples are given below to show how test items can be related to the more functional objectives in various areas of common learning:

IN THE AREA OF STUDY SKILLS[5]

Objective: Ability to differentiate between fact and opinion.
Directions: In the list below, some of the sentences are statements of *fact,*

---

[5] Horace T. Morse and George H. McCune, *Selected Items for the Testing of Study Skills,* Revised Edition, National Council for the Social Studies, National Education Association, Bulletin No. 15 (Washington: The Association, 1949). By permission of the publisher.

and others are statements of *opinion*. Indicate to which class you think each statement belongs by placing the proper letter in the space provided for it. *Do not* try to decide if each statement is true or false, but only whether it should be classified as a statement of *fact* or of *opinion*.

F — Fact
O — Opinion

(O)   55. The Democratic party has done more for this country than the Republican party has.

(F)   56. In 1939 there were two World's Fairs held in the United States.

(F)   57. Alaska is northwest of Oregon.

(F)   58. Scientific research often results in the production of new products.

(O)   59. No war has ever accomplished any good for the world.

(O)   60. A high tariff increases the prosperity of the country.

(O)   61. Only his defeat at the Battle of Waterloo prevented Napoleon from making himself master of Europe.

Objective: Understanding of use of common references.

Directions: The degree to which a social-studies library is useful to students is determined partly by the ability of students to obtain needed information. Below are two lists. One contains those books which could compose a Social Studies Reference Shelf. The other contains a list of questions which you might wish to have answered. Do *not* try to answer the questions. Indicate whether you could find the answers by placing beside the *number* of the question the *letter* of the reference work in which you would be likely to find the answer most satisfactorily.

Example: (F) O. How many students are enrolled in American colleges and universities? The answer *F* refers to *The World Almanac,* a handbook of current information.

Reference Shelf:

A. *Dictionary of American History*
B. An atlas
C. A civics text
D. An economics text
E. *Who's Who in America*
F. *The World Almanac*
G. *Reader's Guide to Periodical Literature*
H. Official state government handbook
I. *Dictionary of American Biography*

Questions:

(B)   110. How does North America compare in size with Africa?

(H)   111. Who is the chief justice of your state supreme court?

(F)   112. How many persons were killed by autos last year?

(A)   113. When was the Cumberland Road built?

(H)   114. Who is the official custodian of state laws?

(G)   115. What was the political significance of the last Congressional election?

In the Language Arts[6]

Objective: To organize and express thought logically, clearly, and effectively in sentences or in larger units.

The logical organization of thoughts into clear and effective sentences and paragraphs includes a clearly defined sentence sense based upon an understanding of word meanings and of the use of words as expressive and connective devices. Use tests such as the following:

(1) Are these groups of words sentences? Draw a line under *Yes* or *No*.

(*a*) On the way to school.	Yes	No
(*b*) He has lost his pencil.	Yes	No
(*c*) Please be quiet.	Yes	No
(*d*) Baseball in the park.	Yes	No

(2) In each exercise below part of a sentence has been cut off by a period. Write each sentence correctly.

> The pup grabbed the bone. And ran out into the yard.
> With a cross growl. Dixie started after him.

(3) Put a cross through every *and* that is not needed in the story below. Put in capital letters and periods where they are needed to make good sentences.

> I have a big white rabbit and his name is Bumpo and every morning he sits up and begs for a handful of clover and one day I went to feed him and he was gone and I found that he had dug out of his pen.

(4) Place an *X* before the one sentence in each group of three that represents the best sentence structure.

(*a*) ____ I counted six paintings walking down the stairs.
____ While walking down the stairs six paintings were counted.
____ While I was walking down the stairs I counted six paintings.
(*b*) ____ He dropped the bundle he was carrying to his mother in the mud.
____ The bundle fell into the mud which he was carrying to his mother.
____ Into the mud fell the bundle which he was carrying to his mother.

[6] Harry A. Greene and William S. Gray, "The Measurement of Understanding in the Language Arts," Chapter IX in *The Measurement of Understanding*, Forty-Fifth Yearbook of the National Society for the Study of Education, Part I (Chicago: The Society [distributed by the University of Chicago Press], 1946). By permission of the publisher.

Objective: To clarify meaning by following correct language usage.

Correct usage of pronoun and verb forms and subject-predicate relationships, and the avoidance of miscellaneous errors, such as double negatives, vague antecedents and redundancy, is a matter of correct habit closely related to understanding in expression. Following are examples of appropriate test items:

(1) Rewrite the following sentences selecting the correct pronoun from those in the parentheses.

   (*a*) (He, Him) and (I, me) were born in the same town.
   (*b*) Mother sent (we, us) girls to the store.

(2) Rewrite the following sentences using the correct verb forms from those in the parentheses.

   (*a*) (Was, Were) you at the show last night?
   (*b*) It (doesn't, don't) seem so cold now.

(3) Faulty expressions appear in these sentences. Rewrite the sentences correcting all mistakes.

   (*a*) Where did you see him at?
   (*b*) We haven't hardly no time left.

In Elementary Mathematics[7]

Objective: Interpretation of data presented graphically and in tables.

1. According to the chart, which food changed most in price?

Year	Price of Foods			
	Eggs	Bread	Milk	Roast
Last year	$0.48	$0.11	$0.13	$0.39
This year	0.51	0.11	0.11	0.43

   a) eggs   *b*) bread   *c*) milk   *d*) roast

2. If the prices in the chart above are considered a fair sample of the cost of living, how does the cost this year compare to the cost last year?

   a) the same   *b*) less   *c*) more   *d*) cannot tell

[7] Ben A. Sueltz, Holmes Boynton, and Irene Sauble, "The Measurement of Understanding in Elementary School Mathematics," Chapter VII in *The Measurement of Understanding,* Forty-Fifth Yearbook of the National Society for the Study of Education, Part I (Chicago: The Society [distributed by the University of Chicago Press], 1946). By permission of the publisher.

3. In social studies we have made a line along which we will arrange dates in history. The line begins with the year 1700 and ends at 2000. What letter on the line is at the year 1812?

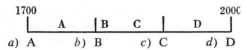

1700   2000

a) A   *b)* B   *c)* C   *d)* D

4. Study the graph of Alberta's weight. During what year did she gain most in weight?

  (*a*) 10 to 11
  (*b*) 11 to 12
  (*c*) 12 to 13
  (*d*) 13 to 14

5. How old was Alberta when she weighed approximately 100 pounds?

  a) 11 years *b*) nearly 12
  c) exactly 12 *d*) a little more
              than 12

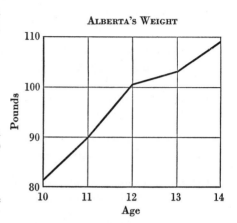

ALBERTA'S WEIGHT

The examples given in the preceding pages illustrate the design of paper-and-pencil tests which go beyond the measurement of mere knowledge and get at understandings such as the ability to interpret and the ability to apply knowledge. In most subjects, particularly academic ones, measurement is largely confined to paper-and-pencil devices. It is possible, however, to use other kinds of tests in some areas like shop, business, homemaking, and agriculture. Here, actual performance can be observed and rated. For example, when a girl is given a recipe for a cake, access to the necessary ingredients and equipment, and is permitted to prepare the cake according to directions, it is possible to observe her behavior and appraise it by means of a check-list, and to judge the product by the use of some kind of a rating device. A series of rating scales for different products of food preparation has been worked out by Clara M. Brown.[8] A sample scale for cake will illustrate the nature of these rating devices:

CAKE (Angel or Sponge)

	1	*2*	*3*	Score
Appearance	1. Sunken or very rounded top	Flat or slightly rounded top		1. _ _ _ _

[8] Clara M. Brown, *Food Score Cards*, (Minneapolis, Minn.: University of Minnesota Press, 1940).

	2. Sugary surface or deep crevices	Slightly rough surface like macaroons	2. _ _ _ _
Color	3. Dark brown or pale	Even, delicate brown	3. _ _ _ _
Moisture Content	4. Dry or insufficiently baked	Slightly moist	4. _ _ _ _
Texture	5. Coarse	Small holes, uniformly distributed	5. _ _ _ _
Lightness	6. Heavy	Very Light	6. _ _ _ _
Tenderness	7. Tough	Very Tender	7. _ _ _ _
Taste and Flavor	8. Flat, too sweet, eggy, or too highly flavored	Pleasing, delicate flavor	8. _ _ _ _

Similarly, in industrial arts, performance and product are easily judged directly when conditions are fairly well controlled. Again, in a typewriting class the teacher can place his pupils in a situation which closely resembles an on-the-job task, such as transcribing a letter, so that he can observe their performance and evaluate the result.

In these areas of teaching it is possible to measure behavior in situations which closely resemble actual working conditions, though it is not easy to do so in the more academic subjects like science or mathematics or history. In such areas the ultimate and more remote goals such as scientific attitudes, problem-solving skills, and good citizenship can often be measured only in a verbalized form. It is generally possible to determine how a pupil *says* he would behave under a given set of circumstances, but it is nearly always difficult — if not impossible — to subject the student to realistic circumstances for measurement purposes. Yet, as the illustrations that we have given demonstrate, considerable progress has been made and more will certainly come. Teachers and others responsible for measurement and evaluation in the schools should keep always before them the ideal of making their practices in this area functional; that is, measurement should be concerned with the appraisal of behavior, as far as possible, rather than with verbalization.

At the same time, teachers and prospective teachers should use or experiment with all current methods of measurement, though, as was pointed out in the beginning of this chapter, paper-and-pencil tests will continue to be the mainstay of the measurement program. Moreover, behavior should not be conceived of in too narrow a sense. When a child solves an arithmetic problem, reads a story with understanding, or interprets a map or a chart, he is exhibiting kinds of behavior that can be adequately measured by paper-and-pencil tests. The teacher's goal should be to make his tests as adequate as possible, and to supplement them whenever possible with a wide variety of other types of measurement and evaluation. The broader and more comprehensive the approach, the better the chances of encompassing in the measurement program all of the important objectives of instruction.

▶ LEARNING EXERCISE ◀

3. In Learning Exercise 1 on page 111 you were asked to select some defined and limited phase of a subject and to state some of the objectives you would consider important if you were teaching. Considering these same objectives, describe in detail, with examples, the kind of measurement techniques you would use to determine how well your goals had been achieved.

ANNOTATED BIBLIOGRAPHY

1. Bloom, Benjamin S., *et al. Taxonomy of Educational Objectives. Handbook I, Cognitive Domain.* New York: David McKay Co., Inc., 1956. A discussion of the problem of classifying educational objectives in a systematic way. Somewhat advanced for the beginner in test construction, but contains many useful ideas.

2. Dressel, Paul L., *et al. Evaluation in Higher Education.* Boston: Houghton Mifflin Company, 1961. Chapter 2: "The Objectives of Instruction," by Walker H. Hill and Paul L. Dressel. A scholarly discussion of the importance of formulating objectives of instruction, considerations in stating objectives, the relation of objectives to content and methods and to the evaluation process. The setting of the discussion is the college level, but the principles presented and elaborated are largely applicable at all levels of instruction.

3. Dressel, Paul L., and Mayhew, Lewis B. *General Education: Explorations in Evaluation.* Washington: American Council on Education, 1954. 302 pp. The report of a cooperative study by nineteen colleges and universities of objectives and methods of evaluation in the areas of social science, communications, science, and the humanities, with emphasis on critical thinking and attitudes. A thorough and comprehensive exploration of goals in general education in higher education.

4. Furst, Edward J. *Constructing Evaluation Instruments.* New York: David McKay Co., Inc., 1958. Chapters 2, 3, and 4. Chapter 2 presents a very thorough discussion of procedures for arriving at statements of educational objectives. Chapter 3 examines the problems of defining objectives in behavioral terms. Chapter 4 considers the matter of devising or arranging situations in which the defined behavior can be observed, that is, of determining the degree to which the educational objectives have been realized.

5. Greene, Harry A.; Jorgensen, Albert N.; and Gerberich, J. Raymond. *Measurement and Evaluation in the Elementary School,* Second Edition. New York: David McKay Co., Inc., 1953.

———. *Measurement and Evaluation in the Secondary School,* Second Edition. New York: David McKay Co., Inc., 1954.
The latter half of each book consists of separate chapters on measurement in the commonly taught subjects in the elementary and the secondary school, respectively. Each chapter presents a statement and discussion of objectives in a subject or subject field.

6. Jordan, A. M. *Measurement in Education.* New York: McGraw-Hill Book Co., Inc., 1953. 533 pp. Chapters 5 through 13 deal with measurement in subject-matter fields such as language, mathematics, social sciences, etc. Each chapter includes a statement and discussion of educational goals in that subject-matter field.

7. Krathwohl, David R., *et al., Taxonomy of Educational Objectives, Handbook II: Affective Domain.* New York: David McKay Co., Inc., 1964. A companion volume to Reference 1, above, dealing with the classification of educational goals in the non-cognitive domain.

8. Lindquist, E. F. (ed.). *Educational Measurement.* Washington: American Council on Education, 1951. Chapter 5: "Preliminary Considerations in Objective Test Construction," by E. F. Lindquist. Chapter 6: "Planning the Objective Test," by K. W. Vaughn. Both chapters, though somewhat advanced in concept for ordinary measurement activities in the classroom, present many good ideas and useful suggestions on objectives and construction of tests.

9. Morse, Horace T., and McCune, George H. *Selected Items for the Testing of Study Skills,* Revised Edition. National Council for the Social Studies, National Education Association, Bulletin No. 15. Washington: The Association, 1949. 81 pp. The first part of this bulletin presents a discussion of the problems involved in formulating objectives and devising tests for study skills. The major portion is given to selected items for these purposes.

10. National Society for the Study of Education. *The Measurement of Understanding,* Forty-Fifth Yearbook, Part I. Chicago: The Society (distributed by the University of Chicago Press), 1946. 338 pp. Emphasizes the importance of trying to teach and test for understanding. The main body of the report consists of twelve chapters, each dealing with a major area of instruction and presenting a discussion and examples of the measurement of objectives in that area. A wealth of ideas for the person concerned with the improvement of objective measures of achievement.

11. Remmers, H. H., and Gage, N. L. *Educational Measurement and Evaluation,* Revised Edition. New York: Harper & Row, Publishers, 1955. Chapter 2. An excellent discussion of educational objectives with suggestions on how to formulate them, and illustrations of objectives of various types for different levels.

12. Ross, C. C., and Stanley, Julian C. *Measurement in Today's Schools,* Third Edition. New York: Prentice-Hall, Inc., 1954. Chapter 5. A brief, practical discussion of the principles of test construction, including planning, preparing, trying out, and evaluating the test.

13. Thomas, R. Murray. *Judging Student Progress,* Second Edition. New York: David McKay Co., Inc., 1960. Chapter 2. A good presentation of the problem of defining educational goals and devising methods of evaluating them. Written primarily with the elementary teacher in mind, though high school teachers can profit from the chapter.

14. Wrightstone, J. Wayne; Justman, Joseph; and Robbins, Irving. *Evaluation in Modern Education.* New York: American Book Company, 1956. Chapter 2. Steps in the process of evaluation, including formulation, definition, and clarification of objectives, and selection of tests for each objective, are briefly discussed.

6

Planning and Constructing

the Teacher-Made Test

STANDARDIZED VERSUS TEACHER–MADE TESTS

The majority of schools in the United States today make use of standardized tests of one kind or another. Most tests of intelligence, aptitude, personality, and interests are standardized tests, made by specialists for a test publisher, and sold by the publisher throughout the country. Few schools or school systems, except in the very large city organizations, attempt to develop such tests for their own use.

The situation with respect to achievement tests is somewhat different. There are, of course, many standardized achievement tests on the market, and literally millions of them are used every year. These include tests in the separate subjects or branches as well as the achievement batteries. However, teachers usually feel that these tests do not adequately measure their own or the local objectives of instruction. While standardized tests are very useful in some ways, they are not usually the principal method of measuring achievement. In general, the classroom teacher himself is relied upon for the formulation of achievement tests. It is important, therefore, that the teacher's professional training include some instruction on effective ways of planning, constructing, and evaluating various measuring instruments.

Clearly, no standardized test of achievement can completely serve the needs and purposes of every local situation. The nature of the requirements for a standardized test is such that the test must be largely confined to the elements of instruction which are common in a large number of schools. Therefore, such a test cannot, if it is to be maximally useful, include all those elements which are peculiar to any one or even a limited number of schools. The most desirable and probably the most common practice is to use both standardized and teacher-made measuring instruments in most situations. Both serve useful though somewhat different purposes, and both are important parts of a well-rounded measurement program.

▶ LEARNING EXERCISE ◀

1. Examine a standardized test of achievement in a subject and grade level that you expect to teach. What objectives does it seem to measure adequately? What objectives do you think you would measure by devices of your own?

Since teacher-made tests play an important part in the evaluation practices of schools, it is well to give some attention to accepted principles of *planning, constructing, using,* and *evaluating* such instruments. These are the four main stages in the process of testing. The stages of planning and constructing will be considered in this chapter, and the use and evaluation of teacher-made tests will be examined in the following chapter.

In developing a standardized test, as, for example, one for first-year algebra, the planning is generally quite extensive and detailed. Textbooks, courses of study, and committee reports are analyzed for common objectives and content; the tests are carefully planned with regard to length, administration, and scoring. When a committee of teachers plans a test for local use some of these same steps will be carried out, though in a less elaborate and formal way. Likewise, a teacher constructing a test or measuring device for his own use does not usually need to go through such a formal procedure. In the first place, he has a certain degree of choice regarding objectives and methods. Then, too, he knows pretty clearly what he wants the test to cover or measure, when he wants to use it, and how much time he can give to it. Finally, he knows what he has been teaching and what testing he has already done so that the proposed test can be fitted into the situation he is familiar with. In other words, much of what constitutes planning in the case of a standardized test is taken care of more or less incidentally and automatically when a teacher devises tests for his own use.

Some aspects of planning have already been discussed in Chapter 5. There, examples were given of test questions designed to measure different kinds of instructional objectives. Also, those examples illustrated different types of test questions. In the rest of this chapter additional consideration will be given the planning of tests and the problems and principles of constructing good questions or items for locally made tests.

▶ LEARNING EXERCISE ◀

2. List some of the decisions a teacher makes in planning a test for his own use. Illustrate each with a specific choice, one which you might make for a test in your field of specialization. For example, assume that your test would be designed to measure achievement in the knowledge and understanding of our solar system that you have been teaching in ninth-grade general science. You might decide to make an objective test, to allow thirty minutes for it, etc.

BASIC QUALIFICATIONS OF THE TEST-MAKER

To make a good objective achievement test requires three somewhat different abilities. In the first place, one must have an adequate knowledge of subject matter. It is not possible to construct a good examination without adequate knowledge of the field, whether it is reading, civics, driver-training, or some other specialty. The person who attempts to construct examinations without such a foundation quickly reveals his deficiencies both to his associates and, sooner or later, to his pupils.

A second requirement for making good objective test items is some degree of knowledge and skill in the techniques of test construction. This, contrary to what some students suppose, is not something that "comes naturally." The techniques of making acceptable test items have been developed by the experience of test experts and teachers over a period of many years, and much of value has thus been learned. Even in the preparation of the essay examination, considerable thought and effort have been expended in finding ways to eliminate some of the shortcomings without sacrificing the good qualities.

The third requisite for the successful test-maker is a knack of putting ideas accurately, concisely, and clearly into words. The ability to apply subject-matter knowledge and test-construction skill to the formulation of items which will be unambiguous and brief, and which will measure accurately what the maker of the instrument intends, is almost an art. The ability to formulate accurate, concise, and clear test items can be developed to some extent by most teachers who possess the first two qualifications and who have a good command of the language and a desire to learn.

In the kind of courses for which this book is intended, little or nothing can be done about the first and the third requirements. Adequate knowledge of subject matter and the ability to put ideas into good, clear English are not the objectives of a course in measurement. However, it is an objective of such a course and of this book to provide some understanding of the basic principles of making good classroom tests and, as far as possible, to give some practice in doing this.

▶ LEARNING EXERCISE ◀

3. Rate yourself on the following scale by placing a check mark on each line indicating where you think you stand with respect to each of the characteristics listed.

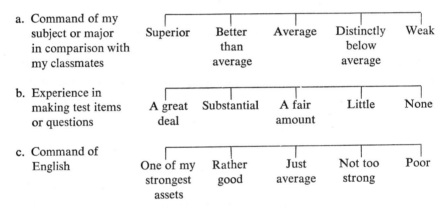

a. Command of my subject or major in comparison with my classmates

|Superior|Better than average|Average|Distinctly below average|Weak|

b. Experience in making test items or questions

|A great deal|Substantial|A fair amount|Little|None|

c. Command of English

|One of my strongest assets|Rather good|Just average|Not too strong|Poor|

Rank yourself on the three characteristics listed above: Best ＿＿ Next best ＿＿ Least ＿＿.

PRELIMINARY STEPS

As we have emphasized in Chapter 5, the first step in planning a test or measuring instrument is to decide what goals or objectives to measure. Having defined his objectives, the teacher then decides what type of test will best accomplish his purposes. Perhaps he decides an essay test will be best, or he may decide on the objective type. If the latter, he must determine what kinds of items to use, i.e., true-false, multiple-choice, matching, short-answer, or possibly some modifications and probably some combinations of these. This decision is usually influenced by the types of items the teacher has had the most success with, and the nature of the content, processes, or skills to be measured. Often it is best not to make a firm decision on this matter in advance, but to construct the kinds of items that seem most suited to the particular objectives and content as one progresses with the construction of the test.

In practice, it is customary to begin by a canvass of the instructional materials and activities in the light of the educational objectives to be measured by the test. These include materials and activities such as reading assignments, problems, experiments performed, films shown, discussions, and field trips. As the teacher reviews these materials and activities, their relationship to important outcomes will be re-emphasized and will probably suggest approaches to evaluation. Assuming that the test-maker decides to use objective techniques, he may find that one phase of the work lends itself to one type of item, whereas another purpose may be best served by a different type. In such cases the test-maker should generally follow his natural inclination and not attempt to make all of his true-false items at once, then all his multiple-choice items, etc. The nature of the knowledge, skill, or outcome to be tested usually suggests and may even determine the kind of item which is most appropriate. On the other hand, it sometimes seems possible to accomplish one's purpose equally well with either of two different types of items. In such cases, other considerations will determine which type to use.

As the items are devised, it is recommended that each be written on a 3″ × 5″ card. When all the items have been written the cards may be sorted and arranged in any way or on any basis desired, such as by type of item, content, length, estimated difficulty, source of the item. As information is obtained on the effectiveness of items through tryout, such data can be entered on the cards, as well as dates of construction and use and cross-references. Cards provide a high degree of flexibility, which is of great value. They are easily filed and grouped. Also, single cards can be easily eliminated without disturbing the rest of the file if any of the items prove ineffective. As the teacher builds up his file of test items, he will be able to select different samples of questions for various tests and purposes.

TYPES OF TEST ITEMS

In this discussion a distinction will be made between the more *subjective* types of questions or items,[1] such as the essay and short-answer, and the

---

[1] The term "item" will be used consistently except in reference to essay, short-answer, and completion types of testing.

more *objective* types such as true-false, multiple-choice, and matching. This is actually a distinction of degree rather than of kind. That is, objectivity is a continuous and variable quality; test items are neither wholly objective nor wholly subjective. For example, the short-answer item is thought of as a variation of the essay question, but is considered somewhat more objective than the "discuss," "explain," or "analyze" forms.

Usually the objectivity of an examination question is judged by the complexity of the pupil's answer and the resulting degree of difficulty in scoring. If the scoring requires judgment and evaluation of the response on the part of the scorer, the question or item is said to be subjective; to the extent that judgment and evaluation are reduced or eliminated from the scoring process, the item is objective. Most standardized tests except those for young children can be scored by clerical workers using a scoring key, or by a test-scoring machine. The process in either case is a mechanical one. Questions of the essay or short-answer variety, on the other hand, cannot be so scored. However, questions of this type can be more or less objective, as will be shown later; they are not all equally or wholly subjective.

The nature of the scoring and the judgment it requires depend also on the nature of the response the pupil is required to make. If the response consists of a number, a "plus" or a "minus" sign, a letter, or a black mark between two printed lines, the scoring can be done mechanically. When the examinee is asked to write out his answer in words, draw a figure, make an outline or something of this nature, the scoring becomes more complex and subjective.

From another standpoint, the more objective type of item is sometimes classified as a *recognition* type in that all of the information necessary for answering is supplied; the short-answer and essay types, on the other hand, are classified as a *recall* type, since the examinee must himself supply the answer. This distinction, though not entirely clear-cut, may be helpful to the student in his thinking about the matter of objectivity.

With these few preliminary observations in mind, we may proceed to a consideration of the various commonly used kinds of examination items, beginning with the more subjective and going on to the more objective types.

▶ **LEARNING EXERCISES** ◀

4. Classifying test items as *objective* or *subjective* is something like trying to classify all people into two groups — tall and short or bright and dull. Is such classification defensible? Justify your answer.

5. Even if one uses nothing but the most objective tests, there are still some subjective elements in the teacher's job of evaluating and marking. Name some of them.

Essay Questions

Although the more objective types of tests have had a very wide acceptance during the last fifty years, the essay question still finds wide use. In a survey[2] of measurement practices of some 2,303 high school teachers in thirty-five states, 13.7 per cent of the teachers questioned said they used no essay tests at all. It seems reasonable to conclude, then, that most of the other 86.3 per cent *do* use them, at least occasionally. Also, 81.2 per cent reported using short-answer or completion items "very often" or "fairly often."

Probably the essay-type question is so well known that it doesn't require definition here; nevertheless, a few words of explanation may serve to clarify or supplement what the student already knows about it. The essay test usually consists of questions beginning with or including such directions as "discuss," "explain," "outline," "evaluate," "define," "compare," "contrast," and "describe." The pupil is allowed comparative freedom with respect to what his answer shall include, its wording, length, and organization. Three examples from typical teacher-made tests follow:

> Discuss the events of the period 1850 to 1861 that led to the outbreak of the Civil War.

> Explain the essential differences between a standardized test and a teacher-made test.

> What are the important steps in processing milk from dairy farm to consumer? Describe each one and explain its function.

Although the essay-type question has continued in favor among teachers for a long time and is stoutly defended by its many advocates, it has also been the object of much criticism. A considerable amount of experimentation, designed largely to show its weaknesses and to prove its unreliability, has been reported in educational literature. The pioneer study of the essay question, at least in the United States, was reported by Starch and Elliott in 1912.[3] These investigators took a typical examination paper

---

[2] Victor H. Noll and Walter N. Durost, *Measurement Practices and Preferences of High School Teachers,* Test Service Notebook No. 8 (New York: Harcourt, Brace & World, Inc., n.d.).

[3] Daniel Starch and Edward C. Elliott, "Reliability of Grading High School Work in English," *School Review,* 20:442–57, September, 1912. Subsequent articles dealing with mathematics and with history in *School Review:* 21:254–59 and 21:676–81, April and December, 1913.

written by a pupil in English and had it graded independently by a large number of teachers of English; the same was done with a geometry paper and a history paper. In each case the results were quite similar: the same paper received marks ranging all the way from nearly perfect to very low failure. Similar results were reported during the next decade by other investigators.

This weakness in the scoring of the essay question has been demonstrated in still another way. One investigator had teachers score the same set of papers twice, with an interval of several months between.[4] The findings pointed to the conclusion that these teachers did not even agree with their own judgments of the quality of the same set of papers when these judgments were made at two different times.

A second principal weakness of the essay examination is that of limited sampling. The typical essay test consists of from five to ten or twelve questions. An objective test which allows the same amount of time for answering questions as the essay test, might well include one hundred or more items. Although the essay questions are larger units, they do not usually constitute as adequate and representative a sample of the field being tested as the one hundred objective items. Therefore, in the case of the essay test, the teacher must base his evaluation of the pupils' accomplishments on a sampling which is much more fragmentary, limited, and sometimes biased. In a one-hundred-item test a pupil's achievement is sampled one hundred times and he is called upon to make that many separate responses or judgments. In an examination consisting of ten essay questions, the person reading the paper has a much smaller sampling of the student's accomplishments upon which to make a judgment; also, if the pupil happens to be weak or deficient on one or two essay questions he is apt to be penalized far more heavily than he would be for equivalent deficiencies on the objective test.

Limited sampling affects the reliability of the essay test and also its empirical validity, since such a test is likely to give lower correlations with other measures of the same abilities than results obtained from measures that sample more adequately.

A third disadvantage of the essay question is the time required to read the answers. While this kind of examination is rather easily and quickly made, judging and scoring the answers is very time-consuming and often tiresome. This, of course, makes the essay test expensive, since it must be read either by the teacher himself or by equally competent scorers. Usually such a test cannot be evaluated by clerical workers or by mechanical methods.

---

[4] Walter C. Eells, "Reliability of Repeated Grading of Essay Type Questions," *Journal of Educational Psychology*, 31:48–52, January, 1930.

The chief advantages claimed for the essay examination may be stated as follows: (1) it is easier to construct than a comparable objective test; (2) it can be used to measure the ability to think, and to organize and apply knowledge; it therefore measures learning of a different kind from that measured by the objective test; (3) it provides exercise in expressing written thoughts clearly, concisely, and correctly — a skill the objective test cannot measure; and (4) it requires a more useful and rewarding kind of study and preparation than that required by the objective test.

On the first point, there probably can be no serious difference of opinion. It is easier and much less time-consuming to prepare ten essay questions and write them on the board than to prepare a one-hundred-item objective test. In practice, the essay examination is often prepared at the last minute, whereas such hurried preparation is not possible in the case of an objective test. It should be recognized, however, that one does not prepare *good* essay questions in this manner. It is possible to dash off a few essay questions on the way to class, but such questions are almost certain to be poor in quality unless this expedient has been preceded by a good deal of thought beforehand. Even then, as will be brought out shortly, much can be done *after* essay questions have been written out to improve their quality and usefulness.

On the second point, we can say only that evidence that the essay examination actually measures mental processes different from those measured by the objective test is hard to find. This is not to deny that such advantages may exist, but simply to point out that no one has apparently been able, or taken the trouble, to find and present evidence to support this assumed advantage of the essay examination. Implicit in the claim is the idea that the objective test does not, or cannot, measure the higher mental processes. Here again, evidence to support this implication seems to be lacking. Some work has been done to develop objective tests that will measure mental abilities of a higher order, such as the ability to interpret data and draw conclusions, and this research suggests that it may be possible to measure such abilities by means of objective tests. Some of this work is described in Chapter 5. Until further research produces some evidence on the question, this claimed advantage of the essay examination will have to be taken largely on faith.

With regard to the third claim, it seems questionable whether the use of essay questions can play a very substantial role in the improvement of a student's writing ability. For one thing, the proportion of total instructional time spent in taking examinations is too small to make very much of an impact. For another, it seems highly unlikely that a student, under the pressure of an examination, will be able to do his best writing, or that he will pay much attention to this skill at all. A more logical and probably more effective procedure for the teacher would be to emphasize good expression, both oral and written, consistently, correcting all mistakes made by his students in this area. Perhaps most important of all, the correct and effective use of our language should be the concern of every teacher, whether he teaches English or shop or mathematics. When students learn that high standards in composition and oral expression are expected, their writing and speech will improve. Too often only the English teacher is concerned with the quality of a student's expression, and, as a result, students practice good English in his classes but are careless or indifferent about it elsewhere.

The fourth advantage, namely, that of different preparation for essay tests than for more objective ones, seems not to be unequivocally supported by evidence. Some studies have been reported showing that when students expect an objective test they study for details, while in preparing for an essay test they focus attention upon relationships, trends, and organization.[5] However, a more recent study by Vallance[6] failed to confirm these findings.

▶ LEARNING EXERCISE ◀

6. Can you think of any other important advantages or serious shortcomings of essay tests? Consult some of the references at the end of this chapter for evidence.

Improving Essay Questions

Having reviewed the main lines of discussion and criticism of the essay question, we might ask what can be done about it. Is the essay question a type that can be recommended for general use? Perhaps a sensible point of view for the student of measurement might be expressed as follows: the essay question is believed by its advocates to have a number of unique advantages over the more objective types; apparently, these advantages have been neither fully proved nor disproved, though some of the basic weaknesses have been clearly demonstrated; nevertheless, since the essay type of questions is used regularly by many teachers, we should try to improve its use in every way possible.

Suggestions for improvement of the essay question are usually directed

[5] See, for example, Paul W. Terry, "How Students Review for Objective and Essay Tests," *Elementary School Journal,* 33:592–603, April, 1933. Also, Harl R. Douglass and Margaret Tallmadge, "How University Students Prepare for New Types of Examinations," *School and Society,* 39:318–20, March 10, 1934.

[6] Theodore R. Vallance, "Comparison of Essay and Objective Examinations as Learning Experiences," *Journal of Educational Research,* 41:279–88, December, 1947.

at two aspects of the process, namely, the preparation of the questions and directions and the scoring or evaluation of the answers. A good deal of helpful material has been written on these two points. Although a complete review of such material is not appropriate or necessary here, a summary of the most useful ideas should be helpful. With respect to planning, constructing, and using essay questions, the following recommendations are often used as guides:

1. Define and restrict the field or area to be covered by the question. For example, in high school chemistry one might say,

> Describe the contact process for making sulfuric acid.

However, it would be better to say,

> Write the equations for the contact process for making sulfuric acid.
> Name all the substances used, and the products.
> Draw a labelled diagram showing where each step of the process occurs.
> What are the by-products of the process and how are they used?

2. The teacher should give more time and thought to the preparation of essay questions. It is logical and obvious that if essay questions are to measure higher thought processes adequately, some amount of forethought must be involved in the planning of the questions. As has already been mentioned, it may seem easy to write a few questions on the board on the spur of the moment, but it is almost impossible to produce really good questions without fairly extensive preparation.

Furthermore, after essay questions have been written out well in advance, careful study and editing are necessary. The teacher must ask himself, and answer, such questions as, What am I really trying to measure with this question? Will my students understand exactly what I am trying to get at? Is this something they can reasonably be expected to know or to do? Only when these criteria of careful preparation and editing have been met can the teacher be satisfied that he has prepared as good an essay question as he can.

3. Students should be told in advance what type of examination they will be given. Whether or not students prepare differently for different types of tests, they should have the privilege of doing so if they wish.

4. The value or weight of each question on an essay examination should be indicated. This is true regardless of whether all questions have the same weight or different weights. The student is entitled to know what he is working for in terms of score or mark.

5. The quality of handwriting, spelling, grammar, punctuation, and clarity of thought should be checked and should carry weight in the evaluation of every essay or composition assigned by English or foreign-language teachers. This is one of the reasons for requiring writing; students will not learn correct usage if their mistakes are not pointed out.

6. Errors in spelling, grammar, usage, etc. should be checked in students' written work by every teacher but should not affect the mark or grade except in language classes. Consistent with the viewpoint espoused above, one of the claimed advantages of essay tests over objective tests is that they provide practice in writing. Such practice loses most, if not all, of its value, if the students' errors are not corrected. However, if a student's work in mathematics, science, or any subject other than language is accurate and correct, the pointing out of such errors should be sufficient.

7. Prepare enough questions to sample the learning of the students adequately. Do not use an essay examination consisting of only one or two questions. When this is done, either the questions must be so broad and general as to cause difficulties in interpretation and delimitation by the student or the sampling outcomes to be measured must be extremely limited.

8. Optional questions giving pupils a choice should not be provided. Such questions reduce the comparability of the sampling of pupils' learning and therefore of the basis for scoring. When pupils have a choice of questions, the lessened comparability of the individual papers affects the accuracy of grading and makes it much more difficult to evaluate the papers on a common basis.

Improving the Grading of Essay Questions

Suggestions for improving the scoring of essay questions are rather generally agreed upon by those who have studied the matter. The following represent some of the more frequently mentioned suggestions:

1. Determine in advance standards for each question to be used on the examination. This is usually done most satisfactorily by writing out a set of model answers. The answers written by pupils can then be compared with the key. The preparation and use of such a key is valuable in at least two ways: it requires the teacher to think through the implications of each question, and it provides a standard with which all papers can be compared for evaluation. It is desirable to prepare such a key *before* the questions are used, because during this preparation the teacher may discover faults which will suggest improvements in or elimination of a question.

2. Remove or cover all pupil-identifying data on the papers to be read. It is not always easy for the teacher or scorer to avoid being influenced by irrelevant matters when he knows the identity of the pupil whose paper he is reading. The evaluation should be based, as far as possible, only on what the pupil has written, and other factors should not be permitted to influence the scorer's judgments. Pupils may be instructed to fasten sheets together and write identifying data only on the back of one page.

3. Read all papers for one question at a time instead of reading each paper in its entirety. In other words, if there are five essay questions answered by thirty pupils, the scorer should read the answers to the first question on every paper, then all the answers to the second question, and so on; then he should give a score to each answer on each paper. Thus, if the question carries a maximum of 10 points, each student's answer is graded on this basis. The same is done with every other question on the examination and after all questions on all papers have been read and scored, the sum of the points on each paper constitutes the student's score on the test.

There are a number of advantages to this procedure. In the first place, the scorer's attention and judgment are focused on one question at a time, and this facilitates a more accurate evaluation of each question than is obtained when the answers to a number of different questions are judged in close succession. Second, this procedure encourages the rating of answers on a comparative basis, each answer being compared with all the other answers to the same question.

4. If a number of different factors — for example, accuracy, methods used, possibly correctness and felicity of expression — are to be taken into account, evaluate each separately. Reliability of grading will be increased if one factor is considered at a time. Lumping two or more together in evaluating responses almost certainly encourages fuzziness and inaccuracy in judgment.

5. After a set of papers has been graded lay them aside for several hours or a day and then look them over again. This often reveals small but possibly important points that may have been overlooked during the first grading. This does not suggest a complete re-scoring — few teachers have time for that — but merely a second "once-over" to catch obvious slips or inaccuracies.

▶ **LEARNING EXERCISES** ◀

7. Criticize the following as an essay question:
    Discuss the historical background of present-day intelligence tests.

8. Revise this question in the light of your criticisms, retaining its good features as an essay question.

9. Write out a model answer for your revised question. Compare the answer with some of the source material given in the references at the end of Chapter 2, pages 36 and 37.

Short-Answer Questions

As the term suggests, the short-answer item consists of a question which can be answered with a word or short phrase. It may be in the form of a direct question as,

    What is the capital of Switzerland? _ _ _ _ _ _ _ _ _ _ _ _ _ _ _ _ _ _

or it may be in the form of an incomplete statement as,

    The capital of Switzerland is _ _ _ _ _ _ _ _ _ _ _ _ _ _ _ _ _ .

In general, high school teachers seem to favor the short-answer type of question, probably because they think it has some of the claimed advantages both of essay and objective test questions. It is relatively easy to construct; it requires the pupil to supply the answer; it is not difficult to score or mark (certainly much easier than the essay question); and time and space requirements will usually permit the use of a large number of such questions in a test, thus obtaining for the teacher an improved sampling without making the test too laborious for the student.

While short-answer questions have the above-mentioned advantages to a greater or lesser degree, they have certain disadvantages as well. One of the foremost of these is the concentration upon specific, often unrelated, facts. In testing for such bits and pieces of knowledge as the capital of Switzerland, the number of ounces in a pound, the opposite of "big," or the discoverer of the Pacific Ocean, the teacher may lose sight of and fail to measure more important objectives. Furthermore, it is often difficult to phrase the short-answer question so that only one or even a few answers will fit. Unless the teacher succeeds fairly well in this, it will be impossible to anticipate the variety of answers which pupils will think of, and which will have to be judged as acceptable or not acceptable.

Since the short-answer type of question has some advantages and is favored by many teachers, we shall consider ways of planning and improving the construction of such items. Listed below are some suggestions which should prove useful.

1. Select and state the questions in such a way that they can be answered with a word or a short phrase. Avoid such questions as,

> What is the best method of making angel-food cake?

Although it might be possible to answer such a question by one word (a name for a method), there is nothing to prevent the willing pupil from writing a paragraph or two describing the best method. It would be better to say,

> List the *chief* ingredients of an angel-food cake.

2. Select and phrase short-answer questions so that only one or a very small number of answers will be correct. Do not say,

> Name the major cause of high prices of consumer goods.

To such a question a dozen or more answers could probably be given, each supported with cogent arguments. Better to say,

> The price support of wheat is fixed by present law at _ _ _ _ _ _
> per cent of _ _ _ _ _ _ _ _ _ _ _ _.

Such a question calls for a definite, specific, and probably undebatable answer. If the teacher wishes to ask a question relating to the cause or causes of high prices, he should probably not use the short-answer form. It would be preferable in such an instance to use the essay form, or perhaps the multiple-choice form wherein the pupil is required to choose the best of a limited number of alternatives.

Short-answer items are, on the whole, easy to construct, though one should not expect to make good short-answer items by taking statements verbatim from the text and merely omitting a word or two. The item should consist of a rephrasing of the idea or point being tested, or an entirely original statement of it. Short-answer questions are useful primarily in testing knowledge of facts and quite specific information. However, because of the shortcomings mentioned earlier, this type of item is not frequently used in standardized tests.

▶ LEARNING EXERCISE ◀

10. Construct five short-answer questions dealing with some objective of a subject you are likely to teach. Try these out, if possible, on one of your fellow students. Do the results bring out any weaknesses and suggestions for improvement?

Completion Questions

What has been said about the short-answer question applies also to the completion form. However, in the short-answer type the blank is nearly always at the end, whereas in the true completion type the blank or blanks may occur anywhere in the statement. It is particularly important in this case to phrase the statement in such a way that only a single answer will be correct. Indefiniteness of the statement or other conditions permitting a variety of defensible answers will multiply the difficulties encountered in the scoring process. Listed below are a few suggestions for the construction of good completion questions:

1. Omit only significant words from the statement. Do not omit articles, prepositions, conjunctions, or similar words unless the purpose is to test the usage of such words (as in the case of a grammar test). If the statement to be used is,

> Democracy is that form of government in which the whole people or some numerous portion of them exercise the governing power through deputies periodically elected by themselves.

one might devise two questions as follows:

> Democracy is that _ _ _ _ _ _ _ _ _ of government in which the whole people or _ _ _ _ _ _ _ _ numerous portion of _ _ _ _ _ _ _ _ exercise the governing power _ _ _ _ _ _ _ _ deputies periodically elected _ _ _ _ _ _ _ _ _ _ _ _ _ _ _ _ _ _.

or,

> Democracy is that form of _ _ _ _ _ _ _ _ _ _ in which the whole _ _ _ _ _ _ _ _ or some numerous portion of them exercise the governing _ _ _ _ _ _ _ _ through _ elected by _ _ _ _ _ _ _ _ _ _.

In the second case, the essential and important ideas of *government,* by the *people, power, representation, periodical* elections are tested; in the first, inconsequential words like *form, some, them, through, by themselves* are required, and it is quite apparent that such words have no significant relationship to the important ideas the statement conveys.

2. In omitting significant words, leave enough clues to enable the competent person to answer correctly. If this principle is not adhered to, filling in the blanks becomes either impossible or just a guessing game. To illustrate, do not say,

> _ _ _ _ _ _ _ _ _ _ _ _ _ _ _ _ discovered _ _ _ _ _ _ _ _ _ _ in _ _ _ _ _ _.

It is impossible to answer this item with assurance because dozens of discoveries might fit the statement. However, if the statement were to read,

Columbus discovered _ _ _ _ _ _ _ _ _ _ _ _ _ in _ _ _ _ _ _ _ _ _.

it would be more definite. Most children who have learned a few basic facts of American history could answer this item correctly, though several answers might still be possible. The effect of excessive deletions is even more marked as statements become more complex.

3. In scoring short-answer and completion items it is generally most satisfactory to allow one point credit for each blank, unless the item requires several words or a phrase. For example,

In woodworking, the device used most commonly for cutting molding and small lumber at 45° angles is called a   *mitre*
box   _ _ _ _ _ _
_ _ _ _ _ _ _.

Here, although two words are needed to complete the statement, only one point should be allowed in scoring, and no partial credit should be allowed for either word alone. Neither is correct by itself, and both are necessary to convey the essential idea.

In the following example, however, four points would be given, one for each correct response:

The four seasons are _ _ _ _ _ _ _ _, _ _ _ _ _ _ _ _, _ _ _ _ _ _ _ _,
and _ _ _ _ _ _ _ _.

This system simplifies scoring and avoids many difficulties arising from methods whereby partial credits are given.

▶ LEARNING EXERCISE ◀

11. Completion questions have been more widely used in mental ability or general intelligence tests than in any other kind of tests. Can you explain why?

True-False Items

In the early days of objective-test development the true-false item was very popular. Some of the first published tests consisted entirely of this type of item. In recent years its popularity has declined to such an extent that one finds it used only rarely in standardized tests. There are at least two reasons for this trend: the inherent weakness in the item itself, especially with regard to the large element of chance or guessing that may enter into the answering, and the fact that it appears deceptively easy to make good true-false items.

The true-false item usually consists of a declarative sentence, to which the examinee responds by marking it true or false, thus:

( ) The capital of Michigan is Lansing.

or,

( ) The first Continental Congress met in New York in 1798.

A variety of modifications of the true-false item have been tried, nearly always in an attempt to lessen the effect of its chief weakness — the element of chance success through guessing. One possible modification is to have the pupil correct the false item by crossing out the word or part that makes it false, and writing in the word or phrase that will make the statement correct. For example, an item appears on the mimeographed or printed test as follows:

( ) A pair of scissors is an example of a lever of the second class.

The pupil marks it "false" and corrects it, thus:

                                    first
(*F*) A pair of scissors is an example of a lever of the ~~second~~ class.

The statement is false because scissors are an example of first-class levers. The item is correctly marked, as shown above, by crossing out the underlined word "second," and writing above it the word "first." Or one might underline the phrase "pair of scissors," draw a line through it, and write in an example of a second-class lever, thus:

                nutcracker
(*F*) A ~~pair of scissors~~ is an example of a lever of the second class.

This arrangement might be a little less satisfactory than the preceding one. In that instance only one word, "first," would be an acceptable answer, while in the variation above a large number of examples of second-class levers would have to be accepted. In both instances, statements which are true are simply marked "true" with the designated symbol; nothing further need be done.

Every true-false question calls for a choice between two alternatives. A statement is either right or wrong, true or false. Hence, the possibility of guessing the right choice, mathematically speaking, is one in two, or 50 per cent. Therefore, with one hundred such items it should be possible to get half of them right on the basis of pure chance alone. The pupil whose results on the test show that he has answered half of the one hundred items right and half wrong can thus be assumed to have done no better than a pupil who has guessed his way through the entire test. To eliminate the element of guesswork, it is common practice to score such tests by the formula of $S = R - W$, where S = score, R = number of true-false items answered correctly, and W = number of true-false items missed.[7]

In the case cited, this would work out as follows: $S = 50 - 50 = 0$. If Robert, on the other hand, gets seventy right and thirty wrong, his score would be $70 - 30$, or 40. Items not attempted are usually disregarded in the scoring. For example, if James omits twelve items out of the one hundred, and gets sixty right and twenty-eight wrong of the remaining eighty-eight, he would receive a score of $60 - 28$, or 32, the twelve omitted being disregarded in arriving at the score.

In the case of Robert, the assumption is that if he knows the answers to forty items and guesses on the remaining sixty, he would get half of these, or thirty, right purely by chance. Consequently, his correct score, 40, is obtained by use of the formula, $S = R - W$, or $S = 70 - 30 = 40$.

$$40 + 30$$

James, however, is quite uncertain about twelve items and omits them; he knows the answers to thirty-two and guesses on the remaining fifty-six, getting half of them (twenty-eight) right and the same number wrong. In this case, the omitted items must first be allowed for, so that $100 - 12 = 88$, the number attempted. Of these, he knows the answers to thirty-two and guesses on the remaining fifty-six, getting half, or twenty-eight, right and the same number wrong. His score, then, is $60 - 28 = 32$, the num-

$$32 + 28$$

ber he actually knows, according to the original assumption.

In this connection, it should be noted that if all students attempt, or answer, every item, the correction for chance success makes no difference in the ranking of scores on the test. For example:

Student	R	W	R–W Score	Rank R	R–W
J	70	30	40	3	3
R	60	40	20	4	4
T	88	12	76	1	1
W	76	24	52	2	2

[7] To eliminate the possibility of chance success in objective tests, the general formula for correction is $S = R - \dfrac{W}{n-1}$. Here, n equals the number of choices. In a true-false item $n = 2$, so the formula becomes $S = R - W$.

However, suppose students are instructed not to guess but to omit items they are uncertain about. Under these circumstances the results might be as follows:

Student	R	W	O	Score R–W	Rank R	R–W
J	65	25	10	40	3	4
R	56	14	30	42	4	3
T	80	12	8	68	1	1
W	70	24	6	46	2	2

Thus we can see that the R–W system of scoring works to the advantage of the cautious, conservative student, in this case, R. By attempting only seventy items of which he is comparatively certain and omitting thirty, the answers to which he doesn't know, he obtains a higher rank by the R–W formula than on the basis of R alone.

Such a lengthy discussion of the scoring of true-false items may seem unnecessary, and, as far as the practice of the typical classroom teacher is concerned, this may be true. He will generally score his true-false items on the basis of right answers alone and let it go at that. Very few students are happy when papers are returned with true-false items scored R − W. Nevertheless, this does happen, especially in college classes, and what we have done here is to present in brief form the rationale for the correction for chance in such items. Since the possibility of chance success, or guessing, is obviously greatest in true-false items, this seemed the appropriate point to explain the procedure, the reasoning behind it, and the effects of following or not following it.

Another factor that has reduced the prestige and use of this type of item is the tendency of inexperienced and relatively untrained persons to fall into the error of assuming that good true-false questions are easy to construct. The inexperienced teacher will often lift sentences verbatim from the textbook, insert a negative, or introduce some other slight modification, and expect therewith to produce a good true-false item. It should be emphasized that superior items are almost never formulated in this manner. The true-false question requires very careful planning and construction; it is hoped that the suggestions below will help the student materially in avoiding many of the common weaknesses of this type of item.

1. Do not include more than a single idea in one true-false item, particularly if one idea is true and the other is false. Except in special situations where the testing may be directed toward unusual objectives, it is considered better to make each true-false item deal with one idea, and to use a statement which is either wholly true or wholly false. Otherwise, the item is sure to be ambiguous. For example,

( ) Lincoln spent six weeks planning his Gettysburg Address before delivering it on November 19, 1863.

This statement is ambiguous because the facts are all correct except the amount of time spent in preparation of the speech. It probably would be better to make two items, thus:

( ) Lincoln spent six weeks planning his Gettysburg Address.

( ) Lincoln delivered his Gettysburg Address on November 19, 1863.

This makes both items acceptable since one is clearly true, the other clearly false, and neither sentence is ambiguous.

2. Avoid negative statements wherever possible. If they are used, the word or phrase that makes the statement a negative one should be emphasized by italics or underlining. A false negative statement results in a double negative — or positive — statement, and such statements will nearly always be confusing. Since our primary purpose is to test learning, not to confuse students or test their ability to solve puzzles, there seems little justification for the use of ambiguous statements. The statement,

( ) A true-false question should *not* be negatively stated.

is true and the word which makes it a negative is italicized. Consider, however, the following item, a perfectly straightforward positive statement:

( ) Washington is the capital of the United States.

Nearly everyone would mark this correctly as a true statement. In the form given, it poses no special problems. If, on the other hand, the statement is changed to read,

( ) Washington is *not* the capital of the United States.

confusion may result because of the double negative thus introduced. The pupils' hesitancy in reacting to this kind of item is easily demonstrated. First, write a true positive statement on the board and ask the class to say orally whether it is true or false. There will be a chorus of "True!" Erase the positive statement and write the negative one in its place. Now ask for a response, true or false. Usually some will say "False," some "True," and the majority will say nothing.

3. An approximately equal number of true and false items should be used. Any great preponderance of either true or false statements might enable the student to detect a trend as he progresses with the test.

4. Avoid long, involved statements, especially those containing dependent clauses, many qualifications, and complex ideas. These factors tend to cause the items to test reading comprehension rather than achievement in a subject. A better technique is to break up such long statements into two or more separate items which will be more easily understood and which will yield more exact and specific information concerning the student's attainments.

5. Use the true-false form only with statements or ideas which are clearly and indubitably true or false as stated. It should be obvious that a test item, the correct response to which is uncertain or debatable, is not suited for use as a true-false item, simply because no scoring key can be devised. A teacher may wish to use arguable matters for purposes of class discussion, but these topics have no place in an objective test. Consider, for example, the following:

( ) The greatest woman in history was Madam Curie.

Immediately we hear: How about Catherine the Great? Elizabeth the First? Cleopatra? Florence Nightingale? etc., etc. The answer would never be agreed upon.

▶ LEARNING EXERCISES ◀

12. It has been suggested by some authorities that true-false questions are better stated in the form of a question, as, "Is a cow a biped?" rather than in the positive form, as, "A cow is a biped." Can you see any justification for this point of view? Do you think it has merit?

13. Construct ten true-false items in a field or area of your own choosing. Check these against the suggestions given in the preceding section. How good a job have you done?

Matching Items

This type of item is employed widely in situations where relationships of more or less similar ideas, facts, or principles are to be examined or judged. For example:

(4) carbohydrate	1. butter
(1) fat	2. lean meat
(2) protein	3. salt
	4. sugar
	5. water

Here, an example of each of several nutrients in the first column is to be found in the second column. The pupil indicates the correct choice in each case by writing the number of the correct example in the parentheses preceding the name of the nutrient the example represents. In practice, the lists are usually longer than in the brief illustration given above.

A modification of the matching question is the classification item, which may also be used to advantage in some cases. For example, in the illustrative matching set below, a list of terms is given, together with a key to be used in identifying or classifying the terms:

1. bird	2. mammal	3. fish	4. amphibian

( ) eagle	( ) cow
( ) mouse	( ) whale
( ) alligator	( ) pike
( ) bat	( ) frog

The matching type of item lends itself well to testing knowledge of words, dates, events, persons, formulas, tools, and many other such matters involving simple relationships or categories. Matching questions are less well suited to the testing of broader concepts such as the ability to organize and apply knowledge, however. The suggestions which follow have been found helpful in improving the quality and usefulness of matching items.

1. A matching exercise usually should not contain more than ten or twelve items. That is, the number of terms, names, etc., to be identified or matched should not exceed ten or twelve, because longer lists will become quite burdensome and tiring to the person taking the test. Where there are more than a dozen items to be tested, it is usually better to construct two or more separate matching exercises.

2. The number of items in the column from which matching terms or formulas are to be selected should always exceed the number of items in the opposite primary column or list. In other words, there should be a number of optional choices or alternatives from which to choose items for matching. For example, instead of this,

(*c*) fast	a. forte
(*a*) loud	b. pianissimo
(*b*) very softly	c. presto

use this:

(*e*) fast	a. forte
(*a*) loud	b. legato
(*c*) very softly	c. pianissimo
	d. poco
	e. presto

In this way, the opportunity for chance success is decreased because there is less chance of arriving at choices by the process of elimination. In the first instance, if the pupil knew two of the three terms he would get the third one automatically; in the second instance, he would still have to choose from among three remaining terms. If there are ten terms in the first column, there should be twelve to fifteen possible choices in the second column.

3. There should be a high degree of homogeneity in every set of matching items. All of the items or terms in each exercise should belong to the same category; otherwise, those which do not will be much easier to match than the rest. To illustrate:

(*f*) capitals	a. at end of direct query
(*g*) comma	b. used to show possession
(*c*) period	c. at end of declarative sentence
(*a*) question mark	d. after expression of strong feeling
(*e*) semicolon	e. used to show balance between coordinate sentence elements
	f. begin all proper nouns
	g. sets off non-restrictive clauses

In the above example the category of the word "capitals" is different from that of the others because it is not a punctuation mark. By looking at the list of options, the intelligent pupil can easily determine which one fits. He will quickly reason that *f.* is the only choice which could possibly fit "capitals," since all other options deal with matters of punctuation, and he will observe that "capitals" is the only plural form in the first column and that "begin" is the only verb in the second column which requires a plural subject. Both errors are easy to commit unknowingly in making sets of matching items.

4. The terms in both lists or columns of a matching exercise should be arranged alphabetically, or in any other logical or systematic order, wherever possible. Such an arrangement will facilitate finding items in the lists, and reduces the searching or reading task. When items consist of phrases, clauses or sentences, or material of a non-verbal character such as chemical formulas, numbers, algebraic terms, and the like, alphabetizing is out of the question. However, whenever some systematic arrangement that does not furnish clues to correct choices is possible, it should be followed.

5. Use the classification type of matching item as a variation of the standard form, particularly in testing such objectives as the ability to apply or interpret. For example:

a. Adjective   d. Interjection   g. Pronoun
b. Adverb   e. Noun   h. Verb
c. Conjunction   f. Preposition

(*f*) 1. We went *over* the river on the bridge.
(*b*) 2. Turn your paper *over*.
(*h*) 3. We have been *over* that once before.
(*e*) 4. John scored a *run*.
(*h*) 5. Mary said she would *run* fast.
(*e*) 6. *Running* is hard work.

Here, a variety of situations are provided in which the pupil may apply what he has learned about parts of speech.

6. Pictorial items can often be used advantageously as a variation in the matching type of item.

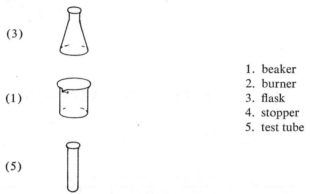

(3)

(1)

1. beaker
2. burner
3. flask
4. stopper
5. test tube

(5)

Such items may be used in subjects where apparatus, equipment, or tools are used. Pictures of objects may be matched with their names, uses, or other characteristics.

7. The same response may be used more than once; but there should not be more than one correct choice for any term.

Do:

(3) adjective   1. and
(2) noun   2. run
(2) verb   3. slow
  4. to
  5. when

Don't:

(4)   adjective   1. and
(2 or 3)   noun   2. boy
(3)   verb   3. run
  4. slow
  5. to

8. Directions for matching items should indicate (a) the basis of match-ing or relationship; (b) the method of indicating answers; (c) whether the same choice or term may be used more than once. Clear, explicit directions for matching items are among the most difficult to write. The test-maker should prepare them carefully and study them to make certain that the above points are provided for.

Although matching items are used quite frequently in informal and locally made tests, their use in published, standardized tests seems to be declining. This type of item does not seem to be popular with professional test-makers for reasons which are not altogether clear. One reason prob-ably is the limited usefulness of the matching item; another reason may be the lack of research data on its value as a measurement device. Neverthe-less, for informal tests made locally, matching items furnish a useful varia-tion and will probably continue to be used by many teachers and other persons who are interested in broadening and improving their own measur-ing techniques.

▶ LEARNING EXERCISES ◀

14. What kinds of learning outcomes might be efficiently measured by matching questions in:

          a. seventh-grade English
          b. third-grade reading
          c. ninth-grade civics
          d. trigonometry
          e. biological science

15. Prepare a set of matching items in a field or subject with which you are familiar. Try them out on a classmate.

Multiple-Choice Items

The percentages of high school teachers reporting the use of multiple-choice items "fairly often" or "very often," in the survey previously cited,[8] are 50.6 and 16.4, respectively, or a total of 67 per cent. The multiple-choice item apparently is the most popular of the objective types. (Cor-responding percentages for the matching type of item are 45.1 and 16.0, a total of 61.1; for true-false the percentages are 37.4 and 11.3, or 48.7 per cent.)

The multiple-choice item usually consists of an incomplete declarative

[8] Noll and Durost, *op. cit.*

sentence followed by a number of possible responses, one of which is clearly correct or best. For example:

> A plane figure of four sides and four angles is called *(1)* a tetrahedron *(2)* a pyramid *(3)* a quadrilateral *(4)* a cube *(5)* an octagon

or again, it may be in the form of a question, thus:

> Which of the following was the leading character in a famous play by the same name? *(1)* Cyrano de Bergerac *(2)* Silas Marner *(3)* Nathaniel Hawthorne *(4)* Betsy Ross *(5)* Shylock

These two examples represent items in which the response to be chosen is clearly in the category of "correct." In the first, only (3) "a quadrilateral," is correct; the others are wrong. In the second, only the answer, "Cyrano de Bergerac" is correct. However, multiple-choice items may be devised in which the examinee is asked to compare the quality of various choices and make a judgment as to which is *best*. Consider, for example, the following:

> From the standpoints of versatility, objectivity, and all around usefulness, the best type of test item is the
>
> 1. Essay
> 2. Matching
> 3. Multiple choice
> 4. Short answer
> 5. True-false

Here no single answer can be *proved* to be correct; however, such an item would provide an opportunity for the examinee to weigh various factors and arrive at the *best* answer in terms of what he had learned through reading, class discussions, and consideration of all relevant factors. Where such items are used in standardized tests the "best" answer must be one agreed upon by competent authorities or judges.

Still another variation of the multiple-choice item is that in which the instructions are to choose the answer which doesn't belong with the others. For example:

> One of the following tools differs from the others in a fundamental characteristic. Which tool?
>
> (1) Axe
> (2) Chisel
> (3) Hatchet
> (4) Knife
> (5) Saw

Here the obvious answer is "saw," since it has a serrated edge, unlike the others. In using this type of item, however, great care must be taken to make certain that only one basis of comparison or relationship is possible. Consider the following example:

Which of the following does not belong with the rest?

  (1) Glass
  (2) Salt
  (3) Soda
  (4) Sugar
  (5) Water

The author of this hypothetical item might have in mind "glass" as the correct answer, since the others are chemical compounds and glass is a mixture. However, in another dimension, "water" could be supported as the correct answer since the others are solids and it is a liquid. Still another possibility might be "sugar," since it is the only organic compound in the list.

Other variations of the multiple-choice form have been devised but the ones described here are those commonly used.

The multiple-choice item is probably the most versatile of the objective recognition types. It lends itself to a wide variety of situations, objectives, and content. It can be quite objective in its scoring, it provides opportunity for wide coverage in the choice of alternatives, and it is not conducive to chance success or guessing. It is so generally regarded as the best and most widely applicable type of item that it has become the stock-in-trade, the basic type, for most standardized tests today.

A number of suggestions and some examples of good techniques for multiple-choice items are given below.

1. Probably the most important skill in making multiple-choice items is in the framing of alternatives. One choice must be clearly the best, but the others must appear plausible to the uninformed, perhaps even more so than the correct choice. To illustrate:

> The capital of the United States is *(1)* Washington *(2)* New York *(3)* Chicago *(4)* St. Louis *(5)* Los Angeles

Each of these choices would probably function, that is, be chosen as the answer by pupils at different levels, living in different parts of the country. As it stands, this might be a good question for Grade Four. But if we change the alternatives we might have this:

> The capital of the United States is *(1)* Washington *(2)* Atlantic City *(3)* Reno *(4)* Milwaukee *(5)* San Antonio

The item is now easier because the four wrong choices are somewhat more obvious than those in the first example. Going still further in this direction, the item might become:

> The capital of the United States is (*1*) Washington
> (*2*) Rome (*3*) Tokyo (*4*) Paris (*5*) London

This item is probably even easier than the others because most children in school who have studied any social science, whether they know that Washington is the answer or not, could probably arrive at it by the process of elimination. The item can also be made absurdly easy:

> The capital of the United States is (*1*) Washington
> (*2*) wheat (*3*) China (*4*) air (*5*) birds

The above illustrations are intended to show how the selection of alternatives will affect the difficulty of a multiple-choice item and the functioning of the choices themselves. An alternative which does not seem plausible or which appeals to no one serves no purpose. If there is one such alternative in a five-response multiple-choice item, the item becomes, in effect, a four-response item. If there are two such alternatives, it becomes a three-response item, and so on. The maker of multiple-choice items will not be successful, regardless of what other capabilities he may have, unless he develops skill in formulating choices which are functional — choices which, even though incorrect, are plausible enough to be chosen.

2. *A multiple-choice item should not have more than one acceptable answer.* Some teachers have a liking for items in which more than one of the choices is acceptable. The difficulty with such items lies in the scoring, for which no generally acceptable method has been devised. For example:

> She has never liked (*1*) this (*2*) them (*3*) that (*4*) those
> (*5*) these -------------- kind of stories.

In this case both (*1*) and (*3*) are acceptable choices, but how shall the item be scored in the following instances? (It is assumed that pupils have been instructed that one or more choices are acceptable.)

> A chooses (*1*) and (*2*) — one right, one wrong.
> B chooses (*1*) and (*3*) — two right.
> C chooses (*4*) and (*5*) — two wrong.
> D chooses (*1*), (*2*), (*3*), and (*4*) — two right, two wrong.

PUPILS	RIGHTS	RIGHTS – WRONGS
A	1	0
B	2	2
C	0	−2
D	2	0

If scoring is based on "rights" alone, B and D get the same score, although B makes no errors while D makes two; also, D gets a higher score than A, who makes fewer errors.

If scoring is based on Rights–Wrongs, C gets a negative score, though this is undesirable; if no score lower than zero is given, C scores the same as A and D, who get one and two right, respectively.

It is generally far more satisfactory to make two items — in this case, one with "this" as the acceptable choice, and the other with "that." Care must be taken, however, to vary the foils so that the correct answers will not be immediately obvious, as they are here:

> a. She has never liked (*1*) this   (*2*) them   (*3*) those
>   (*4*) these _ _ _ _ _ _ _ kind of stories.
>
> b. She has never liked (*1*) that   (*2*) them   (*3*) those
>   (*4*) these _ _ _ _ _ _ _ kind of stories.

Here, the fact that three of the choices are the same in both items would lead the pupil to deduce that the correct choice in *a.* must be "this" and in *b.*, "that." Such clues which lead to a correct answer, but which are irrelevant to the real purpose of the item, should be avoided.

3. The choices in an item should come at or near the end of the statement. When the item is stated as a question, the choices usually occur near the end naturally. For example, if the question is,

> Which of the following sentences is grammatically correct? _ _ _ _
>   (*1*) . . . . .   (*2*) . . . . .   (*3*) . . . . .   (*4*) . . . . .   (*5*) . . . . .

the most natural way of presenting the alternatives seems to be as indicated. However, one could state the item thus:

> (*1*) . . . . .   (*2*) . . . . .   (*3*) . . . . .   (*4*) . . . . .   (*5*) . . . . .
> _ _ _ _ is the only grammatically correct sentence.

Or again, the question might be stated in this form:

> Of the following sentences, the only grammatically correct one is
>   (*1*) . . . . .   (*2*) . . . . .   (*3*) . . . . .   (*4*) . . . . .   (*5*) . . . . .

It is usually considered preferable to place the alternatives at the end of the item, because the more natural sequence is to have the question or problem followed by the suggested answers, and that arrangement is likely to cause little confusion for the person taking the test.

4. In multiple-choice items the best or correct answer should be placed equally often in each possible position. That is, if there are five choices in each item and a considerable number of items in the test, the best answer should occur with approximately the same frequency as *1, 2, 3, 4,* and *5.*

If the best answer appears much more often in one position than in others, its position might serve as an irrelevant clue. It is also essential to have the best-answer position randomized; that is, the first 20 per cent of the items should not all be *1*'s, the next 20 per cent should not all be *2*'s, etc. If, as multiple-choice items are constructed, the best answer of the first one is placed in the number 1 position, the best answer of the next in the number 2 position, and so on, an equal distribution will be obtained. When the items are finally arranged, usually according to difficulty, the order of correct choices will automatically be randomized.

5. Choices should be in parallel form wherever possible. For example:

> The first activity on a cold wintry morning was
>
>   1. to gather wood and build a fire
>   2. eating a hearty breakfast
>   3. fishing for mackerel
>   4. go for fresh water
>   5. a dash around the yard

This item is improved if the wording is changed to

> The first activity on a cold wintry morning was
>
>   1. gathering wood and building a fire
>   2. eating a hearty breakfast
>   3. fishing for mackerel
>   4. going for fresh water
>   5. dashing around the yard

6. Choices should fit the stem grammatically. For example:

> If a straight line forms a right angle with another straight line
> it is said to be
>
>   1. parallel
>   2. straight
>   3. perpendicular
>   4. equal
>   5. adjacent   . . . to that line.

Obviously, choice 2. does not fit the concluding phrase, grammatically speaking, and thus could not possibly be the best answer.

7. The length of the item and the length of the choices should be determined by the purpose of the item. For example, in a test for knowledge and understanding of words, an item might read:

> The word that means the same as "vanished" is
>
>   1. broadened   4. changed
>   2. disappeared   5. narrowed
>   3. decreased

On the other hand, understanding of the theme or main idea of a story might be tested as follows:

> The lesson the speaker learned from his friends was that
> 1. old age can be the happiest, most useful time of life
> 2. it is not desirable for old people to wish to become young again or to behave in the carefree manner of youth
> 3. seeking the fountain of youth is well worth the effort
> 4. it is impossible to make a magic potion that will make people permanently young
> 5. you are as young as you feel and act

8. The number of choices in multiple-choice items should be at least four; the generally preferred number is five. It can be assumed that as the number of choices is reduced the chance factor increases. Theoretically, with four choices there is one chance in four of guessing the answer; with three choices the chances become one in three; and with two alternatives the chances are mathematically the same as in a true-false item. Common practice in standardized tests has been to use five choices or responses, although more recently there appears to be some tendency to use only four. The basis for this is not seemingly well established. It is, of course, more difficult to devise five choices than four, and there is some feeling that the difference in chance success between four and five choices is not great enough to warrant the additional effort required to devise a fifth choice. There is no question, however, that four is the minimum acceptable number. It is also a generally accepted procedure to provide the same number of choices for each item in a given test or set.

9. Words that would be repeated in each response should be part of the stem. For example:

> In national elections in the United States, the President
> 1. is chosen by the people, directly
> 2. is chosen by the members of the Senate
> 3. is chosen by the members of the Cabinet
> 4. is chosen by the members of the House of Representatives
> 5. is chosen by the Electoral College

In the above illustration, the words "is chosen by the" should be made part of the stem so that it would read:

> In national elections in the United States, the President is chosen by the
> 1. people, directly
> 2. members of the Senate
> 3. members of the Cabinet
> 4. members of the House of Representatives
> 5. Electoral College

10. Use "none of the above" and "all of the above" as a choice only occasionally as a variation from the usual pattern. Use them sparingly, however. Where "none of the above" is the correct choice, there should be no possible doubt that the other choices are all clearly incorrect. For example:

The area of a rectangle is equal to

1. the sum of its sides
2. the square of its shorter side
3. the square of its longer side
4. one-half the product of its
   shorter and longer sides
5. none of the above

"All of the above" is probably less desirable as an alternative than "none of the above." It is not easy to devise items of this type which stand up under critical analysis. The choices are either so obvious that the item becomes too easy or it is used simply as a filler to avoid the effort required to find another good choice. Where either of these two choices is used, care should be taken to see that it is the correct answer in a few instances but not all.

The suggestions and examples of the multiple-choice item presented above should serve to orient the beginning classroom teacher, counselor, or supervisor to the construction and evaluation of this most widely used and versatile type of objective test item. When carefully and thoughtfully constructed, it provides the best means of measuring outcomes of instruction so far devised. Its use is by no means confined to achievement testing; it is used in measuring intelligence, aptitudes, interests, and other qualities or traits, which attests to its wide usefulness. The test-maker will generally find practice in the construction and use of multiple-choice items rewarding and satisfying.

▶ **LEARNING EXERCISE** ◀

16. Construct a multiple-choice item to measure each of the following:

    a. Knowledge of the capital city of your state.

    b. Understanding of a rule of punctuation, e.g., the comma.

    c. Ability to interpret a graph or a table showing the relationship of height of children to their weight.

    d. Skill in defining a problem in general science, e.g., how should a high school boy or girl who is overweight proceed to reduce?

Situational or Interpretive Items

A type of item which has found considerable favor among test-makers is one which presents a reading selection, describes a situation, or provides a chart, a table, or a map or sketch to fit the subject matter and the objectives, followed by several items based on the material presented. These items are generally in multiple-choice form, though true–false may also be used. Examples of the situational type may be seen on page 115, in Chapter 5. Here we have a map of a section of a community on which are based a number of multiple-choice items which can be answered by referring to the map. Another example appears on page 120 of the same chapter in the form of a graph showing changes in Alberta's weight with two multiple-choice items following.

Although the situational test is not a type of item in the same sense as matching or true–false, it represents an approach having certain distinct characteristics and assumed advantages. Among these are *first,* that it attempts measurement in what might be called a more global or inclusive fashion than isolated objective test items. *Second,* it reduces differences between individuals in background knowledge and information, since these are supplied to all. *Third,* it purports to measure more complex outcomes of instruction such as the ability to interpret information, to draw valid conclusions, and to make applications.

Situational or interpretive exercises require a higher order of skill to prepare than most other types of objective test items. The matter on which the objective test items are based must be most carefully prepared, generally by the test maker. It is seldom possible to find a selection (except perhaps in literature) or a table that lends itself satisfactorily to the intended purpose or the outcome to be measured. Further, the objective test items must be constructed with great care, so that the answers are not obvious from a mere searching of the material on which they are based. If they are obvious, the unique advantages of this type of item will not be realized. The situational type of exercise has great potential value, which can be realized if the test maker is willing to take the time and make the necessary effort. Most of what has already been said concerning the construction of true-false and multiple-choice items applies with equal force here.

▶ LEARNING EXERCISE ◀

17. Examine some standardized tests in natural science, social studies, or a reading test for examples of interpretive exercises. What objectives do they purport to measure in each instance? What advantages do they seem to have over the more conventional types of objective test items?

OBJECTIVE TEST ITEMS: GENERAL SUGGESTIONS

Many suggestions have been offered in the preceding pages for planning and constructing different types of test questions or items, from the essay to the most objective. An attempt has been made in this presentation to include suggestions primarily relevant to the type of item under consideration. However, there are some basic principles or ideas which apply to all types. It is these which we now present and discuss briefly in concluding this chapter. Some of the statements will already have been touched upon in the discussion of particular types of items, but they bear repetition here since they are most important.

1. Avoid ambiguity, a common fault of tests. One of the most common weaknesses of test items of all types is ambiguity. This means that the meaning of the item is not clear or that it may be interpreted in more than one way. This fault is easy to commit but often difficult to detect in advance, so that it may be evident only when the item has been actually used. Nevertheless, there are some suggestions which, if conscientiously adhered to, will help to avoid ambiguous or unclear items:

a. Strive for clear-cut, concise, exact statements. Long, complicated statements are more difficult to comprehend. Qualifying statements may make an item less ambiguous, but they can also have the opposite effect.

b. Avoid negative statements, particularly in true-false items, where a false negative statement results in a double negative, which can be very confusing. Occasionally, an idea or objective being tested seems to lend itself best to the negative form; in that case, emphasize the word which makes it negative as much as possible by capitalizing or underlining it (i.e., NOT).

c. Have another teacher or counselor look over your test items critically. Teachers are often reluctant to show their tests to a colleague, but having a friendly critic check them can be very helpful. Another's viewpoint is often valuable in detecting faults which the maker of the test has overlooked.

d. The surest way to detect ambiguity in test items is to try them out in actual practice. Of course, it may then be too late to do anything about it, but if the test is to be used again some repairs may be possible. An ambiguous item will nearly always show up when the results of the test are analyzed (to be explained in the next chapter). An item that is missed more often by the best students than by the poor students is often ambiguous.

2. Statements to be used in test items ordinarily should not be taken verbatim from the textbook or other instructional material. Sometimes there may be a need to test for knowledge and understanding of the exact wording of a text, but this will probably not occur often. If one wishes to measure the extent to which pupils know, understand, and use what has been taught, it is desirable to test by rephrasing, reorganizing, and restating the content so that the exact wording of the original is not reproduced. Instead of using the key sentence of a paragraph as a test item, the teacher who is testing for the understanding of any central thought or principle should use a form or words that are different from those used in the textbook. In so doing, the teacher will discourage memorization of the words of a textbook and will be able to determine more adequately whether or not a pupil really understands and can apply what he has read.

3. Restrict the number of types of items used in any given test. Although it was stated earlier in this chapter that the type of item used is determined in part by the purpose of the test or the objective being measured, it is generally desirable to restrict to two or three the kinds of items used in the same test. The purposes of the test can usually be achieved with a few types of items, and the use of too many different ones may confuse and disturb some pupils.

4. Avoid giving irrelevant clues. Unless it is carefully constructed, a test item may, in itself, furnish an indication of the correct or expected answer. For example, the following item is subject to criticism because of the similarity of the word "parallel" in the item and "parallelogram," the answer:

A four-sided figure whose opposite sides are parallel is called

1. a trapezoid	4. an octagon
2. a triangle	5. a hexagon
3. a parallelogram	

The teacher in his preparation of test items must always be on guard against inadvertently providing such clues. Listed below are several other ways in which irrelevant clues are commonly — though unintentionally — provided in the test item:

a. There is a tendency for longer statements or choices to be true or correct more often than not.

b. True-false items containing universals such as "always," "never," "all," and "none" are likely to be false, while those containing "generally," "usually," "some," "many," and "sometimes" are usually true. If such terms are used, the correct response should not be in line with the specific determiner; that is, more often than not the statements containing "always," "never," etc. should be true and those containing "some," "usually," etc. should occasionally, at least, be false.

c. The correct (or incorrect) answer to one item should not be given by another item. To illustrate from a teacher-made, true-false test in United States history, two items were stated as follows:

( ) The Eighteenth Amendment gave women the right to vote.
( ) Repeal of the Eighteenth Amendment occurred during the administration of Franklin Roosevelt.

Here, the correct answer to the first item may be deduced from the second item, for if the student knows that the second item is true, he also knows that the first must be false.

5. *Do not make an item difficult by requiring unnecessarily exact or difficult operations.* In mathematics, for example, if the understanding of a principle is the objective being tested, the calculations in solving a problem should be made as simple as possible without being obvious. The examinee should not miss the item because of mistakes in calculation if he knows the principle. A similar caution is pertinent in science. To illustrate:

The molecular weight of H_2SO_4 is
    a. 64
    b. 32
    c. 98
    d. 96
    e. 196

This item could be made needlessly subject to errors in calculation if the answers provided were based on exact atomic weights, and therefore included decimals, when all that presumably is being tested is whether the student knows how to determine the molecular weight of a compound.

6. *The difficulty of an item should be appropriate to the level of the students being tested.* Beginners in test construction are apt to overestimate what their students can do. They often construct tests that are too long or tests in which the individual items are too difficult to read or to answer. Any teacher can construct a test which will "fail" most, if not all of his students, but this helps neither students nor teacher. The purpose of a test is to find out what the students have learned or can do as well as what they have not learned or cannot do. In a test of appropriate difficulty, all students should find some items they can answer correctly and the best students should be challenged to the limit of their ability. Furthermore, a test of achievement should not be above the reading level of the group for whom

it is intended. To make it so introduces an extraneous factor in the evaluation of the results since, for example, one cannot know whether a student has done poorly because of lack of ability in the subject or because of reading difficulty.

ANNOTATED BIBLIOGRAPHY

1. Furst, Edward J. *Constructing Evaluation Instruments.* New York: David McKay Co., Inc., 1958. 334 p. Part I is a discussion of the objectives of testing. Among the considerations included are the determination of what to evaluate, the definition of behavior, the selection of situations in which to observe or measure, and criteria for sound measurement. Part II presents a detailed discussion of how to plan and construct a test, how to reproduce and use it, and how to analyze the results. The treatment is probably more extensive than necessary for beginners, but the book constitutes a sound reference on the subject.

2. Gerberich, J. Raymond. *Specimen Objective Test Items.* New York: David McKay Co., Inc., 1956. The nature of test items and their applicability to the measurement of various objectives in different subject-matter areas are illustrated in this book by the presentation of thousands of objective test items of different types. Excellent as a source of ideas but not recommended as a source of items for the teacher's own tests.

3. ———; Greene, Harry A.; and Jorgensen, Albert N. *Measurement and Evaluation in the Modern School.* New York: David McKay Co., Inc., 1962. Chapters 9–12. These four chapters deal with constructing and using oral, essay, and short-answer tests; informal objective tests; performance tests; and evaluative tools and techniques. The discussion is practical and detailed.

4. Lindquist, E. F. (ed.). *Educational Measurement.* Washington: American Council on Education, 1951. Chapters 5–13, inclusive. The most thorough and, on the whole, most scholarly discussion of the construction of achievement tests available. All aspects of the problem, from such preliminary considerations as selection of objectives and planning the test, to the final reproducing of the test, are fully discussed. Chapter 13 deals with the essay examination. Not primarily for beginners in the field of test construction.

5. Micheels, William J., and Karnes, M. Ray. *Measuring Educational Achievement.* New York: McGraw-Hill Book Co., Inc., 1950. Chapters 5–14, inclusive. The major purpose of this volume is to "present the how of making and using tests and other instruments of appraisal." The chapters noted above deal with general principles of test construction, with each of the commonly used types of objective test items, and then with other types of measurement and evaluation such as performance and observation. Most of the illustrative material is drawn from the field of industrial arts, but the principles and techniques can be applied in other fields as well.

6. Morse, Horace T., and McCune, George H. *Selected Items for the Testing of Study Skills,* Revised Edition. National Council for the Social Studies, National Education Association, Bulletin No. 15. Washington: The Association, 1949. 81 pp. The main part of this bulletin consists of examples of objective test items designed to measure a variety of study skills such as evaluating sources of information, constructing and reading graphs and tables, drawing inferences, etc. There is also some discussion of the teaching of study skills and constructing tests for the evaluation of such skills.

7. National Society for the Study of Education. *The Measurement of Understanding,* Forty-Fifth Yearbook, Part I. Chicago: The Society (distributed by the University of Chicago Press), 1946. 338 pp. A useful volume emphasizing the measurement of outcomes other than specific knowledge and skills. There are separate chapters on measurement in each of the commonly taught subject fields, with many examples of test items to illustrate practical applications.

8. Remmers, H. H., and Gage, N. L. *Educational Measurement and Evaluation,* Revised Edition. New York: Harper & Row, Publishers, 1955. Chapters 3, 4, 7. A good discussion of the selection and construction of common types of short-answer items in terms of instructional objectives. Chapter 3 includes a review of the advantages and disadvantages of essay tests, and Chapter 7 presents suggestions for improving them.

9. Ross, C. C., and Stanley, Julian C. *Measurement in Today's Schools,* Third Edition. New York: Prentice-Hall, Inc., 1954. Chapters 5, 6, 7. The major topics discussed are: the planning, preparation, tryout, and evaluation of the test; general principles of test construction; the construction of specific types of objective tests; and the construction and use of essay examinations.

10. Thorndike, Robert L., and Hagen, Elizabeth. *Measurement and Evaluation in Psychology and Education,* Second Edition. New York: John Wiley & Sons, Inc., 1961. Chapters 3, 4. Chapter 3 discusses planning a test, compares essay and objective tests, pro and con, and offers suggestions for the improvement of the former type. Chapter 4 deals with the preparation, use, and analysis of the results of objective tests.

11. Travers, Robert M. W. *How To Make Achievement Tests.* New York: The Odyssey Press, 1950. 180 pp. A practical handbook for teachers and research workers on the preparation of tests for classroom use. Begins with the planning of an objective test and discusses the construction of commonly used types of objective questions. Also includes useful suggestions on the assembly, administration, and scoring of objective tests and a discussion of the significance of test scores.

12. Weitzman, Ellis, and McNamara, Walter J. *Constructing Classroom Examinations.* Chicago: Science Research Associates, Inc., 1949. 153 pp. A practical handbook on the planning, construction, scoring, and analysis of results from objective tests in the fields of mathematics, science, English, and social studies. Includes a brief treatment of elementary statistical methods as used in analyzing test results and test items. Primarily useful for teachers at the senior high school and college levels.

7

Trying Out and Evaluating

the Teacher-Made Test

When the teacher or test-maker has constructed the test items and edited and recorded them, either on cards, as suggested in the preceding chapter, or in some other manner, he is ready to arrange them preparatory to having the test reproduced. In the case of an essay test, the sequence of questions presents no problem since such a test usually involves writing the questions on the board at the time of the examination. For tests employing items of a more objective nature, however, the requirements are different. In the following section we shall discuss some of the problems relating to the organization of an objective test.

Arranging the Items

A number of factors have a bearing on the arrangement of items in an objective test. Among these are (1) difficulty, (2) type of item, (3) content, and (4) anticipated use of the scores. Ordinarily, in a standardized test the items are arranged in accordance with most or all of these criteria at the same time. For example, in nearly all such tests the items are arranged in order of difficulty, from the easiest to the most difficult. This system has two advantages. First, it encourages the person taking the test by starting him on items he can easily manage. Second, it tends to avoid the possibility of the student's getting stuck on a difficult item which might not leave him time enough to answer many easier ones that follow. Of course, the difficulty of individual test items is determined on the basis of responses by groups, and does not necessarily coincide with the item-difficulty pattern of any particular individual. The assumption which must be made is that the average difficulty based on responses of the group is the best available difficulty index for the individuals in the group.

It is customary to group items according to type — that is, to place true-false items in one group, multiple-choice in another, etc. — and then to arrange the items within each category according to difficulty, as just described. If there are a great many items of one kind, they may, of course, be divided into two or more groups according to some other criterion such as content. For example, if there are fifty multiple-choice items and fifty true-false items to be arranged, each type might be subdivided into two groups of twenty-five each, particularly if there is some obvious and logical basis for such a division. If, in an arithmetic test, half of the true-false items deal with fractions and half with decimals, the items might be divided on that basis, and similarly the multiple-choice questions. In instances in which part scores on these aspects of arithmetic are desired, such an arrangement will make it easier to obtain them.

Basically then, in most objective tests items are arranged according to type and within the type groups, according to difficulty. The amateur test-maker, as distinguished from the professional, usually has no basis for determining the difficulty of individual test items except his personal judgment. Whereas the producer of standardized tests tries out the items in preliminary forms to determine difficulty, the classroom teacher almost never has the opportunity to do this. Therefore, he does the best he can by grouping the items according to his own estimate of their difficulty. Parenthetically, a word might be added here concerning the grouping of items according to type. This practice is now almost universal and the reasons are fairly obvious. In the first place, it facilitates scoring, since items all of the same type are easier to score than a mixture of various types. In the second place, a test in which items are grouped according to types of items is usually more agreeable to the examinee.

Arranging items within the type groups according to estimated difficulty cannot be a very exact process, and the test-maker will usually have to rely upon his own experience and judgment in this matter. It is sometimes quite satisfactory to arrange items according to length, placing the shortest first. Length is never a basis for judging difficulty, but an arrangement of this sort may encourage the examinee by leading him to assume that the hardest items will come at the end of the test.

Items may be arranged according to content, as in the example of the arithmetic test given above. In every field of concern to him, the teacher has certain ideas or plans for organization of the subject matter. Usually, subject matter is organized by units and by areas within the units. For example, a unit on transportation may be organized according to historical periods or according to kinds of transportation — land, sea, and air, or mechanical and animal. Items in such divisions as these may in turn be arranged according to type, difficulty, and content simultaneously, provided, of course, that there are enough items. For short tests of twenty-five items or less, the grouping of the items on any basis except type is not often practical or useful.

There is one other situation in which the grouping of items is important, namely, when diagnosis is the purpose of the test. Let us assume that in arithmetic, or in English, or in reading the examiner wishes to identify specific strengths and weaknesses in the pupils' grasp of fundamentals. The first step in constructing a test for diagnostic purposes is to make a careful analysis of the rules and skills that are basic to progress in the subject. The next step is to construct an adequate number of items on each rule or skill and then arrange them in the test so that each group constitutes a measure of understanding of one of these. Thus, when the test results are available the responses of each pupil, as well as of the entire class, to items testing a particular rule or skill will be easily determined. Advance arrangement of items for such purposes will facilitate diagnosis and remedial instruction. This will be discussed and illustrated in more detail in Chapter 14.

▶ LEARNING EXERCISES ◀

1. What are the main factors to be considered in arranging items in an objective test? Discuss each briefly, emphasizing the relationships between them. Can you think of any considerations other than those discussed above?

2. What are the advantages of grouping items according to type? Are there any advantages to an omnibus or spiral arrangement of items? (Note: In this arrangement items occur in cycles. For example, a true-false item is followed by a multiple-choice item and a short-answer item, and that cycle is repeated throughout the test or part.)

Preparing Directions

When the arrangement and grouping of the test items has been determined, the next step is to prepare directions. Before the test is duplicated directions should be prepared for the test as a whole, as well as for the sub-tests or parts. If the test is to be used as a semester- or year-end final examination, a title page may be used. This gives the test a more finished appearance; also, if pupils are not to start work on it until preliminary directions have been given, a title page serves to cover the test proper until the directions have been read and the pupils told to begin. If there is to be a title page, it may be set up in a form similar to Figure 8 below.

If the examination is a cooperative effort and is given to classes under the supervision of several different teachers, there should be space for the pupil to indicate his section and his teacher's name, so that the papers can be readily sorted.

If a title page is not used the essential information can be put at the top of the first page of the test.

FIGURE 8 • Typical Title Page for a Teacher-Made Test

Score	Name _ _ _ _ _ _ _ _ _
Part 1 _ _ _ _	Date _ _ _ _ _ _ _ _ _
Part 2 _ _ _ _	Section _ _ _ _ _ _ _ _ _
Total _ _ _ _ _	Teacher's Name _ _ _ _ _ _ _ _ _

Final Examination

English 10A

DIRECTIONS: Do not turn the page until you are told to do so. The examination consists of two parts. Part 1 is True-False and Part 2 is Multiple-Choice. Directions are given in the test for each part. Please read them carefully and follow them exactly. You will have forty minutes to work on the test. Try to answer every question, but if you do not know the answer to a question go on to the next ones and come back to it later. Do not "skip around." Begin at the beginning and work straight through. Your score on the test will be the number answered correctly.

Directions for each part should come at the beginning of the part, as follows:

> *Directions:* The statements in this part are either True or False. Read each one carefully. If you think it is *true,* place a + in the parentheses in front of the statement; if you think it is *false,* place 0 in the parentheses.

If the scoring is to be on the basis of right answers minus wrong answers, the following should be added:

> If you are not sure of the correct answer, but can make an intelligent guess, mark the statement; if not, omit it. Your score on this part of the test will be the number of right answers minus the number of wrong answers.

If the scoring is to be based on the number of right answers only, the following should be added:

> Mark every statement. Your score will be the number right.

If locally duplicated answer sheets are used (see page 171), the directions given first above should be modified in part as follows:

> If you think it is *true,* place a + on the answer sheet opposite the number which corresponds to the number of the statement. If you think it is *false,* place a 0, etc.

If machine-scored or printed answer sheets are used, the directions should be:

> If you think it is *true,* make a heavy black mark (with the special pencil) between the dotted lines in Column 1 opposite the number which corresponds to the number of the statement. If you think it is *false,* blacken the space between the pair of lines in Column 2.

In similar fashion, directions for multiple-choice, matching, or short-answer items should be worked out and reproduced on the test paper so that the directions will precede the part to which they apply.

With younger pupils especially, and in any case where pupils are not accustomed to objective-type tests, it is well to include a sample item with the directions. For example, the following could be used after the directions for matching items:

EXAMPLE:

(*3*) paint	1. compound
(*1*) water	2. element
	3. mixture

Paint is a mixture, so the figure *3* has been placed in the parentheses before *paint;* water is a compound, so the figure *1* has been placed in the parentheses before *water.* Mark the items below in the same way. Notice that there are more items in the right-hand column than in the left, so that after all the blanks have been filled you will have some on the right that you have not used. Some of the items in the right-hand column may be used more than once.

Directions for the test and the sub-tests or parts should be carefully worked out in advance and incorporated into the test. The ideal to strive for is to make the test as nearly self-administering as possible, so that the pupil understands what he is to do with a minimum of supplementary explanations. This is especially desirable if the test is to be used by more than one teacher, and it is advantageous in any case because a test which is nearly self-administering makes for uniformity and objectivity of administration. Otherwise, there is a danger that supplementary instructions will not be identical when given to various pupils or groups at different times.

▶ LEARNING EXERCISES ◀

3. Write out a set of directions for multiple-choice items for a test for a fifth-grade. Include an example.

4. Prepare directions for a set of matching items including an example like the one above. The directions should be clear without the example, however. Submit the directions to the class for criticism.

Reproducing the Test

In most cases, teacher-made tests are duplicated in the school office. Copy is prepared by the teacher, often in handwritten form. It is important to make clear to the typist such matters as capitalization, punctuation, spacing, and provisions for marking answers. Capitalization and punctuation generally do not cause any difficulty, provided the test-maker knows and indicates clearly what he wants. Words to be emphasized should be written in capitals, or underlined, or both.

The matter of spacing is important in setting up objective tests. All material on the page should be arranged and spaced in a manner which will make it as clear and legible as possible for the pupil. This procedure should be followed at all grade levels, and especially when preparing tests for younger children. If answers are to be written or marked on the test itself, sufficient space should be provided and it should be clear that the space left is for this purpose. For example, when answers are to be marked within parentheses they should be spaced thus ( ), not thus (). If words or phrases are to be written, ample space for writing them should be provided. This is usually accomplished by leaving a ruled space, thus, —————————————————, as in short-answer or completion items. If the teacher desires to do so he can give a clue to the length of the word by the amount of space provided. This is not generally recommended, however, since it provides what might be considered an irrelevant clue.

There should always be a full space between successive test items. It is poor economy to crowd them together; however, the statement of each item itself may be single-spaced. In the case of multiple-choice items, general practice favors setting them up in this manner:

( ) The study of living things is called

> 1. physics
> 2. chemistry
> 3. biology
> 4. geology
> 5. astronomy

The above method is generally preferred to the plan of listing choices thus:

( ) The study of living things is called (*1*) physics   (*2*) chemistry   (*3*) biology   (*4*) geology   (*5*) astronomy

Items should be numbered consecutively through the entire test rather than consecutively within each part. The latter procedure results in having two or more items with the same number, as two number *1*'s, two number *2*'s, etc. If there are several parts, there will, of course, be an item numbered *1* in each, and so on. This leads to confusion, particularly if locally made answer sheets are used. Most teacher-made answer sheets are set up with numbered spaces in columns, as shown in Figure 9.

Pupils will become confused if the numbers on the items do not correspond with the numbers on the answer sheet. When the numbering of items in different parts of the test begins in each case with number *1,* no standard answer sheet can be used; instead, each test must have its own answer sheet with numbers coinciding with those on the test. The consecutive arrangement shown in Figure 9 is nearly always followed with answer sheets accompanying standardized tests.

Any study or analysis of individual test items is also facilitated by a consecutive numbering system, since each number quickly identifies a par-

FIGURE 9 • Sample of a Teacher-Made Answer Sheet

Subject	_ _ _ _ _ _ _ _ _ _ _ _	Score	Name _ _ _ _ _ _ _ _ _ _

Subject _ _ _ _ _ _ _ _ _ _ _ _   Score   Name _ _ _ _ _ _ _ _ _ _

_ _ _

Instructor _ _ _ _ _ _ _ _ _ _ _   Date _ _ _ _ _ _ _ _ _ _ _

1. _ _ _ _ _ _ _	26. _ _ _ _ _ _ _	51. _ _ _ _ _ _ _	76. _ _ _ _ _ _ _
2. _ _ _ _ _ _ _	27. _ _ _ _ _ _ _	52. _ _ _ _ _ _ _	77. _ _ _ _ _ _ _
3. _ _ _ _ _ _ _	28. _ _ _ _ _ _ _	53. _ _ _ _ _ _ _	78. _ _ _ _ _ _ _
4. _ _ _ _ _ _ _	29. _ _ _ _ _ _ _	54. _ _ _ _ _ _ _	79. _ _ _ _ _ _ _
5. _ _ _ _ _ _ _	30. _ _ _ _ _ _ _	55. _ _ _ _ _ _ _	80. _ _ _ _ _ _ _
6. _ _ _ _ _ _ _	31. _ _ _ _ _ _ _	56. _ _ _ _ _ _ _	81. _ _ _ _ _ _ _
7. _ _ _ _ _ _ _	32. _ _ _ _ _ _ _	57. _ _ _ _ _ _ _	82. _ _ _ _ _ _ _
8. _ _ _ _ _ _ _	33. _ _ _ _ _ _ _	58. _ _ _ _ _ _ _	83. _ _ _ _ _ _ _
9. _ _ _ _ _ _ _	34. _ _ _ _ _ _ _	59. _ _ _ _ _ _ _	84. _ _ _ _ _ _ _
10. _ _ _ _ _ _ _	35. _ _ _ _ _ _ _	60. _ _ _ _ _ _ _	85. _ _ _ _ _ _ _
11. _ _ _ _ _ _ _	36. _ _ _ _ _ _ _	61. _ _ _ _ _ _ _	86. _ _ _ _ _ _ _
12. _ _ _ _ _ _ _	37. _ _ _ _ _ _ _	62. _ _ _ _ _ _ _	87. _ _ _ _ _ _ _
13. _ _ _ _ _ _ _	38. _ _ _ _ _ _ _	63. _ _ _ _ _ _ _	88. _ _ _ _ _ _ _
14. _ _ _ _ _ _ _	39. _ _ _ _ _ _ _	64. _ _ _ _ _ _ _	89. _ _ _ _ _ _ _
15. _ _ _ _ _ _ _	40. _ _ _ _ _ _ _	65. _ _ _ _ _ _ _	90. _ _ _ _ _ _ _
16. _ _ _ _ _ _ _	41. _ _ _ _ _ _ _	66. _ _ _ _ _ _ _	91. _ _ _ _ _ _ _
17. _ _ _ _ _ _ _	42. _ _ _ _ _ _ _	67. _ _ _ _ _ _ _	92. _ _ _ _ _ _ _
18. _ _ _ _ _ _ _	43. _ _ _ _ _ _ _	68. _ _ _ _ _ _ _	93. _ _ _ _ _ _ _
19. _ _ _ _ _ _ _	44. _ _ _ _ _ _ _	69. _ _ _ _ _ _ _	94. _ _ _ _ _ _ _
20. _ _ _ _ _ _ _	45. _ _ _ _ _ _ _	70. _ _ _ _ _ _ _	95. _ _ _ _ _ _ _
21. _ _ _ _ _ _ _	46. _ _ _ _ _ _ _	71. _ _ _ _ _ _ _	96. _ _ _ _ _ _ _
22. _ _ _ _ _ _ _	47. _ _ _ _ _ _ _	72. _ _ _ _ _ _ _	97. _ _ _ _ _ _ _
23. _ _ _ _ _ _ _	48. _ _ _ _ _ _ _	73. _ _ _ _ _ _ _	98. _ _ _ _ _ _ _
24. _ _ _ _ _ _ _	49. _ _ _ _ _ _ _	74. _ _ _ _ _ _ _	99. _ _ _ _ _ _ _
25. _ _ _ _ _ _ _	50. _ _ _ _ _ _ _	75. _ _ _ _ _ _ _	100. _ _ _ _ _ _ _

ticular question and its corresponding answer and distinguishes that question and answer from all others on the test.

Tests may be reproduced by a number of different processes, each of which has some advantages. If more than one method is available, the choice will be determined by local needs and circumstances. Objective tests should *always* be duplicated. Although some attempts have been made to administer objective tests orally by reading the questions aloud, this method is not recommended. The pupil is entitled to have the test before him and should not be expected to keep the questions in mind or make snap decisions in his choice of correct answers at the moment the questions are read aloud.

Tests reproduced by processes available in most schools should be duplicated on one side of the sheet only. It is generally not satisfactory to use
both sides because, unless extra-heavy paper — and extreme care — are
used, some of the print will show through and make the material difficult
to read. Also, when a test consists of several pages fastened together, it is
easier for the pupil to handle if print appears on only one side of each page.
This is especially true when tablet-arm chairs are used and when answers
are marked on the test itself rather than on a separate answer sheet.

For ease in scoring, the test should be set up and duplicated so that
answer spaces appear in a straight line, all at the same margin. This is
easily arranged for true-false, multiple-choice, and matching items by
placing parentheses before the number of each item. With short-answer and
completion questions a plan similar to the example below may be used:

> 15. The surrender of _____(1)_____ took place   *1.* _____
>
> at Yorktown in the year _____(2)_____ .   *2.* _____

Here all answers are written in the numbered spaces at the right-hand
margin. Also, since all the answer spaces are of the same length, there is
no irrelevant clue to the length of the correct answer.

If answers are written on the test itself, enough copies of the test must be
made so that there will be a new one for each examinee every time the test
is administered. If separate answer sheets are used, the tests themselves
can be used repeatedly. When the same test is used with several groups it
is important to collect all copies each time it is used, for if copies get into
circulation the examination will obviously lose its usefulness as a testing
or measuring instrument. It is helpful to number all copies and require
each pupil to write the number of the copy he is using on the answer sheet,
provided separate answer sheets are used. In this way, missing copies of
the test can be traced and usually recovered. It is also necessary, if tests
are used more than once, to scan them after each use and erase all marks
made on them by the previous users.

In arranging objective tests for duplication it is not desirable to have a
question continue from one page to the next; starting a question on a new
page is preferable to dividing it. *This is particularly important with matching questions,* for the examinee would become justifiably annoyed if he
constantly had to turn a page back and forth to consult the two parts of
each list on two separate pages.

The Scoring Key

When answers are to be marked on the test proper and the blanks are
spaced in the manner suggested above, the preparation of a scoring key is

simple. The scoring key usually consists of a strip of heavy paper or cardboard about an inch and a half wide and as long as the answer column on the test page. The correct answers are entered on this strip, spaced to match exactly the spacing of the items on the test page. Then the strip is laid alongside the column of answers and the scorer checks the wrong or the right answers, whichever he has decided to use in scoring. The answers on the key should be typed or printed near the edge of the strip so that when it is laid on the test the correct answers will be close to the answer spaces on the test.

When locally made answer sheets are used, the same type of scoring key is usable, since the spaces on these answer sheets are usually arranged in columns — usually four to the page — of about an inch to an inch and a half wide. One hundred such spaces can easily be typed, double spaced, on an ordinary sheet of paper, with twenty-five items in each of the four columns, as shown on page 171.

When the machine-scorable type of answer sheet is scored by hand, the most convenient key is one made of a sheet of cardboard the same size as the answer sheet. At each place where a correct answer mark should appear on the answer sheet a small hole is punched in the cardboard. This makes a stencil which can be laid over the answer sheet. Scoring is then done by simply counting the number of marks that appear through the holes in the stencil. This type of scoring stencil is usually provided by publishers of standardized tests. It may be used for hand-scoring as well as for machine-scoring. When using such a scoring stencil, it is necessary to scan the answer sheet before covering it with the stencil to see that only one space is marked for each item. Where more than one space is marked, such items should be counted wrong unless, of course, there is more than one correct answer to the items in question.

If answers are marked on the test itself, spaces for recording scores should be provided either on the title page as shown on page 171 or at the top of page 1 of the test. If part-scores are determined, they should be recorded separately and added to obtain the total score. If derived scores of some type, such as ranks or standard scores are calculated, they should also be recorded in additional spaces provided for the purpose. The same principles apply if separate answer sheets are used, but the scores are recorded on the answer sheets, not on the tests.

ANALYZING THE RESULTS

After a test has been tried out and scored the results may be analyzed in two ways. One is from the standpoint of what the results reveal about the pupils' learning or how successful instruction has been. This means far more than simply tabulating total scores on the test, since high scores may result from an easy test as well as from good teaching, and conversely, low scores may be caused by a difficult test or by inferior teaching. Thorough analysis of test results involves some attempt at diagnosis, even though the test may not have been set up with this purpose clearly in mind. It is always desirable to formulate some kind of analysis showing the degree of success with specific items and parts of the test in order to appraise the efficacy of teaching and learning. Unless an attempt at such analysis is made, the results of the test cannot be put to maximum use.

A simple analysis of the results of a test for diagnostic purposes can be performed in two ways: (1) the teacher can tabulate the responses to each item, which will tell him how often each item was missed, or (2) he can return the scored tests or answer sheets to the students and ask for a show of hands on each item by those who missed it. (In either case, it should be noted, the scoring should be done by checking *wrong answers*.) In this way it is possible to analyze the performance of the students on the test and to identify individual points and areas of content or objectives that have not been well learned. The results of such analysis may provide a basis for re-teaching or remedial work with individual students.

Another type of analysis has for its purpose the evaluation of the test as a measuring instrument. How effective is the test and how well does it function? Although careful analytical appraisal is an essential part of the process of producing a standardized test, this is not generally practiced by classroom teachers in test-making. Yet some evaluation of this sort might well be a part of every teacher's measurement program. Unless teachers are willing to "test the test," the effectiveness of their measurement techniques cannot be satisfactorily determined.

The rest of this chapter will be devoted to an explanation of a few simple techniques which any test-maker can use with a test of his own construction to appraise its worth as a measuring instrument.

Validity

It will be remembered that validity refers to the degree to which a test measures what it is intended to measure. How can a teacher appraise the validity of his own tests? Obviously, curricular validity is one measure. If the teacher has constructed the test on the basis of his instructional objectives, and if the test covers or measures what he has been teaching, the test may be said to have a degree of curricular validity; that is, it is valid because it tests what the teacher has been teaching.

If the teacher wishes to go beyond curricular validity, he can compare the test scores with scores on other tests he has given, with marks based on class and laboratory work, and with other measures of achievement such as standardized tests in the same subject. Correlation is the usual method of determining the extent of such relationships. (This is explained in Chapter 3 and Appendix A.)

The discrimination power of individual items on a test is a valuable index for evaluating their quality. It has been regarded by some authorities as an indicator of validity, or lack of it. The argument runs something like this: One must assume, first, that scores on the whole test have some validity and, second, that scores on a particular valid item should agree with scores on the whole test. Let us examine these assumptions. The first usually implies that the test has curricular validity. There may be other evidence of validity, but generally when item-discrimination is used as a means of establishing validity, the test, which is in this case the criterion of validity, is assumed to have curricular validity because it measures what has been taught. The second assumption is tested by comparing results on a given test item with scores on the whole test. Since the test is assumed to have some validity, an item which agrees with the scores on the test also has some validity. That is, an item which is answered correctly by a higher proportion of those who make high scores on the test than of those who make low scores is functioning in a manner consistent with the scores on the whole test. Whether or not we accept this line of reasoning as justification for regarding the discrimination power of items as evidence of validity, the technique is a widely used and generally accepted method of identifying "good" items and culling out "poor" ones.

To consider how this is done, let us assume that a test has been given and scored and that the papers have been arranged in order of score, from highest to lowest. We may call the highest one-fourth of these the "high group" and the lowest one-fourth the "low group." In a class of forty, the highest ten on the test would constitute the high group, and the lowest ten, the low group.

Now let us consider that the results of a hypothetical test item are as follows:

Item No. 15

	Answered correctly by
High Group	7 (of the top 10)
Low Group	3 (of the lowest 10)

We may conclude that this item discriminates as it should; that is, 70 per cent of the pupils in the high group get it right, while only 30 per cent in the low group do so. Such an item is said to have a positive discrimination value, or to discriminate positively. On the other hand, not every test item will discriminate positively. For example:

ITEM NO. 16

Answered correctly by

High Group	4 (of the top 10)
Low Group	7 (of the lowest 10)

This item is said to discriminate negatively because a higher proportion of the low group get it right than of the high group. Items showing negative discrimination are not uncommon, though it is the aim of the good test technician to identify and eliminate them whenever he can.

The following item is one that actually discriminated negatively in a national tryout:

(2) Temporary teeth in children do *not* include

1. incisors
2. bicuspids
3. canines
4. molars

In trying out this item with about fifteen hundred students in Grades 7, 8, and 9, it was found that Number 2, "bicuspids," the correct answer, was chosen by 11 per cent of the lowest fourth and by only 8 per cent of the highest fourth. Moreover, for some reason, 67 per cent of the top fourth and 42 per cent of the bottom fourth chose Number 4, "molars," as the right answer. Of all the students tested, only about 10 per cent answered the item correctly. There is no factor here of ambiguity, since Number 2 is unquestionably the right choice. It is simply a matter of difficulty. The item was not included in the final forms of the test because of its negative discrimination.

The usual explanation for negatively discriminating items is ambiguity in the statement of the item itself. In such items the abler, more thoughtful pupil may see some implications which the maker of the test himself has overlooked, and may thus be led to choose an answer that has not been labeled as the correct one. The less able pupil, on the other hand, considering the item on a more superficial basis, arrives at the answer which has been keyed as correct.

Sometimes the maker of a test feels that a question missed by a substantial proportion of his class is a bad item or that it reflects on his teaching ability. Consider the following typical results:

ITEM NO. 37

Answered correctly by

High Group	30 (Per Cent)
Low Group	10 (Per Cent)

This item is answered correctly by less than one-third of the high-scoring pupils and by 10 per cent of the low scorers. Of the class as a whole, probably about one-fifth would get it right. However, the item appears to be a good one since it discriminates clearly between the high and low groups in a positive direction. It is an item of more than average difficulty and is therefore justifiable, since a test with adequate range of difficulty should include items ranging from quite easy to fairly difficult.

It should be kept in mind that most item-discrimination techniques start with all the members of the group that have taken the test. Suppose, for example, the teacher has given a test to four classes in first-year algebra. There are 120 students in the four classes. After scoring the test he arranges the test papers in order from highest score to lowest score. Then, starting at the top he takes off the first thirty (top 25 per cent), and starting with the paper having the lowest score he counts off thirty (another 25 per cent) from the bottom. These are, respectively, the high and low fourths of all (120) who took the test. Now, beginning with item Number 1 he counts the number in the high group that answered it correctly and the number in the low group that answered it correctly. These two numbers are the basis for determining the discriminating power for that item.

A simple formula for determining the discriminating power of a test item is $d = \dfrac{n_H - n_L}{N}$, where d = the discrimination index, n_H = the number in the high group answering the item correctly, n_L = the number in the low group answering the item correctly, and N = the total number in either high or low group (N = 25 per cent of all who took the test). For example, if $n_H = 20$, $n_L = 10$ and $N = 30$, $d = \dfrac{20 - 10}{30} = \dfrac{10}{30} = .33$. This index has a possible range from $+1$ to -1. An item answered correctly by all the highs and missed by all the lows would have an index of $+1$. Conversely, an item answered correctly by all the lows and missed by all the highs would have an index of -1. An item answered correctly by equal numbers of highs and lows has an index of 0. A reasonable criterion in using this index would be a value of .25. An item having an index lower than this would be considered a poorly discriminating item.

Functioning of Choices

There is another type of analysis which professional test-makers apply to multiple-choice items, namely, the determination of how the choices in each such item function. As was mentioned in Chapter 6, a choice which no examinee chooses as the correct answer is simply filler or "dead wood."

In determining the quality of multiple-choice items it is customary to determine how often each choice is marked as the correct answer. In the case of a positively discriminating item the *correct* answer must be chosen more often by the high group than by the low group; but each of the wrong choices, or distractors, should be chosen by some.

Thus, a complete analysis for a multiple-choice item might look like this:

ITEM NO. 10:	CHOICES (PER CENT)				
	1	*2*	*3**	*4*	*5*
Highs	10	12	50	7	21
Lows	13	17	31	11	28
* Correct answer.					

Here it can be seen that 50 per cent of the "highs" answered the item correctly as compared with 31 per cent of the "lows." All choices function, i.e., all were marked correct by some examinees. Consider, however, the following example:

ITEM NO. 11:	CHOICES (PER CENT)				
	1	*2**	*3*	*4*	*5*
Highs	5	84	0	11	0
Lows	14	70	4	12	0
* Correct answer					

This item is also a "good" item in that it discriminates positively, as does Number 10 above. However, note that choice *3* was marked correct by only 4 per cent of the lows and none of the highs and that choice *5* is chosen by none of either group. This item would probably be carefully studied and the third and fifth choices would be revised or replaced, since they are so obviously wrong that they are contributing little or nothing to the usefulness of the item.

The teacher who makes a test for repeated use can carry out a simple item-analysis as explained here, and enter the results on the item card. Items which do not discriminate positively — that is, which are not answered correctly by a larger proportion of the best pupils than of the less able ones — should be studied for clues to the reason for the negative discrimination. Unless negatively discriminating items can be shown to have other important values, or can be made positively discriminating, there is little reason to retain them, for they will detract from the validity of the test as a whole.

▶ **LEARNING EXERCISES** ◀

5. An item on a test in general science, given to eighty students, is answered correctly by ten students in the high one-fourth and by five in the low one-fourth. Using the formula above, find the discrimination index of the item. Another item on the same test is missed by twelve of the top fourth and eight of the bottom fourth. What is its discrimination index?

6. If you can obtain copies of a test which has been given either to your class in measurement or elsewhere, and which has been scored, it will be interesting to make an analysis of some of the items. You should have at least ten papers in the highest fourth of the class and ten in the lowest fourth. Set up a table such as the following one and enter the data:

ITEM	HIGHEST FOURTH NUMBER RIGHT	LOWEST FOURTH NUMBER RIGHT	DISC.
1.			
2.			
3.			
4.			
5.			
etc.			

Using the formula given, find the discrimination indexes of the first ten items. Would you retain all of them? If not, which ones would you discard? Justify your answer.

Difficulty

Closely related to considerations of the discrimination values of test items is the question of difficulty. Except for special and unusual reasons, items which are answered correctly or which are missed by all pupils are not considered good, for such items make no discrimination whatever in the class or group being tested. A test made up entirely of such items would result in everyone's getting the same score, either perfect or zero. Obviously, such a result tells nothing about differences in achievement among members of the class. Rather, it demonstrates that the test was either entirely too easy or too difficult, and thus reflects unfavorably on the test-maker's ability.

The only exception to this position might occur if one were testing for mastery. That is, if the teacher had been drilling on certain combinations in addition or perhaps the multiplication tables, his goal might be complete mastery or 100 per cent accuracy. In such an instance he would expect most of his pupils eventually to achieve this goal. Ordinarily, however, we do not expect or get 100 per cent mastery or perfection on any educational objective; our tests are designed to challenge the best students and at the same time to provide ample opportunity for the poorest to show what they can do.

The simplest way for the teacher to determine whether his test is appropriate in difficulty for the group tested is to study the distribution of scores on the test. If the mean is at or near the middle of the range and if there are no perfect or zero scores, the teacher may be fairly certain that the test is suitable for that group. For example, on a test containing eighty questions it is found that the mean score is 42 and the range of scores is from 11 to 75. Such facts indicate that the test was suitable in range and difficulty for this class. Let us suppose, however, that with another class or grade the same test shows an average score of 69 and a range from 50 to 80; obviously the test was too easy for this group. If, on the other hand, the mean is 15 and the range from 0 to 40, the test would have been too difficult.

Thus it may be inferred that difficulty has a bearing on the discrimination value of a test — that a test which is too hard or too easy will not discriminate between individuals of different levels of achievement as well as one which is more appropriate for the range of abilities in the group.

Though absolutely fixed points for acceptable averages or range can rarely be established, the following general principles may serve as a useful guide to the student:

1. Items which are missed or answered correctly by every pupil are not discriminating in that group.

2. On a test which is appropriate in difficulty for a given group, the mean should be near the middle of the range of possible scores.

3. On a test suitable for a group of the usual variability, the range of scores should be as wide as possible, short of zero or perfect scores.

4. Tests which give zero scores or perfect scores are not discriminating for the individuals who make such scores.

▶ LEARNING EXERCISE ◀

7. In Exercise No. 6 on page 179 you found discrimination values for certain test items. Find the difficulty values for these items by averaging the per cent right in the top fourth and the per cent right in the bottom fourth. Do you find a satisfactory range of difficulty from quite easy to rather difficult?

8. Find the mean and the range of scores on the test. Do they indicate that the test was suitable for the group, too easy, or too difficult?

Reliability

Another characteristic of importance to the test-maker is reliability. This is a measure of the consistency with which a test measures whatever it is intended to measure. Various methods for determining reliability — the test-retest, equivalent forms, and the split-half methods — are described in Chapter 3 and in Appendix A. However, test reliability may be estimated by a shorter method which is accurate enough for classroom tests and other ordinary situations. It requires the calculation of only two measures, the mean and the standard deviation of the distribution of scores on the test. The formula follows:[1]

$$r_t = \frac{n\sigma_t^2 - M(n - M)}{\sigma_t^2(n - 1)},$$

where r_t = reliability of the test, n = number of items in the test, σ_t = standard deviation of the scores on the test, and M = mean of scores on the test.

An example will help to clarify the use of this formula. Suppose that a teacher has given a test of fifty items and has found the mean to be 30 and the standard deviation 6. Though circumstances make it inconvenient for him to use any of the usual methods of determining test reliability, he wants to estimate the reliability of this test. To do so, he uses the formula given above, substituting these values: $n = 50$, $M = 30$, and $\sigma_t = 6$:

$$r_t = \frac{[50 \times (6)^2] - [30(50 - 30)]}{(6)^2(50 - 1)}$$

$$= \frac{[50 \times 36] - [30 \times 20]}{36 \times 49}$$

$$= \frac{1800 - 600}{1764}$$

$$= \frac{1200}{1764}$$

$$= .68$$

Thus the teacher finds that his test has a reliability of .68, which is not very high. However, he can take some comfort from the knowledge that this formula nearly always gives an underestimate of true reliability, and that his test therefore probably has a reliability at least as high as .68.

---

[1] G. Frederic Kuder and M. W. Richardson, "The Theory of the Estimation of Test Reliability," *Psychometrika*, 2:151–60, September, 1937.

Knowing the reliability of his test enables the teacher to determine how much reliance he can place on the scores yielded by it.

▶ **LEARNING EXERCISE** ◀

9. Obtain the results of a standardized test given to a class or group of pupils and calculate the reliability coefficient by the method shown above. In the manual that accompanies the test you should find a reliability coefficient given. How does the value you obtained compare with that given in the manual? Is the difference significant? How do you account for any difference found?

There are many refinements and technical details of test analysis which, because they are beyond the scope of the usual first course in educational measurement, are not mentioned here. The average teacher or counselor, however, should be able to follow the suggestions and procedures presented here; certainly if he does use such procedures he will achieve steady improvement in the construction of his tests and in his whole measurement program, and will thus experience a sense of genuine satisfaction in this important part of his job.

ANNOTATED BIBLIOGRAPHY

1. Adkins, Dorothy C., *et al. Construction and Analysis of Achievement Tests.* Washington: U.S. Government Printing Office, 1947. Chapter 4. A detailed and lengthy discussion of the analysis of test results, including item analysis, critical scores, norms, and equivalent forms. Most of the material is suitable for the advanced undergraduate and graduate level.

2. Bean, Kenneth L. *Construction of Educational and Personnel Tests.* New York: McGraw-Hill Book Co., Inc., 1953. Chapter 7. The entire book deals with the planning and construction of tests and thus is a valuable reference for use with this chapter and the one preceding. Chapter 7 deals particularly with the review and tryout of a test and with item analysis.

3. Davis, Frederick B. *Item Analysis Data,* Harvard Education Papers No. 2. Cambridge, Mass.: Graduate School of Education, Harvard University, 1946. 42 pp. Presents a method of item analysis which takes into account correction for chance and which gives an index of discrimination.

4. Furst, Edward J. *Constructing Evaluation Instruments.* New York: David McKay Co., Inc., 1958. Chapter 13. Presents a brief and fairly nontechnical discussion of procedures for evaluating a test, including logical analysis, validation, item-analysis techniques, reliability, and simple statistical analysis.

5. Lindquist, E. F. (ed.). *Educational Measurement.* Washington: American Council on Education, 1951. Chapters 8, 9, and 11. These chapters deal respectively with the experimental tryout of test materials, item selection techniques, and reproducing the test. They contain much that is useful to the beginner as well as to the experienced maker of tests.

6. Ross, C. C., and Stanley, Julian C. *Measurement in Today's Schools,* Third Edition. New York: Prentice-Hall Inc., 1954. Appendix B. A simplified item-analysis procedure is presented, explained, and illustrated. Problems are worked out showing the application of the procedure to test data.

7. Thorndike, R. L., and Hagen, Elizabeth. *Measurement and Evaluation in Psychology and Education,* Second Edition. New York: John Wiley & Sons, Inc., 1961. Chapter 4. The latter part of this chapter deals with analyzing and using the results of objective tests and explains the discrimination value of items.

8. Weitzman, Ellis, and McNamara, Walter J. *Constructing Classroom Examinations.* Chicago: Science Research Associates, Inc., 1949. Chapters 8 and 9. A good discussion of the preparation and use of a teacher-made test and analysis of items. Material is presented in non-technical language with many examples and illustrations.

8

Measuring Achievement in

the Elementary Grades

In this chapter and the following one we shall discuss the measurement of achievement in the elementary and secondary grades and describe the types of instruments most commonly used. Since there are hundreds of standardized achievement tests available, it is obviously beyond the scope of this book to attempt to describe all or even a substantial number of them. Nevertheless, we shall describe in some detail examples of each of the important types and list other major tests which are available in the same areas. No claim is made here that the tests or other measures chosen for detailed description in these chapters are necessarily the best of their respective types. Rather, an attempt has been made to select representative or typical instruments and avoid emphasizing the product of any single publisher. Unquestionably, in many cases other equally good and equally representative samples might be chosen for illustration. Above all, it is the writer's intention to make his descriptions of the tests as instructive as possible by the selection of examples varying widely in organization, approach, format, techniques, methods of scoring and interpretation, etc. It is hoped that those tests described, taken together, will constitute a reasonably representative sample of the better achievement tests available today.

A check-list or schedule is followed in the test descriptions in this chapter and the next so that the descriptions will be systematic and comparable from test to test. The items or categories in the check-list are as follows:

1. Names of test and author(s).
2. Nature and purpose of test.
3. Grade level.
4. Number of forms.
5. Publisher and date of publication.
6. Cost.[1]
7. Content: source, nature, types of sub-tests, types of items.
8. Time required to administer.
9. Directions for and ease of administering.
10. Validity: nature of data.
11. Reliability: nature of data.
12. Manual: nature of, adequacy, clarity, simplicity.
13. Scoring: methods, ease, objectivity, scores.
14. Norms: type, adequacy, usability.
15. Format: paper, printing, arrangement.

In addition to the information presented about a particular test in the check-list, comments of a general nature will be made where it seems appropriate and wherever such comments will be helpful in giving the student a better understanding of the test being discussed.

SURVEY BATTERIES

Survey batteries have long been used for a number of purposes. When an over-all measure of achievement in the common branches or subjects of instruction is needed for purposes of grade placement, promotion, or

[1] As we have pointed out in Chapter 4, cost is not the most important factor to be considered in choosing a test. However, it is generally of interest to all test users. For this reason, we have included prices in the listings and detailed descriptions of the tests. These prices will provide a basis of comparion of different tests on a factor which may be decisive, other things being equal. They will also make it possible for the prospective user to obtain some idea of the total cost of materials for a measurement program. The prices listed are taken from the latest available catalogs of test publishers at the time of publication of this book. They are subject to change, of course, and do not, as a rule, include the cost of separate answer sheets, scoring stencils, and other accessories. Test prices do not include the cost of shipment from publisher to purchaser. The reader is strongly urged not to order tests on the basis of price information given in this book; instead, he should use the latest catalogs of the test publishers.

grouping, the survey battery is most often used. It is also useful in comparisons among classes, schools, or school systems, among individual pupils, or in comparisons of the individual pupil with norms for his age or grade. The survey battery may be employed to good advantage in analyzing and comparing a pupil's achievement in the different subject-matter areas, thereby revealing his strengths and deficiencies. For example, a pupil may be at or above the grade norms in certain areas such as reading and social studies, but below the norms in certain others such as arithmetic. The survey battery is a convenient instrument for revealing such differences, and the deficient areas may be followed up with diagnostic tests to identify specific weaknesses. Survey batteries have a further advantage: the norms for the sub-tests are based on the same population sample and are therefore directly comparable. Generally speaking, the norms will not be comparable when separate tests are used in different subjects.

It is important to keep in mind that such comparisons, for example, by the use of individual profiles, must always be made and interpreted with caution. The sub-tests of a battery are often quite short, which means that the reliability of scores on them may be quite low. Consequently, differences between scores on sub-tests are often chance differences which have no statistical significance. Publishers of test batteries have the obligation to provide information on the reliability of sub-scores and to furnish the necessary data to determine the reliability of differences between them.

Survey batteries have found widest use in the elementary grades where there is much uniformity of objectives and content in fundamental areas. The makers of these tests have generally had to confine the scope of the test items to the knowledge and skills which are common to virtually all textbooks and courses of study in a particular subject for a given grade level in order to meet the practical limitations on time for the use of such tests. In spite of these restrictions, many survey batteries have found extensive use over a long period of time, which indicates that the tests have met the needs of many teachers and administrators.

Stanford Achievement Test

The first of its kind to be published, this test appeared in 1923. Revised editions appeared in 1929, 1940, and 1953, and the present edition was issued in 1964. It has held a position of leadership in the field for forty years, and is still probably one of the best-known and most widely used survey batteries in existence.

1. Name of test and authors. *Stanford Achievement Test.*[2] Authors: Truman L. Kelley, formerly Harvard University; Richard Madden, Sonohma State College; Eric Gardner, Syracuse University; Herbert C. Rudman, Michigan State University.

2. Nature and purpose. Survey battery of achievement tests in common branches of the elementary curriculum. To provide dependable measures of knowledge, skills, and understanding commonly accepted as desirable outcomes.

3. Grade level. Middle of Grade 1 through Grade 9. (High School Battery in preparation.) Primary I Battery, Grades 1.5–2.4; Primary II Battery, Grades 2.5–3.9; Intermediate I Battery, Grades 4.0–5.4; Intermediate II Battery, Grades 5.5–6.9; Advanced Battery, Grades 7.0–9.9.

4. Number of forms. W, X, Y, and Z for each Complete and Partial Battery.

5. Publisher and date of publication. Harcourt, Brace & World, Inc., 1964.

6. Cost. Primary I Battery (Complete), $5.65 for a package of 35 copies; Primary II Battery (Complete), $5.80 for a package of 35 copies; Intermediate I or II Batteries (Complete), Advanced Battery (Complete), $9.75 for a package of 35 copies; Intermediate I or II Batteries (Partial), Advanced Battery (Partial), $8.25 for a package of 35 copies.[3]

7. Content. The Primary I Battery (Complete) includes tests of *Word Reading, Paragraph Meaning, Vocabulary, Spelling, Word Study Skills,* and *Arithmetic.*

The Primary II Battery (Complete) includes tests of *Word Meaning, Paragraph Meaning, Science and Social Studies Concepts, Spelling, Word Study Skills, Language, Arithmetic Computation,* and *Arithmetic Concepts.*

The Intermediate I Battery (Complete) includes tests of *Word Meaning, Paragraph Meaning, Spelling, Word Study Skills, Language, Arithmetic Computation, Arithmetic Concepts, Arithmetic Applications, Social Studies,* and *Science.*

[2] Quotations in test description by permission of the publisher. From *Stanford Achievement Test* by Truman L. Kelley, Richard Madden, Eric Gardner, Herbert C. Rudman. Copyright 1964 by Harcourt, Brace & World, Inc., New York.

[3] Almost all standardized tests today for grades above the third or fourth are planned for use with separate answer sheets. These are available in many forms and from various sources in addition to the publisher of the test. It is impossible to provide information on all these in a listing such as this. The reader is advised to consult publishers' catalogs.

The Intermediate II Battery (Complete) includes tests of *Word Meaning, Paragraph Meaning, Spelling, Language, Arithmetic Computation, Arithmetic Concepts, Arithmetic Applications, Social Studies,* and *Science.*

The Advanced Battery (Complete) includes tests of *Paragraph Meaning, Spelling, Language, Arithmetic Computation, Arithmetic Concepts, Arithmetic Applications, Social Studies,* and *Science.*

The Intermediate and Advanced Partial Batteries contain all the tests included in the Complete Batteries except *Social Studies* and *Science.*

The following are examples of typical items from some of the tests in the Primary I Battery:

a. *Word Reading:*

Find the word that tells what the picture is.

not ○
him ○
sun ○
sit ○

b. *Vocabulary:*

Which of these three words means something to wear?

1. picture ○   2. coat ○   3. dream ○

c. *Word Study Skills:* Items measure the ability to recognize beginning and ending sounds of words, entire words spoken as part of a sentence, and rhyming.

d. *Arithmetic:* (1) Concepts such as "nearest," "farthest," "most," numbers, and amounts, e.g., "Make a cross on the *tallest* flower" and (2) problem solving, including simple addition and subtraction and a bit of multiplication and/or division.

Items typical of some of the tests in the Primary II Battery are the following:

a. *Paragraph Meaning:*

> Billy did a trick.
> He stood on his head.
> His _____ went up in the air.
> hands   head   ball   feet

b. *Spelling:* In all forms of the Primary Batteries a word is pronounced, a sentence containing the word is read, and the word is pronounced again. The pupil writes the word:

fire   The fire crackled cheerily.   *fire*

c. *Science and Social Studies Concepts:*

A large body of ice is
> a planet   O
> the pole   O
> a glacier O

The Pilgrims came from

> Europe   O
> Africa   O
> Asia   O

d. *Language:* The pupil makes a cross (x) over the correct answer:

(1) *Capitalization.*
> mary and tom are going   (T)   (t)

(2) *Punctuation.*
> are you going to school   (.)   (?)   (N)

(3) *Usage.*
> 1 set
> Joe   in the chair   (1)   (2)   (N)
> 2 sat

Typical items from some of the tests in the Intermediate I Battery are:

a. *Spelling:* Finding the misspelled word:

> 1 this   2 kap   3 cold   4 tell

> 1 2 3 4
> O O O O

b. *Word Study Skills:*

(1) Finding the word that has the same sound:

ride

1 sick   2 fine   3 wish   O O O
                                  1 2 3

(2) Syllabification:
   kitten

1 ki tten   2 ki tt en   3 kit ten   4 kitten   1 2 3 4
                                                         O O O O

c. *Arithmetic Applications:*

Joe, Fred, and Don are saving money for a trip. Here are some of their problems:

(1) Joe has saved $2.50, Fred has saved $1.35, and Don has saved 90¢. How much have all three boys saved?

a $3.75   b $3.85   c $4.75   d $4.85   e NG   a b c d e
                                                    O O O O O

d. *Social Studies — Content*

Money to pay the cost of a new public school comes from:

1 dues   2 taxes   3 stamps   4 mints   1 2 3 4
                                                O O O O

Columbus probably took with him on his trip to America a man who knew much about:

1 stars   2 radio waves   3 motors   4 Indians   1 2 3 4
                                                       O O O O

Social Studies — Study Skills

Items based on graphs and maps, requiring their reading and interpretation:

Use the graph below in answering questions 25–29.

Size of the Great Lakes

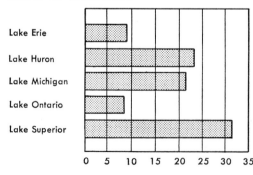

26. Which lake is the smallest?
   1 Superior   3 Ontario
   2 Erie   4 Michigan
        1 2 3 4
        O O O O

in thousands of square miles

e. *Science:*

As water boils, it changes to:

1 ice   2 dew   3 steam   4 snow

1 2 3 4
○ ○ ○ ○

The following are typical items from some of the tests in the Advanced Battery:

a. *Paragraph Meaning:*

We went up in an airplane. At first we flew near the __A__ where we could see people and animals. Later we could not see them. Our plane was too __B__ .

A   1 houses   2 ground   3 town   4 hills

A 1 2 3 4
   ○ ○ ○ ○

B   5 high   6 low   7 far   8 fast

B 5 6 7 8
   ○ ○ ○ ○

b. *Dictionary Skills:*

Check (chek) 1. n. A pattern in squares of different colors. 2. v. To prove true or right. 3. n. A mark showing that something has been examined or compared. 4. v. To hold back or control.

A. Miss Jones made a check beside each sample.

A 1 2 3 4
   ○ ○ ○ ○

B. The word *check* in the sentence above is:

a a noun   b a verb   c an adjective
d an adverb

B a b c d
   ○ ○ ○ ○

c. *Arithmetic Concepts:*

Which number comes next in this set?
35   30   26   23

e 22   f 21   g 20   h 19

e f g h
○ ○ ○ ○

d. *Arithmetic Applications:*

A box contains a black, a white, and a yellow marble. What are the chances that Jerry, without looking, will draw out the black marble first, then the yellow, and finally the white one?

a 1/2   b 1/3   c 1/6
d 1/8   e N G

a b c d e
○ ○ ○ ○ ○

e. *Social Studies — Content:*

Which of these four nations achieved the greatest increase in world influence following World War II?

1 England   2 Germany   3 France   4 Russia

1	2	3	4
O	O	O	O

f. *Science:*

If you want to know whether an animal is an insect, you look for:

1 head, mouth, and gills
2 color, size, and sound
3 mouth, feelers, and gills
4 head, thorax, and abdomen

1	2	3	4
O	O	O	O

Sometimes telephone men string wire very loosely. They are *least* likely to do this when the air is:

1 warm   2 cold   3 humid   4 dry

1	2	3	4
O	O	O	O

The preceding examples are chosen essentially at random to give a picture of the nature of the items, their appropriateness for the different levels, and their content. It should be clear that not all tests in a battery for a given level have been sampled. Also, no items from Intermediate II were included, since Intermediate I and II are quite similar.

8. Time required to administer. The total time for each battery and recommended sittings are as follows:

Batteries	Total
Primary I — Five sittings — 22, 30, 40, 32 and 36 minutes	2 hr. 40 min.
Primary II — Seven sittings — 20, 33, 41, 35, 37, 33, 35 minutes	3 hr. 54 min.
Intermediate I Complete — Seven sittings — 48, 41, 47, 56, 41, 28 minutes	4 hr. 59 min.
Intermediate I Partial — Five sittings — 48, 41, 47, 38, 56 minutes	3 hr. 50 min.
Intermediate II Complete — Seven sittings — 18, 51, 54, 38, 58, 56, 28 minutes	5 hr. 3 min.
Intermediate II Partial — Five sittings —18, 51, 54, 38, 58 minutes	3 hr. 39 min.
Advanced Complete — Six sittings — 53, 52, 35, 61, 58, 28 minutes	4 hr. 47 min.
Advanced Partial — Four sittings — 53, 52, 35, 61 minutes	3 hr. 21 min.

Each test in each battery may be given at a separate sitting if desired, but the tests can be administered most efficiently by following the schedule outlined above. The tests are not speeded and time limits are considered ample for most classes.

9. Directions for and ease of administering. Directions are clear and complete, both as to general administration and specific directions for each sub-test. No special training or experience is required to administer the batteries. It is assumed that the examiner will become thoroughly familiar with the test and all directions and that he will follow them exactly. Directions to pupils are carefully worked out and include sample items and/or practice items preceding each test in a battery.

10. Validity. The evidence on validity of the *Stanford Achievement Test* is entirely curricular in nature. The manual states:

> A major goal in the preparation of this edition of the Stanford was to insure that the content of the test would be in harmony with present objectives and measure what is actually being taught in today's schools. To make certain that the test content would be valid in this sense, the construction of the new edition . . . was preceded by a thorough analysis of the most widely used series of elementary textbooks in the various subjects, of a wide variety of courses of study, and of the research literature pertaining to children's concepts, experiences, and vocabulary at successive ages or grades.

The tests were constructed according to outlines based on these analyses. Subject-matter specialists were consulted at each step in the development of the tests.

For each item in the experimental forms an item profile was constructed showing the per cent of pupils at each grade level answering the item correctly. The extent to which success on each item correlated with progress through school was regarded as an important index of item validity and was used as one basis for the selection of items for the final forms.

The authors of the battery believe that the *Stanford* measures a substantial sampling of the important outcomes or goals of instruction in the common branches at the elementary level. It would have been helpful if at least some of the sources used had been specifically named.

11. Reliability. Reliability data include odd-even split-half and Kuder-Richardson reliability coefficients, and standard errors of measurement by grades for each sub-test of each battery. The results are summarized below:

Battery	Range of Coefficients	Trend	Range of S.E.	Trend
Primary I	.79–.95	High .80's	.5–2.5	±1
Primary II	.66–.94	Middle .80's	2.0–6.0	±3
Intermediate I	.86–.94	± .90	2.5–5.0	±4
Intermediate II	.77–.95	High .80's	4.0–6.0	±5
Advanced	.76–.94	High .80's	7th Gr. 5.0– 9.0	
			8th Gr. 8.0–12.5	
			9th Gr. 8.0–13.0	

It is apparent that with few exceptions reliability coefficients of the sub-tests are in the .80's and .90's. The exceptions are *Science* and *Social Studies Concepts* in Primary II; *Arithmetic Concepts* in Intermediate II, Grade 5; and *Arithmetic Applications* in Advanced, Grades 7 and 9. These coefficients are in the high .60's and .70's.

Standard errors of measurement, expressed in grade score units (see number 13 below) increase from about 1 in Primary I to about 10 in Advanced, Grade 9.

On the whole, the reliabilities, except as noted, are entirely satisfactory, especially in view of the fact that each is calculated for a sub-test within a single grade, where both the shortness of the tests and their restricted range have a depressing effect on reliability coefficients. The reliability of any total battery would almost certainly be at least .95. Each coefficient is based on a random sample of one thousand cases drawn from a given grade.

12. Manual. There are separate manuals for each battery. All are clear and complete.

13. Scoring. Primary Batteries are hand-scored by stencil keys. For the Intermediate and Advanced Batteries a booklet may be hand-scored or be used with separate answer sheets for machine scoring by IBM or MRC process. In the latter case, booklets are reusable. Directions for scoring are complete and not difficult to follow.

Scores are obtained as the number right on each sub-test. These are converted to "grade scores" by means of a table of equivalents at the end of each sub-test. Grade scores are grade equivalents without decimals. Thus a grade score of 58 equals a grade equivalent of 5.8. Grade equivalents may be converted to percentiles and stanines. All three types of scores are recorded for each sub-test on the title page of the test booklet or the answer sheet if booklets are not consumed. A profile may be constructed for each pupil based on his stanine scores.

14. Norms. Essentially three types of norms are provided, as indicated above, namely, grade, percentile, and stanine. "All norms are based on the total enrollment in regular classes at each grade level except for a small group markedly atypical as to age." The grade equivalents represent the average score made by pupils at a specified grade placement. Percentile ranks corresponding to grade scores are provided for beginning, middle, and end-of-year testing. Finally, stanine equivalents are provided for defined ranges or bands of percentile ranks and grade scores.

15. Format. Paper, printing, and general organization of tests and accessories are excellent. The use of coordinated color for each battery and accessories is a new and attractive feature. In addition to manual and scoring key, accessories include a *Class Record* and *Analysis Chart*. These are useful for studying results of the testing for a class as a whole.

▶ LEARNING EXERCISES ◀

1. What are some of the chief uses of survey batteries in the elementary schools? What are their limitations?

2. Select an elementary survey battery for study. Read reviews of it in one of the *Mental Measurements Yearbooks*, but be sure to examine a specimen set. Write a five-hundred-word appraisal of it.

Other Survey Batteries

1. *American School Achievement Tests*. 1960. Forms D and E, all levels. Also F and G for Intermediate and Advanced. Primary I, Grade 1. *Word Recognition, Word Meaning, Numbers*. $4.00 per 35. 35 (50) minutes.[4]

Primary II, Grades 2–3. *Sentence and Word Meaning, Paragraph Meaning, Arithmetic Computation, Arithmetic Problems, Language,* and *Spelling*. $5.75 per 35. 85 (105) minutes.

Intermediate Battery Complete. Grades 4–6. *Reading, Arithmetic, Language, Spelling, Social Studies, Science*. $8.50 per 35. 127 (147) minutes.

Advanced Battery Complete. Grades 7–9. *Reading, Arithmetic, Language, Spelling, Social Studies, Science*. $8.50 per 35. 147 (170) minutes.

---

[4] Wherever possible, two times are given for every test; the first is the actual working time, and the second is the estimated total time required to administer the test. Where only one time is given, it is the actual working time without allowance for reading directions, etc.

Intermediate Battery Partial. Grades 4–6. *Reading, Arithmetic, Language, Spelling.* $7.00 per 35. 117 (137) minutes.

Advanced Battery Partial. Grades 7–9. *Reading, Arithmetic, Language, Spelling.* $7.00 per 35. 137 (157) minutes.

All answers are marked on test booklets and hand-scored. A machine-scored form is also available, Forms D–G, for Intermediate and Advanced levels. Complete, $6.50 per 35. Partial, $5.00 per 35.

The Bobbs-Merrill Company, Inc.

2. *California Achievement Tests.* 1957 Edition. 1963 Norms. (Previous edition still available.) *Reading Vocabulary, Reading Comprehension, Arithmetic Reasoning, Arithmetic Fundamentals, Mechanics of English, Spelling.*

Lower Primary. Grades 1–2. Areas same as above. Forms W ('57), X ('57). $5.60 per 35. 89 minutes.

Upper Primary. Grades H2–L4. Areas same as above. Forms W ('57), X ('57). $5.95 per 35. 178 minutes.

Elementary. Grades 4, 5, 6. Areas same as above. IBM. Forms W ('57), X ('57), Y ('57), Z ('57). $6.65 per 35. 178 minutes.

Junior High Level. Grades 7–9. Areas same as above. IBM. Forms W ('57), X ('57), Y ('57), Z ('57). $6.65 per 35. 178 minutes.

Advanced. Grades 9–14. Areas same as above. IBM. Forms W ('57), X ('57), Y ('57). $5.60 per 35. 178 minutes.

California Test Bureau.

3. *Coordinated Scales of Attainment.* 1948–50. One battery for each grade, 1–8. Battery 1, *Picture-Word Association, Word-Picture Association, Vocabulary Recognition, Reading Comprehension, Arithmetic Experience, Number Skills, Problem Reasoning, Computation.* Forms A and B. $2.65 per 25.

Battery 2, same as Battery 1 plus *Spelling.* Forms A and B. $2.65 per 25.

Battery 3, same as Battery 2. Forms A and B. $2.65 per 25.

Battery 4, *Punctuation, Usage, Capitalization, Reading, History, Geography, Science, Literature, Computation, Problem Reasoning, Spelling.*

Forms A and B. $3.60 per 25.

Batteries 5, 6, 7, and 8, same areas as Battery 4. Forms A and B. Prices same as for Battery 4.

Testing time: Batteries 1, 2, and 3, 100 minutes each; Batteries 4–8, 256 minutes.

American Guidance Service.

4. *Gray-Votaw-Rogers General Achievement Tests.* 1934–63. Grades 1–3, 4–6, 7–9. Primary: *Reading Comprehension, Reading Vocabulary, Spelling, Arithmetic Reasoning, Arithmetic Computation.* Intermediate, same as for Primary plus *Science, Language, Literature, Social Studies, Health and Safety.* Advanced, same as Intermediate. Abbreviated Edition, Grades 5–9: *Science, Social Studies, Literature, Language, Reading, Arithmetic.*

Forms A, B, C, D. $3.75 per 25; Abbreviated, $2.50 per 25. Primary, 70–80 minutes; Intermediate, 170 minutes; Advanced, 170 minutes. Abbreviated, 80 minutes.

Steck Company.

5. *Iowa Every-Pupil Tests of Basic Skills,* New Edition. 1940–50. Elementary, Grades 3–5; Advanced, Grades 5–9.

Forms L, M, N, O, each consisting of Test A, *Silent Reading Comprehension;* Test B, *Work-Study Skills;* Test C, *Basic Language Skills;* Test D, *Basic Arithmetic Skills.* Elementary tests, $3.60 per 35; advanced tests, $3.75 per 35.

Houghton Mifflin Company.

6. *Iowa Tests of Basic Skills.* 1956. Multi-level edition for Grades 3–9. *Vocabulary, Reading Comprehension, Language Skills, Work-Study Skills* and *Arithmetic Skills.*

Forms 1 and 2. $.84 per copy. 4 hours, 39 minutes.

Houghton Mifflin Company.

7. *Metropolitan Achievement Tests.* 1959. Primary I, Grade 1. *Word Knowledge, Word Discrimination, Reading, Arithmetic.* Forms A, B, C. $6.25 per 35. 105 minutes.

Primary II, Grade 2. *Reading, Vocabulary, Arithmetic Fundamentals, Arithmetic Problems, Spelling.* Forms A, B, C. $8.00 per 35. 2 hours.

Elementary, Grades 3 and 4. *Reading, Vocabulary, Arithmetic Fundamentals, Arithmetic Problems, Language, Spelling.* Forms A, B, C, D. $8.00 per 35. 2 hours, 45 minutes.

Intermediate, Grades 5–6. Complete: *Reading, Vocabulary, Arithmetic Fundamentals, Arithmetic Problems, English, Literature, Geography, History, Civics, Science, Spelling.* Forms A, B, C, D. $11.00 per 35. 3 hours, 30 minutes.

Intermediate, Grades 5–6. Partial: *Reading, Vocabulary, Arithmetic Fundamentals, Arithmetic Problems, English, Spelling.* Forms A, B, C, D. $9.00 per 35. 3 hours, 30 minutes.

Advanced, Grades 7–9. Complete: areas same as intermediate complete. $11.00 per 35. 4 hours, 15 minutes. Partial: Same as intermediate partial. $9.00 per 35. 3 hours, 45 minutes.

Harcourt, Brace &'World, Inc.

8. *Sequential Tests of Educational Progress.* 1956–57. Grades 4–6, 7–9, 10–12, 13–14. *Reading, Writing, Listening, Essay Test, Mathematics, Science, Social Studies.* Four levels in each subject area.

Forms A and B for each level. $4.00 per 20 of any test except *Essay,* $1.00 per 20. 70 minutes (two 35-minute units) for each test except *Essay,* 35 minutes complete.

Educational Testing Service.

9. *S.R.A. Achievement Series.* New Edition. 1956. First level, Grades 1–2. *Reading, Arithmetic.* Form A. $3.50 and $2.50 per 20 booklets. Approximately 6 hours.

Second, third, and fourth levels, Grades 2–4, 4–6, and 6–9. *Reading, Arithmetic, Language Arts, Work-Study Skills.* Forms A and B. $2.00 and $2.15 per 20 booklets. Batteries 2–4 and 4–6, 8 hours; battery 6–9, 6 hours.

Science Research Associates, Inc.

MEASUREMENT OF THE THREE R'S

Traditionally, the Three R's has meant reading, writing, and arithmetic. At one time these subjects constituted the curriculum in the grammar school, and the curriculum was unadorned and unhampered by any "fads and frills." In a very real sense they are still the backbone or basic core of all instruction, not only in the elementary grades, but also at higher levels. They represent the means of communicating ideas and concepts without which such exchange is limited to word-of-mouth expression. In primitive societies transmission by word of mouth is used to convey folk-lore and some rudiments of culture from generation to generation, but no society has ever achieved a high degree of civilization without having first progressed beyond oral communication.

Every modern educational program is based on the assumption that pupils must know how to read, write, and "cipher." It is hard to imagine how schools could function today without these rudimentary skills. If teachers had to teach without them it seems evident that our whole system of education as we know it, and our whole civilization, would break down. There would be no books, no newspapers or magazines, no mail, no mathematics, science, or history; probably none of our modern systems of communication like the telegraph, telephone, or radio would have been invented. Societies that have not developed systems of written communciation have remained primitive.

It is not surprising, therefore, that schools everywhere place great emphasis on the development of these skills. In the kindergarten an attempt is made to develop reading readiness, number concepts, and skill in using crude writing tools such as chalk and crayon. If the child does not attend kindergarten, but has his first school experience in first grade he still, as a rule, has opportunities to develop some of these rudimentary but important skills and concepts through children's story books, games, and toys. He learns to associate words with objects and pictures, orally at first by naming them, and later by recognizing the printed word; he learns to count blocks, or kittens, or soldiers; and he learns to hold and use crayons or other writing tools by coloring, copying, or drawing pictures.

The concept of the Three R's has broadened somewhat to include more than reading, writing, and arithmetic.[5] What are now considered basic tool-subjects include, in addition to these three, spelling and language arts (capitalization, punctuation, grammar, and sentence structure), as well as oral communciation. To be sure, instruction in most of these other subjects was a related part of the Three R's in earlier days, but the others were not generally regarded as separate subjects or areas of instruction. In the section which follows, consideration will be given to measurement practices and techniques in reading, writing, arithmetic, spelling, and the language arts, where these have resulted in some generally accepted and widely used instruments, e.g., standardized tests.

Reading and Reading Readiness

Reading is perhaps the most important of the tool-subjects mentioned above, for it comes close to being the basis of our civilization. Illiterate persons cannot progress far in our society, nor can they be effective citizens. It is not surprising, therefore, that reading is the first accomplishment the school attempts to give the child. Until he can read, the child cannot become educated according to our concepts of education. If he does not learn to read well he is constantly handicapped in his progress through the schools. Because of the importance accorded to reading, much research and study have been done on the nature of the reading process, on methods of teaching reading, on the causes and remedies for reading disabilities, and, together with all of these, on the development of tests and techniques

[5] Gertrude Hildreth, *Learning the Three R's; A Modern Interpretation,* Second Edition (Minneapolis, Minn.: Educational Publishers, Inc., 1947).

for measuring reading ability and skill. Literature in educational research contains a wealth of material on this subject. Much of this material is of interest and concern to every teacher, from the kindergarten to the university level.

Reading tests have been mainly concerned with three areas of measurement. One of these areas is reading readiness. It has become pretty generally accepted that readiness to learn to read is, at least in part, a maturational process. That is, a child is ready to learn to read when he has developed intellectually and in other ways to a given level of maturity. Authorities differ on the exact level required, but it is generally agreed that it is not below the mental age or maturity of the average six-year-old. Some place the minimum a half year or so higher. Whatever the minimum is, and it probably varies somewhat under different circumstances, it seems clear that it is very difficult and usually useless to try to teach a child to read before he has reached this minimum maturity level. A good deal of work has been done to develop tests which will give a fairly accurate measure of a child's readiness in a short time.

Another area of measurement in reading concerns achievement. Reading achievement tests are available for use at all levels from first grade upwards. They generally are directed toward the measurement of reading comprehension and speed of reading. Reading comprehension is usually thought of as the power to understand and remember what is read, while speed of reading refers to the amount that is read in a given time without measureable loss in comprehension. Both are important reading skills, and most reading achievement tests are designed to measure both, either directly or indirectly.

The third area of measurement in reading involves diagnostic testing. This is most useful with the slow reader or the reader who has difficulties of one sort or another. The diagnostic reading test is designed to identify such difficulties or weaknesses and to suggest ways of overcoming them. One approach to this — more in the nature of a tool than a test — involves a machine that photographs the eye movements of the reader as he reads. This device has made it very clear that one demonstrable and consistent difference between good and poor readers is in the number of pauses the eye makes. The good reader makes relatively few pauses and his eyes take in long fragments without stopping; the poor reader, on the other hand, reads jerkily, his eyes pause much more often and take in only a word or, at best, a few words between pauses. While the apparatus for photographing eye movements is not a test in the usual sense, it is a measuring instrument that yields information which has been found very useful in helping poor readers to improve.

Gates Testing Program in Reading

In order to orient the student to the area of measurement in reading, we shall describe in detail the comprehensive testing program by Gates.[6] The Gates program is unique in that it provides a continuous and related series of reading tests from kindergarten to tenth grade. It includes tests of every type found in this area, with the possible exception of study skills. The student who gains some familiarity with, and understanding of, the Gates tests will have a good orientation not only to the types of tests commonly used but also to a wide variety of techniques of measurement in reading. The first tests in the *Gates Testing Program* are the *Reading Readiness Tests.*

1. Name of tests and author. *Gates Reading Readiness Tests.*[7] Arthur I. Gates, Teachers College, Columbia University.

2. Purpose. To determine which children are ready to begin reading; how rapid their progress is likely to be; what specific abilities required in learning to read need development.

3. Grade level. End of kindergarten and beginning of first grade.

4. Number of forms. One.

5. Publisher and date of publication. Bureau of Publications, Teachers College, Columbia University, 1939.

6. Cost. $2.25 per 35.

7. Content. *Picture Directions:* Three line drawings — a farm scene, a town scene, and the interior of a general merchandise store. The examiner makes oral comments and asks the children to carry out certain instructions by marking the pictures.

Word Matching: Marking two words that are the same in each of several groups of four words.

Word Card Matching: A word on a flash card is shown for five seconds. The word is then found and marked in a group of four words in the test booklet.

Rhyming: Selecting from groups of four pictured objects one whose name rhymes with a key word given orally; e.g., the objects — hat, dog, cup, and horse — are pictured and the examiner asks for the one that sounded like "pup."

[6] Arthur I. Gates, *Gates Testing Program in Reading* (New York: Teachers College, Columbia University, 1939–1962).

[7] Quotations in the present description of the *Gates Testing Program in Reading* by permission of the publisher.

Reading Letters and Numbers: This is given individually. The child is asked to name capital letters, lower case letters, and numbers from 0 to 9, which are printed on the test blank.

Ability to Grasp the Structure and Substance of a Story: This is not a part of the Readiness Test as such, but is recommended as a valuable adjunct. The first half of a good story from about the middle of a primer is read aloud. Then the child is asked to tell what happened next. The child's account is recorded and judged on general merit.

8. Time required. The tests are non-timed and it is not required that all five tests be given. If all are given, the total time is about one hour. In any case, it is recommended that tests 1, 2, and 5 be given in the first period and that tests 3 and 4 be given later.

9. Directions for and ease of administering. The tests are easily and simply administered by any competent teacher who will follow directions.

10. Validity. The tests were selected on the basis of several extensive research studies using many kinds of tests to identify those most useful for measuring reading readiness. The most promising were tried out with an entire entering-school population in a small city, and on the basis of these results a revised test was given further trial in another group of schools. On the basis of these data the present test was constructed.

11. Reliability. The reliabilities of the five parts of the test are as follows: *Picture Directions, .84; Word Matching, .78; Word Card Matching, .82; Rhyming, .84; Reading Letters and Numbers, .96.* The reliability coefficient of the whole test is .97.

12. Manual. The manual is complete and clear. Besides descriptions of the tests, and directions for administering and scoring the tests and interpreting scores, there are helpful suggestions for remedial work in the various abilities measured, and for predicting reading progress on the basis of scores on the test. The manual contains numerous footnote references to studies, and a selected bibliography.

13. Scoring. The tests are generally scored by counting the number of correct answers. No prepared scoring keys are provided, but directions are given for making simple scoring keys. The scoring, which is essentially a process of counting the number of exercises correctly marked, is quite objective.

14. Norms. Separate tables of percentile norms are provided for kindergarten and for first-grade testing for each of the five sub-tests or parts.

15. Format. The tests are printed on good quality paper in an 8½″ × 11″

booklet of eight pages. The manual is a 6" × 9" booklet of thirty-one pages.

The next tests in the series are the *Primary Reading Tests*. A description of these tests follows:

1. Name of tests and author. *Gates Primary Reading Tests*. Arthur I. Gates.

2. Purpose. These tests are intended to measure level and range of ability in *Word Recognition, Sentence Reading,* and *Paragraph Reading.*

3. Grade level. Grade 1 and first half of Grade 2.

4. Number of forms. Forms 1, 2, 3.

5. Publisher and date of publication. Bureau of Publications, Teachers College, Columbia University, 1958.

6. Cost. $1.50 per 35 copies of each of the three types of tests.

7. Content. Type PWR: *Word Recognition* consists of forty-eight exercises, each of which is made up of a picture followed by four words. The task is to select the one word in each exercise that "tells the most about the picture." For example:

Type PSR: *Sentence Reading* consists of forty-five exercises, each including three sentences marked respectively I, II, and III, and followed by drawings of six objects, three of which are answers to the sentences. Thus:

The child marks the drawing of the boy with *I;* that of the girl, *II;* that of the box, *III*.

Type **PPR**: *Paragraph Reading* consists of twenty-six exercises, each containing three drawings followed by a sentence (in the first third of the exercises), or a short paragraph directing the child to do something with the drawings. For example:

3. Draw a line under the little book.

The hardest exercises contain paragraphs consisting of several sentences, usually describing the drawings or telling a little story. Following the directions requires an understanding of the sense of the paragraph.

8. Time required. *Word Recognition,* 15 minutes; *Sentence Reading,* 15 minutes; *Paragraph Reading,* 20 minutes.

9. Directions for and ease of administering. These are simple and easily followed. Mainly, the task is to make sure that pupils understand what they are to do and do their best. The teacher is encouraged to do anything that helps to achieve this purpose, short of telling anyone the answer to any exercise. Also, no deviation from the established time limits is permitted.

10. Validity. The tests are said to measure different phases of reading ability and to be diagnostic. The validity could be said to be essentially construct in nature. It is hypothesized that reading ability has essentially three different components, namely, word recognition, the ability to read sentences and the ability to read paragraphs. Using this construct as a basis the author has devised test items to measure each of these aspects of it. There is also some empirical evidence in the form of correlations with other reading tests, all from the *Stanford Achievement Battery*. These correlations range from .53 to .86, increasing generally with the increase in grade level tested.

11. Reliability. Extensive data on reliability are given in the form of alternate form reliability coefficients. For the *Primary Reading Tests,* such correlations are in the range of .86 to .89. Standard errors of measurement for *Word Recognition* are about 4.4; for *Sentence Reading* about the same; and for *Paragraph Reading* about 2.2.

12. Manual. The manual provides all essential information for use and interpretation of results for the tests. It includes a rather detailed consideration of the interpretation of differences between scores and a discussion of methods of improving word recognition and reading comprehension.

13. Scoring. The score in type PWR is the number right minus one-third the number wrong. In types PSR and PPR, the score is the number right. A strip key is provided for PWR, and there are translucent overlays for scoring PSR and PPR. Scoring is done strictly according to directions, with reasonable allowances for motor limitations, but none for other failures such as using a different type of mark than that called for.

14. Norms. Grade and age norms are provided for each of the three types of tests. For type PWR, a table of percentile equivalents for raw scores is also provided. These are based upon the scores of approximately 2,400 pupils in Grades 1.4–4.5 in twenty carefully selected schools in various parts of the country.

15. Format. The format of the tests in the revised edition has been made attractive by the use of color and better typography. Tests and manual are the standard 8½″ × 11″ size.

The third set of tests in the Gates series are the *Advanced Primary Reading Tests.* These are similar in organization and content to the *Primary Reading Tests* except that they include only Type AWR, *Word Recognition,* and Type APR, *Paragraph Reading.* They are designed for the second half of Grade 2 and Grade 3.

Type AWR contains forty-eight exercises consisting of a picture and four words, from which the pupil chooses one describing the picture. These differ from those in the *Primary Tests* in that they reach considerably higher and more abstract levels of difficulty.

Type APR consists of twenty-four paragraphs with pictures as in Type PPR of the *Primary Tests.* Again, the exercises in the *Advanced Primary* are more difficult than those in the *Primary Tests.*

In all other respects — tests, manual, administration, scoring, norms, etc. — the two sets of tests are the same or quite similar. The *Primary*

Tests require fifty minutes for three sub-tests; the *Advanced Primary* require forty minutes for the two sub-tests. Reliability coefficients were .89 for Type 1, and .87 for Type 2, predecessors of the 1958 revision. Age and grade norms and percentile norms are given. These are based on 3,300 cases. The manual is very similar in completeness to that for the *Primary Tests,* and many sections are identical. The cost of the separate tests in the two sets is the same.

The *Gates Basic Reading Tests* come next in this series.

1. Name of tests and author. *Gates Basic Reading Tests.* Arthur I. Gates.

2. Purpose. These tests are planned to provide a comprehensive survey of basic reading abilities.

3. Grade level. Second half of Grade 3 through Grade 8.

4. Number of forms. Forms 1, 2, and 3.

5. Publisher and date of publication. Bureau of Publications, Teachers College, Columbia University, 1958.

6. Cost. $1.50 per 35 copies of any one type. The tests, though printed separately, are designed to be used as a team.

7. Content. Type GS, *General Significance,* is a combination of two tests in the previous edition — the test of *Reading to Get the General Significance* and the test of *Reading to Predict the Outcome of Given Events.* It consists of twenty-four paragraphs, each of which is followed by a comprehension exercise in which the pupil marks one of five words which seems to him to indicate in a stipulated way the main idea or meaning of the passage.

Type UD, *Understanding Directions,* measures the ability to comprehend a set of directions with accuracy and exactness. It consists of twenty-four paragraphs, each followed by a brief explanation of what the picture is about. The statement ends with a direction to do something with the picture to show that it is properly interpreted and that the instructions are understood. For example, one picture shows a circle, a triangle, and a square. The statement calls attention to the fact that the circle has no corners, the triangle has three, and the square has four. The pupil is directed to draw a line from the shape that has three corners to the other shape that has corners.

Type ND, *Noting Details,* tests the ability to understand several details in a paragraph but requires a less definitely organized grasp than Type GS and less exact memory for details than Type UD. There are eighteen paragraphs each followed by three statements, each of which is in the form of a multiple-choice item. The examinee answers these three items according to his understanding of the material in the paragraph.

Type RV, *Reading Vocabulary,* is a new test in the series. It consists of sixty-five multiple-choice items, each consisting of a key word followed by five other words. The task is to find the word which means the same or nearly the same as the first word. Pupils are allowed enough time to finish.

Type LC, *Level of Comprehension,* consists of twenty-eight passages arranged in order of increasing difficulty. For example:

> Some dogs love the water. When they see a pond, they
> love to <u>A</u> in and <u>B</u> around.
>
> A. eat   bark   jump   sleep   drink
> B. climb   swim   chew   sing   swing

Again pupils are allowed time to finish, the very slow pupils being permitted to finish alone. Thus the factor of speed, which enters into Types GS, UD, and ND, is not present. The test is designed to measure the degree of comprehension with which the child can read complex and difficult material.

8. Time required. Type GS, 10 minutes for Grades 3 and 4; 8 minutes for Grades 5 and above. Same for Types UD and ND. Type RV, 20 minutes, more or less, as needed. Same for Type LC.

9. Directions for and ease of administering. The tests are practically self-administering. The examiner reads the directions on the title page with the pupils, and starts and stops the test. Directions to pupils are clear and complete.

10. Validity. The new *Basic Reading Tests* are said to "provide a well-diversified and well-balanced appraisal of very important reading skills and abilities. They measure not only vocabulary and power or level of comprehension, but also speed and accuracy of reading in each of three important types of material." As in the case of the other tests in the series, the evidence for validity is essentially logical or construct in nature. Correlations of the five types with *Stanford Reading* range from .53 to .73 for *Paragraph Meaning* (Types GS, ND, UD and LC) and from .83 to .85 for *Word Meaning* (Type RV).

11. Reliability. Alternate form reliability coefficients and standard errors of measurement for the five types for each of grades 3 to 8 are given. The coefficients are all in the .80's and the standard errors range from 1.58 to 4.19. Considering that alternate-form reliability coefficients are generally lower than split-half, and that all these coefficients are based on results in a single grade range, they are quite impressive. Again, the matter of the reliability of differences between individual test scores is discussed.

12. Manual. The manual is complete and detailed. Particular attention is given to scoring and interpreting. There are many suggestions for use of the test results as a basis for diagnosis and remedial work.

13. Scoring. All types are scored with strip keys except Type UD, for which a translucent overlay key is provided. Types GS, UD, and ND are scored on the basis of number correct (called the raw score) and percentage correct of the items attempted. This method of scoring takes into account both speed and accuracy. Types RV and LC are scored on the basis of right answers minus one-fourth the wrong answers. In general, responses are marked "wrong" unless executed exactly according to directions; however, every effort is made to determine the pupil's intentions and give him the benefit of the doubt.

14. Norms. Reading grade, reading age, and percentile norms are provided for each type and for the ten-minute and eight-minute time limits where these apply. Accuracy scores are further classified into the levels "Very High," "High," "Medium," "Low," and "Very Low." All norms are based on 6,800 cases, although by a process of getting "equivalent scores," the number is increased to what are designated 22,900 "effective numbers."

15. Format. Test booklets are 8½″ × 11″ in size and attractively printed in two colors. The manual is similar in format.

The next test in the Gates series is a measure of over-all or general reading ability but in briefer form than the *Basic Tests*.

1. Name of test and author. *Gates Reading Survey.* Arthur I. Gates.

2. Purpose. To provide a shorter and more economical substitute for the *Basic* series. It is considered particularly suitable for a city-wide survey and is available in both hand-scored and machine-scored editions.

3. Grade level. Grade 3 through Grade 10.

4. Number of forms. Forms 1, 2, and 3.

5. Publisher and date of publication. Bureau of Publications, Teachers College, Columbia University, 1958.

6. Cost. $2.75 per 35.

7. Content. *Speed* and *Accuracy* are measured by thirty-six paragraphs of equal difficulty constituting a combination of Types GS, UD and ND of the Basic series.

Reading Vocabulary consists of sixty-five items essentially the same as Type RV of the *Basic* Series.

Level of Comprehension consists of twenty-one paragraphs arranged in order of difficulty. It is essentially a shorter version of Type LC of the Basic series.

8. Time Required. *Speed and Accuracy,* 6 minutes for Grades 3, 4, and 5; 4 minutes for Grade 6 and up. *Vocabulary* and *Level of Comprehension* are not strictly timed but it is suggested that about 20 minutes for each should be sufficient.

9. Directions for and ease of administering. The tests are easy to administer and directions are clear and easily followed. It is necessary to adhere strictly to the time limits for *Speed* and *Accuracy*.

10. Validity. What was said above with reference to validity of the *Basic Reading Test* applies equally to the *Reading Survey Test*. The extent to which these tests measure what they purport to measure is determined by the author's concepts of the components of reading ability and his success in devising tests of these components. In fairness to these tests, it should be said that they are similar to other tests in the same field in many respects and therefore are not out of line with current ideas in measuring reading ability. They do vary in certain respects from other existing tests in this field, for example, in the comparative simplicity of approach. Whether this contributes to their validity is a matter of opinion. Certainly it is an advantage to the user.

11. Reliability. Reliability coefficients and standard errors of measurement are reported for this test as in the case of the Primary and Basic series. Coefficients are all in the .80's and S.E.$_m$ ranges from 1.94 to 3.66.

12. Manual. The manual for the *Reading Survey* follows closely in content and organization that for the *Basic* series.

13. Scoring. *Speed* and *Accuracy* are scored on the basis of number of items correct (called raw score) and the percentage correct of items attempted. *Reading Vocabulary* and *Level of Comprehension* are scored $R - \dfrac{W}{4}$. Strip keys are provided for hand scoring. Scoring stencils and IBM 805 answer sheets for the machine scored edition must be purchased separately.

14. Norms. Age and grade norms are provided for raw scores; percentile norms for the accuracy scores. The norms are based upon 18,600 cases which, by the method of "equivalent scores," were increased to 23,100. These were drawn from school systems of varying sizes and compositions in Vermont, New Jersey, and New York. Also included were groups with varying ethnic, regional, and socio-economic backgrounds in New York City.

15. Format. The tests and manual are identical in appearance and materials to the others in the *Gates* series.

The last tests to be described in the *Gates* series are the *Gates-McKillop Reading Diagnostic Tests*.

1. Name of tests and authors. *Gates-McKillop Reading Diagnostic Tests.* Arthur I. Gates and Anne S. McKillop.

2. Purpose. This is an individual test designed to identify specific strengths and weaknesses in a child's reading skills.

3. Grade level. No grade limits are set for the usefulness of this test. However, it probably is most appropriate in the primary grades when a child's reading skills are being developed.

4. Number of forms. Forms 1 and 2.

5. Publisher and date of publication. Bureau of Publications, Teachers College, Columbia University, 1962.

6. Cost. Pupil Record Booklet, $.20 per copy. Test Materials, $1.25 per set (reusable). Manual, $.25 per copy. Tachistoscope, $.10.

7. Content. The tests included are (I) *Oral Reading;* (II) *Word Pronunciation: Flash Presentation;* (III) *Word Pronunciation: Untimed Presentation;* (IV) *Phrases: Flash Presentation;* (V) *Knowledge of Word Parts: Word Attack;* (V–1) *Recognizing and Blending Common Word Parts;* (V–2) *Giving Letter Sounds;* (V–3) *Naming Capital Letters;* (V–4) *Naming Lower Case Letters;* (VI) *Recognizing the Visual Form or*

Word Equivalents of Sounds; (VI–1) *Nonsense Words;* (VI–2) *Initial Letters;* (VI–3) *Final Letters;* (VI–4) *Vowels;* (VII) *Auditory Blending;* (VIII) *Supplementary Tests;* (VIII–1) *Spelling;* (VIII–2) *Oral Vocabulary;* (VIII–3) *Syllabification;* (VIII–4) *Auditory Discrimination.*

8. Time required. The only tests in which time is a factor are the two flash presentation tests. In these, the words or phrases are flashed at a speed of two per second. In all others the test proceeds at the speed at which the child can work. It is estimated that to give all tests in the battery would require several hours. They would not be given all at one sitting, however, especially with younger pupils, nor would all the tests necessarily be used. The important thing is to use the tests according to their appropriateness for individual diagnosis.

9. Directions for and ease of administering. The directions are probably as clear and complete as they can be. The tests are numerous and varied; their administration is necessarily complicated, resembling in some respects the administration of a *Binet* or *Wechsler* individual intelligence examination. Anyone using them will need first, careful study and preparation and second, some practice.

10. Validity. For a battery such as this the question of validity in the usual sense is not easily answered. The authors have developed a series of measures in accordance with a logical plan (construct) of the basic elements of reading ability. That these tests do differentiate between individual children with respect to the abilities measured seems evident. Whether the results of the tests agree with other criteria of reading ability (or disability) such as teachers' judgments, other tests, or grade progress, etc., the manual does not say. On the whole, the validation of a battery such as this must rest primarily on evidence of how well it serves its purpose, and such evidence is probably not yet available.

11. Reliability. No information was found in the manual or elsewhere on this point.

12. Manual. The manual is a twenty-page booklet giving the rationale of the battery, detailed directions for administering the tests, and for recording results, and tables of norms and directions for scoring and interpreting results. It is detailed and complete.

13. Scoring. The recording of a child's responses in the *Pupil Record Booklet* is an important part of the use of the battery, essential to accurate scoring and meaningful interpretation. This record is the basis for determining a score but, more important, it is carefully studied to determine types of errors made. The manual gives clues and suggestions regarding the most common types of errors in the various tests. In almost all instances the raw score is the number correct. (*Oral Vocabulary* — Raw

$$\text{Score} = \text{R} - \frac{\text{Errors}}{3}\text{).}$$

14. Norms. For all tests, grade score norms are provided. These are further classified as normal progress, low, and very low for most tests.

15. Format. All materials are well-designed, and they are printed on good paper and durably bound. In this respect, they are the equal of any other tests.

▶ LEARNING EXERCISES ◀

3. Does the *Gates Testing Program* described here provide an adequate set of measurements of all the important outcomes of reading? If not, which are inadequately provided for or omitted?

4. Present-day reading instruction seems to stress silent reading more than oral reading, which formerly was emphasized a great deal. What are some of the reasons for this change in emphasis? Is the change desirable, in your opinion?

5. If you were interested in making an objective test of oral reading ability, how would you proceed?

Other Reading and Reading Readiness Tests

READING TESTS

1. *Durrell Analysis of Reading Difficulty.* 1956. Grades 1–6. *Silent and Oral Reading, Listening Comprehension, Word Analysis, Phonetics, Faulty Pronunciation, Writing,* and *Spelling.*
One form: individual. $4.00 per examiner's kit. Additional forms and record blanks, $4.15 per 35. 30–45 minutes.
Harcourt, Brace & World, Inc.

2. *Durrell-Sullivan Reading Capacity and Achievement Tests.* 1955. Primary, Grades 2.5–4.5; Intermediate, Grades 3–6.
Capacity: *Pictorial — Word Meaning* and *Paragraph Meaning* — measured by *Oral Language.* Achievement: *Word Meaning, Paragraph Meaning, Spelling,* and *Written Recall.* Primary, $5.50 per 35; Intermediate, Capacity, $3.30 per 35; Achievement, $4.20 per 35.
Harcourt, Brace & World, Inc.

3. *Gray Oral Reading Tests.* 1963. Grades 1–12. *Standardized Oral*

Reading Paragraphs. Forms A, B, C, D. Reading Passages — each form — $1.60; record booklets — $3.20 per 35.

The Bobbs-Merrill Company, Inc.

4. *Iowa Silent Reading Tests.* 1956. Elementary, Grades 4–8; Advanced, high school, and college. *Rate of Reading, Comprehension,* and *Skills in Locating Information.*

Forms AM, BM, CM, and DM. Elementary, $4.10 per 35; Advanced, $5.50 per 35. Elementary, 49 minutes; Advanced, 45 minutes.

Harcourt, Brace & World, Inc.

5. *Kelley-Greene Reading Comprehension Test.* 1952. Grades 9–13. *Reading Comprehension, Directed Reading,* and *Retention of Details.*

Forms AM and BM. $5.95 per 35. 63 minutes.

Harcourt, Brace & World, Inc.

6. *Lee-Clark Reading Test, First Reader.* 1958. Grades 1, 2. *Vocabulary, Following Directions, Sentence Completion, Inference.*

Forms A and B. $2.80 per 35. 25 minutes.

California Test Bureau.

7. *Nelson-Denny Reading Test.* 1960. Grades 9–16. *Vocabulary* and *Reading Comprehension.*

Forms A and B. $4.20 per 35 tests and self-marking answer booklets. 30 minutes.

Houghton Mifflin Company.

8. *Nelson Reading Test.* 1962. Grades 3–9. *Vocabulary, Reading Comprehension, Ability to Note Details, Ability to Predict Outcomes.*

Forms A and B. $4.95 per 35 tests; $2.55 per 35 self-marking answer booklets. 30 minutes.

Houghton Mifflin Company.

9. *Stroud, Hieronymus, and McKee Primary Reading Profiles.* 1953, 1955, 1957. Grades 1 and 2. *Aptitude for Reading, Auditory Association, Word Recognition, Word Attack, Reading Comprehension.*

Levels 1 and 2. $3.75 per 35 tests, plus a *Manual for Administration,* a *Class Record Sheet,* and a set of *Scoring Keys.*

Houghton Mifflin Company.

10. *Traxler High School Reading Test.* 1938. Grades 10, 11, and 12. Part I, *Rate of Reading and Comprehension at That Rate;* Part II, *Finding Main Ideas in a Paragraph.*

Forms A and B. 45 minutes. $4.20 per 35. Manual, $.25.

The Bobbs-Merrill Company, Inc.

11. *Traxler Silent Reading Test.* 1934–42. Grades 7 to 10. *Rate of Reading; Story Comprehension; Word Meaning; Power of Comprehension.*
Forms 1, 2, 3, and 4. 46 minutes. $4.20 per 35. Manual, $.25.
The Bobbs-Merrill Company, Inc.

READINESS TESTS

1. *American School Reading Readiness Test.* 1955. Kindergarten, Grade 1. *Vocabulary, Discrimination of Letter Forms and Letter Combinations, Recognition of Words, Discrimination of Geometric Forms, Following Directions, Memory of Geometric Forms.*
Form D. $4.00 per 35.
The Bobbs-Merrill Company, Inc.

2. *Harrison-Stroud Reading Readiness Profiles.* 1950, 1956. Kindergarten Grade 1. *Visual Discrimination, Using the Context, Auditory Discrimination, Using Context and Auditory Clues, Using Symbols.*
One form. $4.20 per 35. 79 minutes.
Houghton Mifflin Company.

3. *Lee-Clark Reading Readiness Test.* 1951. Kindergarten, Grade 1. *Visual Discrimination in Letters, Conceptual Maturity, Vocabulary, Following Instructions, Word Forms.*
One form. $.09 per copy in packages of 35. 20 minutes.
California Test Bureau.

4. *Metropolitan Readiness Tests.* 1949–50. Kindergarten, Grade 1. *Word Meaning, Listening, Matching, Numbers, Copying.*
Forms R and S. $4.00 per 35. 60 minutes.
Harcourt, Brace & World, Inc.

Handwriting

Writing and speech are sometimes referred to as the "expressive language arts," as contrasted with reading and listening, which are called the "receptive language arts." Of these, reading and writing are the ones considered here. Although tests measuring reading ability are extensive — as we have learned in the preceding section — few tests for the measurement of speech or listening abilities have been published.

There has been considerable change in emphasis in the teaching of writing in recent years. Attention and effort in teaching have shifted from mechanics to function. That is, in the teaching of handwriting a generation ago considerable attention was devoted to the pupil's development of a beautiful script. Much time was spent on practice from copy and on imitation of symmetrical handwriting. More recently, interest has shifted to the development of speed with legibility, and emphasis has been placed on handwriting as a means of communication and self-expression. Writing is regarded as a developmental process which presupposes the ability to think clearly. The objective is the ability to express ideas clearly and legibly; little attention is given now to the artistic qualities of handwriting. This is not to say that inartistic writing is encouraged or condoned; indeed, those who insist upon expressing their individuality through their handwriting — to the point where their writing is practically illegible — should be discouraged from this practice.

In measuring handwriting we find a number of attempts to produce what is sometimes referred to as a *product scale*. One of the earliest of these was the *Thorndike Scale for Hand-Writing of Children*.[8]

The scale reproduces samples of writing varying in quality from four (the worst writing of fourth-grade children) to Quality 18 (nearly the best writing of eighth-grade children). Each level of quality differs from the next highest or lowest by one-tenth of the difference between the best and the worst of the formal writings of one thousand children in Grades 5 to 8, as ranked by competent judges. A few samples follow:

Quality 6:

Quality 11:

[8] Edward L. Thorndike, *Handwriting* (New York: Teachers College, Columbia University, 1910). Samples reproduced by permission of the publisher.

Quality 16:

*Then the carelessly dressed gentle-
man stepped lightly into Warren's
carriage and held out a small*

Standards are given in terms of the number of letters (of familiar material) written per minute without substantial loss of quality, for not more than three minutes; the quality of writing when the pupil is writing naturally; and the quality of writing when the instructions are to write as well as possible. The pupil's samples of handwriting are compared with the scale to find that level of quality in the scale which his writing most closely resembles.

Another scale similar to that of the Thorndike is the *Ayres Scale,* often referred to as the *Gettysburg Edition.*[9] This was one of the most widely used scales ever devised, more than six hundred thousand copies having been printed between 1917 and 1935. It derives its name from the fact that the opening lines of Lincoln's "Gettysburg Address" are used as the subject matter. The teacher writes on the board the first three sentences of this address and instructs his pupils to read and copy until familiar with it. They then copy it, writing with ink on lined paper for exactly two minutes. The scale includes eight samples of levels of quality, graded from 20 to 90. The pupil's writing is compared with the samples for quality, and the total number of letters written in the two minutes is counted.

Norms are given for both speed and quality for Grades 2 to 8. There are also distributions of quality and rate scores for each grade from 5 to 8, inclusive. The norms show a relatively constant and substantial relationship between speed and quality, and steady progression in both from grade to grade.

Other scales for measuring handwriting are those by Freeman[10] and Hildreth.[11] The Freeman scale may be used for diagnostic purposes to identify handwriting faults in the areas of slantedness or straightness (too slanted or too straight), weight (too heavy or too light), regularity (too much variation in letter forms), and spacing (too much or too little space between letters or words). The Hildreth scale measures the quality of

[9] Leonard P. Ayres, *Measuring Scale for Handwriting: Gettysburg Edition* (New York: Russell Sage Foundation, 1917).

[10] Frank N. Freeman, *Handwriting Measuring Scale* (Columbus, Ohio: Zaner-Bloser Company, 1930).

[11] Gertrude Hildreth, *Metropolitan Primary Handwriting Scale.* Copyright 1933, copyright renewed 1960 by Harcourt, Brace & World, Inc., New York. Sample reproduced by permission of the publisher.

manuscript writing, i.e., printing, on a scale of ten to seventy. The quality of fifty is shown below:

Come To my garden

In Spring Time and hear

Birds Sing

Lateral dominance or handedness may affect a child's ability to learn to write. It is a rather common observation that left-handed children have more difficulty in learning to write and in actual writing than right-handed children. Sometimes the difficulty results from the fact that the teacher is right-handed, and consequently, she and the left-handed pupils have a different orientation and approach to the task. Another source of difficulty grows out of attempts to change the left-handed to right-handed. The effects of such pressures, psychologically speaking, are not completely understood. Emotional difficulties often seem to be associated with them, and handwriting, a finely organized and complex sensory-motor skill, often seems affected adversely.

Teaching a left-handed child to write with his right hand should be undertaken only after a careful study of the individual concerned reveals that such a course would be desirable and wise from a psychological point of view. In any case, tests of lateral dominance should be given to determine the status of the child in this trait before any decisions are made about changing his handedness.

▶ **LEARNING EXERCISE** ◀

6. See if you can find in educational literature any accounts of tests of lateral dominance. What is their nature; that is, what kinds of tasks or questions do they consist of? Is a right-handed person also likely to be right-eyed, right-footed? What significance has this for learning sensory-motor skills like handwriting?

Arithmetic

Except for reading, probably no subject in the elementary curriculum has been studied and investigated more than the teaching of arithmetic.

Many books and articles have been written about it. Perhaps a few almost axiomatic observations about arithmetic will be useful before considering problems of measurement in this subject. In the first place, it is quite generally agreed that arithmetic is a comparatively difficult subject. It calls for thinking of a rigorously exact nature, understanding rather than memory, and the ability to apply principles in different though analogous situations. These objectives are not easily attained, and most pupils do not seem to come by them naturally.

In the second place, arithmetic is not a popular subject, partly because it is difficult. Pupils do not generally elect courses in mathematics, once they pass the required ones, unless they have a special interest in it or unless their educational or vocational objectives require it.

The above statements might be interpreted to mean that arithmetic is inherently difficult and distasteful to many. This may be a safe assumption, yet it should be remembered that through improved teaching it may be possible to make arithmetic better liked and less difficult. Many students of the problem maintain that arithmetic has been poorly taught. It is said that the emphasis has been on memorizing and mechanical learning rather than on functional use and understanding. The problems and activities used in the teaching of arithmetic have often had little relationship to the lives and activities of people. It is believed that a reorientation and reorganization of the teaching of arithmetic to emphasize meaning, understanding, and applications would do much to make it more functional, less difficult, and consequently less distasteful. Many of the more recent textbooks and courses of study show evidences of thought and effort in this direction.

There are numerous published, more or less standardized, tests in arithmetic. Many of these are older tests, published twenty-five years ago or more, but still available. In the *Fifth Mental Measurements Yearbook* more than thirty tests in arithmetic, not including the older tests just mentioned, are reviewed. Even in most of the recent tests, however, the pattern of organization and types of exercises are not substantially different from those found in the older ones. There is some indication in a very few cases of an attempt to break away from this pattern, but such departures are not typical. This may not be the fault of those responsible for producing the tests; it is quite possible that teachers themselves are not yet ready to use tests that depart significantly from established or traditional patterns. Also, a test which is characterized by more or less extreme deviations from the traditional might reveal inadequacies in the pupils' learning about which the teacher may be somewhat sensitive.

Coordinated Scales of Attainment: Arithmetic

The test of arithmetic to be reviewed here is not radically different from conventional types. It is, however, a basically good example of the kind of arithmetic tests that are found in the catalogs of nearly every test publisher and that are being used by the great majority of teachers in our schools today.

1. Name of tests and author. *Coordinated Scales of Attainment: Arithmetic.*[12] L. J. Brueckner, University of Minnesota.

2. Purpose. This is part of a battery covering all the common branches, but is available as a separate test. It is designed to measure important outcomes of instruction in two areas: computation and reasoning.

3. Grade level. Grades 4–8, inclusive.

4. Number of forms. Forms A and B.

5. Publisher and date of publication. American Guidance Service, Inc., 1946–54.

6. Cost. $1.50 per 25 test booklets. Answer sheets required; $.75 per 25. Scoring key, $.10.

7. Content. *Arithmetic Computation.* The answer sheet has forty-five problems involving the fundamental operations with whole numbers, decimals, fractions, percentage, and mensuration problems.
Samples:

Multiply

$$.47 \times .06$$

Write as a decimal   3.12%

Subtract

15 min.	17.5 sec.
− 2 min.	22.8 sec.

Divide $13 \div 20 =$

The problems are worked on the answer sheet. For each problem there is an answer line followed by five spaces for marking as in the usual printed answer sheet, thus:

```
    1    2    3    4    D
   ::   ::   ::   ::   ::
   ::   ::   ::   ::   ::
   ::   ::   ::   ::   ::
```

[12] Quotations in test description by permission of the publisher.

On the test blank there is a matching page of answers for the forty-five problems. The pupil works all of them or as many as he can and then compares his answers with those on the matching page. There are four answers given for each problem. If his answer corresponds to one of those given he indicates this on the answer sheet; if not, he marks the "D" space. There are five problems of the forty-five which have no correct answer given and that should be marked "D." The manual states that these are included "to discourage attempts at illegitimate ways of getting the answer." They are not counted in the score.

Problem Reasoning. In this part there are forty problems which are intended to measure ability to select from four suggested solutions the correct solution to each problem.

Samples:

A. Bill had 14 marbles after he gave 2 to Paul. How many marbles did Bill have at first?

  1. Subtract 2 from 14.
  2. Add 14 and 2.
  3. Multiply 14 by 2.
  4. Divide 14 by 2.

B. Jean shared her 8 cookies equally with 3 friends. How many did she give to each friend?

  1. Add 8 and 3.
  2. Subtract 3 from 8.
  3. Multiply 8 by 4.
  4. Divide 8 by 4.

The exercises involve common problems such as interest, taxes, profit and loss, commissions, installment-buying charges, ratio and proportion.

The problems are typical of the kinds of problems that have been used in textbooks and tests in arithmetic for many years. The type of response called for is unusual in that the pupil does not actually have to work the problem to the point of getting an answer.

8. Time required. The tests are not timed and are said to be power tests. Work is stopped when 90 per cent of the pupils have finished, but the slower pupils may be brought back for a special session at a later time to complete their work. The estimated time for the *Computation* is 45 minutes, and for the *Reasoning,* 30 minutes.

9. Directions for and ease of administering. Directions are complete and quite clear, but administration of the *Computation* is complicated because of the use of the matching-answers feature described above. This seems likely to confuse some pupils, especially at lower grade levels where separate answer sheets are not widely used or recommended. Since the tests are not timed and directions are adequate, the test is easy to administer.

10. Validity. The validity of the test rests upon two bases. The first is the result of an analysis of some forty-five state and city courses of study. This analysis revealed a common core of material being taught at each grade level, and the tests were based on this common core. Experimental forms were constructed and administered to a representative sample of pupils in the grade for which the test was intended, and the grades immediately below and above it. The papers in the middle 20 per cent of the scores of each of the three grade groups were selected for analysis. Each item was evaluated on the criterion of a higher percentage of passes by the grade for which it was intended than by the grade below. In the final forms, only items meeting this discrimination criterion and falling within the middle 50 per cent of the difficulty range were retained.

Second, in the case of the *Reasoning* test, further evidence of validity is inferred from correlations between scores on it and (1) a standardized computation test and (2) a control test equivalent in every way to the *Reasoning* test except that pupils actually worked out solutions to the problems instead of merely identifying the correct method. The correlation with the standardized computation test was .46; with the control test, .46; between the control test and the computation test, .87. These results are interpreted to indicate that the *Reasoning* test measures a function somewhat different from that of the conventional type of test in which the pupil works the problem and gets an answer. In other words, since the correlation between the control test and the computation test is substantially higher than that between the *Reasoning* test and these two, the control test and the computation test are judged to be measuring much the same thing; yet neither one measures to as great an extent what the *Reasoning* test measures. It is stated in the manual that

> these results provide strong evidence that the traditional arithmetic problems test measures to a great extent the same abilities as does the computation test and that a score on such a problems test provides an inaccurate measure of the reasoning abilities involved in arithmetic problem solving. The new type of problem reasoning measurement used in the experimental tests was, therefore, adopted for use in preliminary and final forms of the present tests because it separates more distinctly the measurement of problem reasoning abilities from measurement of computational abilities.[13]

As indicated, the preceding statement is quoted from the *Master Manual*.

[13] *Master Manual* for *Coordinated Scales of Attainment*, p. 23.

The critical user of the tests may be inclined to question the interpretation suggested, since a different one is possible.

11. Reliability. The corrected correlations by odd-even halves of the airthmetic tests are:

TESTS	GRADES	
	4, 5, 6	*7, 8, 9*
Computation	.961 ± .002	.955 ± .002
Reasoning	.913 ± .005	.844 ± .008

The probable error of measurement is reported to be "less than two score units."[14]

These data indicate a high reliability, with the exception that the *Reasoning* test in Grades 7, 8 and 9 is somewhat below desirable standards for a test of this sort.

12. Manual. There are three booklets accompanying these tests. One is a set of directions for administering and scoring. This is clear and complete.

The second booklet is the *Master Manual* for the entire battery, of which the arithmetic tests are a sub-test. This also contains directions for administering and scoring, but in addition it gives directions for interpreting the scores, discusses norms and the preparation of a cumulative record form for individual pupils, presents data on the preparation of the tests and their validity and reliability, and introduces the analysis of errors as a feature of the tests.

The third booklet, the *Guide to Remedial Work,* takes up the analysis of errors in detail. An analysis of the content of each test is given and specific test items are identified with respect to the particular content they test. If the errors and omissions of the pupil are checked against this analysis his particular weaknesses will be revealed. If the errors and omissions for a class or group are tabulated on the *Class Analysis Chart,* a picture of the common weaknesses is obtained. This is recommended as a basis for remedial instruction.

Altogether, these manuals provide a complete and practical guide to the use of the battery and, to a lesser degree, to any sub-test.

13. Scoring. The tests may be scored manually or by machine. A column or strip key may be used where a small number of pupils have been tested; a cut-out stencil to fit over the answer sheet is provided for hand or machine scoring. The scoring throughout is on the basis of right answers only.

14 *Op. cit.,* p. 19.

The score on each test is converted to a Scaled Score, the basis of which is not explained in any of the booklets. It is implied that this is a scale of approximately equal units along the whole range of raw scores. It is called simply "the score."

14. Norms. More than fifty thousand pupils — "a carefully selected sampling of pupil attainment in all sections of the country" — constituted the normative population for the entire battery. In Grade 4, 4,691 pupils were tested; in Grade 5, 7,754; in each of Grades 6 through 8, over nine thousand. Schools were carefully chosen on the basis of such factors as size and type of community, socio-economic levels, and geographical location, to constitute a representative sample of the total population. Schools in forty states were included.

Norms are of two types, namely, grade equivalents and percentile rank. The scaled scores mentioned above are converted into either type of norm by means of tables of equivalents. The grade equivalents appear on the profile chart which, very conveniently, is on the back of the pupil's answer sheet. Percentile ranks are determined by use of a Percentile Rank Indicator which fits over the profile chart.

15. Format. The tests and manuals are well printed on good stock in 8½" × 11" booklets. The answer sheets differ somewhat from established patterns and do not appear to meet the best standards. The arrangement by which the computation problems appear on the answer sheet, which, after working, must be matched with a set of answers in the test booklet, is somewhat unusual. The manual states that this arrangement has caused no difficulties in administering the test, however.

Scoring keys are printed on heavy stock. They are not very accurately cut for placement on the answer sheet, and, in general, are somewhat less professional in appearance and workmanship than comparable ones of the same type.

Test accessories, in addition to those already mentioned, include a class record sheet, a normal progress chart (a cumulative attainment record for the individual pupil from Grades 4 to 8), and a score tabulation sheet for making a frequency distribution of scores.

▶ LEARNING EXERCISES ◀

7. There seem to be more standardized tests in arithmetic than in any other subject in the elementary curriculum, except possibly reading. How do you account for this?

8. We have not discussed in this section any so-called diagnostic test in arith-

metic. If you can obtain a specimen set of such a test, examine it carefully, especially the manual. How does it differ from the one described here? What makes a test diagnostic?

Arithmetic Tests

1. *Brief Survey of Arithmetic Skills.* 1947–53. Grades 5–12. *Computation, Reasoning.*
   Forms A and B. $3.15 per 35. 20 (25) minutes.
   The Bobbs-Merrill Company, Inc.

2. *Brueckner Diagnostic Arithmetic Tests.* 1926, 1943. Grades 4–8, 5–8. *Whole Numbers, Fractions, and Decimals,* each in a separate booklet.
   One form. $2.35 per 25. Individual Diagnostic Sheets, $1.85 per 25. 25–30 minutes per test.
   American Guidance Service.

3. *Diagnostic Tests and Self-Helps.* 1955. Grades 3–12. Screening tests in *whole numbers, fractions, decimals,* and *arithmetic,* plus twenty-three tests covering *addition, subtraction, multiplication, division,* and all the major areas (*fractions, decimals, per cent,* etc.) diagnostically, with self-helps on the back of each test.
   One form. $.02 per test; $1.00 per 50. Untimed; complete set would require several hours.
   California Test Bureau.

4. *Functional Evaluation in Mathematics.* 1952. Elementary Level, Grades 4–6; Upper Level, Grades 7–9. *Quantitative Understanding, Problem Solving* and *Basic Computation.*
   One form. $1.35 to $2.45 per 25. (The three areas are in the form of separate tests at each level — six separate tests in all.) 25 (30) minutes.
   American Guidance Service.

5. *Kansas Arithmetic Tests.* Grades 1–3, 3–5, 6–8. *Computation, Reasoning.*
   Forms A and B. $1.20 per 25.
   Bureau of Educational Measurements.

6. *Los Angeles Diagnostic Tests.* 1925–26. Grades 2–8, 3–9.
   Fundamentals of Arithmetic. Grades 2–8. Fundamental operations with *whole numbers, fractions,* and *decimals.*
   Forms 1 and 2. $2.80 per 35. 40 minutes.
   Reasoning in Arithmetic. Grades 3–9. One-Step problems, two-step

problems, *denominate numbers, percentage,* etc. Forms 1 and 2. $2.80 per 35. 30 minutes in Grades 3–5; 40 minutes in Grades 6–9.

California Test Bureau.

7. *Madden-Peak Arithmetic Computation Test.* 1954–57. Grades 7–12. *Fundamental Operations, Fractions, Decimals, Per Cent, Mental Computations,* and *Estimation.*

Forms A and B. $3.80 per 35. 49 minutes.

Harcourt, Brace & World, Inc.

8. *New York Test of Arithmetical Meanings.* 1956. Grades 1.9–3.1. *Pre-Measurement* and *Numerical Concepts.* Two Levels.

One form. Level One, $4.00 per 35. Level Two, $3.30 per 35. 60 minutes.

Harcourt, Brace & World, Inc.

9. *Number Fact Check Test.* 1946. Grades 5–8. *Addition, Subtraction, Multiplication and Division Facts.*

Forms A and B. $.05 per copy, plus $.60 for scoring stencil. 25 minutes.

California Test Bureau.

10. *American School Achievement–Arithmetic Readiness Test.* 1941–55. Kindergarten-Grade one. *Numbers.*

One Form. $4.00 per 35.

The Bobbs-Merrill Company, Inc.

Spelling

The process of spelling seems not to be fully understood from a psychological point of view. It involves memory, sensory-motor functions including vision, hearing, and muscular coordination, intelligence, phonics, and perhaps an indefinable (or at least a not-well-defined) sense of letter and word combinations, to name only the more obvious factors. It is intimately associated with reading and writing, both of which depend in part on the ability to spell and at the same time contribute to this ability. Individuals differ widely in spelling ability within the same grade, the same I.Q. group, and the same age level.

The measurement of spelling ability raises such questions as what words to test, how many, how to choose them, etc. Usually, words for this purpose are chosen from lists such as Thorndike's *The Teacher's Word Book,*[15] a compilation from many sources of words found most frequently

---

[15] E. L. Thorndike, *The Teacher's Word Book* (New York: Bureau of Publications, Teachers College, Columbia University, 1921).

in running discourse, classified by frequency into the first, second, and third thousands, etc., up to ten thousand. Other lists of a similar nature are also available. The assumption is that an educated person's needs in spelling are related to the frequency with which words are found in English usage, and that the more difficult words are found, by and large, in the less frequently occurring groups.

In setting up tests of spelling, a random sample of words or even a dictionary will generally provide a list which covers a wide range of difficulty and frequency of use. The difficulty can be determined by trying out the words with pupils of varying ages and levels of development. After difficulty has been determined, the words are arranged in order of difficulty in what is usually called a *spelling scale*. In testing, the words are presented in this order, proceeding from easiest to hardest. The scale may be segmented so that a list of one hundred words is divided into a number of overlapping groups of perhaps twenty words each, the first twenty constituting the test for the lowest level, those from the eleventh to the thirtieth word, the next level, and so on to the highest level, the eighty-first to the hundredth.

Various methods are employed to make the testing of spelling ability more objective than simply having the person write the word as it is pronounced. One method is to present groups of four or five different words, one of which may be misspelled; another is to present several spellings of the same word, from which the correct one is chosen. A less objective though probably more common practice is to pronounce the word, use it in a sentence, pronounce it again, and then have the pupils write it. For example:

crowd — There was a large *crowd* at the game. — crowd

Since a spelling test was described in the earlier part of this chapter in the discussion of survey tests, and since spelling tests do not occupy a particularly important place among standardized tests and are all essentially the same, at least for the elementary grades, no further detailed description of such tests will be given. The following list may be useful for reference purposes, however.

Spelling Tests

1. *Davis-Schrammel Spelling Test.* 1935. Grades 1–9. Words chosen from well-known sources; twenty words per grade.

Forms A, B, C, D. $.30 per copy of four forms. (None needed by pupils.) Untimed: about 15 minutes per form.

Bureau of Educational Measurements.

2. *The New Iowa Spelling Scale.* Undated. Grades 2–8. Contains 5,507 words chosen from the writings of children and adults or from the Thorndike-Lorge *Teacher's Word Book.* All words are said to be of high social utility.

One form. $.65 per copy.

Bureau of Educational Research and Service.

3. *Lincoln Diagnostic Spelling Tests.* 1942–57. Intermediate, Grades 5–8; Advanced, Grades 9–12. *Pronunciation, Enunciation,* and *Use of Rules in Spelling.*

Forms A and B. $3.15 per 35. 50 minutes.

The Bobbs-Merrill Company, Inc.

4. *Morrison-McCall Spelling Scale.* 1922. Grades 2–8. Eight lists of fifty words each, ranging from easy to difficult.

One form. $.25 per copy. (None needed by pupils.) Untimed (about 15 minutes).

Harcourt, Brace & World, Inc.

▶ LEARNING EXERCISES ◀

9. What is the correlation or relationship between spelling ability and I.Q.? Can you find any reports of studies that throw light on this question?

10. Is it true that some people who seem otherwise competent, in and out of school, have difficulty with spelling? If so, why? Can you find any evidence to support your opinion?

Language Arts

The concept of the language arts generally includes language skills other than reading, handwriting, and spelling, although the latter is often included in tests labeled "language arts." Broadly speaking, the concept may also include oral expression and listening comprehension as expressive and receptive language arts.

Since a conventional test measuring skills in spelling, punctuation, capitalization, phonics, syllabification, usage, dictionary skills, and sentence sense has already been described as part of the *Stanford Achievement Test,* another test of communcation skills will be described below. This is the test of Listening, a part of the *Sequential Tests of Educational Progress* series. This type of test is somewhat different from the usual test of language arts in that it attempts to measure what might be referred to as a receptive skill.

1. Name of tests and authors. *Sequential Tests of Educational Progress: Listening.*[16] Staff of Cooperative Test Division, Educational Testing Service, and national planning committee of educators.

2. Nature and purposes. The purpose of this sub-test of the *STEP* series is to measure developed educational abilities. The tests in the series are intended to measure the ability of students to solve problems requiring the application of knowledge and skills. The Listening test attempts to measure the abilities to remember, comprehend, interpret, evaluate and apply the main ideas, significant details, and meanings of selections read aloud to the students.

3. Grade level. The *STEP* series covers Grades 4 through 13 in four levels. The test described here is Level 4, for Grades 4, 5, and 6.

4. Number of forms. A and B.

5. Publisher and date of publication. Cooperative Test Division, Educational Testing Service. 1957.

6. Cost. $4.00 per 20.

7. Content. The test at each level consists of a series of selections on which multiple-choice items are based. Those in Level 4A include directions, exposition, narration, argument or persuasion, and aesthetic materials.

Sample:

> The old man hurried back to his house, and his mind was
> full of many things. When he suddenly saw a fat, yellow
> cat sitting in his best armchair, he could only stand there
> rubbing his eyes and wondering whose house he was in.

The above is read aloud at a specified rate to the students by the examiner. The student listens. When the selection is finished he answers questions such as the following, which are printed in his test booklet but also read aloud to him:

> When the old man saw the yellow cat in his best armchair,
> how did he feel?
>> A. Pleased
>> B. Surprised
>> C. Sad
>> D. Angry

There are forty multiple-choice items in each of Part One and Part Two.

[16] Quotations in test description by permission of the publisher.

8. Time required. Exact amount of time for the various selections is not specified. However, the entire test requires approximately 90 minutes.

9. Directions for and ease of administering. The directions are detailed and complete. They include preparations for testing, suggestions for handling students with hearing loss, and directions for the actual administering of the test. Since this requires considerable activity on the part of the administrator in reading selections, the directions are somewhat longer than those for a typical standardized achievement test. Practice in reading and administering the test is essential.

10. Validity. The validity of this, as of all tests in the *STEP* series, is strictly content in nature. That is best assured (in the words of the manual, entitled *Technical Report*) "by relying on well-qualified persons in constructing the tests." Validity studies relating test scores to suitable criterion measures are planned. The correlation between scores on the *Listening Test* and total scores on the *School and College Ability Test* at this level is .66.

11. Reliability. Reliability coefficients for Form 4A, Grade 5, determined by the use of the Kuder-Richardson Formula 20, average .93. It is stated that the reliability based on a single grade within a school would probably be about .03 lower.

12. Manual. There are several manuals. There is one entitled *Directions for Administering and Scoring* and one entitled *Manual for Interpreting.* There is a *Teacher's Guide,* which analyzes the test's content and objectives in detail and offers suggestions to the teacher for analyzing test results and using them for further instruction. There is also a *Technical Report,* which describes the planning, constructing, and standardizing of the tests, statistical characteristics, and norming. All are clear and adequate.

13. Scoring. The answers are marked on printed answer sheets, which may be scored by hand or machine. The same scoring stencil is used for both methods. The score is the number of right answers. This is changed to a type of scaled score called a "converted score."

14. Norms. The manuals provide means and standard deviations by sex and grade for each test. Norms are provided for each test and grade in the form of converted scores, a type of standard score, and percentile bands. Norms for Listening are based on approximately one thousand students per grade in schools in thirty-six states over the entire country.

15. Format. The tests are attractively printed in two colors.

▶ **LEARNING EXERCISE** ◀

11. Should speech be included in the language arts? If so, what aspects of this subject could be measured with paper-and-pencil tests? What kinds of measuring techniques would be suitable, for example, in evaluating a debate as a speech activity?

Other Tests of Language Arts

1. .*Essentials of English Test.* 1960. Grades 7–12. *Punctuation, Capitalization, Sentence Structure, Correct Usage.*
Forms A and B. $2.50 per 25. 45 minutes.
American Guidance Service.

2. *Hoyum-Schrammel English Essentials Tests.* 1955–56. Grades 3–4, 5–6, 7–8. *Sentence Recognition, Capitalization, Punctuation, Correct Usage, Alphabetization* (or *Reference Materials*).
Forms A, B, C, D. $1.25 per 25. 40 (50) minutes.
Bureau of Educational Measurements.

3. *Language Skills.* Sub-test of *Iowa Every-Pupil Tests of Basic Skills.* 1943–47. Grades 3–5. *Punctuation, Capitalization, Usage, Spelling, Sentence-Sense.*
Forms L, M, N, O. $3.60 per 35. 46 minutes.
Houghton Mifflin Company.

MEASUREMENT IN SOCIAL STUDIES AND SCIENCE

In addition to the fundamental tool-subjects taught in all elementary grades, there is always some instruction in social studies and, to a growing extent, in natural science. Social studies has long been an important part of the elementary curriculum, but elementary science, as it is understood today, is relatively new — at least under that name. Its predecessor, nature study, had a long period of usefulness, but has now been largely replaced by a more systematic and scientific type of instruction concerned with helping the child to understand the natural world, and giving him an understanding of the methods by which science has advanced and improved human living.

Social Studies

Recent emphases in the social studies have been on (1) world geography and a world point of view, (2) social studies as a means of interpreting the past and understanding current events, (3) citizenship in a democracy, its responsibilities as well as its privileges, and (4) the scientific study of man and his civilization. As in the case of the other subjects already discussed, these trends represent departures from the history and geography that emphasized learning facts about dates, discoveries, battles, boundaries, capitals, seaports, exports, and imports and memorizing speeches, parts of the branches of government, etc. Not that a knowledge of such matters is unimportant; it is, of course, necessary to know facts if one is to learn to think, since facts are the basis of thinking and of ideas. But it is most important that the process does not stop with the learning of facts. To be useful, such learning must proceed to the interpretation, integration, and application of these facts. Of what value is it if a pupil knows many facts about the organization of government, has memorized the Constitution and the Bill of Rights, but fails to vote at elections, or violates one of the articles in the Bill of Rights without ever relating his actions to the meaning of that article?

Present-day textbooks and courses of study reflect the trends listed above to a greater or lesser degree. Certainly no modern textbook in history, geography, or civics ignores them. Today's pupils seem increasingly to get out of the classroom and into the community to see how governments actually work. The greater mobility of our age makes geography and history much more real and meaningful. Standardized tests reflect to some extent the trends in social studies, although tests tend to be somewhat more conservative than the best teaching — a fact that is also true of other areas, as has been noted. The tests to be described as examples are probably typical of many others in the field.[17]

California Tests in Social and Related Sciences: Social Sciences

1. Name of tests and authors. *California Tests in Social and Related Sciences: Social Studies I* and *Social Studies II.*[18] Georgia Sachs Adams and John A. Sexson.

2. Nature and purposes. *Social Studies I* includes Test 1, *The American Heritage,* and Test 2, *People of Other Lands and Times. Social Studies II* includes Test 3, *Geography,* and Test 4, *Basic Social Processes.*

Test 1 deals with (A) Exploration and Colonization of America, (B)

---

[17] The tests reviewed here are reprinted as a *Survey Test in Introductory American History* and a *Survey Test in Geography,* without content change, from appropriate parts of the *California Tests in Social and Related Sciences.* For prices, see the latest catalog of the California Test Bureau.

[18] Quotations in test description by permission of the publisher.

The Westward Movement, (C) Later Development of the Nation, and (D) Understanding of Democracy.

Test 2 deals with (A) People of Other Lands (Latin America, the Orient, and European countries commonly studied in elementary grades), and (B) People of Other Times (early civilizations of China, Egypt, and Greece), with emphasis on their contributions to the culture of today.

Test 3 deals with (A) Geography of the U.S., (B) World Geography, (C) Map Reading and Knowledge of Geographical Terms, and (D) Effects of Geography on the Life of Man.

Test 4 deals with (A) Food, Clothing, and Shelter, (B) Transportation and Communication.

3. Grade level. The Elementary Test is designed for use in Grades 4–8.

4. Forms. AA and BB.

5. Publisher and date. California Test Bureau. 1946–1953.

6. Cost. Part I, Tests 1 and 2, or Part II, Tests 3 and 4: $.08 per copy. $2.80 per 35.

7. Content. Test 1, Section A, consists of twenty-two multiple-choice items.
Sample:

The first president of the United States was

   a Lincoln *b* Washington
   c Jackson *d* Wilson

Test 1, Section B, consists of eight true-false items and twenty multiple-choice items.
Samples:

  Many of the pioneers built small houses
  or shelters on their flat boats.   *T* *F*
   When the pioneers camped at night on their trail to the West, they arranged their wagons in a circle. Their chief reason for doing this was to provide

  a a central place for eating, singing, and dancing
  b better protection against Indians
  c heat from a central fire
  d protection against rain

Test 1, Section C, consists of five true-false items, and fifteen multiple-choice items dealing with the Civil War and more recent events, including World War I.

Test 1, Section D, consists of twelve true-false items, seven multiple-choice items similar to the samples already given, but dealing with democracy and its principles. In addition to these nineteen items, there are six items to be marked "U.S.," if the item is more often found in the United States; "D," if found more often in dictatorships; and "O," if the pupil thinks it is found in neither.

Sample:

> Studying the laws of a city in order to suggest
> improvements _

Test 2, Section A, consists of fourteen true-false and sixteen multiple-choice items dealing with life and conditions in other countries today.

Test 2, Section B, consists of ten true-false and ten multiple-choice items dealing with the civilizations of ancient times and the Middle Ages.

Test 3, Section A, consists of thirty-five multiple-choice items dealing with geography of the United States. The last fifteen items are based on a map of the United States and deal with the location of large cities, certain states, and some important bodies of water.

Test 3, Section B, consists of six true-false and twenty-four multiple-choice items dealing primarily with the geography of regions other than the United States. The last twelve of the multiple-choice items are based on a Mercator projection of the world and test for knowledge of locations of larger cities, certain countries, and bodies of water.

Test 3, Section C, consists of twenty three-response multiple-choice items testing knowledge of terms such as weather, longitude, etc. and the ability to read a map with symbols for capital cities, distances, etc.

Test 3, Section D, consists of twenty three- or four-response multiple-choice items testing knowledge and understanding of the effects of altitude, latitude, etc. on climate, crops, location of cities, etc. The first six items are based on the same map used in Section C.

Test 4, Section A, is made up of eight true-false and twenty multiple-choice items dealing with food, how and where it is grown, and clothing and shelter under different conditions and times.

Test 4, Section B, includes eighteen true-false and fourteen multiple-choice items on transportation and communication in modern times and their importance.

In all, Test 1 consists of twenty-five true-false and sixty-four multiple-choice items; Test 2, of twenty-four true-false and twenty-six multiple-choice items; Test 3, of six true-false and ninety-nine multiple-choice items; Test 4, of twenty-six true-false and thirty-four multiple-choice items.

8. Time required. If answers are marked on test booklets: Test 1, 33 minutes; Test 2, 17 minutes; Test 3, 32 minutes; Test 4, 18 minutes. When "Scoreze" or separate answer sheets are used: Test 1, 40 minutes; Test 2, 20 minutes; Test 3, 38 minutes; Test 4, 22 minutes. These are suggested actual working times; they do not include time for passing out and collecting materials, reading directions, or answering questions.

9. Directions for and ease of administering. Directions are complete and clear.

10. Validity. Evidence of the validity of the tests rests on three bases:

    a. Analysis of courses of study and textbooks for content to be used in making preliminary test items.
    b. Try-out and statistical analysis of preliminary items.
    c. Rating of items by teachers and supervisors as to degree of importance of the information or concept tested.

Items were selected for the tests on the bases of statistical criteria and ratings.

11. Reliability. Reliabilities (Kuder-Richardson) were computed for each of Grades 4–8 and for each part of each test. They are given in terms of correlation coefficients and standard errors of measurement. The reliability coefficients are generally in the .80's, and, in the seventh and eighth grades, mostly in the .90's. Considering the restricted range, the method used for calculating the correlation coefficient, and the standard errors of measurement, these values are quite satisfactory for scores on the four tests. The user is cautioned not to place much reliance on scores on the sub-tests or parts of each test, since their reliabilities are often below the level necessary for use in individual diagnosis.

12. Manual. The manual for the *Tests in Social and Related Sciences* is excellent. It provides the information needed to administer and score the tests and to interpret the results. This includes the completion, on each test booklet, of a diagnostic profile for that pupil, based on the scores on each of twelve parts or sub-tests of the four tests in social science. Suggestions are given in the manual for use of the test results in appraising needs of an entire class or grade and the needs of pupils transferring from another school.

13. Scoring. The tests may be used and scored in three ways. If the pupil marks his answers on the test booklet, the scoring is done by hand with a printed strip scoring key. Machine-scorable answer sheets may be used and scored by machine or by hand. "Scoreze," double carbon-backed answer sheets, are also available for each part of the tests.

The score throughout is the number right. No correction is made for chance, even though true-false and some three-response multiple-choice items are used.

14. Norms. The normative population for the tests came from eleven states in the northern half of the United States. The population was selected to give a median I.Q. of 100 with a standard deviation of 16; 70 per cent of the pupils were making normal progress, 20 per cent were retarded a half year or more, and 10 per cent were accelerated a half year or more. About 85 per cent were white and the remainder consisted of Mexicans, Negroes, and members of other minority groups.

Percentile norms are provided for each sub-test or part of the four tests in Social Science. There are also grade equivalents and age norms for each of the four tests.

15. Format. The physical appearance, printing, arrangement, and general organization of these tests leave little to be desired. The booklets are attractive and convenient in size. Accessories include a class record sheet.

▶ **LEARNING EXERCISES** ◀

12. Good citizenship is a generally accepted goal of social studies instruction. Do you know of, or can you find, any tests of citizenship? If so, describe them.

13. Describe several different approaches to the evaluation of international understanding.

Other Tests in Social Studies

1. *Emporia Geography Test.* 1937. Grades 4–7. Part I: Knowledge of *U.S. geography,* tested by reference to a map. Part II: Sixty true-false items on *world geography.* Part III: Forty multiple-choice items on *world geography.*
Forms A and B. $1.20 per 25. 30 minutes.
Bureau of Educational Measurement.

2. *Emporia United States History Tests.* 1937. Test I, Grades 5 and 6; Test II, Grades 7 and 8. Test I consists of thirty-four true false and twenty-six multiple-choice items in *U.S. history.* Test II consists of sixty-

four true-false, twenty-five multiple-choice, a set of twenty-six matching, and five *historical sequence* items.

Forms A and B. $1.20 per 25. 40 minutes.

Bureau of Educational Measurement.

3. *Greig Social Studies Test.* 1957. Grades 6–8.

One Form. $3.20 per 35. 40 (50) minutes.

Scholastic Testing Service.

Natural Science

Since elementary science is comparatively new and not completely established in the curriculum, few standardized tests have been developed. This is not entirely surprising, for not all elementary schools offer science; it is not widely taught in every grade, or as a regular subject where it is taught. Rather, it is still offered in many schools on an incidental and irregular basis. Under such conditions, it is very difficult to develop tests that will meet with the approval and fit the needs of many teachers. The content must be either quite general and therefore weak, or extremely limited, in order to satisfy any substantial number of situations. Nevertheless, a few standardized tests are on the market. Most of them are subtests or tests drawn from parts of elementary batteries, but a few are published independently. Part III of the *California Test in Social and Related Sciences* is described below.[19] Parts I and II have been described in the preceding section.

California Tests in Social and Related Sciences: Related Sciences

1. Name of tests and authors. *California Tests in Social and Related Sciences.*[20] Georgia Sachs Adams and John A. Sexson.

2. Nature and purposes. *Related Sciences* includes Test 5, *Health and Safety,* and Test 6, *Elementary Science.*

Test 5 deals with (A) Eating for Health, (B) Other Health Information, and (C) Safety Information.

Test 6 deals with (A) The World About Us and (B) Man's Conquest of Nature.

3. Grade level. The Elementary Test is designed for use in Grades 4–8.

[19] The tests reviewed here are reprinted as a *Survey Test in Introductory Science,* a *Survey Test in Physical Science,* and a *Survey Test in Biological Science,* without content change, from appropriate parts of the *California Tests in Social and Related Sciences.* For prices, see the latest catalog of the California Test Bureau.

[20] Quotations in test description by permission of the publisher.

4. Forms. AA and BB.

5. Publisher and date. California Test Bureau. 1946–1953.

6. Cost. Test booklets, $2.80 per 35.

7. Content. Test 5, Section A, consists of nine true-false and sixteen multiple-choice items.

Samples:

A camel makes long journeys on the
desert without stopping for water.　　*T*　　*F*
One of the best sources of calcium is

　　a white bread　　　*b* milk
　　c oatmeal　　　　 *d* raisins

Test 5, Section B, includes thirteen true-false and seventeen multiple-choice items dealing with teeth, disease, health habits, alcohol, and tobacco.

Test 5, Section C, consists of thirteen true-false and seven multiple-choice items dealing with safety practices and first aid.

Test 6, Section A, consists of fifteen true-false and twenty-five multiple-choice items measuring knowledge and understanding about plant and animal life and the solar system.

Test 6, Section B, is made up of ten true-false and fifteen multiple-choice items concerned with man's early efforts to control nature and modern means of conserving and developing resources and power.

8. Time required. If answers are marked on test booklets: Test 5, 21 minutes; Test 6, 19 minutes. If "Scoreze" or separate answer sheets are used: Test 5, 27 minutes; Test 6, 23 minutes. These suggested times are actual working times only.

9. Directions for and ease of administering. Directions are complete and clear.

10. Validity. As discussed under *Social Sciences* test, page 234.

11. Reliability. See page 234.

12. Manual. See page 234.

13. Scoring. See page 234.

14. Norms. See page 235.

15. Format. See page 235.

▶ LEARNING EXERCISES ◀

14. There are few standardized tests of elementary science. How do you account for this?

15. Can children in the primary grades learn to solve problems by use of the scientific method? If your answer is "yes," give some examples. If "no," justify your answer. How would you test for this?

Other Tests in Elementary Science

1. *Metropolitan Science Tests.* 1959. Grades 5–9. *Science Information, Generalizations,* and *Understandings.* Intermediate and Advanced.
Forms AM, BM, CM. $4.00 per 35. 20 minutes.
Harcourt, Brace & World, Inc.

2. *Sequential Tests of Educational Progress: Science.* 1957. Grades 4–6. *Applications of Scientific Knowledge.*
Forms A and B. $4.00 per 20. 70 minutes.
Educational Testing Service.

ANNOTATED BIBLIOGRAPHY

1. Buros, Oscar K. (ed.). *The Sixth Mental Measurements Yearbook.* Highland Park, N.J.: The Gryphon Press, 1965. (See also earlier editions of the *Mental Measurements Yearbook.*) The most complete and useful review of measuring instruments and books on measurement in education and psychology. The reviews give factual information as well as criticisms. Reviews in earlier editions are cited in each of the subsequent *Yearbooks.*

2. Buros, Oscar K. *Tests in Print.* Highland Park, N.J.: The Gryphon Press, 1961. This volume provides a comprehensive test bibliography and index of tests published in English-speaking countries. Titles, examinees and levels, publication dates, number of scores, authors, publishers, foreign adaptations, and pertinent special comments are given for each entry. In addition, cross references within the volume and also to the *Mental Measurements Yearbooks* are included. The entries are classified by purpose of the test or subject matter tested.

3. Committee on Test Standards, American Educational Research Association, National Education Association, and the National Council on Measurements Used in Education. *Technical Recommendations for Achievement Tests.* Washington: The NEA, 1955. An authoritative statement concerning the kinds of information test manuals should supply. Written primarily with test authors and publishers in mind, but a useful reference for students.

4. Greene, Harry A.; Jorgensen, Albert N.; and Gerberich, J. Raymond. *Measurement and Evaluation in the Elementary School*, Second Edition. New York: David McKay Co., Inc., 1953. Chapters 15–22. A complete discussion of achievement tests for elementary schools. Approximately one-third of the volume is devoted to a discussion of objectives and measurement procedures in each of the common branches of instruction. Reference is made almost wholly to published, standardized tests and the problems of developing such instruments in each subject.

5. Jordan, A. M. *Measurement in Education*. New York: McGraw-Hill Book Co., Inc., 1953. Chapters 5–13. Contains nine chapters dealing with measurement in reading, spelling and handwriting, language and literature, social sciences, foreign languages, mathematics, science, business education, fine arts, manual arts, physical education, and health, respectively. Each chapter discusses objectives and describes tests for elementary grades and high schools in each of the respective fields.

6. National Society for the Study of Education. *The Measurement of Understanding*, Forty-Fifth Yearbook, Part I. Chicago, Ill.: The Society (distributed by the University of Chicago Press), 1946. 338 pp. Describes and gives excerpts from many standardized tests in social studies, science, mathematics, language arts, fine arts, health education, physical education, home economics, agriculture, technical education, and industrial arts. Also gives many helpful suggestions for the improvement of locally made tests in these areas.

7. Torgerson, Theodore L., and Adams, Georgia Sachs. *Measurement and Evaluation for the Elementary School Teacher*. New York: Holt, Rinehart & Winston, Inc., 1954. Chapters 11–16. These six chapters deal with measurement in reading, oral and written communication, handwriting and spelling, arithmetic, social studies and science, and fine arts at the elementary grade level. In each area there is a discussion of methods of teaching and diagnosis and a discussion of methods of measurement and evaluation.

8. Wrightstone, J. Wayne, Justman, Joseph, and Robbins, Irving. *Evaluation in Modern Education*. New York: American Book Company, 1956. Although this book is devoted mainly to evaluative procedures, it contains one chapter dealing very briefly with the measurement of achievement in social studies, natural sciences, music and art, foreign languages, and industrial arts and business education, and one devoted to measurement in language arts and mathematics.

See also catalogs of the test publishers listed in Appendix C.

9

Measuring Achievement in the

Secondary Grades

The problems of producing standardized achievement tests for secondary school classes are somewhat different from those encountered by the maker of tests for the elementary grades. In the first place, there is not such a well-established core in the high school program as there is at the elementary level. The most common areas of study in high school are English, social studies, science, and mathematics. Almost all high school pupils take courses in English and social studies, but content and emphases vary widely. For instance, social studies courses may include anything from civics to ancient history and may be taught in a year's time or over a period of four years.

Prior to Sputnik it could be said that perhaps half the secondary school population took some kind of a course in science before graduation, usually as an elective, and a similar situation held in the field of mathematics. Many graduated from high school without having taken any mathematics at all in the secondary grades. During the past decade the situation has changed. There is today a greatly increased emphasis on science and mathematics in secondary schools, largely as a reflection of a drive for more technically trained persons but also as a result of a reaction against so-called "Mickey Mouse" courses.

No other academic subjects in the high school curriculum are as common as those mentioned, yet there is a great variety of other subjects offered in most schools; all of these subjects provide an opportunity to produce many different tests. Nor does the diversity in high school subject areas end with the names of courses; it extends also to objectives and content. Here again, there is a contrast with the situation in the elementary grades, where objectives and content are much more standardized. An extreme example of such diversity in secondary school subjects is in the field of literature, where it is practically impossible to construct a test whose content will satisfy all or a majority of English teachers. In varying degrees, this same principle applies in other subject-matter areas.

Makers of achievement tests for the secondary grades usually attempt to solve this problem in one or both of two ways. The first and more usual practice is to base the tests on the common essentials as determined by an analysis of leading textbooks and courses of study, putting into the tests only such content and skills as are found in all or nearly all such curricular material. The second approach is to make a test that measures the ability to use the knowledge and skills learned, rather than just knowledge and skills, per se. A test of this sort might include measures of a wide variety of objectives besides knowledge, such as study skills, or the ability to apply or interpret knowledge.

While no sharp line of demarcation can be drawn to identify all current standardized tests with one type or the other, the tendency is away from the currently predominant first type, and toward the second, which may be called the functional approach. Most modern tests for high school subjects lean in this direction, though they nearly always have a definite content orientation as well. This combination is certainly not undesirable and is probably necessary, for it is difficult to conceive of anyone interpreting and applying knowledge which he does not possess. On the other hand, it seems entirely reasonable to assume that if one is successful on a test of applications, one would also do well on a test of knowledge. Both types of objectives are valuable, and an ideal test should measure both.

Time is another factor which complicates the situation for the maker and user of standardized tests in high schools. The elementary school program is much more flexible in this respect than that of the high school. Usually, the elementary teacher remains all day in the same room with the same pupils, and if she wishes to devote several hours of one day to a particular activity, whether this be testing, classwork, or a field trip, the matter of scheduling presents no serious problems. There are no fixed periods and no rigid schedules; generally speaking, no other teachers must be consulted about a change in procedure for the day. The high school program, on the other hand, is nearly always on a fixed schedule of class periods, averaging perhaps forty-five minutes in length. To detain a given group or class for more than one period for testing or other reasons on any given day nearly always requires consultation with others, adjustments in schedules, and approval of arrangements by several persons. As a result, high school tests sometimes seem to be constructed to fit a time schedule rather than to adequately measure important instructional goals. Most batteries, of course, are designed so that they can be given in several sittings, and this arrangement makes possible adherence to a school schedule and yet provides reasonably adequate measurement in each subject.

Finally, since there is such a wide variety of individual study patterns and subjects in the high school, most standardized achievement tests must include items covering a wide range of difficulty and content in order to satisfy a majority. To formulate a test which is inclusive and which samples an area adequately poses difficult problems for those who construct or use standardized tests at the secondary level. The situation is reflected by high school teachers in their most frequently voiced criticism of standardized tests, namely, that "they don't measure what I teach."[1]

In this chapter, as in the preceding one, the study of the types of achievement tests will depend principally on prototypes or examples. There are so many standardized tests for high school subjects, especially in the common or core subjects, that it would be impossible to describe and discuss even a substantial proportion of them in a volume such as this. However, lists of tests will be found at the end of each section, briefly noting such matters as date of publication, cost, content, publisher, number of forms, and time required.

Survey batteries are discussed in the first section, then tests in the specific subject areas of English, social studies, science, and mathematics. The annotated bibliography at the end of the chapter lists a number of books which include discussions and descriptions of tests in many other fields.

SURVEY BATTERIES

The problems that have just been discussed are of particular importance to teachers and to those who construct survey batteries for use in the high school grades. The variety of courses, the fixed schedules, and the wide

[1] Victor H. Noll and Walter N. Durost, *Measurement Practices and Preferences of High School Teachers,* Test Service Notebook No. 8 (New York: Harcourt, Brace & World, Inc., n.d.).

range in content and difficulty all affect the survey battery even more than they affect a test in a single subject, and these factors provoke such questions as the following: To which fields or subject-matter areas should such a battery be confined? How extensively can the battery sample each area, and how simple must some of the exercises be in order that every pupil may find something at which he can succeed? How wide an area can the battery cover before it becomes so thin and superficial that its users will have no confidence in it? Above all, how can an adequate job of measurement be done in a time short enough to enable schools to use the instrument?

The authors of most high school survey batteries meet these questions and situations by confining the tests to the subjects of English, social studies, science, and mathematics. When they venture beyond these areas of knowledge, it is usually to measure interpretive and applicative abilities related to the content areas. Also, test authors usually attempt to include a wide enough range of difficulty in each subject to measure achievement of those pupils who have had from one to eight or more semesters in that area. As a result, the tests are sometimes too difficult for the beginners, or too easy for the bright twelfth-graders.

While conditions and needs at the secondary level vary greatly, they have enough in common to make the survey battery useful for certain purposes. As a measure of a pupil's basic orientation in the broad fields already mentioned, the survey battery is rapid and fairly accurate. Obviously, it does not give adequate measurement in any one subject such as American history or trigonometry. Yet it does reveal inequalities in a pupil's background and achievement among the fields covered and provides a basis for comparison of the achievement of individuals and groups with that of other secondary school pupils. The survey battery is also a useful tool for the guidance worker seeking to assist pupils in making decisions about courses and curriculums. It should be remembered that test batteries differentiate only roughly and should always be used with full regard for their limitations and in conjunction with other more sensitive measuring instruments.

Iowa Tests in Educational Development

The high school survey battery to be described here as an example was first published in 1942. In this first edition, the tests were rented and not sold, and no separate forms of the individual tests were available. This service, which is still available at $1.25 per test includes scoring, tabulating, and analysis of results. The tests were revised in 1952 and have since been available for purchase both as a complete set in one booklet, which is scored by the publisher, and as separate booklets, one for each of the nine sub-tests. The separate booklets are scored manually by the user.

This survey battery represents an outstanding example of an attempt to use the functional rather than the content-centered approach. Other survey batteries for high school use, some of equal quality, are listed at the end of this section.

1. Names of tests and authors. *Iowa Tests of Educational Development.*[2] E. F. Lindquist and L. S. Feldt, General Editors. Test 1: *Understanding of Basic Social Concepts,* J. W. Maucker. Test 2: *General Background in the Natural Sciences,* Robert L. Ebel. Test 3: *Correctness and Appropriateness of Expression,* John Gerber. Test 4: *Ability to Do Quantitative Thinking,* Paul Blommers. Test 5: *Interpretation of Reading Materials in the Social Studies,* K. W. Vaughn. Test 6: *Interpretation of Reading Materials in the Natural Sciences,* K. W. Vaughn. Test 7: *Interpretation of Literary Materials,* Julia Peterson. Test 8: *General Vocabulary,* K. W. Vaughn. Test 9: *Use of Sources of Information,* K. W. Vaughn. All authors are now or were formerly associated with the State University of Iowa.

2. Nature and purposes. The general manual for the battery states:

> These tests are not based on an analysis of individual high school subjects. Rather, they are designed to measure relatively broad and generalized intellectual skills and abilities that are continuously developed in every student throughout all of the years that he is in school. This design makes the tests appropriate for administration to all high school students in all grades regardless of the subjects they are taking.
>
> The battery as a whole is concerned not so much with what the student *knows* as with what he can *do.* The student's performance on these tests indicates not only how much he has accomplished to date, but also how much he can profit from further instruction, or how well he is prepared to continue his own education. The major purposes of the Iowa Tests are:
>
> First, *to enable teachers and counselors to keep themselves more intimately and reliably acquainted with the educational development of each high school student.* Such knowledge makes it easier to adapt instruction and guidance to each student's peculiar and changing needs.
>
> Second, *to provide the school administrator with a more dependable and objective basis for evaluating the total educational offering of the school.* The test results point up any need for curriculum revision that may exist. They also facilitate a wiser distribution of supervisory efforts.

3. Grade level. The manual states that the battery is designed for Grades 9–12, though the tests probably have enough range to make them usable with college freshmen.

[2] Quotations in test description by permission of the publisher.

4. Number of forms. Forms X-35 and Y-35. Each test in each form may be used as the "full length version" with the longer time limit. A smaller number of items of the same test, marked off by a line of stars, may be used as a "class period version" with a 40-minute time limit.

5. Publisher and date of publication. Science Research Associates, Inc., 1957.

6. Cost. (*a*) Each test, 1–9:

20 test booklets	$2.40
100 hand- or machine-scoring answer sheets	5.00
Complete specimen set	3.00
Specimen of each test	.50

(*b*) Single booklet containing all tests and including scoring service: $1.25 per pupil.

7. Content. Test 1, *Understanding of Basic Social Concepts.* Consists of ninety multiple-choice items, "designed to measure general knowledge and understanding of contemporary social institutions and practices."
Sample item:

What is meant by a "left wing" political party?

    a. A party which has recently been defeated
    b. A party which wants to make rapid changes
    c. A party which has only a few members
    d. A party which makes a lot of noise but
       has no real power

Actual working time on Test 1, full-length version, 55 minutes; class-period version, 40 minutes. This does not include time for passing out booklets, reading directions, etc.

Test 2, *General Background in the Natural Sciences.* Consists of ninety multiple-choice items, "designed to measure general knowledge of scientific terms and principles, of common natural phenomena and industrial applications, and of the place of science in modern civilization."
Sample item:

What determines how much heat is used in changing a solid metal ball into liquid metal?

    a. Only the size of the ball
    b. Only the material from which the ball is made
    c. Both the size and the material
    d. The size, the material, and the temperature of
       the applied heat

Actual working time on Test 2, full-length version, 60 minutes; class-period version, 40 minutes.

Test 3, *Correctness and Appropriateness of Expression.* Part I consists of a letter and three prose selections, each containing errors of capitalization, punctuation, and usage and inappropriate expressions. The pupil is to identify these and indicate how each may be corrected or improved. There are eighty-eight items in this part.

Sample item:

He would not be able to see *nothing.*
> *a.* no change
> *b.* nowhere
> *c.* anything

Part II consists of fifteen spelling items.
Sample item:

> *a.* laboratory
> *b.* petroleum
> *c.* advertisement
> *d.* miscellaneous
> *e.* none wrong

Actual working time on Test 3, full-length version, 60 minutes; class-period version, 40 minutes.

Test 4, *Ability to Do Quantitative Thinking.* Consists of fifty-three problem situations in the form of multiple-choice items. "The criterion applied in the selection of the problem situations was that the typical man-on-the-street would readily agree that each of the problems was a very *practical* one which *every* high school graduate should be able to solve."

Sample item:

A home worth $10,000 is insured by an ordinary fire insurance policy for $6,000. It is damaged by fire to the extent of $2,000. How much insurance should the company pay the owner?

> *a.* The amount of the policy, $6,000
> *b.* Three-fifths of the damage, $1,500
> *c.* The amount of the damage, $2,000
> *d.* The value of the home, $10,000
> *e.* Correct answer not given above.

Actual working time on Test 4, full-length version, 65 minutes; class-period version, 40 minutes.

Test 5, *Interpretation of Reading Materials in the Social Studies.* Consists of eighty multiple-choice items intended to measure the "ability to interpret and evaluate reading selections taken from social studies textbooks and references, from mazagine and newspaper articles on social problems, and from the literature of the social studies in general." This includes the ability to understand what is stated and what is implied in a selection and the ability to evaluate it critically.

Sample item (following a paragraph on social insurance):

> With what social issue is this paragraph concerned?
>
> > *a.* Should there be government ownership of life insurance companies?
> > *b.* Should the government make life insurance compulsory?
> > *c.* Should the government be responsible for the economic security of its citizens?
> > *d.* Should the government make it easier to effect reforms?

Actual working time on Test 5, full-length version, 60 minutes; class-period version, 40 minutes.

Test 6, *Interpretation of Reading Materials in the Natural Sciences.* This test measures the ability to interpret and evaluate reading materials "selected from textbooks and references used in the natural sciences, from scientific articles in newspapers and periodicals, and from relatively non-technical or popular and semi-popular scientific literature in general." The test consists of eighty multiple-choice items.

Sample item (following a selection of approximately 450 words dealing with mimicry in animals and plants):

> Which of the following may we infer is especially favorable to the development of mimetic resemblances in insects?
>
> > *a.* The effect of similar functions
> > *b.* Bright coloration
> > *c.* Small size
> > *d.* Short life

Actual working time on Test 6, full-length version, 60 minutes; class-period version, 40 minutes.

Test 7, *Interpretation of Literary Materials.* This test is intended to measure "most of the measurable understandings that high school students derive from the reading of literary materials." Included are such elements as understanding of detail, comprehension of characterization, recognition of mood, tone, emotion, writer's purpose or viewpoint, imagery, figures of speech, grasp of main thought(s) of a passage, and awareness of outstanding qualities of style or structure. The test does not purport to measure appreciation or literary worth, which are subjective and vary from reader to reader.

The test consists of eight selections of prose and three of poetry, on which eighty multiple-choice items are based.

Sample item:

> Loveliest of trees, the cherry now
> Is hung with bloom along the bough,
> And stands about the woodland ride
> Wearing white for Eastertide.

What feeling does the poet express in this passage?

> *a.* Delight in beauty
> *b.* Religious faith
> *c.* Fear of death
> *d.* Enjoyment of old age

Actual working time on Test 7, full-length version, 50 minutes; class-period version, 40 minutes.

Test 8, *General Vocabulary.* The test is intended to measure (1) general aptitude for school work and (2) recognition of word meaning. Ninety per cent of the words were selected from the *Thorndike Century Senior Dictionary* basic list of twenty thousand words. The remainder are in this dictionary but not in the list. The test consists of seventy-five multiple-choice items of which the following is a sample:

	a. formal
Its *ornate* exterior	*c.* plain
	b. highly decorated
	d. bleak

Actual working time on Test 8, 22 minutes.

Test 9, *Use of Sources of Information.* The purpose of this test "is to evaluate the student's ability to utilize the important sources of information available to high school students, or his ability to turn to the source of information which is most likely to contain the solution to a particular problem." Specific objectives measured include:

(1) Knowledge of the best procedures for turning to sources of information; (2) knowledge of the purposes and nature of particular sources of information; (3) knowledge of the specific contents of the more common sources of information, such as dictionaries, encyclopedias, and yearbooks; (4) ability to interpret bibliographical references; and (5) ability to use a card index efficiently.

The test consists of sixty multiple-choice items, such as the following:

Where would you look to find the location of Orange County, Indiana?
   a. In an encyclopedia.
   b. In an atlas.
   c. On a globe.
   d. In a gazetteer.

Actual working time on Test 9, 27 minutes.

8. Time required. It is recommended that the full-length version be administered in four half-day sessions of approximately two and one half hours each, a total time of about ten hours. This includes time for distribution of booklets, instructions, breaks, and the collection and checking of materials. The recommended sequence is Tests 1 and 4, Tests 2 and 5, Tests 7, 8, and 6; and Tests 3 and 9. The class-period version should also be given in four sittings in the following sequence: Tests 8, 1, and 4; Tests 2 and 5; Tests 7 and 6; and Tests 3 and 9. The total time is about six hours.

9. Directions for and ease of administering. The tests are easily administered. All are preceded by a sample item marked on the answer sheet, so that the pupil can see one question answered and marked correctly. The directions for administering each test are clear and complete and include all necessary details regarding room requirements, materials needed, use of answer sheets, proctors, and timing. There are no subparts requiring separate timing in any test.

10. Validity. A large number of items were prepared for each test and, on the basis of preliminary tryouts on 3,500 pupils in eight Iowa high schools, the discriminating power and difficulty of each item were determined.

Correlations between scholarship average in the first year of college and four measures, including composite score on the *ITED,* were calculated for 282 Iowa high school seniors who took the tests in 1946 and the next fall entered one of the three state institutions for higher education in Iowa. The correlations were as follows:

High school grade point average
   with college freshmen average 61
Percentile rank in high school graduating class
   with college freshmen average 58
Composite score on *ITED* at entrance to ninth grade
   with college freshmen average 57
Composite score on *ITED* at entrance to twelfth grade
   with college freshmen average . . . . , ...62

Thus it appears that the results of the *ITED* are as good predictors of success in first-year college, as measured by marks, as the record of four years in high school.

The average of the correlations between each of the nine tests and each of the other eight, and the composite, is .71. This seems to suggest that the nine tests are measuring substantially the same things, though the manual states that this coefficient "constitutes objective and conclusive evidence that the various tests in the Iowa battery really do measure different things."

Finally, it is stated that the ultimate test of validity is whether or not the tests measure what the prospective user considers to be desirable outcomes of a program of general education. It is suggested that he take the tests and then decide for himself whether they are valid or not. In a sense, this implies either that the majority, at least, would have substantially the same ideas of desirable outcomes, or that the tests can be all things to all men. The former seems clearly the only practical alternative.

11. Reliability. Reliability coefficients based on correlations between split-halves (odd-even items) corrected by the *Spearman-Brown Formula* are reported in the form of the average coefficients for separate grade groups within each school. This tends to restrict the variability or range and lower the coefficients. Nevertheless, all the average reliability coefficients are between .81 and .94. Most are in the neighborhood of .88 to .92, which is quite satisfactory. The probable error of measurement of a single standard score is reported as one point.

12. Manuals. There is a general manual for the entire battery giving information on development and standardization, and other important facts about the tests. There is also a *General Manual* for the separate booklet edition, which includes a discussion of purposes; directions for administering; descriptions of the individual tests; directions for organizing, reporting, and interpreting test results; and 1962 norms. An *Examiner's Manual,* which includes directions for administering and scoring the separate booklet edition, is also available. Finally, there is a separate manual entitled *Using the Iowa Tests of Educational Development for College Planning.*

13. Scoring. The tests may be scored manually or by machine. All items are multiple-choice in form and scoring is entirely objective. There is no correction for chance, the score on each test being the number right.

Scores on each of the nine tests can be converted into standard scores based on the same standard scale. The standard scores are said to be comparable from grade to grade, providing that the tests are administered at the same time each year.

14. Norms. The present norms were based on the scores of approximately sixty thousand high school students tested in September, 1962. These students were enrolled in 136 schools constituting a national stratified sample. No other data on the nature of the sample are given. Norms are expressed in standard scores and percentile ranks. The raw score on each test may be converted to a standard score, which in turn may be converted to a percentile rank. It is recommended that the standard scores be used to measure growth from one testing to the next but that percentile norms be used for comparisons between tests. A composite standard score based on tests 1–8 inclusive may also be determined from the sum of the standard scores on the separate tests. The percentile rank equivalents of the composite standard scores may also be compared with the percentile ranks on the individual tests. Profile charts are provided, which are usable both for individuals and for school averages.

15. Format. The material and workmanship of the *Iowa Tests of Educational Development* are of high quality. The tests are expensive in comparison with similar survey batteries, however — especially in the separate-booklet edition — which may tend to restrict their use.

Other Survey Batteries

1. *California* (formerly *Progressive*) *Achievement Tests.* Grades 7–9, 9–14.
Junior High School and Advanced Batteries. 1957. *Reading Vocabulary, Reading Comprehension, Arithmetical Reasoning, Arithmetic Fundamentals, Mechanics of English and Grammar, Spelling.* Forms W, X, Y, and Z. $6.65 per 35; $.50 per specimen set; approximately 3 hours.
California Test Bureau.

2. *Cooperative General Achievement Tests,* Revised Series. Grades 9–13. 1947–51. Separate tests of *Social Studies, Natural Sciences,* and *Mathematics;* Forms XX and YZ, $4.00 per 25; $1.00 per specimen set. 40 (45) minutes.
Educational Testing Service.

3. *Essential High School Content Battery.* Grades 10–12. 1950. *Mathematics, Science, Social Studies,* and *Language and Literature.* Forms Aм, Bм, $9.90 per 35; $.60 per specimen set. 205 (225) minutes.
Harcourt, Brace & World, Inc.

4. *Metropolitan Achievement Tests: High School Battery.* 1962. Grades 9–12. *Reading, Spelling, Language, Language Study Skills, Social Studies Study Skills, Social Studies Vocabulary and Information, Mathematical*

Computation and Concepts, Mathematical Analysis and Problem Solving, Scientific Concepts, Understandings and Information.

Forms Aᴍ and Bᴍ. $10.50 per 35. $1.00 per specimen set. 5 hours, 15 minutes.

Harcourt, Brace & World, Inc.

5. *Sequential Tests of Educational Progress,* 1956–57. Grades 10–12, 13–14. *Reading, Writing, Listening, Essay Test, Mathematics, Science, Social Studies.*

Forms A and B. $4.00 per 20 of each subject test except Essay, $1.00 per 20. 70 minutes (two 35-minute units) for each test except Essay, 35 minutes complete. Specimen set, complete, $5.00.

Educational Testing Service.

6. *Tests of Academic Progress.* Grades 9–12. 1963. *Social Studies, Composition, Science, Reading, Mathematics, Literature.*

Forms 1 and 2. $.84 per booklet containing the six tests. $2.25 per specimen set. 5 hours, 30 minutes.

Houghton Mifflin Company.

ACHIEVEMENT TESTS IN SPECIFIC SUBJECTS

English

Many standardized tests in English are available for junior and senior high school grades. There are tests in the fundamentals of English grammar, sentence structure, capitalization, and punctuation; tests to measure knowledge and appreciation of literature; scales to measure composition or writing ability; and tests of vocabulary and spelling ability. As before, only one test will be described in detail as an example in its field, but others will be listed for reference. This list is not complete or exhaustive, but it includes representative examples of the variety of tests available in this broad field.

Cooperative English Test

1. Name of test and authors. *Cooperative English Tests.*[3] Authors: Clarence Derrick, David P. Harris, and Biron Walker.

2. Nature and purposes. These tests are designed to measure compe-

---

[3] Quotations in test description from *Cooperative English Tests* by Clarence Derrick, David P. Harris, and Biron Walker. Copyright © 1960 by Educational Testing Service. Reprinted by special permission of the Educational Testing Service.

tence in reading and written expression. *Reading Comprehension* includes a test of *vocabulary* and one measuring *speed and comprehension. English Expression* includes a test of *effectiveness* and a test of *mechanics of written expression.*

3. Grade level. Level 1 is for college freshmen and sophomores. Level 2 is for grades 9 through 12.

4. Number of forms. Forms 1A, 1B, and 1C for college students. Forms 2A, 2B, and 2C for high school students.

5. Publisher and date of publication. Cooperative Test Division, Educational Testing Service. 1960.

6. Cost. Separate booklets, *Reading Comprehension* and *English Expression,* $4.00 per 20 of each. Single booklet edition, $6.00 per 20. Answer sheets, $1.00 per 20 (either IBM or SCRIBE). Scoring stencils for IBM answer sheets, $.25.

7. Content. Test 1, *Reading Comprehension, Part I: Vocabulary,* consists of sixty multiple-choice items such as:

Boast

A sew	C brag
B suffer	D lift

Part II: Reading, consists of sixty multiple-choice items based on selected reading passages. The score on the first thirty items is called Level of Comprehension, since experience has shown that most students have time to try all of them. The score on all sixty items is called Speed of Comprehension since it depends on speed as well as accuracy of performance.

Test 2, *English Expression, Part I: Effectiveness,* consists of thirty items testing the ability to recognize and select the word or phrase which precisely conveys the intended meaning of a sentence.

Example:

As far as his spending of money is concerned, his acquaintances consider him (   ).

A shabby	C stingy
B ignoble	D contemptible

Part II: Mechanics, consists of sixty items testing the ability to recognize errors in usage, spelling, punctuation, and capitalization.

Examples:

A When all the marks were
B added together, his standing   A B C O
C was forth in the class   O O O O

The letter "C" is marked on the answer sheet.

E He had not known
F that she lived in   E F G O
G Topeka, Kansas   O O O O

Here the fourth space, "O", is marked to indicate no error.

8. Time required. Test 1, *Reading Comprehension, Part I: Vocabulary,* 15 minutes; *Part II: Reading* (Level of Comprehension and Speed of Comprehension combined), 25 minutes.

Test 2, *English Expression, Part I: Effectiveness,* 15 minutes; *Part II: Mechanics,* 25 minutes.

9. Directions for and ease of administering. Directions are concise and clear. Tests are simple and easy to administer, with a minimum of participation by the examiner.

10. Validity. Evidence for the validity of the *Cooperative English Tests* is of two kinds. First, is content validity. The tests were constructed and reviewed by an impressive group of experts in English and technicians on the staff of Educational Testing Service. Data from the use of millions of earlier forms of the tests provided an experiential basis for revision of both content and organization. Second, a substantial number of studies of the predictive value of earlier forms of the tests have been carried out and repeated. These studies, generally conducted at the college-freshman level, have shown low to moderate correlations between scores on the tests and such criteria as grades in English, grade-point average, and teachers' ratings. On the whole, the evidence for the validity of these tests, while relying in part on data accumulated through the use of earlier editions, is quite satisfactory.

11. Reliability. Alternate form reliability coefficients for the sub-tests of *Reading* based on combined groups of schools range from .71 to .89, with a median of approximately .83. The coefficients for total score on *Reading* range from .91 to .94. Standard errors of measurement range from 2.64 to 6.18 with a median of approximately 4. Alternate form reliabilities for *English Expression,* total scores, range from .81 to .86 with standard errors of measurement of about 4. Standard errors are in converted-score units. It is estimated that the reliability coefficients are from .03 to .10 higher than if they were based on cases within one average school. Although alternate form reliability coefficients are usually lower than corrected split-half coefficients, those reported here, particularly for part scores on Test 1 and total scores on Test 2 leave something to be desired.

12. Manual. The manuals for the *Cooperative English Tests* are excellent. There is one entitled *Directions for Administering and Scoring,* one called *Interpreting Scores,* and a *Technical Report.* Each is complete for its purpose. There is also a form called the *Student Report Profile.*

13. Scoring. Two types of answer sheets may be used with these tests, namely, standard IBM 805's and the ETS SCRIBE. The former may, of course, be hand- or machine-scored. The SCRIBE is the ETS version of the new electronic scoring process which does not require an electrographic or mark-sensing pencil and which is much faster and more complete than the standard IBM process.

14. Norms. Raw scores are converted to standard scores, with a mean of 150 and a standard deviation of 10 for the eleventh-grade population. Percentile rank equivalents for "converted scores" are also provided. A new feature, percentile bands, provides a useful means of estimating the accuracy of individual percentile ranks. A percentile band is the range of one standard error on each side of a given score. Thus a teacher or counselor may interpret a student's score in relation to his probable "true score."

Norms for the college level tests are based on scores of 751 freshmen enrolled in 105 colleges widely distributed geographically and representative of different types of higher institutions. Sophomore norms are based on 558 students enrolled in seventy-eight of the same colleges.

High school norms are based on scores of 8,839 ninth-graders, 8,327 tenth-graders, 7,041 eleventh-graders, and 5,341 twelfth-graders. These students were enrolled in ninety-five schools located in all parts of the country.

For those who wish to equate scores on the 1960 tests with those on earlier editions, a table of equivalents is provided for each sub-test on *Reading* and between the 1960 *English Expression* score and *Mechanics of Expression* score on earlier forms.

15. Format. In appearance, quality of materials, and printing, these tests and accessories are the equal of any on the market and superior in many ways to most competing tests.

Other Tests in English

1. *Barrett-Ryan-Schrammel English Test.* New edition, 1956. Grades 9–13. *Functional grammar, punctuation, parts of speech, vocabulary,* and *pronunciation.*
    Forms DM and EM. $4.00 per 35. 60 minutes.
    Harcourt, Brace & World, Inc.

2. *Campbell-Guiler Test in English Fundamentals.* 1957. Grades 9–12. *Spelling, punctuation, capitalization, sentence organization and structure, grammatical usage and terminology.*
    Forms 3 and 4. $3.50 per 35. 33 minutes
    The Bobbs-Merrill Company, Inc.

3. *Cooperative Dictionary Test.* 1951–52. Grades 7–12. Tests ability to use a dictionary in finding various kinds of information quickly and accurately. Also tests knowledge of *alphabetization, pronunciation, derivation, spelling,* and *meaning of words.*
    Form A. $4.00 per 25. 30 minutes.
    Educational Testing Service.

4. *Cooperative English Test.* (*Usage, spelling, vocabulary.*) 1950. Grades 7–12, and college. *Grammar, punctuation, capitalization, sentence structure, spelling,* and *word knowledge* are tested.
    Forms OM and PM. $4.00 per 25. 70 minutes.
    Educational Testing Service.

5. *Cooperative Literary Comprehension and Appreciation Test.* 1935–51. Grades 10–12, and college. Measures *grasp of content, perception of author's viewpoint, recognition of literary devices,* and *appreciation of style and rhythm in poetry and prose selections.*
    Forms R and T. $4.00 per 25. 40 minutes.
    Educational Testing Service.

6. *Davis-Roahen-Schrammel American Literature Test.* 1938. Grades 9–12, and college. Based on standard selections by American authors. Covers *content, authorship, recognition, and understanding of quotations,* and *appreciation of literary values.*
    Forms A and B. $1.20 per 25. 60 minutes.
    Bureau of Educational Measurements.

7. *Essentials of English Tests.* 1939. Grades 7–13. *Spelling, grammatical usage, word usage, sentence structure, punctuation, and capitalization.*
    Forms A and B. $2.50 per 25. 45 minutes.
    American Guidance Service.

8. *Greene-Stapp Language Abilities Test.* 1951. Grades 9–13. *Capitalization, spelling, punctuation, sentence structure and applied grammar,* and *usage and applied grammar.*

FormsAM and BM. $6.00 per 35. 120 minutes.

Harcourt, Brace & World, Inc.

9. *Pressey Diagnostic Tests in English Composition.* Junior and Senior High School Grades. *Capitalization, punctuation, grammar, sentence structure.*

Forms 1, 2, 3, and 4 of each test. $2.45 per 35. 15 minutes.

The Bobbs-Merrill Company, Inc.

10. *Purdue High School English Test.* 1962. Grades 9–12. *Grammar, punctuation, effective expression, vocabulary, spelling.*

Forms 1 and 2. $4.20 per 35. $2.49 per 35 answer booklets. 36 minutes.

Houghton Mifflin Company.

11. *Rinsland-Beck Natural Tests of English Usage.* 1957. Grades 9–13. *Mechanics of English, Grammar, Rhetoric.*

Forms C and D of each test. $4.55 per 35.

The Bobbs-Merrill Company, Inc.

12. *Test of English Usage.* 1950. Grades 10–13. *Capitalization, use of apostrophe, and punctuation; word usage, building sentences and paragraphs.*

Forms A and B. $3.50 per 35. 100 minutes.

California Test Bureau.

13. *Tressler English Minimum Essentials Test.* 1932–1956. Grades 8–12. *Grammatical correctness, vocabulary, punctuation and capitalization, sentence structure, sentence sense, inflection and accent spelling.*

Forms A, B, C. $2.90 per 35. 40–50 minutes.

The Bobbs-Merrill Company, Inc.

Social Studies

The field of social studies at the secondary level generally includes civics, ancient history, modern European history, world history, United States history, and a course often called problems of democracy or American government. Standardized tests are available in each of these subjects, and most leading publishers have offerings in at least several. One standardized test in American history will be described in detail, and others in the various subjects will be listed for reference.

Crary American History Test

1. Name of test and authors. *Crary American History Test,*[4] Ryland W. Crary, University of Pittsburgh.

2. Nature and purposes. The test is intended to measure the achievement of pupils with respect to the important objectives of a high school course in American history. The objectives and the number and proportion of items emphasizing each are as follows:

Factual Information, 28 items (31 per cent)

Important dates 5
Important laws 4
Important ideas 5
Important treaties 5
Advancement in democracy . . . 5
Advancement in science 4

Skills, 16 items (18 per cent)

Sources of information 4
Time relationships 4
Map skills 8

Interpretation of Historical Information, 8 items
(9 per cent)
Understanding of Historical Processes, 26 items
(29 per cent)
Reasoned Inferences, 12 items (13 per cent)

3. Grade level. No particular grade level is specified, but it is intended to be given at the end of a year's course in American history in the high school.

4. Number of forms. Aᴍ and Bᴍ.

5. Publisher and date of publication. Harcourt, Brace & World, Inc., 1951.

6. Cost. $3.40 per 35. Separate answer sheets required. $1.35 per 35.

7. Content. The first fifty items in the test consist of sets of matching questions. These deal with dates of important events, sources of information, methods and processes in democratic government, accomplishment of important treaties and constitutional amendments, etc.

---

[4] Quotations in test description by permission of the publisher. From *Crary American History Test: Forms A and B* by Ryland W. Crary. Copyright 1951 by Harcourt, Brace & World, Inc., New York.

Sample:

Column I	Column II
a. developments in radio	1. Edison
b. atomic energy research	
c. combine thresher	2. Marconi
d. incandescent lighting	
e. mass production	3. Urey
f. wireless telegraphy	
g. radar development	4. Fleming
h. penicillin research	

Although the test is not divided into parts, the second section consists of multiple-choice items with a few true-false items based on a reading selection. Part of the multiple-choice items are based on an outline map of the United States and test for knowledge of important cities and localities identified by what makes them important rather than by their names.

Sample:

The chief automobile manufacturing center of America is represented on the map by

    a. 1   *b.* 4   *c.* 6   *d.* 11
         e. none of the above

The true-false questions represent conclusions which are correct or incorrect according to statements in the passage read. These conclusions are not all factual, some being in the nature of inferences. The next twenty-one items are in multiple-choice form and bear on the entire range of objectives for the test, but they emphasize thought and understanding rather than knowledge alone. The last three items are a variation of multiple-choice in which the statement or question is followed by five or six choices, which in turn are followed by five answers, each representing a different combination of the choices.

Sample:

What conditions contributed to the economic depression of the early 1930's?

1. The lack of farm prosperity in the 1920's.
2. The decline of foreign markets after World War I.
3. The lack of purchasing power of low-income groups.
4. The large military budgets of the 1920's.
5. The lack of industrial capacity and natural resources.

      a. 1, 2, 3
      b. 1, 2, 4
      c. 2, 3, 5
      d. 1, 4, 5
      e. all of the above

8. Time required. 40 minutes.

9. Directions for and ease of administration. Directions for administering are very brief but complete; the test is practically self-administering.

10. Validity. Evidence for the validity of the *Crary American History Test* rests upon two bases: (a) analysis of textbooks, courses of study, and pronouncements of national committees for the social studies and (b) statistical analysis of items in the preliminary forms after tryout.

Step (a) was employed to determine objectives and emphases, and the weights to be assigned them in the test and in the content of the items.

Step (b) yielded difficulty values and discrimination indexes for each item tried out. In terms of the percentage of pupils passing each item, the mean difficulty value for the items in Form AM was 48 per cent. The mean discrimination index was .46. No data on these criteria are given in the manual for Form BM.

11. Reliability. Corrected split-half reliability coefficients of .87 and .91 are reported, though it is not stated to which form or forms these apply. The standard error of measurement for the test is 4.0 standard score points.

12. Manual. The manual is brief and seems more like a preliminary edition than a final or complete one. Necessary information for using the test is included, but subsequent editions will probably go into more detail.

13. Scoring. The test is easily and quickly scored, either by the use of a hand-scoring stencil or by a test-scoring machine. No spaces are provided on the test for marking answers, so the scoring is always done on printed answer sheets. Raw scores are converted into normalized standard scores having a mean of 104 and a standard deviation of 12.5. These standard scores are as comparable as any type of score generally used with standardized tests. All scores on tests in the Evaluation and Adjustment Series, of which the *Crary* test is one, are expressed in these normalized standard scores. This makes it possible to compare an individual pupil's score on different tests in the series and with his ability level as measured by the *Terman-McNemar Test of Mental Ability*.

14. Norms. Percentile norms are provided for end-of-year administration of the test. They are based upon the scores of 6,178 pupils in fifty-five schools in twenty-one states.

15. Format. The test manual and other materials are excellent in organization, composition, and quality.

Other Tests in Social Studies

1. *California Tests in Social and Related Sciences.* 1946–53. Advanced, Grades 9–12. 1. *Creating a New Nation* (to 1789). 2. *Nationalism, Sectionalism, and Conflict* (1790–1876). 3. *Emergence of Modern America* (1877–1918). 4. *The United States in Transition* (since 1918).

Forms AA and BB. 1 and 2 in a booklet, $.08 per copy; 3 and 4 in a booklet, $.08 per copy. 1 and 2, 45 minutes; 3 and 4, 45 minutes.

California Test Bureau.

2. *Cooperative American History Test.* 1947–49. High school and college. *Basic facts and trends in the economic, social, and political development of the United States.* Approximately one-half the items cover the period since 1865.

Forms Y and Z. $4.00 per 25. 40 minutes.

Educational Testing Service.

3. *Cooperative Ancient History Test.* 1938–39. High school grades. *Fundamentals underlying broad understanding of ancient backgrounds of our civilization.*

Forms O and P. $4.00 per 25. 40 minutes.

Educational Testing Service.

4. *Cooperative Modern European History Test.* 1947–48. High school and college. *Historical development from the Middle Ages to the present.*

Forms X and Y. $4.00 per 25. 80 minutes.

Educational Testing Service.

5. *Cooperative Social Studies Test.* 1948. Grades 7–9. *American and world history, geography, and civics.*

Forms X and Y. $4.00 per 25. 80 minutes.

Educational Testing Service.

6. *Cooperative Test in American Government.* 1947. Upper high school grades. *Organization and background of American government.*

Forms X and Y. $4.00 per 25. 40 minutes.

Educational Testing Service.

7. *Cooperative Test on Foreign Affairs.* 1960. Grades 12–16, Adults. *Interpretation of maps, cartoons,* etc., *sequence of important events, nations and people, world geography, natural resources.*

One Form. $4.00 per 20. 60 minutes.

Educational Testing Service.

8. *Cooperative World History Test.* 1947–49. High school grades. *Major political, social, and economic trends from prehistoric times to the present.*

Forms Y and Z. $4.00 per 25. 40 minutes.
Educational Testing Service.

9. *Cummings World History Test.* 1950. High school end-of-course test. *Major historical events, dates, places, and leaders. History of ancient times, medieval and modern Europe, and the world wars.*

Forms AM and BM. $4.70 per 35. 40 minutes.
Harcourt, Brace & World, Inc.

10. *Dimond-Pflieger Problems of Democracy Test.* 1952. High school end-of-course test. *Government economics, sociology, and international affairs.*

Forms AM and BM. $4.00 per 35. 40 minutes.
Harcourt, Brace & World, Inc.

11. *Hills Economics Test.* 1940. High school and college. *Basic facts, principles, and theories of economics.*

One form. $1.20 per 25. 40 minutes.
Bureau of Educational Measurements.

12. *Peltier-Durost Civics and Citizenship Test.* 1951. Grades 9–12. *Section 1 — Knowledge in civics and citizenship; Section 2 — Civic attitudes.*

Forms AM and BM. $4.10 per 35. 55 minutes.
Harcourt, Brace & World, Inc.

Natural Science

The commonly taught science subjects in junior and senior high schools are general science, biology, chemistry, and physics. Another course, variously named — senior science, consumer science, advanced general science — has also found a place in the high school curriculum. These are, and have been for many years, the courses usually offered. However, as in the case of mathematics, profound changes have been taking place in their content and organization since World War II. The developments in nuclear fission and fusion; the recent growth of space science and technology; and the new discoveries in biochemistry, biophysics, and medicine have had a profound effect on high school science courses. National committees, including the Biological Science Curriculum Study, the Chem-Bond and Chem-Study groups, and the Physical Science Study Committee, have produced courses of study that represent significant changes, both in content and emphasis, in the traditional high school courses in science.

The committees responsible for the development of the new courses of study have had tests constructed to be used by teachers with their instructional materials. These are not usually suitable for use elsewhere, however. Nor are existing tests appropriate evaluative instruments with classes using the new materials. The tendency at present seems to be to revise existing tests or to produce new tests in the sciences which are a compromise between the traditional and the more recent. This will probably continue for some time to come until the changes in science courses become stabilized. Indeed, the content and organization of the courses as they develop will almost certainly represent such a compromise.

One quite recent standardized test in general science is described in detail below.

Read General Science Test

1. Name of test and author. *Read General Science Test,* Revised Edition.[5] John G. Read, Boston University.

2. Nature and purposes. The objectives of the test are to measure the degree to which the following objectives have been attained:

   a. Knowledge of important facts, concepts, and principles of science.
   b. Understanding of such facts, concepts, and principles.
   c. Ability to apply such knowledge and understanding in the solution of new or unfamiliar problems.
   d. Ability to interpret data or situations which are new but to which such knowledge and understanding are relevant.

3. Grade level. Seventh, eighth, and ninth grades.

4. Number of forms. E and F.

5. Publisher and date of publication. Harcourt, Brace & World, Inc., 1964.

6. Cost. $5.25 per 35.

7. Content. Solids, liquids, work and machines, gases, heat, light, sound, electricity, magnetism, electronics, communication — 21.3 per cent; properties and uses of familiar substances, chemical change — 8.0 per cent; characteristics of living organisms, plants, animals, human biol-

---

[5] Quotations in test descriptions by permission of the publisher. From *Read General Science Test: Forms E and F,* by John G. Read. Copyright 1964 by Harcourt, Brace & World, Inc., New York.

ogy, heredity, conservation, ecology — 32.0 per cent; weather, climate, geology, exploration of space — 28.0 per cent; solar system, stars, galaxies — 5.3 per cent; scientific method, scientific attitudes — 5.3 per cent.

The test consists of two forms of seventy-five multiple-choice items each. The selection of content is based on the analysis of leading textbooks and several state and city syllabi in general science for Grades 7, 8, and 9; on research recommendations of national committee reports on elementary and secondary school science; and on the new curricular materials produced by the BSCS, Chem-Bond, Chem-Study, and PSSC committees.

Samples:

The basic substance of all plant and animal life is:

1. lymph
2. protoplasm
3. serum
4. connective tissue
5. Don't Know

A recent discovery which allows many more television programs and telephone messages to be sent at the same time is the:

1. transistor
2. transformer
3. Q-tube
4. laser
5. Don't Know

The response, "Don't Know," is used as a possible fifth choice on the theory that it reduces guessing by students who have no sound basis for answering. The validity of this assumption does not appear to have been established, however.

8. Time required. 40 minutes.

9. Directions for and ease of administering. The test is not difficult to administer. Directions are clear and complete. It may be used as a consumable booklet (the student marks his choices on the test booklet) with IBM answer sheets, both 805 (the standard form) or 1230 (new electronic type) MRC answer sheets, or Harbor answer cards. The variety of answer media requires several sets of directions to the student, making administration somewhat more complicated and time-consuming than it would be if only test booklets or standard IBM answer sheets were used.

10. Validity. The test is designed to reflect current teaching of general science in junior high school Grades 7–9. It is based upon analysis of current instructional materials, pronouncements of national committees, and research studies on the teaching of general science and is therefore held to have a high degree of content or curricular validity.

Students in the standardization population took the *Otis Gamma Mental Ability* along with the experimental forms of the revised *Read*. The correlations between *Otis* I.Q.'s and scores on the *Read* range from .645 to .709. These may be interpreted as indication of concurrent validity in that they show a marked tendency for brighter students to make higher scores on the science test than the less able. At the same time, the correlation is not high enough to suggest that the two tests are measures of the same thing.

Another indication of the validity of the revised *Read* is to be found in the consistent differences between the mean scores of Grades 7, 8, and 9. The means are as follows:

Grade 7	Grade 8	Grade 9
32.69	38.11	40.53

Taking all these data into account, the *Read General Science Test* would appear to have a high degree of validity as a measure of current objectives and content of general science as taught in junior high school grades.

11. Reliability. Split-half reliability coefficients for each form by grades are as follows:

	Grade 7	Grade 8	Grade 9
Form E	.896	.908	.908
Form F	.903	.919	.914

The standard error of measurement for both forms and all three grade levels is approximately 4 raw score points.

12. Manual. The manual for the test is quite adequate. It contains information on the development of the test, its validity and reliability, equivalence of forms and norms. Directions for administering, scoring, and interpreting are clear and complete. It also contains some suggestions for the use of test results.

13. Scoring. The *Read* test may be scored by hand or machine. When answers are marked on the test booklet, scoring must be done by hand. Standard IBM answer sheets may be scored either way. If IBM 1230, MRC or Harbor answer cards are used, machine scoring is the only practical method.

14. Norms. Percentile, scaled score, and stanine norms are provided by grade level. The norms are based upon a sampling of 17,958 students enrolled in twenty-seven schools in seventeen states distributed in all sections of the country. Included were 6,172 pupils in Grade 7, 5,779 in Grade 8, and 6,007 in Grade 9.

15. Format. The appearance of the revised *Read General Science Test* has been improved by the use of color and better typography and paper. The over-all format is pleasing.

Other Tests in Natural Science

1. *Anderson Chemistry Test.* 1951. Grades 10–13. End-of-course test for high school chemistry. *Understanding of facts and concepts; understanding and application of functional principles; understanding and application of scientific method; ability to use basic skills in chemistry.*
    Forms Aᴍ and Bᴍ. $4.70 per 35. 40 minutes.
    Harcourt Brace & World, Inc.

2. *Cooperative Biology Test.* 1948. High school classes in biology. *General information in biological science; understanding of, and ability to use, basic principles; ability to interpret materials not generally encountered in textbooks.*
    Forms X and Y. $4.00 per 25. 40 minutes.
    Educational Testing Service.

3. *Cooperative Chemistry Test.* 1950. High school classes in chemistry. *Knowledge of fundamental concepts, terms, reactions, preparations, atomic structure, and chemistry related to daily living. Ability to apply knowledge of chemistry and to interpret scientific information.*
    Forms X, Y, and Z. $4.00 per 25. 40 minutes.
    Educational Testing Service.

4. *Cooperative General Science Test.* 1950. Grade 9. *Understanding of reasons behind familiar scientific phenomena and processes.*
    Forms Y and Z. $4.00 per 25. 40 minutes.
    Educational Testing Service.

5. *Cooperative Physics Test.* 1949. High school classes in physics. *Mechanics, heat, light, sound, and electricity; numerical problems and interpretation of diagrams.*
    Forms Y and Z. $4.00 per 25. 40 minutes.
    Educational Testing Service.

6. *Cooperative Science Test for Grades 7, 8, and 9.* 1948. Grade 9 and superior pupils in Grades 7 and 8. *Informational background, terms,*

concepts, and understanding, interpretation, and ability to apply ideas from scientific reading selections.

Forms X and Y. $4.00 per 25. 80 minutes.
Educational Testing Service.

7. *Dunning Physics Test.* 1951. Grades 11 and 12. End-of-course test for high school physics. *Knowledge and understanding of basic facts, principles, and laws. Mechanics, heat, sound, light, electricity, and modern physics.*

Forms AM and BM. $4.70 per 35. 45 minutes.
Harcourt, Brace & World, Inc.

Mathematics

Since World War II significant changes have been taking place in the mathematics curriculum. The traditional titles of courses — arithmetic, algebra, plane geometry, solid geometry, and trigonometry are still in general use. However, the content of these courses has been undergoing continuous study and revision. Concepts new to high school courses have been introduced. More recently, the development of computers and programming has also begun to have an effect on the content of courses in mathematics.

Also significant is the trend toward moving downward in the mathematics curriculum content which had been traditionally reserved for college and university courses. Analytic geometry and calculus, for example, are being taught in high school mathematics classes, and some experimentation has been carried out in teaching the simpler or basic concepts of algebra, geometry, and even calculus in elementary schools. The entire mathematics program below the college level is in a state of flux.

These changes are not yet stabilized or standardized. Textbooks of the more traditional type are still widely used, although many are now available that reflect some of the "new mathematics." Of course, many teachers are neither prepared nor willing to change to the new mathematics, and it will take some time before the content of high school mathematics courses is firmly established and generally accepted.

The trends in the mathematics curriculum will eventually be reflected in standardized tests but this, too, will take time. At present, a few tests are appearing that incorporate some of the changes, but they represent essentially a compromise between the old and the new. The tests described below are of this type.

New Cooperative Mathematics Tests

1. Name of tests and authors. *New Cooperative Mathematics Tests in Arithmetic, Algebra I, Algebra II,* and Geometry.[6] Educational Testing Service Staff.

2. Nature and purposes. A series of tests for junior and senior high school grades reflecting a blend of some of the newer content and terminology with important aspects of traditional mathematics courses at the secondary level.

3. Grade level. Grades 7–12.

4. Number of forms. *Arithmetic* — A, B, C; *Algebra* and *Geometry* — A and B.

5. Publisher and date of publication. Educational Testing Service. 1962.

6. Cost. $4.00 per 20. Answer sheets, $1.00 per 20.

7. Content. Arithmetic: *Number concepts, fractions, decimals, ratio and proportion, percentage, graphs.* Algebra I: *Equations, inequalities, binomials, factoring, coordinates.* Algebra II: Same as Algebra I plus *linear and quadratic equations, logarithms, powers.* Geometry: *Angles, plane figures, theorems, intuitive solid geometry, rectangular coordinates.*
Samples:

Arithmetic:

> Which of the following will never change the value of a number?
>
> > I. Multiplying it by 1.
> > II. Dividing it by 1.
> > III. Multiplying it by its reciprocal.
> > A. I only.
> > B. II only.
> > C. III only.
> > D. I and II only.
> > E. I and III only.

Algebra I:

> What number must be added to $x^2 - 6x + 4$ in order to make it a perfect square?

[6] Quotations in test description by permission of the publisher.

A. −4
B.   0
C.   2
D.   5
E. 32

Algebra II:

The graphs of two linear equations are distinct and do *not* intersect. How many solutions do these two equations have in common?

A. None.
B. One.
C. Two.
D. An unlimited number.
E. It cannot be determined
   from the information given.

Geometry:

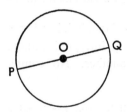

The figure above is a circle with center at O. The path once completely around the circle from P back to P is about how many times the path from P straight across through O to Q?

A. 1

B. $\dfrac{4}{3}$

C. $\dfrac{3}{2}$

D. $\dfrac{5}{2}$

E. $\dfrac{22}{7}$

8. Time required. 40 minutes (Geometry, two parts — 40 minutes each.)

9. Directions for and ease of administering. Directions for administering are clear and complete. The tests themselves are practically self-administering. All answers are marked on IBM answer sheets.

10. Validity. Content outlines for the tests were reviewed by a committee of mathematics educators and curriculum specialists. Outstanding classroom teachers and mathematicians participated in the preparation of test items. Validity must therefore rest on the judgment of persons involved in the production of the tests.

11. Reliability. Kuder-Richardson Formula 20 was used to determine estimates of reliability and standard errors of measurement. For *Arithmetic* single-grade coefficients range from .80 to .91; S.E. measurement is approximately 3 raw score points. For *Algebra I,* K–R reliability coefficients range from .82 to .85; S.E. measurement, about 2.65. For *Algebra II,* K–R coefficients range from .80 to .85; S.E. measurement, about 2.70. For *Geometry, Part I,* K–R coefficients range from .79 to .84; S.E. measurement, about 2.50. *For Geometry, Part I* and *Part II,* K–R coefficients range from .82 to .85; S.E. measurement, about 3.65.

12. Manual. Directions for administering and scoring are printed in one booklet and preliminary interpretive data, including information on reliability and norms, in another. No complete manual with technical data is available.

13. Scoring. One stencil is used for hand or machine scoring. Score is the number right.

14. Norms. Only percentile ranks based on a limited sampling of suburban, urban, and rural schools are at present available. The manual states that a national standardization program is under way which will provide scaled score and percentile band norms.

15. Format. Tests in this edition are less attractive than other *Cooperative* tests. The format, although fairly good, is not up to the best standards.

Other Tests in Mathematics

1. *Becker-Schrammel Plane Geometry Test.* 1934. Test I, first semester, Test II, second semester, of plane geometry. *Geometrical reasoning, computation, proofs,* and *constructions.*
  Forms A and B. $1.20 per 25 of either test. 40 minutes.
  Bureau of Educational Measurements.

2. *Blyth Second-Year Algebra Test.* 1951. End of second-year algebra course in high schools. *Symbolic expression, factoring, radicals, ex-*

ponents, logarithms, simple progressions, linear and quadratic equations, and *graphic methods.*

Forms AM and BM. $3.80 per 35. 45 minutes.

Harcourt, Brace & World, Inc.

3. *Colvin-Schrammel Algebra Test.* 1937. Test I, first semester, Test II, second semester, of high school algebra. Test I, *formulas, signed numbers, equations, monomials,* and *polynomials.* Test II, *the same,* and *also simple quadratic equations soluble by factoring, fractions, literal equations,* and *simultaneous linear equations.*

Forms A and B. $1.20 per 25 of Test I or Test II. 40 minutes.

Bureau of Educational Measurements.

4. *Cooperative Algebra Test: Elementary Algebra Through Quadratics.* 1950. High school classes in elementary algebra. Covers *basic knowledge, skills and applications of elementary algebra.* Includes *interpretation of graphs and charts.*

Forms T, Y, and Z. $4.00 per 25. 40 minutes.

Educational Testing Service.

5. *Cooperative Intermediate Algebra Test: Quadratics and Beyond.* 1950. High school classes in intermediate algebra. *Quadratics, exponents, factoring, progressions, logarithms, imaginary numbers, radicals, simultaneous equations, graphs, right triangle* (*trigonometric*) *relationships,* and *proportion.*

Forms T, Y, and Z. $4.00 per 25. 40 minutes.

Educational Testing Service.

6. *Cooperative Mathematics Pre-test for College Students.* 1950. For students beginning mathematics in college. *Mastery of skills in arithmetic, algebra, plane and solid geometry, and trigonometry. Most of the test deals with algebra.* (The distribution of this test is restricted to colleges and universities.)

Forms X and Y. $4.00 per 25. 40 minutes.

Educational Testing Service.

7. *Cooperative Mathematics Test for Grades 7, 8 and 9.* 1951. *Skills; facts, terms and concepts; applications; appreciation.*

Forms X and Y. $4.00 per 25. 80 minutes.

Educational Testing Service.

8. *Cooperative Plane Geometry Test.* 1950. High school classes in plane geometry. *Knowledge of theorems concerning circles, triangles, polygons, and constructions; application of pertinent theorems in deductive*

reasoning and computational situations; ability to analyze the formal proofs of original problems.

Forms T, Y, and Z. $4.00 per 25. 40 minutes.

Educational Testing Service.

9. *Cooperative Solid Geometry Test.* 1954. High school classes in solid geometry. *Mastery of essential formulas of solid geometry and ability to apply them.*

Forms O and P. $4.00 per 25. 40 minutes.

Educational Testing Service.

10. *Cooperative Trigonometry Test.* 1950. High school and college classes in trigonometry. *Basic definitions, formulas, computations, and applied work problems.*

Forms U and Y. $4.00 per 25. 40 minutes.

Educational Testing Service.

11. *Davis Test of Functional Competence in Mathematics.* 1951–52. Grades 9–13. *Consumer problems, graphs and tables, symbolism, equations, ratio, tolerance, etc.*

Forms AM and BM. $4.70 per 35. 80 minutes.

Harcourt, Brace & World, Inc.

12. *Functional Evaluation in Mathematics.* 1952. Upper Level, Grades 7–9: Test 4, *Quantitative Understanding;* Test 5, *Problem Solving;* Test 6, *Basic Computation.*

Form A. Test 4, $2.45 per 25; Tests 5 and 6, $1.35 per 25. Manual, $1.00. 25 minutes.

American Guidance Service.

13. *Garman-Schrammel Third-Semester Algebra Test.* 1934–40. *Quadratic equations, functions, ratios, proportion and variation, radicals, exponents, imaginary numbers, logarithms, arithmetic and geometric progressions,* and *the binomial theorem.*

Forms A and B. $1.20 per 25. 40 minutes.

Bureau of Educational Measurements.

14. *Illinois Algebra Test.* 1956–58. Test I, first semester; Test II, second semester; Test III, one year's work. *Manipulative and mechanical skills.*

One form. $2.80 per 35 of each test. 37 minutes.

The Bobbs-Merrill Company, Inc.

15. *Illinois Plane Geometry Test.* 1957. Tests 1–4 for one semester mid-term and final, second semester mid-term and final.

One form. $3.15 per 35 of each test. 37 minutes.

The Bobbs-Merrill Company, Inc.

16. *Lane-Greene Unit Tests in Plane Geometry.* Revised, 1944. High school plane geometry. Test 1, *Fundamental Ideas of Geometry;* Test 2, *Parallel Lines and Triangles;* Test 3, *Rectilinear Figures;* Test 4, *The Circle;* Test 5, *Proportion and Similar Polygons;* Test 6, *Areas of Polygons.* Available in a thirty-two page booklet only.

Forms A and B. $3.75 per 25. Each test requires from 35 to 38 minutes.

Bureau of Educational Research and Service.

17. *Lankton First-Year Algebra Test.* 1951–52. End-of-course in first-year algebra. *Vocabulary, meaning and use of symbols, fundamental operations, formulas, equations, simple algebraic fractions, radicals, ratio, proportion, variation, graphs, trigonometric functions, and algebraic solution of problems.*

Forms AM and BM. $4.00 per 35. 40 minutes.

Harcourt, Brace & World, Inc.

18. *Larson-Greene Unit Tests in First-Year Algebra.* Revised, 1947. First-year algebra in high schools. Tests 1, 2 and 3 for first semester; Tests 4, 5 and 6 for second semester. Available in a 24-page booklet only.

Forms X and Y. $3.75 per 25. Each test requires from 36 to 40 minutes.

Bureau of Educational Research and Service.

19. *Rasmussen General Mathematics Test.* 1942. High school and college. *Basic facts, principles, theories, and "problems common to six reputable texts in this field."*

Forms A and B. $1.20 per 25. 40 minutes.

Bureau of Educational Measurements.

20. *Rasmussen Trigonometry Test.* 1940. High school and college. *Basic facts, principles, theories, and problems commonly included in elementary textbooks.*

Forms A and B. $1.20 per 25. 40 minutes.

Bureau of Educational Measurements.

21. *Schrammel-Reed Solid Geometry Tests.* 1950. High school and college. Catalog states: "a comprehensive and thoroughly objective test in solid geometry."

Forms A and B. $1.20 per 25. 50 minutes.

Bureau of Educational Measurements.

22. *Seattle Algebra Test.* 1951. End of first half-year of algebra in high school. *Understanding of basic terms, fundamental processes with signed quantities, sequence of numerical operations, practical formulas, multiplication of binomials, solution of equations of the first degree by the rules of equality, solution of simple simultaneous equations, algebraic representation, and problems.*

Forms AM and BM. $3.40 per 35. 40 minutes.

Harcourt, Brace & World, Inc.

23. *Seattle Plane Geometry Test.* 1951. End of first half-year of plane geometry. *Vocabulary of geometry, knowledge of simple geometric construction, computational skills, and ability to reason from a figure.*

Forms AM and BM. $4.00 per 35. 45 minutes.

Harcourt, Brace & World, Inc.

24. *Shaycoft Plane Geometry Test.* 1951–52. End of one-year course in plane geometry. *Fundamental concepts, lines and rectilinear figures, the circle, proportions, area of polygons, and geometric-reasoning.*

Forms AM and BM. $4.00 per 35. 40 minutes.

Harcourt, Brace & World, Inc.

25. *Snader-General Mathematics Test.* 1951–52. End of one-year course in general mathematics. *Arithmetical concepts and processes, informal geometry, graphic representation, algebraic principles and skills, and numerical trigonometry. Measures not only computation and manipulation skills, but also application through problem situations.*

Forms AM and BM. $4.70 per 35. 40 minutes.

Harcourt, Brace & World, Inc.

▶ LEARNING EXERCISES ◀

1. If you were to have a part in planning and constructing a standardized test in a subject in your major field, how would you proceed? Prepare an outline of your procedure and be prepared to explain how you would carry out each step.

2. What are the advantages and disadvantages of a state-wide testing program such as those in New York, Ohio, or Iowa? Can you find any surveys or studies in educational literature that give evidence on this question?

3. Is the content of fifth-grade arithmetic more standardized than that of ninth-grade algebra? How would you find out?

4. Examine a specimen set of an achievement test in a high school subject, studying carefully the test, manual, and other accessories. Does it seem to you

an adequate instrument for measuring important outcomes in that subject? Give your reasons. After you have done this, consult one of *The Mental Measurements Yearbooks* to see how well you and the experts agree in your appraisal.

ANNOTATED BIBLIOGRAPHY

1. Buros, Oscar K. (Ed.). *The Sixth Mental Measurements Yearbook.* Highland Park, N.J.: The Gryphon Press, 1965. The most complete and useful review of measuring instruments and books on measurement in education and psychology. Reviews give factual information as well as reviewers' criticisms. Reviews in earlier editions are cited in each subsequent edition.

2. Buros, Oscar K. *Tests in Print.* Highland Park, N.J.: The Gryphon Press, 1961. (See reference to this volume following Chapter 8.)

3. Committee on Test Standards of the American Educational Research Association, National Education Association, and the National Council on Measurements Used in Education. *Technical Recommendations for Achievement Tests.* Washington: NEA, 1955. 36 pp. An authoritative statement concerning the kinds of information test manuals should supply. Written primarily with test authors and publishers in mind, though it is a useful reference for students.

4. Greene, Harry A., Jorgensen, Albert N., and Gerberich, J. Raymond. *Measurement and Evaluation in the Secondary School,* Second Edition. New York: David McKay Co., Inc., 1954. Chapters 15–25. Approximately one-third of the volume is devoted to a discussion of objectives and measurement procedures in each of the common branches of instruction. Reference is made almost wholly to published standardized tests and the problems of developing such instruments in each subject.

5. Jordan, A. M. *Measurement in Education.* New York: McGraw-Hill Book Co., Inc., 1953. Chapters 5–13. Nine chapters dealing with measurement in reading, spelling, handwriting, language and literature, social sciences, foreign languages, mathematics, science, business education, fine arts, manual arts, and physical education and health, respectively. Each chapter discusses objectives and describes tests for elementary grades and high schools in a particular subject area.

6. National Society for the Study of Education. *The Measurement of Understanding,* Forty-Fifth Yearbook, Part I. Chicago: The Society (distributed by the University of Chicago Press), 1946. 338 pp. Describes and gives excerpts from many standardized tests in social studies, science, mathematics, language arts, fine arts, health education, physical education, home economics, agriculture, technical education, and industrial arts. Also gives many helpful suggestions for the improvement of locally made tests in these areas.

See also catalogs of test publishers listed in Appendix C.

10

The Measurement of Capacity:

General Intelligence

The term "capacity" as used here includes both intelligence and aptitude. This chapter deals with the measurement of intelligence, and the following one deals with the measurement of aptitude.

Numerous attempts have been made to define intelligence, yet educators and psychologists have never been able to come to complete agreement on the term or on the concepts which it involves. Substantial progress has been made in the measurement of intelligence, however; such progress has resulted from attempts to find measures that would differentiate feeble-minded from normal children, or pupils successful in school work from those who are less successful, as judged by their teachers. Actually, our definition of intelligence is circular, since we are in effect saying that intelligence is what intelligence tests measure, and that it is what makes for success in academic work. This is true, at least insofar as the schools are concerned.

A second type of capacity to be considered in Chapter 11, is often referred to as "aptitude." As used here, the meaning of the term differs from intelligence in one important respect. Aptitude refers to capacities in special fields, such as music, art, or mechanics. Intelligence tests have sometimes been referred to as tests of "scholastic aptitude," but the term "aptitude" is probably more applicable to tests that are narrower in scope and more specialized. In this chapter intelligence tests will be described and illustrated, and their theoretical bases and uses will be discussed briefly.

For a long time psychologists have been interested in the measurement of intelligence, and the history of the development of intelligence tests closely parallels the development of psychology as a science. Moreover, intelligence measurement is an area of study that is not without its controversial aspects. Also, it must be recognized that the use of intelligence tests requires in many instances a considerable amount of technical knowledge and training, and in no instance can one expect to use such tests properly without at least some preparation. The first part of this chapter treats these three aspects of intelligence testing: the background of the movement, its associated problems, and its current procedures.

HISTORICAL BACKGROUNDS OF INTELLIGENCE MEASUREMENT

Persent-day intelligence tests are based on the work of a French psychologist, Alfred Binet. Associated with him were, first, V. Henri, and later, Théodore Simon. There can be no doubt that Binet was the shining light and genius of this most important contribution to modern psychological methods, even though many others contributed to the developments which culminated in his work.

For instance, the work of Francis Galton (1822–1911), an English scientist, did much to stimulate interest in individual differences and their measurement. He devised various tests of sensory discrimination involving weights, tones, and mental imagery, and made important contributions to the advancement of statistical methods. He is generally regarded as having been the first to use standard scores and correlation.

In the United States a number of psychologists became interested in the possibility of measuring intelligence. At this point it must suffice to mention only one, James McKeen Cattell, who had more to do with early developments along these lines than anyone else in this country. Cattell studied psychology under the famous German, Wilhelm Wundt, who was not very favorably disposed toward the "new psychology" — that is, the measurement of mental abilities. However, Cattell became actively interested in the measurement of intelligence, and when he returned to this country did much to stimulate interest in it. In 1896 he devised and administered to students at Columbia University a series of tests largely of the sensory-motor type. These tests measured such traits or abilities as keenness of vision and hearing, reaction time, mental imagery, and perception of weights, colors, and tones. For the most part, the tests were simple, objective, and easily administered. Almost without exception, however, the results showed little relation to teachers' estimates of their students' intelligence, or to the students' success in school work as measured by marks or by other means.

Binet also experimented with most of these tests and dozens of others with similarly unsatisfactory results. He and his co-workers became convinced that the value of such tests for measuring intelligence was extremely limited. Gradually, however, he developed a new approach to the problem, and began to make real progress. Binet based his theory on the assumption that success would depend on the measurement of complex mental processes rather than specific traits. In 1905, after years of research and experimentation, he published his first scale of intelligence, developed primarily for the purpose of identifying subnormal children in the schools of Paris. This scale represented a distinct departure from previous efforts. In the first place, Binet's tests were arranged in order of increasing difficulty, and thus they constituted a scale for measuring the individual's level of mental development. In the second place, although the tests were of considerable variety, they were intended to measure a complex, central factor in intelligence which Binet called "judgment." Of course, Binet recognized that the thirty tests in the scale could not all be demonstrated to measure this one factor; nevertheless, the originality and purpose of the tests were clearly evident. Some of the items required the student to execute simple orders such as "Close the door," to name objects designated in a picture, to cite from memory the differences between pairs of familiar objects or materials such as wood and glass, and to construct a sentence embodying three given words such as "Paris, gutter, fortune."[1]

This first scale was followed in 1908 by a revision in which the tests were grouped at ages or levels, a marked improvement over the serial order of the original scale. In 1911 a second revision was published. This was the culmination of Binet's work, since he died in the same year at the age of fifty-four. This third scale was more complete, more carefully standardized, and more systematically scored than either of its predecessors.

During Binet's lifetime several psychologists, most of them Americans, translated and used the first and the second scales, and criticized them, largely to Binet's benefit. However, the basic principles were established

---

[1] See Joseph Peterson. *Early Conceptions and Tests of Intelligence* (New York: Harcourt, Brace & World, Inc., 1925), pp. 172–74.

by Binet, and it was clearly demonstrated that the third scale in particular was an instrument superior in usefulness, accuracy, and scope to anything that had preceded it. The need now was for further translations and adaptations of the scale for use with children of different nationalities, cultures, and languages, and this need was soon fulfilled, at least in the United States.

Three Americans are most closely associated with the development of the Binet tests. Henry Goddard translated both the 1905 and the 1907 scales into English and used them in his work at the Vineland, New Jersey, Training School for the Feeble-minded. In a similar way, Fred Kuhlmann used the early scales at an institution for the feeble-minded at Faribault, Minnesota. He published the first translation and thoroughgoing revision of Binet's scales for use with American children in 1912. This edition has been revised several times subsequently, and still finds some use in certain sections of this country.

The major work in adapting the Binet scales for use with English-speaking subjects was done by Lewis M. Terman, who had carried on some experimentation with tests independently, but had not gone very far when the Binet scales appeared. He set to work at once on these and in 1916 published what became the most widely used and accepted intelligence test, known as the *Stanford Revision of the Binet Scale*. This was a careful translation and revision, involving a complete standardization on American children and adults. There were tests at Years III, IV, V, VI, VII, VIII, IX, X, XII, XIV, and for levels called Average Adult and Superior Adult. Terman rearranged many of the tests from the positions established by Binet, added new tests, especially at the upper end of the scale, and eliminated others. This became the standard instrument for the measurement of intelligence in the United States and other English-speaking countries for more than twenty years.

In time, certain shortcomings and weaknesses in Terman's scale became apparent, and in 1937 he and Maud R. Merrill published their revision of the *Stanford-Binet Scale* which remedied most, if not all, of these faults. The chief faults were a lack of equivalent forms, gaps in the scale, notably at Years XI and XIII, and incompleteness at both ends of the scale. The 1937 Revision appeared in two equivalent forms; it provided tests for the missing years; it extended downward to age two, with tests at half-year intervals from age two to age six, thus providing a far more thorough testing at these levels; and it extended upward to a much higher level by adding three sets of tests, Superior Adult I, II, and III, giving the scale more "top" or "ceiling" for use with adults. Also, the normative population was more adequate and more carefully selected than in the earlier scale.[2] A few samples from Form L of the *Revised Stanford-Binet Tests of Intelligence* will serve to show its nature.

YEAR III–6. **Drawing Designs: Cross**

Procedure: Give the child a pencil and as you draw a cross making diagonal lines about two inches in length (X) say to him, "You make one just like this." Illustrate once only. Give one trial.

Score: "Requirement is that child shall make two lines that cross each other. We disregard the angle of crossing and the straightness and length of the lines."

YEAR VIII. **Comprehension IV**

Procedure: Ask

(*a*) "What makes a sailboat move?"

(*b*) "What should you say when you are in a strange city and someone asks you how to find a certain address?"

(*c*) "What should you do if you found on the streets of a city a three-year-old baby that was lost from its parents?"

Score: 2 plus. Sample answers are given. In (*a*) for instance, "wind," "wind and water," "wind and sails," are acceptable; "water," "the motor" are not.

SUPERIOR ADULT III. **Repeating 9 Digits**

Procedure: Say, "I am going to say some numbers and when I am through I want you to say them just the way I do. Listen carefully, and get them just right." Before each series repeat, "Listen carefully, and get them just right." Rate, one per second. Avoid accent and rhythm.

(*a*) 3 — 7 — 1, etc.
(*b*) 7 — 3 — 9, etc.
(*c*) 8 — 5 — 2, etc.

Score: 1 plus. The series must be repeated in correct order without error after a single reading.

The administration of this scale requires training, practice, and skill. No one should attempt it except as a learner under expert supervision until he has all three requisites. The examiner should be so thoroughly familiar with the procedure that he can give major attention to the presentation of the tasks, recording of responses, and legitimate encouragement of the subject. Assuming that the user has attained satisfactory skill and has estab-

---

[2] Lewis M. Terman and Maud R. Merrill, *Measuring Intelligence* (Boston: Houghton Mifflin Company, 1937). Quoted by permission of authors and publisher.

lished rapport with the subject, the procedure for administering the scale is as follows:

1. Establish the basal mental age. This is the highest level on the scale at which the subject passes all the tests.
2. Proceed to give all the tests at successively higher levels, recording successes and failures at each level.
3. Stop at the level at which the subject fails all the tests.
4. Calculate the intelligence quotient.

The procedure may be illustrated with the example of Mary, aged eight years and six months. The examiner starts at the seven-year level at which he finds she passes all the tests; she does the same at eight; at the nine-year level she passes five out of six; at ten, three out of six; at eleven, two out of six; at twelve, one out of six; and none at the thirteen-year level. To summarize:

Mary, Age 8–6

Basal M.A., 8 years

Nine year level passes	$5 \times 2^3 =$	10 months
Ten year level passes	$3 \times 2 =$	6 months
Eleven year level passes	$2 \times 2 =$	4 months
Twelve year level passes	$1 \times 2 =$	2 months
		22 months

Mental Age: 8 years + 22 mos. = 9–10

$$\text{I.Q.} = \frac{\text{M.A.}}{\text{C.A.}} \times 100 = \frac{9\text{–}10}{8\text{–}6} \times 100 = \frac{118}{102} \times 100 = 116$$

The tests are placed at age levels such that the standardization population yields an I.Q. very close to 100 at each level. Assuming the sample to be representative of the total population, this is as it should be. Earlier, Binet and others had placed tests at age levels where approximately three-fourths of the standardization population of a given age passed the test. This method was not entirely satisfactory and has been superseded by the method mentioned above. Under ideal circumstances, however, the two methods yield about the same results.

After nearly a quarter century of use of Forms L and M of the 1937

---

[3] Since there are six tests at each year level at this part of the scale, each test is given a weight of two months, that is, $12 \div 6$. At earlier levels there are six tests every half year. These count for one month each. At higher levels tests have a weight of three or more months each.

scale, still another revision was published in 1960.[4] It was made up of those items of Forms L and M which had proved to be most reliable and valid and whose content had not become out-of-date. Items which met these criteria were given a final tryout with several thousand cases and the best ones were combined into Form L–M. The 1937 Forms L and M are still available and widely used but the best of them has been put into a new form. Since this is so, Form L–M is superior in certain respects to its predecessors though there is no equivalent form to go with it.

The new scale also provides tables of Deviation I.Q.'s which can be read directly without calculations when the chronological age is known and the mental age has been established by administering either form of the 1937 scale or the 1960 L–M scale.

The Binet scales and their counterparts in other countries had one limitation, the significance of which was that only one person could be tested at a time by a trained examiner. This is a time-consuming procedure, although it has, nevertheless, certain desirable features, including the opportunity to establish rapport between subject and examiner and to observe the subject while being tested; also, when properly administered, it yields a very dependable appraisal. However, some American psychologists, notably Arthur S. Otis of The World Book Company, W. S. Miller of the University of Minnesota, Rudolf Pintner and E. L. Thorndike of Columbia University, and Terman himself, soon began experimenting with the adaptation of certain types of tests to group testing. In 1917, the entry of the United States into World War I gave this movement the impetus it required for success. Large numbers of men were being inducted into military service and the need for and potential usefulness of some kind of rapid, accurate, mental measurement of men soon became apparent. The government asked a number of psychologists to develop a test for this purpose. The result was *Army Alpha,* the first single, unified group test of intelligence. Its counterpart, *Army Beta,* was also constructed for use with illiterates and those who could not read well enough for *Army Alpha,* which presupposed about sixth-grade reading ability. Nearly two million men were tested by *Alpha* during the war, and in subsequent years it was widely used in schools and colleges.

Soon after *Army Alpha* and *Beta* were produced, many group tests were published, some very closely patterned after the army tests, and none differing materially from them. *Alpha* had been designed for use with adults; most of the new tests were adaptations for use with children and adolescents.

[4] Lewis M. Terman and Maud A. Merrill, *Stanford-Binet Intelligence Scale,* Third Revision (Boston: Houghton Mifflin Company, 1960).

Although *Army Alpha* is rarely used today, it will be interesting and revealing to examine it a little more closely. It consisted of eight subtests or parts, each closely timed. The working time for the entire test was forty minutes. Some samples follow:

ARMY ALPHA — FORM 6

Test 3. This is a test of common sense. Below are sixteen questions. Three answers are given to each question. You are to look at the answers carefully; then make a cross in the square before the best answer to each question, as in the sample:

Sample:

Why do we use stoves? Because

☐ they look well

☒ they keep us warm

☐ they are black

Here the second answer is the best and is marked with a cross. Begin with No. 1 and keep on until time is called. Time: 1½ minutes.

Test 7.

Sample:

> sky — blue::grass — **table green warm big**
> fish — swims::man — **paper time walks girl**
> day — night::white — **red black clear pure**

In each of the lines above, the first two words are related to each other in some way. What you are to do in each line is to see what the relation is between the first two words, and underline the word in heavy type that is related in the same way to the third word. Begin with No. 1 and mark as many sets as you can before time is called. Time: 3 minutes (for 40 analogies).

The other tests in *Army Alpha* were *Following Directions, Arithmetic, Opposites, Scrambled or Disarranged Sentences, Number Series Completion,* and *General Information.* The items in each test were arranged in order of difficulty, closely timed, and speeded — that is, speed was strongly emphasized.

Army Beta was designed as a counterpart to *Army Alpha,* but it did not require the ability to read. It could be given without spoken directions, so it was strictly a non-verbal examination. It had the same number of parts as *Alpha* and was designed to parallel in purpose, but pictorially, most of the parts or sub-tests of *Alpha*. *Army Beta* was not nearly as extensively used as *Alpha,* either during the war or subsequently.

Although hundreds of group intelligence tests have been developed since 1917, those which have been successful do not differ in fundamental respects from *Army Alpha*. This is not a criticism of newer tests, but rather, a recognition of the basic soundness of this first venture, which, of course, was essentially an adaptation of Binet's ideas to group testing. The importance of Binet's contribution to the development of mental tests is obvious. Undoubtedly a genius, he established the basic principles and devised the appropriate techniques which have been followed, without material change, to this day.

▶ LEARNING EXERCISES ◀

1. Besides those mentioned in the brief historical sketch just given, others have been prominently identified with the early days of mental testing. Find five of these and give in a sentence or two the chief contribution of each. (Note: See references at the end of this chapter. Do not confine yourself to Americans.)

2. Binet died in 1911 at the age of fifty-four. Look up his biography and make an outline of the main events of his professional life and his major contributions to psychology.

3. Examine a copy of *Army Beta* along with one of *Army Alpha*. See if you can pair the tests in the former with their counterparts in the latter. How would you set up an experiment to determine the extent to which *Alpha* and *Beta* were equivalent.

BASIC CONCEPTS AND PRINCIPLES OF INTELLIGENCE MEASUREMENT

Before discussing current procedures in measuring intelligence we should consider some of the fundamental ideas and associated problems of this field. Most of these problems are theoretical and do not affect to any great extent the actual use of the tests. Nevertheless, it is important for the user to understand this theory so that he can be more realistic in his approach and more aware of the strengths and limitations of the instruments he uses. In instances where the topics discussed are controversial issues, we have tried to present some of the facts on both sides.

Theories of Intelligence

Binet, like many in his field, revised his thinking as he gained more experience and witnessed the results of his tests. It will be recalled that at the time of the publication of his first scale in 1905 he believed "sound judgment" to be the central factor. This was in sharp contrast to the views held by most of his predecessors and contemporaries, who believed that intelligence consists of a large number of specifics. The tests of reaction time, acuity of vision, hearing, and so on, were consistent with this latter view, but they did not prove very useful in distinguishing between feeble-minded and normal children, or in identifying those who were considered brighter by their teachers, or those who did relatively poorly in school or college.

Binet's definition of intelligence included three factors or capacities: ability in thinking (1) to maintain a definite direction or to "stay on the track," (2) to choose appropriate means to ends, or to adapt procedures to goals sought, and (3) to evaluate objectively one's own actions (autocriticism). In general, Binet held that the mind is unitary and possesses one overriding function: effective adjustment to environment.

More precisely defined theories of intelligence have been advanced by various people contemporary with and following Binet. The first of these is the *two-factor theory* developed by Charles Spearman, an English statistician. On the basis of correlation studies, he proposed a theory that intelligence consists of two factors: a general factor, g, and many specific factors, s_1, s_2, etc. The g enters into all intellectual activities, while each particular activity is also subject to one or more specific factors.

In contrast with the two-factor theory is one which has been referred to as the *multi-factor theory,* the beginnings of which are generally associated with the name of E. L. Thorndike.[5] His theory holds that intelligence consists of a very large number of specific factors or functions ($s_1 + s_2 + s_3 + \ldots . . s_n$) and casts doubt on the existence of any g, or general factor. This is consistent with Thorndike's theory of learning called *connectionism,* which holds that learning consists of forming connections or bonds between specific stimuli and responses and that a person's learning increases with the number of connections formed. Consequently, his degree of intelligence would be determined by the ease with which bonds are formed and by their strength and number.

A third theory, somewhat between these two, is called the *group-factor theory,* usually associated with the name of L. L. Thurstone, an American

[5] E. L. Thorndike, *The Measurement of Intelligence* (New York: Teachers College, Columbia University, 1927).

psychologist and statistician. According to this theory, intelligence consists neither of *g* and *s,* nor of many *s*'s, but of six to ten primary or group factors. The six named by Thurstone are number, verbal, space, word fluency, reasoning, and rote memory. While none of these factors is completely distinct from the others, statistical evidence has been presented to justify the assumption that they are not the same. The Thurstone theory is, in a sense, a compromise or middle ground between the other two.

In developing the theory of group factors, or Primary Mental Abilities as Thurstone called them, he used the technique referred to earlier (Chapter 2) as factor analysis. By this statistical procedure, based on intercorrelations between tests, the factor analyst arrives at a limited number of factors which appear to be fairly distinct entities. Taken together they comprise what, in this instance, is called general intelligence or general mental ability.

Although all three of the theories discussed are based on statistical foundations, they illustrate the inevitable fact that different individuals will occasionally interpret the same or similar data differently. Present-day thinking leans toward the group-factor theory as being probably most consistent with the facts, but it recognizes the probability of the existence of a general factor also.

The Intelligence Quotient

Apparently Binet did not come to the concept of the I.Q. himself, but he clearly saw and expressed the mental-age concept at the time of the publication of his first scale, and the idea emerged clearly with the 1908 revision. A German psychologist, Wilhelm Stern, seems to have been the first to formulate the concept of the intelligence quotient, in 1912, a year after Binet's death. The intelligence quotient, or I.Q., as it is generally known, was quickly adopted by Terman and others, and today is the generally accepted means of expressing intelligence, at least of persons below adulthood.

The ratio I.Q., as has been shown already, is the ratio of mental age or level to chronological or life age. Thus, it is reasoned that a child developing normally should have a mental age equivalent to his chronological age and therefore an I.Q. of 1, or, as it is commonly expressed, 100: The mental age or level for any given chronological age up to maturity is determined by testing a representative sample of children of that age. The mental age of nine, for example, is determined by giving that test to a representative sample of nine-year-old children. The average score in a group test made by these nine-year-olds is the mental-age norm for that life age.

Subsequently, any child who makes that score is said to have a mental age of nine. On the other hand, this same score (and mental age) may be earned by children of varying life or chronological ages. Thus, John who is twelve may earn a score typical of nine-year-olds; therefore, his I.Q. is $\frac{9}{12} \times 100 = 75$. Again, Jean may be ten and if her mental age is nine, her I.Q. is 90; still another child with an M.A. of nine may be only seven, in which case his I.Q. is about 130. Thus, the I.Q. represents the ratio of mental age to chronological age or the rate of mental development compared to age. In the first instance above, there is, on the average, three-quarters of a year of mental growth per year of life; in the second, nine-tenths of a year; and in the third, 1.3 years mental gain for every year lived. The same facts may be shown in a different way by comparing children of the same age who have different mental ages.

The ratio I.Q. concept has been under fire from various quarters for a number of reasons. For example, it does not have the unqualified approval of educational statisticians because it does not have the same meaning at all levels or points on the scale. An I.Q. of 120 represents the ratio of $\frac{6}{5}$ in a five-year-old and the ratio of $\frac{12}{10}$ in a ten-year-old. Obviously, in the first case the difference between M.A. and C.A. is one year; in the second, two years. However, this disadvantage is inherent in any ratio and applies to the I.Q. to no greater extent than it does to any other.

Another criticism of the ratio I.Q. is that such I.Q.'s are not comparable from one test to another. This was early pointed out by W. S. Miller[6] who gave ten different intelligence tests to a group of fifty-seven ninth-grade pupils and found that there was a range of more than three years in the mean M.A.'s on the ten tests. Thus a child might have an I.Q. of 116 on one of the tests and 130 on another. Miller showed that this was largely due to differences in the tests themselves and differences in the standardization population. He suggested a method of equating such differences by converting the I.Q.'s to standard scores, as described in Chapter 3.

Another shortcoming of the ratio I.Q. resides in the assumption of a constant rate of mental development for a given individual. This assumption, although true, relatively speaking, for many, is not true for all. Research has shown that rate of mental development, as measured by existing tests, is not constant but fluctuates rather markedly in some instances.

[6] W. S. Miller, "Variation and Significance of Intelligence Quotients Obtained from Group Tests," *Journal of Educational Psychology,* 15:359–66, September, 1924; "Variation of I.Q.'s Obtained from Group Tests," 24:468–74, September, 1933.

One other aspect of the ratio I.Q. concept, also in the nature of a limitation, should be mentioned here. Experience has shown that the functions or capacities measured by existing intelligence tests reach their maximum about the same time as physical maturity is reached, which seems to be somewhere between the ages of fifteen and twenty, as reported in various studies. In some respects this would appear to be quite consistent, since we do not expect an individual to grow taller or to acquire more teeth or stronger eyesight once he is mature. On the other hand, most individuals like to think of themselves as gaining in wisdom and stature as long as they live, or at least until they grow quite old. Thus, as far as the ratio I.Q. goes, if we continue to use $\frac{M.A.}{C.A.}$ and the individual's M.A. ceases to increase after a certain age, the I.Q. value declines. To illustrate, if $\frac{M.A.}{C.A.}$ were $\frac{16}{16}$ the I.Q. would be 100. If the M.A. was still 16 when the C.A. was 20, the ratio then would be .80, or, I.Q. = 80. This, of course is an obviously erroneous conclusion, and certainly a demoralizing one. Consequently, it is customary with subjects past the age of sixteen not to calculate I.Q.'s at all, but to express the individual's position relative to others in his group, either by percentile ranks or by standard scores. This is the procedure followed almost entirely with adult groups such as college and university students, men and women in military service, and so on. In effect, this procedure results in an equivalent of the I.Q., since we can assume that these persons have reached maturity. Therefore, the denominator of the $\frac{M.A.}{C.A.}$ ratio is a constant factor and the score or percentile rank is really a measure comparable to the ratio I.Q. rather than simply a measure of rank or relative position.

To overcome the major weaknesses of the ratio I.Q. the so-called deviation I.Q. has come increasingly into use in recent years. As explained in Chapter 3, this is a standard score with an arbitrarily chosen mean and standard deviation. Although any values, such as a mean of 50 and standard deviation of 10 as used for the sigma scores in Chapter 3, could be employed, it has become quite general practice to use a mean of 100 and a standard deviation of 16. The reason for using these values is that they are the mean and standard deviation, respectively, of *Stanford Binet* I.Q.'s. I.Q.'s based on these constants are therefore numerically comparable to *Binet* I.Q.'s. Thus, a ratio I.Q. one standard deviation above the mean of a particular group test becomes a deviation I.Q. of 116; one which is two standard deviations above the mean on this test becomes a deviation

I.Q. of 132; a ratio I.Q. one standard deviation below the mean of the test becomes a deviation I.Q. of 84, and so on.

The comparable values in terms of standard scores, deviation I.Q.'s, and percentile ranks can be seen clearly by reference to Figure 1 in Chapter 3.

Constancy of the I.Q.

One of the continuing points of issue about the I.Q. concept is the question of constancy. Usually this means constancy from time to time in the development of the individual, though it may also mean constancy at different levels or points on the scale. The latter has been touched upon in the preceding section as a function of the ratio I.Q. and is a technical matter beyond the scope of this book. The question of constancy in an individual, however, is one of direct concern to every user of intelligence tests. In essence, this question is, "If I test a child today and he has an I.Q. of 90, what is the result likely to be if I test him again a year or more from now?" This is probably what most persons have in mind when they discuss the constancy of the I.Q.

Numerous longitudinal studies have been reported in which children have been tested annually or semi-annually over a period of years. In one study,[7] sixty-one children were tested at the pre-school ages of one month to five years by the *California Pre-school Schedule,* from six to twelve years and at fourteen and seventeen years by the *Stanford-Binet.* At ages thirteen and fifteen they were tested by a group test, the *Terman McNemar,* and at age sixteen and eighteen, by the *Wechsler-Bellevue.* The study began with sixty-one infants. At the last testing at age eighteen, thirty-seven cases were tested. The results showed that: (1) correlations between tests of children below age six ranged from −.13 to .73 (*California* with *Binet*), and (2) correlations between tests given between age six and eleven ranged from .73 to .93 (*Binet* at all levels).

In another study,[8] 252 children were tested annually from age twenty-one months to eighteen years by the *California Pre-School Schedule,* the *Stanford-Binet,* or the *Wechsler-Bellevue* (an individual scale for adults). The results were similar to those reported by Bayley. In general they indicated that: the (1) results of tests made after age six are much more stable than those of tests made before age six; (2) individual children showed

[7] Nancy Bayley, "Consistency and Variability in the Growth of Intelligence from Birth to Eighteen," *Journal of Genetic Psychology,* 75:165–196, 1949.

[8] Marjorie P. Honzik, Jean MacFarlane, and L. Allen, "The Stability of Mental Test Performance Between Two and Eighteen Years," *Journal of Experimental Education,* 17:309–324, December, 1948.

marked fluctuation in I.Q. over the sixteen-year period (the tested I.Q.'s of 58 per cent of the children changed 15 points or more); (3) the longer the interval between tests, the greater the possibility of change; and (4) the maximum shift in average I.Q. for the group as a whole, between twenty-one months and eighteen years, was from 118 to 123 or 5 points.

Another study[9] is of interest since it examines the question of whether or not deviation I.Q.'s are more stable than ratio I.Q.'s, as has been suggested by some authorities. Fifty boys and girls were tested by the 1937 *Binet* every six months from age two and a half to five and annually from six through twelve years of age. The results showed that: (1) average I.Q.s in the 140–169 range increased over the years by about 30 points; (2) averages below this range tended to be much more stable; (3) variability of I.Q.'s of the entire group decreased between ages three and five, increased between five and ten and declined again between ten and twelve; and (4) no difference was found in the relative variability of ratio and deviation I.Q.'s.

Taken altogether, the evidence on stability of measured I.Q.'s can be summed up as follows: (1) average I.Q.'s for groups remain remarkably stable over many years; (2) I.Q.'s of many individual children often fluctuate by substantial amounts;[10] (3) tested I.Q.'s of children below age six are much less stable than those of the same children after age six; and (4) the results of intelligence tests of many children show remarkable consistency over long periods of time.

Finally, it must be emphasized that a single test, either individual or group, constitutes only a very limited sampling of a child's behavior. Because of this fact, the results from a single testing should always be regarded as provisional and should be supplemented by additional testing whenever possible. It should be pointed out in this connection that many schools include in their testing programs at least two and often three to five testings of intelligence between Grades 1 and 12.

Although it is currently fashionable to criticize all standardized tests, and particularly intelligence tests, there should be no serious question of their over-all value and usefulness. This point of view is epitomized in the words of a leading authority in the field, who says:

> The outstanding success of scientific measurement of individual differences in behavior has been that of the general mental test. Despite the overenthusiasm and occasional errors that have attended its development,

---

[9] Byron W. Lindholm, "Changes in Conventional and Deviation I.Q.'s," *Journal of Educational Psychology*, 55:110–113, April, 1964.

[10] In this connection it should be pointed out that in the Bayley and Honzik studies different tests were used at different age levels. Some of the changes found were almost certainly the result of differences between tests.

the general mental test stands today as the most important single contribution of psychology to the practical guidance of human affairs.[11]

The great majority of counselors and school psychologists know this, as do many teachers. To use these instruments wisely, with full recognition of their strengths and weaknesses, should be an objective of everyone involved in testing in the schools.

Distribution of Intelligence Quotients

Since there is no absolute standard of intelligence or of mental age, the basis for these must be relative. In other words, a mental age of twelve years is determined by what a sampling of children representative of the total population of twelve-year-olds can do on a given test. As has been pointed out, this varies from one test to another because of differences in the tests themselves and differences in the population sample. Nevertheless, distributions both of raw scores and I.Q.'s obtained from adequate population samples quite generally show results closely approximating the normal curve. One such distribution for the *Revised Stanford-Binet* is shown in Figure 10. This is based on a composite I.Q. on Forms L and M

FIGURE 10 • Distributions of Composite L–M I.Q.'s of Standardization Group

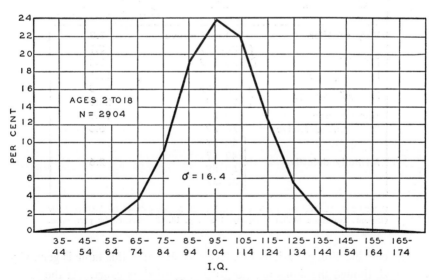

From Lewis M. Terman and Maud A. Merrill, *Measuring Intelligence,* Boston: Houghton Mifflin Company, 1937. Reproduced by permission of the authors and publisher.

[11] Lee J. Cronbach, *Essentials of Psychological Testing,* Second Edition (New York: Harper & Row, Publishers, 1960), p. 157.

of the 1937 Revision for 2,904 subjects, ages two to eighteen, inclusive.

The close approximation to the normal curve in the form of the distribution of I.Q.'s is of considerable importance. If I.Q.'s obtained from intelligence tests did not yield this kind of distribution from adequate population samples, there might be a basis for doubting the validity of such tests, or at least the validity of the particular ones used. The basic assumption is that intelligence is normally distributed in the general population, and tests which do not yield results at least approximating the normal might be open to serious question. Also, this assumption provides a sound theoretical basis for interpreting the significance of any given I.Q. in comparison with the proportion of the general population that has the same I.Q.

When the normal distribution of I.Q.'s is broken up according to the areas under the curve, and a mean of 100 and a standard deviation of 16 are used as the constant values (based on *Stanford-Binet* I.Q. distributions), the proportions of various levels of I.Q. are as shown in Table VIII below.

TABLE VIII • Classification and Proportions of Various Levels of I.Q. in the General Population

Classification	I.Q.	Percentage in General Population
Very superior	140 and above	1.3
Superior	⎰ 130–139	3.1
	⎱ 120–129	8.2
High average	110–119	18.1
Normal average	⎰ 100–109	23.5
	⎱ 90–99	23.0
Low average	80–89	14.5
Borderline defective	70–79	5.6
Mentally defective	⎧ 60–69 ⎫	2.6
	⎪ 40–49 ⎪	
	⎨ 50–59 ⎬	
	⎩ 30–39 ⎭	

From Lewis M. Terman and Maude A. Merrill, *Stanford-Binet Intelligence Scale* (Boston: Houghton Mifflin Company, 1960), p. 18. Reproduced by permission.

The classification of various I.Q. levels as shown in this table is generally accepted, though the limits are not to be regarded as exact. At the lower end of the distribution, the mentally defective have, in the past, been classed as morons, imbeciles, and idiots, in descending order; those whose I.Q.'s are below the lowest limit in the table are usually classed as idiots.

However, it is customary to use more functional designations today, such as "educable" or "trainable mentally retarded." Another recommended set of designations is "mildly retarded" (moron), "moderately retarded" (imbecile), and "severely retarded" (idiot).

Heredity versus Environment

Closely related to the question of the constancy of the I.Q. is the question of the relative influence of heredity and environment. This controversy has raged for years with equally strong support on both sides of the argument. To a considerable degree the argument has been implemented and intensified by the development of intelligence tests. The widespread application of *Army Alpha* and its successors has supplied immense amounts of data, making possible comparisons among different racial, socio-economic, and cultural groups or levels. Implicit in such comparisons, of course, is always the question of to what extent the differences among these groups are due to heredity or environment, or both.

The debate on the relative influences of heredity and environment, while often apparently useless, is nevertheless concerned with a question of fundamental importance to educators and psychologists. Obviously, if a child's capacity for accomplishment were determined solely by inherited traits or abilities, education necessarily would have quite a different outlook and philosophy than it would in a less deterministic frame of reference.

Many investigations and experiments have been made on this question from the time of Galton to the present. One method of investigation involves studies of persons who are obviously brilliant, feebleminded, or degenerate, to determine whether such traits tend to run in families. Most of these studies show that they do. Even with this knowledge, however, the question of whether such characteristics are due more to inheritance or to environment is not satisfactorily answered.

Another type of investigation involves the transplanting of children from a poor environment to a good one. The results of such studies are equivocal; some children show general and marked improvement in intelligence and other traits; others do not. One is almost forced to conclude, that investigators tend to find the results they look for; much of the research showing marked changes has been severely criticized for poor control, careless procedures, or bad statistical treatment of data.

A third type of investigation uses twins as subjects. Identical twins are as nearly alike in heredity and environment as two humans can be. Starting with a large number of pairs of twins, the investigator studies many aspects of their resemblances — physical, mental, and in personality. Most of these studies show remarkable and, in some instances, almost incredible similarities among pairs of identical twins. In the few cases where studies have been made of identical twins reared in different environments, the resemblances have been less close in mental and social traits than in physical traits.

In summary, it may be said that the heredity-environment issue is far from settled. During the last hundred years there appears to have been a gradual shift from a viewpoint strongly hereditarian to one more favorable to the environmentalist point of view. Of course there are extremists who would rule out entirely one or the other point of view, but most educators and psychologists, believing that what the individual becomes is the result of an interaction of heredity and environment, take a middle-of-the-road view on this question. As one writer has put it, "The great mathematician, Sir Isaac Newton, if he had been brought up among African bushmen would probably have become a remarkable bushman but he would never have discovered the laws of motion." Similar statements might be made about a Mozart, an Einstein, or an Edison. In every instance, environmental opportunities were necessary to bring out a remarkable native endowment. On the other hand it is improbable that any conceivable environment could make an Einstein, a Mozart, a Newton, or an Edison of a child having no special talents or unusual endowments.

Recent studies[12] suggest that cultural factors may enter into performance on intelligence tests more than had been supposed. It is maintained that existing group tests penalize children who come from poor homes and whose cultural patterns, parental attitudes, and group standards are not the middle-class ones which are said to dominate school and testing situations. Experimentation and studies are now being carried on to investigate this hypothesis further.

▶ **LEARNING EXERCISES** ◀

4. Solve the following using the formula $\text{I.Q.} = \dfrac{\text{M.A.}}{\text{C.A.}} \times 100$:

$$\text{M.A.} = 7; \text{C.A.} = 10 \qquad \text{I.Q.} =$$
$$\text{M.A.} = 12; \text{I.Q.} = 125 \qquad \text{C.A.} =$$
$$\text{C.A.} = 10; \text{I.Q.} = 90 \qquad \text{M.A.} =$$
$$\text{M.A.} = 10 - 8; \text{C.A.} = 9 - 4 \qquad \text{I.Q.} =$$

[12] Kenneth W. Eells, Allison Davis, Robert J. Havighurst, Virgil E. Herrick, and Ralph Tyler, *Intelligence and Cultural Differences* (Chicago: University of Chicago Press, 1951).

5. Using the following data, calculate the proportion of the total population with I.Q.'s above 116 and the proportion below 84.

$$M = 100 \qquad \sigma = 16$$

(Note: Refer to Chapter 3 and Appendix A.)

6. Assume that Group Test A yields a mean I.Q. of 102 and a standard deviation of 18 for a representative sample of ten-year-olds. Convert the following ratio I.Q.'s into deviation I.Q.'s with a mean of 100 and a standard deviation of 16: (a) 120;   (b) 84;   (c) 75;   (d) 138;   (e) 93.

7. Plan an experiment with guinea pigs to show the effects of differences in heredity under the same environmental condition. Plan another to measure the effects of changed environment with heredity constant. How would you measure the results?

CURRENT PROCEDURES IN MEASURING INTELLIGENCE

Verbal and Non-verbal Material

The content of intelligence tests is generally classified as verbal or non-verbal. Verbal material requires the ability to read or, at the very least, to understand material spoken or read aloud by the examiner. Therefore, a strictly non-verbal examination is one that requires no use of language in its administration or in the pupils' answers. Such a test was referred to earlier in the case of *Army Beta,* where it was stated that the directions for that examination could be given in pantomime. Tests are rarely non-verbal to this extreme; indeed we generally consider an intelligence test non-verbal as long as it does not require any reading ability. This type of test is useful and quite generally necessary in testing young children, illiterates, and the feebleminded.

While non-verbal material may be pictorial, it may also be of the type known as "performance." Formboards, which are a kind of jigsaw puzzle, building blocks, and tracing mazes are typical of the performance type of exercises found in individual intelligence tests. Samples are shown in Figure 11.

In group tests the non-verbal material is generally pictorial, as will be illustrated later in this chapter.

Although the correlation between verbal and non-verbal types of tests of intelligence is far from perfect, it is generally high enough to justify the use of non-verbal material where verbal tests cannot be used. This is found most often in tests for young children. Non-verbal material of the performance type is also used extensively in tests of aptitude.

It should also be noted that many intelligence tests in current use in-

FIGURE 11 • Examples of Typical Performance Tests

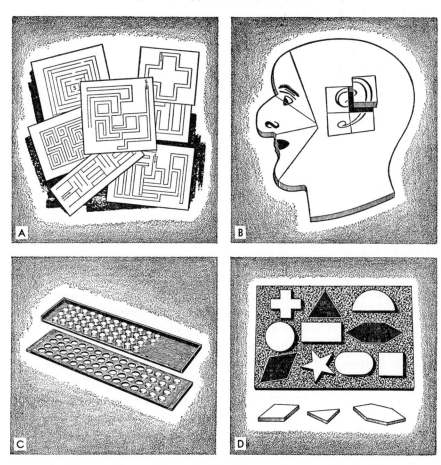

A. Porteus Maze Test. B. Knox-Kemp Feature Profile Test: Pintner-Patterson Modification. C. Minnesota Rate of Manipulation Test. D. Seguin-Goddard Formboard.

Reproduced by permission of C. H. Stoelting Company, publisher.

clude both verbal and non-verbal, that is, non-reading, material. This is true of both individual scales like the Binet and of numerous group tests. In some instances the materials are arranged so as to yield both a verbal and a non-verbal I.Q.

Individual Scales

A brief description has already been given of the nature and the procedure for administering a *Stanford-Binet* examination. The method is essentially the same in others of the *Binet* type, such as the *Kuhlmann,* except that the latter takes both accuracy and speed of response into account. It will be recalled that one of the criticisms of the *Stanford-Binet* (1916) was lack of adequate "ceiling" or "top" for testing adults. Although this was remedied to a large extent in the 1937 Revision, there was still some dissatisfaction on this point.

Another frequently voiced criticism of the *Binet* scale and its revisions was that the scales were designed for use with children, and the adult materials added later were really not essentially different. Consequently, it was said that the scales were not appropriate for adults and not intrinsically interesting to them. To meet these criticisms a scale for measuring adult intelligence was brought out by Wechsler in 1939.[13] This was an individual intelligence scale known as the *Wechsler-Bellevue Intelligence Scale.* It departs in certain important respects from the *Binet*-type scale. The tests are not grouped by age levels and the scale yields standard score or deviation I.Q.'s. It was designed for and standardized largely on adults, but attained some popularity for use with children as well. In 1949 Wechsler published another scale for children, the *Wechsler Intelligence Scale for Children,* along the same general pattern as the adult scale.[14] More recently he has published a revised and improved *Adult Intelligence Scale.*[15]

The *WAIS* consists of eleven sub-tests divided into a Verbal Scale and a Performance Scale. The Verbal Scale includes tests called *Information, Comprehension, Arithmetic, Similarities, Digit Span,* and *Vocabulary.* The Performance Scale includes tests called *Digit Symbol, Picture Completion, Block Design, Picture Arrangement,* and *Object Assembly.* Each test is administered and scored separately; the scores of the Verbal Scale are combined to yield a Verbal I.Q.; the tests of the Performance Scale, to yield a Performance I.Q. All eleven tests combined yield a Full-Scale I.Q. Scores on each sub-test are expressed in standard score units with a mean of 10 and a standard deviation of 3. The I.Q.'s are expressed as deviation I.Q.'s with a mean of 100 and a standard deviation of 15. Five of the sub-tests are scored in terms of both speed and accuracy; the other six are scored on the basis of the number right.

The *WISC* is very similar to the *WAIS* in its composition. It consists of twelve sub-tests also grouped into Verbal and Performance Scales.

[13] David Wechsler, *The Measurement of Adult Intelligence* (Baltimore: Williams and Wilkins, 1939).

[14] David Wechsler, *Wechsler Intelligence Scale for Children* (New York: Psychological Corporation, 1949).

[15] David Wechsler, *Wechsler Adult Intelligence Scale* (New York: Psychological Corporation, 1955).

Most of the sub-tests are of the same type as those in the *WAIS,* but they are easier. Procedures for scoring and calculating I.Q.'s on the two scales are almost identical.

These scales, together with the *Stanford-Binet,* are by far the most widely used individual intelligence tests and are regarded as standard in nearly all work where individual tests are used.

TYPICAL GROUP TESTS OF INTELLIGENCE

There are many group intelligence tests available for use at all levels of human development from kindergarten to adult. Since it would be impossible to make a complete and up-to-date listing of such tests, to say nothing of describing them in detail, only a small number of illustrative ones will be discussed at length, as was done previously with achievement tests. Reference to catalogs of test publishers and to the various editions of *The Mental Measurements Yearbook* will identify many other intelligence tests for those who are interested.

The first group test to be described is one which illustrates many excellent features of construction and standardization. It has come increasingly into general use since its publication.

Lorge-Thorndike Intelligence Tests

1. Names of test and authors. *Lorge-Thorndike Intelligence Tests.*[16] Irving Lorge, Robert L. Thorndike, and Elizabeth Hagen.

2. Nature and purposes. A series of tests of abstract intelligence defined as the ability to work with ideas and the relationships among ideas. The Primary Battery, Levels 1 and 2, is entirely nonverbal. Above these levels, both a Verbal and a Nonverbal Battery are provided.

3. Grade levels. Level 1, K–1; Level 2, 2–3; Level 3, 4–6; Level 4, 7–9; Level 5, 10–12.

4. Number of forms. Forms A and B.

5. Publisher and date of publication. Houghton Mifflin Company, 1954–1964.

6. Cost. Levels 1 or 2, $3.45 per 35; Levels 3, 4, or 5, Verbal or Nonverbal, Consumable Edition, $2.85 per 35, Re-usable Edition, $3.15 per 35. IBM 805 answer sheets, $1.44 per 35; MRC answer sheets $7.50 per 100. Scoring keys and manuals, extra.

---

[16] Quotations in test description by permission of Houghton Mifflin Company, publisher.

7. Content. Subtests of the Primary Battery include *Oral Vocabulary, Pictorial Classification* (the one that doesn't belong) and *Pairing* (the two that go together). The items consist of pictures of familiar common objects or of simple geometrical figures.

The first three drawings are alike in that each has four sides and no lines inside it. The drawing at the right that goes with them is at **D.** It has four sides and no lines inside it. Make a heavy black pencil mark in the **D** answer space for question 0.
Now look at question 00. Find the drawing at the right that goes with the first three.

The Verbal Battery includes sub-tests of *Word Knowledge, Sentence Completion, Verbal Classification, Verbal Analogies,* and *Arithmetic Reasoning.* The Nonverbal Battery includes sub-tests called *Figure Analogies, Figure Classification,* and *Number Series.* No reading is involved.

One word has been left out of each sentence on this page. Choose the word that will make the best, the truest, and the most sensible complete sentence. Look at sample sentence 0.

0. Hot weather comes in the   .

  A fall   **B** night   **C** summer   **D** winter   **E** snow

        A   B   C   D   E

The best answer is **summer.** The letter before **summer** is **C,** so you should make a heavy black pencil mark in the **C** answer space for sentence 0.

Items for all the tests were chosen from a pool of 1,200 on the basis of tryout and statistical analysis of difficulty and item-test correlation.

8. Time required. The Primary Battery, Levels 1 and 2, has no time limits. Working time of 20 minutes and total time of 30 minutes is considered adequate. It is recommended, especially for Level 1, that the test at these levels be administered in two sessions.

For the Verbal Battery, Levels 3, 4, and 5, the working time is 34 minutes with total time not over 45 minutes.

For the Nonverbal Battery, Levels 3, 4, and 5, working time is 27 minutes, total time not over 40 minutes.

Time limits are based on preliminary tryouts and are considered ample for most pupils.

9. Directions for and ease of administering. Directions are clear and complete. However, considering the amount to be read by the examiner, the sample items to be answered, and time required for distributing materials, answering questions, and for taking care of possible exigencies, together with the inexperience in test administration of the average examiner, it seems doubtful that the total times suggested will be adequate. The user should probably be prepared to allow from 5 to 15 minutes more than is suggested.

10. Validity. It is implied that the tests have content validity in that the items generally deal with familiar matters, and success in answering correctly depends primarily on the ability to deal with the relationships among the components.

Construct validity is believed by the authors to result from the facts that the tests deal with abstract and general concepts, require use and interpretation of symbols and relationships among them, require flexibility in organizing concepts and symbols, and test power rather than speed.

Correlations with the *California Test of Mental Maturity,* the *Kuhlmann-Anderson* and the *Otis* tests of mental ability given not more than three years earlier average respectively, .74, .66, and .73. Correlations with the *Pintner-Cunningham,* the *Stanford-Binet,* and the *WISC* range from .44 to .77, with a median of .54. Correlations with the *Stanford Achievement Test, Reading* was .87 and with Arithmetic, .76. In one study, the correlation between the *Lorge-Thorndike,* Level 4, given at the beginning of the year in the ninth grade, and average achievement at the end of the year was .672.

A factor analysis of the sub-tests of the *Lorge-Thorndike* showed a distinct communality for the verbal tests and a similar result for the nonverbal tests.

Taken altogether, the data on the validity of these tests is impressive.

11. Reliability. Alternate forms reliability coefficients for the different levels are as follows: Level 1, .810; Level 2, .761; Levels 3, 4, and 5, Nonverbal, average about .80; Levels 3, 4, and 5, Verbal, average about .87. Odd-even reliabilities are with one exception, above .90. The standard error of measurement for the Primary Battery is approximately 7 points of I.Q.; for the Nonverbal Battery, about 6.5 I.Q. points; for the Verbal Battery, about 4.7 I.Q. points. They range at different score levels and in the three batteries, from 3.0 to 8.3. As would be expected, the lower the score and the lower the level, the larger the standard error.

Correlations between Verbal and Nonverbal batteries average about .65.

12. Manual. *Examiners' Manuals* contain instructions for administering and scoring, information on standardization of the tests, a summary of the nature of the tests, and tables of I.Q. norms, grade percentiles, and grade and age equivalents.

A *Technical Manual* describes in detail how the tests were planned, constructed, and standardized.

Both manuals are clear and complete. They represent a high standard of excellence.

13. Scoring. All levels come in consumable editions which are hand-scored by the use of strip or punched out keys depending on level. Directions are printed on the keys. Levels 3, 4, and 5 are available also in a reusable edition with separate answer sheets, either IBM or MRC. Answer sheets for reusable editions may be hand-scored or scored by machine. Both Verbal and Nonverbal batteries yield deviation I.Q.'s with a mean of 100 and a standard deviation of 16.

14. Norms. More than 136,000 children in forty-four communities in twenty-two states were tested in establishing norms. Communities were selected on the basis of the per cent of adult illiteracy, the proportion of professional workers, home ownership, and home rental value. All pupils in the schools of each community, K–12, were tested.

Besides deviation I.Q.'s for both Verbal and Nonverbal batteries, norms are available in the form of grade percentiles, grade equivalents, and age equivalents. Grade percentiles show the relative position of a pupil in abstract reasoning ability as compared with typical pupils in the same grade tested early in the school year. Grade equivalents are most useful for judging whether or not a pupil's measured achievement, e.g., on an achievement battery, corresponds to his mental ability. Age equivalents are the average raw scores made by pupils of given chronological ages near the beginning of the school year.

15. Format. In makeup, quality of materials, and printing these tests measure up to highest standards. The art work in the Nonverbal items and the arrangement on the page are excellent.

The next group test to be described represents a quite different approach from that used in the *Lorge-Thorndike*. Although designed basically for the same purpose, it uses fewer types of items. It exemplifies in its development, standardization, and subsequent evaluation the highest standards in care and thoroughness of procedures.

Cooperative School and College Ability Tests

1. Names of test and authors. *Cooperative School and College Ability Tests*.[17] Staff members of the Educational Testing Service with the advice and cooperation of many professional educators.

2. Nature and purposes. A series of general mental ability tests designed to measure the capacity of a student to undertake the academic work of the next higher level of schooling. They are, in a certain sense, the descendants of the American Council on Education's *Psychological Tests* for high school seniors and college freshmen. They measure, as did their forerunners, verbal and quantitative abilities.

3. Grade level. Grades 4 through 14: Level 1, 13–14; Level 2, 10–12; Level 3, 8–10; Level 4, 6–8; Level 5, 4–6.

4. Number of forms. A and B.

5. Publisher and date of publication. Educational Testing Service. 1955–57. Supplements, 1958, 1962, 1963.

6. Cost. $4.00 per 20. Answer sheets $1.00 per 20.

7. Content. The content of all levels is of the same nature. There are four types of items.

   a. Sentence understandings:

      We had worked hard all day so that by evening we were quite

   A small   B tired   C old   D untrained   E intelligent

   b. Numerical computation:

$$5413$$
$$-4827$$

   F 586   G 596   H 696   J 1586   K none of these

[17] Quotations in test description by permission of the publisher, the Educational Testing Service.

c. *Word meanings:*

Chilly:

   A tired   B nice   C dry   D cold   E sunny

d. *Numerical problem solving:*

Four $10 bills are equal to how many $5 bills?

   F 20   G 10   H 8   J 40   K 2

The items in the five levels differ only in difficulty. Item types (a) and (c) are combined to yield a Verbal score; (b) and (d) are combined to yield a Quantitative score. All four types combined yield a Total score.

8. Time required. Ninety-five minutes if given in one session; 95–100 minutes if given in two sessions.

9. Directions for and ease of administering. The directions are models of clarity and completeness, both for preparations for testing and for administering. The tests are simple to administer. If they are administered in two sessions, the directions do not include instructions regarding how to prevent students from changing answers marked in the first session when they return for the second.

10. Validity. Evidence for validity is primarily statistical in nature. It consists largely of correlations between scores (V, Q, and T) and teachers' ratings, grades, and scores on standardized tests of achievement. Space limitations prohibit the listing of the results of the many studies of this nature reported in the manuals and supplements. On the average, the correlations are as high or higher than those reported for any tests of a similar nature. The studies range over all grades from fifth through twelfth, and measure predictive value over one-and two-year periods. In another study, scores on *SCAT* earned in the eighth, ninth, tenth, eleventh and twelfth grades were correlated with twelfth grade scores on the *Scholastic Aptitude Test* of the College Entrance Examination Board. These correlations ranged from .68 (*SCAT, Q.* eighth grade with *SAT* Math twelfth grade) to .86 (*SCAT, V.* twelfth grade with *SAT*, Verbal twelfth grade).

11. Reliability. All reliability coefficients and standard errors of measurement are based upon the Kuder-Richardson Formula 20. Coefficients for Verbal scores range from .92 to .94. For Quantitative scores the range is .88–.93. For Total scores all coefficients, Levels 1–5, are .95 except Level 4A, which is .96. All coefficients are based on scores on Form A, but since Forms A and B are very similar in content, it is stated that the reliabilities of Form B are probably very similar. No test-retest or alternate form reliabilities are reported. Standard errors of measurement range from 2.71 to 4.34 raw score units.

12. Manual. Manuals include a Directions for Administering and Scoring, a Manual for Interpreting Scores, a Technical Report, and Supplements for 1958, 1962, and 1963. These provide the necessary directions for using the tests and a wealth of information concerning the development, standardization, and subsequent evaluation of the effectiveness of the tests for the purposes for which they were developed, and supplemental norms.

13. Scoring. Tests may be scored by hand, by an IBM test-scoring machine, or by SCRIBE, the electronic scoring process of the Educational Testing Service. The last-named is by far the quickest method and the most efficient for scoring large numbers of papers. All answers are marked on separate answer sheets. Three scores — Verbal, Quantitative and Total — are obtained for each student. Raw scores are changed to "converted scores," a type of standard score. These in turn are converted to percentile ranks. Comparisons of a student's score with that of other students at the same level or adjacent levels may be made by use of the converted score scale. Percentile ranks are interpreted in terms of percentile bands which represent confidence levels having a range of two standard errors, one on either side of a student's obtained score.

14. Norms. The normative populations for these tests were chosen with great care to make them as truly representative as possible for the various grade levels. To accomplish this, *SCAT* was administered to all the students in at least fifty schools in each grade from 4 through 12 and in each of grades 13 and 14 to twelve students in 120 colleges. The schools and colleges were chosen from nine regions of the United States so as to be proportional to the populations of those regions. The first norms were based on 1955 testing and new or supplemental norms were obtained by testing in 1957. The 1963 Supplement reports norms for grades 4 through 12 based on testing in urban schools in fifty-nine cities with populations of 100,000 or more. Norms relating *SCAT* scores to scores on the *Sequential Tests of Educational Progress* are also available for grades 4 through 12.

15. Format. In quality of materials, printing, and attractiveness of format, the *SCAT* series is of the highest order. The use of color on the covers of all booklets adds to their appeal.

The third type of intelligence test to be described here is one that is unusual and yet representative of a number of attempts to construct a test that is relatively "culture fair." Many persons have been concerned with the possibility that scores on existing intelligence tests are affected by the cultural and educational opportunities of the individual, as we have mentioned earlier in this chapter. The basic assumption in conventional tests is that the material or content used is novel to practically all children being tested, or that the children have had an equal opportunity to learn it. From a test construction standpoint, it is more desirable to use material which is novel to a majority of the children, yet it is most difficult to attain this objective in any absolute sense. It seems safe to say, therefore, that the best current intelligence tests have attempted to provide materials and content which most school children have had ample opportunity to learn, and most tests have succeeded rather well in this. Thus, the degree to which the child has learned that which is within the common experience of children of his age group can be taken as a reflection of his ability to learn, that is, his intelligence.

In the work of Eells and his associates, cited earlier, it was found that some types of content in current intelligence tests seem more affected than others by differences in cultural and socio-economic factors. An attempt was made to identify types of material least affected in this way and to construct a test which would be little affected by such differences. The test to be described is the instrument that was devised as a result of this research. Although its use in the schools has not borne out the expectations of those responsible for its development and standardization, it is described here as an example of an unusual and interesting attempt to solve a recurring problem in the field of mental measurement.

Davis-Eells Test of General Intelligence or Problem Solving Ability

1. Names of test and authors. *Davis-Eells Test of General Intelligence or Problem Solving Ability*.[18] Allison Davis and Kenneth Eells.

2. Nature and purposes. To construct a test of intelligence, free of reading demands, based on common experiences shared by all urban American children. The test is said to consist of realistic problems in the experience of all children and is entirely pictorial except for directions read aloud by the administrator of the test.

3. Grade level. Primary, Grades 1 and 2; Elementary, Grades 3 through 6.

4. Number of forms. One form.

5. Publisher and date of publication. Harcourt, Brace & World, Inc. 1953.

6. Cost. Primary, $4.00 per 35; Elementary, $4.45 per 35.

[18] Quotations in test description by permission of the publisher. From *Davis-Eells Test of General Intelligence or Problem-Solving Ability* by Allison Davis and Kenneth Eells. Copyright 1953 by Harcourt, Brace & World, Inc., New York.

7. Content. One part is called "Best Ways" problems. In each problem, three pictures are presented. Each picture shows a person or group of persons starting to solve a problem in a different way. The task is to find the picture that shows the best way of solving the problem. Example:

Another type of problem is called "Analogies." This consists of pictorial situations like the example shown below.

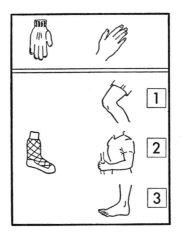

In each case the relationship between the first pair is made clear or suggested by the examiner before the child finds the answer.

A third type of problem is one called "Probabilities." In each case a picture shows a situation which is followed by three possible explanations. The task is to select the most likely explanation.

No. 1: The man *fell down* and hit his head.

No. 2: A ball *came through the window* and hit the man's head.

No. 3: The picture *does not show how* the man got the bump on his head. Nobody can tell because the picture doesn't show how the man got the bump.

Which number was true?

These three types of problems are found both in the *Primary* and the *Elementary* tests. In addition, the *Elementary* test contains some problems called "Money Problems." In these the pupil is required to indicate how a given amount of change could be made from certain available coins. For example, in the problem below the task is to select from the three pictures the one in which the coins on the right could be obtained from the group of coins on the left.

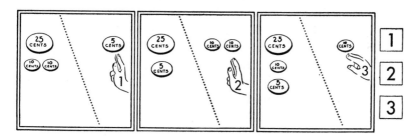

8. Time required. *Primary,* Grade 1: two 30-minute periods. Grade 2: three 30-minute periods. *Elementary:* two 60-minute periods.

9. Directions for and ease of administering. Directions for administering are very detailed and complete. Administration is comparatively complicated and time-consuming. Most of the time required to give the tests is consumed in reading directions and explanations.

10. Validity. The content of the tests is said to be independent of reading skill, in-school instruction, or speed of response. The test purports to be a measure of "over-all capacity to solve mental problems," and not a scholastic aptitude test. These problems are chosen as being of a kind which are encountered by most children. Correlations of the *Davis-Eells Test* with *Otis Quick-Scoring Mental Ability Tests* range from .39 to .66, with a median of .52. Correlations with scores on standardized achievement tests in reading, arithmetic, language, and spelling are in the neighborhood of .40.

11. Reliability. Split-half reliability coefficients corrected by use of the Spearman-Brown Formula average about .83 in Grades 2 through 6; for Grade 1 this coefficient is .68. The standard error of measurement of a score ranges from 2.5 to 3.5. Test-retest coefficients with an interval of two weeks were approximately .70 in Grade 2 and .90 in Grade 4.

12. Manual. The tests are accompanied by *Directions for Administering,* which include directions for scoring, tables for converting raw score to an Index of Problem Solving Ability (IPSA), and percentile equivalents. Information concerning development of the test, validity, reliability, and other statistical data is available in a separate manual. It would be useful to have at least the most important of such information in the booklet accompanying the test.

13. Scoring. Scoring is quite simple. All items are of the three-response type, the pupil marking the number of the choice that seems best to him. Since there are only forty-seven items in the *Primary* form and sixty-two in the *Elementary,* and since these are widely spaced and in large print, it is easy to score the test. No separate answer sheets are provided, though they could be used, at least at the upper grade levels. The score is the number right. Printed scoring keys are provided. The raw score is converted to an IPSA (Index of Problem Solving Ability) by use of the tables previously referred to. Ages are used to the nearest half-year, which gives an approximate value for the IPSA. The IPSA is based on a normalized distribution with a mean of 100 and a standard deviation of 16. The authors state that this Index of Problem Solving Ability may also be called an I.Q.

14. Norms. Means, medians, and standard deviations of raw scores are given for age groups by three-month intervals from 6–0 to 8–5 in Grade 1; from 7–0 to 9–5 in Grade 2; from 8–0 to 13–11 in Grades 3 to 6.

15. Format. The tests are well arranged and well printed. Figures are large and spacing is generous.

Other Intelligence Tests

INDIVIDUAL

1. *Arthur Point Scale of Performance Tests.* 1947. Ages five to fifteen. *Knox Cube Test, Seguin Form Board* (*Arthur Revision*)*, Arthur Stencil Design Test, Porteus Maze Test* (Arthur Printing)*, Healy Picture Completion Test II.*

Revised Form II. Complete set, with manual and 100 score sheets, $73.00. 60–90 minutes.

Psychological Corporation.

2. *Columbia Mental Maturity Scale.* Revised, 1959.

Ages three to 10. One hundred cards each containing a series of drawings from which the examinee selects the one that does not belong.

One form, $35.00 per set including manual. Record blanks, $1.60 per 35. 15–20 minutes.

Harcourt, Brace & World, Inc.

3. *Leiter International Performance Scale.* 1948–52. Ages two to eighteen. Fifty-four tests involving *matching of colors and of objects, picture completion, spatial relations, footprint recognition,* etc.

One form, revised. $187.50 per set of test materials, 100 record blanks, carrying case, and manual. 30 to 60 minutes.

C. H. Stoelting Company.

4. *Minnesota Preschool Scale.* 1940. Ages one and a half to six, inclusive. Twenty-six tests: Verbal includes *pointing to and naming objects; comprehension; naming colors,* etc. Non-verbal includes *copying figures, Knox Cube Test, paper-folding,* etc.

Forms A and B. $38.00 per set. 10–30 minutes.

American Guidance Service.

5. *Revised Stanford-Binet Intelligence Scale.* 1960.

Age two to superior adult. For description see text.

One form. $33.20 per set. Record Booklets, $4.40 per 35.

Manual, $4.48. Printed card material separately, $2.60 or $1.00 per set. 1½ hours.

Houghton Mifflin Company.

6. *Wechsler-Bellevue Intelligence Scale.* 1939, 1946. For adults. *Information, general comprehension, arithmetic reasoning, memory span for digits, similarities, vocabulary, picture arrangement, picture completion, block design, object assembly, digit symbol.*

Form II. $21.00 per set; manual, $2.25. Record blanks, $2.10 per 25. About 1 hour.

Psychological Corporation.

7. *Wechsler Intelligence Scale for Children.* 1949. Ages five to fifteen. Same tests as in *Wechsler-Bellevue* with addition of *optional maze test* and *coding* in place of *digit symbol.*

One form. $25.00 per set, including manual. Record forms, $7.50 per 25. Maze Test, $1.35 per 25. About 1 hour.

Psychological Corporation.

8. *Wechsler Adult Intelligence Scale.* 1955. Ages sixteen to seventy-five. Same tests as in *Wechsler-Bellevue,* Form I, revised and re-standardized.

One form. $24.00 per set, including manual. Record forms, $2.10 per 25. About 1 hour.

Psychological Corporation.

GROUP

1. *Academic Promise Tests.* 1959–62. Grades 6–9. *Verbal, numerical, abstract reasoning, language usage.*

Forms A and B. $4.50 per 25. Accessories at additional cost. 90 minutes.

Psychological Corporation.

2. *Army General Classification Test.* 1948. Grades 9–12 and adults. *Vocabulary, arithmetic and block counting (spatial).*

One form. $10.80 per 20 with manual. Answer pads, $2.40 per 20. Answer sheets for machine scoring, $23.50 per 500. 40 minutes.

Science Research Associates, Inc.

3. *California Test of Mental Maturity.* Revised, 1963.

K–adult. Short form — *opposites, similarities, analogies, numerical values, number problems, verbal comprehension, memory (delayed recall).* Long form — *rights and lefts, manipulation of areas, number series, inferences and immediate recall* added.

One form. Short form, $3.50 per 35. Long form, $6.30 per 35. Accessories at additional cost. Short form, about 50 minutes. Long form, about 1–1½ hours.

California Test Bureau.

4. *College Qualification Tests.* 1955–61. Grades 11–13. *Verbal numerical, information, total.*

Form A; Forms B and C, restricted to colleges and universities. $5.00 per 25. Accessories at additional cost. 80 minutes.

Psychological Corporation.

5. *Henmon-Nelson Tests of Mental Ability,* Revised Edition. 1957–58. Grades 3–6; 6–9; 9–12; College. *Synonyms, analogies, number sequence, arithmetic,* etc.

Forms A and B. $3.60 per 35. Accessories at additional cost. 30 minutes.

Houghton Mifflin Company.

6. *Kuhlmann-Anderson Intelligence Tests.* Sixth Edition, 1952, Tests for K, Grades 1, 2, 3. Seventh Edition, 1960–62, Tests for 4–5, 5–7, 7–9, and 9–12. *Verbal and quantitative.*

One form. $3.00 per 25. Accessories at additional cost. 50–60 minutes.

Personnel Press.

7. *Kuhlmann-Finch Scholastic Aptitude Tests.* 1956–57. Grades 1, 2, 3, 4, 5, 6, 7–9, 10–12. *Verbal and non-verbal materials.*
One form. $2.95 per 25. Accessories at additional cost. 45 minutes.
American Guidance Service.

8. *Ohio State University Psychological Test.* 1958.
Grades 9–13. *Vocabulary, word relationships, reading comprehension.*
One form. $10.80 per 20. Answer pads, $2.40 per 20. Answer sheets, $23.50 per 500. Two hours.
Science Research Associates, Inc.

9. *Otis Quick-Scoring Mental Ability Tests.* Revised, 1954. *Alpha,* Grades 1–4; *Beta,* Grades 4–9; *Gamma,* High School and College. *Alpha* consists of *pictorial items, Beta* and *Gamma* of *verbal material.*
Forms AB of *Alpha;* CM, DM, EM, and FM of *Beta;* AM, BM, EM, and FM *of Gamma. Alpha,* $3.75 per 35; *Beta* and *Gamma,* $3.10 per 35. *Alpha,* 25 to 40 minutes; *Beta,* 30 minutes. Accessories at additional cost.
Harcourt, Brace & World, Inc.

10. *Pintner General Ability Tests.* 1938–46.
Verbal Series: Grades K–2, 2–4, 5–12. Non-language Series, Grades 4–9. All except verbal elementary Scale 2 and intermediate and advanced verbal require no reading.
Forms A, B, C of *Primary Verbal;* A, B of *Intermediate* and *Advanced Verbal;* K, L of *Intermediate Non-Language. Primary,* $3.65 per 35; *Elementary,* $5.00 per 35; *Intermediate* and *Advanced, Verbal,* $4.40 per 35; *Non-language,* $5.65 per 35. 25–55 minutes depending on level.
Harcourt, Brace & World, Inc.

11. *Primary Mental Abilities Test.* Revised 1963.
Grades K–1, 2–4, 4–6, 6–9, 9–12. *Verbal meaning, spatial ability, perception, number facility, reasoning.*
One form, First two levels, $3.00 per 20. Three upper levels, $11.00 per 20. Answer sheets, $5.00 per 100. 55–60 minutes.
Science Research Associates, Inc.

12. *S.R.A. Tests of Educational Ability.* 1957–58.
Grades 4–6, 6–9, 9–12. *Language, reasoning, quantitative.*
One form. $7.00 per 20. Answer sheets, $7.00 per 100. 50–60 minutes.
Science Research Associates, Inc.

13. *Terman-McNemar Test of Mental Ability.* 1941. Grades 7–13. *Information, synonyms, logical selection, classification, analogies, opposites, best answer.*

Forms C and D. $4.00 per 35. 40 minutes.

Harcourt, Brace & World, Inc.

▶ LEARNING EXERCISES ◀

8. If you were responsible for choosing a group intelligence test for use with the fifth and sixth grades, how would you proceed? Describe the steps involved and justify each one.

9. Intelligence tests frequently include tests of vocabulary (same-opposites, word meaning, etc.) and of numerical problems. There are also achievement tests in the same subjects or areas. How do you account for this?

10. Why is an individual examination like the *Binet* generally regarded as more accurate and dependable than a group test?

11. Compare a group test of intelligence with one of those described above. What are their comparative merits?

ANNOTATED BIBLIOGRAPHY

1. Anastasi, Anne. *Psychological Testing,* Second Edition. New York: The Macmillan Company, 1961. 657 pp. This volume consists of four parts. Part I deals with the principles of psychological testing, including basic theory and uses. Part II deals with general classification or general intelligence tests. Part III deals with aptitude tests and includes some discussion of achievement tests. Part IV deals with measurement of personality, including measures of interests and attitudes, and sociometric devices.

2. Cronbach, Lee J. *Essentials of Psychological Testing,* Second Edition. New York: Harper & Row, Publishers, 1960. 650 pp. Part I presents basic concepts, with emphasis on selection and use of mental tests. Part II deals chiefly with measures of intelligence, but also includes consideration of tests of special abilities and achievement. Part III treats personality testing, interest tests, observation techniques, and the assessment of the dynamics of personality.

3. Freeman, Frank S. *Theory and Practice of Psychological Testing,* Third Edition. New York: Holt, Rinehart & Winston, Inc., 1960. 650 pp. Major attention is given to the theory, problems, development, nature, and types of intelligence tests. There are also chapters on aptitude tests and personality tests, including discussion of projective methods.

4. Greene, Edward B. *Measurements of Human Behavior,* Revised. New York: The Odyssey Press, 1952. Chapters 5, 6, 8, 9, 10. This book presents

excellent brief discussions of intelligence and aptitude tests and scales. Chapter 5 deals with tests of early childhood; Chapter 6, with individual tests of ability; Chapter 8, with group tests of ability; Chapter 9, with mechanical and motor tests; and Chapter 10, with tests of special aptitudes.

5. Jordan, A. M. *Measurement in Education.* New York: McGraw-Hill Book Co., Inc., 1953. Chapters 14, 15. A good introductory treatment of the development of intelligence tests and the use of group tests. Emphasis on the uses of intelligence tests.

6. Murphy, Gardner. *An Historical Introduction to Modern Psychology.* New York: Harcourt, Brace & World, Inc., 1929. Chapter 21. A basic text on the history of modern psychology from the seventeenth century. Presents considerable background material on the development of modern intelligence tests and brief accounts of the work of Binet and other pioneers in this movement.

7. Peterson, Joseph. *Early Conceptions and Tests of Intelligence.* New York: Harcourt, Brace & World, Inc., 1925. 295 pp. The definitive book on the history of modern intelligence tests up to the end of World War I. Especially valuable reference on the development of Binet's scales and their successors.

8. Remmers, H. H., and Gage, N. L. *Educational Measurement and Evaluation,* Revised. New York: Harper & Row, Publishers, 1955. Chapters 8–10. These three chapters deal with the nature of mental abilities and the measurement of general mental abilities and of special abilities or aptitudes.

9. Super, Donald E. *Appraising Vocational Fitness.* New York: Harper & Row, Publishers, 1949. 727 pp. A thorough treatment of the use of tests in vocational counseling. Includes consideration of tests of intelligence, achievement, aptitude, interests, personality, and the use of such tests in predicting job success. Many tests are carefully studied, described, and appraised for their value in vocational counseling.

10. Terman, Lewis M., and Merrill, Maud A. *Stanford-Binet Intelligence Scale.* Boston: Houghton Mifflin Company, 1960. 363 pp. Describes in detail the work of developing the third revision, Form L–M. Also includes the complete scale with directions for administering and scoring, and tables of deviation I.Q.'s.

11. Thorndike, Robert L., and Hagen, Elizabeth. *Measurement and Evaluation in Psychology and Education,* Second Edition. New York: John Wiley & Sons, Inc., 1961. Chapter 9 deals with standardized tests of intelligence. It presents a brief but sound discussion of different approaches to the measurement of intelligence and a discussion of the significance of the results of such measures.

11

The Measurement of Capacity:

Special Aptitudes

In the preceding chapter we considered tests of general intelligence which have shown their greatest usefulness as predictors of success in school and college, particularly in academic courses. There is another type of test, also used primarily for prediction, referred to as aptitude tests. These differ from general intelligence tests in that their purpose usually is to predict success in a more restricted field or area such as mechanical or clerical or artistic pursuits. Aptitude tests differ from achievement tests also in that they are designed to measure potential or promise. They do not pre-suppose training in a particular field but purport to measure an individual's capacity to profit by instruction in that field.

Specific aptitude tests are often designed to measure specific skills or knowledge essential to successful performance. Thus a mechanical aptitude test may include such tasks as assembling a dismantled object like an electric bell, and a test of clerical aptitude may measure skill in locating numbers or alphabetizing. Such skills may be based on job analyses which identify the specifics of successful performance in a given occupation or field. If a test is to screen applicants for a certain type of work, let us say that of an electrician, a detailed analysis of the job of an electrician may be made. On the basis of this analysis are determined the specific skills required of a successful electrician. Then a test is constructed to measure these abilities objectively and accurately. Job analysis is one widely used approach to the planning and developing of aptitude tests in special fields.

Another method used in constructing aptitude tests is based upon a theoretical, possibly more or less "armchair," attack. In this case an attempt is made to spell out basic qualities or abilities which are considered to underly all successful, effective performance in a particular field. This approach is illustrated by aptitude tests in such fields as art or music. As we shall see when we examine prototypes of these tests, they purport to measure abilities of a fundamental nature, as for example in tests of art aptitude, a feeling for line, color, balance, and the like in a work of art or in producing the basis for a drawing, painting, or sculpture. Similarly, in tests of musical aptitude we commonly find measures of pitch discrimination, tonality, rhythm, etc. As mentioned earlier, such tests do not presuppose previous training in the field, though it is generally agreed that scores on them are influenced by training.

One other approach is to test knowledge in a particular field. This is based upon the assumption that interest in and aptitude for a particular type of work will cause the possessor of these qualities to read widely in the field of such work, to experiment and work with the "tools of the trade," and thus to accumulate a fund of information which can readily be tested. The amount, depth, and accuracy of knowledge possessed is believed to reflect interest and aptitude. Many illustrations can be cited. The girl who likes to cook or sew, the boy who enjoys tinkering with an old "jaloppy" of a car or radios will naturally accumulate information about these matters which indirectly reveals an interest and possibly an aptitude for cooking, sewing, auto mechanics, or radio, as the case may be. This point of view suggests the use of tests of knowledge in a particular field as elements of aptitude tests. And we often do find tests of knowledge included in aptitude tests as we shall see shortly.

Finally, there are the aptitude test batteries or multi-aptitude tests, a number of which are now available. These tests are designed in some instances primarily to predict success in specific school subjects; others are for the purpose of predicting success in a number of different occupations. An example of the former type will be described in detail later in this chapter. The *General Aptitude Test Battery* of the United States Employment Service is a battery that is widely used to assist in fitting applicants for employment into types of training or work that they seem to have some aptitude for. This is, of course, a very large and difficult task, since there are a multitude of different occupations to be considered.

The aptitude test batteries are based, for the most part on factor analysis, the purpose being to construct a battery of a manageable number of subtests which will, in various combinations, be optimally predictive of success in many different occupations. This constitutes a continuing and never-ending task as new occupations are studied and as additional data accumulate from the use of the tests in the battery.

All the approaches to testing aptitude which have been briefly discussed will be found illustrated in one or another of the tests to be described. There are many aptitude tests in many different fields, but we shall confine our descriptions to a few areas in which the most work has been done and which, in general, are of greatest interest and value to teachers and counselors. It would be impossible to do more in a book such as this within reasonable limitations of space.

▶ LEARNING EXERCISES ◀

1. The terms "ability" and "aptitude" are sometimes used interchangeably. Defend or criticize this practice. (The article by Michael in the *Encyclopedia of Educational Research* cited in the bibliography at the end of this chapter is pertinent.)

2. Compare and contrast tests of readiness, intelligence, and aptitude with respect to (a) purposes, (b) content, and (c) methods of validation.

MECHANICAL APTITUDE

One of the first specialized fields for which aptitude tests were developed is that of mechanical abilities. The reasons are not hard to find. There are many occupations requiring mechanical ability, and they engage large numbers of persons. Men and boys especially seem to have inclinations toward working with machines, mechanical toys, electrical equipment, and tools. It is not surprising, therefore, to find some of the earliest work in the measurement of special aptitudes in this area. Some of the first tests which were developed, like the *Stenquist Mechanical Aptitude Test,* published in 1921, and the *MacQuarrie Test for Mechanical Ability,* published in 1925, are no longer available. However, work in this field has continued, although no new tests have appeared recently.

Many of the older tests of mechanical aptitude included tasks of disassembling and assembling small pieces of equipment, such as an electric bell, as well as paper and pencil problems. These had the disadvantage of requiring individual testing. More recent tests have tended to concentrate largely on paper-and-pencil devices. The one to be described here, the *Minnesota Paper Form Board,*[1] is a paper-and-pencil test measuring spatial perception as indicated by the ability to visualize assembly of two-dimensional shapes into a whole design. For example:[2]

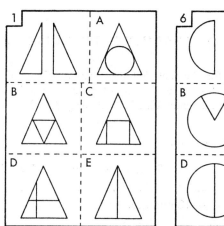 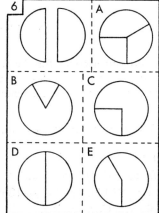

This test is part of a battery of mechanical ability tests developed at the University of Minnesota in the late 1920's. There has probably been more study and research of the *Paper Form Board* than any test ever developed in this field. Consisting of sixty-four items of the type illustrated, it is simple to administer and takes only twenty minutes of actual working time. Reliability of a single form is reported to be .85 and of both forms together, .92.

The test has been validated by correlating scores on it with ratings of performance in shop courses, mechanical drawing, descriptive geometry, and machine drafting. Scores of engineering students have been compared with those of non-engineers. The test has also been given to students in dentistry and to workers in many mechanical pursuits.

Although the correlations between scores on the *Minnesota Paper Form Board* and ratings, grades in courses, production records of workers, and

[1] *Minnesota Paper Form Board,* Revised. 1930–48. Grade 9–Adult. Forms AA, BB (hand scored) or MA, MB (machine scored). Also AA–FE, BB–FE (for French-Canadian use). $2.30 per 25; $3.25 per 25. Answer sheets, $1.90 per 50. New York: Psychological Corporation.

[2] Reproduced by permission. Copyright © 1948. Published by The Psychological Corporation, New York, N.Y. All rights reserved.

scores of criterion groups are not uniformly high or discriminatory, the mass of evidence accumulated about the test is generally quite favorable. It appears to be one of the best tests of a paper-and-pencil type yet devised for predicting success in a wide variety of fields of work that require more or less mechanical abilities. It is, of course, particularly useful for counselors and guidance workers in helping boys and young men to achieve a better appraisal of their fitness for certain occupations.

▶ LEARNING EXERCISE ◀

3. How do you account for the fact that paper-and-pencil tests of spatial relations seem to correlate at least as well with criteria of mechanical performance as do tests requiring the manipulation of objects or gadgets?

Other Tests of Mechanical Aptitude

1. *Bennett Hand-Tool Dexterity Test.* Adolescents and adults. *Proficiency in use of wrenches and screwdrivers.*
   One form. $29.50 per set. 4–12 minutes.
   Psychological Corporation.

2. *Crawford Small Parts Dexterity Test.* 1946–56. Adolescents and adults. *Dexterity in use of tweezers and screwdrivers.*
   One form. $35.50 per set. 9–25 minutes.
   Psychological Corporation.

3. *Detroit Mechanical Aptitudes Examination.* 1939. Grades 7–12. *Tool recognition, motor speed, size discrimination, arithmetic fundamentals, disarranged pictures, tool information, direction and speed of pulley and belt movements,* and *digit-letter substitution.*
   One form. $4.55 per 35. 30 minutes.
   The Bobbs-Merrill Company, Inc.

4. *MacQuarrie Test for Mechanical Ability.* 1925. Grades 7–adult. *Tracing, tapping, dotting, copying, location, blocks,* and *pursuit.*
   One form. $4.20 per 35. 20 minutes.
   California Test Bureau.

5. *Mellenbruch Mechanical Motivation Test.* 1956–57. Grades 6 to adult. *Matching pairs of objects in pictures.*
   Forms A and B. $1.95 per 20. 40 minutes.
   Psychometric Affiliates.

6. *Minnesota Assembly Test.* 1930. Ages 11 and up. Revision of the *Stenquist Assembly Test. Assembly of thirty-three common mechanical devices* such as *push-button, doorbell, etc.* (Abridged form, twenty devices.)

Two forms — Complete and Abridged. $71.00 and $52.00. 60 minutes.

C. H. Stoelting Company.

7. *O'Rourke Mechanical Aptitude Test.* 1939–57. High school and adults. *Mechanical information.*

Forms A and B. $4.50 per 50. 55 minutes.

Psychological Corporation.

8. *Prognostic Test of Mechanical Abilities.* 1946. Grades 7–12 and adults. *Arithmetic computation, reading simple drawings, use of tools, accuracy in measuring and discerning spatial relationships.*

One form. $4.20 per 35. 38 minutes.

California Test Bureau.

9. *Purdue Mechanical Performance Test.* 1957. Ages 17 to adult. *Transfer boards, spatial relations, hub assemblies.*

One form. $175 per set. 20 minutes.

Lafayette Instrument Company.

10. *S.R.A. Mechanical Aptitudes.* 1947. High school and adults. *Tool usage, space visualization,* and *shop arithmetic.*

One form. $10.80 per 20. Answer pads, $2.40 per 20. 40 minutes.

Science Research Associates, Inc.

11. *Stromberg Dexterity Test.* Adolescents and adults. *Precision in placement of disks.*

One form. $42.00 per set. 5–10 minutes.

Psychological Corporation.

12. *Test of Mechanical Comprehension.* 1940–51. Grade 9 and up. *Sixty pictures requiring judgment on mechanical and physical principles.*

Forms AA, AA–F (French), BB–S (Spanish), BB, CC, and W_1 (for women). $4.75 per 25. 30 minutes.

Psychological Corporation.

CLERICAL APTITUDE

The designation above refers to tests in the commercial and business field. There are aptitude tests for general office work, typewriting, bookkeeping, and shorthand. Although extensive work has been done in the testing of these aptitudes, the tests so far developed have not been outstandingly successful as predictive measures, and they have not been widely used by teachers, employers, or counselors.

Detroit Clerical Aptitudes Examination

The *Detroit Clerical Aptitudes Examination*[3] consists of eight parts. Part 1 is a test of rate and quality of handwriting and involves the copying of a short selection. Part 2 consists of a comparison between two sets of numbers to determine whether they are the same or different, e.g., 2 7 3 — 2 7 5. Part 3 contains arithmetic problems. Part 4 is a test of manual dexterity and requires the student to perform such tasks as drawing crosses in circles as rapidly as possible without touching the circles. Part 5 tests miscellaneous knowledge related to office and business. Part 6 is a series of pictures, each presented in several sections or parts of the whole; the task is to indicate their proper order or sequence. Part 7 is a substitution test in which letters are numbered according to a key which is constantly changing. Part 8 is a test of alphabetization.

Each part of the *Detroit Clerical Aptitudes Examination* is timed separately. The test is designed for use with pupils at the intermediate and junior high school grade levels to identify those who will probably succeed in commercial courses in high school. The reliability, test-retest, is .85. The correlation between scores on the test and scholarship in bookkeeping is .563; between test scores and scholarship in shorthand, .366; between test scores and scholarship in typewriting, .317. The *Detroit Clerical Aptitudes Examination* is available in one form only at $3.85 for 35 copies. The handwriting scale used in Test 1 must be ordered separately at $.50 per copy.

Other Tests of Commercial and Business Aptitude

1. *Bennett Stenographic Aptitude Test.* 1939. High school and college. *Substitution of numbers for symbols and symbols for numbers,* and *spelling.*

One form. $2.40 per 25. 25 minutes.

Psychological Corporation.

2. *E.R.C. Stenographic Aptitude Test.* 1944. High school and adults. *Word discrimination, phonetic spelling, vocabulary, sentence dictation,* and *speed of writing.*

---

[3] Harry J. Baker and Paul F. Voelker, *Detroit Clerical Aptitudes Examination, Revised* (Indianapolis: The Bobbs-Merrill Company, Inc., 1944).

One form. $4.00 per 20. 45 minutes.
Science Research Associates, Inc.

3. *General Clerical Test.* 1950. High school and above. *Clerical speed and accuracy, numerical ability, verbal facility.*
One form. $5.00 per 25. 43 minutes.
Psychological Corporation.

4. *Minnesota Clerical Test.* 1933–46. Grades 8–12 and adults. *Speed and accuracy in checking numbers and names.*
One form. $2.15 per 25. 15 minutes.
Psychological Corporation.

5. *O'Rourke Clerical Aptitude.* 1926–58. *Clerical problems and reasoning.*
One form. $1.95 per 50 copies of either part. 25 minutes.
Psychological Institute.

6. *Personnel Research Institute Clerical Battery.* 1945–47. Adults. *(1)* classification, *(2)* number comparison, *(3)* name comparison, *(4)* tabulation, *(5)* filing, *(6)* alphabetizing, *(7)* arithmetic reasoning, *(8)* spelling.
Form A of 1–3; Forms A and B of 4–8. $2.00 per 25 copies of any test. Total time, including time for directions, 100 minutes.
Personnel Research Institute.

7. *Purdue Clerical Adaptability Test.* 1949–56. Applicants for clerical positions. *Spelling, computation, checking, word meaning, copying, reasoning.*
One form. $5.00 per 25. 60 minutes.
Purdue University Bookstore.

8. *Short Employment Tests.* 1951. Adults. *Vocabulary, arithmetic computation, clerical skill.*
Forms 1, 2, 3, 4 (1 is restricted). $2.10 per 25 for each test. 15 minutes.
Psychological Corporation.

9. *Turse Clerical Aptitudes Test.* 1953–55. Grades 8–12, adults. *Verbal skills, number skills, written directions, checking speed, classifying-sorting, alphabetizing.*
One form. $4.00 per 35. 40 minutes.
Harcourt, Brace & World, Inc.

10. *Turse Shorthand Aptitude Test.* 1940. Grade 8 and above. *Stroking, spelling, phonetic association, symbol transcription, word discrimination, dictation,* and *word sense.*

One form. $3.90 per 35. 40 minutes.

Harcourt, Brace & World, Inc.

MUSICAL APTITUDE

Seashore Measures of Musical Talent

Various tests of musical aptitude have been devised, though the total number of such tests is not large. Probably the best-known is the *Seashore,*[4] which consists of tests of *pitch, loudness, rhythm, time, timbre,* and *tonal memory,* all on one phonograph record. The tests are as follows: *pitch* (the higher of two tones); *loudness* (the louder of two tones); *rhythm* (comparison of two rhythmic patterns); *time* (the longer of two sounds); *timbre* (comparison of tonal quality to decide whether two tones are the same or different); *tonal memory* (comparison of two short musical figures differing in one note, to indicate by number which note is different). The tests are said to be applicable from the fifth grade up, but they seem to work best with older subjects. Reliabilities range from .62 to .88 with an average of about .80. The tests require about one hour to administer, and may be given to individuals or groups. They show little relationship to differences in amount of musical training at advanced levels, but when administered in combination with an intelligence test, the *Seashore* shows a definite relationship to success in advanced musical study.

Many musical aptitude tests are largely paper-and-pencil tests which measure knowledge and understanding of musical terms and symbols, though a few include tests of some of the types of performance that are measured by the *Seashore.*

Other Tests of Musical Aptitude

1. *Aliferis Music Achievement Test.* 1954. College freshmen. *Matching melodies, harmonies or rhythms with musical notations.*

One form. $3.00 per 20. (Piano or tape recording necessary.) 45 minutes.

University of Minnesota Press.

2. *Drake Musical Aptitude Tests.* 1954. Grades 3 through college. *Musical memory and musical rhythm.* One 33⅓ LP record.

[4] Carl E. Seashore, *et al.*, *Seashore Measures of Musical Talents* (New York: Psychological Corporation, 1919–1944). Available on one LP record plus 50 answer sheets, $12.00. Answer sheets, $2.30 per 50.

Forms A and B. $5.95 per record and manual; answer pads, $6.00 per 100. 80 minutes.

Science Research Associates, Inc.

3. *Farnum Music Notation Test.* 1953. Grades 7–9. *Detection of changes in pitch, rhythm, or time in melodies.*

One form. $6.75 per 78 rpm. record and 50 test blanks. 20 minutes.

Psychological Corporation.

4. *Musical Aptitude Test.* 1950. Grades 4–10. *Rhythm recognition, pitch recognition, melody recognition, pitch discrimination, advanced rhythm recognition.*

One form. $3.00 per examiner's booklet. (Piano necessary.) 40 minutes.

California Test Bureau.

ART APTITUDE

Another area of aptitude testing in which considerable work has been done is the field of visual or graphic arts. A number of tests have been developed which purport to get at potential along these lines. As in other specialized areas, the distinction between achievement and aptitude in art is not easy to make or maintain. In some instances, as has already been pointed out, so-called aptitude tests have measured information or learned abilities on the theory that such outcomes are indicative of interest and possibly aptitude as well. This is perhaps less relevant in the measurement of art aptitude than in some other areas since the most successful of the tests so far developed deal with abstractions. Some, however, are in the nature of work samples testing the ability of the subject to draw or to create.

The test of art aptitude to be described is the *Meier Art Judgment Test,*[5] one of the best and most widely used tests of its type. It consists of one hundred pairs of pictures in which the task is to select the better in each pair. One of the pair is a picture of a work of established merit. The other is the same except that the picture has been altered in some way to impair a fundamental and universal principle of art contained in the original (see Figure 12).

The material used was chosen from the works of old masters and contemporary artists. Three hundred pairs of pictures were tried out and eventually reduced to one hundred. The pairs were submitted to twenty-five art experts and were responded to by 1,081 persons ranging in age

[5] *Meier Art Judgment Test.* 1928–42. Grades 7–12 and adults. One form. Test booklets. $1.40 per copy. Answer sheets, $2.70 per 100. Manual and scoring keys, $.70. Iowa City, Iowa: Bureau of Educational Research and Service.

FIGURE 12 • Sample Pair of Figures from the *Meier Art Judgment Test*

Reproduced by permission of the author, Norman C. Meier.

from eleven years to past middle life. Final selection of item pairs was based upon favorable critical reaction by the experts and a 60 to 90 per cent preference by the 1,081 subjects. Scores on the final one-hundred-item test differentiated consistently between various groups in expected directions. Correlations between scores on *Meier Art Judgment* and intelligence are generally low, averaging close to zero. Reliability, split-half, and Spearman-Brown range from .70 to .84. Norms are based upon students in junior and senior high schools, primarily those interested in art.

The usefulness of the test as a measure of art aptitude is based upon the principle or theory that aesthetic judgment is an important factor in the complex of factors that make up this aptitude. This factor, said to be the product of ancestry and experience, is the unfailing response to a work of art embodying good principles of line, proportion, balance, and the like.

▶ **LEARNING EXERCISES** ◀

4. Against what criteria are tests of musical aptitude validated?

5. Tests of musical aptitude and art aptitude do not usually have very high reliability coefficients. How could these be raised?

6. For what fields or subjects other than those discussed in this chapter have aptitude tests been developed? Consult Buros' *Mental Measurements Yearbooks* for examples.

Other Tests of Art Aptitude

1. *Graves Design Judgment Test*. 1948. Grades 7–16 and adults. Ninety sets of two- and three-dimensional designs calling for *discrimination on the basis of eight principles of art*.
One form. $1.50 per booklet. 20–30 minutes.
Psychological Corporation.

2. *Horn Art Aptitude Inventory*. 1951. Grades 12–16 and adults. *Outline drawings of simple objects* and *creative composition*.
One form. $5.25 per set. 50 minutes.
C. H. Stoelting Company.

FOREIGN LANGUAGE APTITUDE

In recent years interest in foreign languages has increased materially for reasons which are fairly obvious. The growing importance of international relations, improved means of travel, and the great increase in foreign travel have all affected foreign language instruction. The support of such instruction by the Federal government through the National Defense Education Act has encouraged such developments. Instruction in foreign languages has been added to the curriculums of many elementary schools, and colleges and universities have greatly expanded their offerings in this field.

As a result there is an awakened interest in the measurement of aptitude for learning a foreign language. A few tests of this nature have been developed over the years but these have not been widely used. Some new tests have been developed, one of which will be described. It is called the *Modern Language Aptitude Test*.[6] Although its title suggests that it is designed primarily as a measure of an individual's probable degree of success in learning a modern foreign language, it is claimed to be useful also in measuring potential success in Latin and Greek.

The test has five parts. "Number Learning" is intended to measure memory. "Phonetic Script" measures the ability to learn correspondences between speech sounds and orthographic symbols. "Spelling Clues" presents words spelled in disguised form as "luv" for "love." The task is to

[6] John B. Carroll and Stanley M. Sapon, *Modern Language Aptitude Test*. 1955–58. Grade 9 to adult. One form. Tape recording, $7.50. Reusable booklets, $3.50 per 25. Answer sheets, $3.60 per 25. 70 minutes. New York: Psychological Corporation.

select from a group of five words the one which means the same or nearly the same as the disguised word, e.g. affection. "Word In Sentences" tests the ability to identify a word in a test sentence which has the same function as a designated word in another "key" sentence. For example:[7]

LONDON is the capital of England.
He liked to *go fishing* in *Maine.*
A B C D E

Here, the word "he" has the same function in the second sentence as LONDON has in the first.

The last part is called "Paired Associates." It measures the ability to learn and recognize a short set of equivalents of English words in a foreign language.

All directions for the tests are given by tape recording. A short form consisting of Parts III, IV, and V may be given either by use of the tape or with oral instructions in about thirty minutes. The test may be scored either by hand or machine.

Validity of the *Modern Language Aptitude Test* was determined on the basis of correlations between scores on it and course grades in Latin, Spanish, French, German, Russian, Chinese, and Indo-European. These correlations range from .13 to .83, with the majority in the range of about .35 to .65. Included were classes in foreign languages in Grades 9–11, college classes, and intensive courses for adults. The coefficients with scores on the total test and the short forms are generally almost identical, differing in most instances by less than .05.

Odd-even reliabilities for the total test are above .90; for the short form, slightly less, ranging from .83 to .93. Norms are based upon approximately nineteen hundred students beginning the study of a foreign language in Grades 9–12 in fourteen high schools and approximately thirteen hundred students in ten colleges and universities. No students of current enrollment who had studied a language previously were included.

This test represents a praiseworthy attempt to develop a valid and reliable predictive instrument in the field of foreign language study. It has many features that make it outstanding among those of its type.

Other Tests of Foreign Language Aptitude

1. *Luria-Orleans Modern Language Prognosis Test.* Grades 7–12. One form. $3.60 per 35. 76 minutes.
Harcourt, Brace & World, Inc.

---

[7] Reproduced by permission. Copyright © 1958, The Psychological Corporation, New York, N.Y. All rights reserved.

2. *Orleans-Solomon Latin Prognosis Test.* 1926. Grades 8–13.
One form. $3.70 per 35. 50 minutes.
Harcourt, Brace & World, Inc.

3. *Symonds Foreign Language Prognosis Test.* 1930. Grades 8–9.
Forms 1, 2. $7.35 per 100. 65 minutes.
Bureau of Publications, Teachers College, Columbia University.

APTITUDE BATTERIES

A comparatively recent development in measuring aptitudes is the aptitude battery, or what is sometimes called the *differential* or *factored* aptitude battery. Such batteries have grown out of the development of factor analysis discussed earlier in this chapter. The attempt to isolate and identify specific factors in general intelligence has carried over into the measurement of particular aptitudes. It was reasoned that test batteries could be devised which would measure a number of important abilities or traits that enter into many types of work or activities. Then if the scores on the parts of the battery could be related to specific occupations or groups of occupations, these part scores could be differentially weighted according to their importance in such occupations.

In addition to the impact of factor analysis, the growing number of persons engaged in educational and vocational guidance or counseling has increased the interest in and the demand for such batteries. Obviously, no counselor could test his client with all aptitude tests to determine how to advise him. Therefore, a single battery or group of tests would be very useful.

Broadly speaking, one might include in the category of aptitude batteries the *Primary Mental Abilities Test* and any others which yield part scores that can be demonstrated to have *low intercorrelations*. Obviously, if the parts of a battery have high correlations with each other they are measuring the same thing to a substantial degree and thus have little "differential" value. Not many test batteries meet this criterion very well. We are concerned here with batteries developed to meet the criteria as outlined above and those which are designed primarily for general counseling purposes. Several such batteries are now available, and a typical one will be described below.

Differential Aptitude Tests

The *Differential Aptitude Tests*[8] were some of the first of this type. They consist of tests of *Verbal Reasoning* (analogies), *Numerical Ability* (arith-

[8] G. K. Bennett, H. G. Seashore, and A. G. Wesman. *Differential Aptitude Tests.* 1963 Edition. Grades 8–12 and adults. Forms L and M Booklet 1 — V, N, A, C;

metic computation), *Abstract Reasoning, Space Relations, Mechanical Reasoning, Clerical Speed and Accuracy,* and *Language Usage* (spelling, grammar, punctuation).

The *Abstract Reasoning* consists of items like the following:[9]

PROBLEM FIGURES   **ANSWER FIGURES**

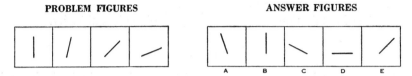

The task is to select from among the Answer Figures the one that should come next in the series of Problem Figures.

Space Relations consists of items in which a pattern that can be folded into a figure is followed by five figures, one or more of which can be formed from the pattern. The task is to identify the figure which can be formed from the pattern at the left.

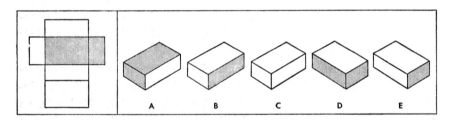

Mechanical Reasoning consists of a series of problems like the following:

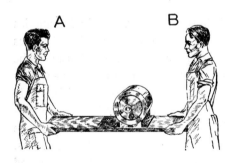

X

Which man has the heavier load?
(If equal, mark C.)

Clerical Speed and *Accuracy* consists of sets of letter and number combinations in pairs. In the first set one combination is underlined. The task is to find the same combination in the second set.

Booklet 2 — M, S, L, U. $7.75 per 25 of either booklet. Answer sheets, $4.50–$5.50 per 50. Separate test booklets, $2.25–$3.75 per 25. Answer sheets, $2.00 per 50. New York: Psychological Corporation.

[9] All sample items from *DAT* reproduced by permission. Copyright © 1963, The Psychological Corporation, New York, N.Y. All rights reserved.

TEST ITEMS	SAMPLE OF ANSWER SHEET

V.	<u>AB</u>	AC	AD	AE	AF	V	AC :::::	AE :::::	AF :::::	AB ▰	AD :::::
W.	aA	aB	BA	Ba	<u>Bb</u>	W	BA :::::	Ba :::::	Bb ▪	aA :::::	aB :::::
X.	A7	7A	B7	<u>7B</u>	AB	X	7B ▰	B7 :::::	AB :::::	7A :::::	A7 :::::
Y.	Aa	Ba	<u>bA</u>	BA	bB	Y	Aa :::::	bA ▰	bB :::::	Ba :::::	BA :::::
Z.	3A	3B	<u>33</u>	B3	BB	Z	BB :::::	3B :::::	B3 :::::	3A :::::	33 ▰

Originally, the eight tests in the battery were printed in separate booklets as Forms A and B, and each was separately administered. Later these were issued in three booklets containing (1) *Verbal Reasoning* and *Numerical Ability,* (2) *Mechanical Reasoning, Language Usage and Space Relations,* and (3) *Clerical Speed and Accuracy,* and *Abstract Reasoning.* In 1963 a new edition with new norms was issued in a two-booklet format. Booklet 1 contains the *Verbal, Numerical, Abstract Reasoning,* and *Clerical* tests. Booklet 2 contains the *Mechanical, Space* and *Language Usage,* 1 and 2, tests. There are two forms, L and M, with which either IBM or MRC answer sheets may be used. There is also a booklet containing the *Verbal Reasoning* and *Numerical Ability* tests only.

The tests are designed for use in junior and senior high schools, but may also be used with young adults in employment counseling. Reliability coefficients (split-half) for the eight sub-tests are generally in the .80's and low .90's except for *Mechanical Reasoning* when used with girls, where the average is about .70.

Ideally, in a battery such as this the correlations between the sub-tests should be low. They range from .06 to .67 and the authors believe that these correlations indicate that what the separate tests measure is sufficiently different to warrant the inclusion of every test in the battery. By statistical analysis it is shown that the separate tests meet a rather high standard of differentiating power.

A continuing program of validation of the test battery for predictive purposes is being conducted by the authors and publishers. The studies reported are concerned principally with correlations between the sub-tests of the battery and grades in a wide variety of courses, tests of intelligence, other aptitude batteries, and objective achievement tests. In general, these results show that the tests do exhibit a differential relationship to achievement in various subject matters and to mental ability levels.

The tests are accompanied by a detailed *Interpretative Manual* and a casebook, *Counseling from Profiles,* which includes a small number of individual case histories.

▶ **LEARNING EXERCISES** ◀

7. Examine a specimen set of an aptitude battery other than the *DAT*. Compare it with the *DAT* with respect to (a) purpose, (b) content, and (c) validity.

8. In what respects does the *Lorge-Thorndike* test resemble an aptitude battery? In what ways does it differ? Could the two be used for the same purposes?

Other Aptitude Batteries

1. *Aptitude Tests for Occupations.* 1951. Grades 9–13. *Personal-social, mechanical, general sales, clerical routine, computational,* and *scientific aptitudes.*
   One form. Six booklets, $2.10; $3.50 per 35. 107 minutes.
   California Test Bureau.

2. *Flanagan Aptitude Classification Tests.* 1953. High school and adults. *Inspection, coding, memory, precision, assembly, scales, coordination, judgment and comprehension, arithmetic, patterns, components, tables, mechanics, expression.*
   One form. Each of the 14 tests, $2.55 per 20. All tests in two booklets, $.80. Two half-day sessions, each with ten-minute break. Total time, including time for directions, 2 hours, 46 minutes, and 2 hours, 42 minutes.
   Science Research Associates, Inc.

3. *General Aptitude Test Battery.* 1947. Ages 16 and up. *Intelligence, verbal, numerical, spatial, form perception, clerical perception, eye-hand coordination, motor speed, finger dexterity, manual dexterity.*
   One form. $54.65 per complete set. 135 minutes.
   United States Employment Service, United States Department of Labor.

4. *Holzinger-Crowder Uni-Factor Tests.* 1954. Grades 7–12. *Verbal, spatial, numerical, and reasoning.*
   Forms AM and BM, $7.00 per 35. Total time, 90 minutes.
   Harcourt, Brace & World, Inc.

5. *Multiple Aptitude Tests.* 1954. Grades 7–13. *Word meaning, paragraph meaning, language usage, routine clerical facility, arithmetic reasoning arithmetic computation, applied science and mechanics, spatial relations — two dimensions, and spatial relations — three dimensions.*
   One form. Four booklets, $4.90 per 35. 177 minutes.
   California Test Bureau.

OTHER APTITUDE TESTS

In addition to the aptitude tests described or listed in this chapter, a number of such tests have been developed in other fields. A perusal of Buros' *Fifth Mental Measurements Yearbook* shows listings of one or more tests or batteries in each of the following areas: medicine, nursing, dentistry, law, engineering, selling, accounting, dental hygiene, firefighting, driving and traffic safety, business management, law enforcement, carpentry, coach operation, and truck driving. This is not a complete list but it indicates the variety of purposes for which such tests have been devised.

The use of aptitude or prognostic tests was given considerable impetus during World War II. Large numbers of men and women were inducted into service with little or no training or experience that could be used in the armed forces. These people had to be screened and assigned either to training or to jobs, and this had to be done quickly. The need for reasonably accurate, objective, and rapid methods for appraising an individual and assigning him was obvious. Consequently a great deal of effort was expended on the development of aptitude tests, some of which have continued to be used in civilian life.

The development of aptitude tests or batteries is a challenging task. Research and development in this field are likely to continue, particularly in business and industry. Perhaps the most promising development is that of the factored aptitude batteries, but these require great expenditures of talent and money as exemplified by the *General Aptitude Test Battery* of the United States Employment Service. They also demand continuing research and appraisal to meet changing requirements in occupations. However, valid and reliable aptitude tests are well worth what they cost if they save time, money, and energy and if they help to avoid frustration and disappointment for millions of young people faced with the necessity of making decisions about their life's work.

ANNOTATED BIBLIOGRAPHY

1. Anastasi, Anne. *Psychological Testing,* Second Edition. New York: The Macmillan Co., 1961. Part 3 deals with the differential testing of abilities and includes discussions of aptitude batteries, special aptitude tests and achievement tests. Many tests are described, illustrated, and evaluated.

2. Buros, Oscar K. *Tests in Print.* Highland Park, N.J.: The Gryphon Press, 1961. Lists multi-aptitude batteries and special aptitude tests with essential information and references to reviews of each in the *Mental Measurements Yearbooks.*

3. Cronbach, Lee J. *Essentials of Psychological Testing,* Second Edition. New York: Harper & Row, Publishers, 1960. Chapters 9, 10, 11. These chapters deal with factor analysis, aptitude test batteries, and special aptitude tests. The discussions present an overview of each topic but the major emphasis is on interpretation of results from the use of these instruments in guidance.

4. Darley, John G., and Hagenah, Theba. *Vocational Interest Measurement: Theory and Practice.* Minneapolis: University of Minnesota Press, 1955. 279 pp. Deals with the procedures and results of standardizing the *Strong-Vocational Interest Blank,* the relationship between scores on interest inventories and personality tests, and theories of the development and measurement of interests.

5. Freeman, Frank S. *Theory and Practice of Psychological Testing,* Third Edition. New York: Holt, Rinehart & Winston, Inc., 1962. Chapters 17, 18, 19. The topics treated are multi-factor test batteries; special aptitude tests; and tests for the professions of medicine, law, teaching, and science and engineering. Each chapter concludes with an evaluation.

6. Greene, Edward B. *Measurements of Human Behavior,* Revised. New York: The Odyssey Press, 1952. Chapters 9, 10. Although brief, the discussion of mechanical and motor tests and tests of other special aptitudes in these two chapters provides useful background reading.

7. Michael, William B. "Aptitudes," in the *Encyclopedia of Educational Research.* Third Edition. New York: The Macmillan Co., 1960. pp. 59–63. A brief discussion of aptitudes, including a consideration of the meanings frequently attached to the term, some historical background, an evaluation of present status, and a bibliography.

8. Super, Donald E. *Appraising Vocational Fitness.* New York: Harper & Row, Publishers, 1949. 727 pp. The use of tests in vocational counseling. Many tests are fully described and appraised.

9. Thorndike, Robert L., and Hagen, Elizabeth. *Measurement and Evaluation in Psychology and Education,* Second Edition. New York: John Wiley & Sons, Inc. 1961. Chapter 10. Includes aptitude batteries, reading readiness tests, and brief discussions of professional-school aptitude batteries and tests of musical and artistic aptitude.

12

The Measurement of Personality and

Adjustment: Self-Report Techniques

Among college and university students personality is often considered to be synonymous with popularity. The individual who knows a large number of people, who is present at all functions, and who is persuasive in his dealings with others is said to have a "wonderful personality." While there is undoubtedly some slight basis for this point of view, it is quite inadequate as an acceptable definition of personality. In a deeper sense, personality is the most inclusive frame of reference in which an individual can be judged. It includes the sum of all his characteristics and his behavior — his intelligence, knowledge, attitudes, interests, and his responses to and interaction with his environment. Personality thus broadly conceived is the total of all of these qualities, together with the effects of the combination of them on what he thinks, feels, says, and does.

If we can accept such a broad definition of personality, we may go a step further and suggest that personality has two aspects: inner and outer. The inner phase refers to the adjustment of the individual within himself. That is, does he have a realistic and satisfying self-concept? Is he confident, sure of his personal worth? Has he set suitable and challenging goals for himself, keeping in mind his own limitations as well as his strengths?

Is he satisfied with his occupation? Of course there are many more factors which importantly affect one's inner personality, but these are among the chief elements.

The outer or interpersonal phase of personality concerns the individual's relationships with other people. Is he a useful member of family and community groups? Does he have the respect and affection of his associates? Is he capable of enjoying group activities? Such questions point up the social or interpersonal aspect of personality as it is conceived here.

We cannot emphasize too strongly the importance of adjustment in the definition of personality. Indeed, the individual who is well adjusted is most likely to be happy and to have a personality which makes a favorable impression on others. Conversely, the poorly adjusted person, almost by definition, is unhappy, and consequently his relationships with others will tend to be strained and difficult. Thus, one's personality is not some superficial characteristic that may be briefly adopted; rather, it is a reflection of a person's innermost self, and it influences and becomes a part of everything he does.

There are two fundamental approaches to the measurement of personality or adjustment. In the simplest terms, the first approach involves asking the individual himself what he thinks, feels, says, and does; the second involves finding out about the individual from others who have known him. The first may be called the *self-report* approach; the other, the *observational* approach. The examiner who uses the self-report technique asks questions or presents stimuli to which the individual being measured responds. From the replies obtained, the examiner can formulate some idea of the subject's personality or certain aspects of it. The examiner using the observational technique asks someone who knows the subject well to express opinions about him. Both of these methods are widely used. Self-report techniques may be distinguished from observational by the fact that the former are more often tests or other devices which yield scores. Thus, personality inventories, tests of attitudes, and tests of interests are typical self-report instruments, whereas rating scales, anecdotal records, and sociograms are examples of the observational type of report.

The nature, advantages, and disadvantages of self-report techniques will be discussed in this chapter, and those of the observational techniques will be treated in Chapter 13.

PERSONALITY INVENTORIES

The typical personality inventory of earlier years was an instrument planned in terms of some rationale conceived either in terms of areas of activity such as school, home, and job, or a set of psychological constructs conceived by the author. In the latter case an author's constructs might include such traits as sociability or confidence. As a matter of fact, most inventories, past and present, represent one or the other of these two basic patterns of organization.

More recently, two developments in measurement theory have been applied to the construction of self-report inventories, one of which is *factor analysis*. Considerable research has been done in the application of this technique to the development of these instruments. The results have been promising in that the technique has helped to isolate a limited number of fairly distinct factors or traits of personality.

The other development is the so-called *"forced choice"* technique. One of the nagging concerns of those who use any type of self-report device is the possibility of the subject's faking or slanting responses. Presumably, the individual, by judicious selection of his responses, can create an impression that is false but favorable to himself. The forced choice technique purports to eliminate or at least reduce the possibility of such faking. Typically, it presents a choice between pairs of equally complimentary or equally uncomplimentary alternatives. One of each pair, however, is a more significant response than the other with respect to some criterion such as emotional stability. The subject is required to choose one response which he considers to be most like him and one least like him. Since both of one pair sound equally complimentary and both of the other pair sound equally uncomplimentary, his chances of faking are believed to be greatly reduced. The forced choice technique was developed during World War II and has found considerable application in fields in which measurement depends on self-report. An example of forced choice items is presented below in connection with the discussion of the personality inventory prototype.

Gordon Personal Profile — Personal Inventory

The *Gordon Personal Profile* and *Gordon Personal Inventory*[1] are companion pieces designed to measure eight factors of personality. Those included in the *Profile* are *ascendancy, responsibility, emotional stability,* and *sociability*. The *Inventory* covers *cautiousness, original thinking, personal relations,* and *vigor*. These eight traits or aspects of personality are reported to have been arrived at and identified through several successive factor analyses.

[1] *Gordon Personal Profile* and *Gordon Personal Inventory*. 1953–63. High school, college, and adult. One form each. $3.15 per 35 booklets (hand score); $2.90 per 35 (answer sheet edition). Harcourt, Brace & World, Inc.

Data presented in the manuals for the two tests tend to support, at least in part, the claim that the tests measure significantly different aspects of personality. Intercorrelations among the four scales of the *Profile* range from −.18 (sociability with emotional stability) to .71 (ascendancy with sociability). The correlation between emotional stability and responsibility is about .50. Other intercorrelations for the *Profile* are low positive or low negative.

Intercorrelations among the four scales of the *Inventory* range from .42 (cautiousness with personal relations) to −.45 (cautiousness with vigor).

Intercorrelations among scales of the *Profile* and scales of the *Inventory* range between .47 (emotional stability with personal relations) and −.21 (sociability with cautiousness). Most of the coefficients are between zero and .40.

The forced choice type of item is used in both instruments. A sample item follows:

> 1. Likes to work primarily with ideas.
> 2. Does things at a rather slow pace.
> 3. Very careful when making a decision.
> 4. Finds a number of people hard to get along with.[2]

Here the first and third items are judged to be equally complimentary, the second and fourth, the opposite. The person taking the test is to mark one that is *most* like him and one that is *least* like him in each tetrad or group of four. Each set of four consists of one item related to each of the four scales or traits. Thus, one item of a tetrad in the *Profile* pertains to cautiousness, one to original thinking, etc., and similarly with the *Inventory*.

Extensive studies of the validity of both tests have been reported. They consist mainly of reports of scores of groups expected to differ as, for example, males, females, clerks and stenographers, foremen, executives, and many other occupational groups. Comparisons between students in various curriculums in high schools are also reported. Correlations between scores and personality ratings by peers, counselors, teachers, supervisors and with scores on other personality measures are reported in a substantial number of investigations. The data on validity are more extensive than usual with instruments of this type and, on the whole, are quite encouraging, especially in the case of the *Profile*. Those for the *Inventory* are less extensive though no less convincing.

---

[2] From *Gordon Personal Inventory* by Leonard V. Gordon. Copyright 1956, 1955 by Harcourt, Brace & World, Inc., New York. Reproduced by permission.

Reliability of the two tests is reported in terms of split-half coefficients. They are typically in the high .70's and .80's. In one study involving several hundred high school students the separate reliabilities of the four parts of the *Profile* were found to be about .60.

Percentile norms are provided for college students, high school students, and adult groups in various occupations. Norms are provided in each case by sex. On the whole, the *Gordon Profile* and *Inventory* are promising devices. They were developed by use of the best available techniques and have been extensively evaluated by independent researchers. Either of the pair may be used alone or they may be used together, seemingly without substantial overlap or duplication.

The Mooney Problem Check Lists

The Mooney Problem Check Lists[3] yield data on problems or difficulties in such categories as *Health and Physical Development, Home and Family, Morals and Religion, Sex, Economic Security, School or Occupation,* and *Social and Recreational.* Obviously, this represents a different approach or analysis from that of the Gordon tests. A number of other personality inventories yield scores that are indicative of adjustment in similar areas.

The Mooney Problem Check Lists are available in different forms for the junior high school, high school, college, and adult levels. The areas covered are esssentially the same in each form, although there are differences in the items at the various maturity levels. The person responding is asked to read the list of several hundred items, underline those problems which are troublesome to him, and indicate the two or three which are of real concern. The items are so arranged that a count can easily be made of the check marks in each of the different areas. In the junior high form the areas are *Health and Physical Development; School; Home and Family; Money, Work, and the Future; Boy and Girl Relations; Relations with People in General;* and *Self-Centered Concerns.* In the high school and college forms these same areas are included, with additional ones such as *Morals and Religion,* and *Curriculum and Teaching Procedure.* The check lists can be completed by most persons in fifty minutes or less. The following samples from the junior high school form show the nature of the arrangement:

[3] Ross L. Mooney and Leonard V. Gordon, *The Mooney Problem Check Lists* (New York: The Psychological Corporation, 1950). $1.75 per 25; reusable booklets, $2.40 per 25. Answer sheets, $1.90 per 50. Examples from the *Check Lists* used by permission of the publisher.

	1. Often have headaches
Health	2. Don't get enough sleep
and	3. Have trouble with my teeth
Physical	4. Not as healthy as I should be
Education	5. . . . .

	6. Getting low grades in school
	7. Afraid of tests
School	8. Being a grade behind in school
	9. . . . .
	10. . . . .

	11. Being an only child
Home	12. Not living with my parents
and	13. Worried about someone in the family
Family	14. . . . .
	15. . . . .[4]

In the junior high school form there are 210 items in seven areas; in the high school, college, and adult forms there are 330 items in eleven areas. In every area there are thirty items.

The Mooney Problem Check Lists are not tests in the usual sense, and do not yield scores. However, they do provide a useful tool for teachers and especially for counselors in locating problem areas which may then be investigated by the use of more refined techniques. The *Mooney Lists* can also be used as a basis for guidance and orientation programs, and as a foundation for increasing teacher understanding in the classroom.

Pintner's *Aspects of Personality*

One other inventory of the self-report type is Pintner's *Aspects of Personality*,[5] which is designed for use with subjects younger than those tested by either the *Gordon* or the *Mooney,* being suitable for Grades 4 to 9. The aim of this test is to reveal something significant about a child's personal adjustment in the areas of *Ascendancy-Submission, Introversion-Extroversion,* and *Emotional Stability.* The items are modifications of those in leading adult inventories, stated in language appropriate to the fourth-grade level.

The child's responses to the items of the inventory are on a "same-different" basis. Thus, the child indicates his agreement or disagreement with an item such as, "When some child tries to push into line ahead of me, I

---

[4] Reproduced by permission. Copyright © 1950, The Psychological Corporation, New York, N.Y. All rights reserved.

[5] Rudolf Pintner, *et al., Aspects of Personality* (New York: Harcourt, Brace & World, Inc., 1938).

am not afraid to tell him to get back."[6] A low score on the Ascendancy-Submission part may indicate that a child is shy and retiring; a high score may indicate that he is domineering and bullying. A low score on Introversion-Extroversion may indicate a tendency on the part of the child to withdraw, dodge responsibility, and live in a world of fantasy. Children scoring low on Emotional Stability are likely to be flighty and easily upset.

It is suggested that *Aspects of Personality* may be used as a screening device to identify children who need psychiatric advice, as an aid in educational and vocational guidance, and as a guide for the psychologist or psychiatrist in studying and diagnosing cases of maladjustment.

Several questions are perennially raised concerning the self-report type of personality inventory. One of these has to do with its validity and reliability. A second, already mentioned, relates to the problem of the subject's faking or simulating responses. A third question concerns the usability of such inventories in schools. How much use should be made of them? By whom should they be used? Full discussions of these questions are beyond the scope of this book, but a few statements will be made to provide some information on each point.

First, concerning validity, a little reflection will make it clear that the usual methods of establishing validity cannot apply to personality inventories. It is not possible to establish validity of personality inventories by correlating the scores with age, grade, or I.Q., except possibly in a negative way by showing a lack of relationship between such measures. One criterion often used is a comparison of scores with teachers' ratings of adjustment; another is a comparison of scores with case histories to see if those who make poor scores on the inventory show a history of maladjustment, problem behavior, and personality disorders. On the whole, such studies show the self-report inventory to have fairly satisfactory validity as a screening device. Although these instruments generally do not reveal minute differences in adjustment, they serve to identify most of the serious cases of maladjustment.

As to reliability, data vary widely. Some inventories report reliability coefficients as high as .90. Some, as in the case of the *Mooney,* do not yield scores and thus do not lend themselves to statistical analysis. In general, the reliability of personality inventories is lower than that of good standardized tests of intelligence or achievement. The reliability coefficients range from the .60's to the .80's, with the average falling somewhere between

[6] *Ibid.* Quotation used by permission of Harcourt, Brace & World, Inc., publisher.

.70 and .80. In this connection, it must be kept in mind that it is not the subject's response to one or even a few items that is meaningful, but rather, the *trend* of his responses to a large number of items. For example, in the *Gordon* there are seventy-two items in each of the two tests; in the *Mooney* there are more than two hundred; and even in the *Aspects of Personality* there are 105.

On the problem of faked or simulated responses there is some evidence from research.[7] The information obtained from some of these studies may be summed up briefly as follows:

1. It is possible to fake or slant answers on a self-report inventory.

2. It is not as easy to do this as might be supposed, especially to take and maintain consistently a pose. Ability to slant answers is affected, among other things, by (a) the sophistication of the subjects, (b) the subtlety of the statements on the inventory, and (c) the number of items.

3. Some individuals cannot consistently fake answers in a desired direction even when told to do so.

It is obvious that a personality inventory differs from a test of achievement in this respect. In the latter case there is little chance for faking or bluffing if it is a good test, while in the former, the value of the responses depends on the subject's willingness to be truthful and on his ability to give accurate representations of his behavior and feelings. Unless he is cooperative, the responses are of no value.

As to the question of whether personality inventories should be used in schools, it may be said, first of all, that they should be used very conservatively. Whereas the average classroom teacher can handle standardized tests of achievement and intelligence with some help and guidance from the counselor or school psychologist, this is seldom the case with personality tests. The use and interpretation of these tests require more training and experience than most teachers possess. As a rule, the personality test should be given on an individual basis rather than on a school-wide basis. When a child asks his teacher or counselor for help, or shows symptoms of maladjustment, the use of a personality inventory certainly may be indicated. It is important that the results be held in strictest confidence and used only with caution by a person qualified to interpret them. Even a tool like the *Mooney Check Lists* should probably be used selectively rather than on a school-wide basis, and the results should be made available only to guidance workers or school psychologists. When these principles are not

---

[7] See, for example, Victor H. Noll, "Simulation by College Students of a Prescribed Pattern on a Personality Scale," *Educational and Psychological Measurement,* 11:478–88, Spring, 1951; also, Bernard M. Bass, "Faking by Sales Applicants of a Forced-Choice Personality Inventory," *Journal of Applied Psychology,* 41:403–404, December, 1957.

adhered to, the results will often prove detrimental to pupil morale as well as to the parents' confidence in the method used. This, in turn, may decrease the value of the inventory as a whole.

There are many self-report-type personality inventories. A few typical examples are listed below.

Other Personality Inventories

1. *Adjustment Inventory.* 1934–38; student form revised 1962. Grades 7–16 and adults. *Home, health, social, emotional, hostility, masculinity-femininity.*

Student form and adult form. Student form, $3.40 per 25; adult form, $3.20 per 25. 30 minutes.

Stanford University Press.

2. *A–S Reaction Study.* A scale for measuring ascendance-submission in personality. 1928. College students and adults. Measures the *tendency to dominate or be dominated in face-to-face relationships.*

Form for men and form for women, $3.40 per 35. 20 minutes.

Houghton Mifflin Company.

3. *California Test of Personality.* 1953. Primary, K–3; Elementary, 4–8; Intermediate, 7–10; Secondary, 9–College; Adults. *Self-adjustment and social adjustment.*

Forms AA and BB. $3.50 per 35. 50 minutes.

California Test Bureau.

4. *Detroit Adjustment Inventory.* 1942–53. Ages 5–8, Grades 3–6 and 7–12. Adjustment in four areas: *self, home, school, and community.*

Forms Delta, Gamma, Alpha. $4.50 per 35. 30 minutes.

The Bobbs-Merrill Company, Inc.

5. *Edwards Personal Preference Schedule.* 1953–57. College and adults. *Achievement, deference, order, exhibition, autonomy, affiliation, intraception, succorance, dominance, abasement, nurturance, change, endurance, heterosexuality, aggression.*

One form. $3.50 per 25. 45 minutes.

Psychological Corporation.

6. *Guilford-Zimmerman Temperament Survey.* 1949. Grades 9–16 and adults. *General activity, restraint, ascendance, sociability, emotional stability, confidence, personal relations, home satisfaction.*

One form. $3.75 per 25. 45 minutes.

Sheridan Supply Company.

7. *IPAT Anxiety Scale.* 1957. Ages 14 and up. *Self-sentiment development, ego strength, paranoid trend, guilt proneness, ergic tension.* One form. $3.00 per 25. 10 minutes.
Institute for Personality and Ability Testing.

8. *Minnesota Counseling Inventory.* 1953–57. Grades 9–12. *Family relationships, social relationships, emotional stability, conformity, adjustment to reality, mood, leadership.* One form. $3.50 per 25. 50 minutes.
Psychological Corporation.

9. *Minnesota Multiphasic Personality Inventory.* 1951. Age 16 and up. *Hypochondriasis, depression, hysteria, psychopathic deviate, masculinity and femininity, paranoia, psychasthenia, schizophrenia, hypomania,* and *social introversion.*
Individual form and group form. Individual, $15.00 per set, plus $1.50 per manual; scoring keys and manual, $8.50. Group, $5.50 per 25, plus $1.50 per manual. Scoring keys and manual, $4.65. 60–90 minutes.
Psychological Corporation.

10. *S.R.A. Junior Inventory.* 1951–55. Grades 4–8. *Getting along with others, my home and family, my health, about myself, my school,* and *things in general.*
Form A, $10.80 per 20; Form S, $2.30 per 20. 40 minutes.
Science Research Associates, Inc.

11. *S.R.A. Youth Inventory.* 1949. Grades 7–12. *My school, looking ahead, about myself, getting along with others, my home and family, boy meets girl, health, things in general.*
Form H, $10.80 per 20; Form S, 2.40 per 20.
Science Research Associates, Inc.

12. *Study of Values.* Revised, 1951. College and adult. Aims to measure the relative prominence of six basic interests or motives in personality: *the theoretical, economic, aesthetic, social, political,* and *religious.*
One form. $4.00 per 35. About 20 minutes.
Houghton Mifflin Company.

PROJECTIVE TECHNIQUES

Another type of self-report is the projective test, which is a clinical instrument to be used only by psychiatrists or clinical psychologists. It derives its name from the fact that in his responses the subject "projects" his feelings, emotions, conflicts, and problems. The projective tests are less structured than the personality inventories in that the questions, items, or stimuli are less definite and specific, and the subject is far more free to make responses in his own words.

The Rorschach Ink-Blot Test is a well-known example of a projective test. It consists of a series of what purport to be inkblots, some black, some in color (see Figure 13). These are shown to the subject one at a time, and he is asked to tell what they suggest or remind him of. From the subject's responses the psychiatrist can determine much about the presence and nature of deep-seated emotional conflicts and maladjustments which the subject himself may not understand or even be conscious of. Obviously, such a test requires much training and experience to administer and interpret.

FIGURE 13. • Holtzman Inkblot (Similar to Those in the *Rorschach Ink-Blot Test*)

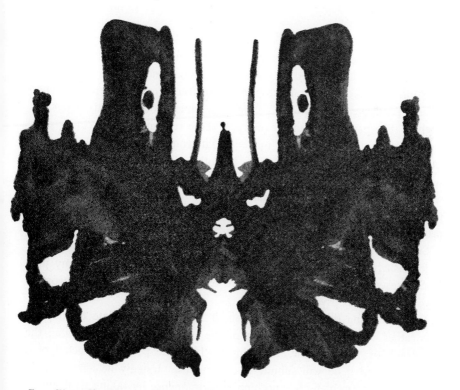

A simpler form of projective technique, and one probably antedating such instruments as the *Rorschach,* is the word-association test. The procedure in this type of test is to present a list of words one at a time to the subject, asking him to give the first word that comes to mind in each case. Some of the words are "loaded," that is, they may carry emotional aspects for some individuals under certain circumstances. To be more specific, suppose a teacher or psychologist presented the following list of words to a group of fifth-grade children and asked each pupil to tell or write the first word that came to mind in each instance. Let us assume that the list of words has been used in this way with many children and that certain conventional or non-emotional responses have been identified. The results might reveal that two pupils responded as follows:

STIMULUS WORD	PUPIL A	PUPIL B
House	big	white
Apple	eat	sour
Paper	write	burn
Teacher	lady	ugly
Sky	blue	high

On the basis of the previous trials of these same words the responses of Pupil A might be regarded as quite conventional and normal. In the case of Pupil B, however, certain responses are found to be different in character. To apple, he responds "sour"; to paper, "burn"; and to teacher, "ugly." The psychiatrist might interpret these responses as reflecting some factors in Pupil B's emotional makeup that would warrant further investigation. Not only the response itself, but other considerations as well, have significance. For example, long hesitation before responding to a given word may be a sign of emotional blocking. Such a word list is a simple projective device in that the subject often "projects" his complexes or problems in the responses he makes.

Some projective tests consist of pictures of people, and still others use objects such as toys or simple mechanical devices. There are many projective tests and devices and they are especially popular with European psychologists and psychiatrists.

Before closing this brief discussion, it may be appropriate to mention one rather well-known application of the association technique, i.e., the polygraph or "lie detector." By this method, the person suspected of a crime is asked if he will submit to such a test. Usually he agrees to do so. If he is innocent he has nothing to fear or lose by taking it; if guilty, he is afraid that refusal will reflect on him adversely, so he generally agrees to take it with the hope of "beating" it. The test depends upon the known effect of strong emotion on blood pressure, pulse rate, and amount of palmar sweating, all of which are increased by heightened emotion. Normal rates of each are established for the subject under simple and innocuous questioning, then loaded questions are introduced. If the pulse, blood pressure, and palmar sweating increase, it is judged that the subject is not telling the truth. This, of course, is not accepted as proof of guilt, but the results, when shown to a guilty suspect, often bring about a confession. In general, specialists in crime detection are of the opinion that the results of lie detector tests are quite reliable, and that few persons are successful in beating the test. The harder the individual tries and the more determined he is to beat it, the more pronounced are the tell-tale signs when a loaded question or some significant piece of evidence is suddenly introduced.

For those interested in the further study of projective tests and procedures, certain references in the bibliography at the end of this chapter should prove helpful.

▶ LEARNING EXERCISES ◀

1. Define (*a*) personality, (*b*) adjustment.

2. How might the results of personality tests be used by (*a*) classroom teachers, (*b*) guidance workers, and (*c*) school psychologists?

3. Is there any place for projective tests in the school? If so, under what circumstances?

4. Graphology, the attempt to study personality through handwriting, is much favored in some European countries. How would you set up a scientific experiment to test the accuracy of analyses of handwriting of different individuals?

INTEREST INVENTORIES

Though interest inventories are not measures of personality and adjustment in a technical sense, it seems appropriate to consider such inventories at this point, since a person's interests reflect his personality and are a part of it; moreover, his interests in relation to his abilities, opportunities, and background may have a definite bearing on his adjustment. Interest inventories are useful tools for counselors and school psychologists in helping the individual to make appropriate educational and occupational choices; inappropriate or unsuitable choices often lead to maladjustment and serious loss of time and energy.

The interest inventory is based on the theory that a dependable picture of a person's interest pattern can be obtained by asking him to express likes and dislikes of a large number of diverse activities and things. It is assumed, furthermore, that persons successful in the same occupation or field of work will have patterns of interests that are similar. Thus, a successful motion picture actor will have patterns of interests that are similar to the patterns of other successful actors. Finally, it is assumed that the patterns of interests of persons successfully engaged in one occupation — teaching, for example — will differ from those of persons in another field, such as engineering or chemistry. These three assumptions are at the root of the development of interest inventories. Two typical inventories of this type will be briefly described. The total number of such inventories is not large, as compared with the number of tests in other types of personality measurement.

Strong Vocational Interest Blanks

One of the earliest and best-known interest inventories was developed by Strong. It consists of items listed under such topics as "Occupations," "School Subjects," "Amusements," "Activities," and "Peculiarities of People." In each group of items the individual is asked to express a preference, either in terms of "Like," "Indifferent," or "Dislike," or an order of preference for the items. For example, in "Part I — Occupations":[8]

```
        1. Actor  .  .  .  .  . L  I  D
        2. Advertiser .  .  . . L  I  D
        3. Architect  .  .  . . L  I  D
        4. Army Officer .  . . L  I  D
        5. Artist  .  .  .  . . L  I  D
```

the subject encircles "L" if he would like or be interested in that occupation, "D" if he would dislike it, and "I" if he is indifferent toward it.

Again, in "Part VI — Order of Preference of Activities":

---

[8] Sample items reprinted from *Vocational Interest Blank for Men* and *Vocational Interest Blank for Women*, by Edward K. Strong, Jr., with the permission of the publishers, Stanford University Press. Copyright 1938 and 1946 by the Board of Trustees of Leland Stanford University. Distributed by Psychological Corporation. Hand Score edition, $4.15 per 25. Machine Score edition, $6.20 per 25. Answer sheets, $2.65 per 50. Scoring keys at extra cost.

Indicate by checking in Column 1 the three activities you would enjoy most; in Column 3 the three you would enjoy least; and the remaining four in Column 2.

	1.	*2.*	*3.*	
311.	( )	( )	( )	President of a Society or Club
312.	( )	( )	( )	Secretary of a Society or Club
313.	( )	( )	( )	Treasurer of a Society or Club
314.	( )	( )	( )	Member of a Society or Club
315.	( )	( )	( )	Chairman, Arrangements Committee
316.	( )	( )	( )	Chairman, Educational Committee
317.	( )	( )	( )	Chairman, Entertainment Committee
318.	( )	( )	( )	Chairman, Membership Committee
319.	( )	( )	( )	Chairman, Program Committee
320.	( )	( )	( )	Chairman, Publicity Committee

There are separate blanks for men and women. The categories in the blank for women are the same as those for men, but of course the activities, occupations, etc., are those appropriate for women. Each blank contains four hundred items to be checked. On the basis of the responses a profile is constructed for each individual, showing the resemblances and differences between the examinee's pattern of preferences and patterns of successful people in particular occupations. The blank for men can be scored for fifty-four occupations; that for women, for thirty. The scoring is rather complicated and laborious when done manually. It is best done by the use of prepared answer sheets and the test-scoring machine.

The Strong blanks are probably the most carefully constructed and validated instruments of this type. In addition to the occupational scales, scoring keys have been worked out for six occupational groups such as scientific or linguistic, and for certain non-occupational interests. The individuals on which scoring scales for the various criterion groups are based have been carefully selected from among persons successfully engaged in their present respective occupations for at least three years. They number in most instances two hundred cases or more. The reliabilities of the separate scales for men are nearly all above .80 and a substantial proportion are above .90. The reliabilities of the scoring scales for the women's blank average .86. All were calculated by the split-half method.

Validity is determined by the fact that men or women entering a particular occupation make higher scores on the scale for that occupation than on any other; that men or women continuing in an occupation suggested by the Strong blanks make higher scores than men or women entering an occupation other than that suggested; that men or women continuing in a suggested occupation make higher scores than those who change from that occupation to another one; and that a person changing from some other occupation to occupation X ten years later made higher scores as a college senior on the scale for occupation X or one other occupation than he did on the scales for eighteen other occupations.[9] While such data do not show that scores on the blank predict success in an occupation, they do indicate that scores are related to occupational preference as judged by entrance into and persistence in an occupation.

Kuder Preference Records — Vocational and Personal

Another well-known and widely used set of interest inventories are the *Kuder Preference Records — Vocational C, Vocational B, Personal A,* and *Occupational D.*[10] *Vocational C* measures ten broad areas of educational interest: *outdoor, mechanical, computational, scientific, persuasive, artistic, literary, musical, social service,* and *clerical. Vocational B* measures all these except *outdoor interest.* The *Personal A* measures five different kinds of personal preferences referred to as *sociable, practical, theoretical, agreeable,* and *dominant.* The newest form, *Occupational D,* relates preferences to specific jobs, and the publishers state that scoring keys for fifty occupations may be obtained. These inventories call for choices among a wide range of activities as does the Strong, but the choices are not grouped into categories such as occupations, subjects, etc. The alternatives are presented in groups of three; in each group the subject selects the one alternative which he would most prefer and the one which he would least like. For example:

P. Exercise in a gymnasium
Q. Go fishing
R. Play baseball

S. Cook for a hotel
T. Cook for people on camping trips
U. Cook for a family

The activities in each group are not necessarily in the same category, though in most groups they are. The blanks are scored for preferences in terms of the areas or fields as listed above and for specific occupations.

The scoring of the *Kuder Preference Records* is very simple. By means of a special type of answer booklet the scores of each individual on the

[9] Edward K. Strong, Jr., *Manual for Vocational Interest Blank for Women* (Stanford University, Calif.: Stanford University Press, 1947), p. 14.
[10] G. Frederic Kuder, *Kuder Preference Records — Vocational, Occupational, and Personal* (Chicago: Science Research Associates, 1948). Sample items reproduced by permission of the publisher.

group or area scales can be readily determined and the scores transmuted into a profile. Machine scorable answer sheets may also be used.

A large amount of research bearing on the validity of the *Kuder Records,* particularly *Vocational C,* has been published. The general trend of such studies has been to show marked differences in scores on the separate scales for different occupational groups and for different college majors and curricula, and definite relationships to job satisfaction. The reliabilities of the various scales, determined by the Kuder-Richardson Formula, are mostly between .85 and .90.

Although interest inventories are very useful in certain situations, especially in guidance and counseling, the results obtained by their use can be overgeneralized if certain facts are not kept clearly in mind. In the first place, the inventories are not aptitude tests. Although a similarity-of-interest pattern such as that of persons successfully engaged in a given occupation is undoubtedly a desirable attribute for one considering that occupation as his life's work, such resemblance is not a guarantee of success in the occupation. An inventory might reveal a pattern of interests which resembles very closely that of successful engineers, for example, but much more than an interest pattern is needed to achieve success in such work; the same is true of any other profession or occupation. Teachers and counselors should guard against becoming uncritical, over-enthusiastic users of these instruments; students should not be advised to choose a given occupation solely on the basis of scores on an interest inventory.

In the second place, it should always be kept in mind that interests change, particularly for persons below the age of twenty-five years. When an interest inventory is given in the junior high school, for example, the results should be considered as very tentative and likely to change markedly, perhaps more than once, before the individual "settles down." It is common knowledge that many persons change their goals even after leaving college. The results of an interest inventory should always be regarded as provisional, at least until the individual has attained full maturity.

Finally, it should be recognized that few persons have the breadth of knowledge and experience to make valid choices among such a wide range of activities as these inventories present, and that many such choices must, at best, be based upon questionable or very limited information. Moreover, when the inventories are used with children in junior high schools it seems likely that many of the words used in them may pose vocabulary problems. If a pupil does not know the meanings of the words or terms, he certainly cannot make intelligent choices.

In the light of these considerations, the use of interest inventories with subjects below the senior high school level seems questionable. When they are used, it should always be with full cognizance of the limitations and safeguards that have been pointed out. Interest inventories are valuable tools and their use can be recommended particularly for counselors and guidance workers provided the results are interpreted and used with appropriate caution.

Other Interest Inventories

1. *Brainard Occupational Preference Inventory.* 1945. Grades 8–12 and adults. *Commercial, personal service, agricultural, mechanical, professional, aesthetic,* and *scientific.*
   One form, $3.25 per 25. 30 minutes.
   Psychological Corporation.

2. *Cleeton Vocational Interest Inventory.* 1943. Grades 9–16 and adults. *Biological sciences, sales, physical sciences, social sciences, business, literary, mechanical, finance and accounting, artistic, elementary teacher, high school teacher, personal service, household and factory, homemaking.*
   One form for men, one for women. $2.50 per 25. 50 minutes.
   Bureau of Educational Research and Service.

3. *Guilford-Schneidman-Zimmerman Interest Survey.* 1948. Grades 9–16 and adults. *Artistic, linguistic, scientific, mechanical, outdoor, business, social, personal, office.*
   One form. $4.00 per 25. 50 minutes.
   Sheridan Supply Company.

4. *Occupational Interest Inventory.* 1956. Intermediate, Grade 7 to average adult; Advanced, Grades 9–12, college, superior adult. *Personal-social, natural, mechanical, business, arts, sciences, verbal, manipulative, computational.*
   One form, $5.25 per 35. 40 minutes.
   California Test Bureau.

5. *Thurstone Interest Schedule.* 1947. High school and college. *Physical science, biological science, computational, business, executive, persuasive, linguistic, humanitarian, artistic, musical.*
   One form, $2.10 per 25. 15 minutes.
   Psychological Corporation.

▶ **LEARNING EXERCISES** ◀

5. Would you expect the *Strong Interest Blank* to be more appropriate for persons above the age of eighteen, and the *Kuder Preference Record* to be more suitable for high school ages? If so, why?

6. Does the fact that interests of adolescents are often not stabilized make the use of interest inventories inadvisable? What are some ways in which they can be used to advantage with high school pupils?

7. Compared with other types of tests, there are relatively few interest inventories. Can you give some reasons for this?

THE MEASUREMENT OF ATTITUDES

Attitudes may be considered to be one phase of personality. They are closely associated with feelings and emotions, and are a large factor in determining our reactions and behavior. An attitude may be thought of as a response pattern, or a tendency to think or act in a particular way under a given set of circumstances. Thus, a person has established attitudes towards certain activities, geographical regions, political parties, and towards particular individuals such as the principal of his school, his homeroom teacher, his classmates, etc. When situations arise in which one or another of these is involved, he tends to react in each case in a certain way. His attitude toward Communists may be strongly antagonistic; toward his principal, neutral; and toward the football coach, strongly favorable. In the first instance the attitude may be generalized to include all Communists; in the second and third the attitude is specific with respect to a single individual. In every case there is likely to be some emotional reaction, however slight.

It has already been pointed out that attitudes condition behavior. An unfavorable attitude will usually cause a reaction either of avoidance or of aggression; a neutral attitude, indifference; and a favorable attitude, a seeking behavior. Of course, not all attitudes can be neatly classified as unfavorable, neutral, or favorable. Attitudes range by degrees from one extreme to the other, and the use of the three terms is merely for convenience.

The Method of Equal-Appearing Intervals

The measurement of attitudes is carried out by self-report methods. One method is to present to the subject a list of statements expressing attitudes varying widely from very favorable to neutral to very unfavorable; the subject is asked to check those with which he agrees. This method, known as the method of *equal-appearing intervals,* was devised some years ago by Thurstone and Chave.[11] A large number of statements of attitude toward something, e.g., the Republican Party, are collected. These statements must vary by fine degrees in the attitudes they express, from extremely favorable to extremely unfavorable. A number of competent judges sort the statements into eleven piles or groups according to the shade or degree of opinion expressed. All statements in one pile are those judged to be expressive of the same attitude. Each pile differs from the adjoining ones above and below by apparently equal intervals or equal differences in attitude. Each judge sorts the statements independently.

Next, the judges together select from each group the two or three statements which they regard as most typical of that group and which express most nearly the same degree of attitude. When these are assembled there are generally twenty-five to thirty statements varying in expressed attitude from very favorable through neutral to extremely unfavorable. Each statement has a scale value according to its position or grouping. Thus, those at the most unfavorable end of the scale may each have a scale value of 11, the neutral ones, 6, and the more favorable ones, 5, 4, 3, 2, and 1, in that order. The statements are reproduced in random order and the person whose attitude toward the Republican Party is to be measured is asked to check those statements with which he agrees. His score or attitude is based on the average scale values of those he checks.

To illustrate this type of scale, a few statements from a scale constructed to measure attitudes toward vocational education in secondary schools are given below.

> I think that for his own good, every high school student should be required to take one shop course. (2.9)
>
> I think that one course is as good as another. It all depends on what you can do and are interested in. (5.4)
>
> Students in a regular high school should have an opportunity to take vocational courses if they want to. (4.2)
>
> Vocational subjects are taken by many students because they require very little homework and outside study. (8.0)
>
> I think that academic courses should all be elective and that only vocational courses should be required. (1.0)
>
> I see no value to anyone in vocational subjects; they are an absolute waste of time. (10.5)
>
> I think that vocational subjects are usually spoiled by the practice of "dumping" failures from other subjects into them. (7.7)

[11] L. L. Thurstone and E. J. Chave. *The Measurement of Attitude* (Chicago: University of Chicago Press, 1929).

These statements represent a sampling from some thirty that constituted a scale of attitudes toward vocational subjects in high school. The scale value of each statement is given in the parentheses following it. These values are generally not shown on the scale that is checked by the person taking the test. This scale, one of four devised for use with high school students, was developed by following very closely the procedure of Thurstone.

The Likert Method

The Likert method[12] of measuring attitudes is somewhat less time-consuming than that just described. It, too, begins with a considerable number of statements of attitude toward something. However, in this case they are either decidedly favorable or decidedly unfavorable. Each statement usually has five possible responses: "SA" ("Strongly Agree"); "A" ("Agree"); "U" ("Undecided"); "D" ("Disagree"); and "SD" ("Strongly Disagree"). The person taking the test reacts to *every* statement by marking one of the five possible responses. The responses have weights of 5, 4, 3, 2, and 1 for favorable statements, and 1, 2, 3, 4, and 5 for unfavorable ones. The subject's score is the sum of the weights of the responses he checks. A high score indicates a highly favorable attitude, a low score, the opposite.

The Likert method eliminates the sorting by judges and therefore it requires less time to prepare a scale than the method of equal-appearing intervals. It also uses more statements, as a rule, and the subject is required to check all of them, both of which factors tend to increase the reliability of scores but also the time required.

A sample set of statements set up by the Likert method might read as follows:

SA A U D SD	All Mexicans are dirty.
SA A U D SD	Mexicans are intelligent, industrious people who have not had opportunity to develop.
SA A U D SD	Mexicans should not be permitted to enter the United States.

Other methods used for measuring attitudes require the subject to react to pictures, and still another method requires a series of choices from paired alternatives such as "salesman and mechanic," "banker and professor," "owner and operator," etc. However, the two methods that have

[12] Rensis Likert, "A Technique for the Measurement of Attitudes," *Archives of Psychology,* Volume 22, No. 140 (1932).

been described above are probably the best of those developed to the present time. Both give fairly high reliabilities for the type of measurement. Correlations between scores on comparable scales of the two types are reported to be quite high.[13]

One of the chief problems in connection with attitude scales is their validity. As with all self-report instruments, the value of the score is dependent upon the cooperation of the person taking the test. It is very easy for him to simulate an extreme attitude if he wishes to do so, simply by checking all the strong statements one way or the other, or by strongly agreeing or strongly disagreeing with all the statements of one type or another. Generally this is much easier to do in an attitude scale than in a personality inventory. In the latter the implications of specific statements are not always obvious. Unless the subject is honestly trying to cooperate when he checks the attitude scale the results are of little or no value.

In the second place, what a person agrees or disagrees with on paper is not necessarily a reflection of how he really feels or acts. There is no way of determining whether or not the subject is honestly expressing what he believes. Furthermore, what he endorses on the test is one thing, but his actual behavior in the same or a similar situation may not be consistent with his verbal responses. Some research has been done on this with widely varying findings. Some studies report substantial correlations between scores on an attitude scale and observed behavior; others report negligible correlations. Corey, for example, found practically no correlation in a college class between scores on a scale of attitude toward cheating and actual behavior in an examination.[14]

Much of the research suggests that there is a positive correlation in the neighborhood of .50–.60 between scores on attitudes scales and actual performance or behavior. This is not a close relationship, but it does indicate a substantial tendency. The ultimate validity of attitude scores depends on how well they correlate with action. It may be interesting and in some instances useful to know what an individual's verbalized attitudes are, but unless they can be used to predict how he will act, such data are of limited value for practical purposes. In this respect there is still much to be accomplished in the area of attitude measurement.

[13] Allen L. Edwards and Kathryn C. Kenney, "A Comparison of the Thurstone and Likert Techniques of Attitude Scale Construction," *Journal of Applied Psychology*, 30:72–83 (February, 1946).

[14] Stephen M. Corey, "Professed Attitudes and Actual Behavior," *Journal of Educational Psychology*, 28:271–80 (April, 1937).

▶ LEARNING EXERCISES ◀

8. List some matters such as school subjects, athletics, high marks, or senior trips, toward which a high school faculty might wish to test attitudes. Name some that elementary teachers might be similarly interested in.

9. Select one of the above and write out ten statements expressing different attitudes toward it that might become part of a scale, following either the Thurstone or the Likert plan.

10. What are some of the issues for which scales of attitudes have been devised? Find in the literature on educational measurement a report of one such project and prepare an abstract of it.

11. Can attitudes be changed? If so, how? Of what value are tests or scales of attitude in such attempts?

ANNOTATED BIBLIOGRAPHY

1. Anastasi, Anne. *Psychological Testing,* Second Edition. New York: The Macmillan Co., 1961. Chapters 18–20 present discussions of personality inventories, measures of interests and attitudes, and projective techniques, with roughly equal emphasis on each. The discussions are quite complete.

2. Anderson, H. H., and Anderson, Gladys L. *An Introduction to Projective Techniques and Other Devices for Understanding the Dynamics of Human Behavior.* New York: Prentice Hall, Inc., 1951. 720 pp. A thorough survey of projective techniques.

3. Bell, John E. *Projective Techniques.* New York: David McKay Co., Inc., 1948. 533 pp. A volume that reviews the literature on projective techniques and describes a large number of such instruments and the methods for their use.

4. Cronbach, Lee J. *Essentials of Psychological Testing,* Second Edition. New York: Harper & Row, Publishers, 1960. Chapters 14 to 19, inclusive. A detailed discussion of measurement of personality and adjustment, including all the usual techniques plus interests, attitudes, and observational procedures. Especially good for its review of research in this field.

5. Edwards, Allen L. *Techniques of Attitude Scale Construction.* New York: Appleton-Century-Crofts, Inc., 1957. A scholarly discussion of the different methods of constructing scales for the measurement of attitudes. Also presents methods of evaluating scales derived by each method described.

6. Freeman, Frank S. *Theory and Practice of Psychological Testing,* Third Edition. New York: Holt, Rinehart & Winston Inc., 1962. Chapters 21 to

26 inclusive. A thorough coverage of rating methods, situational measures and devices, self-report inventories, interests, attitudes, values, and projective methods of various types.

7. Greene, Harry A.; Jorgensen, Albert N.; and Gerberich, J. Raymond. *Measurement and Evaluation in the Elementary School,* Second Edition. David McKay Co., Inc., 1953. Chapter 11 discusses the nature of personality and the measurement of personality, attitudes, interests, and emotional adjustment, and the use of anecdotal records, projective techniques, sociograms, and measures of total personality. The treatment is necessarily brief and limited.

8. Jordan, A. M. *Measurement in Education.* New York: McGraw-Hill Book Co., Inc., 1953. Chapters 16, 17, 18. Chapter 16 is a discussion of the measurement of interest by interest inventories, by direct observation of behavior, and by testing information as a reflection of interest. The approach is stimulating and unusual. Chapter 17 is a good discussion of the measurement of attitudes. Chapter 18 deals with self-report inventories and rating scales. Validity and reliability are discussed in each of the three chapters.

9. Remmers, H. H., and Gage, N. L. *Educational Measurement and Evaluation,* Revised. New York: Harper & Row, Publishers, 1955. Chapters 12, 13, and 14 offer a general but thoughtful presentation on evaluation of emotional and social adjustment. All the common techniques are briefly discussed and evaluated. Chapters 13 and 14 deal with the nature and measurement of attitudes.

10. Super, Donald E. *Appraising Vocational Fitness.* New York: Harper & Row, Publishers, 1949. Chapters 16–19, inclusive. A thorough, scholarly discussion of the nature of interests and their measurement and a briefer treatment of the measurement of personality, including self-report and projective instruments.

11. Thomas, R. Murray. *Judging Student Progress,* Second Edition. New York: David McKay Co., Inc., 1960. Chapter 6. There is some discussion of personality inventories, but the bulk of the chapter deals with projective techniques. The presentation is non-technical and is directed primarily at teachers in elementary schools. Emphasizes that such instruments must be used only by clinically trained persons.

12. Thorndike, Robert L., and Hagen, Elizabeth. *Measurement and Evaluation in Psychology and Education,* Second Edition. New York: John Wiley & Sons, Inc., 1961. Chapter 12 is concerned with self-report devices including attitude tests and interest inventories. Chapter 15 deals with projective techniques. Each chapter includes an evaluation of the methods presented.

13. Travers, Robert M. W. *Educational Measurement.* New York: The Macmillan Co., 1955. Chapters 9, 10, and 11. Chapter 9 presents a theory of personality and various approaches to the measurement of personality including rating, personality inventories, and projective techniques. Chapter 10 deals with the measurement of attitudes, and Chapter 11 with assessment of interests.

14. Wrightstone, J. Wayne; Justman, Joseph; and Robbins, Irving. *Evaluation in Modern Education*. New York: American Book Company, 1956. Chapters 9, 10, 16, 18, and 19. Chapter 9 deals with check lists and rating scales, and emphasizes their use in the improvement of teaching. Some attention is given to their construction. Chapter 10 describes personal reports and projective techniques without emphasis on matters of technique. Chapter 16 deals with evaluation of interests, Chapter 18 with personal-social adjustment, and Chapter 19 with attitudes and values.

13

The Measurement of Personality and

Adjustment: Observational Techniques

In Chapter 12 various self-report approaches to the measurement of personality and adjustment were presented. In this chapter we shall continue and conclude the discussion of the measurement of personality and adjustment with a consideration of observational techniques. Observational techniques employ information supplied by sources other than the individual being studied. The techniques which will be discussed here are rating scales, systematic observation, anecdotal records, and sociometric methods. Each will be described and illustrated. There will also be a brief discussion of the effective use and the particular advantages and disadvantages of each technique.

RATING SCALES

The basic purpose of rating devices is to obtain systematically and objectively a sampling of opinion on certain characteristics of a given individual. Such judgments should be obtained from people who are well acquainted with the person being rated and who can express accurate and dependable opinions. In order to obtain satisfactory results it is essential to follow certain well-established and tested procedures. Among other things, it is necessary to define the traits or characteristics on which the ratings will be based, to provide some kind of scale or range by which the rater can indicate his judgment of the amount or degree of the trait, and to give the rater some specific and carefully worked out instructions regarding the purposes and use of the instrument. In addition, it is highly desirable to meet with the persons who are going to do the rating in order to discuss the use of the device with them, and, if possible, to give them some practice in using it. Instruction and information in addition to that which is printed on the scale *must* be given to persons untrained in the use of rating scales if the results are to be valid and reliable.

In constructing a rating scale the first step is to divide the broad area to be analyzed into specific traits or characteristics. To ask for ratings in such wide areas as "personality" or "adjustment" would give results that are almost meaningless. Therefore, the concept of "personality" should be broken down into more specific and definable terms such as "persistence," "cheerfulness," "aggressive tendencies," "generosity," or "resourcefulness."

When such an analysis has been made, the next step is to define each of these traits in terms which will be meaningful to the rater and which will convey similar meanings to the various persons using the scale. This is a difficult task and, of course, it is never possible to be sure that one has succeeded. However, if the traits are clearly defined in terms of *behavior,* rather than vague abstractions, it helps materially to insure that those using the scale will have common understandings of the traits being rated.

Finally, the specific traits should be defined in such a way that the definitions provide descriptions of the varying degrees of each trait and lead the rater to make quantitative judgments rather than vague, meaningless generalizations.

The most widely used form of rating device is generally referred to as the *graphic rating scale.* In this form each trait is represented not only by descriptions of varying degrees of the trait but also a line divided into the same number of equal segments as there are trait descriptions. The rater expresses his judgment by placing a check mark on the line to indicate his estimate of the person being rated. An illustration of this technique might be as follows:

Trustworthiness

5	4 ✓	3	2	1
Completely dependable in all situations	Can nearly always be relied upon to honor commitments	Can be relied upon in most situations	Not dependable. Often slips up on responsibilities	Irresponsible. Can never be relied upon

A check mark placed as shown indicates the rater's appraisal of the person being rated, in this case, between average and somewhat above average. This rating could be given a numerical value of 3.5 if desired.

BEC Personality Rating Schedule

An excerpt from a graphic rating scale of personality is shown in Figure 14. It clearly illustrates the principles of construction and organization that have just been discussed.

This rating scale, or rating schedule, as it is called, provides opportunity for ratings on twenty-nine traits grouped in eight categories: *Mental Alertness, Initiative, Dependability, Cooperativeness, Judgment, Personal Impression, Courtesy,* and *Health.* A score may be obtained on each trait and these scores may be averaged within each category or for all twenty-nine traits, if desired.

Michigan Department of Mental Health Rating Scale for Pupil Adjustment

Another rating scale, set up somewhat differently, is the *Michigan Department of Mental Health Rating Scale for Pupil Adjustment.*[1] This provides for letter ratings on eleven characteristics or traits: *Over-all Emotional Adjustment, Social Maturity, Tendency Toward Depression, Tendency Toward Aggressive Behavior, Extroversion-Introversion, Emotional Security, Motor Control and Stability, Impulsiveness, Emotional Irritability, School Achievement,* and *School Conduct.* In addition, there is an opportunity to check physical conditions of the child such as height,

---

[1] *Michigan Department of Mental Health Rating Scale for Pupil Adjustment* (Chicago: Science Research Associates, Inc., 1953). Quotation from this scale by permission of the publisher.

FIGURE 14 • Excerpt from *BEC Personality Rating Schedule*

V. JUDGMENT	5	4	3	2	1	0
1. *Sense of Values*	Is unfailingly keen of insight in distinguishing the important from the unimportant in classwork 5	Generally distinguishes the important from the unimportant in classwork even when confusion might be easy 4	Distinguishes satisfactorily between the important and the unimportant in classwork 3	Occasionally confuses the important with the unimportant in classwork 2	Commonly neglects crucial issues in classwork through attention to the unimportant 1	0
2. *Deliberativeness*	Always considers carefully all aspects of problem situation before proposing solution 5	Usually considers all important aspects of problem situation before proposing solution 4	Seldom proposes solution to important problem situation without some preliminary analysis 3	Sometimes proposes solutions to problem situations without any preliminary analysis 2	Is constantly jumping at conclusions 1	0
3. *Tact*	Extremely gifted in discerning the best thing to do or say when dealing with others; never gives any offense 5	Usually says or does the suitable thing when dealing with others 4	Only rarely gives any offense through ill-considered speech or action 3	Sometimes says or does the wrong thing when dealing with others 2	Frequently gives offense through lack of discernment in speech or action 1	0
4. *Worth of Opinions*	His opinion invariably sought by colleagues in deliberative assemblies	His opinion usually valued by colleagues in deliberative assemblies	His views generally accorded a courteous reception	His opinion not generally sought by colleagues	His opinions accorded little esteem in deliberative meetings	

Reprinted by permission of the publishers from Philip J. Rulon and others, *BEC Personality Rating Schedule*; Cambridge, Mass.: Harvard University Press. Copyright, 1936, by The President and Fellows of Harvard College.

weight, and physical handicaps and defects. The sample below shows how this scale is set up.

IX. Emotional Irritability

(Definition: Tendency to become angry, irritated, or upset.)

A. Usually good-natured.
B. Good-natured — rarely irritable.
C. Fairly good-natured — occasionally irritable.
D. Moderately irritable — frequently shows *moderate* irritation.
E. Extremely irritable — frequently shows *marked* irritation.

A   B   C   D   E

Obviously, this is not a *graphic* rating scale in the usual sense of the term. There is no line or continuum upon which a check mark can be placed anywhere according to the rater's best judgment. Instead, there are five levels for each trait, and the rater simply checks the one of these which is most appropriate. He cannot signify an in-between rating. In the opinion of some persons this is a disadvantage in that it does not permit as much differentiation as the graphic scale.

A score is obtained on each trait by multiplying *A* ratings by 5, *B*'s by 4, *C*'s by 3, *D*'s by 2, and *E*'s by 1. These products are added to get a total score. The authors state that the best index of *Total Emotional Adjustment* is a score based on a combination of four traits, namely, *Overall Emotional Adjustment, Social Maturity, Emotional Security,* and *Impulsiveness.* It is recommended that this score be used as the adjustment criterion until results of further research on validity are available. Ratings on various combinations of traits may be used to obtain scores in other areas such as Aggressive Behavior or Inhibitory Control.

This rating scale is suggested for use as a screening device. After pupils have been rated by their teachers and the scores have been calculated, a distribution of scores is made. Pupils scoring in the lower third or lower fourth of the distribution may be referred to the proper clinical services for further study and therapy. The proportion suggested for referral will depend on a number of factors such as the quality and availability of clinical services, and the character of the school population with respect to such factors as culture, socio-economic status, and geographical area.

Rating scales and devices may be used for purposes other than rating personality and adjustment. For example, they may be used to rate performance on a job, the quality of a product such as a cake or a lampstand made by a pupil, or the quality of handwriting. The use of rating scales for such purposes has already been discussed in a previous chapter.

In closing the discussion of rating scales it may be helpful to present a few suggestions regarding their effective use. We mentioned earlier that it is not safe to assume that anyone can use a rating scale properly and effectively without instructions; indeed, it is generally recognized that some instruction is necessary if the results are to be of value.

Some of the common errors in using rating scales may serve as a starting point in developing suggestions for effective use. A frequent cause of error is the *halo effect,* the tendency of the rater to let his general, over-all impression of the person being rated influence his ratings on every trait. If he likes the subject, he will tend to rate him favorably on everything. Contrariwise, a rater's dislike of a subject will tend to color all his ratings.

Another common error is the tendency to avoid the ends of the scale, that is, to avoid rating persons very high or very low. This is sometimes referred to as the *error of central tendency* and is likely to occur where raters are not well acquainted with the persons being rated. A similar type of tendency is known as the *generosity error,* which refers to the practice of rating everyone average or above. When this happens no one gets a rating below the middle of the scale, a fact which is manifestly unrealistic in most situations since there are usually as many below the average in a given group as there are above.

Another common error is called the *stereotype error,* which means that some raters will have preconceived ideas regarding members of certain groups — racial, religious, economic, or occupational — and will tend to rate them accordingly.

There are other types of errors in using rating scales, but the foregoing are among the most common and serious. The suggestions listed below should help to counteract, if not entirely overcome, such tendencies toward error.

Suggestions for Users of Rating Scales

1. Rate each member of a group in comparison with all the others in his group. If only one person is being rated compare him mentally with others of his same level, class, occupation, etc. Do not rate him on the basis of some ideal that exists only in your imagination, or on the basis of some unrealistic and unattainable standards.

2. Rate each person on one trait before going to the next. For example, if there are thirty-five pupils to be rated on ten traits, rate all thirty-five on Trait 1, then all thirty-five on Trait 2, and so on. This is believed to

make ratings more accurate and dependable in that the rater concentrates on one trait at a time and compares each member of the group with all the others on the same trait before considering another trait.

3. Wherever possible use multiple ratings. That is, have several teachers or observers rate the same pupils without consulting each other. Ratings which are made independently by several raters and then considered collectively are much better than single ratings by one individual.

4. In making ratings try to think of the individual's behavior in as many different situations as possible. Isolated incidents, although they may be very striking, are not always typical of his usual behavior.

5. Do not rate individuals on traits or categories for which you cannot cite specific evidence or behavior to support your rating. If you have no basis for making a judgment, *do not rate*. Rather, leave that item unmarked and use "NOTO" (No Opportunity To Observe). A false or inaccurate rating is worse than none at all.

6. If you are responsible for obtaining ratings, give those who are to make them some instruction and assistance. A staff meeting or two could well be devoted to the development and discussion of such points as the five preceding.

▶ LEARNING EXERCISES ◀

1. Devise a short graphic rating scale for the five traits of Industry, Perseverance, Courtesy, Emotional Stability, and Sociability. Try to define degrees of each trait in terms of observable behavior.

2. Write out a set of instructions which will help fifth-grade teachers use the scale correctly.

Other Rating Scales

1. *Haggerty-Olson-Wickman Behavior Rating Scale.* 1930. Grades K–12. *Intellectual, physical, social,* and *emotional traits.*
One form, $3.00 per 35.
Harcourt, Brace & World, Inc.

2. *KD Proneness Scale.* 1950. Grades 7–12. *Delinquency proneness (truancy record, home background, attitude toward school, club membership, family mobility, etc.).*
One form, $3.45 per 35. 25 minutes.
Western Psychological Services.

3. *Pupil Adjustment Inventory.* 1957. Grades K–12. Consists of a rating scale for each of a number of *academic, social, emotional, physical, interest, school,* and *family-background characteristics* as they are related to the adjustment of the pupil.

Short and long forms. $2.70 per package of 35 short forms, 5 long forms; long form, $.06 per copy.

Houghton Mifflin Company.

4. *Vineland Social Maturity Scale.* 1946. Birthday to maturity. *Self-help, self-direction, occupation, locomotion, communication,* and *socialization.*

One form, $1.65 per 25. 30 minutes.

Educational Test Bureau.

OBSERVATION

Although each of the methods described in this chapter involves observation, there is an *observation technique* which has several features that merit individual consideration. The observation technique has been developed primarily in connection with child study. Nursery schools and kindergartens, particularly where these are part of a laboratory or demonstration school, are commonly equipped with one-way-vision screens so that children may be observed without their seeing the observers or knowing that they are being observed. Some efficient and dependable procedures for making and recording such observations have been developed through experience and research, and these procedures will be considered briefly as a means of evaluating behavior, personality, and adjustment.

As in the case of rating scales, one basic principle in observation is to define the behavior to be observed. It has not been found very useful or satisfactory just to "observe" children. It is much more productive first to define what is going to be observed and then to concentrate on observation in terms of the definition established. For example, suppose one were interested in making a study of personality traits in a group of four- and five-year-olds. The first step would be to identify and define the traits to be observed — such traits, for example, as cooperative behavior. What constitutes cooperative behavior at this age? Probably a dozen or more kinds of behavior (sharing toys, helping the teacher, picking up, etc.) could be thought of that would be evidence of cooperation among five-year-olds.

When the particular characteristic in question has been analyzed and divided into specific acts or behavior patterns, these elements are listed on a schedule or check list which the observer uses as a means of recording observations. Each time a particular behavior is observed it is recorded on the check list. In addition, cooperative behaviors not listed can be added as they occur.

A second principle is that there should be frequent and distributed observations. This means that it is better to divide the total observation time per child into smaller amounts for frequent observation than to use it all in one or two observations. Assuming, for example, that the observer has two hours of observation time per child, what is the best way to use it? It can be used in one two-hour block, two one-hour periods, and so on, down to 120 one-minute observations. Although no arbitrary, hard-and-fast rule can be given, it is generally agreed that a total of two hours divided into twenty-four five-minute periods would be preferable to longer and less frequent observations. Some investigators would use shorter and more frequent periods than this. In general, expert opinion seems to favor frequent, short observations distributed over a period of several weeks and falling at different times of the day. The chief advantage of such a plan is that it is likely to yield a more adequate sample of a child's behavior and thus reduce the chances of getting erroneous impressions from a long observation on what might be a very non-typical day. Rotating the time of observation so that the same child is not observed at the same time of day each observation period reduces the probabilities of getting consistently biased samples of behavior at a particular time of day, such as just before lunch.

It must be recognized, of course, that longer observation periods may be preferable under certain conditions or for certain purposes. This is particularly true where sequence of behavior is to be studied and where the development from beginning to end of certain behavior situations is to be observed.

Instead of defining and concentrating the observation on a specific behavior, one may keep a continuing or running account of the total behavior of a given child over a period of several days. This procedure, often used by clinicians, has the advantage of giving a more complete picture of the child, though it usually lacks the objectivity of the other method and it does not yield data which can readily be expressed in quantitative terms, such as a count of the number of times the defined behavior occurred.

Much depends on the training and the skill of the observer. He must be able to observe and record objectively, keep personal bias out of his observations, and distinguish clearly between observation and interpretation. He should record only what happens and do so as promptly as he can so that he does not have to rely too long on memory for important data. It is generally best to concentrate on obtaining a complete and accurate record at the time of observation and to make interpretations of the record later when there is more time for careful study.

An illustration or two of the observation method should serve to make it more definite and meaningful. One of the earliest applications of the *time-sampling* method of observing behavior in young children was a study reported by Olson in 1929.[2] He observed nervous habits in elementary school children by using five-minute observation periods for each child and recording the incidence of nervous habits (such as nose-picking, twitching, etc.). Although later investigators have improved upon and refined his procedure, Olson's was one of the first to yield quantitative data based on systematic time samples of children's observable behavior.

Another illustration of the observation technique will show how it can be used for evaluative purposes in the classroom. An experiment was conducted in seventy elementary schools in New York City to compare the effects of "activity programs" with a more conventional type of program.[3] The methods used to evaluate the results of the experiment included a wide variety of tests, anecdotal records, and observations. The observers, after a period of orientation and training, carried out a series of half-hour observations on each class in the experimental and control schools. The observer recorded by use of a code each occurrence of pupil activity which the experiment was designed to encourage. The number of observations varied from six to fourteen per class. When observations were checked by having two observers present at the same time, a substantial amount of agreement (averaging above 85 per cent) was found. The results of the observations showed a distinct superiority for the activity-program schools in the number and variety of pupil activities. The control classes showed a reliable superiority in recitational behavior.

It should be mentioned before closing this discussion of the observational method that the importance of training and skill in observation can scarcely be overemphasized. People vary greatly in their ability to observe and report accurately on what they have seen. It is well known, for example, that witnesses to an accident may give diametrically opposite accounts of what took place. Even under less strained conditions observers

[2] Willard C. Olson, *The Measurement of Nervous Habits in Normal Children,* Institute of Child Welfare Monographs, No. 3 (Minneapolis, Minn.: University of Minnesota Press, 1929).

[3] A. T. Jersild, R. L. Thorndike, B. Goldman, and J. J. Loftus, "An Evaluation of Aspects of the Activity Program in the New York City Public Elementary Schools," *Journal of Experimental Education,* 8:166–207, December, 1939.

in a laboratory or in a theater may differ in the accuracy of their observations, even though they have witnessed the same circumstances or events.

In research the observers are usually carefully selected on the basis of tests, and they are thoroughly trained. Furthermore, their reports are checked against those of other observers for agreement and consistency. Data gathered under such conditions are likely to be acceptable in validity and reliability. However, there are many situations in which such precautions and safeguards are impractical, even though systematic observations are desirable. Observations must often be made by classroom teachers who are relatively untrained for this work. Not only where educational experiments are being conducted in the schools, but in the daily activities in the classroom, much of our information about pupils and activities is based on observation by teachers. Observation by classroom teachers is generally informal and unsystematic and is carried on without benefit of check lists or planned procedure. Anything that can be done to make teachers more reliable and accurate observers should add to our understanding of children, which in turn should contribute to better adjustment and more wholesome personalities. To become better observers teachers must first of all have a genuine interest in improvement; they must be willing to accept instruction and assistance, and they must be willing to have their observations checked for accuracy and dependability. Students of science are trained constantly and rigorously in careful observation. It seems quite as important that prospective teachers be given similar training, since much of what is known about child behavior is based upon observation by their teachers.

▶ LEARNING EXERCISES ◀

3. Devise a record sheet in the form of a check list that might be used in observing and recording evidence of aggressive behavior in kindergarten children.

4. Devise a similar form for recording observations of changes in behavior as a result of instruction in a unit on personal hygiene in ninth-grade general science.

ANECDOTAL RECORDS

The method discussed in the preceding section is a systematic procedure for gathering observational data and is used more often in research than in everyday classroom situations. A method used more frequently and informally is the anecdotal record, which is the teacher's written record of an occurrence or incident involving a child. For example, the following might be typical:

GRADE 5 — MISS JONES

9/15/57 A new boy, Jimmy Long, came to school this morning. He is large and strong for his age. I heard him telling some of the other boys during recess about his dad who is a professional baseball player. (He didn't seem to be boasting — just proud of his dad.)

9/18/57 Jimmy, the new boy, got into an argument with Bob about a percentage problem dealing with baseball batting averages. Later, Jimmy hit John with a ruler and John cried. I made Jimmy say he was sorry. (Jimmy may be inclined to bully. Time will tell.)

These are samples of what Miss Jones might record as significant anecdotes concerning a new pupil. They illustrate some of the generally accepted principles of making anecdotal records.

First, it should be noted that the record is in two parts — the incident itself and, in parentheses, Miss Jones's interpretation. This is desirable and important if the records are to be maximally useful. When fact and interpretation are mingled it makes the records less objective and more difficult to interpret. Also, different persons may interpret an anecdote differently.

Second, the examples suggest that Miss Jones will keep a continuing record on Jimmy over a period of time and in a variety of situations. By this means she will secure a more complete and accurate picture of Jimmy's personality and will certainly be in a good position to give him help if he needs it.

Third, the samples indicate what Miss Jones considers to be significant aspects of Jimmy's behavior. There are undoubtedly other occurrences which she might have recorded, but these seemed to her to give the most insight into his personality during the first few days of school.

It is not easy to know what is significant and worth recording. Teachers inevitably have preferences and dislikes among their pupils, often without being fully aware of them, and these biases tend to influence the choice of children about whom anecdotes are recorded, as well as the nature of the anecdotes. It is quite natural, also, to overlook the shy, quiet child and to record anecdotes only on the more aggressive children. The observation that "Ruth sat in her seat and looked out the window while the other children came up to the desk to see the turtle," may be just as significant as the fact that "David brought a live turtle to school today which attracted a great deal of attention to him as well as to the turtle."

A recurring question on the matter of anecdotal records concerns the number of children on whom to keep such records and the number of anecdotes to record. Some authorities advocate that anecdotes should be regularly recorded for all children.[4] Ideally this is certainly desirable, but in most situations it would be impractical for busy teachers. A goal of only one anecdote per week per pupil would mean something like thirty-five or forty per year per pupil. Thus a teacher with thirty-five pupils in her room would have 35 × 35, or 1,275 anecdotes per year to record, which would be no small task in itself, to say nothing of the time required for the interpretation and use of the anecdotes. In this connection it should be noted that keeping anecdotal records presents quite different problems for the elementary and high school teacher. The former usually has about twenty-five to thirty pupils in her room all day every day, which provides ample opportunity to observe significant happenings. The high school teacher, on the other hand, may see 150 pupils every day for only one period each. Observing and recording significant anecdotes in this case is obviously more difficult.

In most situations it is probably best to begin by keeping records on a few pupils. As the teacher gains some experience and confidence he can undertake the recording of anecdotes on additional pupils. Even with a modest beginning, however, the teacher should take care to avoid the common mistake of keeping records on "problem cases" only. As we have already suggested, the shy, reticent child may be just as much in need of study and help as the one who is always causing trouble. In the beginning, when records are kept on only a few children, it would be well to select the children with a view to including some of the less obvious cases as well as some who demand attention.

Records of anecdotes should be made as soon as possible after the incident has been observed, but never so that pupils are aware that this is being done. Many teachers find it best to make a few notes at the first opportunity and then to make a complete record during free time at noon or after school. Anecdotes should always be recorded on the day of their occurrence if at all possible, for the longer the time lapse between the occurrence and the recording of it, the less distinct and accurate one's memory of the incident becomes. Anecdotes are probably best recorded on cards. Each anecdote may be recorded on a single small card, or, as is sometimes preferred, several anecdotes may be recorded on one large card. The latter system makes the interpretation of trends or developments a

---

[4] Arthur E. Traxler, *The Nature and Use of Anecdotal Records,* Educational Records Bureau Supplementary Bulletin D, Revised (New York: Educational Records Bureau, 1949).

little easier for some teachers. In any case, cards are the most convenient means of record-keeping since they are easy to file, sort, handle, and arrange.

To be most useful, anecdotal records on a pupil should be kept over an extended period of time. To obtain a reliable sample of a child's behavior and to make any useful assessment of changes that may occur, it is essential that an adequate number of anecdotes or observations be made. These principles apply here no less than in the case of systematic observations discussed in the preceding section. It is of little value to record an anecdote or two about an individual and then neglect him for a month. By observing him long enough to see how he functions in a variety of situations from day to day it is possible to gain much better insight into his personality and whatever difficulties he may have. The only exception to this principle might be in a school system where anecdotal records are a part of the regular cumulative records kept on all pupils. In such a system it would probably be impossible to record anecdotes frequently and regularly on every child; occasional anecdotes would have to suffice. Nevertheless, the principle still holds that, other factors being equal, the more frequent and regular the anecdotes recorded for a given individual, the more dependable the results will be.

If anecdotal records are to be valuable they must be used, and if they are to be used they must first be interpreted. To interpret the records it is of course necessary to study and summarize them. Several anecdotes on a single pupil must be studied and compared. They tell a story, reveal characteristic behavior, show the individual in his interaction with others in a natural setting. In these respects anecdotal records have certain advantages over other methods such as ratings or systematic observation. However, the task of summarizing and interpreting is not an easy one, and it invariably takes much thought and time. Ordinarily, summarizing should be done often enough to keep abreast of typical behavior and developments of the individual, and yet not so frequently that the process will become too much of a chore. Perhaps two or three times per year is often enough under ordinary circumstances. However, in individual cases it may be desirable to summarize and interpret more frequently.

Summarizing and interpreting are usually best done by the teacher who has written the anecdotal record, though this may also be done by a committee of two or three teachers, especially in difficult cases. The guidance teacher, counselor, or the school psychologist may be brought into the picture if needed.

The anecdotal record and summaries should be passed on to successive teachers as the pupil progresses so that each teacher will have the benefit of previous observations and can add to them. By this means a quite complete and valuable "behavior journal" of a pupil may be built up over a period of years.

It probably goes without saying that anecdotal records should always be related to all the other available information concerning a given child. Information on home conditions, health, ability, success in schoolwork, participation in extra class activities, etc., should be considered along with the anecdotal records, and the whole taken into account in any interpretations that are made.

One factor which often causes difficulty in maintaining a system of anecdotal records is the clerical work involved. Reference was made earlier to the time involved in recording even one anecdote per pupil per week. Where a schoolwide program involving hundreds of children is maintained, the total amount of time and labor can grow to large proportions. Nevertheless, some programs of this nature have been tried and found feasible. In one school system six teachers in Grades 4 to 7 recorded anecdotes for three months on every pupil.[5] During this time an extensive testing program was carried out with the same pupils. At the end of the three months the anecdotal records were compared with test results to determine how well the two types of data agreed. Although the findings are too extensive to cite in detail here, it was found that teachers could keep such records without too much difficulty and that they were able to judge the social relations of their pupils accurately by comparing anecdotal records with test results. Among the most significant conclusions were: (1) The success of anecdotal records depends in large measure on the outlook of the teachers. Those having a formal, academic viewpoint will probably find little use for anecdotal records, and those they write will be of little value. (2) Unless the child has opportunity for many varied experiences it is probable that little useful information about that child will be found in anecdotal records. (3) Classes enrolling from seventeen to twenty-eight pupils show no appreciable difference in the number of anecdotes recorded.

The results of this study are encouraging. They suggest that keeping anecdotal records, at least in the elementary grades, is not an inhuman task, that teachers who are interested in studying problems of pupil adjustment can do it, and that the results seem to bear significant relationships to other measures of personality and adjustment.

[5] Arthur E. Hamalainen, *An Appraisal of Anecdotal Records*, Contributions to Education, No. 891 (New York: Teachers College, Columbia University, 1943).

▶ LEARNING EXERCISES ◀

5. What are the purposes of anecdotal records?

6. What are the advantages and disadvantages of anecdotal records in comparison with other methods of personality appraisal?

7. Write out five or six imaginary anecdotes about a pupil who is shy and withdrawn. Do the same for one who is overly aggressive. Write your interpretations of each set.

SOCIOMETRIC METHODS

The last of the observational methods to be discussed are those known as *sociometric,* sometimes referred to as *interpersonal,* methods. The instrument usually associated with these is called a *sociogram.* It is a pictorial or graphic representation of relationships of a specified nature among members of a group, and is based on information gathered from members of the group. Thus it differs from other observational methods discussed in this chapter in that the data are collected about individuals from their peers, rather than from teachers or other observers.

The use of sociometric techniques probably dates from the now famous work of Jacob L. Moreno, first published in 1934.[6] Much study has been made of the sociogram during the last thirty years, and it has been widely used in schools. The sociogram has proved valuable when properly used, but it has definite limitations and some dangers in the hands of those not adequately prepared.

A sociogram is generally based upon the written answers to a question put to members of a group. For example, a fifth-grade group might be told that they were about to begin work on a certain project and that they were to be grouped for this into committees of three. They might then be asked to list the names of two pupils with whom they would like to work as a committee. Or, they might be asked to indicate a first choice and a second choice.

The question can also be put in a way that requires the individual to react to every member of the group in a form of rating, as in a social distance scale. In this form each member of a group places every other member in one of several categories as, "Like very much," or "Okay," or "Don't want to be with him any time." However, the data obtained by use of the latter type of scale do not lend themselves readily to organization into a sociogram as do those obtained by the first type of question.

[6] Jacob L. Moreno, *Who Shall Survive?* (Washington: Nervous and Mental Disease Publishing Company, 1934).

Once the data have been collected, the next step is to tabulate them in a form that is useful. Two forms are commonly employed, the table and the sociogram. Either or both may be used with a given set of data. An illustration will help to make this clear. Suppose a fifth-grade teacher has asked seventeen pupils to nominate their first and second choices of members of the class to work with on a certain project. The responses of the pupils might be tabulated as shown below:

Chooser	First Choice	Second Choice
Ken	Guy	Fran
Jack	Kevin	Len
Helen	Fran	Kathy
Ted	Mike	Kevin
Fred	Ken	Karl
Fran	Jane	Milly
Jean	Kathy	Kevin
Sally	Milly	Jane
Jessie	Helen	Fran
Karl	Fran	Ken
Mike	Jean	Kevin
Len	Fran	Ken
Guy	Karl	Ken
Milly	Fran	Jane
Kathy	Helen	Jean
Jane	Sally	Fran
Kevin	Ted	Jean

These choices may be organized into a chart somewhat like the one shown in Figure 15. Here each pupil's first choice is indicated by a *1* under the name of the pupil chosen, and the second choice by a *2*.

The number of times each pupil is chosen as a first choice and as a second choice is shown at the bottom. Those not chosen at all have no numbers in the columns under their names. Mutual choices are indicated by an asterisk. For example, Guy is Ken's first choice, and Ken is Guy's second choice.

A better way of showing the relationships in this group is by the sociogram shown in Figure 16, page 376.

There are several methods of constructing such a chart, but to discuss these in detail is beyond the scope of this book. One of the easiest and most practical methods is described in a publication dealing explicitly with this matter,[7] and any teacher or counselor can learn the method with a little study and practice.

[7] Horace Mann–Lincoln Institute of School Experimentation, *How to Construct a Sociogram* (New York: Teachers College, Columbia University, 1947).

FIGURE 15 • Pupils' Choices of Class Members to Work on Project

	Ken	Jack	Helen	Ted	Fred	Fran	Jean	Sally	Jessie	Karl	Mike	Len	Guy	Milly	Kathy	Jane	Kevin
Ken						2							1*				
Jack											2						1
Helen						1									2*		
Ted												1					2*
Fred	1					2											
Fran														2*	1*		
Jean														1*			2*
Sally														1	2*		
Jessie		1				2											
Karl	2					1											
Mike							1										2
Len	2					1											
Guy	2*							1									
Milly						1*									2		
Kathy		1*					2*										
Jane						2*			1*								
Kevin				1*		2*											
First choice	1	2	1			4	1	1		1	1		1	1	1	1	1
Second choice	3					3	2			1		1		1	1	2	3

A conventional terminology has come to be used in interpreting a sociogram, which may be illustrated by reference to Figure 16. A "star" is an individual who is chosen by many. Fran is an example; so are Kevin and Ken. A "chain" is a sequence of choices in a line, none of whom is chosen by many; an example here is the Jessie–Helen–Kathy–Jean–Mike–Ted alignment. An isolate is one not chosen; examples are Jack, Jessie and Fred. The term "island" refers to a small, more or less self-contained, group or clique; an example is Milly, Sally, Fran, and Jane; another is Ken, Karl, Guy, and Fred. Such cliques are often the cause of concern to the teacher and may have an undesirable effect on the relations of the group as a whole.

So far, we have dealt with methods of collecting sociometric data and ways of tabulating and summarizing them. Perhaps a more important question concerns the purposes for which the results may be used. A further question concerns the advantages and disadvantages of a sociogram.

It may be said that a sociogram is probably the best instrument yet devised to reveal the social structure of a group. It shows interrelationships

FIGURE 16 • Sociogram Showing First and Second
Choices of Seventeen Fifth-Grade Pupils

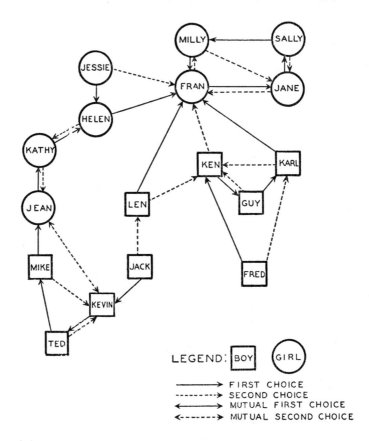

LEGEND:

──────────▶	FIRST CHOICE
------------▶	SECOND CHOICE
◀─────────▶	MUTUAL FIRST CHOICE
◀------------▶	MUTUAL SECOND CHOICE

among individuals and relationships of each individual to the entire group.
It provides a teacher or group leader with information that will help him
to understand the behavior of the group and to function more effectively
in working with that group. There are many relationships and sub-groups
within any class or group which are not apparent on the surface.

It is important that appropriate action be taken soon after the sociogram has been completed and examined.[8] If the teacher has asked pupils
to tell with whom they would like to work, groupings should be formed
on the basis of what the children have requested, as far as that is possible.
The effect on pupils of carrying through is very wholesome. It goes without saying that not to do so has the opposite effect, and that pupils will

[8] Helen H. Jennings, *Sociometry in Group Relations* (Washington: American
Council on Education, 1948).

lose interest in sociograms if they come to believe that nothing happens as a result of their expressions of preference.

The booklet mentioned earlier[9] suggests the following uses of a sociogram:

1. To identify mutual choices, stars, isolates, chains, islands, and triangles or circles.

2. Studying race or nationality in relation to group structure. In this case racial groups may be coded by use of different shaped figures [as was done for sex in Figure 16].

3. Studying age or maturity in relation to group structure.

4. Studying the relation of total group structure to out-of-school groupings, as scouts, sororities, etc.

5. Studying the effect of certain experiences. In this case there should be a sociogram "before and after." Thus it may be used to study the effect of various methods of choosing committees on the structure of the group.

In the same publication some limitations of sociograms are mentioned. First, it is pointed out that sociograms are only as valid as the rapport between teacher and pupils will permit. Pupils must sign responses if the results are to be useful, and if there is resistance to doing this or to answering the questions the responses are not likely to be worth much.

Second, it is pointed out that since group structure, especially among younger children, is quite fluid, the reliability of a single sociogram may not be very high.

Third, the way in which the data are gathered may force responses which are misleading. For example, the sociogram does not reveal differences between strong and weak feelings, or even hostility. The point is made that to require three choices may force the nomination of someone for whom there is really no feeling of attraction and for whom there is perhaps even a feeling of dislike.

Fourth, it is important to remember that a sociogram merely reveals conditions; it does not give answers or solutions. A teacher may decide that acceptance of an isolate by other members of a group must be brought about by authority, if necessary. Measures taken to accomplish this, even though subtle, may result in stronger feelings of rejection instead of greater acceptance. The solution or amelioration of conditions revealed by a sociogram depends upon the use of other techniques such as anecdotal records, interviews with individual children, and further careful study of the total situation. Perhaps the status of sociograms is best summed up by this quotation from the same bulletin:[10]

[9] Horace Mann–Lincoln Institute of School Experimentation, *op. cit.*
[10] *Ibid.,* p. 12.

Once a sociogram has been plotted, it is a beginning, not an end. It raises questions rather than answers them. Perhaps its greatest value is that it directs the attention to certain aspects of group structure which will lead to further observation of individual and group behavior. To date, we have few, if any, generalizations which can be applied in the interpretation of sociograms, although we are beginning to find certain tentative hypotheses. We are in great need of carefully reported anecdotes of group behavior recorded by teachers who are sensitive to problems of group behavior. If the making of sociograms encourages such observation and recording, they shall have fulfilled an important function.

▶ **LEARNING EXERCISES** ◀

8. Using the following data, construct a sociogram:

Chooser	First Choice	Second Choice
Jerry	Jim	Harry
Bill	Bob	Sam
Carl	Jack	Jerry
Jim	Harry	Sam
Jack	Bob	Sam
Ed	Sam	Harry
Sam	Bill	David
Harry	Jim	Ed
David	Bill	Sam
Frank	Bill	Jack
Bob	Bill	David
Tom	Frank	Bob

Suggestions: Start with Sam and Bill and place around them those pupils who chose them, and then work in the rest. Try to construct a graph which has straight, right-angle lines, and no lines crossing each other. Use a solid line for first choices and a broken line for second choices.

9. Can you identify any stars, isolates, chains, or cliques in your chart?

10. If you were dividing this group into four subgroups or committees of three each, how would you proceed? Give reasons for your groupings.

ANNOTATED BIBLIOGRAPHY

1. Freeman, Frank S. *Theory and Practice of Psychological Testing,* Third Edition. New York: Holt, Rinehart & Winston, Inc., 1962. Chapters 21 and 22. Personality rating scales are described and illustrated in Chapter 21, with an evaluation at the end of the chapter. Chapter 22 discusses situational tests including sociograms and other sociometric methods.

2. Krugman, Judith I., and Wrightstone, J. Wayne. *A Guide to the Use of Anecdotal Records.* Educational Research Bulletin, No. 11. New York: Board of Education, 1949. 33 pp. A very helpful presentation of the values and basic principles of anecdotal records. Tells how to use such records, from the selection of children to be observed to the interpretaton and application of the results. Includes sample records and an annotated bibliography.

3. Remmers, H. H., and Gage, N. L. *Educational Measurement and Evaluation,* Revised. New York: Harper & Row, Publishers, 1955. Chapter 12 includes brief, practical discussions of sociograms, anecdotal records, and rating methods.

4. Thomas, R. Murray. *Judging Student Progress,* Second Edition. New York: David McKay Co., Inc., 1960. Chapters 8, 9, and 11. Anecdotal records and observation are briefly discussed in Chapter 8, and sociograms are fully treated in Chapter 9. In Chapter 11 check lists and rating scales are described and illustrated, and their uses and limitations are presented in a practical way. The entire presentation is directed primarily at the elementary teacher.

5. Thorndike, Robert L., and Hagen, Elizabeth. *Measurement and Evaluation in Psychology and Education,* Second Edition. New York: John Wiley & Sons, Inc., 1961. Chapters 13 and 14. Chapter 13 is devoted largely to a discussion of rating techniques but includes a brief treatment of sociograms. Chapter 14 includes discussions of behavioral or situational tests, observation, and anecdotal records.

6. Traxler, Arthur E. *The Nature and Use of Anecdotal Records.* Educational Records Bureau Supplementary Bulletin D, Revised. New York: Educational Records Bureau, 1949. 41 pp. A summary of research and recommendations by students of the method of anecdotal records. Brings together what was generally accepted as being well-established practice up to 1949.

7. Wrightstone, J. Wayne; Justman, Joseph; and Robbins, Irving. *Evaluation in Modern Education.* New York: American Book Company, 1956. Chapters 7, 9, and 11. Good, practical treatment of observation and anecdotal records in Chapter 7; check lists and rating scales are briefly discussed in Chapter 9; sociometric methods are presented in Chapter 11, with major attention to the sociogram. The discussion throughout emphasizes practical applications in the classroom and school.

14

The Measurement Program

WHAT IS A MEASUREMENT PROGRAM?

Reference has already been made in Chapter 2 to large-scale or national testing programs. These are quite generally referred to as "external testing programs" because they are directed and administered by agencies outside the local school authorities. Among the most prominent of such programs are those of the College Entrance Examination Board, the National Merit Scholarship Qualifying Examinations, the American College Testing Program, and the state-wide testing programs. The criticisms of testing, some of which were cited in Chapter 2, have been directed mainly, though not exclusively, at such programs. Enough has been said in that chapter concerning this matter for the purposes of this book.

The type of measurement or testing program with which we are concerned in this chapter is the locally initiated and directed, systematic use of tests to meet local needs, solve local problems and contribute to the attainment of local educational goals. If such a program serves wider purposes, so much the better, but its focus is basically on meeting the needs of a particular school or school system.

Without the support and cooperation of teachers and counselors, the results of a measurement program can scarcely be utilized to the fullest extent. When some action is to be taken as a result of the program, whether it is grouping, counseling, remedial work, or some other, teachers and counselors may defeat the very purposes for which the testing was done by not cooperating in the program. If the program has been "dictated" by authorities rather than carried out with their advice and cooperation, it is possible that those involved will not respond wholeheartedly. Unfortunately, administrators, though fully aware of this fact, do not always take the trouble and time to secure the support of their staffs. The result is that the programs sometimes fall far short of attaining their maximum usefulness, or fail entirely.

On the other hand, it must be recognized that it is not always easy to stimulate the active cooperation and interest of teachers in the systematic use of measuring instruments. Some teachers resent the interruption it may cause in their usual routine, some do not appreciate the extra demands on their time and energy, and a few are prejudiced against "outside" tests of any kind. They do not like the idea of having their pupils examined by any means other than those which they themselves have devised. Where such attitudes exist, they must be changed before a measurement program can be carried on with any reasonable assurance of cooperation and success. It may take some time to accomplish this, yet there are a number of ways of creating more favorable attitudes: selected teachers can be sent to summer school to take courses in measurement, professional libraries can be built up, and teachers can be urged to participate in workshops and institutes dealing with problems of measurement and evaluation. In-service training programs may also focus attention on measurement as a means of facilitating curriculum revision and improving instruction.

A measurement program of any consequence is always undertaken with the cooperation and responsibility of more than one person. The program may involve only classroom teachers and their supervisors or principals, or the work may be planned and carried out with the cooperation of the entire staff of a school or school system. In the latter case it is customary to entrust most of the actual direction to one qualified person or to a representative committee. As we have said, it is almost axiomatic that unless a measurement program has the active cooperation and support of all concerned it cannot achieve its maximum usefulness. When a measurement program is carried out to meet needs or to solve the problems which the teachers themselves regard as important, and when those teachers participate actively in planning and carrying out the program, it will have a good chance of succeeding. It is also helpful to have parents understand the reasons for measurement so that they too will support the program. If parents can see that the results of measurement help to bring about better learning and adjustment on the part of their children, their confidence in the usefulness of measurement and their faith in the school will be increased.

PLANNING A MEASUREMENT PROGRAM

Purposes

A measurement program will be successful to the extent that it accomplishes the purposes for which it is designed and carried out. Therefore, it must be planned in accordance with those purposes. This is a matter for cooperative endeavor by all concerned. Although many teachers are not well acquainted with standardized tests and techniques of measurement and appraisal, most will know what the educational problems are, and they will know of many situations in which measurement may be helpful. School psychologists, counselors, directors of research, and other personnel with more specialized training can usually supply the leadership, the technical knowledge, and the skills needed for setting up a measurement program.

Whereas in a smaller school or community the planning of a measurement program may be undertaken by the entire staff, such a procedure will generally be too cumbersome or unwieldly in a larger system. In the latter case it is generally better to have a committee made up of representatives of various groups, grade levels, schools, or districts to assume responsibility for planning and carrying out the program. This is not to say that the entire staff loses contact with the program. On the contrary, general teachers' meetings from time to time may be devoted to over-all planning, progress reports, discussions, and implementation of results. Furthermore, occasional reports to the community may be used as a means of improving relations between the schools and the parents.

Listed below are some of the major purposes for which a measurement program may be carried on. A more extensive discussion of each of these purposes, together with practical suggestions on using test results, will be found in the next chapter.

PURPOSES OF MEASUREMENT PROGRAMS

1. Placement and promotion
2. Homogeneous grouping
3. Diagnosis and remedial work
4. Counseling and guidance
5. Marking

6. Motivation
7. Identification and study of exceptional children
8. Interpreting schools to the community
9. Improvement of school staff
10. Educational research

The above list is based on various studies and reports of the use of measurement in schools, and, while not exhaustive, it probably includes most of the common purposes for which educational measurement is used.

Time of Year for Testing

When the purposes of the measurement program have been decided upon, several other considerations immediately come to the fore. One of these is the time of year for giving the tests. Often this matter resolves itself into a choice between giving the tests at the beginning of the school year or near the end. The decision on timing will usually depend largely upon the purposes for which the tests are intended. For example, diagnostic testing and testing for purposes of grouping or grade placement will most profitably come early in the school year, while testing for purposes of promotion, educational counseling, marking, and comparison of achievement with norms will usually occur near the end of the term or year. On the other hand, some of the purposes for which measurement programs are carried on are unrelated to the time of year. (See above list.)

Frequency and Grade Levels of Testing

Questions which must be decided upon early are the frequency of the testing and the grade levels at which particular tests are to be given. In part, these matters are determined by the purposes for which the testing is intended. For example, if tests are to be given for counseling purposes there will generally be less emphasis on and less need for testing below the secondary level. On the other hand, diagnostic testing in arithmetic or reading will almost certainly be started in the earlier grades of the elementary school.

The frequency of testing also depends on the purposes, but it is further affected by such considerations as the kinds of measuring instruments being used and the amount of money and time available for the work required. Many a measurement program, undertaken with enthusiasm and high hopes, has failed because those responsible greatly underestimated the expense, the time, and the effort necessary to carry it through. The initial cost of standardized tests is frequently the smallest item of expense;

getting the tests properly administered, scored, and interpreted requires much time and effort. It is far better to undertake a modest program and complete the work required to put the results to effective use than to try to carry on a more extensive and ambitious program, only to have it bog down.

A Minimum School- or Community-Wide Measurement Program

No program can be prescribed which will fit every situation. Nevertheless, some suggestions will be made to help the prospective teacher, counselor, or administrator set up a kind of priority list for the planning of a testing program.

If only one type of test is to be given, at least as a beginning, the first choice should almost certainly be a group intelligence test. If no standardized tests have been used before, it is desirable to give a group intelligence test to every pupil. Since the I.Q. based upon one group test is not completely reliable, any cases which raise serious questions or present discrepancies with other known facts about an individual should be tested as soon as possible with *another form of the same test*. This point is important because two forms of the same test will give results which are directly comparable, whereas I.Q.'s obtained through the use of two different tests must be equated by standard scores or similar derived scores before they can be directly compared.

The recommendation of a test of intelligence as the essential minimum is based on several considerations. In the first place, the I.Q. of a pupil cannot be accurately determined without such a test. In the second place, for educational purposes this information about a pupil is probably the most useful and important that we can learn. The I.Q. gives more insight into his work, achievement, and general mental ability than any other single fact about him can provide.

If testing is to be done at regular intervals after the first year in which a measurement program is started, it would be advisable to give intelligence tests in the second grade and again in the fourth grade; they should be given again in the sixth grade if there is a junior high school, or in the eighth grade if the system is organized on the 8–4 plan; and again in the tenth grade. The results of these measurements should always be made a part of the cumulative record which accompanies the pupil as he progresses through the elementary and secondary grades.

If more than one type of test can be given, and the results put to use, a reading readiness test should be administered at the end of the kindergarten year or early in the first grade, an achievement battery in the third or fourth, and sixth or seventh grades, and an interest test or inventory in the ninth and twelfth grades. These tests will supplement the results of the intelligence tests at critical points in the pupil's school career in ways which are most useful and appropriate at those points.

The use of other types of tests, such as diagnostic, personality, aptitude, reading, and those in specific school subjects should be undertaken where necessary, with a view to the available resources of the school and to the other factors peculiar to each situation. In every case, the purposes of the measurement program should be the dominating factor in determining its nature and extent.

A tabulation of a recommended minimum school- or community-wide annual testing program is given here:

Grade Level	Type of Test
K or 1	Readiness
2	Intelligence
3 or 4	Intelligence
3 or 4	Achievement Battery (including reading)
6 or 8[1]	Intelligence
6 or 7	Achievement Battery (including reading)
9	Interests
10	Intelligence
12	Interests

This program amounts to nine separate tests given annually at various levels throughout the usual grades of the elementary and high schools. An achievement battery may also be given in the eleventh grade if time and resources permit, although separate subject-matter tests may be preferred for various reasons. Where two tests are recommended for use in either of two grades, it probably would be best, other things being equal, to distribute the burden by giving one test in each grade instead of giving both tests at the same grade level. This is particularly desirable where the scoring is done by teachers, and it also requires less of the pupils' time for such testing in any given grade.

Such a program should not be undertaken lightly. It will require much time and work, although the results should be worth the effort many times over. The cost may safely be reckoned on an average of twenty-five cents

---

[1] Depending on whether 6 or 8 is the last grade in the elementary school.

per pupil annually, provided that scoring the tests and tabulating and interpreting the results will not necessitate additional expenditures, and provided that most test blanks can be used over and over again with separate answer sheets.

Larger school systems often carry on testing programs far more extensive than the one outlined. With a central staff organized for such work, and ample financial support, a great deal more can be done. However, the above plan will provide a good foundation, and it represents the type of program that most schools with limited funds for measurement can carry.

It will take three or four years under this plan for every pupil to be reached unless a group intelligence test is given to every pupil the first year. If a school-wide test is given the first year of the program, there will be information available on every pupil as soon as the tests can be given and scored, and this will be a real advantage to teachers. The regular program may be launched the second year. Even if the school-wide intelligence test is not given the first year, there will still be test results available at four important levels of the child's progress through the school. This will be a useful beginning and will help to introduce the program gradually so that those responsible will more easily be able to absorb the load.

SELECTING AND OBTAINING THE TESTS

Selecting the Tests

Chapter 4 contains a discussion of the important criteria for judging the quality of tests. Here we need only stress the point that in planning a measurement program one should use the best available instruments for it. The criteria of *validity, reliability, objectivity, ease of administration, scoring,* and *interpretation,* availability of *equivalent forms, adequate norms,* and *economy* provide a sound basis for appraising any measuring instrument, although, as has been mentioned, all of these criteria do not necessarily apply to every type of instrument.

In addition to the criteria mentioned above, a number of less tangible considerations usually influence the selection of instruments. In the case of standardized tests, for example, the deciding factor may be simply a general impression of the whole test. If those responsible for the selection like an instrument, if it seems to measure objectives which are important, and if they think it is suitable for their situation, that test or instrument will often be chosen in preference to one that meets the technical criteria more adequately. Probably the best that can be hoped for is an objective choice based on careful consideration of *all available information* about the test and the situation in which it is to be used.

In a measurement program the task of selecting tests may be delegated to a committee. Sometimes the tests are selected by a member of the supervisory or administrative staff and occasionally by the director of research or by the counseling staff. However, if the program is to be of the type outlined above for all-around basic purposes, the tests should be selected by a committee on which teaching, counseling, research, supervisory, and administrative personnel all have representation.

This committee should have full responsibility and authority to obtain, examine, select, and purchase the tests in the quantities needed. It should also have the authority and the initiative to encourage local groups to develop measuring devices for local needs where commercially available instruments are not adequate. The committee should feel free to consult with experts and with any school personnel in making its choices, yet its decisions should be final and should be accepted as such by all concerned. That is, as long as all elements of the school staff have representation on the committee, and as long as the committee makes a thorough study of available instruments in relation to the purposes of the program, its choices should not be subject to veto by administrative authorities or other groups except in the most extraordinary circumstances. If the committee responsible for the over-all program is a large one, smaller sub-committees may be appointed to look after various phases of the program. The selection of tests might well be done by such a sub-committee.

Obtaining the Tests

It is common practice for test publishers to put up tests in packages of twenty-five or thirty-five. Each package contains the specified number of copies of the test, a manual of directions, a scoring key, a class record sheet, and any other materials necessary for proper use of the tests, except answer sheets, which are nearly always sold separately. Test publishers, as a rule, will not break packages of tests; in ordering, therefore, it is advisable to request a number which can be shipped in unbroken packages. For example, if tests are needed for 170 pupils, one would ordinarily order 175 (seven packages of twenty-five each or five packages of thirty-five each). The same is true of answer sheets. Prices are usually quoted for quantities of twenty-five or more.

Of course, the above applies only to paper-and-pencil tests. If the program involves the use of other types of materials such as sets of pictures, toys, nuts and bolts, phonograph records, etc., such equipment will usually have to be bought in single complete sets. Such material is not consumable, and the same instruments therefore may be used repeatedly.

Handling the Tests Prior to Administration

The committee or person responsible should take charge of all measurement materials when they are received and keep them in a safe place until they are to be used. The assumption in the use of a standardized test is that everyone who takes it has an equal chance and that no one has an unfair advantage. Although classroom teachers are usually most scrupulous in such matters, their enthusiasm and eagerness to see pupils do well will sometimes lead them to give assistance which they should not give.

The story is told about a high school principal and the teacher of mathematics who had agreed that a certain test should be given in the plane geometry classes. The tests were ordered, received, and turned over to the teacher for safe-keeping until the time set for the testing. A few days before the tests were to be given, the principal dropped into the room to speak to the mathematics teacher, and he was surprised to find several problems from the test copied on the board and the teacher discussing these problems with his pupils. After the class had been dismissed, the principal asked the teacher to explain. The teacher replied, "I was so anxious to see what they would do with the problems that I couldn't wait. I just had to try them out on a few." While this teacher's enthusiasm and interest were highly commendable, it is clear that his understanding of the purposes and use of standardized tests left much to be desired.

Answer Sheets

The use of printed answer media has developed greatly in recent years, as have techniques and services for scoring them. Several different types of answer sheets and answer cards are commercially available, and the organizations that produce them usually also offer a scoring service. The most advanced of these, using electronic equipment, not only score the answer sheets but also provide distributions of scores and part scores, intercorrelations between scores, percentile and standard score equivalents, and almost any type of analysis desired. For larger systems or large-scale testing programs such services are both efficient and economical. A sample of the electronically scored answer sheet is shown in Figure 17.

Some type of separate answer sheet is now available with nearly all standardized tests for Grade 4 and higher. For testing in grades below this level it is still customary to have answers written or printed by the children in the test booklets. Research has shown that separate answer media may be safely used beginning at about the fourth- or fifth-grade level. Although marking answers in test booklets adds to the expense of

FIGURE 17 • Facsimile of a Portion of an Electronically Scored Answer Sheet

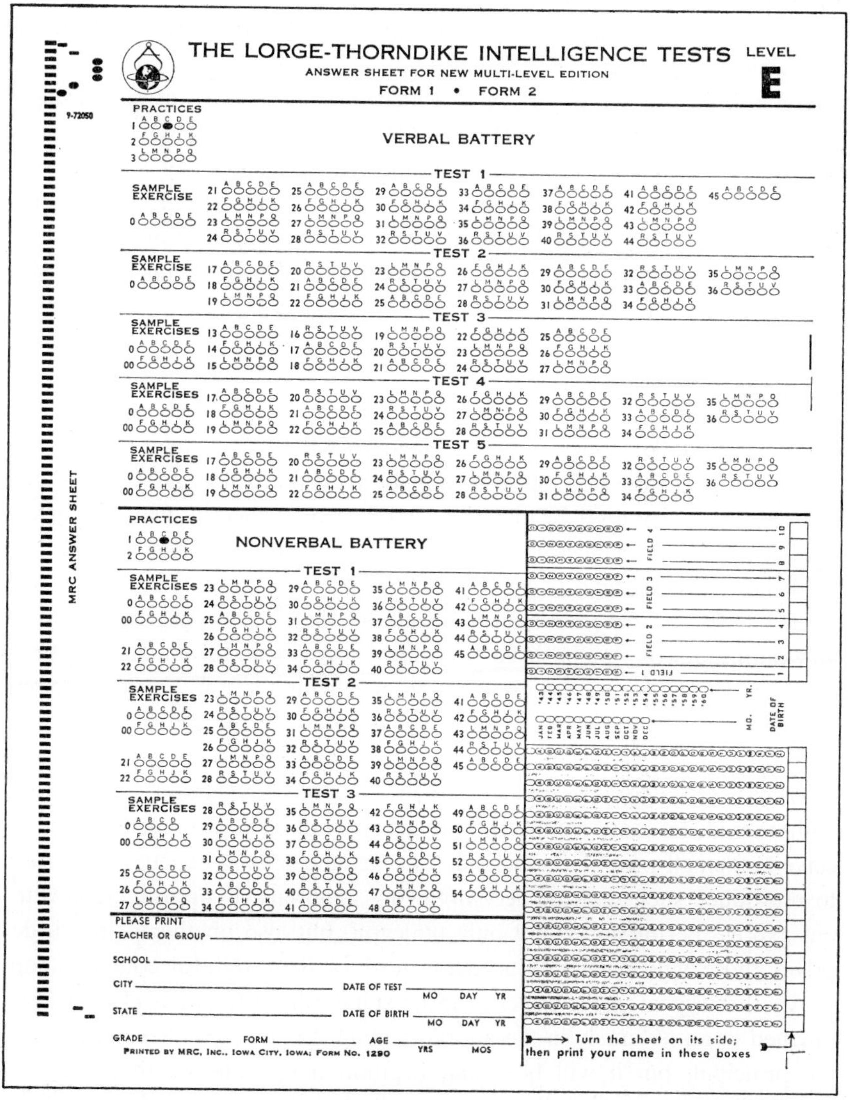

MRC Answer Sheet for the *Lorge-Thorndike Intelligence Tests,* Multi-Level Edition, Level E., by Irving Lorge and Robert L. Thorndike (Boston: Houghton Mifflin Company, 1964). All rights reserved. Reproduced by permission.

testing, since the booklets cannot be used again, this practice has certain advantages. First, of course, is the removal of the possibility of confusion on the part of the children taking the test if a separate answer sheet is used. Probably of equal importance is the value to the teacher, who scores the papers, of seeing which items each child answers correctly or misses. Teachers often feel that this type of information is the most valuable result achieved by testing.

A facsimile of one of the most widely used types of answer sheets is shown in Figure 18, page 391. This form, known as IBM 805, though designed primarily for use with multiple-choice items, may also be used with true-false items by using only the first two spaces — 1 for true and 2 for false. It may also be used for the 3 x 5 type of matching item described in Chapter 6. It may be scored by hand with a punched overlay stencil or by machine.

Ethics

A word on the ethics of using standardized tests may be appropriate at this point. In the first place, it must be recognized that published standardized tests are copyright material. No part of such tests may be copied, duplicated, or reproduced in *any form* without written permission from the holder of the copyright. To do so is to violate copyright law. Aside from the legal aspects, there is a moral obligation which is equally great. Authors and publishers of standardized tests must expend large amounts of time, professional competence, and money in producing these tests. A single test may have involved the work of several persons for three to five years, as well as the cooperation of dozens of other people and the expenditure of thousands of dollars. Except for the professional recognition accorded the authors and, to some extent, the publishers, the only recompense they receive is a small profit from the sale of tests and answer sheets. Therefore, to reproduce such tests or accompanying materials or parts thereof without express permission is not only unlawful, but also unethical since it deprives those who have produced the tests of their rightful compensation.

Another aspect of the ethics of using standardized tests has already been touched upon obliquely in the anecdote about the mathematics teacher and the principal, but it will bear amplification here. The continued use of standardized tests of intelligence and achievement requires that their nature and content be kept confidential until the tests are administered. Obviously, if persons who are to be tested have prior knowledge of the contents of a test, standardized or otherwise, the results are invalidated. Such prior knowledge is even more undesirable if some individuals have it but

FIGURE 18 • Portion of the IBM 805 Answer Sheet

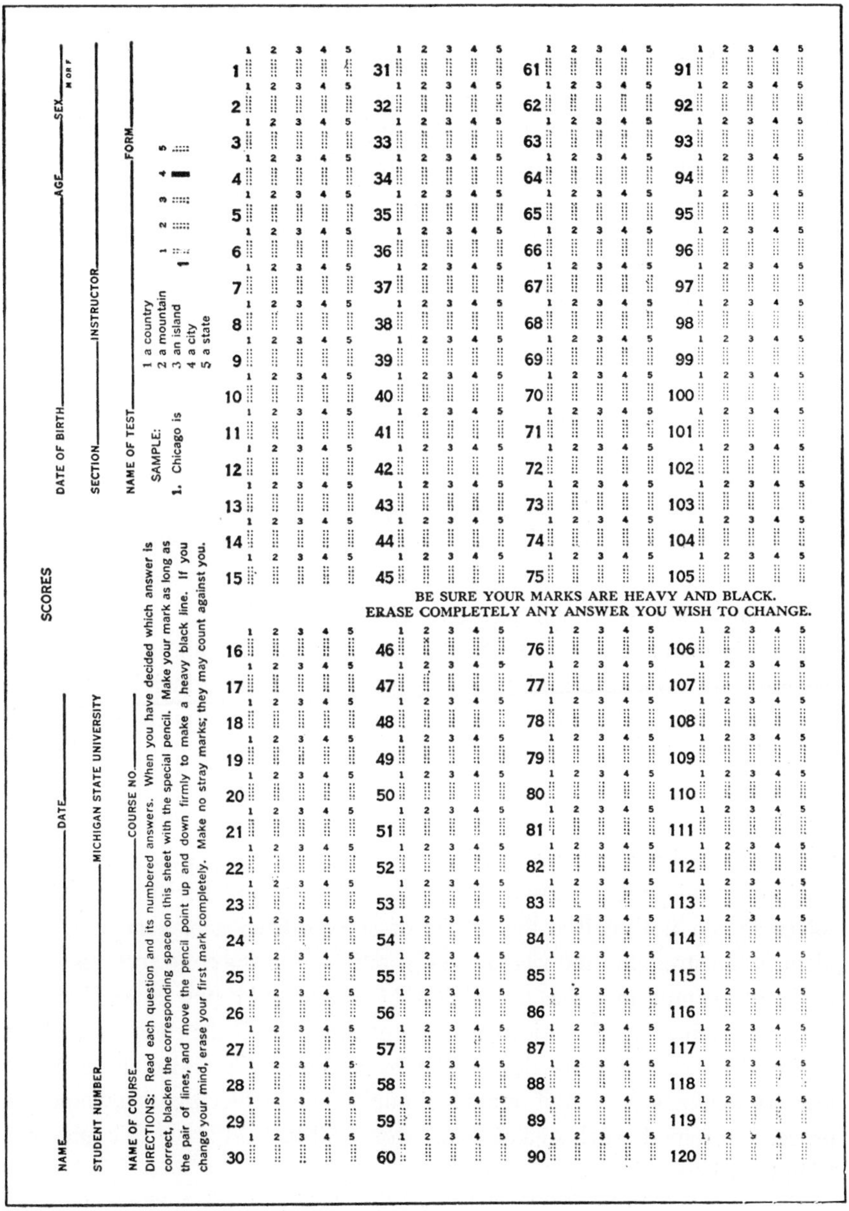

not all. In either case, the results are meaningless and no comparison with norms is possible. The continued use of standardized tests with meaningful, dependable results requires that the content must not be passed along from one person who has seen the test to another who has not. Consequently, it is axiomatic that tests should be safe-guarded by their users as confidential material if their use *as tests* is to be continued.

The only possible exception to this principle is the standardized diagnostic test. With this type of instrument it may be permissible under certain circumstances to go over the test with the individual pupil so that he can see his errors, but even here it is usually possible to accomplish the same objective in other ways. The manual of directions for such tests contains specific instructions regarding how the results of a diagnostic test may be used most effectively in remedial work. If the user adheres to these directions and suggestions he will usually be successful *and* ethical.

If pupils are permitted to go over their diagnostic test papers for the purposes mentioned above, the teacher should always make sure beforehand that two or more equivalent forms of the test are available. Then, if retesting is to be done, a different form can be used, thus minimizing the effect of familiarity with specific details of the form first used. What we have said about achievement tests applies with even greater force to tests of intelligence and personality, and to evaluative devices such as ratings, sociograms, and anecdotal records. The results of these as well as the original instruments are to be held in strict confidence and should be accessible only to authorized school personnel. These principles of usage may seem strict, especially to the inexperienced student and user of standardized tests, but they are not unduly so. Psychologists and educators involved in the production and proper use of measuring instruments are genuinely concerned with this problem and have published a code of ethics which includes recommendations for the proper use of psychological tests.[2]

Nothing said above should be interpreted to mean that teachers themselves should not analyze the results of standardized achievement tests to identify the strengths and weaknesses of pupils. On the contrary, this is one of the most important uses to which test results can be put. A teacher may thus determine which objectives or outcomes of instruction have been achieved to a satisfactory degree and by which pupils. Also, he can also identify weaknesses both of individual pupils and of the class as a whole and proceed to remedy such weaknesses. More will be said about this matter in Chapter 15.

[2] American Psychological Association Committee, *Ethical Standards for Psychologists* (Washington: American Psychological Association, 1953), pp. 143–55.

▶ **LEARNING EXERCISES** ◀

1. Assume that you have been given the responsibility for planning a testing program for an elementary school enrolling three hundred pupils, K — Grade 8. List your major concerns in this assignment and explain briefly how you would proceed with each.

2. As a counselor you are responsible for planning and directing a testing program in Grades 9–12. How would you determine (a) what tests to use, (b) the grade in which each is to be given, and (c) how the results would be put to use?

SCHEDULING THE TESTS

Day of Week and Time of Day for Testing

Considerations relating to the time of year for testing have already been mentioned. It is also necessary to decide when each test is to be given, particularly if a school-wide or community-wide program is planned. This involves a decision on the day of the week and the time of day for testing. It is usually best to have the tests administered to all pupils at the same time, for such a plan causes less disruption of the school program and has the added advantage that pupils' discussions of the tests will not work to the benefit of some and to the disadvantage of others. It also reduces or eliminates entirely the period of worry and dread which some children inevitably suffer if they know in advance that they are to take some tests.

With regard to the matter of pupil concern about forthcoming tests, it has been the writer's experience that it is best to give standardized tests without any previous announcement to pupils. This eliminates all fear in advance of the testing, it eliminates hasty "cramming," and pressures on the teacher for hints on the nature of the tests. Nothing is gained by announcing such tests in advance, and much suffering and annoyance may result.

It is probably best to give the tests in the morning because pupils are likely to feel more alert then than later in the day. There is a psychological advantage in this, if not an actual, measurable difference in performance. It is also desirable, generally speaking, to give tests near the middle of the week. Monday is often "blue Monday," and Fridays are likely to be crowded with activities of more compelling interest. While none of these factors may have a demonstrable effect on test performance, they may all have some effect on the state of mind of pupils, their attitudes towards the program, and their concentration. A favorable attitude towards the testing is advantageous to the teacher and to the pupil. Ideally, the pupil should feel that he has been able to do his best on the test.

Since absentees create additional problems, it is well to give the tests when absences are likely to be at a minimum. If the tests require more than one sitting, it may be necessary to spread the testing over a period of several days. Some achievement batteries require several hours of testing time, which will require several sittings, especially for younger pupils. If there are large numbers to be tested it is probably best to arrange a schedule of sessions to which every class or group will adhere. If a small number of pupils are involved — perhaps one or two classes — the schedule can be arranged to suit the convenience of those concerned.

Ordinarily, it is desirable to plan a schedule for the administration of tests in a testing program. This increases the efficiency of the program and helps to avoid the intrusion of personal preferences of the individual teachers. When the time for giving tests is left to the choice of the individual teacher, it is advantageous to require that the testing be completed within a specified number of days. Otherwise, there may be delays and postponements which will hold up the entire program.

Place of Testing

The choice of the place for testing will depend on circumstances. With younger pupils it is generally best to administer the tests to the pupils in their usual surroundings if they provide the proper conditions for testing. It is also better, if possible, to test very young pupils in small groups of fifteen or less. With older pupils location is probably not so important. Testing pupils in their own home-rooms eliminates the problem of working out a room-assignment schedule and considerably simplifies this aspect of the work. On the other hand, if large numbers are to be tested, it is more efficient to test as many pupils at one time as facilities will permit. It is obviously more efficient to test two hundred pupils at once than to test five groups of forty separately. The number that can be tested properly at one time is limited by the facilities available and by the organizational ability of those in charge. With the necessary facilities and assistance, one thousand pupils can be tested just as easily as one hundred or fewer.

The place of testing should provide conditions and facilities necessary to the correct and most satisfactory administration of the test. In part, the choice of location will depend upon the factors of accessibility and availability.

ADMINISTERING THE TESTS

It is essential that standardized tests be given exactly according to directions, which may be long and complicated. No one should expect to be able to pick up a manual just before the test is to begin, and, without previous experience and study, step into the job with complete assurance. Time and study are a necessary part of the preparation for giving a standardized test, even for the experienced examiner. The inexperienced examiner may profitably have a more experienced person help him review instructions and procedure beforehand.

If a considerable amount of testing is to be done, the best plan may be to have all of the administration handled by only a few people. They can be given fairly intensive training by the person best fitted to do it — the school psychologist, research director, counselor, or other qualified person. This small group of specially trained teachers can then administer all the tests. Such a plan is almost sure to increase accuracy, uniformity, and efficiency.

With very young pupils it is sometimes preferable to have the testing done by their own teacher, for children frequently will be more at ease and will respond better with someone they know and like than with a stranger. However, when teachers administer tests to their own pupils it is important that the testing be done objectively and that the instructions for administering the tests be adhered to.

Qualities of a Good Examiner

Most teachers and counselors can learn to administer standardized tests successfully, yet a few seem constitutionally unfitted for the task. A list of qualities which the successful administrator of standardized group tests should possess would almost certainly include the following:

1. *Ability to understand and follow directions.* The person who is to give a standardized test must have the ability to follow directions exactly. Sometimes test directions require the performance of complicated activities by the pupil and accurate timing by the examiner. Not every person likes to undertake involved procedures of this nature, and not everyone is qualified to perform these tasks and supply students with the needed guidance and assistance. The examiner must be willing to read and study the directions until he understands them thoroughly. He should work through the entire test himself before he attempts to administer it so that he will be thoroughly familiar with every part of it.

Once in a discussion among teachers about the uses of tests in the class-room, one member of the group, a middle-aged teacher, raised a problem: she stated that on a certain English test which she had used for a number of years her pupils invariably made scores well above the norms for the grade. This puzzled her, since the pupils were not otherwise unusual or exceptional, and she was unable to account for their very high attainment on this test. No one in the group was able to explain it, and the matter was dropped for the time being. The conference proceeded to other matters, but sometime later the same teacher brought up the problem again. This time, however, she happened to mention that when she administered the English test she ignored the time limits set in the directions and permitted her pupils to work on the test as long as they wished! The teacher seemed quite innocent of any notion of error on her part.

Thorough study of the test and directions for its use and careful adherence to instructions in every detail are the essentials for successful administration of a standardized test. Most teachers and school personnel can meet these requirements without undue difficulty. As teachers gain in experience and confidence, the administration of standardized tests becomes fairly easy and often stimulating and enjoyable.

2. *Ability to maintain the attention and whole-hearted cooperation of a group.* The administrator of a standardized test must be able to command the attention of a group and draw from each member his best efforts. If the test is a good one the tasks it involves and the instructions to the pupils will help the examiner hold the pupils' attention. Perhaps most important, the examiner himself must give an impression of serious attention and an attitude of regard for the importance of the task at hand. Many a well-meaning examiner, in his attempt to set pupils at ease, has spoiled the entire effort by such remarks as, "Don't take this too seriously," or, "It doesn't mean anything." Certainly children should not suffer unnecessary emotional strain in taking a test, yet a test is a test and if the child is to do as well as he possibly can, he must be urged to give his undivided attention and cooperation. The examiner must avoid instilling in his pupils either an attitude of extreme emotional tension, which may prevent a child from doing his best, *or* an attitude of careless indifference, which will defeat the very purpose of the test.

3. *Ability to read directions aloud clearly and distinctly.* Reading aloud is something of a lost art for the emphasis in the teaching of reading has shifted almost completely to silent reading. The administration of a group test usually requires that the directions be read aloud, clearly and distinctly. This requires a good voice and the ability to use it effectively. It is neces-

sary for every examiner, even the experienced one, to practice reading the directions aloud before giving a test for the first time. Through such rehearsal he will learn the proper inflections, pronunciations, and phrasing. Sometimes the wrong intonation can change the meaning of a sentence and cause confusion or misunderstanding.

By practicing reading the directions aloud the examiner can also gain sufficient familiarity with them so that he can make the reading more pleasant and meaningful to his audience. He should be able to take his eyes off the printed page occasionally, not only to see if all the pupils are paying attention and following him, but also for the good effect this will have on his audience. It may be necessary for the examiner to interrupt his reading occasionally in order to explain an example given in the directions or to make sure that all pupils understand what they are to do. A thorough mastery of the directions helps to smooth such breaks and avoid awkward pauses.

4. *Ability to be objective.* A teacher measuring her own pupils with a standardized test may find it very difficult to be objective because she is aware that the test results may often seem to conflict with her own judgment. She observes Johnny struggling unsuccessfully with a test problem and she feels that she must give him "just a tiny hint to help him solve it," for she has seen him solve similar problems many times. The "tiny hint" may not even be expressed in words. As she looks at Johnny's answer sheet over his shoulder, a frown or a surprised expression may be all that is needed to set him on the right track. This may make both Johnny and the teacher happy at the moment, but it destroys the objectivity of a good testing situation and it may later prove harmful to all concerned.

If one is having the antifreeze solution in the radiator of his car tested when the temperature is below freezing and falling rapidly, he does not ask the service-station attendant to make the measurement sound better than it actually is in order to save the cost of a quart of antifreeze. To do so might prove very expensive and even disastrous. In a situation of this sort we want as objective and accurate a report as possible so that we may know what to do to be safe. In the same way, we should seek objectivity and accuracy when using standardized tests. To say that the hydrometer the garage mechanic uses or the tests that educators use are not exact instruments merely beclouds the issue. We do not disregard the report on our antifreeze because the mechanic's instrument is not as accurate as those of the scientist who is dealing with very minute quantities in theoretical physics, or because there is some variation in the grades of antifreeze manufactured by different companies. We know that any instrument —

mechanical or educational — that is properly selected and used will give results which are reasonably accurate, or which are at least more dependable and accurate than subjective opinion or plain guessing. The point here is that educational tests should be used as objectively and carefully as possible, with full realization of their limitations and with regard for the fact that using them carelessly or inaccurately may make the results quite valueless or misleading. Of course, the person administering standardized tests or other measuring instruments should demonstrate warmth, understanding, and every attitude calculated to encourage pupils to enjoy taking tests and to do their very best; yet the examiner in his desire to see his pupils do well must do nothing that will invalidate the results of the testing, and he must not deviate from the test instructions.

Physical Conditions of Testing

The examiner should observe a few simple rules concerning the physical conditions of testing. First, the room should be comfortable. It should be well-lighted, well-ventilated, and well-heated. The seats should be comfortable and of appropriate height. It is not uncommon to enter a room where testing is going on to find it crowded, the temperature too high or too low for comfort, all windows tightly closed, and the air almost unbearable. Frequently, the occupants of the room are entirely unaware of these conditions. Again, when pupils are shifted to a different room for testing, the desks in the new room may be totally unsuitable for them — too large or too small, for example. Such conditions can usually be avoided by calling them to the attention of responsible persons before the testing begins.

It is also a good idea to place a sign on the door of a room being used for testing. This will keep out those whose business is not urgent and will reduce the number of interruptions.

The room should be large enough to permit the spacing of pupils in such a way that the temptation to copy will be minimized. If the desks are movable they can usually be placed at a suitable distance from each other without much trouble. If there are too many pupils to be properly accommodated in a single room the teacher or examiner should try to divide the pupils so that the test can be given in two or more rooms. If the desks are fixed it is desirable to seat pupils at alternate desks and, if possible, in alternate rows. If tables and chairs are used pupils should be seated so that there is no temptation to compare papers. Such measures do not reflect on the honesty of pupils; rather, they are intended to reduce to a minimum the opportunity and temptation to cheat.

Duties of the Examiner

The person in charge of administering a standardized test is responsible for the proper conduct of the examination. He should have one or more proctors or assistants if the group is large, but the over-all responsibility is his. He needs a good stop watch or at least a watch with a sweep second hand. Many standardized tests require accurate timing and this is always the examiner's responsibility. If he has a stop watch he should know exactly how to operate it beforehand. Stop watches of different makes and quality vary somewhat in technique of operation. After the testing has begun, it may be impossible to correct an error in timing resulting from the faulty manipulation of watch controls.

If the examiner has only a watch with a second hand the following procedure is recommended:

1. The examiner should synchronize the second hand and the minute hand so that both are together, that is, at the end of a minute at the same time.

2. At the moment he finishes reading the directions for a timed test and says "begin," or "go," he should glance at his watch, looking at the *second hand first,* and then the minute hand, immediately *writing down* the time, thus: 9–42–21, which means that the pupils began work on that part at forty-two minutes and twenty-one seconds past nine o'clock.

3. Then, if the time allowance for that part of the test is two minutes and thirty seconds, he adds that to the starting time, thus:

$$9\text{–}42\text{–}21$$
$$\underline{2\text{–}30}$$
$$9\text{–}44\text{–}51$$

4. Forty-four minutes and fifty-one seconds past nine is the time when he should give instructions to stop, turn over the page, or whatever may be indicated.

No examiner should rely on his memory for the time of beginning or attempt to figure out by mental arithmetic the time of stopping. It is impossible for most persons to do this accurately. Furthermore, during the administration of a standardized group test there are many things to do which are more useful and important than trying to calculate and remember times of starting and stopping.

The examiner should be alert to everything that goes on in the room during testing. It is his responsibility to see that the proper conditions for testing are maintained and to note and record any unusual happenings such as extreme nervousness, accidents, or illness. If the group is large these responsibilities are discharged with the help of his assistants or proctors, but the examiner is still the person ultimately responsible for the proper conduct of the test.

▶ LEARNING EXERCISE ◀

3. You are administering a group mental ability test to seventy-five ninth-graders. You suddenly discover that you have allowed them five minutes too little on Part I and they are now working on Part II. What do you do?

Proctors

Thirty or fewer pupils in a standardized testing situation can usually be handled by one person if the physical conditions, such as seating arrangements, are right. If the number being tested is between thirty and sixty, one proctor will be needed, from sixty to ninety, two, etc. The duties of proctors are to see that the pupils follow the directions given by the examiner, to see that pupils have pencils and other necessary equipment, to distribute and collect test blanks, answer sheets, and other necessary materials at the proper time, and to help the examiner in every way to carry out his job as effectively as possible.

The examiner should assign his proctors or assistants to definite sections of the room or to specific parts of the group being tested, and each proctor should be held responsible for his section or part throughout the test. The proctor should stay with that portion of the group and be available to its members at all times for any legitimate assistance. Inexperienced proctors occasionally make mistakes which can easily be avoided. For example, they sometimes line up at the front of the room while the examiner is reading directions. They should avoid this, remaining as much as possible at their stations or in the background. The examiner should be the sole focus of attention when instructions are given or directions read. As far as possible, nothing should divert the attention of the pupils from the task at hand.

If the testing is not being done by the pupils' own teacher, he should endeavor to be as inconspicuous as possible; he should either leave the room or sit quietly at the back while the testing is in progress. This may sometimes create a little awkwardness, but it can usually be handled through the principal of the school a day or two before the testing begins. The presence of the teacher in the formal testing situation may have effects which are not conducive to the best efforts of the pupils.

Finally, proctors should remain alert and interested in what is going on during the entire test. Sometimes they tend to feel that once the test has successfully gotten under way no further attention on their part is needed. That may be just the time when they should be most alert; a pupil breaks his pencil, his pen runs dry, he turns two pages at once, or something else happens which the alert proctor can remedy immediately. To be most useful, the good proctor should also be thoroughly familiar with the test and the details of its administration. Without this knowledge he cannot actively and properly assist in carrying out the administration of the test.

In connection with the administration of standardized tests the question of how far one may go in giving help often comes up. A good rule to follow is to allow no assistance of any kind with the problems or tasks of the test proper. Also, it is generally considered good practice not to answer any questions regarding the test after work on it has actually begun. Though everyone is anxious for each pupil to do his best, the ideal standardized test situation requires uniformity of conditions for everyone being tested. Any act that gives one pupil more help or explanation than is given to all is not permissible. In some tests understanding and following directions are *part of the test,* and in such cases no explanation of directions other than what is provided by the manual is allowed. The manual of a well-standardized test is usually quite explicit regarding what to say and read in giving the test, and it is not permissible to add to or depart from such instructions *in any way.*

SCORING THE TESTS

Who Shall Score the Tests?

After the tests have been given, the next task is to get the scoring done. If arrangements can be made for having the tests scored by machine there is usually no problem. In many situations, however, hand-scoring is still the common procedure. The labor involved in scoring by hand has been greatly reduced by the better arrangement of test items on the page, by the use of separate answer sheets with scoring stencils, and by the development of self-scoring techniques and other aids. However, we are still a long way from entirely relieving teachers of this job. If funds are available some of the work may be done by clerks, but of course this adds to the cost of testing.

If teachers do the scoring it is very desirable to make some adjustment in their regular duties to give them adequate time for the work. Some of their classes may be dismissed or assigned temporarily to other teachers or substitutes, or they may be excused from some of their non-teaching duties for the time. These adjustments will not only help to get the scoring done quickly, but will also help to create favorable attitudes toward the testing program. Furthermore, there is the advantage that the scoring task will thus not become an extra burden for busy teachers.

Suggestions for Efficient Scoring

In hand-scoring standardized tests there are certain methods and principles which can contribute much to the speed and accuracy with which the work is accomplished.

Although the suggestions which follow are particularly appropriate where large numbers of tests are to be scored, most of them are applicable to every test-scoring task or situation.

In the first place, it is well to divide the task so that each person may develop speed and accuracy on a particular part of the scoring. For example, if there are eight pages or parts of a test it is more efficient to have one individual score one page or part on all the tests than to have him score each test in its entirety. If there are enough workers to assign one page or part to each, an assembly-line procedure can be set up to good advantage. If not, each scorer should concentrate on one page or part at a time and then go on to the next, as each is finished. By this method the scorer sometimes is able to quickly memorize the scoring key so that he can dispense with it entirely. This contributes to both speed and accuracy since the scorer can concentrate on the scoring without the necessity of manipulating scoring keys or checking the keys with answers written on the paper. Moreover, with this system the scorer does not need to constantly shift his attention from one part of the test to an entirely different part. He concentrates on one until it is finished.

The task of arriving at part scores and adding them to get the total score should also be done by one person. The transforming of raw scores into percentiles or standard scores should be the separate responsibility of another individual, or, if it seems convenient and efficient, the one who works out part scores and total scores can also do this, but again, it is probably more efficient for him to do one part of the job at a time.

The assembly-line procedure should be planned and carried out so that test blanks can move along the line smoothly without piling up at any one point. This requires that the work be assigned according to the difficulty of the separate tasks and the particular skill of each individual. A slow worker will necessarily be given a smaller or easier job; otherwise, he may delay others. The person in charge of the scoring must experiment with his helpers and the task at hand until an efficient and agreeable procedure is worked out.

Second, it is generally better to do the work of scoring in a group than to let individuals take tests away with them to score at their convenience. When the scoring is done in a group it is possible to settle questions about procedure, allowable answers, etc., on the spot. Also the scoring is more interesting and stimulating for those participating and delays are avoided. On the other hand, it is sometimes difficult to find the time or a suitable place for assembly-line scoring. However, it is often possible to find time when six or eight teachers can work together if, as has been suggested, the work is done during school hours.

The place for scoring of tests should be relatively quiet and free from interruptions, and the workers should be able to talk with each other freely without fear of disturbing others. If possible, there should be a large table or several smaller ones that can be put together so that all the scorers can work comfortably in a group.

Third, all hand-scoring — the entire operation, from beginning to end — should be carefully checked for accuracy. Every step should be systematically checked, and the person in charge should also check the accuracy of his individual workers. Wide variations will nearly always be found in the work of particular individuals; some will perform their tasks with few errors, while others will seem unable to score accurately, no matter how much they practice.

Checking the scoring is best done by re-scoring a sampling of papers. It may be desirable at the beginning to re-score entirely the first few papers, perhaps five or ten, to see what mistakes are being made by individual scorers and to help correct these mistakes. After this, a sampling of every fifth paper or perhaps every tenth paper should be completely re-scored as a continuous check on the accuracy of the work. If it is found that errors are frequent in all parts of the tests, it will be necessary to re-score all papers. If errors are consistently found only in certain parts of the test or in certain phases of the work, it will suffice, as a rule, to re-score only those parts where error is found.

There is one basic fact often overlooked by users of standardized tests, namely, that errors occur in all such work, and it is therefore absolutely essential that continuous and systematic checking take place. The less experienced the workers, the greater the probability of error, but regardless of the experience of the scorers, the scoring should not be accepted as final or the results recorded until every step of the process has been checked. To permit inaccurate scoring is a waste of time and money, and it may cause grave injustice to the pupils.

Finally, it is important to train workers in the scoring process. One does not usually put scorers to work until they have had some prior instruction. It is usually desirable first to have prospective scorers read the manual, or at least the part dealing with scoring, so that they will understand what they are to do and how to do it. Then the person in charge should help score enough papers so that there is no doubt that the work is being done correctly. In this way one may be reasonably sure that the correct procedure is being followed.

RECORDING AND ANALYZING RESULTS

Recording Test Results

After the tests have been scored and checked, the results must be made a part of the permanent records of the pupil and the school. Most schools have some sort of permanent record for each pupil, usually in the form of a folder providing for the recording of information such as personal and home background data, schools attended, marks, honors, disciplinary or other special actions, and results of various tests. Many such record systems have been devised, some by national agencies, some on the state level, and some by the larger city school systems. In Figure 19, one such sample permanent record form is reproduced. Although the data in the sample record were gathered some time ago, they exemplify the full and complete use of the form and are as appropriate for illustrative purposes as though they had been gathered yesterday.

Whatever the type of permanent record, it is important that there be one, that the test results be recorded as soon as possible after they are available, and that this record be readily accessible to those entitled to use it. The entering of test data upon the record form may be done by teachers for their own pupils or by clerks if such help is available. These records are confidential and should not be available to pupils or other unauthorized persons.

It is probably most advantageous to keep the permanent cumulative records of pupils in some central place such as the principal's office. In some schools records are distributed to teachers so that each will have in his custody the records of his own pupils. It may also be found desirable to have the records filed in the office of the counselor, if there is one. There are arguments for and against centralized and distributed record systems, but they need not be reviewed here. The important thing is that the records be used — not just filed — and it should be determined in each situation what arrangement is best for all concerned.

▶ **LEARNING EXERCISE** ◀

4. Your testing program is proceeding nicely, with tests given as scheduled, scoring done promptly and accurately, and results tabulated and analyzed. However, you must see that the results are entered on the pupils' individual record forms. You have no money for clerical help. How will you get the records completed?

Analyzing Test Results

Before anything can be done as a follow-up of testing there must be an analysis of the results. The analysis may be very simple in nature, as when a pupil's rank in the class is determined, or it may be more complicated, as in the case of large-scale testing programs involving hundreds of schools and thousands of pupils in a large city system. Whatever is done, the basic procedures and techniques are usually statistical. A brief survey of statistical techniques, especially as they apply to educational and psychological test results, is given in Chapter 3 and Appendix A. By the application of these techniques a teacher or counselor can make all of the usual types of analysis without going too far into technicalities. For analysis of a more advanced nature one of the standard works in statistical methods should be consulted.

It may be appropriate to say a word here on profiles and other graphic methods. It is sometimes erroneously assumed that when we make a profile, a percentile curve, or some other graphic record of test results, we are making a further statistical analysis of test results. It is possible that a graphic representation of data may clarify a statistical situation or even give new insight into its meaning, but a graph or chart simply expresses statistical data in another form. A profile is merely a graphic representation of data which are already known. By extending or extrapolating a curve we may extend the data, but the results of such procedures are always hypothetical. Moreover, the same results may be determined statistically as well as graphically.

The reason for emphasizing this matter is that users of tests and test results sometimes are led to believe that profiles, distribution curves, and other graphic methods add something which statistical data do not yield. Profiles and other graphic methods are often very helpful, but principally because they express findings in a way which is more readily grasped than mere statistics. They do not, as a rule, tell us anything about John or Mary which the numbers do not already say.

Cumulative School Record

LAST NAME	FIRST	MIDDLE	NICKNAME	RELIGION	DATE AND PLACE OF BIRTH	SEX	COLOR
Anderson	MARY	MARGARET	MAE	BAPTIST	Amden, Mass. Feb. 12, 1923	M (P)	W

ADDRESS AND TELEPHONE: 25 Irving Terrace, Circle 5600 — 2104 Kayes Ave. East 0415

PHOTOS (Dated)

PREVIOUS SCHOOL RECORD: Names and Types of Schools Attended, Achievement in Subjects and Activities, School Difficulties Encountered, Summary of Test Results

Attended Parmount elementary school including Kindergarten. Very good record throughout. Citizenship always marked excellent. Work has always been commensurate with mental test scores which indicate intelligence quotients above 130. Tested reading performance above eighth grade level while in sixth grade. Superior performances in Art, Music, and Arithmetic. Family very cooperative with school and much interested in achievements of children. Excellent health and attendance records. Mary should wear her glasses in school.

Name and Type of School Attended	West Jr. High	West Jr. High	Same	Same	Amden Sr. High	Same	Same
COUNSELOR	Miss Watson	Miss Watson	Mr. Robinson	Mr. Robinson	Mr. Rones	Miss Cowan	Miss Cowan
AGE (As of Sept. 1)	12-7	12-7	13-7	14-7	15-7	16-7	17-7
SCHOOL YEAR AND GRADE	1936 / 7		1937 / 8	1938 / 9	1939 / 10	1940 / 11	1941 / 12

ACADEMIC ACHIEVEMENT

These columns are for analyses of development in fields indicated. Headings might include work habits, ability to think logically, mastery of technique, oral and written communication and some estimate of achievement. In this school S indicates satisfactory and U unsatisfactory progress in consideration of ability of pupil. An X indicates serious lack of progress.

Column sub-headings per year: WH (Work Habits), T (Thinking Technique), Comm, Mark

Subject	1936 WH/T/Comm/Mark	1937 WH/T/Comm/Mark	1938 WH/T/Comm/Mark	1939 WH/T/Comm/Mark	1940 WH/T/Comm/Mark	1941 WH/T/Comm/Mark
English — Lit. and Comp.	S S S B	S S S U	S S S B	S S S B	S S S B	S S S A
Oral						
Grammar	S S S A	S S S S	S S U A	S S S B	S U S S	S S S A
Lang. — French	S S S B	S S S B	S S U B		U S U S	X X X Dropped
Latin			S S U	S U X C	S S S	
Math — Arithmetic	S U S B		S S S B	S S S A	S S S	
Algebra			S S S B	S S S		
Geometry						
Advanced Math.			S S S A		S U S	S U S S
Science — Chemistry		S S U A		S S S X	S S S X	
Social Studies — Soc. Studies	S S S A		S S S B		U U U	U S S
American Hist.					C	
Other Subjects — Practical Arts	S S S A		S S S A			
Drawing	S S S A		S S S A			S S S A
Music	S S S A		S S S A		Chorus	S S S S
Spelling	S S S A		S S S A			
Physical Education		B		A	A	A

TEST RECORD / READING

Year	TEST	Mo. Score	%ile
1936	Henmon-Nelson	S	(I.Q.-129)
	Stanford Ach.		
	Paragraph M.	S 113	98
	Word Meaning	S 105	77
	Spelling	S 102	85
1937	Kuhl-Anderson	S	(I.Q.-131)
	Stanford Ach.		
	Paragraph M.	S 115	89
	Inglis Vocabulary	S 76	92
1938	Kuhl-Anderson	S	(I.Q.-136)
	Stan-Binet (L)	N	(I.Q.-142)
	Stanford Ach.	S	
	Paragraph M.	S 115	84
	Word Meaning	S 109	74
1939	Kuhl-Anderson	S	(I.Q.-130)
	Iowa Reading (A)	S	
	Comprehension	S 140	87
	Speed	S 39	85
	W. Vocabulary	S 43	78
1940	Kuhl-Anderson	S	(I.Q.-130)
	A.C.E. Psych.	N 117	
	Iowa Reading		
	Comprehension	N 185	94
	Speed	N 43	89
	W. Vocabulary	N 46	80
1941	Kuhl-Anderson	S	(I.Q.-140)
	A.C.E. Psych. (College Form?)	O 154	96
	Coop. Reading		
	Level	O 66	90
	Speed	O 68	93
	W. Vocabulary	O 60	89

ACADEMIC APTITUDE (Use M. and I.Q. if Preferred)

READING

ACHIEVEMENT AND OTHER TESTS

Test			
	S 107 71		Minnesota Clerical
History-Civics	S 100 65	History-Civics S 93 53	Names N 136 87
Geography	S 89 32	Geography S 96 36	Numbers N 156 92
Phys.-Hygiene	S 95 80		
Arith-Reasoning	S 100 72	Arith-Reasoning S 105 70	Arith-Reasoning S 110 77
Arith-Computation	S 95 47	Arith-Computation S 101 57	Arith-Computation S 105 54
		M-S Art Judgment S 102 85	Min. P. Form Board S 42 79
Coop. French S 52 76	Coop. French N 66 74	Minnesota Clerical O	
Coop. Latin S 65 62	Coop. Chemistry N 64 77	Names 0 148 85	
Coop. Math. O 30 80	Coop. Math. N 40 85	Numbers 0 169 97	
Min. P. Form Board N 47 75		Coop. Am. History 0 53 51	
		Coop. Math. 0 51 95	

INTERPRETATION OF TEST RECORD AND ITS RELATION TO ACADEMIC ACHIEVEMENT
(In the interpretation of test scores consider differences in norms used. In transferring records indicate basis of norms)

Superior in ability to do school work and frequently finds that work is not challenging enough for her. When this occurs she keeps busy with so many out-of-school activities that she neglects some school assignments

Enthusiastic and exceptionally efficient reader. Can work accurately and fast on objective tests but finds teachers' tests based on cumulative drill work very difficult. Could do much better in languages if she could see more reason for doing them.

Although Mary continues to make high scores on objective tests of ability she has difficulty with cumulative subjects where her background work is irregular and spotty. Finds it hard to settle down to drill which teachers recommend. 'A' student if she would do assignments. Performance in advanced Math very good despite fact that she had not covered all prerequisites. Mother advised her to carry on all co-curricular activities and have a full pleasant senior year.

ATTENDANCE (Reasons if irregular)

Absent 10 days - colds	No Absences	Same	Same	Missed occasional classes for rehearsals and clubs

INTERESTS REPORTED BY STUDENT

Art- Lettering, drawing; Group sports; Vocal music	Art - copy; Baseball + hockey teams; Music	Art; Any activity which brought contact with other people	Art ← Same; said she had read "all the books in the library".	Any opportunity to work or play with others	← Same; clubs, dates, games

EXPERIENCES IN SCHOOL

Choir	Art editor school paper; Glee club; Chorus	Designed cover for annual; Glee club; Chorus	Glee club	Glee club- president; Lead in Gilbert+Sullivan	Glee club - chorus; Duchess in Gondoliers

OUT OF SCHOOL AND SUMMER EXPERIENCES

Sunday school regular attendance; Scouts; Played at home in summer	Church choirs	Church choir; Designed original greeting cards	Church choir; Leader church student group	Church choir	Church choir; Chairman missionary group in church

WORK EXPERIENCES
NOTE TYPE, DURATION, HOURS PER WEEK, EARNINGS AND OTHER SIGNIFICANT FACTS

NONE	NONE	Assistant to secretary of school. No pay. Efficient worker	NONE	Care of children in evenings. Paid $4 for 12 to 16 hours per month; Demonstrator- food show one week $15	← Same

SIGNIFICANT ACTIVITIES AND ACCOMPLISHMENTS THAT GIVE EVIDENCE REGARDING INTERESTS AND POWERS

FINANCIAL AID (Type and amount)

NONE	NONE	NONE	NONE	N.Y.A. clerical $6 monthly; 20 hours	N.Y.A. clerical $6 monthly; Teaching math. or work in statistics.

Educational and Occupational Plans {Pupil, Parents, Counselor}

Go to college- then get married; None stated; Wait till school performance observed	Many vague ideas; None stated; Encouraged to continue many activities as try-outs	Commercial artist; Father discouraged choice of career in comm. art; consider any career requiring college training	Commercial artist ← Same	Commercial artist ← Same	Secretary in position where math. is used and then marriage.; Free to choose own career but parents agree with above; Good compromise; further study of possibilities and professions recommended

HEALTH AND PHYSICAL CHARACTERISTICS
(Vigor or lack of; assets, disabilities or limitations)

Should wear glasses for reading; No marked presence or absence of vigor; Rather plump	Vigorous - Peppy; Radiant health; Beautiful blonde hair and fine color of complexion	Stopped wearing glasses because she thought they detracted from appearance; Same	Will not wear glasses. Excellent health and much vigor	SAME → Same → Same → Same

DISCIPLINE {Academic, Personal}

NONE	NONE	Some make-up time required to get home-work done.	NONE	NONE

FIGURE 19 •

Typical Permanent Record Form

Reproduced by permission of the National Association of Secondary School Principals, National Education Association, and the American Council on Education.

ILLUSTRATIVE MEASUREMENT PROGRAMS

To complete this discussion of measurement programs we shall offer a few illustrations representing actual practice in school systems of different sizes. All these programs have been developed through local leadership and experience. Therefore they are practical, and their scope is such that they can be managed at the local level without undue expense or labor. Included are programs for (1) a small community school with no secondary grades, (2) a larger school including all grades from kindergarten through the twelfth grade, and (3) a city system comprising a large number of elementary schools, plus junior and senior high schools.

A Typical Program for the Small School

The first measurement program to be described is one which any small elementary school enrolling three hundred or fewer pupils can manage without outside help. It follows closely the minimum program presented earlier in this chapter. It happens to be one which has been successfully administered for a number of years at the Stoner School near Lansing, Michigan. Some of the students in the writer's classes in educational measurement have participated in the program, have helped to administer and score the tests and analyze the results, and have had the opportunity to discuss with the teachers ways of putting the results to use.[3] This has helped the teachers and the school and has provided important practical experience for a number of university students.

STONER SCHOOL TESTING PROGRAM

Grade	Test	Time
K	Reading Readiness	May
1 or 2	Intelligence	February
3 or 4	Achievement Battery	October
5	Intelligence	February
6	Achievement Battery	October

This program is simple and it is limited enough to be managed by the regular staff of the school without outside assistance. The results are used in various ways, including identifying exceptional children, both the slow-learning and gifted, counseling with parents, sectioning or grouping, diagnosing, and comparing test results with national norms.

[3] Victor H. Noll and Marvin D. Glock, "Functional Courses in Measurement and Evaluation," *School and Society*, 70:339–40, November 26, 1949.

The program gives information of several types, all useful in improving instruction. It reveals the stage of development or readiness of beginnners for learning the fundamentals, it gives several appraisals of each child's general capacity for school work, and it provides a reasonably adequate survey of each pupil's progress in the common branches of the elementary school curriculum. The entire cost of the program, including test material and some clerical assistance for recording the results, can be kept to less than twenty-five cents per pupil per year. This allows nothing, of course, for the time of the school staff or for any outside help. However, when teachers become educated to the value of the results of their work and feel that they have a real part in the program, they are usually glad to contribute a reasonable amount of time and energy to the work of carrying it through.

▶ LEARNING EXERCISE ◀

5. Compare the minimum testing program outlined on page 385 and that of the Stoner School above. Are there any differences which you consider significant? If so, what are they? Outline what you would consider a practical testing program for a similar situation.

A Typical Program for the Larger School

The program to be described next is one that might fit a school system of almost any size, though its scope is such that it can be managed by a school of moderate size without a particularly large specialized staff. It calls for one part-time coordinator at the elementary level and one coordinator each at the junior and senior high school levels. Each of these coordinators may be a counselor or guidance person, or a teacher whose schedule of regular work has been adjusted for this purpose and who has had some instruction in measurement.

MEASUREMENT PROGRAM: TWELVE GRADES[4]

Grade	Test	Time
K	Reading Readiness	May
1	Intelligence	January
3	Achievement Battery	October
4	Achievement Battery	April
5	Achievement Battery	October
6	Intelligence	April
8	Achievement Battery	October
8	Algebra Aptitude	April

[4] Courtesy of Okemos, Michigan, Public Schools.

8	Intelligence	April
9	Vocational Interests	October
9	Intelligence	April
9	Personality (limited use as appropriate)	
10	Achievement Battery	October
11	Vocational Interests	October
11	Intelligence	April
11	Personality (limited use as appropriate)	
11	Aptitude tests (clerical, mechanical, etc., in individual cases)	

To summarize, two tests measuring a pupil's general mental ability, plus a reading readiness test, are given in the elementary grades; three surveys of achievement are also given. In the secondary school three more tests of intelligence, two measures of vocational interests, two achievement tests, and an algebra aptitude test are given. In addition, the secondary school counselor uses a personality test at his discretion in individual cases. Some tests of special aptitudes are also given by the counselor to individual pupils in the eleventh grade, as seems desirable. The entire cost of this program for 2150 pupils, including all materials, supplies, and some clerical services, is about $1150 per year, or fifty-four cents per pupil.

It will be seen that the schedule is so arranged that practically all of the testing comes in October and April. This has the advantage of causing less disruption of the regular schedule than if the testing were scattered throughout the year. It enables the staff and administration to plan regularly for the testing and to concentrate on it at stated times. It may also have the advantage that pupils are not taking the same or similar tests at different times — a condition which sometimes gives those who take the tests later an advantage over those taking them first.

The administration of this measurement program is in the hands of the Assistant Superintendent for Instruction. The tests are administered by the counselors, or under their supervision. Tests are machine scored whenever possible. The hand-scoring is done by clerks, some of whom are high school students who work under careful supervision during free school hours and after school. Where such help is used the test papers are coded so that the pupils' papers cannot be identified. After the tests are scored the raw scores are converted to appropriate derived scores, and profiles are constructed by the teachers. The results are recorded in the pupils' permanent record folders. The records for the first six grades are kept in the classroom for use by the teacher, and the secondary school pupils' folders are kept in the guidance office.

The results of this program are used in many ways, such as for the identification of retarded and gifted children for special instruction. The reading readiness testing usually reveals a number of pupils in the kindergarten who are not ready to begin first-grade work, and special provisions are made for such cases. The reading tests at the higher grade levels serve to identify pupils who have reading difficulties. The school maintains a reading improvement service with the full-time help of a reading specialist.

The algebra aptitude test is used to determine whether or not pupils are ready to take algebra. If not, they are advised to take a course in general mathematics instead. When the general course is completed satisfactorily, and a pupil still wants to take algebra, he is then enrolled in that course.

The intelligence and achievement tests are used in sectioning pupils according to capacity and past performance, wherever this is feasible and advisable. The interest inventory is used as a starting point for high school freshmen in a class in sociology. Here, pupils examine their own interest profiles and make studies of occupations which the inventory suggests should be of particular interest. The studies may include visits to places of business, industrial plants, hospitals, schoolrooms, etc., according to the occupations being considered.

The results of the measurement program are used to identify individuals who may need psychiatric or clinical services, in educational and vocational guidance, and to assist in bringing about better understanding and better relationships among school personnel, pupils, parents, and in the community in general. These results serve many particular purposes, but the most important purpose is the improvement of the educational program and the consequent improvement in the functioning of the entire school system and its contribution to the community. It is believed by those responsible that the measurement program in this community contributes substantially to these purposes.

A Typical Program for a City System

The third program to be described is one that has been developed by the Long Beach, California, school system, enrolling approximately seventy-five thousand pupils in elementary schools and in the junior and senior high schools. Altogether, seventy-two schools are involved, of which fifty-three are elementary, Grades K–6; fourteen are junior high schools, Grades, 7–9; and five are senior high schools, Grades 10–12.

The basic program followed throughout the district is shown below:

LONG BEACH PUBLIC SCHOOLS

Grade	Test	Week
4	Local Spelling Test	3
5*	Intelligence	4–5
5*	Achievement Battery	5–9
5	Geography	10
3	Intelligence	12–13
3	Reading; Arithmetic	20–21
6	Reading; Arithmetic; Spelling	24–26
6	Local Geography Test	30
4	Local Spelling Test	31

Junior High Schools

Grade	Test	Week
8	Local Spelling Test	3
7	Intelligence	4–5
8*	Intelligence	5
8*	Achievement Battery	5–9
9	Reading	25
7	Local Spelling Test	31
9	Written English	35–36

Senior High Schools

Grade	Test	Week
10	Intelligence	3–4
10	Study Skills	4–5
11*	Intelligence	5
11*	Achievement Battery	6–9
12	Written English	35–36

The tests in the basic program are administered to all pupils at the levels and at the approximate times indicated. Tests are usually administered by counselors or by teachers, though sometimes in an elementary school they are administered by the principal. The few tests which require hand-

---

* California law requires the giving of intelligence tests and achievement tests in selected grades. For the period 1962–63 through 1964–65, the pattern of state-required testing consisted of intelligence tests and tests of reading, arithmetic or mathematics, and language or English in Grades 5, 8, and 11. (Students taking an approved mental test in Grades 4, 7, or 10 were not required to take the same test the following year. The Long Beach system prefers to give an intelligence test to its seventh- and tenth-graders as they enter junior and senior high school; it then administers the same tests in Grades 8 and 11 in order to test new students who missed the original surveys in the previous grades.)

scoring — mainly tests for pupils of the lower elementary grades — are scored by the clerks, teachers, and counselors at the individual school sites; where machine-scorable answer sheets are used, the scoring is done in a central office and the scores are returned to the school for a tabulation of results. In general, tabulations of all test results are sent to the office of the Director of Research, but the scored tests are kept at the school. Test results are recorded in each pupil's cumulative record.

The Long Beach Director of Research has developed a series of mimeographed instruction sheets which supplement the manuals for the various tests, and these instruction sheets provide teachers with practical suggestions on administering and scoring tests, tabulating, analyzing, and recording results, and reporting them to the office of the Director. Such carefully worked-out instruction sheets are essential in a large program such as this where personal contact with all cooperating teachers is impossible.

In addition to the district-wide or required program of testing, which begins with the fourth grade, each school has an opportunity to select additional standardized tests for optional use in any grade or classroom. These tests are selected by the personnel of the individual schools, and vary considerably from one school to the next. Test requests by teachers of a school are channeled to the offices of the counselor and school principal; they are then forwarded to the district's Research Office for final review before the materials are delivered or requisitioned for later delivery.

Most of the elementary schools choose to give a mental or readiness test in Grade 1. By common agreement among the junior high schools, every ninth-grade student is given a vocational interest test and a battery of differential ability tests. In the senior high schools those seniors who are not planning to enter college are given another battery of multiple-aptitude tests. General ability and achievement tests that are part of national testing programs are given to a high percentage of those juniors and seniors who plan to enter college.

Many of the junior and senior high schools elect to give standardized achievement tests that are not required on a district-wide basis, particularly in the fields of foreign language, mathematics, and science. Schools that are making unusual efforts to develop reading skills often request standardized reading tests that help measure gains during a specified instructional period. Teachers make frequent requests, too, for reading tests (and sometimes for tests in other areas of skill) that are designed to offer clues concerning the specific learning deficiencies of individual pupils.

The Research Office does not purchase the pencil-and-paper personality tests or adjustment inventories which may occasionally be requested by a school. This is the only broad limitation on the selection of tests by school personnel except for the restrictions imposed by the status of the district's test supply budget.

The program of testing in Long Beach — the required or district-wide schedule and the near-uniform testing by common agreement — may be summarized as follows:

Grade in Which Test Is Given

Test	1	2	3	4	5	6	7	8	9	10	11	12
Intelligence	x		x		x		x			x		
Multiple Aptitude									x			x
Vocational Interest									x			
Study Skills										x		
Merit and Pre-College											x	x
Reading			x		x	x	x	x		x		
Language–English					x		x	x		x		x
Arithmetic–Math.			x		x	x	x			x		
Spelling				x	x	x	x					
Geography					x	x						

A pupil attending the Long Beach Public Schools from Grade 1 through Grade 12 will take five different measures of general scholastic ability as he moves through the grades. In Grade 9 he will be given some assistance in his early search for a career choice by taking both a multiple-aptitude battery and a measure of his vocational interests. Toward the close of his high school career he will take a second battery of aptitude tests if he does not plan to attend college; if he does plan to attend college, he will probably take one or more tests of the usual pre-admission type. Skill in locating needed information and in handling common references is checked in the early part of the tenth grade, shortly after admission to senior high school.

In line with the existing pattern of required testing throughout California in the mid-1960's, the Long Beach Public Schools give a battery of achievement tests covering the "three R's" in Grades 5, 8, and 11. The bulk of the achievement testing that is not state-required is concentrated in Grades 3, 6, and 9. Each of the grades in which several achievement tests are given is a crucial year, and the information derived from the measurement program thus becomes available at a time when it will be most useful. By the time a Long Beach pupil finishes high school, he will have had at least six standardized measures of reading achievement, five measures of language or written English, and five tests of arithmetic or mathematics. In addition, he will have had four spelling tests and two tests in geography.

Such a program requires the leadership and assistance of a central co-ordinating agency; in the case of the Long Beach school system the supervisor of the program is the Director of Research, though the major share of the work is divided among the teachers and counselors so that no one will be overburdened. The results are reported to the central office, but the scored tests are kept in the respective schools where they may be interpreted and put to use. This program, moreover, is not an expensive one.[5]

The results of the Long Beach testing program are used in various ways, including the following:

1. *To assist the central office staff — particularly those in the Division of Instruction — in identifying curricular fields of strength and weakness for the total district.* If the district-wide test results in a given field are not satisfactory, it means that special effort must be made to analyze the causes and then to correct conditions which are believed to be responsible for the weakness in pupil achievement.

2. *To provide school administrators with one basis for evaluating pupil achievement in individual schools of the district.* For example, each principal is expected to maintain a set of tables or graphs on which the record of the test achievement of pupils in his school is shown for previous years and for the current year. By examining these tables or graphs a newly appointed principal can see what the past record of his school has been on reading tests, for example, and he has a basis for judging whether the current year's test scores are in line with those of previous years.

3. *To identify those pupils in the district who rank in the upper 2 per cent of general scholastic aptitude, so that these "mentally gifted" pupils can be given individual counseling and instruction adapted to their abilities. Similarly, to identify those pupils in Grades 9 to 12 who rank one standard deviation above the mean in general scholastic ability, so that these "academically talented" students may be counseled concerning the kinds of high school courses best suited for those planning to take four years of college. Another related use: to identify those who may be admitted to certain elective courses designed for pupils in accelerated programs.*

4. *To identify pupils who should be re-tested individually in order to determine whether they should be placed in special classes for the slower learners.*

[5] Dr. Anton Thompson, Director of Research in the Long Beach, California, school system, reports in a personal communication that the cost for tests and materials per pupil in average daily attendance in the elementary schools was twenty-five cents in 1963–64; for high schools it was thirty-nine cents per pupil. This does not include cost of services such as scoring, recording, and statistical analysis.

5. *To furnish teachers and counselors with test data needed for student counseling.*

6. *To provide data needed by counselors and administrators in grouping high school students by ability and achievement in certain required subjects such as tenth-grade English.*

7. *To give teachers an objective basis for judging pupil progress in achievement.* For example, the senior high teacher of English can compare the achievement of his students with that of other pupils in the nation who were in the norm group.

8. *To supply teachers with certain instructional clues.* Following some surveys, an analysis of the pupils' answers (an "item-count") in a sample of test papers is made. A report is then prepared so that teachers can learn which types of skills and understandings seem to have been satisfactorily mastered and which types appear to be in need of strengthening.

9. *To maintain public confidence in the local schools.* During a given week thousands of pupils tell their parents that they have just taken a standardized reading test. Many parents are impressed with the fact that the school system not only teaches reading (and the other basic skills), but also checks up on its teaching efforts. Another important use in public relations: the district-wide data can be used by school administrators to provide a factual answer to an occasional critic making an unfounded charge concerning the general level of achievement of local pupils. A citizen sometimes bases his criticism of a school's educational program upon extremely limited evidence, perhaps on his subjective judgment regarding the academic accomplishment of a few pupils or graduates he has met. In such circumstances a skillful administrator can use the results of the district's testing program to build and maintain public confidence. He might tactfully show the critical citizen (assuming the critic is a reasonable person) that according to the results of a recognized achievement test given to the total school population of many thousands in a grade the district median represents a satisfactory level of accomplishment.

Other testing programs in similar-sized communities could be described, and these would differ in such details as grade placement of tests, and areas tested. However, the three programs we have described have been found workable and useful in their respective communities. They are not extremely elaborate, and they are modest in cost. They serve to illustrate the principles discussed in the first part of this chapter and should be suggestive of what can be done by other communities with similar needs and purposes

It is probably unnecessary to state that in any measurement program the teacher or supervisor should anticipate the necessity for re-testing in doubtful cases and that provision should be made for this on an individual basis. Accidents will happen to prevent pupils from finishing a test; there will be surprisingly low, or sometimes surprisingly high, scores, and of course there will always be absentees. Whenever a child misses the testing, or when there is good reason to believe that he has not been adequately or accurately measured, a make-up test is in order. Whenever an alternate form of the same test is available, it should be used in such cases, especially when a child has started a test, but has been unable to finish. It is usually more satisfactory to have him take the entire test in another form than to have him attempt to go on from the point where he stopped.

It should be understood that the discussion in this chapter has been concerned entirely with group tests. It is recognized that in some cases an individual examination like the *Binet,* the *Wechsler,* or other individual tests may be used. However, such examinations must be administered by a person with special training since most classroom teachers have not had the necessary instruction in the use of these instruments. Where such tests are needed and used it is assumed that qualified persons are available to administer them, and that the tests will be given as necessary.

▶ LEARNING EXERCISES ◀

6. Make a careful analysis of the Okemos testing program. What suggestions can you offer which you feel would strengthen it? Does the program have any unique or unusual features? If so, what are they?

7. Give your judgment or rating of the Long Beach program on the following factors: (a) Comprehensiveness; (b) practicality; (c) economy; (d) usefulness; (e) acceptability to teachers, counselors, and administrators.

ANNOTATED BIBLIOGRAPHY

1. Bauernfeind, Robert H. *Building a School Testing Program.* Boston: Houghton Mifflin Company, 1963. 343 pp. A general treatment of basic principles of testing and the uses of different types of tests. The attention given to the actual planning and carrying out of a school testing program is a relatively minor feature of the book.

2. Durost, Walter N. *What Constitutes a Minimal Testing Program for Elementary and Junior High School,* Test Service Notebook No. 1, Revised. New York: Harcourt, Brace & World, Inc., 1956. Discusses the major phases of

planning, conducting, and using the results of a testing program in a practical manner.

3. Lindquist, E. F. (ed.). *Educational Measurement.* Washington: American Council on Education, 1951. Chapter 10: "Administering and Scoring the Objective Test," by Arthur E. Traxler. An excellent discussion of two phases of a testing program. It is aimed, for the most part, at the large-scale user of tests. The bibliography is excellent, but is limited almost entirely to scoring problems.

4. National Society for the Study of Education. *The Impact and Improvement of School Testing Programs.* Sixty-Second Yearbook of the Society, Part II. Chicago: The Society (distributed by the University of Chicago Press), 1963. 304 pp. A comprehensive treatment of the subject by a Committee of the Society. Includes the consideration of different types of testing programs, their impact on the schools and on individuals, the function of programs in college preparation and guidance, and the selection and use of tests.

5. Public School Publishing Company. *The Testing Program,* Test Bulletin No. 1. Indianapolis: The Bobbs Merrill Company, Inc., 1958. 20 pp. A brief discussion of the use of different kinds of tests and their purposes in a testing program.

6. Ross, C. C., and Stanley, Julian C. *Measurement in Today's Schools,* Third Edition. New York: Prentice-Hall, Inc., 1954. Chapter 8 consists of an excellent discussion of a testing program for the beginner in his work. Contains many helpful ideas and references. Especially good on planning, selecting, administering, and scoring.

7. Traxler, Arthur E. "Fifteen Criteria of a Testing Program," *The Clearing House,* 25:3–7, September, 1950. A brief and practical discussion containing a useful set of criteria for judging the efficiency and value of a testing program.

8. ———. *Techniques of Guidance,* Revised Edition. New York: Harper & Row, Publishers, 1957. Chapters IX, X, and XI. These chapters deal respectively with the topics of planning and administering a testing program, scoring, organizing and reporting test results, and using tests to improve instruction and counseling.

9. ———, et al. *Introduction to Testing and the Use of Test Results in Public Schools.* New York: Harper & Row, Publishers, 1953. A manual for those responsible for planning and carrying out a testing program. Although directed primarily toward the large-scale program in cities, it is a practical reference for all users of standardized tests.

10. Womer, Frank B. *Testing Programs in Michigan Schools.* Ann Arbor: Bureau of School Services, University of Michigan, 1963. 64 pp. A survey of testing programs in Michigan schools as of January, 1963. Presents information on who is responsible for the program, who does the work, the tests used, and how the results are interpreted and implemented.

15

Using the Results of Measurement

In preceding chapters many kinds of measuring instruments have been described and evaluated. We have suggested or discussed the uses of these instruments in many instances. In Chapter 14 we emphasized that measurement programs should be planned and carried out in the light of definite purposes. In that chapter also, a number of broad objectives or purposes for a measurement program were cited, and it was stated that these would be discussed in some detail later. Listed below are the objectives mentioned there:

1. Placement and promotion
2. Homogeneous grouping
3. Diagnosis and remedial work
4. Counseling and guidance
5. Marking
6. Motivation
7. Identification and study of exceptional children
8. Interpreting schools to the community
9. Improvement of school staff
10. Educational research

These are probably the main purposes for which tests and other measuring instruments are used in the schools today. Certainly they seem important and worthy of careful consideration; it will be the aim of this chapter, therefore, to discuss these purposes and to show how measurement can contribute to the attainment of each.

INTERPRETATION OF TEST RESULTS

Basic to using the results of measurement is the interpretation of scores. As was pointed out in Chapter 3, a test score is merely a number, devoid of meaning in and by itself. Not until it is related to something does it become meaningful and thus useful. Much of Chapter 3 is concerned with the procedures by which test scores are given meaning. Before we proceed with a discussion of the various uses of test results, it would be well to take another look at a device which facilitates interpretation and to which reference has already been made in Chapter 14. This is the profile, a graphic method of depicting the results of the testing of individuals and of groups. The profile typically shows the results of an achievement battery such as the *Stanford,* an aptitude battery, such as the *Differential Aptitude Tests,* or scores on an interest inventory for various occupations, such as the *Strong.* Although a profile actually adds nothing to the information given by scores, norms, and statistical interpretations, it does facilitate comparisons and interpretations by presenting results graphically and all in one package, as it were, for a given individual or a group. Several examples of profiles are shown here as illustrations.

Figure 20 shows the scores of an individual pupil on the sub-tests of the *Stanford* battery and his median score. His profile shows the comparative score on each sub-test. The chart also shows his standing on each sub-test in terms of grade equivalents, age equivalents, and percentile ranks and in relation to the grade norm. The medians for the class on each sub-test could also be added to produce a group profile, if desired. Additional profiles and class analysis charts are shown in Figures 21 and 22.

Figure 21 depicts results on the *Metropolitan Achievement Test* for a homogeneous second-grade class. Individuals' scores on the sub-tests of the battery are located by numbered circles; results on a learning capacity measure are shown in column 8; all scores are expressed in stanines; and median stanines for each sub-test and the capacity measure are shown at the bottom. It will be apparent that this class is quite homogeneous in both ability and achievement: no pupil is below the fourth stanine. Median stanines on the *Metropolitan,* based on national norms, are all 7 or 8. The median stanine on the *Pintner-Durost* is 6, suggesting that the achievement of this class is consistent with its measured capacity to learn.

FIGURE 20 • A Pupil's Completed Profile Chart, Based on his Scores on the *Stanford Achievement Test, Advanced Battery*

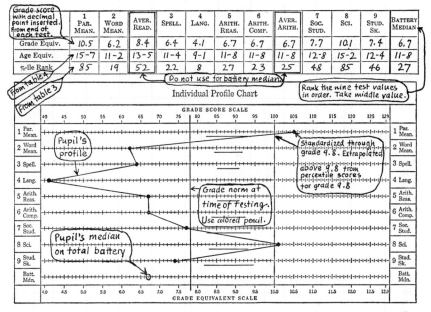

Grade score with decimal point inserted from end of each test.	1 PAR. MEAN.	2 WORD MEAN.	AVER. READ.	3 SPELL.	4 LANG.	5 ARITH. REAS.	6 ARITH. COMP.	AVER. ARITH.	7 SOC. STUD.	8 SCI.	9 STUD. SK.	BATTERY MEDIAN
Grade Equiv.	10.5	6.2	8.4	6.4	4.1	6.7	6.7	6.7	7.7	10.1	7.4	6.7
Age Equiv.	15-7	11-2	13-5	11-4	9-1	11-8	11-8	11-8	12-8	15-2	12-4	11-8
%-ile Rank	85	19	52	22	8	27	23	25	48	85	46	27

From *Stanford Achievement Test: Forms J–N* by Truman L. Kelley, *et al.* Copyright 1953 by Harcourt, Brace & World, Inc., New York. Individual Profile Chart from *Directions for Administering Intermediate and Advanced Complete Batteries*. Reproduced by permission.

Figure 22 shows results for a Grade 6 heterogeneous class on the *Metropolitan* and the *Pintner* Intermediate tests. The first and most obvious difference from the Grade 2 chart is the much greater range in ability and achievement. Pupils range in both from the first stanine to the ninth. Median stanines are all 5's. Individual profiles for a few pupils are again shown by connecting lines revealing, in some cases, wide fluctuations from one sub-test to another, in other cases, extremely consistent performance.

Such class analysis charts and profiles provide teachers with valuable information and facilitate interpretations of test results for most of the purposes for which tests may be used.

PLACEMENT AND PROMOTION

One of the primary uses of test results is placement of pupils at particular grade levels, promoting, accelerating, or holding them as may be judged appropriate. Ideally, pupils should be placed at levels where they can learn without being unduly discouraged, overworked, or bored.

FIGURE 21 • Class Analysis Chart — Homogeneous Second Grade Class

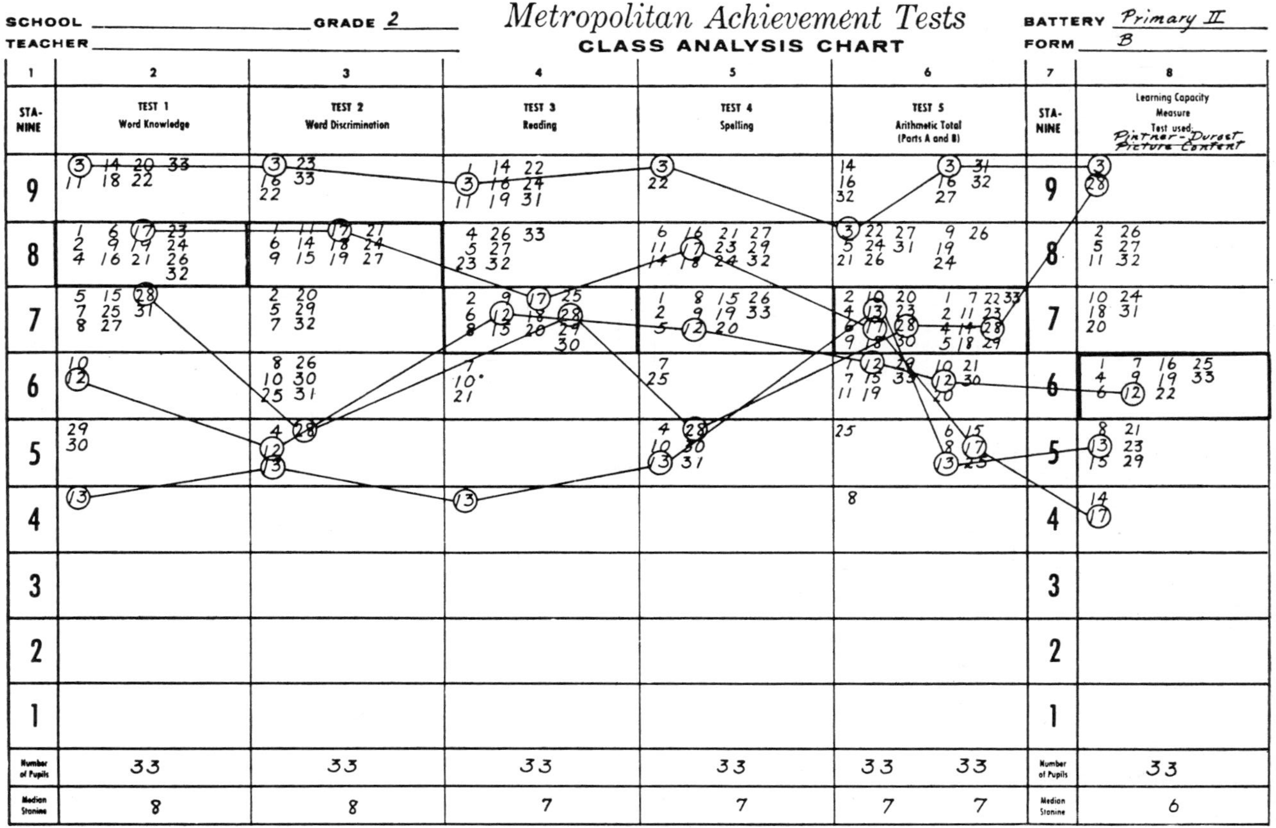

From *Metropolitan Achievement Tests, Manual for Interpreting* by Walter N. Durost. Copyright © 1962 by Harcourt, Brace & World, Inc., New York. P. 30. Reproduced by permission.

FIGURE 22 Class Analysis Chart — Heterogeneous Sixth-Grade Class

Metropolitan Achievement Tests **CLASS ANALYSIS CHART** *Intermediate* **BATTERY** *Grade 6*

1	2	3	4	5	6	7	8	9	10	11	12	13
STA-NINE	TEST 1 Word Knowledge	TEST 2 Reading	TEST 3 Spelling	TEST 4 Language Total (Parts A-C)	TEST 5 Language Study Skills	TEST 6 Arithmetic Computation	TEST 7 Arith. Prob. Solv. & Conc.	TEST 8 Soc. Studies Information	TEST 9 Soc. Studies Study Skills	TEST 10 Science	STA-NINE	Learning Capacity Measure Test used: *Pintner Inter.*
9	5	22 32		15 22	15 22	2 22	14		14 15 22	15 20 32	9	15
8	12 15 32	5 15 29		12	5 29 32	14	15 20 22 32	15 32		16 29	8	12 14 22
7	2 22 24	20 24	2 12 32 4 15 5 22 11 29	5 24 13 29 14	2 14 24	10 32 15 16 29	2 27 9 24	3 22 7 16 17	3 18 27	3 14 5 24 7 12	7	5 20 24 32 27
6	14 29 16 20	2 12 17 3 13 27 8 14	8 24 9 13 14	2 16 32 4 19 10 21 11 25	16 21 28	1 12 33 3 24 5 25 11 27	3 12 8 16 10 18 11 29	5 8 9 20 12 27 14 29	1 19 2 20 12 16	4 17 18 22	6	2 21 9 16
5	3 9 18 23 4 13 19 27 7 17 21	1 9 19 28 4 10 21 7 16 23	3 21 18 23 19 28 20 31	1 20 28 3 23 31 9 27	10 18 11 19 12 20 13 31	9 19 28 13 20 34 17 21 18 26	1 21 28 5 23 33 13 25 19 26	1 2 13	4 13 28 5 23 29 7 24 32 10 26	2 23 8 27 10 21	5	13 26 17 29 18 19
4	8 25 10 28 11 31	11 18 26	1 16 6 17 7 25 10	7 26 8 18	1 8 25 3 9 27 4 17 34 7 23	4 8 31	4 17 34	11 24 19 25 21 34 23	8 25 9 34 11 17	1 25 9 26 11 28 13	4	1 8 31 3 10 4 11
3	1 26	25 31 34	26 27	17	26	7 23	7	4 6 8 28	21 31	19 31	3	7 34 23 28
2	6 34	6	33 34	6 33 34	33	6	6 31	10 26 31	6 30 33	6	2	6 33
1	30 33	30 33	30	30	6 30	30	30	30 33		30 33 34	1	25 30
Number of Pupils	34	34	34	34	34	34	34	34	34	34	Number of Pupils	34
Median Stanine	5	5	5	5.5	5	5.5	5.5	5	5	5	Median Stanine	5

From *Metropolitan Achievement Tests, Manual for Interpreting* by Walter N. Durost. Copyright © 1962 by Harcourt, Brace & World, Inc., New York. P. 29. Reproduced by permission.

Placement at particular grade levels may be thought of as *vertical* classification, as contrasted with *horizontal* grouping which will be discussed shortly. The most useful test for such classification or grade placement is probably a general school achievement battery. As noted above, these batteries have grade norms for the separate subject tests, norms for the battery as a whole, and norms for converting the scores into age levels. With these three types of norms it is possible to determine fairly accurately a pupil's grade level with regard to achievement in school subjects.

When a pupil transfers from one school to another, particularly when he moves to a different school system or state, a standardized achievement battery is one of the most dependable tools for determining his level of achievement. It is probably more accurate to speak of *levels* of achievement, since these will not always be the same in different subjects or parts of the test battery, and, as we have seen, the profile, based on scores on the different subject tests, will generally not be a straight line.

It is usually desirable in classifying pupils to give a general intelligence test in addition to achievement tests so that both educational and general mental development can be taken into account in placing the pupil. Then, knowing his grade level of achievement, his chronological age, his mental age, and his I.Q., it is possible to arrive at a decision based on objective data rather than guesswork. If the pupil's previous school record is available, this too should be taken into consideration, though for grade placement with respect to subject-matter achievement the test battery is probably the more accurate measure.

Thus, for example, if a pupil is nine years, six months of age, with an over-all achievement of the seventh month of the fifth grade, and a mental age of ten years, eight months, we can form a fairly accurate estimate of his level of development and achievement. His ratio I.Q. is 10–8 (or 128 months) divided by 9–6 (or 114 months) × 100, or 112. Assuming school entrance was between 5–6 and 6–0 (which can usually be checked), we have the following data:

Age	*M.A.*	*Grade Level*	*I.Q.*	*Year in School*
9–6	10–8	5–7	112	5th

In this case the picture is fairly clear. The pupil is somewhat above average in mental age and intelligence and is at grade for his age and years in school. He could properly be placed in the fifth grade and encouraged to do extra work and outside reading to satisfy his accelerated mental development.

In cases involving retardation or acceleration the same types of information about the individual will be useful. The weight of evidence and opinion seems to be against holding pupils back, particularly at upper grade levels.[1] Studies show that most pupils repeating a grade do just as badly or worse than they did the first time. If this is generally true, there seems little to be said in favor of holding back over-age pupils. However, tests can be very useful in determining a slow learner's level of achievement and his mental level. A pupil aged twelve years with a reading level of third grade, a mental age of nine, and an I.Q. of 75 will almost surely flounder hopelessly if he tries to do sixth-grade work. He will probably never go beyond the eighth grade and can hardly be expected to do satisfactory work as compared with average pupils; yet he can be helped through special instruction in reading, arithmetic, and other subjects, by the use of material at the third-grade level in difficulty but suitable in content for a twelve-year-old. The necessary preliminary information for the proper adjustment of a program to individual differences in ability and achievement is provided most quickly and efficiently by standardized tests.

The question of acceleration is related to that of non-promotion. If it is undesirable to hold back slow pupils, the same argument applies in the case of bright ones. When a very able pupil is kept *at grade* for his age we are in effect not promoting him just as surely as when we make a dull pupil repeat a grade. Pressey has made a thorough review of the substantial evidence on this point.[2] The evidence shows clearly that students who are accelerated by extra promotions in school, or who are permitted to finish college in less than the usual time, seem to do well in their studies and are well adjusted socially; they seem not to suffer in health and not to be handicapped otherwise as a result of their acceleration. Nevertheless, many school authorities are reluctant to adopt such practices. Parents also often wish their children to remain with "their group," and are fearful of what acceleration might do to their children's social adjustment. It is unfortunate that high school and college students who are both mentally and physically advanced for their age are generally required to sit through all the regular lessons and classes when they could proceed much faster in the environment of a more advanced grade or class level. Not only would acceleration save much valuable time, but it would also help to avoid the boredom and the bad study habits which may be developed by a bright pupil who is required to wait while the slowest in the group catches up.

When achievement tests and mental tests reveal that a pupil is accelerated in achievement and mental development, and if he has no physical or social handicaps, he should be carefully considered for extra promotions

[1] Henry J. Otto, "Pupil Failure as an Administrative Device in Elementary Education," *Elementary School Journal*, 34:576–89, April, 1934; see also, John I. Goodlad, "To Promote or Not to Promote," *Childhood Education*, 30:212–215 January, 1954.

[2] S. L. Pressey, *Educational Acceleration: Appraisals and Basic Problems*, Bureau of Educational Research Monograph No. 31 (Columbus, Ohio: Ohio State University, 1949).

and adjustment of work to his level. Moreover, he should be encouraged to progress through school and college as rapidly as he can, and at every level the tasks presented him should be in keeping with his abilities and should require appropriately high standards of work. Able students are needed in the world of today, perhaps more than ever before. To hold them back on the basis of fears which seem quite unsubstantiated by the available evidence is an injustice to them and to society.

HOMOGENEOUS GROUPING

Various methods of grouping pupils according to ability are widely practiced, particularly in the elementary grades. The grouping may be done informally and more or less subjectively, as when a teacher of second grade forms her thirty pupils into reading groups of ten to fifteen on the basis of reading ability. Or it may be done formally, as when a hundred pupils in the fifth grade are divided into three classes according to general mental ability.

This type of classification, by which pupils in the same grade are grouped according to ability, may be thought of as *horizontal,* in contrast with the *vertical* grouping already discussed. Ability classification, or homogeneous grouping in one form or another is common in the elementary schools where pupils read, recite, and do other academic work in groups whose members are usually judged by the teacher to be somewhat alike in ability. However, in the elementary school pupils are not sectioned and separated as high school pupils usually are, and therefore the objection that grouping at the elementary level is undemocratic does not apply, or at least seems less important. There is ample opportunity in the elementary classroom for social intercourse among all pupils in a class, even if they are grouped according to ability in reading, arithmetic, and other academic work.

Grouping has been a somewhat controversial practice. Its opponents have charged that pupils placed in fast groups are likely to become "conceited," while those in the slow group are stigmatized as "dumbbells." They have also held that there is no such thing as a homogeneous group and that when pupils are grouped on the basis of one criterion, such as I.Q., they are still heterogeneous with respect to other, perhaps equally important, criteria, such as achievement. Furthermore, it is said that individual pupils vary widely in different skills or abilities. The profile charts shown on pages 421, 422, and 423 throw some light on this point. It is apparent that, while a given pupil does not perform at exactly the same level on each sub-test of the achievement battery, there is much consistency of performance in many cases. It is also clear that the range of performance on the *Metropolitan* is much smaller in the homogeneous class than in the heterogeneous class.

Recent years have seen a greatly increased emphasis on quality in education and greatly increased interest in providing stimulating and challenging opportunities for the superior pupil. It is felt that we have permitted the most able pupils to go along at "half speed" as it were, with a resultant loss of interest and accomplishment. Advocates of homogeneous grouping believe that providing a more rewarding and challenging education for gifted pupils can be done more easily and successfully if such pupils are grouped or sectioned so that they can have an enriched program and can also proceed at an accelerated pace. It is also maintained that homogeneous sections for slow learners are advantageous for them in that the instruction can proceed at a pace more suited to their abilities. Furthermore, it is felt that the slower learners in a class of similar capacity and interests avoid the discouragement and failure that often are their lot when they are instructed in classes with pupils who are much more able academically.

A great deal of research has been done on the question of homogeneous grouping. One of the earliest reports[3] dealt largely with the question of reactions to the practice. The conclusion on this point was that where such grouping was practiced the majority of parents, pupils, and teachers were happy and satisfied with it. Similar reports seem to indicate that the slow learners, who are quite often the main concern of opponents of the practice, much prefer homogeneous to heterogeneous classes. A study in point was conducted by Drews.[4] This was a carefully designed, controlled experiment involving 432 ninth-grade pupils enrolled in English classes in four junior high schools. The pupils were sectioned into Superior, Average, and Slow groups on the basis of (1) achievement in reading and language, (2) I.Q., (3) school marks, and (4) teacher judgment. The performance of homogeneous classes was compared with that of equivalent heterogeneous classes. Each of the latter classes included the full range of abilities represented in the three levels of homogeneous groups.

On a questionnaire of attitudes toward homogeneous and heterogeneous classes, 83 per cent of the slow students in homogeneous classes gave positive reactions toward homogeneous classes as against 60 per cent positive

[3] *The Grouping of Pupils,* Thirty-Fifth Yearbook of the National Society for the Study of Education, Part I (Chicago: The Society [distributed by the University of Chicago Press], 1936), pp. 302–303.

[4] Elizabeth M. Drews, "The Effectiveness of Homogeneous and Heterogeneous Ability Grouping in 9th Grade English Classes with Slow, Average, and Superior Students Including the Investigation of Attitudes, Self-Concept, and Critical Thinking" (Unpublished manuscript, College of Education, Michigan State University, East Lansing, Michigan, 1961).

reactions toward heterogeneous classes by slow students in such classes. On the same questionnaire superior students in homogeneous classes gave 73 per cent positive reactions toward such classes as against 33 per cent positive reactions of superior students in heterogeneous classes toward such classes.

A summary of research studies of homogeneous grouping[5] indicates that the results, taken altogether, are inconclusive. The findings in about half the studies are favorable to the practice and an equal number are unfavorable. In any case, wherever homogeneous grouping is used several factors have a most important bearing on the success of the practice. First, it must be recognized that what teachers do in adapting content and method to different ability groups largely determines how effective the grouping will be in terms of increased learning and attainment of goals. To form different groups according to ability without making modifications in the methods and materials used with those groups is not likely to result in any advantage.

Second, in any scheme of grouping there should be provision for the shifting and adjustment of individual pupils. No pupil should feel that he is finally and permanently attached to a particular group. The able pupil must demonstrate his ability to stay in a faster group, while the slow pupil should always be made to feel that he can change his status by doing better work. Such flexibility, though perhaps difficult from the administrative standpoint, would go far toward meeting one of the most frequently voiced objections to ability grouping, namely, that it is not democratic. Moreover, it would provide excellent motivation for pupils at all levels and in every group.

Third, as the same profiles have clearly shown, a pupil's achievement in different academic areas is often uneven. Consequently, it may be appropriate to have him in a fast section in one subject, an average section in another, and perhaps even in a slow section in a third. For example, the pupil whose profile is shown in Figure 20 is above the grade norm in Paragraph Meaning and Science, at the grade norm in Social Studies and Study Skills, and far below in Language. If ability grouping were practiced he would presumably be in fast, average, and slow sections in these respective areas. Any system of grouping to be effective should take such differences into account in placement of pupils.

It seems reasonable to assume that such flexibility would help to eliminate or at least reduce any tendency to stigmatize pupils, since the same pupil would probably be in different groups for different subjects or activities.

[5] Ruth B. Ekstrom, *Experimental Studies of Homogeneous Grouping: A Review of the Literature* (Princeton, N.J.: Educational Testing Service, 1961).

▶ LEARNING EXERCISES ◀

1. Distinguish between vertical classification and horizontal classification. What are the common bases or criteria for each?

2. Summarize the arguments *and the evidence,* pro and con, for each of the following: (*a*) classification by grade versus non-graded classification; (*b*) homogeneous versus non-homogeneous (or heterogeneous) grouping.

3. If you were to form three ability sections in ninth-grade general science, how would you proceed? Assume that one hundred pupils have elected the course.

DIAGNOSIS AND REMEDIAL WORK

In contrast to the two areas of usefulness just discussed, the employment of tests for diagnosis is an instructional function rather than an administrative one. The purpose of a diagnostic test is to find the specific weaknesses and strengths of a pupil in a particular area of study or subject matter. In a survey of measurement practices and preferences of high school teachers[6] it was found that diagnostic testing and remedial work are the most frequently mentioned uses of standardized test results. Between 40 and 50 per cent of the teachers using standardized tests reported these as their purposes in giving such tests.

The process of diagnosis in education may be thought of as a progression from broad, general areas to narrower and more specific knowledges or skills. For example, one might begin by giving to a class of seventh-grade pupils a survey battery, including tests of language arts, social studies, mathematics, and science. After these tests are scored and the results analyzed, it might appear that the class as a whole is up to or above acceptable standards in all areas tested except language arts. Further testing in the language arts might show that vocabulary, reading, and spelling are acceptable, but that there are serious weaknesses in fundamentals of grammar, sentence structure, punctuation, and capitalization. Knowing of these weaknesses, one can then proceed to give diagnostic tests in these areas to determine which fundamentals have been inadequately mastered and are in need of further study and drill. The real diagnosis is done only at this last level of measurement, although all which precedes it is basic to the last step. However, a teacher may begin at this point without going through the earlier steps. That is, he may give his pupils a diagnostic test at any time to discover strengths and weaknesses in pupil learning so that

[6] Victor H. Noll and Walter N. Durost, *Measurement Practices and Preferences of High School Teachers,* Test Service Notebook No. 8 (New York: Harcourt, Brace & World Inc., n.d.).

he may review and improve points not mastered through previous teaching and study.

A truly diagnostic test should be planned and constructed with this function in mind. Many achievement tests may be used for diagnosis, but much time and energy are saved and a more systematic analysis is possible when a test is designed and built with diagnosis in mind, if that is to be its function. There are several important steps to be followed in the diagnostic testing procedure.

First, *there should be a careful analysis of the rules, principles, knowledges, or skills which the test is intended to measure.* In the example cited above, this would mean analysis of the rules or principles of good usage with respect to grammar, sentence structure, punctuation, and capitalization in English. The Pressey *Diagnostic Tests in English Composition*[7] are good examples of tests based on this kind of analysis. The test in each of the four areas covers the basic rules in that area. For example, the punctuation test covers such rules as, "Every declarative sentence should be followed by a period." The capitalization test covers such rules as, "Begin every proper name with a capital letter," and similarly appropriate rules are covered in the tests of grammar and of sentence structure.

Second, *a good diagnostic test is planned and constructed so that every rule or principle is adequately and equally tested by objective items.* For example, in the Pressey test on capitalization each of seven basic rules is covered by four objective test items. By this method, no point of importance is slighted or over-emphasized, and the user of the test can be sure of reasonably adequate and systematic coverage.

Third, *the test items are generally arranged in groups to facilitate the analysis and diagnosis.* That is, if there are four items on each rule, those dealing with the same rule will be placed together rather than scattered throughout the entire test. This makes it simpler, in analyzing the results, to determine specific areas of strength and weakness.

In addition to the above-mentioned principles, diagnostic tests are usually accompanied by a chart similar to the one reproduced in Figure 23. This permits the diagnosis of strengths and weaknesses of the class or group as a whole, as well as of individuals.

The diagnostic chart for Miss Jones' seventh-grade class reveals the standing of individuals and of the class. Reading across the page, it is possible to determine individual needs in capitalization. Jane Allen, for example, misses only five items out of twenty-eight, and these deal with Rules 4, 5, 6, and 1, respectively. On the other hand, Mary Brady ap-

[7] S. L. Pressey, *et al. Diagnostic Tests in English Composition* (Indianapolis: The Bobbs-Merrill Company, Inc., 1924).

Reproduced by permission of the publishers, The Bobbs-Merrill Company, Inc.

Grade 7th School Roosevelt City Smithport State Pa. Date 11/15/55 Examiner Miss James

Form of Test 1 (1, 2, 3 or 4)

Capitalization Test

Pupil's Name	Sentence → columns 1–28	Total
1 Allen, Jane		23
2 Bedford, Jim		14
3 Brady, Mary		8
4 Clark, Mary Jane		15
5 Cole, Henry		12
6 Drake, Alice		13
7 Ferguson, Charles		10
8 Grost, Marjorie		17
9 Gray, Bob		9
10 Holan, Elmer		10
11 Holt, John		12
12 James, Albert		12
13 Jones, Kenneth		10
14 Lane, Susan		13
15 Miller, Paul		21
16 Nelson, Fran		9
17 Reed, Henry		11
18 Ross, Bill		11
19 Scott, Bill		11
20 Watson, Ann		13
21 White, Frank		15

Total right—each sentence →: 17 15 16 13 | 6 10 7 6 | 9 8 7 8 | 5 6 7 8 | 5 10 9 11 | 10 4 7 8 | 5 14 14 13 18

Rule illustrated (Forms 1 and 3): Rule 2 | Rule 3 | Rule 4 | Rule 5 | Rule 7 | Rule 5 | Rule 7 | Rule 1 | Rule 1

Rule illustrated (Forms 2 and 4): Rule 6 | Rule 2 | Rule 4 | Rule 5 | Rule 4 | Rule 7 | Rule 3 | Rule 6 | Rule 7

Compare with rules in column to left. Notice what rules are most frequently violated. Teach each child what he does not know.

CAPITALIZATION TEST RULES COVERED BY TEST

1. Capitalize the first word of every sentence. Capitalize also the first word of every line of poetry, and the first word of a direct quotation. However, if the quotation is indirect do not use the capital.

2. Capitalize the names of persons, with their titles; however, do not capitalize titles when they are not part of a name.

3. Capitalize the names of countries, states, cities, streets, buildings, of mountains, rivers, oceans, or any word designating a particular location or part of the world; however, do not capitalize the points of the compass, or such terms as 'street, river, ocean,' when not part of a name.

4. Capitalize the names of business firms, schools, societies, or other organizations; however, do not capitalize such words as company, school, society, when not part of a name.

5. Capitalize words derived from the names of countries, places, or organizations or persons.

6. Capitalize the days of the week, the months of the year, and holidays; however, do not capitalize the seasons.

7. Capitalize the first word, and all other important words, in titles (and sub-titles and headings) of themes, magazine articles, poems, books, of laws or governmental documents, and the trade names of commercial products.

FIGURE 23 •

Analysis Chart Showing the Results of a Seventh-Grade Class on the Pressey Diagnostic Test in Capitalization

Norms (November testing)

Grade	Median Forms 1 & 2	Median Forms 3 & 4
7	16.8	18.0
8	20.6	19.7
9	21.5	20.5
10	22.8	21.3
11	23.3	22.1
12	23.8	22.5
College	24.0	23.0

Class Record

Score	No. of Pupils
28	
27	
26	
25	
24	
23	1
22	
21	1
20	
19	
18	
17	1
16	
15	1 1
14	1
13	1 1 1
12	1 1 1
11	1 1 1
10	1 1 1
9	1 1
8	1
7	
6	
5	
4	
3	
2	2
1	
0	
Total	21
Median	12

pears to be very weak on capitalization, for she has answered correctly only eight out of twenty-eight and has missed most of the items relating to every rule except No. 2.

Reading the chart vertically, by groups of items relating to each rule, we see that the class as a whole is strong on Rules 2, 7, and 1, and is comparatively weak on Rules 3, 4, 5, and 6 — especially the latter two. This gives Miss Jones information which will be useful in planning remedial work and drill for the whole class.

At the side of the chart the individual scores are tabulated and the median is determined. By comparison with seventh-grade norms it is evident that this class is quite deficient in knowledge and understanding of the rules of capitalization and will need thorough review and practice on fundamentals. Sometime later, another form of the test may be given to measure improvement. Since there are four forms of the test, the teacher may test and teach, test and teach, several times without giving the same test twice.

Equivalent forms are very advantageous for diagnostic tests, perhaps even more than for standardized tests in general. The most widely accepted method for the use of diagnostic tests calls for testing, remedial instruction, retesting, further remedial instruction, etc., until adequate mastery is attained. For this process it is highly desirable to have available several equivalent forms of each test so that the second and subsequent testings may be done with different forms covering the same objectives. This avoids the repeated use of exactly the same questions and thus greatly reduces or practically eliminates gain in scores due to familiarity with the questions.

Another example of a truly diagnostic test is the *Doren Diagnostic Reading Test,*[8] designed for use at the end of the second grade or beginning of the third grade. It is based on the theory that reading difficulty occurs mainly because of deficiency in skills of word recognition. Unless a child possesses these skills to an acceptable degree he will not be able to develop the higher level skills of understanding or comprehension necessary to acquire information, apply it as in study, or read for enjoyment.

The test is based on the analysis of word recognition skills as found in five basic reading programs. The skills arrived at through the analysis are the following:

1. Letter Recognition
2. Beginning Sounds

[8] Margaret Doren, *Doren Diagnostic Reading Test of Word Recognition Skills* (Minneapolis: American Guidance Service, Inc., 1956).

3. Whole Word Recognition
4. Words Within Words
5. Speech Consonants
6. Ending Sounds
7. Blending
8. Rhyming
9. Vowels
10. Sight Words
11. Discriminate Guessing (ability to supply missing words
    from a clue given by other words in content).

Each of the listed skills is measured by a separate part of the test, thus enabling the teacher to identify for each pupil his specific weaknesses in skills of word recognition. The test is designed to be given to pupils in groups, thereby saving much time over what would be required for individual diagnosis. It may, of course, be given to individual children. The total time required is three hours.

The test has been carefully standardized. Correlations with scores on a reading achievement test range from .77 in Grade 1 to .92 in Grade 4. Mean scores show substantial growth in word recognition skills in Grades 1 and 2 with smaller increments, as might be expected, in Grades 3 and 4. Reliabilities of the eleven sub-tests range from .53 to .83 with most in the .70's and .80's. As sub-test reliabilities go, these are good.

The manual is very complete. It includes a detailed account of the rationale and development of the test, instructions for administering and scoring, and technical data. In addition, there are many practical suggestions for remedial activities in each skill tested and a class analysis chart similar to the one shown in Figure 23 for the Pressey test.

It should be recognized that a diagnostic test does not necessarily reveal the *causes* of weaknesses. A diagnostic test in arithmetic may reveal certain specific deficiencies, let us say, in the multiplication of two-place numbers by two-place numbers, as 87×34. These weaknesses may be the result of a lack of correct knowledge of multiplication tables, or of carrying, or of adding, or of some other process. But knowing that a pupil does not perform one or the other of these operations correctly is no guarantee that remedial work and drill on the specific processes will produce the desired improvement. Deficiencies in learning may be due to various causes, such as defective hearing or vision, poor home conditions, unsatisfactory relations with classmates or teacher, lack of ability, and so on. In all diagnostic and remedial work it is essential to attempt to identify the basic causes of deficiencies and to work on those. Otherwise, remediation is likely to be a waste of time and energy.

▶ LEARNING EXERCISES ◀

4. How does a diagnostic test differ from a conventional achievement test? Answer by comparing a standardized achievement test, perhaps in fundamentals of English, with one like the *Pressey*.

5. If you were selecting a test for diagnostic purposes in the fundamentals of multiplication in arithmetic, what would you look for?

6. Why are there more diagnostic tests available for the elementary school than for the high school or college?

COUNSELING AND GUIDANCE

Broadly stated, the function of the counselor or guidance worker is to help pupils achieve satisfactory and satisfying solutions to their problems. Darley,[9] as a result of a survey of high school seniors in a large city, classified these problems in a descending order of frequency, as follows: (1) vocational, (2) educational, (3) social or personal, (4) financial, (5) family adjustment, and (6) health. The emphasis might be different at lower grade levels or in different communities, but the categories seem to encompass the major areas of concern to adolescents, as well as to people in general.

The most common problems under these respective categories were: (1) discrepancy between vocational goal and abilities, (2) discrepancy between educational goal and abilities, (3) feelings of inferiority, (4) too much outside work, and inadequate finances, (5) family conflicts over educational and vocational plans, desire for independence, personality and age differences, and (6) poor health. Under educational problems (2) should probably be added those related to the choice of subjects (such problems, for example, as whether to take algebra or homemaking), and those related to the choice of a curriculum or course of study.

Among the "tools" available to, and used by, the counselor, tests are central in importance. This is recognized in the National Defense Education Act of 1958, which provides financial support for testing in programs of guidance and counseling. The extensive use and the value of tests in counseling and guidance is also attested by the requirement of courses in tests and measurements in training programs for counselors and by the

[9] John G. Darley, *Testing and Counseling in the High School Guidance Program* (Chicago: Science Research Associates, Inc., 1943), pp. 140–41.

publication of books dealing specifically with the use of tests in the counseling process.[10]

It is difficult to imagine how a guidance program could function without the use of measures of intelligence, achievement, aptitudes, interests and personality. Where discrepancies exist between goals and abilities, intelligence test results tactfully and confidentially discussed with the pupil may help to bring about a readjustment of plans more closely in line with his talents. Marks and test scores representing the student's achievement in school work will often bring a student to face realities and help him decide that perhaps he does not want to be an electrical engineer after all, in view of the advanced mathematics and physics required. Together with the results of measures of general academic ability, such data, when discussed sympathetically with the pupil, and his parents, have great value in bringing about an acceptance of educational and vocational goals that are more consistent with abilities. Such counseling procedures often avoid frustration and unhappiness for those most concerned.

When a pupil seeks guidance in educational or vocational matters, tests of aptitudes and interests provide useful tools. The nature of such instruments has already been discussed in Chapter 11, and the applications of these instruments in guidance and counseling are obvious, particularly with reference to educational and vocational decisions.

An aptitude test is a useful tool in counseling if the results are properly understood and used. A high score on a test of mechanical aptitude does not guarantee success in an occupation requiring mechanical ability any more than a good score on a test of musical aptitude guarantees that the person who made the score will become a great musician. Many other factors besides aptitude enter into success; interest, effort, persistence, and opportunity all contribute. Yet the counselor can encourage the person making a high score on an aptitude test by saying that he seems to have the talent if he will develop it, and can help him to determine whether or not he has the other qualities needed for success in the field in question.

On the other hand, the counselor can speak with more assurance in the case of a low score on a test. It is safe and pertinent, in such instances, to point out to the individual that statistics show that perhaps only one person in ten with his score is successful in this particular vocation. The choice of a life work should certainly not be based on the results of a single aptitude test, yet the information this provides may be one of the

[10] See, for example, Leo Goldman, *Using Tests in Counseling* (New York: Appleton-Century-Crofts, Inc., 1961); see also, Ralph F. Berdie, *et al., Testing in Guidance and Counseling.* (New York: McGraw-Hill Book Co., Inc., 1963).

deciding factors when all other data concerning the particular occupation and person do not seem to point to a clear-cut decision.

The interest inventory provides a useful supplement to other kinds of tests. It should be emphasized again, perhaps even more strongly than in the case of aptitude tests, that a particular pattern of interests or preferences is not in any sense a guarantee of success in a given field. All one can say is that the interest score or pattern of the individual tested resembles or does not resemble that of successful persons in a particular occupation or field of work.

Interest tests are widely used, especially at the senior high school and junior college level. The results of such tests, when carefully studied and discussed with the counselor, have considerable usefulness, particularly in giving the student more insight into his own potentialities and causing him to think more carefully about his own decisions and choices. Used in conjunction with the results of other tests, and information about home background, financial status, scholastic record, and health, they help to round out the picture of the individual.

Student problems frequently occur also in the areas of adjustment and personality. The survey reported by Darley[11] revealed that feelings of inferiority, lack of confidence, and personality clashes in the home were among the most common problems of high school seniors. The use of personality measures will sometimes reveal the existence of such problems when interviews and other means have failed to bring them to light.

Personality measures of various types may be used with groups to identify more or less serious cases of maladjustment. In every hundred pupils there will be, on the average, from two to five who need help and who should be referred to a clinic or to someone trained to deal with such cases. Tests of this nature can also be used by counselors to shed additional light on the cases of pupils who come for advice and help, either on personal problems or on educational or vocational problems. With the pupil who is having difficulties in school or at home, a personality test often gives a helpful insight into the situation. The test may be supplemented by interviews, anecdotal records, ratings, and other information, all of which will usually provide a basis for understanding and help.

Personality tests may be used to help a pupil make the most of his talents, and they may help him get along better with others and attain better adjustment by giving him and the counselor more insight into his emotional and social behavior. In short, these tests help to give the individual a better understanding of himself, and thus expain why he behaves as he does in certain situations.

[11] *Ibid.*

Concerning financial problems and poor health, the counselor will obtain information about problems of this nature through means other than tests. These difficulties, particularly the health problems, usually require expert advice and treatment, and the responsibility of the counselor is mainly to identify such cases and refer them to the proper authorities. There may be many things a counselor can do to help a pupil earn money in after-school hours, or to help the one that is working too many hours outside, but these are not matters in which tests will generally play a significant role. Yet a knowledge of a student's I.Q. may be useful in helping the counselor and the student decide how much work he can take on to earn money without doing an injustice to his school work.

▶ LEARNING EXERCISES ◀

7. What are the major types of problems of adolescents that a counselor is likely to encounter?

8. As a high school counselor, what types of measuring instruments would you expect to find most useful? Give reasons for your choices.

9. Is there a place for counseling and guidance in the elementary grades? If so, what measuring instruments should prove useful?

10. What uses would a counselor have for achievement test results?

MARKING

It was stated early in this book that measurement and evaluation are a part of the job of teaching. Every teacher has the responsibility for making the best judgments he can about his pupils' achievement and development in subject matter, maturity, citizenship, character, and in other areas. These judgments may be expressed in various ways, but marks are the commonest. As our schools and educational programs are constituted, marks are an integral part of the system. Pupils, parents, and administrators expect them. They are the terms in which appraisals of a pupil's accomplishments are communicated. It is therefore only sensible for the teacher to try to do the best possible job of evaluating and marking, to strive constantly to improve the marking system, and to do his best to keep abreast of improvements in marking practices.

That measurement has an important function in marking is self-evident. Teachers regularly use tests and examinations of their own devising as a basis for marking, especially when measuring achievement in subject matter. However, tests of capacity such as the intelligence test are also useful in marking in that they provide a basis for judging whether or not a pupil is working up to capacity. It has been suggested that two marks be given, one expressing actual achievement in terms of A, B, C, D, or E, and the other in terms of S or U, expressing whether the pupil is doing satisfactory or unsatisfactory work in relation to his ability. Thus, one pupil of high intelligence might get a B and a U in algebra, while another less able pupil might receive a C and an S. In at least one community where this has been tried, the system has worked well.[12]

A perennial question in arriving at marks has to do with the propriety of using standardized tests of achievement for this purpose. It may be said at once that the use of such tests as the sole basis for marks is seldom justified, since no standardized test is likely to provide adequate measures of all the outcomes of a course in a particular school or community. Few teachers would be satisfied to base the evaluation of their pupils' accomplishments solely or even substantially on standardized test scores. Nevertheless, it is true that such tests may be useful in helping to arrive at a semester's or a year's mark in a given course. That is, when a standardized test is judged by the teacher to be an adequate measure of one or more of the locally determined goals of instruction, there would seem to be no valid reason for not using it, together with other measures, for marking purposes. A standardized test can supplement or contribute in a useful way to evaluation based on the teacher's own measurement procedures. A goal of every teacher should be the best possible evaluaton of each pupil's accomplishments. It is only good sense to make use of every practical device that helps achieve this objective. It may even be that a carefully constructed standardized test will at times provide a better measure of certain outcomes of instruction than the average teacher can make for himself, as, for example, in the case of skills tests in elementary grades. The school assumes some responsibility for the all-around development of each pupil to the extent of his capacity and desire to achieve. This includes not only achievement in subject matter, but also development of character and personality, physical development and health, maturity in selecting and planning for his future vocation, choosing a life partner, and so on. In any of these areas the teacher may be called upon to express some judgment or evaluation of the pupil's status and development. In every one measurement has something to contribute. Personality measures, in-

---

[12] Irvin A. Keller, "A More Comprehensive and Significant Marking System," *Bulletin of the National Association of Secondary School Principals,* 36:70–78, January, 1952.

terest inventories, measures of physical development, and records of health and physical examinations are all useful in making evaluations, whether they are expressed in the form of a mark or in some other manner. Measurement can and should enter into every aspect of the process of evaluating pupil accomplishment and growth.

The problem of what proportion of various marks to give — how many A's, B's, C's, etc. — is one that is often vexing to teachers. The conscientious instructor tries to do justice to all his pupils and at the same time attempts to conform with good principles of marking. There is no simple method to recommend that will satisfy both purposes. Recommendations on this point may be based on the concept of the normal curve. In any group or class, unless it is a very small one numbering less than twenty, abilities and achievement are likely to be distributed in a fashion approximating the normal distribution. If this assumption is appropriate, then the distribution of marks should approximate the proportions of the normal curve, which means that the largest proportion should be average, which is usually C. Smaller proportions will be somewhat above and below the average, and these would be marked B and D, respectively. Approximately equal and quite small percentages would be found at the upper and lower extremes, and these would receive marks of A and E or F, as the case might be.

These principles can be embodied in a number of different systems or proportions, one of the most widely used being based on the standard deviation, which is illustrated in Figure 24.

It can be seen that the middle group, or C, extends one half standard deviation on either side of the mean, which area under the normal curve includes approximately 38 per cent of the total. One additional standard deviation beyond these limits on either side will include another 24 per cent in each case; and another standard deviation beyond the $+1.5\ \sigma$ and

FIGURE 24 • Distribution of Marks Based on Standard Deviation

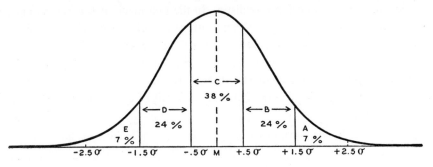

$-1.5\ \sigma$, extending to $+2.5\ \sigma$ and $-2.5\ \sigma$, will include approximately 7 per cent more. The total $38 + 24 + 24 + 7 + 7 = 100$.[13]

Although the results of measurements of most classes will not be distributed in exactly these theoretical proportions, they will quite generally approximate them if (1) the classes are not highly selected, and (2) the measures used are adequate for all levels of ability represented in the group. No teacher will want to force his distribution of marks into these theoretical proportions, particularly if he has reason to believe that the nature of the group or the measuring instruments used do not justify it. Nevertheless, the concept of a normal distribution as applied here can be a very useful guide to a teacher in giving marks and can help him to avoid giving marks that are clearly out of line with sound principles.

What has been said so far and the facts that are known about the distribution of human abilities and achievements provide a basis for some useful generalizations about marking and the use of measurement in marking. A brief statement of these principles is given below. In reading and thinking about them the student is cautioned to remember that no hard and fast rules can be laid down for every teacher to follow in giving marks. Each teacher will have to use his own best judgment in his own situation, since marking, generally speaking, is a responsibility that cannot be shared with anyone else. The one unequivocal principle, if there is such, is that justice be done to *every pupil* insofar as possible, and that none be favored above any other.

1. *It is generally agreed that marks should be assigned on a comparative basis.* That is, the best pupils should receive the highest marks, the next best, B's, etc. In most school situations this practice is certainly preferable to setting some arbitrary and perhaps unrealistic standard and failing those pupils who do not attain it.

2. *Practice now generally favors the use of letter marks rather than percentages.* Letter marks have several advantages: they are easier to use, easier to interpret, and more realistic. In the first place, it is easier to mark a group with a five-point scale than with one having a hundred divisions. Letter marks are easier to understand for the same reason. It may be said with confidence that not many people can make the fine distinctions of judgment that percentage marks imply. It has been demonstrated that teachers can discriminate among five or six levels of quality or achievement, but not one hundred!

[13] Theoretically, the curve touches the baseline only at infinity, so that within $2\frac{1}{2}$ standard deviations above and below the mean there will be only 98.76 per cent of the total area under the curve. For all practical purposes, we may assume that 100 per cent of the cases or scores will fall between these limits.

3. *Marks should be based as much as possible on objective measurements.* Enough has been said in earlier discussions to show the unreliability of teachers' judgments of essay examinations. It may be assumed that what was demonstrated in those experiments applies with equal force to other subjective judgments or processes. It may not be possible to find or construct objective measures of all desirable outcomes, but the aim should be to move constantly in this direction and to increase the objectivity of our measurements as much as possible.

4. *As far as possible, marks should express accomplishment of specific goals rather than the results of global or omnibus appraisal.* A marking system which does not provide for some precise differentiation as, for example, between knowledge and skills, is less informative than one which does. Also, one should not atttempt to combine in one mark achievement in subject matter and such other traits as courtesy, punctuality, or effort. The measurement of these traits is important, but if the pupil is given a B in arithmetic the *mark should denote his accomplishment in that subject.* If desired, he may be given credit for courtesy, effort, and other important matters, but these should be expressed in *separate marks.* Otherwise, two pupils may receive B's in arithmetic, one of the marks representing achievement of A and effort of C, the other representing an achievement of C and effort of A. To give them the same mark of B is an injustice to both pupils as well as to their next teacher, their parents, and any others who have no way of knowing what the marks really represent.

This principle applies also to the appraisal of growth or improvement. Such outcomes should not be combined in one mark with status or level of accomplishment. To illustrate, let us assume that marks are being given to two girls taking typewriting. X starts at ten words per minute and progresses by the end of the year to forty words per minute. Y starts at thirty words per minute and goes to fifty words per minute. X made a gain of thirty words while Y gained only twenty. Yet Y is a more efficient typist than X. Would it be fair to give X a better mark than Y, because she had made a numerically greater gain? It would not seem so. Certainly anyone seeking to employ a typist would be misled if both girls received even the same mark. Here, as in cases already cited, it would be most accurate and fair to use two marks, one for status and another for improvement. Then the picture might be as follows:

PUPIL	STATUS	IMPROVEMENT
X	C	B
Y	B	C

Knowing these facts, the prospective employer or any other person concerned would be able to make an intelligent choice, assuming, of course, that other aspects of the two cases are equal.

In substance, this principle states that marks should mean and stand for what they are intended to mean and stand for. If a mark is given in English it should represent accomplishment in English and, if possible, should be differentiated to designate accomplishment in composition, American literature, English literature, or some other specific course or part of a course. If evaluations of other important qualities such as effort, citizenship, personal traits, and the like are desired, these should be reported separately with adequate labels so that they will not be confused or misunderstood. The use of objective measurements should contribute to the attainment of this principle in practice.

5. *Finally, better marking can be attained by using a wide variety of measures.* The more measures of a pupil's achievement that are employed and the more varied in approach and design they are, the better the sampling of his behavior is likely to be. Even if the tests are quite similar in nature the combined results of several of them should give a more accurate appraisal than any one of them alone. This is simply an application of the principle of sampling: the more samples taken the more accurate the measurement will be, always providing, of course, that there is no consistent bias operating. Furthermore, by use of a variety of measuring instruments we are likely to obtain a wider sampling than we otherwise would. In measuring the results of instruction in civics, for example, a teacher may find it desirable to use not only tests, but also rating scales, anecdotal records, and systematic observations of behavior — all of these contributing to the appraisal of achievement in civics.

An example showing assignment of marks to a college class in tests and measurements will serve to illustrate the principles just enumerated.

There were thirty-six students enrolled in the class, most of whom were juniors and seniors preparing to teach in elementary or secondary schools. The assignments and tests included a set of simple statistical problems; a blueprint or two-way chart showing content and objectives to be measured by an objective test; the test itself, constructed by the student; an objective mid-term test of seventy-five items on the first half of the course; and an objective final examination of seventy-five items covering the second half. The assignments were marked by the instructor personally, either in points (in the case of the statistical problems) or in letter grades. The letter grades were converted to points on the basis of $A = 50$, $B = 40$, etc. The mid-term and final were scored on the basis of number right. Thus, in the end, each student's marks or accomplishment were expressed in points. These points were added to obtain a total for each student.[14] The totals were then arranged in a frequency distribution and assigned marks as shown in Table IX.

A number of points are at once apparent. First, the distribution is not "normal" in the sense of producing, if it were graphed, the bell-shaped curve. It is, in fact, bi-modal because of the fact that some students did additional work on some assignments to obtain graduate credit. Second, the assignments and tests did produce a spread or range. Some students

TABLE IX • Distribution of Total Points and Marks Earned by Thirty-Six Students in a Course in Educational Measurement

Totals		f*	Marks
200–204	///	3	
195–199	//	2	5 A's = 14%
190–194	//	2	
185–189	///	3	
180–184	//	2	12 B's = 33%
175–179	⧸⧸⧸⧸	5	
170–174	//	2	
165–169	///	3	
160–164	/	1	14 C's = 39%
155–159	⧸⧸⧸⧸	5	
150–154	///	3	
145–149		0	
140–144	/	1	
135–139	/	1	3 D's = 8%
130–134	/	1	
125–129		0	
120–124		0	
115–119	/	1	
110–114		0	2 F's = 6%
105–109		0	
100–104		0	
95–99		0	
90–94	/	1	
N = 36			

* Frequency.

[14] The writer has found by experience and empirical trial that considerations of variability in the separate point scores, where the number of possible points on each assignment or test is approximately the same, do not affect the comparative standing of students sufficiently to justify a system of differential weighting.

did twice as well, in terms of total points earned, as others. Thus there is a clear basis for differentiation. Third, it is obvious that the proportions of the different marks assigned are not in accord with any theoretical distribution. There are more than twice as many A's as F's and four times as many B's as D's. Here, the facts that the course is an upper-level elective for prospective teachers and one enrolling graduate students as well as undergraduates have a bearing. This is clearly shown by the top-heavy nature of the distribution and is recognized in the proportions of the various marks given.

It should also be noted that the "breaks" between different marks are placed, insofar as possible, at points where there are gaps in the distribution. This is clearly the case between C and D and between D and F.

It must be admitted that no system of assigning marks is entirely objective. Even when the teacher adopts some arbitrary system such as 7 per cent A's, 24 per cent B's, 38 per cent C's, etc. he is making a decision based on his judgment or belief that that system is the right one. In the example above, the chief element of subjectivity comes at the choices of division points between marks. In this case, other factors as mentioned above also introduce elements of subjective judgment. Nevertheless, a review of the process illustrated will show that it adheres to and applies each of the principles of good marking enumerated earlier. In larger classes, at lower levels with less selected and more heterogeneous students and in required courses, it is possible by such a system of appraisal and marking to come much closer to theoretical proportions of marks based on the concept of a normal distribution. However, it must always be kept in mind that the fundamental purpose of marking is not to follow some theory but to communicate as accurate, unbiased, and true appraisal of a pupil's achievement as possible.

▶ LEARNING EXERCISES ◀

11. State your viewpoint on the place of marking in the schools. How would measurements enter into it?

12. Name some situations in which the selection of persons completing training on the basis of improvement alone, without reference to level of skill attained, would be dangerous, e.g., airplane pilots. Name some in which the amount and nature of improvement would be more important than level of proficiency.

13. The following forty-nine scores on a general science test are taken from Appendix A: 71, 68, 67, 61, 60, 58, 58, 55, 54, 52, 50, 49, 47, 47, 46, 45, 44, 44, 44, 43, 43, 43, 42, 41, 41, 40, 40, 39, 38, 38, 38, 37, 36, 36, 36, 33, 33, 32,

28, 27, 25, 24, 22, 21, 18, 15, 13, 8, 3. Assign a mark to each score by the method shown in this chapter. What proportion of A, B, C, D and E does this yield? How closely does this conform to theoretical proportions? Explain the reasons for any divergencies.

MOTIVATION

It is generally assumed that the prospect of taking a test motivates pupils to study. There is no doubt that most people make some preparation, if they can, when faced with the prospect of taking a final examination in a course. There are other aspects of the problem of motivation, however. For example, there is the question of whether pupils do better on a final examination if they have had occasional tests during the term or semester than they would without having had such periodic tests. The question is complicated by various factors such as the kinds of periodic tests used in relation to the kind of final examination given, whether students are simply told their scores on the tests or are permitted to go over them afterwards, and whether the tests are announced in advance or are given without warning.

The question of motivation is not a simple one, and it is likely that many teachers and others assume the motivational value of tests without giving much thought to the various problems involved. It is a generally accepted principle of psychology that the practice of a skill with a knowledge of results — that is, of errors, successes, and over-all improvement — produces much more progress than practice wherein such information is withheld from the learner. Indeed, there is evidence that the practice of a simple skill such as drawing a straight line just two inches long without knowledge of the accuracy of the preceding efforts or trials does not bring about any improvement in accuracy. In other words, practice under such conditions — far from making perfect — does not even result in slight improvement. It is a widely accepted fact that only when the learner knows his errors and knows when he performs well does practice bring about noticeable improvement.

There is considerable experimental evidence on the effect of occasional testing on achievement as measured by success on final examinations. In most such experiments two groups, equal in ability and previous preparation, are formed. Both are taught by the same teacher using the same materials and methods. Both take the same final examination. The only difference is that one group, which may be called the experimental group, is given tests at intervals throughout the semester or term while the control group is not. Any difference in achievement as measured by the final examination can then be ascribed to the single variable of periodic tests.

The results of these experiments indicate on the whole that achievement on final examinations is not appreciably affected by the use of periodic or occasional written tests.[15]

Although many experiments have been conducted along the lines just indicated, there seem to be few reports of studies where the effects of regular testing on problem assignments, as in the teaching of arithmetic, have been investigated. One study of this nature[16] conducted with pupils in fourth-grade arithmetic provides some light on this question. Two groups of pupils in fifty-six different classes were used as subjects. A total of 358 were used as the experimental group, matched with 358 used as controls. The instruction of both was the same except that the experimental group was encouraged to compare their achievement on drill units with a set of standards, while the control group was not given access to such standards. On the final test the experimental group made an average score substantially higher than that of the control group. These findings are in agreement with what would seem like a reasonable expectation. When pupils can go over their test papers and find out *what they did wrong and why,* it would appear safe to assume that many of them, if not all, would not make the same mistakes again.

Teachers will probably go on using tests, particularly those of their own devising, at least partly to stimulate pupils to greater achievement, in the belief that the tests function in that way regardless of the findings of experimental studies. In this connection, it must always be remembered that situations and circumstances differ from one teacher and class to another, and that the use of tests for motivational purposes will depend on the individual teacher's judgment and experience of what is effective for him and his students.

The use of tests for motivation is confined largely and quite naturally to achievement tests. There is little that an individual can or should do beforehand in trying to improve his score on tests of intelligence, aptitude, interests, or personality. On those, we are interested in motivating the person tested to put forth his maximum effort at the time of testing, and we are interested also in eliminating any coaching, study, or previous knowledge of the test which might give a pupil an unfair advantage and which might result in an inaccurate and misleading measurement of that pupil's ability. Achievement tests have as their basic purpose the measurement of the results of teaching, and anything that can be done legitimately

[15] Victor H. Noll, "The Effect of Written Tests upon Achievement in College Classes: An Experiment and a Summary of Evidence," *Journal of Educational Research,* 32:345–58, January, 1939.

[16] Isidoro Panlasigui and F. B. Knight, "The Effect of Awareness of Success or Failure," in the *Twenty-Ninth Yearbook of the National Society for the Study of Education* (Chicago: The Society [distributed by the University of Chicago Press], 1930), Chap. XI, pp. 611–19.

to improve such learning is desirable. Therefore, if periodic testing serves to stimulate interest and motivate the pupil to greater effort and accomplishment, there is justification for the use of tests for that purpose.

▶ LEARNING EXERCISES ◀

14. Would you expect the effect of tests announced in advance to be the same as that of unannounced tests? Give reasons for your answer.

15. Should a teacher go over standardized tests of achievement, after they have been scored, with pupils in order to discuss questions missed? If so, under what circumstances?

IDENTIFICATION AND STUDY OF EXCEPTIONAL CHILDREN

The majority of pupils in our schools fall within what may be thought of as the normal range. However, in nearly every class or group there are those who are outside this range in some respect. They may be exceptionally bright or dull; they may have more or fewer than the usual number of adjustment problems, or their problems may be unusually severe or mild; some may be exceptional in physical qualities — either unusually gifted or perhaps handicapped in some way that interferes with normal participation and success in activities of various sorts. Such children are referred to in educational literature as exceptional children.

For those who are exceptional intellectually, tests have been found over many years to provide the best basis for screening and identification of both gifted and retarded.[17] The procedure that seems most effective is to use group tests of mental ability, along with nominations by teachers as the initial basis for screening. Those thus located are then tested by a school psychologist or psychometrist with an individual examination such as the *Stanford-Binet*. In the study by Pegnato seven different procedures for identifying gifted children were used and evaluated. The procedure found to be most efficient was an initial screening by the use of group intelligence tests followed by individual testing for actual identification of the gifted.

In recent years much attention has been given to the study of creativity and there have been attempts to devise tests of creativity. The best known

[17] See, for example, Carl W. Pegnato and Jack W. Birch, "Locating Gifted Children in Junior High Schools — A Comparison of Methods," *Exceptional Children*, 25:300–304, March, 1959; see also, Marion J. Erickson, "Current Trends and Practices in the Education of the Mentally Retarded," *Educational Administration and Supervision*, 44:297–308, September, 1958.

work in this field is by Guilford.[18] Based on factor analysis, the study identifies an area Guilford calls "divergent thinking," a kind of thinking which is not inhibited by the usual constraints but which goes off in different directions. To measure this type of thinking he has devised tests of word fluency, ideational fluency, associational fluency, expressional fluency; and tests of flexibility and originality. These tests are still in the experimental stage but they represent an interesting attempt to get at some factors or traits which may be associated with creativity in many fields.

Children with obvious physical handicaps such as those who are crippled, those having nervous disorders as a result of brain damage, and the like pose no problem as far as identification is concerned. The exact nature of the disability will be diagnosed and treatment prescribed by medical means. Less obvious but often equally serious handicaps, as far as school learning is concerned, are defects of vision and hearing. These often go unnoticed by teachers and even parents. Children are apt to try to hide such defects and in rare instances may themselves be unaware of them. They can be detected and measured quite accurately, however, by standard tests.

Visual acuity can be checked by devices such as the Snellen Chart; color vision or color blindness can be measured by various tests designed for the purpose; and a thorough measurement of all visual functions can be made by such instruments as the Ortho-Rater, Sight Screener and the Telebinocular.

Hearing acuity or hearing loss can be measured roughly by whisper or watch-tick. The examiner simply determines the greatest distance from which the child can hear a whisper or the tick of a watch. A more accurate and thus more reliable measurement of auditory acuity or defect is made with the audiometer. Such instruments as the pure-tone audiometer measure the hearing loss of an individual by determining how much louder the tone must be made for him to hear it than is required with normal hearing.

For use with physically handicapped children the typical paper-and-pencil test of school achievement must often be modifield in some way. Larger print for the visually handicapped, oral or Braille instructions for blind children, modification of directions for the deaf or hard-of hearing, and various adaptations of test procedures for use with crippled children represent ways in which tests have been modified for use with the handicapped child. Individual tests such as the *Stanford-Binet* have also been modified for use with handicapped children.

Tests may also be very useful in measuring results of special programs. Usually after a handicapped child has been identified and his case diag-

18 Joy P. Guilford, "Creative Ability in the Arts," *Psychological Review,* 64:110–118, 1957.

nosed there is an attempt to do something about his handicap and make adjustments for it. Special schools, special classes, remedial work, therapy of various kinds, and correction of defects by more radical means are used as each case may require. The amount of improvement — educational, psychological, or emotional — may be gauged by the use of suitable tests, either tests designed for the purpose or modifications of existing tests.

In working with exceptional children it is only natural that the handicapped should receive the most attention. A child who is blind, deaf, feeble-minded, or crippled naturally calls forth sympathy and assistance. This is as it should be. However, there is another type of exceptional child, the gifted child, who is often neglected and given even less attention than a normal child. Because a child is gifted it is easy to ignore him or leave him to his own devices while energy and help are directed toward the others. The gifted child can usually be depended upon to "come through" without much help from anyone. Not to give him special attention and encouragement is, however, a short-sighted policy. Our future leaders in science, industry, and public affairs will come largely from the ranks of these gifted children, and it is to society's advantage to help them in every way to make the most of their unusual talents. Not to do so is to risk depriving society of great benefits. There is considerable evidence that schools and society in general are becoming increasingly aware of the importance of giving special attention to gifted children, and that they are now providing rich opportunities for these children to develop their unusual gifts to the fullest.[19]

The development of standardized intelligence tests and, to a lesser degree, standardized achievement tests has made it possible to identify and measure more accurately than ever before these gifted children in our schools. Personality tests have made it possible to study their personal and social characteristics and have demonstrated that, contrary to belief among some persons, children who are gifted intellectually are usually normal and well-adjusted, at least as much so as the general population. The use of tests with gifted children has opened a whole new field of study and research which should result in benefits of considerable importance to society as a whole.

The research on creativity referred to earlier, the National Merit Qualifying Examinations, the Advanced Placement Programs, the testing of high school seniors by selective service, the many scholarships offered by public and private agencies and loan funds for students are some of the ways in

[19] Elise H. Martens, *Curriculum Adjustments for Gifted Children*, U.S. Office of Education Bulletin 1946, No. 1 (Washington: Government Printing Office, 1946); also, Arno Jewett, J. Dan Hull, *et al., Teaching Rapid and Slow Learners in High School,* U.S. Office of Education Bulletin 1954, No. 5 (Washington: Government Printing Office, 1954).

which individuals who have exceptional ability are being encouraged and assisted to obtain as much education as they can take and to develop their talents to the fullest possible extent. Such provisions are advantageous not only to the person who is helped but also to his family, his community, his state, and the nation.

▶ **LEARNING EXERCISES** ◀

16. What kinds of measurements would you use to identify gifted children? How would you decide, on the basis of scores on each type, what your criteria for "gifted" would be?

17. Make a list of the various kinds of handicaps found among school children. Cite one or more types of measurement useful in each case.

18. What adaptations in a paper-and-pencil test must be made for (*a*) the deaf, (*b*) the blind, (*c*) the feeble-minded, (*d*) spastics?

INTERPRETING SCHOOLS TO THE COMMUNITY

There seems to be a growing interest, on the part of the public, in the activities and problems of the schools. The verb "seems" is used because it is evident from many records and from the history of education in this country that parents have always taken an active interest in the schools, at least as long as their own children were enrolled. With improved communication and transportation the public is probably better informed about the schools today than at any previous time. This, of course, is highly desirable; the more the public knows about the schools the better its understanding and support are likely to be.

Letters to parents, reports to the public through meetings, discussions, and the press, can explain and justify the aims of the schools and give the public an opportunity to react to the ideas presented. Tests and other kinds of evaluative instruments and techniques can also be very useful in explaining what the schools are trying to accomplish, and they are particularly useful in showing how well these purposes are being realized.

To illustrate how tests have helped to interpret the schools in one community, a self-survey was conducted by lay committees with the help of professional educators as consultants. Standardized tests of reading, arithmetic, and language arts were given in the primary grades and standardized batteries in the upper grades; also, tests in English, social studies, science, and arithmetic were given in the junior and senior high schools. The results were compared with national norms and analyzed in relation to local goals, ability of pupils, and other factors. The findings were presented in pamphlet form and discussed by parents, teachers, and professional educators at public meetings. As a result of this survey the community had a better knowledge and understanding of its schools, and most of the citizens were much more interested in supporting a program of improvement than they might otherwise have been.

In recent years the schools have been criticized rather frequently on the grounds that they are neglecting fundamentals, that children are not learning to read, write, spell, and "cipher" as well as they used to, and that training in courtesy, industry, and punctuality is being neglected. It is obviously difficult to prove or disprove such accusations. For one thing, the use of standardized tests of achievement is a fairly recent development, and without results of such tests from earlier periods objective comparisons are very difficult, if not impossible. In one investigation, however, it was possible to repeat certain tests that had been given seventy-five years earlier.[20] In about half the instances the average scores of the modern generation of pupils were better than those of the earlier generation, and in the other half they were not as good. In 1845 children generally performed better on questions of rote memory and abstract skills, and less well on "thought" questions, than children in 1919. On the whole, the children did at least as well in 1919 as those in 1845.

As time goes on, it will be possible to make comparisons of the achievement of pupils at any desired intervals. It is important not only that such studies measure the achievement of pupils, but also that the results be interpreted in relation to the measurement of the pupils' intelligence and other factors that have a bearing on their achievement. It seems fairly certain, for instance, that comparisons of the intelligence of today's high school pupils with that of similar pupils of a century ago would show the latter to be a more highly selected group. Only a small proportion of children of secondary school age had the opportunity then to attend a secondary school, whereas today almost all children who desire it may go to school until they are at least part way through high school. Most states require school attendance until age sixteen, which serves to get most children at least into, if not through, some type of secondary school. Comparisons of achievement, no matter how good the tests, would be open to serious question unless it were possible either to assume equality of ability or to submit evidence that it existed.

It seems clear, therefore, that tests and other measurement devices and techniques can be highly useful in interpreting the schools to the commu-

---

[20] Otis W. Caldwell and S. A. Courtis, *Then and Now in Education* (New York: Harcourt, Brace & World, Inc., 1925), Chap. 7.

nity. As more adequate measures of the great variety of objectives of our educational programs are developed, they should increasingly serve to bring about better rapport and understanding between teachers, pupils, and parents. The respect of pupil and parent for the teacher and for the importance and complexity of his task will grow. At the same time, the teacher should be able to do a better job because the results of tests will give him a better insight into the nature of his pupils and will assist him in explaining what his purposes and his successes are.

▶ LEARNING EXERCISES ◀

19. Assume that you are responsible for public relations between the schools and the public in a community of fifteen thousand. How would you use the results of measurement to interpret your program to the community?

20. If you had to deal with a parent who took the attitude that all tests are bad, how would you proceed to change his viewpoint?

IMPROVEMENT OF SCHOOL STAFF

The use of tests and other measuring techniques can contribute substantially to the professional development of teachers in several ways. In the first place, putting on a measurement program can result in professional growth through the cooperative planning, organizing, and conducting of such a project. In order to participate actively, teachers must learn something about available tests, the characteristics of good measuring instruments, methods of determining whether a test is a good one or not, and sources of information which will provide a basis for making such a determination. Some teachers must also learn how to administer, score, and interpret tests, and how to put the results to good use. All of these experiences and skills can come out of participation by teachers in a measurement program.

Another way in which measurement contributes to staff improvement is through the construction of tests and other measures for local use. In this activity a teacher must identify objectives of instruction and try to construct instruments which will measure progress toward them. This will direct attention not only to the objectives, but also to methods and materials for attaining them. It will also bring the pupil into the picture since, in constructing tests, the teacher will constantly be thinking of ways in which to measure pupil changes resulting from instruction.

After the results of measurement are known, these will promote professional growth in the teacher by revealing what has worked well in his instruction and what has not. An appraisal of the apparent effectiveness of his methods and materials will cause him to examine these with new insight. Measurement programs may also help teachers to learn from each other by revealing individual strengths and weaknesses and by encouraging them to exchange ideas much in the same manner as housewives improve their cooking by exchanging their best recipes with one another.

Educational measurements may also contribute to the professional growth of a school staff by giving the teacher better insight into the individual pupil's capacities, interests, achievements, personality problems, and needs. Such improvement in understanding will almost certainly make the teacher more useful and effective as a teacher and as a friend and adviser.

Knowledge and use of measuring procedures may contribute to professional growth of the school staff through the development of a better understanding of the problems involved in accurate measurement of human traits and greater appreciation of the efforts of pioneers in this area. Also, such study and investigation by teachers should help to bring about improvement in their own tests and measuring instruments. The better the evaluative procedures used by teachers and counselors, the more effective will be their teaching and counseling.

Finally, the use of measuring instruments should be helpful to the administrator and supervisor in many ways. Tests may be used to help select personnel for teaching and other positions. Tests of pupil achievement, observations, and rating scales will be useful to the supervisor in the inservice education of teachers. Various measuring and evaluative devices such as check lists and score cards may also be useful in arriving at sounder judgments concerning physical facilities.

▶ LEARNING EXERCISES ◀

21. What are some ways in which a teacher may grow as a result of participation in planning and carrying out a measurement program?

22. Should scores on achievement tests of pupils be used by supervisors in assisting teachers to improve their effectiveness? If so, in what ways might this be done?

23. Of what benefit to teachers might self-rating be?

EDUCATIONAL RESEARCH

Although research is not generally thought of as one of the major functions of the average school or school system, it is true that in a modest sense most schools perform research of one kind or another. In many of these research activities tests play an important role. If comparisons are desired between grades, schools, or systems, tests provide an objective, reliable basis for making them. In fact, standardized tests are the only type which permits local comparisons and also comparisons with national norms.

In school surveys tests are useful tools for studying such problems as the grade placement of pupils, achievement in basic fundamentals, the relationship of the offerings of the school to the needs of the community, and the degree of success attained in realizing the educational goals of the school or of the community. Measuring instruments are not available yet for all of the educational goals a school or community may set for itself, but the use of most existing instruments is comparatively simple. This is true, for example, of educational goals expressed in terms of subject matter and, to a lesser extent, of such goals as attitudes, desirable habits of work and study, and participation in school and community activities. In other areas such as social adjustment or citizenship it may be necessary to devise original measures. This in itself is a worthwhile type of research activity for teachers, particularly if they have the advice and help of specialists.

Tests may also serve research purposes in the schools in conjunction with comparative studies of different methods of teaching. Most teachers are keenly interested in finding the most effective ways of doing things, not only because of the improved efficiency and consequent saving of time and energy, but also because better methods result in better learning or achievement by the pupil. A common type of educational research is to form two equated or equivalent classes or sections and to compare the relative effectiveness of two methods of instruction, one class being taught by one method, the second by the other method. If the two groups are equal at the beginning, then any difference at the end may be ascribed to the differences in method, provided, of course, that all other factors that might affect the results are held constant. In all such experiments measurement plays an important part. It is used to measure and equate the status of groups before the experiment is begun, and to measure the results after it is completed.

▶ LEARNING EXERCISES ◀

24. List three examples of research in which classroom teachers might engage and which would require the use of measurement.

25. Would research interests and problems of counselors differ from those of classroom teachers? If so, give some examples of possible interests and problems of each group and indicate what kinds of tests they would utilize.

26. The larger school system generally has a bureau of research. What measurement functions and activities would such an organization perform?

ANNOTATED BIBLIOGRAPHY

1. Berdie, Ralph F. *et al. Testing in Guidance and Counseling.* New York: McGraw-Hill Book Co., Inc., 1963. Chapters 5, 6, 7, 8, and 15. The nature and uses of tests in counseling; the organization of a testing program; the administration of tests; national testing programs. Chapter 15 consists of descriptions of a large number of tests used in counseling.

2. Darley, John G. *Testing and Counseling in the High School Guidance Program.* Chicago: Science Research Associates, Inc., 1943. Chapters 6 and 7 deal with the identification of students' problems and ways to help students solve them. The use of tests is but one approach discussed, and there is considerable emphasis on interviewing.

3. Durost, Walter N., and Prescott, George A. *Essentials of Measurement for Teachers.* New York: Harcourt, Brace & World, Inc., 1962. 167 pp. A capsule treatment of the major areas of educational measurement from the standpoint of the needs of the classroom teacher. Emphasizes the use of stanines in test interpretation.

4. *The Education of Exceptional Children.* Forty-Ninth Yearbook of the National Society for the Study of Education, Part II. Chicago: The Society (distributed by the University of Chicago Press), 1950. Chapter 3. The identification and diagnosis of exceptional children and the uses of tests and other methods of doing this are discussed. In other parts of the volume the values and uses of tests in the education of exceptional children are presented and discussed.

5. Froelich, Clifford P., and Darley, John G. *Studying Students: Guidance Methods of Individual Analysis.* Chicago: Science Research Associates, Inc., 1952. Chapter 9. Most of this book deals with the use of various techniques for gathering data about individuals and the use of such data. The major emphasis is on individual counseling, but there is much of value to teachers, school psychologists, and others concerned with measurement in the schools.

6. Goldman, Leo. *Using Tests in Counseling*. New York: Appleton-Century-Crofts, Inc., 1961. Except for Chapters 8, 9, and 10, the entire book deals with the use of tests in counseling and guidance. Every phase of the subject is covered from "purposes of testing" to "test reporting." The three chapters excepted deal with the question of the comparative merits of statistical versus clinical prediction.

7. *The Grouping of Pupils*. Thirty-Fifth Yearbook of the National Society for the Study of Education, Part I. Chicago: The Society (distributed by the University of Chicago Press), 1936. Chapters 11, 12, 13. The chapters cited contain descriptions of various schemes for homogeneous or ability grouping of pupils in elementary and secondary schools.

8. *Guidance Handbook for Elementary Schools*. Los Angeles: Division of Research and Guidance, California Test Bureau, 1948. Chapters 8–14. A discussion of how to use test data in grouping, motivating, and helping handicapped pupils. Also treats the problems of using such data in the community and for professional training of school personnel.

9. *Guidance Handbook for Secondary Schools*. Los Angeles: Division of Research and Guidance, California Test Bureau, 1948. Chapters 3, 4, 5, 6, 7, 8. A companion volume to the one cited above. Discusses the same problems, but with emphasis on the secondary level.

10. Lindquist, E. F. (ed.). *Educational Measurement*. Washington: American Council on Education, 1951. Chapters 1–4. A somewhat advanced treatment of the functions of measurement in the facilitation of learning, improving instruction, counseling, and educational placement. Suitable for, and stimulating to, the more advanced student.

11. Lyman, Howard B. *Test Scores and What They Mean*. Englewood Cliffs, N.J.: Prentice-Hall, Inc., 1963. 223 pp. A brief treatment of educational measurement including most of the topics usually discussed in more comprehensive books. The emphasis is on interpretation of test scores. Useful as a supplement to the regular textbook in courses in measurement or guidance and as the basis for a refresher course.

12. Ross, C. C., and Stanley, Julian C. *Measurement in Today's Schools*, Third Edition. New York: Prentice-Hall, Inc., 1954. Chapters 11–16. The six chapters cited are devoted to detailed discussions of major areas of usefulness for measurement in instruction. These areas are, respectively, motivation and practice, diagnosis, classification and promotion, guidance, evaluation of schools, and public relations.

13. Traxler, Arthur E. *Techniques of Guidance*, Revised Edition. New York: Harper & Row, Publishers, 1957. Chapter 10. A brief but excellent discussion of administrative and supervisory uses of tests. The main emphasis is on instructional and counseling uses of test results. The chapter also gives some of the limitations of tests in these areas and some suggestions on how to improve their usefulness. There is a good bibliography at the end of the chapter.

APPENDIX A

Further Statistical Computations

The problems in this appendix utilize as far as possible the data presented in Chapter 3. The chief purpose of this section is to supplement Chapter 3 by providing an opportunity for the student to learn and practice the actual steps in computing the usual statistical measures and by giving him a deeper insight into the meaning and significance of these measures in interpreting the results of measurement.

FREQUENCY DISTRIBUTION

Ordinarily, a teacher works with classes or groups numbering between twenty-five and forty pupils. In most such cases the scores can be handled individually without any special arrangement or grouping. However, it is often advantageous to arrange the scores in some systematic order; where the number of scores or cases is large, perhaps fifty or more, such grouping is practically a necessity.

A frequency distribution is merely a method of arranging scores into groups, or class intervals, as they are generally called, for ease in handling the figures. Since most statistical work is done with scores arranged in such a frequency table or distribution, it is helpful to be able to construct or read one.

On the arithmetic test cited in Chapter 3 (page 40), the scores of John's class were as follows: 44, 21, 14, 18, 46, 45, 52, 30, 39, 36, 31, 22, 23, 38, 33, 33, 29, 38, 32, 29, 42, 28, 26, 33, 25. These were arranged in order from the highest to the lowest, producing this sequence: 52, 46, 45, 44, 42, 39, 38, 38, 36, 33, 33, 33, 32, 31, 30, 29, 29, 28, 26, 25, 23, 22, 21, 18, 14.

John's score of 36, as we know, was ninth in the class; the arithmetic mean was 32.3 and the mid-score was 32. These results are easily obtained without any further rearrangement of the scores. However, we can make a frequency table from these scores by the following steps:

1. Choose some convenient class interval, say five. If the range of scores is small (the range is the difference between the highest and lowest scores), use a smaller class interval; if the range is large, use a larger interval, perhaps ten. In any case, use an interval large enough so that the table will not be too long for convenience in working with it and yet small enough to represent the scores with reasonable accuracy. In this case we have used an interval of five.

2. Make a table of class intervals that will serve to include all scores in the class or group. In general, the class interval used should be of such a size as to give a distribution containing not less than eight nor more than sixteen intervals. By using the interval of five in the example below (see Table X), we establish nine such categories.

3. Tally the scores one by one in the proper class intervals.

4. Add the tallies and write the sum opposite each interval. These sums are called frequencies. The total of all of the frequencies (N) gives the number of students tested.

TABLE X • Frequency Distribution

Class Intervals	Tallies	Frequencies
50–54	/	1
45–49	//	2
40–44	//	2
35–39	////	4
30–34	HHT /	6
25–29	HHT	5
20–24	///	3
15–19	/	1
10–14	/	1
		$N = 25$

Although we have gone through the essential steps in setting up a frequency table, we have not considered adequately some basic questions underlying this method. To use the method correctly and intelligently these questions must be considered and answers agreed upon. The first of these concerns the class interval.

Limits of Class Intervals

A score on a test is usually a whole number, such as 22. Generally we do not deal with fractional scores in educational measurement. However, it is necessary to give some consideration to the actual value of a whole number. For example, we can consider the score of 22 as representing a range of all possible values from exactly 22.0 *up to but not including* 23.0. In this case the score of 22 should really be written 22.5, since that would be the most probable value, assuming the possibility of values ranging from 22.0 to 23.0.

On the other hand, we can consider the score of 22 as representing a range of all possible values from 21.5 *up to but not including* 22.5. In this case the score of 22 is taken to mean 22.0, which is the most probable value. The latter concept is the one most generally favored in statistical work.

The use of decimal places here is arbitrary. *Exactly* 22 would mean 22 followed by an infinite number of zeros; *exactly* 22½ would mean 22.5 followed by an infinite number of zeros. When we write 22.0 we assume the rest of the zeros if we mean *exactly* 22. A similar assumption holds in the case of 22.5.

The same principles apply in the interpretation of the limits of class intervals. If we are dealing with a class interval of five we may indicate this in several different ways:

25–30	25–29	24.5–29.49 . . .
or	or	
20–25	20–24	19.5–24.49 . . .

The first, seldom used, is the least desirable since the limit 25 appears in two successive intervals and may thus lead to errors in tabulation; the second has the advantage over the third of simplicity, and does not have the obvious fault of the first; the third, although the most exact in statement, is cumbersome. The second method is therefore recommended with the admonition that the value of a score be remembered as explained above. Then the interval 20–24 really means from 19.5 to 24.5. This constitutes an interval of five which contains all whole number scores of 20, 21, 22, 23, and 24, or any score from 19.5 up to, but not including, 24.5.[1]

Mid-Point of Intervals

In statistical work with frequency distributions it is often necessary to use the mid-point of an interval. There are two steps in determining the mid-point:

[1] It must be borne in mind that the whole numbers (20, 24, etc.) are *integral limits* as distinguished from the *real limits* (19.5, 24.5, etc.).

1. Find one-half the class interval.

2. Add this to the real lower limit or subtract it from the real upper limit of the interval whose mid-point is desired.

Let us take as an example the interval 20–24. The interval is, of course, five, and so halfway through it would be 2.5. Then if we begin at the upper (24.5) or lower (19.5) real limits of the interval and add or subtract 2.5 steps or score points we get $19.5 + 2.5 = 22.0$, or $24.5 - 2.5 = 22.0$. This must be the mid-point since it is equidistant from the upper limit and the lower limit of the class interval.

▶ **LEARNING EXERCISE** ◀

1. Find the mid-points of the following class intervals: (*a*) 50–59; (*b*) 27–29; (*c*) 30–35; (*d*) 13–14; (*e*) 96–101. (59 includes from 58.5 up to, but not including, 59.5; 29 includes from 28.5 up to, but not including, 29.5, etc.

One basic assumption is made in working with mid-points of class intervals. The interval 20–24 has a mid-point of 22; if nine cases fall in this interval, we assume that these nine scores are evenly distributed throughout the interval, or, in any event, that the average of these nine scores is equal to the mid-point of the interval.

What we have said concerning class intervals can be presented graphically as follows:

```
                              X
                x             X             X
      x         x             X             x             x
  |_____|
      .    .    .    .    .    .    .    .    .
 19.5  20.0 20.5 21.0 21.5 22.0 22.5 23.0 23.5 24.0 24.5
```

The actual or real limits of the interval are shown at the ends of the line, the mid-point, 22, at the center; the nine scores in the interval balance so that any average of them would give 22. Any distribution of the nine scores which gives an average equal to the mid-point of the interval will satisfy the assumption. In actual practice this assumption tends to be reasonably well met. This is particularly true when the number of cases is large and the class interval chosen is fairly small. The larger the class interval and the smaller the frequencies, the greater are the chances of introducing error. It is also likely that error introduced as a result of cases piling up at one end of a particular interval will be balanced by an opposite tendency in another interval, the two sources of error thus tending to balance or neutralize each other.

Making a Frequency Distribution

A simple frequency distribution was shown on page 458, with a brief statement of the steps involved in making it. Let us now take a series of scores and carefully work through the steps required to make a frequency distribution of them. The following scores represent actual scores of forty-nine pupils on a general science test: 33, 42, 47, 61, 43, 52, 71, 21, 43, 37, 60, 43, 54, 68, 13, 50, 38, 40, 67, 3, 45, 47, 49, 58, 38, 46, 58, 36, 44, 55, 15, 38, 44, 40, 28, 27, 44, 36, 41, 39, 22, 36, 18, 41, 24, 32, 8, 33, 25.

1. Choose a class interval of suitable size. This is usually done by (a) finding the range of scores (here it is $71 - 3 = 68$), and (b) dividing the range by a convenient class interval to see if it gives a number of intervals between 8 and 16. In this case:

$$68 \div 4 = 17$$
$$68 \div 5 = 13+$$
$$68 \div 6 = 11+$$
$$68 \div 7 = \ \ 9+$$

In practice we seldom use class intervals of four, six, or seven. The most commonly used intervals are two, three, five, ten, or, if necessary, twenty. Here we shall use five as our class interval since it is of a convenient size and, as we shall see, it actually gives fifteen class intervals.

2. Next, set up a frequency table designating the class intervals. Note that we have chosen the lower limits of our intervals in such a way that they are multiples of the interval size, that is, of five. We use these limits here for the sake of convenience, but it would be just as satisfactory statistically to use limits which are not multiples of the interval. Some authorities recommend choosing the limits in such a way that the mid-points of the intervals are multiples of the interval, but this seems a less natural way of thinking about class intervals. The two methods are illustrated as follows:

A. Limits are Multiples of the Interval		B. Mid-points are Multiples of the Interval	
Limits	*Mid-points*	*Limits*	*Mid-points*
25–29	27	23–27	25
20–24	22	18–22	20
15–19	17	13–17	15

Since our scores range from 3 to 71 we will need a series of intervals that will include these extremes and all possible scores in between. Using system A, above, we arrive at the series of intervals given below, showing intervals for the complete range of scores from 3 to 71 and all possible scores in between.

3. Tally the actual scores in the proper class intervals, adding the tallies in each class interval. These are the frequencies:

Class Intervals (*c.i.*)		Frequencies (*f*)
70–74	/	1
65–69	//	2
60–64	//	2
55–59	///	3
50–54	///	3
45–49	₩₩	5
40–44	₩₩ ₩₩ /	11
35–39	₩₩ ///	8
30–34	///	3
25–29	///	3
20–24	///	3
15–19	//	2
10–14	/	1
5–9	/	1
0–4	/	1
		$N = 49$

The sum of the frequencies (N) should be equal to the number of scores in the group. This is a rough check on the accuracy of the tabulation. However, the most common error in making a frequency distribution is the tabulation of a score in the wrong class interval. It is easy to make this mistake, and the only way to detect such errors is to tabulate the scores *twice* and see whether the frequencies in each class interval check. The second tabulation may be done alongside the first one or by placing a dot over each tally when going through the second time, thus:

$$\overset{\cdots\cdots\ \ \cdots}{35\text{--}39\ \ \text{₩₩}\ ///.}$$

▶ **LEARNING EXERCISES** ◀

2. Make a new frequency table using the forty-nine scores on page 461, but with a class interval of three.

3. Make a frequency table of the reading test scores given in Chapter 3, page 49.

MEASURES OF CENTRAL TENDENCY

Mean

In Chapter 3 the mean and median were discussed and calculated with twenty-five ungrouped scores. Let us now see how the mean and median are determined from a frequency distribution of the forty-nine scores on the science test on the preceding page.

The steps illustrated in Table XI are as follows:

1. Select an arbitrary origin. It is generally best to select a point near the center of the distribution, although any interval may be used without affecting the result. Here we chose the interval 40–44 whose mid-point, 42, we call the *assumed mean.*

2. In the *d* column mark off steps by intervals above (+) and below (−) the *A.M.* (*d* = deviations from the interval containing the assumed mean, in units of the class interval).

3. Multiply these steps by the frequencies in the respective intervals and enter these products in the *fd* column.

4. Add the positive *fd*'s (44) and the negative *fd*'s (−66) separately. Algebraically add the +*fd*'s and −*fd*'s to find Σ*fd*. The Σ*fd* divided by *N*

TABLE XI • Calculation of Mean Using Forty-Nine Scores on Science Test

c.i.	f	d	fd	
70–74	1	6	6	$M = A.M. + \left(\dfrac{\Sigma fd}{N} \times c.i.\right)$
65–69	2	5	10	
60–64	2	4	8	
55–59	3	3	9	M = Mean
50–54	3	2	6	A.M. = Assumed mean
45–49	5	1	5	Σfd = Algebraic sum of devia-
			(44)	tions about assumed mean
40–44	11	0	0	N = Number of scores
35–39	8	− 1	− 8	c.i. = Class interval
30–34	3	− 2	− 6	
25–29	3	− 3	− 9	
20–24	3	− 4	− 12	$M = 42.0 + \left(\dfrac{44 - 66}{49} \times 5\right)$
15–19	2	− 5	− 10	
10–14	1	− 6	− 6	$= 42.0 + \left(\dfrac{-22}{49} \times 5\right)$
5– 9	1	− 7	− 7	
0– 4	1	− 8	− 8	
	N = 49		(− 66)	$= 42.0 + \left(\dfrac{-110}{49}\right)$
				$= 42.0 - 2.2$
				$= 39.8$

gives the correction, that is, the amount expressed in units of the class interval by which our assumed mean differs from the actual value or mean.

5. The formula $M = A.M. + \left(\dfrac{\Sigma fd}{N} \times c.i.\right)$ simply converts the correc-

tion from units of the class interval to score units and applies this correction to the assumed mean, giving us the corrected value for the mean.

▶ LEARNING EXERCISES ◀

4. Check the value 39.8 (Table XI) by adding the forty-nine scores and
dividing by 49. Is there a difference? Why?

5. Check this value further by assuming the mean to be in some interval
other than 40–44, and re-calculating the mean. Does it agree with the value
already obtained?

6. Calculate the means of the scores on the arithmetic test and the reading
test using the frequency distributions shown in Table X and prepared in Learning Exercise 3, p. 462.

Mid-Score and Approximate Semi-Interquartile Range

Where data are not grouped into class intervals of a frequency distribution it is often sufficiently accurate to use the middle score of the series as
the average, and approximate values of the third and first quartiles in finding the semi-interquartile range (Q) as a measure of variability.

The mid-score may be determined by use of the formula $\dfrac{N + 1}{2}$. For

example, if one had six papers scored 80, 70, 60, 50, 40, and 30, $\dfrac{N + 1}{2}$

$= \dfrac{6 + 1}{2} = 3.5$. The 3.5th score is half way between the third (60) and

the fourth (50) scores, or 55. If we add one score to the series, say 90,

$\dfrac{N + 1}{2} = \dfrac{7 + 1}{2} = 4$. Our 4th score is 60. This is the mid-score.

Table XII shows the calculation of mid-score and Q's from ungrouped
data.

Median

When data are grouped in a frequency distribution the calculation of
the median requires the determination of a point above and below which
50 per cent of the scores or cases lie. This may be an actual score but

TABLE XII • Determination of Mid-Score and Semi-Interquartile Range Using Ungrouped Data: Twenty-Five Arithmetic Test Scores and Twenty-Five Reading Test Scores

Arithmetic Scores		Reading Scores
52	$N = 25$	111
46		102
45		94
44		92
42		91
39		87
38	← Q_3 (Approx.) nearest whole number →	86
38	above which 25% of cases	81
36	$\left(\dfrac{N}{4} = \dfrac{25}{4}\right) = 6.25$) lie	80
33		77
33		77
33		76
32	← —————— Mid-score —————— →	75
31		73
30		72
29		70
29		69
28		68
26	← Q_1 (Approx.) nearest whole number →	66
25	below which 25% of cases lie	65
23		62
22		59
21		56
18		48
14		46

$$Q = \frac{Q_3 - Q_1}{2} \qquad\qquad Q = \frac{Q_3 - Q_1}{2}$$

$$= \frac{38 - 26}{2} \qquad\qquad = \frac{86 - 66}{2}$$

$$= 6 \qquad\qquad\qquad = 10$$

more often it is not. Table XIII shows the steps in calculating the median from a frequency distribution.

These steps are:

1. Divide the total number of cases by two. This gives the half sum or the number of cases above and below the middle of the distribution. In this example $\frac{N}{2} = 24.5$.

2. By inspection determine in which class interval this point will be. Since there are only twenty-two cases below the interval 40–44, and since

TABLE XIII • Calculation of the Median from a Frequency Distribution of Forty-Nine Science Test Scores

c.i.	f	cum. f		
70–74	1	49		
65–69	2	48	Median $= l.l. + \left(\dfrac{\dfrac{N}{2} - F}{f_m} \right) \times$ c.i.	
60–64	2	46		
55–59	3	44	$l.l. =$ lower limit of class	
50–54	3	41	interval within which	
45–49	5	38	median falls	
40–44	11	33	$\dfrac{N}{2} =$ one-half of the scores	
35–39	8	22		
30–34	3	14	$F =$ sum of all scores	
25–29	3	11	below $l.l.$	
20–24	3	8	$f_m =$ number of scores within	
15–19	2	5	interval in which	
10–14	1	3	median falls	
5–9	1	2	c.i. $=$ size of class interval	
0–4	1	1		

$N = 49$

Median falls in this interval (brackets 40–44 and 35–39)

$$\text{Median} = 39.5 + \left(\frac{\frac{49}{2} - 22}{11} \right) \times 5$$

$$= 39.5 + \left(\frac{24.5 - 22}{11} \right) \times 5$$

$$= 39.5 + 1.1$$

$$= 40.6$$

Adapted from Henry E. Garrett, *Statistics in Psychology and Education,* Fifth Edition; New York: David McKay Co., Inc., 1958. Pp. 28–33.

the number of scores *below* the *next* interval, 45–49, is thirty-three, we know the 24.5 point must be somewhere in the interval, 40–44.

3. Subtract the number of cases below this interval as shown in the cumulative frequency column from 24.5. This gives us the number of cases needed out of the interval in which the median falls. In this instance it is $24.5 - 22 = 2.5$ cases.

4. Divide this number by the total number of cases in the *interval.* Here, this is 11. $2\frac{1}{2} \div 11 = .23$. Thus we determine how far through the interval we must go to get the proportion of the cases needed. (Remember the assumption mentioned earlier that all scores in an interval are evenly distributed throughout the interval.)

5. Multiply this ratio by the size of the class interval to ascertain *score points* for this proportion of the interval. In our problem this gives 1.1 score points.

6. Add this to the lower limit of the interval containing the median. This gives the median: that point below and above which an equal number of cases or scores fall. As in the example, it is usually a theoretical point rather than an actual score, because of the method used in finding it.

▶ LEARNING EXERCISE ◀

7. Using the frequency distributions of the scores shown in Table X and those prepared in Learning Exercise 3, calculate the median in each case.

The Mode

There is one other measure of central tendency which should be mentioned. It is a crude, inspectional average called the mode. This may be defined as the score occurring with greatest frequency. In a frequency table the mode is the mid-point of the interval having the largest frequency. In Table XIII it is 42.

The mode is of little importance, statistically speaking. Its chief use is to show the point of the greatest concentration of scores.

Comparison of Mean and Median

As pointed out in Chapter 3, there are some important differences between the mean and the median. The mean is a *weighted average* in that it is affected by the actual amount or size of every score in the distribution. The median, however, is a *counting average,* or average of position. It is not so affected by the size of extreme scores. This was illustrated in Chapter 3, on page 43. In a symmetrical distribution[2] the mean and median are identical. Therefore, the degree of asymmetry or lack of symmetricalness of a distribution can be gauged by the extent to which the mean and median differ.

For most situations in which an easily calculated measure of central tendency is all that is needed, the median or even the mid-score serves the purpose. On the other hand, if careful statistical analysis is planned it is well to calculate the mean, or both the mean and the median.

---

[2] A symmetrical distribution is one in which the frequencies on each side of the average are the same. Generally these frequencies gradually increase from both ends to the middle. The distribution of scores on the science test (page 462) is roughly symmetrical.

MEASURES OF VARIABILITY

The importance of measures of variability in describing a series of scores has already been discussed in Chapter 3. It will be the purpose here to supplement that discussion by showing how to calculate the two most commonly used measures of variability or dispersion using the frequency distribution of forty-nine science test scores already presented.

Range

The range is a rough measure of variability. It is simply the difference between the highest and lowest scores in a distribution. It has been used earlier in determining the size of class interval. Since the range is based on only two scores it is not a very stable measure and is little used in statistical work.

Semi-Interquartile Range

This measure is quite common in educational statistics. It is obtained by taking one-half the difference between the 75th percentile (Q_3) and the 25th percentile (Q_1). This can be expressed by the formula $Q = \dfrac{Q_3 - Q_1}{2}$. We have already learned how to calculate the necessary values in connection with our calculations of the mid-score and Q in Table XII, and the median in Table XIII. Using the same method we can calculate Q_3 and Q_1, the 75th and 25th percentiles, respectively. This is illustrated in Table XIV.

One may ask why the formula for Q calls for one-half the range between Q_3 and Q_1. This is because a true measure of variability is based on the deviations of scores from some measure of central tendency and is expressed as a distance on either side of that measure. To express the interquartile range in somewhat similar terms, it is halved. Although the semi-interquartile range is not based on deviations of individual scores from an average and is therefore not a true measure of variability, it is roughly comparable to such measures. In a symmetrical distribution Q may be added to and subtracted from the average, and it will include the middle 50 per cent of the cases. In an asymmetrical distribution there is usually some variation from this proportion.

When a series of scores is quite homogeneous, Q will be smaller than when the differences between scores or individuals is greater. This principle is illustrated in Figure 25.

TABLE XIV • Calculation of the Semi-Interquartile Range from a Frequency Distribution of Forty-Nine Science Test Scores

c.i.	f	cum. f	
70–74	1	49	
65–69	2	48	
60–64	2	46	
55–59	3	44	
50–54	3	41	
45–49	5	38	Third Quartile: $Q_3 =$ 75th Percentile in this interval
40–44	11	33	
35–39	8	22	
30–34	3	14	First Quartile: $Q_1 =$ 25th Percentile in this interval
25–29	3	11	
20–24	3	8	
15–19	2	5	l.l. = lower limit of class interval within which quartile point falls
10–14	1	3	
5– 9	1	2	
0– 4	1	1	$F =$ sum of all scores below l.l.
	$N = 49$		$f_m =$ number of scores within interval in which quartile point falls

$$Q_3 = \text{l.l.} + \left(\frac{\frac{3N}{4} - F}{f_m} \right) \times \text{c.i.}$$

$$= 44.5 + \frac{(36.75 - 33)}{5} \times 5$$

$$= 48.25$$

$$Q_1 = \text{l.l.} + \left(\frac{\frac{N}{4} - F}{f_m} \right) \times \text{c.i.}$$

$$= 29.5 + \frac{(12.25 - 11)}{3} \times 5$$

$$= 31.58$$

$$Q = \frac{Q_3 - Q_1}{2}$$

$$= \frac{48.25 - 31.58}{2}$$

$$= 8.33$$

FIGURE 25 • Comparison of Q Values of Two Distributions Differing in Spread

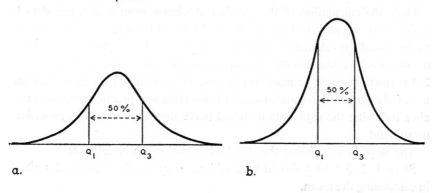

a.

b.

In a. the spread of scores is greater than it is in b. Consequently, the Q_1's and Q_3's are farther apart and the Q is larger in a. than in b. In other words, it is necessary to take in a wider range or variation of scores in a. than in b. to include the middle half (50 per cent) of the cases in each distribution.

Standard Deviation

If we take each score in a class or series separately, find the difference between it and the mean, and add these differences without regard to sign, our result will be a number which gives some measure of the extent to which all the scores tend to vary from the mean. Obviously, if all the scores are the same, all of the differences between the scores and the mean will be zero, and the variability will also be zero. The larger the sum of these deviations from the mean, the greater the dispersion or variability. This is the principle upon which the calculation of most measures of variability or dispersion is based.

In calculating the standard deviation (σ), we square the deviation of each score from the mean. This has the effect of eliminating minus signs from the deviations of scores below the mean and it gives the standard deviation more stability as a measure of variability than any similar measure. We further divide the sum of the squared deviations by the number of cases or scores, which gives us the mean of these squares. Finally, we extract the square root of this mean. The quotient is called the standard deviation.

Table XV shows the steps by which the means and standard deviations of the arithmetic scores and the reading scores used in Chapter 3 were calculated. For the sake of simplicity, the results were used there without a demonstration of how they had been obtained. Each step of the work is shown in Table XV, which can probably be interpreted without further explanation.

Once the calculation of the standard deviation from ungrouped data is understood, we may proceed to Table XVI. This table demonstrates the method used for calculating σ from grouped data, that is, from a frequency distribution. Fundamentally, the process is the same as for ungrouped data, but corrections must be made for the use of an assumed mean and for the use of class intervals. Careful study of this table and practice with the exercises following the explanation should make these differences in procedure meaningful.

The steps in calculating the standard deviation are as follows:

Steps 1, 2, 3, and 4 should be familiar. They are the same as described in calculating the mean.

TABLE XV • Calculation of the Mean and Standard Deviation Using Ungrouped Data: Twenty-Five Arithmetic Test Scores and Twenty-Five Reading Test Scores

| | ARITHMETIC | | | READING | |
| | Deviations from | | | Deviations from | |
Scores	Mean	d^2	Scores	Mean	d^2
52	19.7	388.09	111	35.7	1274.49
46	13.7	187.69	102	26.7	712.89
45	12.7	161.29	94	18.7	349.69
44	11.7	136.89	92	16.7	278.89
42	9.7	94.09	91	15.7	246.49
39	6.7	44.89	87	11.7	136.89
38	5.7	32.49	86	10.7	114.49
38	5.7	32.49	81	5.7	32.49
36	3.7	13.69	80	4.7	22.09
33	.7	.49	77	1.7	2.89
33	.7	.49	77	1.7	2.89
33	.7	.49	76	.7	.49
32	− .3	.09	75	− .3	.09
31	− 1.3	1.69	73	− 2.3	5.29
30	− 2.3	5.29	72	− 3.3	10.89
29	− 3.3	10.89	70	− 5.3	28.09
29	− 3.3	10.89	69	− 6.3	39.69
28	− 4.3	18.49	68	− 7.3	53.29
26	− 6.3	39.69	66	− 9.3	86.49
25	− 7.3	53.29	65	− 10.3	106.09
23	− 9.3	86.49	62	− 13.3	176.89
22	− 10.3	106.09	59	− 16.3	265.69
21	− 11.3	127.69	56	− 19.3	372.49
18	− 14.3	204.49	48	− 27.3	745.29
14	− 18.3	334.89	46	− 29.3	858.49
$\Sigma m = 807$		$\Sigma d^2 = 2093.05$	$\Sigma m = 1883$		$\Sigma d^2 = 5923.45$
$N = 25$					

M = mean	d = deviations from mean
Σ = sum	N = number of scores or cases in group
m = scores or measures	σ = standard deviation

$$M = \frac{\Sigma m}{N} \qquad \sigma = \sqrt{\frac{\Sigma d^2}{N}}$$

$$= \frac{807}{25} \qquad = \sqrt{\frac{2093.05}{25}}$$

$$= 32.3 \qquad = \sqrt{83.72}$$

$$= 9.2$$

$$M = \frac{\Sigma m}{N} \qquad \sigma = \sqrt{\frac{\Sigma d^2}{N}}$$

$$= \frac{1883}{25} \qquad = \sqrt{\frac{5923.45}{25}}$$

$$= 75.3 \qquad = \sqrt{236.94*}$$

$$= 15.4$$

* See Appendix B, page 493, for method for extracting square root.

TABLE XVI • Calculation of Standard Deviation from a Frequency Distribution of Forty-Nine Science Test Scores

c.i.	f	d	fd	fd²	
70–74	1	6	6	36	$\sigma = \sqrt{\dfrac{\Sigma fd^2}{N} - \left(\dfrac{\Sigma fd}{N}\right)^2} \times$ c.i.
65–69	2	5	10	50	
60–64	2	4	8	32	
55–59	3	3	9	27	$\sigma =$ standard deviation
50–54	3	2	6	12	$\Sigma fd^2 =$ sum of squared deviations
45–49	5	1	5	5	of each score from mean
			(44)		$\Sigma fd =$ algebraic sum of deviations
40–44	11	0	0	0	of each score from mean
35–39	8	− 1	− 8	8	c.i. = class interval
30–34	3	− 2	− 6	12	
25–29	3	− 3	− 9	27	
20–24	3	− 4	− 12	48	$\sigma = \sqrt{\dfrac{456}{49} - \left(\dfrac{-22}{49}\right)^2} \times 5$
15–19	2	− 5	− 10	50	
10–14	1	− 6	− 6	36	$= \sqrt{9.3061 - (.45)^2} \times 5$
5– 9	1	− 7	− 7	49	
0– 4	1	− 8	− 8	64	$= \sqrt{9.1036 \times 5}$
	N = 49		(− 66)	456	$= 15.10$

5. Multiply each entry in the *fd* column by its corresponding *d*. This gives the *fd²* values. Enter these in the *fd²* column.

6. Add all the *fd²* entries to get Σfd^2.

7. Substitute the proper values for each expression in the formula and solve for σ, the standard deviation.

It should be noted that $\dfrac{\Sigma fd}{N}$ is the correction which was used in calculating the mean from an assumed origin. Since we follow the same procedure here, it is necessary again to make the same correction, but since it is under the radical with the $\dfrac{\Sigma fd^2}{N}$, it too is squared.

As explained in Chapter 3, the standard deviation is that distance which, laid off above and below the mean, will include the middle 68.26 per cent of the cases or scores. This is exactly true in a so-called normal distribution only. In most situations where *approximately* normal distributions are the rule, one standard deviation on either side of the mean will usually include about two-thirds of the cases.

Again, as pointed out with *Q,* the more variable a group, the larger will be the standard deviation or distance on either side of the mean required to include the middle 68.26 per cent of the scores. This is illustrated in Figure 26.

FIGURE 26 • Comparison of σ's of Two Distributions Differing in Spread

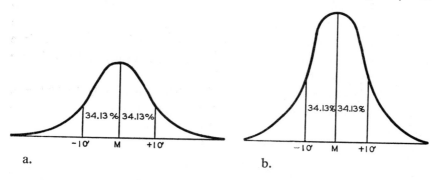

a.   b.

It will be noted that in both a. and b. one sigma (1.0σ) on either side of the mean cuts off 34.13 per cent of the cases, but that the standard deviation in a. is considerably larger than in b. due to the greater spread or variability of the group represented by curve a. It should be emphasized, however, that such comparisons are valid *only* when the same test is administered to two groups or when the same group is tested twice.

The standard deviation is one of the most important and valuable statistical measures, though it is a little more difficult to calculate than some others. It finds many uses, some of which have already been discussed; we shall learn about others shortly. Whenever the most stable and widely useful measure of variability is desired, the standard deviation is the one to employ. It is basic to, or enters into, the calculation of many other statistical measures.

▶ **LEARNING EXERCISES** ◀

8. Draw a curve similar to those shown in Figure 26 and show the relationship (approximate) of the standard deviation (σ) and the semi-interquartile range (*Q*). Which is larger? Is this always so? Why?

9. Calculate the means of the scores on arithmetic and reading using the frequency distributions made earlier in this chapter. Compare them with the values obtained from the same scores ungrouped.

10. Do the same for the standard deviations. What differences do you find? How do you account for them?

PERCENTILES AND PERCENTILE RANKS

In Chapter 3 percentile ranks were briefly discussed along with simple ranks, primarily to show their superiority to simple ranks in comparing standings of individuals when the groups on which the ranks are based differ in size. The method for finding the percentile rank of a score, explained on page 41, gives only approximate results, and where percentile ranks are used extensively more exact methods should be used. Also, since tables of test norms are often presented in the form of percentile ranks, we need to know how these are obtained.

By using the formula for the median (which, of course, is the 50th percentile), we can calculate any desired percentile, that is, the score below which any given percentage of cases lies. All that is necessary is to substitute the desired proportion of cases in this formula for the expression $\frac{N}{2}$. We have already done this for Q_1 by substituting $\frac{N}{4}$ (or 25 per cent of the cases), which was 12.25, and for Q_3 by substituting $\frac{3N}{4}$ (or 75 per cent of the cases), which was 36.75. (See Table XIV.) If the 10th percentile were desired we should use $\frac{N}{10}$, and so on.

The simplest and most practical method of arriving at percentiles or percentile ranks for any given distribution is to construct a cumulative frequency, or ogive, curve. From such a curve percentiles or percentile ranks can be read very easily. Such curves also have other uses which will be discussed later.

There are two methods for constructing such a curve. They are basically the same, the choice of which to use being a matter of preference. The necessary calculations for each method are shown in Table XVII.

Under Method 1 scores have been calculated corresponding to arbitrarily chosen percentiles or per cents of the total number of cases, just as has been shown previously for the median and Q_1 and Q_3. These points are then plotted as shown in Figure 27. They are marked with a circle to distinguish them from the points calculated and plotted by the second method, those points being marked with an X. In the latter we have calculated the percentile ranks corresponding to certain frequencies, using the total number of scores in the distribution as our base. Method I goes from percentages to percentiles or scores, whereas Method II goes from scores to percentile ranks.

It will be noted that the two methods give results that agree exactly, except possibly at the two extremes of the curve. At these places it is permissible to end the two curves at the upper limit of the highest interval and at the lower limit of the lowest interval, calling these points the one hundredth and the zero percentiles, respectively. When this is done the curves obtained by the two sets of calculations representing the two methods will coincide.

TABLE XVII • Two Methods of Calculating Values Needed to Construct a Percentile Graph or Ogive Curve

c.i.	f	cum. f	% of N	n	Percentile	cum. f	Percentile Rank
			METHOD I			METHOD II	
70–74	1	49	100%	49	74.5	49	100.00
65–69	2	48	95%	46.55	65.88	48	97.92
60–64	2	46	90%	44.1	59.75	46	93.84
55–59	3	44				44	89.76
50–54	3	41	80%	39.2	51.50	41	83.64
45–49	5	38	70%	34.3	45.80	38	77.52
40–44	11	33	60%	29.4	42.86	33	67.32
			50%	24.5	40.64		
35–39	8	22	40%	19.6	38.00	22	44.88
			30%	14.7	34.94		
30–34	3	14				14	28.56
25–29	3	11	20%	9.8	27.50	11	22.44
20–24	3	8				8	16.32
15–19	2	5	10%	4.9	19.25	5	10.20
10–14	1	3	5%	2.45	11.75	3	6.12
5–9	1	2				2	4.08
0–4	1	1	0%	0	0	1	2.04
	$\overline{49}$						

SAMPLE CALCULATIONS

Method I

$$\text{5th percentile} = l.l. + \left(\frac{\frac{N}{20} - F}{f_m}\right) \times c.i.$$

$$= 9.5 + \frac{2.45 - 2}{1} \times 5$$

$$= 11.75$$

Method II

Percentile rank of lower limit of interval 5–9

$$= \frac{1}{49} \times 100 = 2.04$$

FIGURE 27 • Percentile Graph Based on Forty-Nine Science Test Scores

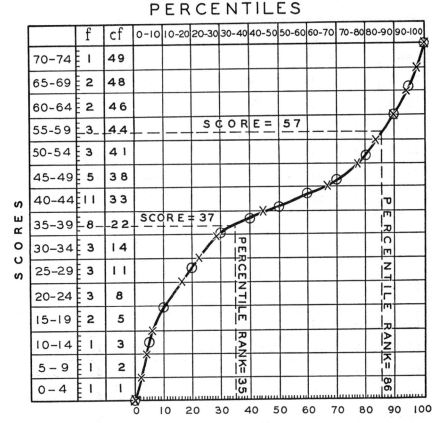

PERCENTILES

⊙   Designates points determined by Method I.
X   Designates points determined by Method II.

With such a curve one may quickly determine the percentile rank of any score by locating the score on the vertical scale, finding the point where the curve crosses the line corresponding to that score, and dropping a perpendicular (visually) to the base line where the corresponding percentile rank may be read. The process is made clear by the broken lines which have been drawn in the diagram. In the use of such a graph, lines such as these are not drawn, of course, but the answers are determined by inspection.

In the curve shown in Figure 27 a score of 37 is found to have a percentile rank of 35; similarly, a score of 57 has a percentile rank of 86. By definition, 35 per cent of the scores lie below 37, and 86 per cent lie below 57. By use of such a curve we may find the percentile rank of any score in the series. Percentile graphs are useful in many other ways, a few of which are mentioned below:

1. Besides obtaining percentile ranks visually, we can easily determine what score corresponds to any given percentile; thus we may estimate the 25th (Q_1), 50th (median), and 75th (Q_3), as well as any other score corresponding to any percentile from 0 to 100, directly from the curve.

2. We can determine the percentage of scores which lie between certain limits. Likewise, it is easy to estimate the range of scores in the upper 10 per cent of the group or the range of the middle 20 per cent.

3. It is possible to construct several percentile curves on the same graph, representing distributions for several different groups, such as successive grades on the same test or the same group on several different tests. With these curves one may compare medians, quartiles, or any other corresponding points on the curves, determine percentage of over-lapping, and make many other useful comparisons.

In tables of norms, percentile ranks are usually given numerically for every possible score, but these values are most conveniently determined by first constructing a curve based on the cumulative frequencies as we have done here.

▶ LEARNING EXERCISES ◀

11. Construct a percentile curve for the twenty-five arithmetic scores and one for the twenty-five reading scores using Method I for arithmetic and Method II for reading. Are these curves like the sample in Figure 27? If not, how do you explain the differences?

12. From Figure 27 determine the following:
   a. The median of the distribution.
   b. The semi-interquartile range (Check with Table XIV).
   c. The proportion (per cent) of scores above 60; below 15; between 20 and 50.
   d. An approximate value for the standard deviation of the distribution (Check with Table XVI.)

THE NORMAL PROBABILITY CURVE

To introduce the discussion of the normal curve, two methods commonly used to depict frequency distributions in graphic form are shown in Figure 28. Both are based on the distribution of arithmetic scores, Table X.

The histogram and the frequency polygon are based on the same data, but the method of construction differs, as does the appearance of the two graphs. In both, frequencies are represented on the vertical axis, class intervals on the horizontal axis. Thus, the height at any point represents

FIGURE 28 • Graphs of Frequency Distribution of Twenty-Five Arithmetic Test Scores

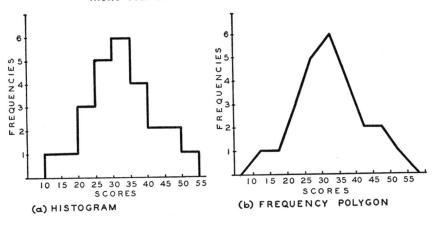

(a) HISTOGRAM   (b) FREQUENCY POLYGON

the number of scores or cases in the interval directly below that point. In the histogram, points are located at the correct height at the beginning and end of each interval. These are connected by a horizontal line, and by vertical lines to the adjacent points in the next higher and lower intervals. The graph ends on the base line at the lower limit of the lowest interval and at the upper limit of the highest interval of the distribution.

In the frequency polygon, points representing the frequencies of each class interval are located directly above the middle of the respective class intervals. These points are connected with straight lines. The graph ends at the base line, as in the case of the histogram, but there is one difference in this respect. It is customary to end the frequency polygon at the mid-point of the interval *just below* the lowest one in the frequency distribution that contains any cases, and at the mid-point of the next highest interval *above* the highest one in the frequency distribution.

These two graphs have certain important features in common which concern us in considering the normal curve. First, they have a form which is generally referred to as humped or bell-shaped. This results from the fact that frequencies are much smaller at the extremes than at the middle. That is, the number of cases increases more or less steadily as we go toward the middle or average from very high or very low scores. Second, the curves or graphs are continuous. There are no gaps, or class intervals with zero frequencies. These two features or characteristics are common to all so-called normal curves.[3]

[3] The term *normal* has a mathematical connotation which has no connection with *normal* and *abnormal* as used in psychology or education. The equation for the normal curve is $y = \dfrac{N}{\sigma\sqrt{2\pi}} \, e^{-\frac{x^2}{2\sigma^2}}$

The normal curve is a limiting curve which is approached by many distributions when a large number of measurements is made, or, as we say, when there is a large number of cases. It is necessary to assume, furthermore, that these measurements or cases are taken at random, or that there is no bias or systematic error. For example, if it were desired to take an unbiased and representative sample of students on a given college or university campus, it would be necessary to plan the sampling procedure in such a way that *every* student would have an *equal chance* of being chosen. If these conditions were met the sample would be an unbiased and representative one.

One method of illustrating the normal curve is by tossing coins or dice. If we represent "heads" by H and "tails" by T, the expression $H + T$ represents the probabilities for any toss of one coin, i.e., equal probabilities of a head or a tail. If we toss the coin one hundred times, the results will approximate fifty heads and fifty tails. If we toss two coins, the possibilities are two heads, head and tail, tail and head, two tails, or, $H^2 + 2HT + T^2$.

If we toss two coins one hundred times we would (theoretically) get $25H^2 + 50\ HT + 25T^2$, or heads twenty-five times on both coins, one head and one tail fifty times, and tails on both coins twenty-five times. Similarly, we can predict the theoretical frequency with which each possible combination of any number of coins tossed simultaneously any given number of times will occur.

In tossing coins, since if there is an equal chance for each coin to fall head or tail each time, every possible combination can occur; however, if we toss ten coins, the probabilities of getting ten heads or ten tails are less than those for getting other combinations. The most probable combination is five heads and five tails, since each coin has an equal chance of falling heads or tails. By expanding $(H + T)^{10}$ we get the probabilities of each possible combination occurring if ten coins were tossed an infinite number of times. The expression becomes $H^{10} + 10H^9T + 45H^8T^2 + 120H^7T^3 + 210H^6T^4 + 252H^5T^5 + 210H^4T^6 + 120H^3T^7 + 45H^2T^8 + 10HT^9 + T^{10}$.

This means that the chances of getting five heads and five tails in tossing ten coins are 252 in 1,024. The probabilities of getting ten heads or ten tails are, respectively, one in 1,024. Where ten coins have thus been tossed, it has been found that the frequencies with which possible combinations do occur approach the theoretical values as limits. For example, Figure 29, which is based upon an actual experiment, shows the results of tossing ten pennies one thousand times.

Although the number of tosses is one thousand instead of 1,024, it is evident that the frequency with which each possible combination actually

FIGURE 29 • Frequency Distribution Based
on Tossing Ten Pennies One
Thousand Times

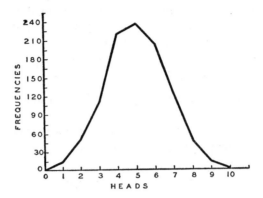

From Daniel Starch, *Educational Psychology;*
New York: The Macmillan Company, 1919. By
permission of the author.

occurred closely approximated the theoretical values. It is presumed that
under ideal conditions, that is, an infinite number of tosses with each toss
exactly like every other, and each coin free to fall heads or tails as chance
dictates, the actual frequencies would coincide with the theoretical.

Another situation in which the typical bell-shaped distribution curve
occurs is in measurement of natural phenomena. Thousands of such measurements have been made of barometric and temperature readings over a
long period at a given locality; of height, weight, and other bodily measurements of humans of the same sex and age; of the distribution of errors of
measurement which are due to chance; and of measures of ability and
achievement, particularly when these are objective and based on large
numbers of cases. Figure 30 shows such a distribution curve for the stature
of men.

In Chapter 10 the distribution of I.Q.'s based on the composite of Forms
L and M of the *Revised Stanford-Binet* is reproduced in Figure 10.

Figure 31 shows the distribution of scores on an objective examination
in educational measurement.

All these distribution curves approximate, more or less closely, the
theoretical frequency curve. The larger the number of measurements and
the more random the sample, the more symmetrical the curves become.

The significance of these results for educational and psychological measurement is great. In the first place, to the extent that human abilities tend
to be distributed normally, we may expect to find relatively small pro-

FIGURE 30 • Frequency Distribution of Stature for 8,585 Adult Males Born in the British Isles

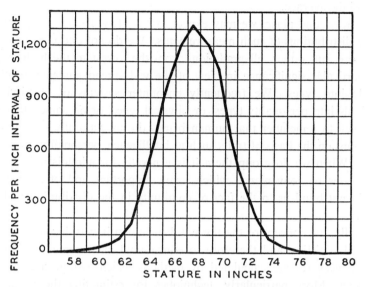

From G. Udny Yule and M. G. Kendall, *An Introduction to the Theory of Statistics,* 14th Edition, Revised; London: Charles Griffin and Company, Ltd., Third Impression, 1958. P. 83. Reproduced by permission of the publisher.

FIGURE 31 • Frequency Distribution of Scores by 138 College Students on an Objective Final Examination in Educational Measurement

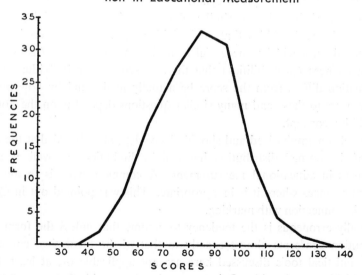

portions in the total population that are very gifted or extremely lacking in ability, and conversely, we may expect the great majority to cluster around the average.

In the second place, we may expect to have few, if any, gaps or breaks in the distributions of such measurements. We do not find classes or types in nature, but rather, all gradations from the lowest to the highest. This has particular significance in view of the widespread tendency to classify people into types. We frequently encounter systems of classifying individuals into personality types, or physical types, or on some other basis. It is well to remember that human beings do not naturally fall into types or groups on the basis of traits such as intelligence, personality, or achievement. When we do group them it is generally for administrative reasons or reasons of convenience which, while important and often necessary, should not blind us to the fact of continuity in the distribution of human traits.

Finally, the concept of the normal distribution is very important to educational statistics, and therefore to educational measurements. Most statistical measures are calculated by methods which assume a normal distribution. More particularly, techniques for estimating the accuracy of measurements rest upon the concept of the normal probability curve. As we have emphasized, the usefulness of tests and evaluative techniques depends in part upon their value for predictive purposes. Such instruments as intelligence, aptitude, and prognostic tests are essentially tests for predictive purposes. Prediction is based squarely on the concept of probability. Given a certain score on a certain test, what will be the probable score if the test is given again? Or, what is the probable score on another test of the same or similar abilities, traits, or potentialities? Or, what are the probabilities that an individual who makes a certain score on a certain test will be successful in a chosen profession? Again, what are the chances (probabilities) that the true score of an individual on an examination differs from the score he actually made, and by how much? The answers to these and many similar questions depend upon the normal probability concept.

It has been emphasized and should always be remembered that the concept of the normal distribution has definite limitations as well as great usefulness in educational measurement. A common error is to apply it in circumstances where it is inappropriate. This was pointed out in Chapter 15 in connection with marking.

Equally erroneous is the tendency to assume that unless the form of a distribution conforms almost exactly to that of the theoretical curve the usual statistical tools discussed here are not applicable or, at least, their use is highly questionable. It is true, as has been said, that a great many statistical procedures, particularly those relating to prediction, are based on the assumption of normality. However, the amount of error introduced by departures from the theoretical are not great enough in most ordinary statistical work to invalidate the results. For the purist, procedures are available which make possible certain corrections for various conditions resulting in departures from the normal distribution.

On the whole, the concept of the normal distribution is a very useful and even indispensable one in educational and psychological measurement. Its usefulness is, however, not confined to measurement. It is basic to an understanding of individual differences in physical and mental qualities and characteristics which measurement serves to quantify. It has been and will undoubtedly continue to be an essential concept both theoretically and practically.

▶ LEARNING EXERCISE ◀

13. Toss four pennies sixteen times and record the number of heads and tails for each toss. Determine the theoretical frequencies of each possible combination by expanding $(H + T)^4$. Compare these with the ones obtained by tossing.

MEASURES OF CORRELATION OR RELATIONSHIP

In Chapter 3 graphic illustrations of correlation were presented in the form of scatter diagrams or two-way tables. These illustrations provided pictorial or graphic representation of the extent of agreement between two variables and also showed whether the relationship was positive or negative. In each case a coefficient of correlation — a quantitative measure of the degree and direction of relationship existing between two (or more) variables — was given. This statistic is very important in that it forms the basis for gauging the efficiency of prediction.

Rank Difference Correlation

Although there are several methods of calculating the coefficient of correlation, only two will be discussed here. The first and simplest of these is based on ranks. Briefly, the theory underlying it is that if two sets of scores are obtained on the same population, and if each individual is ranked on both, the size of the differences between the ranks gives a measure of the extent of agreement between the two tests. To illustrate, let us assume that four pupils, A, B, C, and D have taken two tests, one in geography and one in intelligence. Their scores are as follows:

	A	B	C	D
Geography	25	40	30	20
Intelligence	90	100	95	80

If we rank them, they take the following order:

	A	B	C	D
Rank in Geography Test	3	1	2	4
Rank in Intelligence Test	3	1	2	4

The ranks on the two tests agree perfectly, as may be shown by taking the differences between the two sets of ranks, thus:

	A	B	C	D
	3	1	2	4
	3	1	2	4
	0	0	0	0

Since the agreement is perfect, the correlation will be perfect.

Now let us suppose the scores, ranks, and differences are as follows:

	A	B	C	D
Score in Geography Test	25	30	40	20
Score in Intelligence Test	90	110	100	80

If these are ranked they show the following order:

	A	B	C	D
Rank in Geography Test	3	2	1	4
Rank in Intelligence Test	3	1	2	4
Differences between Ranks	0	1	1	0

Here we have something less than perfect agreement and the differences between ranks are greater than they were in the first case.

One more illustration will help to clarify this principle. Let us assume the following:

	A	B	C	D
Score in Geography Test	40	30	20	15
Score in Intelligence Test	90	100	110	120
Rank in Geography Test	1	2	3	4
Rank in Intelligence Test	4	3	2	1
Differences between Ranks	3	1	1	3

In this case we have a complete reversal of ranks between the two tests, and thus the differences are at a maximum total. This illustration, though greatly simplified, shows how agreement (or lack of it) between ranks gives a measure of the extent of correlation.

An eminent English statistician, Charles Spearman, worked out a method of determining the extent of correlation based on this principle. It is known as the Spearman Rank Difference Method.

TABLE XVIII • Calculation of Rank Difference (ρ) Correlation Coefficient: Scores of Twenty-Five Pupils on Arithmetic Test and Reading Test

Pupil	Scores Arithmetic	Scores Reading	Ranks Arithmetic	Ranks Reading	D	D²
A	44	86	4	7	3	9
B	21	68	23	18	5	25
C	14	48	25	24	1	1
D	18	70	24	16	8	64
E	46	94	2	3	1	1
F	45	102	3	2	1	1
G	52	92	1	4	3	9
H	30	72	15	15	0	0
I	39	91	6	5	1	1
J	36	80	9	9	0	0
K	31	69	14	17	3	9
L	22	62	22	21	1	1
M	23	56	21	23	2	4
N	38	73	7.5	14	6.5	42.25
O	33	66	11	19	8	64
P	33	77	11	10.5	.5	.25
Q	29	75	16.5	13	3.5	12.25
R	38	65	7.5	20	12.5	156.25
S	32	87	13	6	7	49
T	29	46	16.5	25	8.5	72.25
U	42	111	5	1	4	16
V	28	81	18	8	10	100
W	26	59	19	22	3	9
X	33	77	11	10.5	.5	.25
Y	25	76	20	12	8	64
						710.50

ρ = rank difference correlation

D = differences between ranks

N = number of cases

$$\rho = 1 - \frac{6\Sigma D^2}{N(N^2 - 1)}$$

$$= 1 - \frac{6 \times 710.50}{25(625 - 1)}$$

$$= 1 - \frac{4263}{15600}$$

$$= 1 - .27 = .73$$

As can be seen in Table XVIII, we have determined the rank difference correlation between scores in arithmetic and reading for John's class. The results of these calculations, a correlation coefficient of .73, show that there is a substantial degree of relationship between scores on the arithmetic test and scores on the reading test. We can say, therefore, that there is a marked tendency for pupils who do well on one to do well on the other, and vice versa. The correlation is not perfect by any means, and there are individuals who constitute important exceptions to the general trend, for example, in such instances as R, T, and V; and, to a lesser degree, D and O.

Product-Moment Correlation

One of the disadvantages of the Rank Difference Method is that it is practical only with small groups. If there are large numbers of cases the numbers denoting ranks and the possible rank differences become large, and when these are squared they become too cumbersome to deal with conveniently. Aside from the matter of convenience, there are other reasons why statistical workers generally prefer another method of correlation known as the Pearson Product-Moment Correlation. Let us suppose we have measured the heights and weights of some infants and we wish to determine whether there is a correlation between these two variables. In order to simplify the explanation we shall use only five cases which we shall call J, K, L, M, and N.

Deviations from Mean

	Height	Weight	Height	Weight			
	X	Y	x	y	x^2	y^2	xy
J	31	17	1	−2	1	4	−2
K	27	18	−3	−1	9	1	3
L	29	16	−1	−3	1	9	3
M	31	22	1	3	1	9	3
N	32	22	2	3	4	9	6
					16	32	13
Mean	30	19					

A formula (there are many variations) for the Product-Moment Correlation is:

$$r = \frac{\Sigma xy}{\sqrt{\Sigma x^2 \times \Sigma y^2}}$$

Substituting the values obtained for the five cases above gives us:

$$r = \frac{13}{\sqrt{16 \times 32}}$$

$$= \frac{13}{22.6}$$

$$= .57+$$

The Product-Moment coefficient of correlation shows the extent to which variations of individuals from the respective means of the distribution of two traits agree in direction and relative size. For example, M and N are both above the means in height and weight; K and L are below the means in both. Their xy products are all positive, yielding a positive value of r. However, J is above the mean in height but below the mean in weight. The xy product is negative which reduces the Σxy and the size of r. If the sum of the negative xy's equals the sum of the positive xy's, the Σxy is zero and r is zero, showing that there is no consistent tendency for variations of individuals to agree. When the sum of the negative xy's exceeds the sum of the positive xy's the correlation is negative, showing that variations of individuals on the two traits tend to go in opposite directions though similar in relative amount. Various types and degrees of relationships were shown graphically in Figures 2, 3, and 4, Chapter 3.

▶ LEARNING EXERCISES ◀

14. Make a table similar to the one above, using five cases that you think would give a negative correlation. Prove it.

15. Using the twenty-five scores in arithmetic and reading (Table XVIII), calculate the Product-Moment coefficient of correlation. (Suggestion: To reduce the labor of calculation, use 32 as the mean of the arithmetic scores and 75 as the mean of the reading scores.) Compare your answer with that obtained by the Rank Difference Method.

A variation of the formula for r which was used above is:

$$r = \frac{\Sigma xy}{N \sigma_x \sigma_y}$$

This is useful if the standard deviation of each variable (in this case, arithmetic and reading test scores) has already been calculated. All that needs to be done in addition is to calculate the *xy* products, substitute the different values in the formula, and solve for *r*.

The calculation of *r* from grouped data is more complicated than it is as shown here with use of actual scores. For further information on this procedure textbooks in statistical methods may be consulted. A number of so-called "Correlation Charts" have been devised to make this task simpler and more mechanical. These can be obtained from publishers of standardized tests, and they are often very useful, especially if one has a large number of correlations to do. Of course, correlations, as well as other statistics are most efficiently determined today by electronic computers.

USES OF CORRELATION

Validity

In Chapter 4 the criteria of a good measuring instrument were discussed. It was stated that of all such criteria, *validity* is the most important, and different approaches to validating a test were described. One of these was empirical or statistical validity. The extent to which a test (let us say of intelligence) correlates with a criterion, that is, with some accepted measure of intelligence, is a measure of its statistical validity. It is obvious that if the criterion is a valid one and the test under scrutiny does not correlate with the criterion to any noticeable extent, it cannot be regarded as having statistical validity. A test that is supposed to measure the intelligence of ten-year old children, scores on which show the following correlations with other criteria of intelligence, would hardly be said to have statistical validity:

	With school marks over several years	With *Stanford-Binet* mental ages
Correlation of supposed test of intelligence	.17	.28

Such a test would be open to strong suspicion as a measure of intelligence, though it might conceivably prove to have validity as a measure of something else.

In situations where statistical measures of validity are desired, the coefficient of correlation is the measure most frequently used. The correlation between scores on the measure or test whose validity is to be determined, and some established or generally accepted measure of the same quality or trait which the new test purports to measure, is a standard statistical measure of validity.

The criteria used for statistical determination of the validity of a test purporting to measure mental ability would include teachers' marks, scores on standardized tests of achievement or of intelligence, chronological age (in the case of children), ratings of teachers, and possibly measures of socio-economic status. Similar criteria would be used for validating achievement tests. The method of correlation is also used in establishing the validity of other types of tests such as aptitude, interest, and personality tests, though the criteria would necessarily be different. For example, aptitude tests and interest inventories might be validated by correlating scores on them with measures of success in the field of work they were intended to predict. Scores on personality inventories might be correlated with ratings or even clinical diagnoses.

Validity coefficients vary considerably with criteria used. The correlation of scores or I.Q.'s from a mental ability test will typically range from .40 or .50 with teachers' marks to .70 or .80 with standardized tests of achievement. As was mentioned in Chapter 4, the size of the coefficient and its interpretation will depend on the situation.

Reliability

Another important application of correlation techniques is in determining the reliability of tests. Reliability has been defined as the consistency with which a test measures whatever it does measure. There are three commonly used methods of determining reliability or consistency of measurement. The first is to give the same test twice to the same group and calculate the correlation between the two sets of scores. The second is to give two equivalent forms of a test to the same group. The third method is to administer the test once only, score it by the split-half method, correlate the half scores, and apply the Spearman-Brown formula. These methods have been explained and illustrated in Chapter 4, and are mentioned again here only as illustrations of the use of correlation techniques.

Reliability coefficients of standardized tests may be expected to reach or exceed .90, and some published ones exceed .95. This presents a marked contrast with the size of the usual validity coefficients and illustrates the inadequacy of interpreting coefficients of correlation on the basis of magnitude alone. Whereas a validity coefficient of .50 may be quite acceptable, a reliability of .50 would be considered unsatisfactory for almost any test.

Prediction — Standard Error of Estimate

The rank difference correlation between the arithmetic and reading scores in John's class was found to be .73. Now, suppose we ask the question: How can we predict a pupil's score on an arithmetic test, knowing his score on a reading test? Knowing a pupil's score on an arithmetic test, how accurately can we predict his reading score? Answering this question involves calculations which are beyond the scope of this book, but one of the end products is a formula known as the Standard Error of Estimate which is $\sigma_{(est.y)} = \sigma_y \sqrt{1 - r^2}$, where $\sigma_{(est.y)}$ is the standard error of prediction of a reading test score, σ_y is the standard deviation of the reading test scores, and r is the correlation between arithmetic and reading scores. Substituting our calculated values (see Table XV) in this formula we have:

$$\sigma_{(est.y)} = 15.4 \sqrt{1 - (.73)^2}$$
$$= 15.4 \sqrt{1 - .5329}$$
$$= 15.4 \sqrt{.4671}$$
$$= 15.4 \times .68$$
$$= 10.5$$

This tells us that, knowing the score in arithmetic made by John or one of his classmates, we can predict his score in reading with an estimated standard error of 10.5 points, and that the chances are 68.26 out of one hundred that our prediction will not be in error by more than 10.5 points either way. In other words, if the most probable score on reading is 75 for a person scoring 36 on arithmetic, the chances are about two to one that his actual score in reading will fall between 75 − 10.5, or 64.5, and 75 + 10.5, or 85.5.

We may go a step further. Adding and subtracting two standard errors to the obtained score of 75 gives upper and lower limits of 96 and 54 respectively, which tell us that the probabilities are approximately ninety-five to five that John's score in reading will be between 96 and 54. Similarly, we can predict with the probability of ninety-nine chances in one hundred that, given his score of thirty-six on arithmetic, his score on reading will be between 102.3 and 47.7.

Standard Error of Measurement

Similarly, we may wish to know what the standard error of an obtained score is when we have given a test of known reliability. To put the problem in another way, what is the probability that a pupil's true score on a test does not differ significantly from the score which he actually obtains? This is another way of asking how reliable a single test score is.

Here again, we have a formula which is based on correlation, this time on the reliability coefficient. It is $\sigma_{meas.} = \sigma \sqrt{1 - r}$, where $\sigma_{meas.}$ is the standard error of measurement, σ is the standard deviation of the test, and r is the reliability coefficient of the test.

To illustrate the use of this formula, let us assume that we have determinded the reliability of the arithmetic test used in John's class to be .90. We know that the standard deviation is 9.2 (Table XV). Substituting, we have:

$$\sigma_{meas.} = 9.2 \sqrt{1 - .90}$$
$$= 9.2 \sqrt{.10}$$
$$= 9.2 \times .32$$
$$= 2.9$$

This result indicates that the chances are about two to one that the obtained score of any pupil on the arithmetic test will not vary from his true score (whatever it may be) by more than three (2.9) points. More specifically, the chances are two to one that John's true score on the arithmetic test lies somewhere between 33 and 39 (his obtained score of 36 $\pm$ 3). Furthermore, we can say with much greater assurance (with chances of about nineteen to one) that his true score lies between 30 and 42; that is, it does not differ from his obtained score by more than six points; and we can be almost certain that it lies between 27 and 45.

▶ LEARNING EXERCISES ◀

16. Assume the following data:
    a. Correlation between I.Q. and marks in algebra equals .64.
    b. Reliability of test of intelligence equals .91; of teacher's marks in algebra equals .51.
    c. Standard deviation of scores on intelligence test equals 16; of teacher's marks on basis of 4 for A, 3 for B, 2 for C, 1 for D and 0 for E, equals 1.0.
    Using these data, calculate the standard error of measurement of the intelligence test and of the teacher's marks in algebra.

17. Calculate the standard error of estimate for scores on the intelligence test, knowing the pupil's mark. For his mark, knowing his score on the intelligence test.

Extracting Square Root

1. Point off from decimal by pairs in both directions. (Zeros added here in order to round off to one decimal at end.)

$$\sqrt{236.94} = \sqrt{2\ 36.94\ 00}$$

2. Take nearest square root of first number or pair, in this case, $\sqrt{2} = 1+$.

$$\frac{1}{\sqrt{2\ 36.94\ 00}}$$

3. Place this under the first digit or pair and subtract.

$$
\begin{array}{r}
1 \\
\sqrt{2\ 36.94\ 00} \\
1 \\
\hline
1
\end{array}
$$

4. Bring down the next pair of digits.

$$
\begin{array}{r}
1 \\
\sqrt{2\ 36.94\ 00} \\
1 \\
\hline
136
\end{array}
$$

5. Multiply the answer so far obtained by 2, bring down the product, and add a zero.

$$
\begin{array}{r}
1 \\
\sqrt{2\ 36.94\ 00} \\
1 \\
\hline
20\ \ \lfloor\overline{136}
\end{array}
$$

493

6. Use this number as a trial divisor. In this case the tentative quotient is 5.

$$
\begin{array}{r}
1\ 5 \\
\sqrt{2\ 36.94\ 00} \\
\end{array}
$$

$$
\begin{array}{r|l}
 & 1 \\
20 & 136 \\
5 & \\
\end{array}
$$

7. Add the tentative quotient to the doubled figure with zero added and multiply by the tentative quotient.*

$$
\begin{array}{r}
1\ 5 \\
\sqrt{2\ 36.94\ 00} \\
\end{array}
$$

$$
\begin{array}{r|l}
 & 1 \\
20 & 136 \\
5 & \\
\hline
25 & 125 \\
\end{array}
$$

8. Subtract, bring down the next pair of numbers, and repeat the process.

$$
\begin{array}{r}
1\ 5\ 3\ 9 \\
\sqrt{2\ 36.94\ 00} \\
\end{array}
$$

$$
\begin{array}{r|l}
 & 1 \\
20 & 136 \\
5 & \\
\hline
25 & 125 \\
300 & 1194 \\
3 & \\
\hline
303 & 909 \\
3060 & 28500 \\
9 & \\
\hline
3069 & 27621 \\
\end{array}
$$

9. Insert the decimal and round off: 15.39 or 15.4.

* Note that although 20 goes more than 6 times into 136, adding 6 to 20 and multiplying by 6 would have given a product of 156 — too large for our dividend of 136.

A Selective List of Test Publishers in the United States

This list includes those publishers or other organizations whose tests are referred to in this book.

American Guidance Service, 720 Washington Avenue, S.E., Minneapolis 14, Minnesota.

The Bobbs-Merrill Company, 4300 West 62nd Street, Indianapolis 6, Indiana (includes Public School Publishing Company and C. A. Gregory Company).

Bureau of Educational Measurements, Kansas State Teachers College, Emporia, Kansas.

Bureau of Educational Research and Service, State University of Iowa, Iowa City, Iowa.

Bureau of Publications, Teachers College, Columbia University, New York 27, New York.

California Test Bureau, Del Monte Research Park, Monterey, California.

Cooperative Test Division, Educational Testing Service, Princeton, New Jersey.

Educational Records Bureau, 21 Audubon Avenue, New York 32, New York.

Harcourt, Brace & World, Inc., 757 Third Avenue, New York 17, New York.

Houghton Mifflin Company, 2 Park Street, Boston 7, Massachusetts.

Ohio Scholarship Tests, Ohio State Department of Education, Columbus 15, Ohio.

Personnel Press, Inc., 20 Nassau Street, Princeton, New Jersey.

Personnel Research Institute, Western Reserve University, Cleveland 6, Ohio.

Psychological Corporation, 304 East 45th Street, New York 36, New York.

Psychometric Affiliates, Box 1625, Chicago 90, Illinois.

Science Research Associates, Inc., 259 East Erie Street, Chicago 11, Illinois.

Sheridan Supply Company, P.O. Box 837, Beverly Hills, California.

Stanford University Press, Stanford, California.

C. H. Stoelting Company, 424 North Homan Avenue, Chicago 24, Illinois.

Western Psychological Services, 12035 Wilshire Boulevard, Los Angeles 25, California.

Index of Names

Robbins, Irving, 17, 103, 124, 239, 357, 379
Ross, C. C., 17, 37, 70, 103, 123, 163, 183, 418, 456
Ruch, Giles M., 27 n.
Rudman, Herbert C., 187
Rugg, Harold O., 27
Rulon, Philip J., 361
Rummel, J. Francis, 17
Ryan, Teresa M., 73

Sapon, Stanley M., 325 n.
Sauble, Irene, 119 n.
Schrammel, H. E., 73
Seashore, Carl E., 29, 322 n.
Seashore, Harold G., 75, 327 n.
Sexson, John A., 231, 236
Simon, Théodore, 24, 82, 277
Smith, G. Milton, 70
Spearman, Charles, 33, 285, 485
Stanley, Julian C., 17, 37, 70, 103, 123, 163, 183, 418, 456
Starch, Daniel, 27 n., 131, 480
Stenquist, J. L., 29
Stern, Wilhelm, 286
Stone, C. W., 5, 23
Sueltz, Ben A., 119 n.
Super, Donald E., 313, 332, 356

Tallmadge, Margaret, 134 n.
Terman, Lewis M., 27 n., 279, 280 n., 282, 286, 291, 292, 313
Terry, Paul W., 134 n.
Thomas, R. Murray, 123, 356, 379

Thompson, Anton, 415 n.
Thorndike, Edward Lee, 20 n., 22–23, 25, 37, 215 n., 225, 282, 285
Thorndike, Robert L., 14, 17, 102–103, 163, 183, 298, 313, 332, 356, 367 n., 379, 389
Thurstone, L. L., 29, 33 n., 285–286, 352
Thurstone, Thelma Gwinn, 33 n.
Tiegs, Ernest W., 74
Torgerson, Theodore L., 239
Travers, Robert M. W., 163, 356
Traxler, Arthur E., 370 n., 379, 418, 456
Tyler, Ralph, 294 n.

Vallance, Theodore R., 134
Vaughn, K. W., 123, 244
Voelker, Paul F., 28, 320 n.

Wade, Herbert T., 2 n.
Walker, Biron, 67, 252
Walker, Helen M., 70
Weaver, Warren, 17
Wechsler, David, 297
Weitzman, Ellis, 163, 183
Wesman, A. G., 327 n.
Womer, Frank B., 418
Woodworth, R. S., 26, 28
Wrightstone, J. Wayne, 17, 103, 124, 239, 357, 379
Wundt, Wilhelm, 277

Yule, G. Udny, 481

Index of Subjects